FOUNDATIONS OF CHINESE ART

FOUNDATIONS

322 illustrations in colour and black and white
91 maps and line drawings

New York · Toronto · London

OF CHINESE ART

from neolithic pottery to modern architecture

WILLIAM WILLETTS

McGRAW-HILL BOOK COMPANY

COPYRIGHT © 1965 BY THAMES AND HUDSON, LONDON
LIBRARY OF CONGRESS CATALOG CARD NUMBER: 64-66127
BLOCKS MADE IN WESTERN GERMANY BY
KLISCHEE-WERKSTÄTTEN DER INDUSTRIEDIENST GMBH, WIESBADEN
70305

PRINTED IN SWITZERLAND BY BUCHDRUCKEREI WINTERTHUR AG, WINTERTHUR

CONTENTS

This book is a revised, abridged, and drastically rewritten version of my original *Chinese Art* published in two volumes by Penguin Books in 1958. In the Foreword to *Chinese Art* I made an elaborate acknowledgement of indebtedness to all those people who in one way or another had helped me to write it. The present version was written without any such aid; there is no-one I need thank except my editor Stephan Feuchtwang (backed by my publishers), who has followed me through the laborious stages of the book's reconstruction with quite unbelievable forbearance.

In preparing this version, I have tried to make the text more readable for the ordinary reader by cutting out much of the 'medieval disputation' that kept invading the pages of *Chinese Art*, and perhaps also by lightening the style somewhat. I have incorporated some of the new archaeological discoveries of the past two decades, and particularly those which push the history of Chinese bronze art back two centuries to the beginning of the Shang dynasty, about 1500 BC, and which show us its primitive autochthonous beginnings on Chinese soil; a fact previously discredited by so many Western scholars. I have corrected a number of errors without, I hope, introducing new ones, and I have simplified the terminology.

The text figures were drawn by Janet Duchesne, Theodore Ramos, and Lowther Robinson, under the direction of Mr Ramos and in collaboration with the author. The maps were compiled by the author and drawn by John Walkey. Figure 19 was originally drawn by R. J. Charleston and is reproduced with his kind permission. The examples of Chinese script were brushed by Wu Shih-ch'ang, Ca Chit, and C. Su.

This version of my book was written in India.

Singapore, Spring 1965

For my Mother and Sister

INTRODUCTION

Definition

'Art', says Croce, 'is what everyone knows it to be.' That granted, to embark on a long explanation of what I have in mind when I think about art would be neither here nor there, even if I could persuade myself it was anything at all easily put into words. But what is meant by 'art' in the present context is merely a matter of summary definition. To begin with, we do not mean art, the aesthetic expression of feeling and emotion, but rather the vehicles of such expression – that is, the art-forms themselves. And whereas a writer on European art might properly confine himself to the *arti liberali* – the 'free' arts of painting and sculpture – he would be telling only part of the story were he to do so in the case of the arts of the Far East. For all who have come into contact with Chinese art will agree that its masterpieces were no less frequently wrought in materials such as jade, bronze, and pottery than in those of painting and sculpture. Each is an art-form in its own right.

Painting and sculpture came to maturity only relatively late in the wide span of Chinese history. So that were we in fact to confine our survey to painting and sculpture alone, we should find ourselves with practically nothing to say about a period of two thousand and more years of China's prehistoric and early dynastic culture. Is it antiquarian bias that makes us unwilling to ignore this vast tract of ancient time? Such a bias may well be the result of what might be called a contemporary education in Chinese art history. During the last fifty years or so, Westerners have come to realize that the picture of Chinese art as a whole is not at all what Europe of the eighteenth and nineteenth centuries took it to be. The Chinese then showed us only a small part of their artistic inheritance. It was no fault of theirs that the brilliant *œuvre* of the eighteenth century – the lacquers, textiles, porcelains, and so forth, then being made in China – should so completely have satisfied contemporary European taste for the decorative, the exotic, or the merely quaint; or that during much of the last century European fancy was for articles valued chiefly as curios or objects of *vertu*. But they were at no great pains to create a better-informed taste on the part of the West; one doubts whether they believed such a thing possible.

Then, about the turn of the century, a very few Western scholars began to realize that Chinese art extended back into a scarcely credible antiquity. Compared with what was now coming to light, the *chinoiseries* of the eighteenth century began to seem trivial and effete. Lacking critical standards by which to judge so completely unfamiliar an art, those who did not turn their backs on it were forced to see it largely through Chinese eyes, and from much the same historical standpoint as did the Chinese antiquarians who compiled the great Imperial catalogues of Sung and later times. Hence a possible prejudice on the part of the writer for art-forms, other than painting and sculpture, whose interest lies to some extent in their association with China's distant past.

Yet a picture of Chinese art including what we would call 'applied' as well as 'fine' art is, beyond doubt, the only one we can paint. Even for European art a distinction between the two categories is not easily made; in the case of Chinese it breaks down more or less completely. Sculpture, for example, has never in China won for itself the exalted position of sculpture in Europe. So that the distinction, if one insisted on making it, would have to be between painting and calligraphy on the one hand, and the remaining art-forms on the other. Yet the same thread of artistic genius, married to technical mastery of a very high order, runs through them all. It is a vague awareness of this common quality that emboldens us to think and speak of Chinese art as an organic whole.

And the physical elements out of which this picture is built up are almost as complete as they are ever likely to be. It is, of course, true that some phases in the history of each art-form remain still to be discovered, while others are irretrievably lost. The architecture of the early dynasties, for example, can be reconstructed only from indirect evidence, for not a single building from before the time of Christ is known to survive. That, I dare say, is the greatest single loss; although others, such as that of most of the textiles and wood-carvings of the same period, are almost as deplorable. Nevertheless, the range of materials and media in which the aesthetic impulse manifested itself, over a period of upwards of 4,000 years, now seems to be permanently established.

Stephen Bushell, writing his *Chinese Art* in 1904, apparently knew little or nothing of any art in China before the beginning of our era, except from literary sources; the centre of gravity of his book is still the eighteenth century.[1] Despite the great advance that *Chinese Art* undoubtedly marked, and despite Bushell's erudition, one scarcely gets the impression that Chinese art as we know it today was a living reality for him. Credit must, however, go to men such as he; to the great school of French sinologists, among whom Édouard Chavannes, Paul Pelliot, and Henri Maspero were outstanding for their scholarship and catholic taste in art; to explorers such as Sir Aurel Stein and archaeologists like Gunnar Andersson; to collectors like George Eumorfopoulos and Oscar Raphael; to the Chinese archaeologists of the Academia Sinica headed by Dr Li Chi; and to many, many others who helped to build up an immense structure of knowledge and taste, and bequeathed it to the world. In the West the climax was reached with the International Exhibition of Chinese Art held at Burlington House during the Winter of 1935–6. This was undoubtedly the finest display of Chinese art objects ever brought together under one roof, and it proved once for all that Chinese art was equal in magnitude to that of any other of the great divisions of mankind. At the same time it gave an opportunity for measuring the dimensions of each art-form in relation to Chinese material culture as a whole; no major revaluation in this respect has since been made, and, as we have already said, probably none ever will.

Scope

In this book we intend to discuss eight art-forms; namely, those of jade, bronze, lacquer, silk, sculpture, pottery, painting and calligraphy[2], and architecture. Of them, bronze, sculpture, pottery, and painting and calligraphy are, we suppose, automatic choices; and so also would be architecture, were it not for the fact that its theoretical and actual accomplishments are as yet scarcely known to the West. And if the others – jade, lacquer, and silk – seem to us minor arts by comparison, they no longer appear so when placed in their proper contexts in the history of Chinese civilization. If the reader will presently accept the list as it stands, we shall try to explain, in each chapter, the reasons why the art-form there discussed is entitled to its place in a history of Chinese art.

Method

The method of this book will be descriptive. We shall not pass aesthetic judgements on the objects discussed, but shall allow the illustrations to speak on their behalf. Nor shall we try to evoke in the reader the sort of intellectual excitement that Roger Fry and Laurence Binyon were able to stimulate by the compelling force of their prose. Not that 'exclamatory' criticism is necessarily bad. Whatever leads people to explore where they might not otherwise have gone has a value of its own, even when it is very little more than an infectious enthusiasm. But word magic is deceptive, and even if one had the power to perform it, the reader might yet be in danger of confusing verbal imagery with the objects it is meant to embellish. The art historical approach is better suited to our purpose, although the methods of European art history admittedly will not as yet reap comparable rewards when applied to the art of China; we still know far too little about it. But a start has been made – for example, by Swedish archaeologists working on Bronze Age art – and part of our task will be to hand on to the reader some of the results yielded by these first attempts at handling the data of Chinese art history.

*

Everybody is aware of a close connexion between art and the society of which it is an ingredient. A major art-form grows up in response to a social need which it alone can satisfy, a need that can be traced to the nexus of cultural factors that makes up the history of its day and age. Like an organic growth, it contains possibilities of variation. And its coming into flower, should that happen, is the result of a selective process working along a definite line and is not, so to speak, a sudden and unpredictable mutation. The question then occurs, how much meaning can a work of art have for us if we know nothing of the social forces that govern its growth and maturation? I think we would agree, not very much. Binyon himself begins an essay on Chinese painting and calligraphy by remarking: 'If we are truly to appreciate any work of art it is idle to approach it from the outside, bringing with us all our prejudices and preconceptions. We must try to enter into the mind of the man who made it, discover what his aim was, and consider how far he has achieved his aim.'[3] Two comments are perhaps called for here. First, before we can get an idea of the artist's aim, we must have at least some idea of the nature of the society in which he lived and worked. Second, and connected with the first, we *cannot but* approach Chinese art from the outside, however hard we try. For most of us there simply is no means of intuitive *rapport*. With European art it is different; ignorant as we may be of its detailed progress, however little aesthetic significance it may have for us, the content and conventions of European art are part of the tradition in which we grow up. For we are ourselves members of the society of which it is an historical ingredient. I do not think there is any need to stress how foreign are the content and conventions of Chinese art; our approach to it must, in the long run, be analytical.

By this we do not imply anything impersonal, or emotionally detached. The spirit that lives in a work of art can never be merely an object of sober intellection on the part of the beholder. Were there no first liberating shock of pleasure on sensing that spirit, one would have no heart to consolidate and deepen the aesthetic experience. But the shock in this case is surely inevitable. However hedged about we may be with 'prejudices and preconceptions', we cannot encounter a thing so fresh to our eyes as an object of Chinese art without experiencing altogether new reactions. But if an experience is to go beyond mere novelty, if it is not to fade into indifference or even revulsion, it must be deepened by understanding; and part of the process of coming to understand Chinese art necessarily involves understanding the conditions that give rise to it.

*

Writers on the material arts of a given civilization usually adopt one or other of two courses. The theme may be unfolded in a chronological sequence, each chapter being made to correspond to a major historical era, as do the successive episodes of a pageant. Its inherent legibility will be welcomed by the reader. Its drawback is that its treatment of each individual art-form is necessarily discontinuous; if the reader is primarily interested in, say, pottery, he will have to sift material from all over the book in order to gain a clear picture of that particular art-form. Again, with such an approach, emphasis tends to be placed more on social and political history and less on material culture and art.

Following the second method, each chapter may be devoted to a single art-form, whose whole known history is traced therein. Chronological continuity is now forfeited. Dates and names of dynasties have to be repeated over and over again, and so does the description of that great unifying quality common to all the arts of a given period – its historical style. And the social and political background tends to get ignored in the effort to describe technical, typological, and stylistic developments in an art-form with a history of perhaps 2,000 years within the limits of a single chapter.

Both methods suffer from a further defect. Both lay the writer under the necessity, unless he clearly states an alternative intention, of discussing the progress of each art-form over its whole life-span. To do this at all effectively is quite out of the question in the present case; for Chinese art, like every other dimension of Chinese culture, is of appalling magnitude. Nor do we think the reader would be at all grateful if we attempted this task. After all, the progress of each art-form is quite uneven; there are bound to be long periods in its history scarcely worth mentioning, and the best comment on mediocrity is perhaps silence. Such omissions, in fact, may in themselves help to make for a sort of overall evaluation, leaving our attention free to concentrate on the best work that was being done in each successive period.

With these considerations in mind, we have tried to effect a compromise between the two methods just outlined. Chinese history can be made to fit, very loosely, into phases represented here by chapters two to eight. The first known phase of Chinese civilization belongs to the late prehistoric period, roughly 2500–1300 BC, and forms a natural background to chapter two. The Bronze Age, between about 1500 and 500 BC, forms another distinctive social and political phase and is dealt with in chapter three. The social and political character of the period covered by chapter four, roughly 200 BC to AD 200, is in turn quite different from those that precede it: and so on. The historical phases thus follow each other in more or less strict chronological sequence from about the third millennium BC down to modern times; and chapter one, which forms an introduction to the others, takes the story back to the earliest traces of man in China.

But again, each main historical phase has at least one art-form – sometimes only one – which is for one reason or other especially characteristic of that phase; in the case of the period 1500–500 BC, for instance, bronze. True, we know next to nothing of other material arts during this time. But what we *can* claim is that bronze art, represented by the sacrificial vessels with which we mainly deal in chapter three, is absolutely characteristic of the social outlook and aspirations of pre-Han dynastic China; and furthermore, that at no later time did it reach greater beauty or expressiveness. The same is true of the period between the Han and T'ang dynasties (AD 220–618), corresponding to chapter five, when sculpture reached its *floruit* under the patronage of Chinese Buddhism. The craft of pottery underwent certain crucial technical and stylistic developments during the T'ang period. The conventions and categories of classical Chinese painting can best be observed in the context of the Sung: and so on.

I owe it to the reader to repeat that this method is a compromise. For each historical period we take a sample art, while the other arts of the period are considered only when their existence demonstrably influences the character of the sample art chosen. Again, for each art-form we take a sample period in its history, and other historical periods are touched on only when a complete understanding of the art-form in its particular historical context depends on our doing so. It is this choice of art-form and historical period that is arbitrary. We have tried, however, to choose the most 'characteristic' art-form of each period as the sample, and the most 'representative' period in its history in which to describe it. The bibliography and notes on the text will guide the reader in forming a more complete picture of the history of each art-form, while for this new edition a number of illustrations has been added with the same aim in view.

I CHINA: GEOGRAPHY AND EARLY MAN

The Eighteen Provinces (Shih pa shêng)

It is never very easy to say at what point in a nation's history national consciousness comes upon its people. We have ample archaeological evidence to show that advanced societies were living in north China well before the historical period; and no doubt some of these conceived of themselves collectively as a 'We' group united by common social, cultural, and linguistic traits. But there is no reason to suppose that their effective political authority was at all widespread. Nor are political conditions during the early dynastic period at all easily imagined. Judging by the state of affairs late in the Chou period (1027–221 BC), the centres of higher society were scattered, and were separated from each other by pockets of unassimilated barbarian tribes whose society, culture, and speech were relatively foreign.

Orthodox Chinese history leaves us with the names of two overlordships preceding the Chou; namely, the Hsia and the Shang. That the first of these ever existed is archaeologically unproved; the Shang certainly did [p. 73]. At any rate, the term 'Hsia' is used in Chou times not only to name the alleged dynasty, but also to designate the 'We' group in a cultural sense; for the expression *chu Hsia* – 'all the Hsia' – has precisely this meaning in Chou texts, when the superiority and exclusiveness of Chou society *vis-à-vis* the barbarians are being asserted. And if, as some have thought, the Hsia dynasty was a mere myth created by the Chou after their conquest of the Shang in order to equip themselves with a legitimate civilized ancestry, this is surely the best possible reason for concluding that they acknowledged the China of their day as a distinctive, self-contained, and adult society and culture. They were simply securing title-deeds to their newly-won inheritance. The term *hua Hsia*, in which *hua* means something like 'flowering', 'cultivated', or 'cultured', is still in use today as an epithet for China.

The area of effective Chou rule was never very extensive, and within three centuries it had been reduced to a tiny royal domain surrounded by powerful independent states sprung from fiefs originally granted by the Chou to its military aristocracy. These states were of two sorts. All were at loggerheads; but those lying in the region of metropolitan China, around the Yellow River valley, were continually being forced on to the defensive by their powerful and aggressive neighbours in the west, south, and east. Collective security never took practical form; but at least the notion was current that *chung kuo*, or 'the Central States', in some way formed a distinct polity whose traditions and institutions were older and more valid than those of outlying societies. This expression, too, has come to stand as a designation for 'China'. We often translate it, wrongly, 'the Middle Kingdom'.

In 221 BC an aggressor state in the west, Ch'in, succeeded for a time in bringing all China north of the Yangtze under one rule. The dynasty then founded was not destined to endure, but various measures aimed at unification of the country were set on foot [p. 308], and the Ch'in Empire marks a definitive stage in the growth of a politically integrated China.

*

The northern states had long since thrown up defensive walls on their northern frontiers as protection against the horse-riding nomads of the steppes and deserts of what today are Mongolia and Manchuria, peoples who were definitely *not* Chinese either by race or by way of life. Ch'in now undertook to join these walls into one long, defensive chain. This act of integration, whatever its military value may have been, had important political consequences, col. 53 for the Great Wall served to point the contrast between the peoples living inside it – 'south of the Wall' – and the nomadic tribes who lived beyond. Not only did the Great Wall help to weld the Chinese into a nation; it had an equally formative effect on the outsiders. It helped to unify the peoples of the steppes into a great political and military power, and so marked a turning point in the political history of Asia as a whole.

The map of China was still not such as we would recognize today. The 'Chinese' world still stopped more or less at the Yangtze. But the tradition of a centralized government was thereafter never broken; and during the succeeding dynasty, the Han (206 BC to AD 220), imperial control gradually extended until it reached into south Manchuria and Korea in the north-east, Tongking in the south, and Chinese Turkestan in the west. The normal or 'optimum' limits of China Proper had been established for posterity. And, in recognition of this fact, the Chinese still speak of themselves as 'Han', using the word to signify a racial and cultural comity differing significantly from the many minority peoples within the Republic. Today the country is variously named. We in the West speak of 'China', and this word probably has a long descent from the name of the Ch'in state, 'China Proper', 'the Middle Kingdom', and 'the Eighteen Provinces'. We almost always mean the whole area south of the Great Wall. The Eighteen Provinces formed the national polity during the period of Manchu rule, until AD 1907; all of them still exist. They may be conveniently grouped in relation to the three main river systems, as follows:

1. *Yellow River (Huang Ho)*: Kansu, Shensi, Shansi, Honan, Hopei (Chihli), Shantung
2. *Yangtze*: Szechwan, Hupeh, Anhwei, Kiangsu, Hunan, Kiangsi, Chekiang
3. *West River (Hsi Chiang)*: Yunnan, Kwangsi, Kwangtung, Fukien, Kweichow

Map 1 indicates the present political confines of the People's Republic of China. As well as the region comprising the Eighteen Provinces, it shows a number of autonomous areas lying to the west, north-west, and north-east, including Tibet, Chinese Turkestan, Inner Mongolia, and Manchuria. These are regions over which China has exercised political control during expansionist phases of her history, and where her cultural influence has always been strong, and they contain most of her minority or non-Han populations. The cultural differentiation between Han and non-Han Chinese thus corresponds broadly to a territorial division between the Eighteen Provinces and what, to use the Roman analogy, we might call China *in partibus*. The former area is roughly circular in shape; as a help in simplifying our notions of its physiography, we have therefore drawn it on map 1 as a circle having its centre on the Yangtze at the border between the provinces of Szechwan and Hupeh.

Regional divisions of the Eighteen Provinces

If we now divide this circle into a northern and a southern half, we split China into two sharply defined regions, North and South. Marked physical differences, especially in climate,

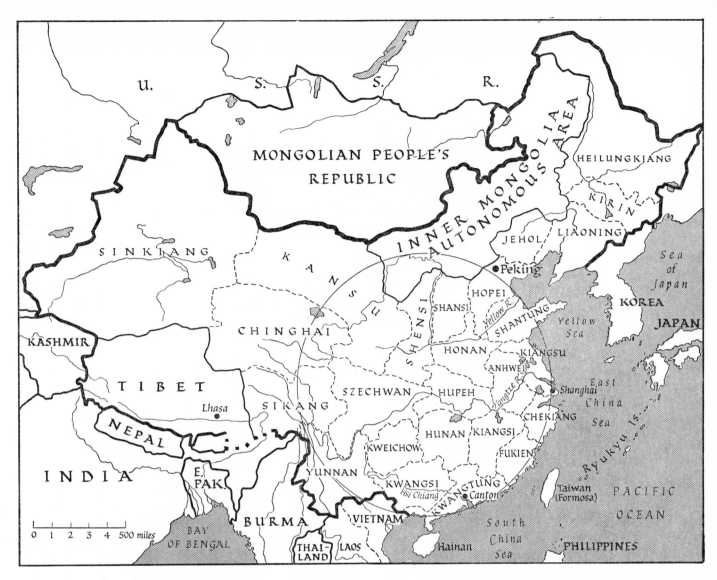

Map 1 China – the Eighteen Provinces

have brought into being two separate Chinas with distinct racial, linguistic, and other traits, while the natural barriers between them have cut them off from each other during long periods in their history. Indeed, not until the Han period (205 BC to AD 220), when the South was for the first time largely brought under control, was its influence on the North more than marginal. It is as near the truth as makes no matter to say that the formative elements in Chinese civilization – its material culture, its written language and literature, its *mores* – all began in the North; and almost everything dealt with in the first two chapters of this book concerns the North alone. The Yellow River valley, its principal feature, has with good reason been called the cradle of the Chinese race. The actual geographical change, we should hasten to add, lies somewhat north of our diameter, around the 34th parallel, and follows the watershed made by a succession of mountain ranges which run from west to east – the eastern extension of the Kun-lun, the Tsing-ling, and the Huai-yang which curves away somewhat to the south-east. In order to show how deep this North–South cleavage is, we have drawn up a

19

table which shows some of its characteristic features. The table is based on material collected by G.B. Cressey in the 'thirties, so that the picture it gives would not be true in certain respects of China today.[1]

I must emphasize that these differences are not absolute. The gap between North and South has been bridged from time to time by powerful unifying forces, of which the present government is naturally the one that comes first to mind. The written language, in a land of diverse dialects, is another; Buddhism was another, and the habit of the Chinese Court of seeking refuge in the South, when threatened by rebellion or invasion from the third century AD onwards, was another. Nor was the early development of Chinese civilization entirely a one-sided affair; well before Han times the state of Ch'u, which lay largely in the South, was making its contribution to the culture of metropolitan China, and by Han times the whole area of the Yangtze basin had been incorporated absolutely into China as a nation. But local tradition, in the absence of first-class communication from one area to another, is a strongly-enduring quantity. The persistence in the South, and especially in the far South, of regional pockets with variations in race, custom, and dialect, and of aboriginal minorities who have never become Chinese, suggests with what difficulty, and how late, south China succumbed to the process of 'sinification' from the North.

NORTH	SOUTH
1. CLIMATE	
Cold winters; hot, dry summers	Cool winters; hot, moist summers
Dust storms	Typhoons
Rainfall often inadequate	Rainfall usually abundant
Prevailing winds north-westerly from Inner Asia	Prevailing winds south-easterly from the Pacific
2. RACE	
Average height 169 cm	Average height 161 cm
Almond eye percentage 11–21	Almond eye percentage 36
Uniform hybrid race	Racial varieties, including many aboriginal pockets
3. LIVELIHOOD	
4–6 months growing season	9–12 months growing season
1–2 crops annually	2–3 crops annually
Dry terrace cultivation	Irrigated terrace cultivation
Kaoliang, millet, wheat, beans	Rice
Frequent famines recorded	Fewer famines, offset by overcrowding of population
Smooth coastlines, poor harbours, little fishing	Irregular coastline, good harbours, much fishing
4. VEGETATION	
Grassless and treeless, brown landscape in winter	Abundant forests, green all year round
Typical tree: pine	Typical tree: bamboo
Parts afforested until c. AD 800	Almost whole area afforested until c. AD 1300
5. TRANSPORT	
Roads, two-wheeled carts	Flagstone trails, coolie transport
Draught animals: donkey, mule, camel	Draught animal: water buffalo
6. SOCIETY	
Classical and conservative, scholars	Radical and restless, merchants
Mandarin dialect spoken	Diversity of dialects
Emigration to Manchuria	Emigration to south-east Asia
Foreign intercourse by land	Foreign intercourse by sea

A second significant division can be made. It is between the north-west and the north-east – that is, between the left and right upper quadrants of our circle. Here China gained her first political and cultural identity, one that may be thought of as the adjustment of forces operating between two highly contrasting natural habitats, Plateau and Plain. The former lies mainly in the north-west, and includes the relatively infertile loess highlands of Kansu, Shensi, and Shansi, while the latter lies in the north-east and contains the abundantly rich alluvial plains of eastern Honan, Shantung, and Hopei. The proximity of these two regions of unequal productivity probably accounts for a general drift of populations from west to east in China, both in prehistoric and early dynastic times. Dr Li Chi conceives of a pre-historic 'We' people of the Plain, and a 'You' of the Plateau. The former had highly developed ceramic techniques. They had that strange totem of Chinese culture, the *li* tripod [p. 85]. They practised scapulimancy [p. 73]. And they built defensive walls of stamped earth round their settlements. On and near the Plateau were the 'You' people. They were of the same ethnic stock as the 'We', and in many ways their mode of life was much the same. They lived in round or rectangular huts, for instance, sunk a few feet below ground level and with the lower walls and floor lime-plastered. Their stone tool industry is also akin. But the hallmark of their material culture is a painted red pottery utterly different in character from the black pottery of the 'We' group [pp. 28–31]. Interpreting their history from the distribution of this red ware, it would seem that in China Proper they at one time spread eastward as far as northern Honan, and there is even reason to suppose that offshoots of their population may have reached south Manchuria, though this must have been well in the historical period in north China. Whether they came into collision with the 'We' people there is no means of knowing. But the later stages of the painted pottery tradition are found far away to the west, in Kansu; and the overall picture is of a cultural invasion on the part of the 'You' people, followed by a withdrawal.

col. 5

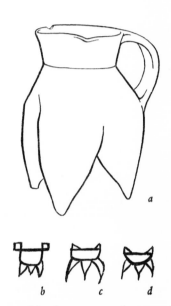

1 *a* prehistoric pottery vessel excavated by Andersson; *b–d* oracle-bone graphs, apparently showing the same type of vessel and equated with the modern character for *li,* 'tripod'

This theory of ebb and flow between Plateau and Plain has been further elaborated by Fu Ssŭ-nien. He points out that traditions concerning the alleged first Chinese dynasty, the Hsia, seem to indicate that it originated in the Plateau region. Its successor, the Shang, is associated with the Plain. The third dynasty, the Chou, had its origin in the west. Half-way through its course the royal house moved east, and from 771 BC onwards took up residence in central Honan. The next rulers of north China, the Ch'in, also came from the west. The successful rebellion that overturned the Ch'in Empire began in the east, in Anhwei and Kiangsu. The Han dynasty had its first capital in the west, and then, half-way through, shifted east as the Chou had done. It is significant that the two great military conquests of pre-Han China, the Chou and the Ch'in, were made by people of western China, and were directed eastwards.

*

In the first edition of this book I introduced readers to an enigmatic creature called *Giganto-pithecus* ('Giant Ape'), whose existence depended on the testimony of three huge molar teeth found in 1935 and 1939 in Hong Kong druggists' shops. The teeth were said to have come from Kwangsi province on the Chinese mainland, and were provisionally assigned to the Lower Pleistocene period. In September 1956 a complete jawbone of a female *Gigantopithe-cus* was recovered from a cave-site in the Lêng-chai Hills of Liu-ch'êng district, Kwangsi, thus confirming the supposed provenance.

Subsequent excavation by Dr P'ei Wên-chung[2] brought to light abundant fossil remains of the animals on which *Gigantopithecus* fed. According to Dr P'ei he was, emphatically, an ape; the tentative name *Gigantothropus* ('Giant Man'), first proposed in 1945 by the anthropologist Franz Weidenreich, must therefore be dropped. At the same time certain features of the jawbone and of the dentition, as well as the fact that the Kwangsi ape was to some extent a meat-eater and not exclusively a vegetarian, as are modern great apes, suggest that he was more closely related to the true hominids than they. Possibly his ancestors were derived from a common stock which they shared with man, not long before the appearance of the first true hominids in the Far East. The individuals whose remains we possess were, in fact, contemporaneous with the first known tool-using hominid of eastern Asia, Peking Man, and lived in the Middle Pleistocene period about 600,000 to 400,000 years ago.

*

In 1918 the Swedish geologist J. G. Andersson visited a Pleistocene cave-site near the village of Chou-k'ou-tien, some 25 miles south-west of Peking, and three years later located neolithic remains at Yang-shao-ts'un in western Honan province.[3] Since then, with increasing momentum, archaeologists have unearthed skeletal and other material remains of prehistoric man from almost every province of China and its environs, corresponding to the chronological and typological phases known as Paleolithic, Mesolithic, and Neolithic.

Excavations at Chou-k'ou-tien (Locality 1), beginning in 1927, had by 1939 brought to light skeletal remains of some forty individuals of a Middle Pleistocene hominid called Peking Man, *Sinanthropus pekinensis*, who lived on the North China Plain about half a million years ago, and who is the oldest certified tool-using man so far discovered, except perhaps those recently reported from East Africa.

He stood about 5 feet 2 inches high. He had the use of fire for cooking, an archaic stone industry comprising flakes and crude cores, and possibly some primitive form of articulate speech. He ate hackberries and wild grains, and the meat of animals; sometimes also he ate human flesh.

Perhaps not long after the disappearance of Peking Man, perhaps during his lifetime, another Middle Pleistocene hominid lived in north China, whose skeletal remains are represented by one lower molar tooth and two upper incisors found in 1954 at a site near Ting-ts'un in the Hsiang-fên district of Shansi province. The incisors have a characteristic 'shovel-shape' formation on the inner face which they share with those of Peking Man and *Pithecanthropus*, and for that matter with those of the historical Chinese race also; the flake industry is more advanced than that associated with the Peking Man of Chou-k'ou-tien (Locality 1), and includes a greater variety of types. It is comparable with a series excavated at Chou-k'ou-tien (Locality 15) between 1934-5, and may date from about 200,000 years ago; that is, before the period of deposition of the 'yellow earth' or *loess* in north China. The Ting-ts'un remains were found in a gravel bed lying directly under the *loess*.

'Yellow earth', which the Chinese call *huang t'u*, is a consolidated eolian dust blown out of Inner Asia by strong north-westerly winds during the Upper Pleistocene period, perhaps between 150,000 and 20,000 years ago. Over much of north-west China it covers the land surface like a blanket, its depth varying between fifty and three or four hundred feet.

Traces of human life in China during the period of *loess* formation, and in the areas where this took place, are at best sporadic. In 1923-4 Fathers Licent and Teilhard de Chardin discovered a cultural stratum almost at the bottom of the *loess*, some forty feet below the actual surface, at a place called Shui-tung-k'ou on the western edge of the Ordos Desert near the east bank of the Yellow River and opposite the provincial capital of Ninghsia. The flake industry, had it been found in Europe, would have been diagnosed as of Mousterian type –

1 *Human head with painted mask, perhaps that of a shaman, and possibly serving as the lid of a mortuary urn; fine polished earthenware painted in slip pigments. Probably from Pan-shan, T'ao river valley, Kansu. Middle Yang-shao Culture (c. 2000–1500 BC). An* appliqué *pottery snake runs up the back of the head and appears on the crown. This is perhaps the same order of being as appears on the Pan-p'o bowl of figure 2. In particular they seem to share the remarkable collar or 'ruff' with serrated border, seen in perspective in the Pan-p'o version. Height: 5 7/8 in. Ostasiatiska Museet, Stockholm.*

2 Funerary urn with a tall neck, t'an, fine polished earthenware painted in slip pigments. From Pan-shan, T'ao river valley, Kan-su. Middle Yang-shao Culture (c. 2000–1500 BC). Height: 15 $^{15}/_{16}$ in. Ostasiatiska Museet, Stockholm.

3 Bowl on tall flared stem, tou, fine dark brown burnished earthenware. From Yang-shao-ts'un, western Honan. Lung-shan Culture (c. 1700–1300 BC). This tou represents the pottery prototype of the corresponding bronze vessel-class [see figure 11]. Its presence on the Yang-shao site, together with other Lung-shan pottery remains, shows a western advance of the culture from its home in Shantung province. Height: 8 $^2/_3$ in. Ostasiatiska Museet, Stockholm.

4 *Bowl*, kang, *with wide mouth, high collar, and high shoulder; fine red earthenware with a lustrous black slip. From Yang-shao-ts'un, western Honan. Lung-shan Culture (c. 1700–1300 BC). Perhaps this might be represented as a successful attempt to imitate the characteristic Lung-shan fabric. Height:* 4³/₈ *in.; greatest diameter:* 9⁷/₁₆ *in. Ostasiatiska Museet, Stockholm.*

5 *Tripod vessel*, li, *with single side-handle. From Ssŭ-wa, T'ao river valley, Kansu. Late Yang-shao Culture (c. 1500–1000 BC). Penetration of the* li *into this remote part of north-west China suggests that Ssŭ-wa is contemporary with the early Bronze Age in eastern China. Height:* 3³/₄ *in. Ostasiatiska Museet, Stockholm.*

that associated with Neanderthaloid Man. It can be ascribed to the Middle Paleolithic period, and its approximate age may be about 50,000 years. No skeletal remains were found.

In places where the accumulation of *loess* was impeded, or temporarily halted, conditions more benign to human life prevailed. So, in the canyon of the Sjarra-osso-gol, a river flowing along the southern edge of the Ordos Desert, and a natural oasis in a sea of sand, were found not only flakes of the Shui-tung-k'ou type, but, mingled with them, tiny cores from which microliths had been struck. In Europe such tools would not be dated earlier than the Magdalenian. We stand here on the vague boundary between Upper Paleolithic and Mesolithic; but it is doubtful whether this cultural frontier was crossed in north-west China. The cold and dessicating wind, the engulfing clouds of dust blowing over the Plateau, must have made it quite unfit for continuous human habitation, and we may perhaps picture north-west China at the end of the loessic phase as a lunar landscape, over which scarcely a living thing moved.

Meanwhile in north-east China human life was still possible, and in the Upper Cave at Chou-k'ou-tien we have evidence of an Upper Paleolithic culture, discovered in 1930. The skeletal remains are those of modern man, but, it has been claimed, of no fewer than three different types – Mongoloid, Melanesoid, and Eskimoid. As well as stone tools, objects in bone such as pendants and a needle were found (this last indicating tailored clothes). A bevy of perforated ornaments included marine shells, fish-bones, teeth of deer and fox, and pebbles that had been stained red with haematite. Haematitic powder was also found sprinkled on and around the skeletal remains. This constellation is reminiscent in every detail of the Cro-Magnon burials in the Grimaldi caves of south-east France. Indeed, one authority professes to see a resemblance between the Upper Cave old man's skull – that dubbed Mongoloid – and the classical 'Old Man's' skull of Cro-Magnon.[4] The date of Upper Cave Man may be about 25,000 years ago, perhaps less.

The peri-Gobi placenta

It is most unwise to generalize on the basis of the meagre facts that constitute our total knowledge of Chinese prehistory – several reputations have been damaged by doing so. The fact remains that we cannot so far point to any indisputable traces of human settlement in north China between about 25,000 and 4,500 years ago, a blank in the archaeological record which Andersson called the 'Neolithic hiatus'. And the generalization I am attempting is that the Late Neolithic society that followed this hiatus, which was the first in China to produce objects recognizable for their aesthetic appeal, had its cultural antecedents largely outside the area in which we discover it today. The Ordos finds do not give us the impression of an indigenous high culture in China at the end of the Paleolithic period. We wait, so far in vain, for any revelation of an art of prehistoric cave-painting in north China[5]; nor are there any signs of an indigenous Mesolithic culture, or of a transitional phase in which Mesolithic and Early Neolithic ingredients are mixed, or of a phase containing exclusively Early Neolithic elements.

On the other hand, this smooth development *can* be traced at sites in the peri-Gobi region, especially those around Lake Baikal, in the upper Yenessei valley, in northern Mongolia, and in northern Manchuria. Not only do these sites represent all the missing cultural stages between the Upper Paleolithic and the Late Neolithic, but, more significantly, the earlier sites are more remote from north China and the later sites nearer, which suggests a movement of population stretching towards the North China Plain from the direction of northern Mongolia and northern Manchuria; but particularly, perhaps, from northern Manchuria.

The four sites which we may use to illustrate this cultural graduation are as follows:

1. Djalai-nor (*c*. 6,000 BC)
2. Ang-ang-hsi (*c*. 5,000 BC)
3. Lin-hsi (*c*. 4,000 BC)
4. Hung-shan-hou (*c*. 2,500 BC)

Djalai-nor is in Inner Mongolia, about 650 miles east of Lake Baikal; Ang-ang-hsi is 300 miles south-east of Djalai-nor in northern Manchuria; Lin-hsi is some 500 miles south-west of Ang-ang-hsi in central Manchuria; and Hung-shan-hou is 150 miles south-east of Lin-hsi in south Manchuria. The total distance from north to south between the four sites is about 550 miles.

At Djalai-nor we find a microlithic industry similar to those scattered round the southern shores of Lake Baikal, whose upper age limit has been estimated to be about 8,000 years. The characteristic tool is the elongated sickle of bone or wood, in which is set a row of triangular microliths acting as the cutting edge. No pottery is present.

At Ang-ang-hsi we again find microliths and the composite sickle, and also bone har-poons strikingly like those of the mesolithic Maglemosian industry of northern Europe, dated between about 6,800 and 5,000 BC. Like the mesolithic inhabitants of Djalai-nor and Lake Baikal, the Ang-ang-hsi people were dune- and lake-dwellers who hunted, and fished, and gathered food-plants. But two new elements in their culture serve to mark the beginning of the Early Neolithic phase in north Manchuria. For the first time, polished stone adzes are found, as well as abundant remains of a coarse, hand-made pottery bearing incised geo-metrical ornament.

The third site, Lin-hsi, also yielded microliths, yet marks a further cultural advance. Large numbers of polished mealing-stones were recovered, demonstrating a regular reliance on grain harvesting unknown at either Ang-ang-hsi or Djalai-nor. The pottery, too, is far superior to that of Ang-ang-hsi. It includes a fine, grey-bodied ware ornamented with stamped geo-metrical patterns; much of it, remarkably, is turned on the wheel.

Lastly at Hung-shan-hou we meet with an entirely new feature, one that links this site with the Late Neolithic culture of north-central and north-west China. I refer to a fine red pottery bearing traces of painting and closely resembling the painted pottery that so excited Andersson when he first came across it at Yang-shao village in western Honan. Hung-shan-hou may therefore represent the critical stage of cultural contact between Manchuria and north China, possibly with some movement of population into the Yellow River valley, half-way through the third millennium BC. As I now see it, the effect of this infusion was to reanimate the exhausted communities that had survived the loessic deluge in north China, thereby laying the foundations of the first recognizable Chinese society and civilization.

Neolithic North China: the Yang-shao Culture

pls 1–10
col. 1, 2, 5 Excavation in north China has revealed two Late Neolithic cultures there, the one located mainly on the Plateau, the other on the Plain. The former is characterized by a fine-bodied, high-fired red ware of which a proportion – rarely more than ten per cent – is handsomely decorated with hand-painted designs of matchless quality, the latter by a black pottery no less distinguished for beauty of form and manufacture. Falling into line with most modern scholars, particularly the Chinese, I shall henceforward refer to the former as the Yang-shao Culture, and to the latter as the Lung-shan Culture. The Yang-shao Culture was first located by Andersson at Yang-shao-ts'un in 1921; the Lung-shan Culture by Wu Gin-ting

at a site called Ch'êng-tzǔ-yai near Lung-shan in Shantung in 1928.[6] The question as to which preceded which is partly answered by excavation at Hou-kang in northern Honan, a site close by the remains of a late Shang capital at Hsiao-t'un [p. 73]. Three layers were uncovered: the lowest layer (Hou-kang 1) contained only red ware; the middle layer (Hou-kang 2) contained only black; and the top layer (Hou-kang 3) yielded a coarse, gritty, grey ware contemporary with the nearby Shang site. Thus in this centrally situated region the Yang-shao Culture preceded the Lung-shan.

Indeed Hou-kang 1 apparently represents the earliest phase of the Yang-shao Culture, and perhaps its beginnings are not later than about 2,500 BC. Vessel-shapes are few, a wide-mouthed shallow bowl of attractive form being most common. The decoration, too, is simple, and usually consists of groups of vertical or oblique stripes laid in darker red pigment on the light red body, and running down from the mouthrim to a level a little below the high shoulder.

pl. 1

*

The immensely rich Middle Phase of the Yang-shao Culture has been dated by Andersson to a period from about 2,200 to 1,700 BC. Two regional aspects can be differentiated, one belonging to Honan, Shensi and Shansi, the other to Kansu. They are separated geographically by the watershed dividing the valleys of the Wei river in Shensi and the T'ao in Kansu. Within the former region is Pan-p'o, in south Shensi. The site is that of an important village two and a half acres in extent. It was excavated in 1954, and is today completely roofed-in by a site museum.[7] The magnitude of Pan-p'o, and the wealth of information it provides on the mode of life of its inhabitants, is winning for it a fame exceeding that of Yang-shao itself, but the two are in fact contemporary and their painted potteries closely related. As at Hou-kang 1, bowls and basins for use in the home predominate, but the painted geometrical patterns are a little more enterprising, and include broad bands, triangles, cross-hatching, circular spots, and concentric circles. Several of the Pan-p'o bowls, but none of those from Yang-shao, are also embellished with queer human masks and a fish motif painted on the inside surface. Possibly we may recognize in the domestic painted pottery of Ma-chia-yao a westward extension of this eastern tradition, notwithstanding it lies within the Kansu zone.

2 Early Yang-shao painted bowl (*c.* 2,500 BC) excavated at Pan-p'o, Shensi province. Note the geometrical mask, with ear ornaments in the form of fish that appear to be whispering into the ears. Note also the 'convict stripe' motif on the rim (*cf.* plate 7)

pl. 2

The Kansu aspect of the Middle Yang-shao Culture constitutes a brilliant episode in the history of Chinese art, and the culmination of the entire painted pottery tradition. Its most celebrated site is the cemetery at Pan-shan on the west bank of the T'ao river, 44 miles south of Lanchow, the provincial capital. Here, in 1923, hundreds of unbroken funerary urns of impressive form were unearthed, and brought for sale to Andersson in Lanchow. Today these urns are to be found in museums all over the world, and few critics, I imagine, would oppose the proposition that they are the finest Neolithic pottery the world has ever seen. They were made by the method of ringing, being trimmed on a slow wheel or turntable in the final stages of manufacture; and they are very thinly potted for their size. The shape is full and 'bursting', and the painted design is disposed as a mantle round the upper part of the pot. It may take the form of a series of horizontal plain bands, zigzag bands, festoons, or rows of small circles; or of four or five large circles, or rhombuses, or large interlocking spirals that seem to chase each other endlessly round the pot. The fields are filled with checker-patterns, cross-hatching, oblique lines, 'railway-lines', and 'wheel-spokes'; and all these elements appear in countless combinations, so that the décor of every pot is unique. The bands and lines, boldly applied on the prepared surface of the pot, show signs of modulation: They were, as a general rule, drawn by hand with a brush; though Wu Gin-ting thought some of the

pls 3–8, col. 2

designs were produced by means of a stencil. The combination of black and purplish-brown colour, derived from iron and manganese pigments, is most restful and very pleasing to the modern eye.

pls 6–7 The Ma-ch'ang ware takes its name from a site not actually in Kansu, although lying very close to its western border near Sining, the provincial capital of Chinghai. It seems, however, to have been well distributed along the *loess* terraces of the upper Yellow River in Chinghai *pl. 8* and Kansu – for instance at the important burial site of Pai-tao-kou near Lanchow, excavated in 1954. The fabric of Ma-ch'ang pottery is not light red but a pale grey, and it is coarser in texture than Pan-shan ware. There is, moreover, a perceptible slackening of form; the change of direction at the shoulder is more gradual, the shoulder itself being lower and more relaxed. The design is less tightly organized, and indeed less carefully drawn, and the whole presentation is more sophisticated than that made by the Pan-shan ware. On the evidence of ceramic form we might be inclined to date Ma-ch'ang later than Pan-shan, and Andersson in fact established a Ma-ch'ang stage between 1700 and 1300 BC. All these dates are in any case conjectural, and Chêng Tê-k'un, whose division of the Yang-shao Culture into three Phases we are adopting here, does not distinguish between Pan-shan and Ma-ch'ang as far as their dates are concerned.[8]

*

The Late Yang-shao Culture is a continuation of the Kansu aspect of the Middle Yang-shao. At Hsin-tien, on the east bank of the T'ao river below Pan-shan, a remarkable type of painted ware was found by Andersson in a thin stratum overlying typical Middle Yang-shao remains. Hsin-tien pottery is therefore later than that of Pan-shan or Ma-ch'ang, and Andersson considered that it represented a stage in the Culture beginning about 1300 BC and ending around 1000 BC. Chêng Tê-k'un puts its beginnings at 1500 BC, perhaps a little on the early side.

Technically Hsin-tien ware shows increasing signs of the degeneration at which we hinted *pl. 9* in the case of Ma-ch'ang. The form nevertheless is exquisite, and altogether unexpected. Urns have tall necks with a concave profile, and the change of direction at the shoulder is sharp; shoulder and mouthrim are usually connected by a pair of prominent, elongated side-handles, balancing the concavity of the neck. Bowls are shallow, with wide mouths and smaller side-handles, but with the same sharply carinated shoulder. The design is sober. Often the upper part of the neck is decorated with a continuous angular meander, while the lower part has two or more pairs of joined upturned hooks – the so-called 'wild sheep's horns' motif. In the interstices tiny figures are sometimes found, looking remarkably like certain archaic Chinese pictograms, as Chêng Tê-k'un observes. The form-language of these Hsin-tien pots, determined by their shape and ornamentation, is severe, elegaic.

After the Hsin-tien stage, the Late Yang-shao Culture disintegrates somewhat, due to intrusion of elements belonging to the historical (Shang) culture as typified by the grey ware of Hou-kang 3 [p. 29]. One such mixed site is Ch'i-chia-p'ing in the T'ao river valley, which was thought by Andersson to be earlier than the Middle Yang-shao Phase, and was represented by him as the oldest stage of the Yang-shao Culture. It has now been conclusively shown to be later than the Middle Phase, and is dated by Chêng Tê-k'un as beginning about 1500 BC. One fine vessel-type is a tall pitcher of grey ware, with a vaulted cover bearing *pl. 18* a cylindrical spout and forming an integral part of the vessel. We are instantly reminded of a *col. 15* version of the bronze vessel called *ho* [p. 92] said to have come from a royal tomb of the Shang dynasty, and there is little doubt but that Ch'i-chia-p'ing is contemporary with the early historical period in north-central China, and was perhaps flourishing around 1000 BC. We are here situated not far from the Chou heartland, whence they launched their successful attack on the Shang overlordship at the end of the second millennium BC.

Ch'i-chia-p'ing may thus be the remnants of an early Chou settlement, as also may be Ssŭ-wa, a site directly opposite Ch'i-chia-p'ing on the east bank of the T'ao river. Ssŭ-wa is characterized by the presence of the *li* tripod, a vessel commonly associated with the grey pottery of northern Honan as found at Hou-kang 3, Hsiao-t'un, and other places all of which are contemporary around 1300 BC; it is unknown in the Early and Middle Yang-shao Culture. The *li* as a ceramic form reached Ssŭ-wa from the east, therefore, probably not long before 1000 BC.

pl. 10
col. 5

*

A resemblance between the painted pottery of the Yang-shao Culture and certain neolithic wares of the Near East and eastern Europe has often been commented on. The connexion least likely to be imaginary is that between the Middle Yang-shao potteries of Kansu (Pan-shan and Ma-ch'ang) and those of the Tripolye Culture of the southern Ukraine, also a loessic area. I shall not expatiate on these parallels, but merely record that most modern authorities are inclined to believe that a connexion between the two centres *did* exist, and that China was probably the recipient of the painted pottery tradition, in however embryonic a form it may first have arrived. I share the view of Watson, namely that the 'small beginnings of the painted pottery tradition may have been inspired from the West', but that its masterly elaboration, as seen at its climax in the Middle Yang-shao, was a purely Chinese achievement, in conception as in execution.[9]

Neolithic North China: the Lung-shan Culture

It has also been claimed that the black pottery of the Lung-shan Culture may in the first instance have been an importation from western Asia, typified by the black pottery of Tepe Hissar in Iran; and that knowledge of its manufacture may have entered north China via Manchuria in the third millennium BC, perhaps as a result of immigration.[10] It will be seen that this view accords with the theory of cultural infiltration developed on pages 27 and 28.

pls 17, 19, 20
col. 3, 4

We have seen that at Hou-kang, near the late Shang capital, a Lung-shan stage preceded the historical phase marked by presence of coarse grey pottery. Since this latter phase opened about 1300 BC, and since a time interval separated it from the preceding Lung-shan stage, we may perhaps conclude that the Lung-shan occupation at Hou-kang ended about 1500 BC. This estimate is reinforced by the stratification at Chêng-chou, the newly revealed Bronze Age site in northern Honan [p. 74]. The Shang occupation at Chêng-chou probably lasted from about 1500 to 1300 BC, and the Lung-shan remains are found immediately below the earliest traces of the Shang. At this point the culture may have been in existence for as long as a thousand years.

Lung-shan is essentially a culture of the Plain, of the 'We' people, to use Li Chi's concept, as opposed to the 'You' of the Yang-shao Culture and the Plateau. It has been located as far north as the Liaotung Peninsula of south Manchuria, and as far south as Chekiang; but its heartland seems to have been Shantung.

Very little can be asserted about the sequence of Lung-shan sites. It has been suggested that one called Liang-ch'êng-chên on the Shantung coast may represent the culture in its earliest and purest form, in which the fine polished black pottery predominates over all other wares. Ch'êng-tzŭ-yai, the type site, may represent a middle stage, in which the proportion of grey pottery has increased to as much as 34 per cent. Hou-kang 2 may represent a late stage, in which the typical black pottery has become comparatively rare.

Several of the Lung-shan pottery shapes are said to be derived from those found at Tepe Hissar and other western Asian sites, among them being a dish on a tall foot, the bronze version of which is called *tou*.[11] It is also said that the *li* tripod is rare at Liang-ch'êng-chên, more frequent at Ch'êng-tzǔ-yai, and takes definite shape at Hou-kang 2.

In spite of these admittedly vague indications, we have only to glance at a set of outline drawings of these crisp, metallic-looking pots, to see immediately that they are the true precursors of the great bronze vessel-classes to be discussed in chapter three. We can feel safe in saying that the bronze classes known as *ting*, *li*, *hsien*, *tou*, *p'an*, and *chia*, all originated in the Lung-shan Culture; and when we take into consideration other items in its material culture which it shares with that of the historic Shang, we shall not hesitate to claim it as the immediate ancestor of the Chinese Bronze Age.

pls 19, 20   The important Lung-shan site at Liang-chu in Chekiang, excavated in 1936 and again in 1954–5, offers a wide range of bronze vessel-shapes executed in the typical black pottery of this culture. In addition to those already mentioned, they include possible ancestors of the *hu* and *tsun* vases and the *kuei* food container. It is however probable that Liang-chu represents a survival of Neolithic culture in this region contemporary with the historical Shang period in northern Honan, and that the vessel-shapes are derived from those of bronze vessels.

*

The black pottery of the Lung-shan Culture is a superb, perfectionist ware, often seeming to express a hankering for the ultimate regularity of form we expect to find in a machine-tooled article. As Chêng Tê-k'un observes, small-scale models of vessels, as well as rattles and toys, reveal the potter's determination to explore fully the plastic possibilities of his materials. The finest variety is jet black, and is burnished to a fine gloss at some stage of its manufacture so that it somewhat resembles Athenian black ware of the fifth–fourth centuries BC. It is wheel-turned, high-fired, and of the utmost delicacy, some of the sherds being no more than a millimetre thick. Surface decoration is confined mainly to horizontal ribs and lines, and the aesthetic appeal of this ware resides largely in the quality of its fabric and the compelling beauty of its forms.

THE EARLY AND MIDDLE YANG-SHAO CULTURE

1 Bowl, *po*, of fine brick-red polished earthenware painted in dark red slip pigment. From Hou-kang, northern Honan. Early Yang-shao Culture (*c*.2500–2000 BC). This bowl comes from the lowest level at Hou-kang (Hou-kang I), and belongs to the earliest known phase of the Yang-shao Culture [see p. 29]. Height: 4 in., diameter: 14 in. Institute of Archaeology of the Academy of Sciences, Peking.

2 Basin, *p'an*, of fine buff earthenware painted in black slip pigment. From Ma-chia-yao, T'ao river valley, Kansu. Middle Yang-shao Culture (*c*.2000–1500 BC). Similar zoomorphic motifs are common on Ma-chia-yao pots, which are all domestic. This motif Andersson called the 'swimming toad' [see p. 29]. Diameter: 12 ¹/₂ in. Ostasiatiska Museet, Stockholm.

3 Jug of fine brick-red polished earthenware painted in black and purplish-brown slip pigments. From Pan-shan, T'ao river valley, Kansu. Middle Yang-shao Culture (*c*. 2000–1500 BC). The pattern on the neck below the cross-hatching is found only on funerary ware. Height: 6 3/8 in. Ostasiatiska Museet, Stockholm.

4 Funerary urn with tall neck, *t'an,* of fine brick-red polished earthenware with cross-hatched gourd-pattern painted in black and purplish-brown slip pigments. From Pan-shan, T'ao river valley, Kansu. Middle Yang-shao Culture (*c*. 2000–1500 BC). Height: 14 9/16 in. Ostasiatiska Museet, Stockholm.

from left to right

7 Funerary urn, *kuan,* fine greyish-pink polished earthenware painted in black and purplish-brown slip pigments on a white ground. From Ma-ch'ang, Lo-tu-hsien, Chinghai. Middle Yang-shao Culture (*c*. 2000–1500 BC). Note the more relaxed form of Ma-ch'ang types compared with that of Pan-shan. The design is anthropomorphic and apparently related to the 'convict stripe' on the rim of the Pan-p'o bowl of figure 2. Height: 8 3/8 in. Ostasiatiska Museet, Stockholm.

8 Funerary urn, *kuan,* fine brick-red earthenware painted in black and purplish-brown slip pigments, of Ma-ch'ang type. From Pai-tao-kou-p'ing near Lan-chou, Kansu. Middle Yang-shao Culture (*c*. 2000–1500 BC). Height: 8 11/16 in. Institute of Archaeology of the Academy of Sciences, Peking.

9 Two-handled urn, coarse greyish-yellow earthenware boldly painted in black slip pigment with an angular meander on the neck and the 'wild sheep's horns' motif on the shoulder. From Hsin-tien, T'ao river valley, Kansu. Late Yang-shao Culture (*c*. 1500–1000 BC). The two motifs presage the squared spiral and 'hook and volute' of bronze décor, and may imply contact with the Shang civilization. The small animals seem to be cows [see p. 30]. Height: 11 3/4 in. Ostasiatiska Museet, Stockholm.

5 Funerary urn, *kuan*, of fine brick-red polished earth-enware with gourd-pattern painted in black and pur-plish-brown slip pigments. From Pan-shan, T'ao river valley, Kansu. Middle Yang-shao Culture (*c.* 2000–1500 BC). Height: 11 ¹³/₁₆ in. British Museum.

6 Funerary urn, fine brick-red polished earthenware painted in black and purplish-brown slip pigments. From Ma-ch'ang, Lo-tu-hsien, Chinghai. Middle Yang-shao Culture (*c.* 2000–1500 BC). Despite its sophistication, the urn represents a decline from the perfectionist stan-dard of Pan-shan. Height: 5 ⅝ in. Ostasiatiska Museet, Stockholm.

10 Amphora, oval in section and with what Andersson called a 'saddle-shaped' mouth; coarse red earthenware freely sketched with animal and geometrical human figures. From Ssŭ-wa, T'ao river valley, Kansu. Late Yang-shao Culture (*c.* 1500–1000 BC) [see p. 31 and col. 5]. Height: 7 1/4 in. British Museum.

11 Bowl, *wan,* red earthenware with an incised *t'ao-t'ieh* mask, visible on this side. From Shih-chia-ho, T'ien-mên-hsien, Hupeh. This is the only known occurrence of the *t'ao-t'ieh* motif in a prehistoric context and perhaps also its earliest recorded appearance in Chinese art. The date of the site, which contains mixed cultural elements, is conjectural but is probably close to the early Shang period. Height: 2 1/16 in. Institute of Archaeology of the Academy of Sciences, Peking.

12 (right) Water vessel, *lei,* fine white kaolinic earthenware. From An-yang, Honan. Shang dynasty (*c.* 1500–1027 BC) [see pp. 90 and 242]. Height: 13 in. Freer Gallery of Art, Washington.

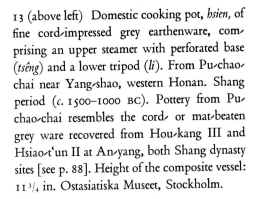

SHANG PERIOD: SOME PROTOTYPES FOR BRONZE VESSELS

13 (above left) Domestic cooking pot, *hsien,* of fine cord-impressed grey earthenware, comprising an upper steamer with perforated base (*tsêng*) and a lower tripod (*li*). From Pu-chao-chai near Yang-shao, western Honan. Shang period (*c.* 1500–1000 BC). Pottery from Pu-chao-chai resembles the cord- or mat-beaten grey ware recovered from Hou-kang III and Hsiao-t'un II at An-yang, both Shang dynasty sites [see p. 88]. Height of the composite vessel: 11 3/4 in. Ostasiatiska Museet, Stockholm.

14 (centre) Steamer, *hsien,* fine grey earthenware moulded in one piece. Said to have come from Manchuria (perhaps from the Liaotung Peninsula). Second half of first millennium BC. A provincial Neolithic survival into historical times. Height: 11 3/4 in. Museum of Science, Buffalo.

15 (below left) Amphora cup, fine grey earthenware. From Pu-chao-chai, near Yang-shao, Honan. Shang period (*c.* 1500–1000 BC). This exquisite shape, strangely like that of the Greek *cantharus,* was apparently never reproduced in bronze. Height: 2 5/8 in. Ostasiatiska Museet, Stockholm.

16 (below right) Domestic cooking pot, *ting,* coarse grey earthenware with cord impressions. From Yang-shao-ts'un, western Honan. Shang period (*c.* 1500–1000 BC) [see p. 86]. Height: 7.9 in. Ostasiatiska Museet, Stockholm.

17 (centre) Stem-cup of highly polished fine black burnished earthenware. Excavated at An-ch'iu-hsien, Shantung. Lung-shan Culture (*c.* 1500 BC). A strikingly beautiful and original ceramic form, but not one reproduced in bronze. Height: *c.* 8 in. The Museum of Chinese History, Peking.

18 (above right) Ewer, *ho,* of fine dark grey earthenware, with domed lid and spout (broken). From Ch'i-chia-p'ing, T'ao river valley, Kansu (*c.* 1500–1000 BC). This lovely ceramic form demonstrates contact with the Shang civilization of eastern China [see p. 92 and col. 15]. Height with spout: 10 ⁹/₁₆ in. Ost-asiatiska Museet, Stockholm.

19 (below left) Food vessel, *kuei,* fine black burnished earthenware. From Liang-chu, Hangchou, Chekiang. Liang-chu, excavated in 1955, is the southernmost site of the Lung-shan Culture so far located [see p. 88]. Height: 4 ¹/₄ in. Institute of Archaeology of the Academy of Sciences, Peking.

20 (below right) Bowl on a tall flared stem, *tou,* of fine burnished black earthenware. From Liang-chu, Hangchou, Chekiang. Late Lung-shan Culture (*c.* 1500–1300 BC) [see p. 88]. Height: 5 ³/₄ in. Institute of Archaeology of the Academy of Sciences, Peking.

THE LUNG-SHAN CULTURE:
MORE PROTOTYPES OF
BRONZE VESSELS

21 Amphora, dark grey burnished earthenware. From Li-fan, Szechwan. Fifth to first centuries BC. This most eloquent pot still speaks the form-language of Hsin-tien and Ch'i-chia-p'ing, perhaps a thousand years antecedent, while by an unaccountable parallelism resembling the work of Mycenean goldsmiths. It would seem that the type, if not this very vessel, was reproduced in bronze in China, for Koop (1924) illustrates a bronze vessel in the Musée Cernuschi which at a glance could easily be mis-taken for this pot, the bronze omitting only the double hatched band below the mouthrim. Koop thought the bronze must date from about the Sung period, but I personally see no reason why it should not be more or less contemporary with the pot. Height: 11 3/8 in. British Museum.

II JADE: THE NEOLITHIC PERIOD

An element in Neolithic Chinese Culture

The first-century AD writer Yüan K'ang conceived that the material culture of China had passed through four historical stages, the first characterized by use of stone for making weapons, the next of jade, the next of copper, and the last of iron.[1] This proposition, so ancient in date, amazingly anticipates the concept of the Three Ages of Man first put forward by C. J. Thomsen in 1836, and may even contain the germ of the idea of a division of the Stone Age into two successive stages, Paleolithic and Neolithic. For when Yüan K'ang contrasted *shih*, 'stone', with *yü*, 'jade', he clearly meant to indicate no more than a phenomenal difference between them – or rather between jade and most other stones, since of course jade *is* stone, as he very well knew. He may, in other words, have been surmising a distant time when weapons were made of stone by the method of flaking, and presented a crude, irregular surface, and a nearer time when they came to be made by other lithic techniques, and presented a neat, smooth, and sometimes highly lustrous surface. Such objects he would habitually call *yü*.

According to Yüan K'ang it was during the reign of the legendary Huang Ti, the Yellow Emperor, that weapons were first made of jade. Huang Ti is traditionally supposed to have ruled China about the middle of the third millennium BC. So here is an early Chinese estimate, if our inferences are correct, of the antiquity of their Neolithic Age. It is startlingly close to that proposed by modern archaeologists.

The Chinese began to use jade late in the Neolithic period and they have used it ever since; so that people have come to think of jade as a beautiful stone that somehow embodies the impalpable qualities of Chinese civilization, its durability, venerability, *mystique*. Here is Andersson's testimony: 'Upon now turning to the use of jade in prehistoric China I feel it my duty to call attention to the fact that the penchant for, not to say the worship of jade, the substance itself, seems to have formed a bond that links prehistoric and dynastic China together, differentiating the Chinese race from the rest of mankind.'[2]

Jade-carving might be called the neolithic craft *par excellence*, for of all stones that can be worked to suit the needs of man it is the most intractable; yet jade-carvings from Neolithic contexts in China are matched in technical and artistic accomplishment only by some of the contemporary pottery. More significant from the technological point of view is the fact that fresh jade is so hard that it can be cut only by one or other of the few stones harder than itself. Steel makes no impression on it, provided it is in fresh condition. In spite of the fact, therefore, that metal tools were probably being used early in the Bronze Age as means by which pastes containing the abrasive stone were brought into frictional contact with the jade, and that rotary tools of iron may have come into use as early as the sixth or fifth century BC, the ultimate contact is still between stone and stone. In this sense jade-carving is, and always has been, a lithic industry. Jade techniques and, I believe, many traditional jade-shapes emerged from a Neolithic background; and it is in association with the Neolithic period in Chinese history that I propose to discuss the craft.

The material

What, then, is 'jade'? Unfortunately this word, like the Chinese *yü*, came into being long before the time of mineralogical analysis, with the result that stones of widely differing physical structure and chemical composition have been called jade.[3] Even among mineralogists today there is no exact agreement as to how it should be defined. Quintessential jade is nephrite, what Chinese today call *chên yü*, 'true jade', as opposed to *fu yü* or 'false jade', which would include serpentines, pyrophyllite, and other hard stones. On the other hand, the substance best known to the West as jade – the translucent emerald- or dark-green stone commonly worked into articles of jewellery – is *not* nephrite, but jadeite. Although superficially this mineral closely resembles true jade, and although the working of it is in the hands of the same Chinese lapidaries, jadeite differs from jade both in composition and microscopic appearance; there is no evidence that it was worked in China before the eighteenth century AD, and we shall not be dealing with it in this account. On the other hand, we can by no means be sure that all objects chosen for illustration here are indubitably nephrite. Very few jades, whether in museums or private collections, have been submitted to the delicate tests needed to prove their true nature. But for present purposes this does not greatly matter, since we are primarily concerned with objects normally made of jade rather than with the material itself or the methods by which it was worked. A recent account of the origin and development of Chinese jade-carving by Professor Hansford deals fully with these related topics.[4]

About AD 100 a certain Hsü Shên compiled a book destined to become one of the most influential ever written in Chinese, *Shuo wên chieh tzŭ*, or 'An Explanation of [Ancient] Figures and an Analysis of [Compound] Characters'. *Shuo wên* is an attempt to account for the structure of Chinese written characters in terms of the constructional principles upon which its author believed they were composed, and it is therefore rather a 'scriptionary' than a dictionary in our sense [p. 308]. Yet it does define words, or at least describes the things they stand for; such, for example, as the entry under the character *yü*, for jade: '*Yü* is the fairest of stones. It is endowed with five virtues. Charity is typified by its lustre, bright yet warm; rectitude by its translucency, revealing the colour and markings within; wisdom by the purity and penetrating quality of its note, when the stone is struck; courage in that it can be broken but cannot be bent; equity in that it has sharp edges which yet injure none.'[5]

Now, as we have remarked, any stone matching such a description would probably have been called *yü*. But Hsü Shên and others who wrote about jade must have been familiar enough with the sensible properties of real nephrite to reserve for it a separate category in their minds, even if, like us, they were not always able to tell it apart in practice. In other cases writers referring to *yü* could hardly have beguiled themselves or their readers into supposing that nephrite was meant. For the word soon took on a eulogistic meaning, so greatly was jade itself valued. It came to denote substances that were not precious stones, nor necessarily minerals at all. The *yü* which, when eaten in powdered form, was said to confer ceremonial purity on rulers, and the *yü* of various sorts used as medicines, whatever they may have been, could not possibly have been mistaken for true jade.

The qualities of true jade are partly described in the paragraph from *Shuo wên* quoted above. In less fanciful language, jade is ice-cold to the touch; it is translucent when cut thin; it is so hard that it cannot be scratched by steel; it emits a musical note when struck; it takes a high, oily polish. Ideally, and in its most prized form, it is white. But presence of chemical elements and compounds, especially of iron, chromium, and manganese, serves to give it a characteristic range of neutral colours; among these, various shades of green are perhaps most common.

Techniques of working jade

The difficulty in working jade is due to its extreme hardness ($6\frac{1}{2}$ on Mohs' scale). It can be cut only with stone harder than itself, such as quartz sand (7), crushed garnets ($7\frac{1}{2}$), and corundum (9). Corundum, or the artificial product carborundum, in the form of a sand thoroughly moistened with water, is generally used today. This semi-liquid abrasive is applied to the edge of the 'cutting' tool while at work, so that the material is very slowly ground through in the required direction. The movement of the tool is rotary, except in the case of saws used for trimming blocks of raw material, which are operated by either one or two men with a back-and-forth motion. Rotary tools made of steel, iron, wood, or leather, and operated by treadle lathes, include a large cutting disc, smaller cutting discs, drills, gouges, and grinding and polishing, or 'buffing', tools. Despite this extensive equipment and despite recent introduction of improved abrasives, the process is still laborious in the extreme. Hansford, who made a first-hand study of the traditional craft as practised to this day in Peking, says that a single cut through a foot-cube block, using the four-handed saw and carborundum as an abrasive, would take several weeks' work.[6]

Obviously the Neolithic worker was far less well equipped. We may assume however that his tools included saws of various sizes and some form of drill. As for the saws, almost any sort of lamina would have served; Hansford suggests that one may have been a well-known type of stone knife which crops up time and again at Neolithic sites inside and outside the Great Wall [p. 53]. This often has two or more small perforations at the back of the blade, and Andersson believes that these were means whereby the knife was 'dressed' with leather to make it more comfortable to hold.

We have just mentioned perforations. These are quite common features of early Chinese jades, and range from a few millimetres to an inch or more in diameter. A drill was, of course, used for making them. Marks of rotary action are to be seen on many, as well as evidence of drilling from both sides; for the borings do not always meet flush, and the holes are often bi-conical in section due to gradual wearing away of the soft drill head; where the perforation has been made from one side only, the hole is usually conical. Objects showing partly drilled and discarded borings have been found among prehistoric material; and in one of these, discovered by Andersson, a circular core still remains – proof that the drill was tubular. Andersson says it was a hollow bone. Hansford, on the other hand, believes that a bamboo tube was used. He has shown that drilling jade by this means is perfectly feasible, by doing so himself using ordinary builders' sand as an abrasive.

Sources of Chinese jade

Jade, as far as we know, is not native to China Proper. Hansford has painstakingly examined all the literary evidence on which rests the claim that it is, or once was; but he concludes that there is no foundation for such a belief. It has arisen through faulty identification of other stones as nephrite, and through habitual use of vague terminology. The actual source of jade *map 2* used in China is in the mountains and river valleys of Khotan and Yarkand in Chinese Turkestan, 2,000 miles or so distant from the centres of early Chinese culture.

In his report in chapter 123 of the first great Chinese history, *Shih chi* [p. 121], the explorer Chang Ch'ien notes much jade-stone in Khotan, which he visited about 125 BC. He adds that Khotanese jade was collected and transported to the Emperor, and implies that the trade was of long standing. The late Professor Haloun has given evidence to show that a traffic in jade existed between the Chinese and their neighbours to the north-west, the Yüeh-chih [p. 123], as early as the fourth century BC.[7]

Chinese Turkestan has certainly supplied the bulk of nephrite for China during the last 2,000 years, and we are bound to agree with Hansford that it probably always did. The only other source of jade that might have been known to the prehistoric Chinese is the area round Lake Baikal. Siberian jade has a rather distinctive appearance owing to the presence of small particles of black graphite embedded in the stone, which leads the Chinese to call it 'spinach jade'. Prehistoric implements made of this material have been found in Siberia near Tobolsk, Barnaul, and Yakutsk, but there is no record of its importation into China until quite recently. On the other hand, among the jades bought by Andersson in the Pan-shan hills are *pls 25, 34* a flat tablet and an annular disc reproduced here on plates 25 and 34, which look as if they might conceivably be made of Siberian jade. We must also admit the possibility that some Siberian jade may not be of the 'spinach' variety.

The beginnings of Chinese jade-carving

If now jade came thousands of miles across central Asia to reach China during prehistoric times, the question arises who brought it, and when? We have given reasons for supposing that at least some of the Neolithic cultures outside the Great Wall are earlier than those of China Proper [pp. 27–28]. The Chinese Turkestan branch of the peri-Gobi Neolithic has been examined by Bergman, who regards it as typical of the whole complex.[8] Among finds from this region he records a few polished jade axes – one or two picked up on the Lop *pl. 22* Nor desert floor by Stein and Hedin, and others purchased by Pelliot at Kucha. If these tools are contemporary with other Neolithic remains in Chinese Turkestan, as there seems no reason to doubt, then they may well represent the earliest jade-craft of the East.

Jade, the material, may thus be a local central Asiatic ingredient in the peri-Gobi culture, which, like some tool-types from the north, filtered into China late in prehistoric times. The combination of jades and painted pottery among the burial furniture at the Pan-shan cemetery may signify that knowledge of the painted pottery, and of jade-carving, reached north China through the agency of a jade-using people of Chinese Turkestan, perhaps half-way through the third millennium BC.

The symbolism of early Chinese jades

With very few exceptions the early jades of China are worked from flat slabs not more than a few millimetres thick, themselves cut either from pebbles and small boulders, or else – and this was almost certainly a later development – from quarried blocks. They fall into two main groups, the first comprising small decorative amulets in the form of beads, buttons, pendants, and plaques to be worn with or sewn on to clothing; and the second a variety of objects whose

44

use, as is generally believed, had to do with ritual and ceremonial. Most common in this group are the tablets traditionally called *kuei*. They are of many shapes, and native tradition attributes various functions to them, but generally seems to have regarded them as tokens of sovereign power and feudal rank.

The shapes of *kuei* and other ritual jades are of a sort that we would call 'abstract' were we to encounter them in contemporary art. Miss Ramsden, comparing them with the work of sculptors such as Barbara Hepworth and Brancusi, says: 'There is, at least, in all of them the same sensuous enjoyment of the material for its own sake, the same interest in its expressive possibilities as a medium, the same exquisite workmanship and austere simplicity.'[9] But we must not because of this resemblance assume that the aims of their creators were at all similar, or that their shapes should be interpreted simply as essays in 'pure form'. How, then, *are* they to be interpreted?

Before we turn to the obvious explanation, let us glance at traditional Chinese and European views on the purpose and meaning of these early jades. Towards the end of the Chou period was written the substance of a book long since known as *Chou li*, or 'Chou Rituals'.[10] This work, which is attributed by tradition to that model administrator of early Chou times, the Duke of Chou, purports to give an account of ceremonial practices as they were carried out during his day, and defines the duties of officials responsible for their upkeep. It is in fact an imaginary reconstruction, as its bias towards formal numerical categories suggests. That such books appeared late in the dynasty is simply because some of China's noblest political aspirants were then making a last despairing attempt to institute law and order at a time of anarchy and force. They therefore invoked tradition. But tradition had been broken, and the history of the early Chou period become mere hearsay. Its social and political conditions were a dim and confused memory; and pretty well the whole of its material culture, as well as that of the Shang dynasty, had been replaced. State ritual had become so corrupted and vulgarized by usurpers not entitled to practise it, that nobody knew what it was supposed to mean.

Under such conditions any systematic inquiry into the part played by traditional jade-forms in early Chou ritual, or any reasonable explanation of their shapes, was out of the question. The *Chou li* compilers invented ceremonial roles for such archaic jades as were known to them, and gave them names. Sometimes they essayed an explanation of a jade's ceremonial role in terms of its shape. More often this was left to the ingenuity of later commentators, who inherited the text but, all too frequently, not the jades described therein. The next stage in the obliteration of the jade's personality was therefore to reconstruct it in imagination, and reproduce it in the form of a drawing; this done, we are confronted with a chimera based on a commentator's interpretation of a ritualist's conception of the role played by a given jade, known to him, in a ritual that may never have been enacted. This was the tradition received by Wu Ta-ch'êng and Laufer, the scholars who fifty or more years ago began afresh the task of equating the ceremonial jades mentioned in classical literature with actual and palpable ancient Chinese jades.[11] To a large extent they succeeded; they swept away the accumulated layers of speculation, and identified many of the jades we now know by their Chinese names. But they did not venture back beyond *Chou li* to the time when the jades themselves were manufactured, and continued to cling to the *Chou li* explanation of their forms. My argument is that before we uncritically accept this principle of formal symbolism underlying jade-shapes, we should first try to discover whether some of them cannot be simply explained as imitations of authentic craft tools or weapons; and whether others may not themselves originally have been designed for actual practical use.

Jade used in imitation of tools and weapons

In his Frazer lecture given at Liverpool University in 1949, Professor Gordon Childe several times spoke of the manner in which craft tools 'made by the application of science and employed for perfectly rational ends' acquire, in primitive societies, magical properties of their own. Proof of this, he said, is that amulets in the form of miniature models of such tools – for example, the polished axe – are widely distributed in Neolithic contexts throughout the Mediterranean area from Egypt to France. The copies, by sympathetic magic, partake of the virtue of the originals.[12]

Many of the ritual jades of China, I believe, are objects of this type. That is, they were first conceived of and made in imitation of functional prototypes whose efficacy they shared. Already at Ang-ang-hsi, presumably dating from the earliest phase of the peri-Gobi Neolithic [p. 27], we find stone implements, specially selected for their fine quality, buried in fixed relation to the corpse. Substitutes made of jade, the most beautiful mineral known in the pre-metal era, and whose value was heightened by rarity and by costs of transport and manufacture, would, I believe, have been thought specially efficacious for ritual and burial purposes. On this assumption the bulk of early Chinese jades, though not necessarily all, may never have been intended for actual use, however strongly their shapes may plead. It is true that jade is very durable and keeps a keen edge. It is also true that a jade object used as a craft tool would be no less efficacious, because it had been so used, when it eventually came to be consigned to the grave. But bearing in mind the intractability and rarity of jade, I find difficulty in believing that it was habitually used for making actual tools; the extreme fragility of many *pl. 32*   specimens – for instance, the 'dagger-axe' of plate 32 – definitely argues to the contrary.

The contention is, then, that the shapes of a great many ritual jades, known to us by the Chou dynasty names of ritual and ceremonial objects with which they have at one time or another been equated, imitate functional precursors that were tools or weapons; and that we need look no further for the explanation of their forms.

Again, my view is that these jades were not originally meant for any purpose other than the *pls 29, 32*   service of the dead. At the same time it would probably be going too far to claim that such *col. 6*   handsome jades as those illustrated on plates 29, 32 and colour plate 6, so obviously derived from tool and weapon prototypes, were made *exclusively* for burial purposes. Ritual and ceremonial use by the living is the traditional role assigned to early Chinese jades; and perhaps an analogy can be found in the dual purpose served by the bronze sacral vessels to be discussed in chapter three. Like the jades, they were modelled in the shapes of actual utensils – in this case domestic pottery; during the lifetimes of their owners they were used ritually, and were buried with them when they died. But allowing the ritual and ceremonial part that jade may have played in prehistoric Chinese society – and that no doubt grew in importance as time went by – the notion that its main role was then to serve the dead still seems to me a right one. By far the finest pots recovered from the Kansu cemeteries were mortuary urns never intended for domestic use by the living – a striking instance of the care with which the prehistoric Chinese attended to the well-being of their dead. Bestowal of jade, I argue, was another.

Classes of Chinese ritual jades

The uses to which were put jades of the classes discussed below may very well have changed during the long period through which they were made; especially, perhaps, during the course

46

of the Chou dynasty. If, as we hold, the earliest of them were simply mortuary objects, it is also probable that many of their descendants were taken over for ritual functions of the sort described by *Chou li*. In the account that follows we therefore follow the convention of calling them all 'ritual' jades. But this is a mere label. Some whole classes of objects may never have been involved in ritual, not even that of burial; for example, the *hsüan chi* and *ts'ung*, which according to one theory were extremely practical astronomical instruments and nothing more.

Again, we are putting forward the view that ritual jades were generally speaking based on implement prototypes. But jades belonging to the last three classes to be described do not readily reveal this ancestry, and in fact may well be *sui generis* and without forebears, made expressly to fulfil some highly specialized function.

The ungrooved polished stone axe is of all craft tools the one most representative of Neolithic culture; dozens of finely-polished specimens have come from Late Neolithic sites in north China, as well as from remote places like Szechwan and Taiwan. The tool is in fact distributed throughout the entire cultural complex of Neolithic eastern Asia, including the Gobi, Sinkiang, and Manchuria. While these axes display classifiable variations in shape, all have one feature in common. Seen in side view, their contours are absolutely symmetrical about the long axis. In other words, they are true axes; as opposed to adzes, in which the plane of the front face turns abruptly in to make the cutting edge, so that the contours are *not* symmetrical about the long axis when seen in side view. Further, in the true axe the cutting edge lies in the same plane as the cutting stroke. Whereas in the adze, whether hafted or not, the cutting edge is always at right angles to the plane of the blow.

CLASS I.
OBJECTS DERIVED FROM
THE POLISHED AXE
pls 22–24

Of the objects chosen to illustrate this class two are Neolithic. The first, bought by Pelliot at Kucha, not very far from the source of jade supply in Khotan, seems to me may well have *pl. 22* been used as an actual tool. On the other hand, the second Neolithic piece, bought by An- *pl. 23* dersson at a place near Hsin-hsien in Honan, was presumably manufactured some 1,500 miles away from the known source of jade, and I think we may assume that this was a mortuary jade; its form is typical of the variety called 'northern rounded' by Andersson. The Chou *pl. 24* piece is presumably derived from a perforated variety of 'northern rounded' axe. It is a most distinguished piece of jade-carving, the material being white nephrite with brown-and-yellow mottling. If we want a clue to the fluid arabesque pattern that covers its upper surface, we have to seek it among the decorative motifs of Second Phase bronze art [pp. 100–102]; they are not of the sort that would naturally occur to the jade-carver, who is obviously happier disposing of purely rectilinear patterns such as those shown on plate 32. Indeed, only com- *pl. 32* plete ascendancy of bronze styles during this phase (ninth to sixth centuries BC) could have induced him to break a stylistic rule in order to undertake so formidable a task.

We can only guess what ceremonial use the Chou piece may have served. Objects resem- *pl. 24* bling it in general shape were identified by Wu Ta-ch'êng as the *yüan kuei* spoken of in *Chou li*. As depicted in Laufer's book [13] they have the same slim and rounded forms as our jade, and two of them are perforated towards the butt end. According to *Chou li*, *yüan kuei*, or 'rounded *kuei*', carried a silk cord – presumably passing through the perforation – and served to 'regulate virtue'. We may perhaps remark that our specimen is 7.8 inches long, a near approximation to the canonical length of 9 Chou inches (= 7.6 English inches) specified by *Chou li* for *yüan kuei*.

Later commentators elaborate the story of *yüan kuei*. One says that the jade was conferred by the ruler on those of his feudatories who gave consistently loyal and virtuous service;

another that it was rounded so that it might serve to arouse virtue and bring good feelings to maturity; the theory being, apparently, that a rounded object symbolized virtue and a pointed one depravity.

A rounded form is characteristic of most types of Chinese polished stone axe. Whether such a tool was really the original model of the *yüan kuei* is uncertain. For who can say definitely what the latter looked like? What *is* apparent is that several of the jades identified by Wu as *yüan kuei* are derived from a stone-axe prototype. And here we get a clue as to the real purport of these jades. Excavation of Neolithic burials in north China shows that, in the case of a male burial, a polished stone axe was commonly placed near the head of the corpse. These mortuary tools, though rarely made of jade, were evidently *objets de luxe* and among the deceased's most valued possessions. Substituting for such objects replicas of them made of jade, the most valuable mineral of all, seems a natural step forward. Burial with the dead was, I conclude, the original role of jade tablets in the shape we associate with *yüan kuei*.

CLASS 2. OBJECTS DERIVED FROM THE HAND ADZE *pls 25, 28* *col. 6*	The small imperforated hand adze or chisel is a tool found in Neolithic contexts in all parts of the peri-Gobi area, for example at Ang-ang-hsi [p. 28]. Such tools may be regarded as forerunners of the splendid jade chisels acquired by Andersson in north China. A group of seven come from burial-sites in the T'ao river valley of southern Kansu; only one of them was excavated by Andersson personally, but the remainder were bought at the site, and there is no reason to suppose that all of them are not genuine Neolithic pieces, contemporary with the magnificent funerary urns recovered from the same place and dating from the Middle Yang-shao [p. 29]. Another jade chisel was excavated at Lo-han-t'ang, a site about 100 miles north-west of the T'ao river, probably contemporary with Ch'i-chia-p'ing [p. 30] and dating from about 1,500 BC. And another group of five comes from the vicinity of Yang-shao-ts'un itself, in Honan.
pl. 25 *col. 6*	All are of one or other of two types. The more common is a flat chisel with relatively broad cutting edge; but another type, to which belongs the object illustrated on colour plate 6, is proportionally much thicker and narrower, and has a high, solid shoulder sloping rapidly in towards the cutting edge. I think it very unlikely that these jades were ever used as tools. Everything points, rather, to their being imitations in precious stone, and for burial purposes, of an authentic and valued craft tool-type.

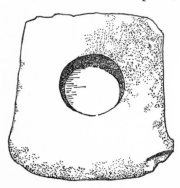

CLASS 3.
OBJECTS DERIVED FROM
THE SHAFT-HOLE ADZE
pl. 27

3 Neolithic shaft-hole adze (*c.* 1,500 BC) excavated at Shih-chia-ho, Hupei province, length 6¹/₄″. Compare with the *chên kuei* of plate 27

This implement, which might have served equally as a flat hammer, mace, or hoe, is characterized by a large central perforation through which the handle passed, so that the plane of the striking edge was at right angles to that of the blow. It is not very common in Neolithic contexts in the Far East, and seems to have made its appearance rather late. It has however been found in male Neolithic burials, for example at the Manchurian site of P'i-tzŭ-wo.

This implement is quite obviously a prototype for certain kinds of ritual *kuei*. I illustrate here a specimen excavated from a site at Shih-chia-ho in Hupei in 1955, for comparison with plate 27 which shows a famous example in dark-brown nephrite mottled with green, formerly in the Eumorfopoulos Collection, and now in the British Museum. What is apparently the very same piece as the latter is illustrated by Laufer, who describes it as a 'jade hammer-shaped symbol of Imperial Power'[14]; Wu Ta-ch'êng identified it with the *chên kuei* described in *Chou li* as a tablet, 12 (Chou) inches high[15], held by the sovereign in his hands when, with the *ta kuei* in his girdle, he offered sacrifice to the morning sun in the spring. This is conceivably true: the fact remains

48

from left to right

6 *Jade chisel, the butt broken off. From the Pan-shan cemetery, Kansu. Middle Yang-shao Culture (c. 2000 BC). Present length: 2 1/2 in. Ost-asiatiska Museet, Stockholm.*

7 *Jade knife, so-called* hu, *with three perforations along the butt. Shang or early Chou dynasty. Not all of the incised ornament is original. Length: 14 3/4 in. Freer Gallery of Art, Washington.*

8 *Jade dagger-axe,* ko, *with median perforation on the tang and decorative lugs. Perhaps early Chou dynasty. The shape is associated with the ya chang (toothed tablet) of Chou li, said to be the token of authority given to military recruiting and training offi-cers. Length: 12 3/4 in. Art Institute of Chicago.*

9 So-called kuei pi, *of jade, the* pi *ornamented with 'comma' pattern. Late Chou dynasty, perhaps third century* BC. *This jade, which combines the forms of the* pi *disc and the* ku kuei [see p. 55], *is of a type said by* Chou li *to have been used in sacrificing to the sun, moon and stars; a constellation has been incised below the point. However, its shape remains enigmatic, and even its date is open to some doubt. Height: 9 ³/₈ in. British Museum.*

10 *Image of the so-called 'ancestor',* wêng-tsung, *in jade. Han dynasty. Height: 6 ¹/₂ in. British Museum.*

11 *Perforated disc,* pi, *of jade ornamented with an outer relief band of nine convoluted animal-forms ending in birds' and tigers' heads, and an inner zone containing ten concentric circles of paired hooks interlocking stepwise. Late Chou dynasty, perhaps fourth century* BC. *Diameter: 8 in. Art Institute of Chicago.*

that the form of the *chên kuei* is based on that of a shaft-hole adze, and that its efficacy was originally that of a craft tool, customarily buried with the dead.

A basic stone tool-type that crops up over the whole Far Eastern area is a knife indifferently describable as rectangular, trapezoid, crescentic, or semi-lunar. In the far north-east of Asia a variety of this knife was until recently in use among the Chukchee Eskimo and the Kuriaks of New Siberia, while others are widely distributed in America, especially in the north-western Eskimo area and that of the Second Laurentian Culture in Ontario, New England, and New York. The knife has also been found at several places in Manchuria, of which the earliest is Ang-ang-hsi and the latest P'i-tzŭ-wo. In China such knives have been found over the entire area of Neolithic occupation in the north, as well as at several Shang sites. Made of iron, they persist in north China to this day, where peasants use them to crop the ripe ears of kaoliang. The prototype has also been compared to the knife used by itinerant tanners in Peking, and by Chêng Tê-k'un to the 'broad kitchen knife of the cook'.

Figure 4 shows a series of knives from different provenances in China and Manchuria, the earliest being that from Ang-ang-hsi and the latest a modern iron knife from north China. The specimens are arranged chronologically, reading down the page, but they are not in-tended to demonstrate an evolution in form. What they do demonstrate is the conservation of form in a basic tool-type. It seems to have bequeathed this form to a type of ritual jade of which many examples are to be found in Western collections, where they are sometimes labelled *kuei*. These jades are usually slimmer than are Neolithic examples made of other ma-terials, and they often have an extra perforation at one end, presumably to hang them up by. The lateral perforations obviously imitate the perforations found in the craft-tool prototype, put there so that a leather handle or hand-guard could be fitted.

Figure 4 h reproduces a drawing made by Wu Ta-ch'êng of a jade object in his collection. Wu believed it to be a jade writing-tablet once used by the Chou sovereign; and this iden-tification Laufer accepted, although he correctly noted the general similarity of the jade to a knife. What Wu's identification was based on is by no means clear. *Chou li* indeed says that records of Imperial audiences were kept on a flat rectangular tablet called a *hu*, but this was made of wood. The fourth-century BC *Li chi*, or 'Record of Rites', says that use of jade for writing-tablets was the prerogative of the ruler, and that such tablets were known as *t'ing*. Then, in the *Tso chuan*, a fourth-century BC history, we find: 'a *t'ing* is a writing-tablet (*hu*) made of jade'.[16]

But can we seriously believe that jades of this form were really designed to be used as writing-tablets, or ever served as such; or, what is more improbable, that they were the ex-clusive property of the Son of Heaven? In late Chou times, assuming they were then still being made, they no doubt served as ceremonial objects symbolical of some sort of feudal authority. But their form proclaims them to be essentially knives; and the symbolical signif-icance that they later acquired, I submit, came because they were once deemed to be suitable objects to be buried with the dead who had used them, or others like them, in life.[17]

A small group of jade objects is made in imitation of the bronze socketed spearhead in use during the Shang dynasty. The spearhead does not seem to have had a prehistoric ancestor in the Far East, nor does the jade appear to have survived into the Chou period. As known to us it is a composite form, the blade alone being made of jade, the socket being of bronze delicately inlaid with tiny bits of turquoise and malachite. There is no telling whether it was made for burial, for ceremonial display, or for both.

CLASS 4.
OBJECTS DERIVED
FROM KNIVES
pl. 29
col. 7

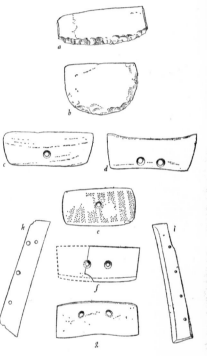

4 The conservation of a tool type. Prehistoric stone knives from Manchuria and north China, compared with two dynastic jades and a modern iron knife: *a* Ang-ang-hsi; *b* Lin-hsi; *c* Lo-han-t'ang; *d* Lo-han-t'ang; *e* Ma-chia-yao (painted pottery sherd); *f* Chu-chia-chai; *g* modern iron knife; *h* jade object identified by Wu Ta-ch'êng as the *hu; i* jade knife of plate 29

CLASS 5.
OBJECTS DERIVED FROM
THE BRONZE SOCKETED
SPEARHEAD
pl. 31

53

CLASS 6.
OBJECTS DERIVED FROM
THE BRONZE DAGGER-AXE,
OR HALBERD
pls 32, 33
col. 8

The weapon called *ko* by the Chinese, on the other hand, has a long and complicated history. Its own evolution in metal, beginning in Shang times, is tortuous enough. But it also gives rise to close and apparently contemporary imitations in jade and bronze combined, or in jade alone, as also to a whole range of later ritual jades the shapes of which are debased versions of the original bronze forms. These are the objects on which the commentators let their imaginations run riot; they are usually labelled *kuei*, like all the other jades we have discussed so far.

The word 'dagger-axe' is a recognized archaeological term for a weapon which has both a point and a cutting edge. As applied to the Chinese *ko*, however, it is perhaps liable to be misinterpreted to mean an axe descended from or in some way related to a long-handled dagger; whereas Karlgren seeks to show that it is derived partly from a slot-hafted axe – of which a single prehistoric example in stone is known – and partly from a knife which he calls the 'inward curving animal-head knife'.[18] Karlgren's drawing shows that two types of halberd emerged, one hafted by means of a vertical tubular shaft-hole, the other by means of a posterior tang that passed through a slot in the handle; lugs above and below acted as tenons that fitted into mortises alongside the main socket, giving extra firm articulation.

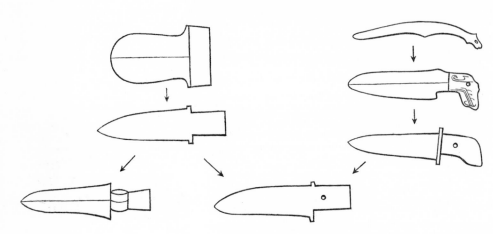

5 The evolution of the bronze dagger-axe according to Karlgren

A number of jade specimens show unmistakable signs of descent, however remote, from the bronze dagger-axe of Shang times. Some have been recently recovered from the main Shang site at An-yang, and are beyond doubt contemporary with the bronze weapons on which they were modelled. Others are known to us because they were given places of honour in the great Chinese collections of the last century, such as that of the Imperial viceroy Tuan Fang, and through the writings of such as Wu Ta-ch'êng. As a rule we cannot tell what was the original provenance of these, and it would be a safe guess that some are archaistic products of the Sung period. Among them are some which are provided with lugs; yet their general appearance is unconvincing. They may be late Chou, Han, or even Sung, but they never give the impression of having been made by craftsmen working direct from original models.

From the point of view of the jade craftsman the lug is an unnecessary inconvenience, and in a piece intended only for burial or ceremonial display it may be dispensed with, being replaced by a much more easily-made perforation. The jade version of a *ko* shown in figure 6a comes from An-yang. It has no lugs, but at the back edge of the tang is a semicircular notch; this, in conjunction with the median perforation on the tang, was a device by which the *ko* was lashed on to its haft. Another jade *ko* from An-yang is shown in figure 6b and here the tang has a number of indentations at the edge. Attempts have been made to explain such notches, found on Neolithic objects of pottery, bone, stone, and jade, as remnants of some system of numeral magic.[19] But even if that were so in the case of a jade such as this, I think the primary purpose of the notches was still to serve as a means of lashing; on the bronze version, which has a vertical shaft-hole, the striped and indented tang is functionless and may, in this case, have been borrowed from a jade example, as suggested below.

fig. 6c

We are now in a position to explain the general shape and significance of the splendid jade *ko* illustrated on plate 32, attributed to the Shang period and quite clearly an *objet de luxe*. The somewhat curved blade proclaims, according to Karlgren's theory, the inward-curving animal-head knife from which it partly descends. The hole on the tang is for articulation with a slotted handle, while the indentations and stripes are the formalized descendants of those on the *ko* of figures 6b and c. This is superb jade technique. The rectilinear carved patterns, especially the band of lozenges and triangles at the base of the blade, are the jade-carver's natural response to difficulties of working his material. Hansford has drawn attention to the characteristic differences that usually exist between styles of decoration suitable for bronzes and those suitable for jades. He nevertheless believes that a number of well-known bronze motifs may have been borrowed, perhaps not early in the history of Chinese bronze-casting, from the repertory of the jade-carver. Among these he puts the squared spiral, the lozenge, and the segmented flanges of bronzes [p. 96]. Two of these devices, as we see, appear on the present specimen.

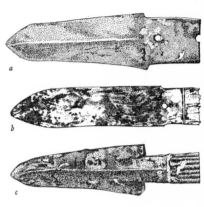

6 Three Shang dagger-axes: *a, b* jade; *c* bronze

Plate 33 shows a composite *ko*, its blade of jade and its tang of bronze inlaid with turquoise.

pl. 33

The jade portion of this type of weapon seems to have bequeathed its shape to the tablet traditionally known as *ku kuei*, '*kuei* ornamented with grain pattern', which *Chou li* says was 7 inches long and was given by the Emperor to his bride-elect. An example appears on a bas-relief of the Han period reproduced in *Chin shih so*, twelve volumes of researches into inscriptions upon bronze (*chin*) and stone (*shih*) objects of antiquity first published in 1822. The cut shows a flat oblong plaque about two and a half times as long as it is broad, with one end carved away symmetrically to a sharp point, covered with a typically Han diaper pattern of lozenges with a nodule at the centre of each.[20]

With this piece in mind, Laufer says of the *ku kuei* that its shape is 'presumably derived from that of a spear', but I have set alongside it in figure 7 the jade portion of a jade and bronze *ko* in the William Rockhill Nelson Gallery of Art, Kansas City, in order to show what I take to be its true affinities. A piece identified by Wu Ta-ch'êng as a *ku kuei* is very similar in shape and also has one side ornamented with diapered lozenges, while the other is decorated with rows of raised knobs typical of the Han period, the so-called 'grain pattern'.

7 *a* jade object of the type called *ku kuei*, redrawn from *Chin shih so*, compared with *b*, the jade portion of a Shang jade and bronze dagger-axe

In a compilation entitled *Po hu t'ung tê lun*, 'Universal Discussions at the White Tiger Lodge', the first-century AD historian Pan Ku seeks to explain away the shape of a *ku kuei* by saying that the upper pointed part of the tablet means the male principle *yang*, and the lower squared section the female *yin* [p. 150]. I cannot see why. Laufer, however, took a fancy to the idea and said: 'This may hint at a possible phallic significance of this emblem...' In view of its probable descent from a halberd blade, there seems to be no good reason to think any such thing of this jade's shape.

We may treat as *pi* all perforated stone discs, other than rings and bracelets on the one hand, and spindle-whorls on the other. A glance at plates 34–36 will immediately inform the reader what we have in mind – the group of jades which Hansford calls, generically, '*pi*-forms'.

CLASS 7.
ANNULAR DISCS; *PI*-FORMS
pls 34–36
col. 11

The *pi* is a most ancient and auspicious object, a classical ingredient in Chinese material culture, one so familiar yet so sublime that it could very well serve, like the *li* tripod, as a distinctive emblem of Chinese society.

8 *a* oracle-bone graph, equated with *b*, modern *jih*, 'sun'; *c* bronze graph, equated with *d*, modern *t'ien*, 'heaven'

fig. 8

pl. 36

fig. 8

pl. 34

What we call a *pi* has probably always been known as such. The idea that it was once used in worship of Heaven (T'ien) is introduced by *Chou li*, which says: 'He [the Master of Ceremonies] pays homage to Heaven with a *ch'ing pi* [a *pi* of greenish or bluish jade]'. But that the actual form of the *pi* in some way stood for Heaven was not mooted until the second century AD, when the commentator Chêng Hsüan remarks with reference to the *Chou li* entry: 'The *pi* is round and symbolizes Heaven.' Broadly speaking, both the *Chou li* description of its function, and Chêng Hsüan's comment on its form, have been accepted by Western and Chinese scholars alike.

How then does the form of the *pi* reveal to us Heaven? Laufer tells us only that the jade disc *pi* is symbolic of the deity Heaven, and again that 'the shapes of these images were found by geometrical construction, a jade disc round and perforated representing Heaven ...'[21] Now Schindler, followed by Karlgren, observes that the form of the *pi* is simply that of the ancient graph for 'sun', and this is of course very plausible. Hansford moreover suggests that both graph and *pi* portray the sun shining in the surrounding vault of heaven. If for a moment we turn to the jade disc of plate 36, on whose surface the milky impurities look like cirrus cloud high in the sky, and if we half-close our eyes until the central hole begins to blaze out like the sun, we shall surely admit the force and beauty of this idea.

Apart from worship of Heaven, *Chou li* prescribes several other ceremonial purposes to which *pi* were put. Is this multiplication of uses merely a symptom of the corruption of ritual practices at the time, and may we conclude that the earlier and original use of the *pi* was in fact in worshipping Heaven? How far back does such worship go?

From what we can deduce about Shang religious practices and beliefs, it appears that they sacrificed to their deified royal ancestors, and to a deity called Shang Ti, or Supreme Ruler. The deity T'ien does not appear till Chou times, and it is significant that the graph for T'ien is no abstract symbol, but quite plainly depicts a person, and one of some consequence. Creel was probably right, therefore, in surmising that the Chou originally conceived of their Heaven, T'ien, as a 'great man', as a deified royal ancestor similar to those of the Shang.[22] The fact is also significant that the Chou called their earthly ruler T'ien Tzǔ, 'Son of Heaven', and that Shang Ti and T'ien are used interchangeably in early Chou texts and bronze inscriptions. It becomes difficult to see what symbolic part the *pi* could have played in a system of worship so attached to anthropomorphic concepts.

As for the prehistoric Chinese, we do not know what were their religious beliefs. *Pi* have, however, been found in neolithic contexts in north China and Manchuria. Seven specimens, three of them beautifully carved in jade, came from the Middle Yang-shao burial-site in the Pan-shan hills [p. 29], and were among the treasures bought there by Andersson in 1924; one of them was said to have been found lying on the chest of a skeleton. Again, in a cave at Wei-k'ên-ha-ta in the Yi-lan district of Heilungkiang, excavated in 1950, many white jade *pi* were found in proximity to skeletons. The cave may be a Neolithic survivor into historical times, but the burial practice was probably traditional.

Coming down to Shang and early Chou times we again find jade *pi* conspicuous among excavated burial furniture; there is moreover a second passage in *Chou li* which specifically names the *pi* among six jades meet to be buried with the dead.

Evidence thus accumulates to show that the primary role of the *pi* was in no way connected with worship of Heaven, but that it was a mortuary object in the same class as the jade axes and adzes of which we have spoken. In that case its prototype was a tool. Can we say what tool? When I first wrote this book I thought it might have been the fly-wheel of a drill. Hentze long ago held the view that it was a mace or disc-shaped shaft-hole axe.[23] Perhaps this is after all the true explanation; many disc-shaped mace heads were recovered from the excavations at Pan-p'o in 1954 [p. 29], so that the mace is now well established as a tool-type of the Middle Phase of the Yang-shao Culture.

CLASS 8.
ANNULAR DISCS WITH
SERRATED EDGE
pl. 37

Wu Ta-ch'êng was the first to identify discs of the sort shown on plate 37 with the astronomical instrument *hsüan chi* spoken of in pre-Han texts; but he made no attempt to explain how such discs might have been used for taking celestial observations. A remarkably ingenious explanation has recently been suggested by Henri Michel, and I propose to summarize it here.[24]

That there was an ancient astronomical instrument called the *hsüan chi yü hêng* has always been known to Chinese scholars. The 'Book of History', *Shu ching*, says it was used to regulate the Seven Governors, and these, according to Ssŭ-ma Ch'ien's *Shih chi*, were the stars of the Great Bear. It is significant that the Chinese still call α, β, γ, and δ Ursa Majoris by the name *hsüan chi*. From *Shu ching* and its various commentaries, we gather the information that the *hsüan chi yü hêng* was a composite affair having one part that could be rotated and another that was a sighting tube. The rotor was the *hsüan chi*, and the sighting tube was the *yü hêng*. You looked through the *yü hêng*, rotated the *hsüan chi*, and made some sort of astronomical observation. Michel's theory involves equating notched discs such as that of plate 37 with *pl. 37* the *hsüan chi*, as proposed by Wu Ta-ch'êng, and the *yü hêng* with a well-known class *pls 38–40* of ritual jade in the shape of a tube, called *ts'ung*. You will notice that *ts'ung* are cut so as to leave a circular collar projecting at either end. The theory is that the *hsüan chi* was mounted upon one of these collars, and the observer looked through the other end. When the *yü hêng* was pointed at the night sky, and the *hsüan chi* rotated until a position was reached where certain stars appeared to fit closely into the notches on its perimeter, then the celestial north pole was at the exact centre of the field of vision within the tube. The *hsüan chi*, in other words, was a stellar template, and the whole instrument a device for fixing the position of the pole.

Owing to the precession of the equinoxes, the pole three thousand years ago was not marked by the presence of a bright star, as it is today. The nearest star was β Ursa Minoris, distant a matter of seven degrees, or fourteen times the moon's diameter. Yet it was vitally important for ancient Chinese astronomers to determine the position of the pole, and from it that of the colure, an imaginary great circle passing through the pole and through the solstitial points on the ecliptic; these are the most northerly and southerly apparent positions reached by the sun in its annual motion, and all calender-making requires the exact determination of their date.

Michel adds some fascinating details, taken from Chinese sources, that give strong corroboration for his most original theory. Of course it does not imply that *all* notched discs were in use as astronomical instruments. Quite obviously a device of such efficacy would have been thought supremely suitable as a burial object, and I have no doubt but that a great many of them were made simply for that purpose. We shall now go on to consider the *ts'ung*, which Michel believes was the sighting tube that accompanied the *hsüan chi*.

The objects thus described are the last ritual jades surveyed here. They are those known to every jade collector since the days of Wu Ta-ch'êng as *ts'ung*, several sorts of which are mentioned in *Chou li*. Three typical examples are illustrated, and it will be seen that although the dimensions and proportions of *ts'ung* vary considerably, the essential form does not. It is that of a rectangular block, square in section. Along one axis, usually the longest, a wide

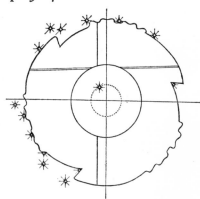

9 Jade object of the type identified as the astronomical instrument *hsüan chi*, showing how it could have been used as a stellar template. The circumpolar stars, around the circumference of the instrument, were α, δ, ε, and ζ Ursa Majoris; ι, ʒ, and φ Draconis; χ Cephei; and α Ursa Minoris, the present Pole Star. The nearest bright star to the pole, β Ursa Minoris, would have appeared to rotate round the inner perimeter of the sighting tube (dotted circle) once in every 24 hours

CLASS 9.
TUBES WITH SQUARE
OUTER AND ROUND
INNER PERIMETER
pls 38–40

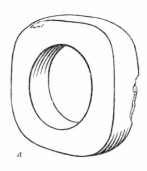

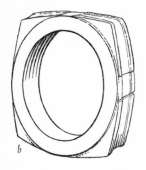

10 *a* jade ring recovered from the Neolithic cemetery in the Pan-shan hills, Kansu, compared with *b,* jade object of the type called *ts'ung*

perforation is drilled whereby the block is converted into a tube with circular bore, open at both ends. Upper and lower ends are normally cut away so that a low collar projects; this collar is usually round but is sometimes squarish in section. The proportions of *ts'ung* vary from those of a tall column to a squat form that is little more than a ring. Many are unorna- mented, but probably more are engraved with geometrical designs, a pattern of horizontal grooves or strapping, with or without 'eyes', being especially favoured. *Ts'ung* seem to have been conceived of as made of nephrite, and many apparently were. But perhaps even more are of other hard stones used as substitutes for true jade.

Ts'ung are the most controversial of all ritual jades. Here are some of the things they have been taken to be. The author of *Ku yü t'u p'u*, 'Illustrated Record of Ancient Jades', believed them to be wheel-naves (*kang t'ou*) off a hypothetical jade chariot owned by the Chou ruler. He did not therefore call them *ts'ung* at all. Wu Ta-ch'êng gets the credit for having first recognized them as the *ts'ung* mentioned in *Chou li* where it says: 'He [the Master of Religious Ceremonies] pays homage to Heaven with the *ch'ing pi*; he pays homage to Earth with the yellow *ts'ung*.' From this, most later scholars have concluded that *ts'ung* in some way symbolize the deity Earth (Ti); they disagree only as to how.

Laufer said that the *ts'ung* was a 'real image of the deity Earth'; this pronouncement rested on a cryptic remark made by the *Chou li* commentator Chêng Hsüan – 'the *pi* is round and symbolizes Heaven; the *ts'ung* is eight-cornered and symbolizes Earth'. How is a *ts'ung* eight- cornered? Because it is a rectangular block, and this, of course, has eight corners. How did a rectangular block symbolize Earth? Because Earth was visualized as a rectangle. Laufer moreover believed that Earth was feminine, which explained why several sorts of *ts'ung* men- tioned in *Chou li* were used in rituals involving women of the royal house. Erkes went a step further and said that the *ts'ung* was the literal and concrete symbol of the feminine deity, since in fact it represented a vagina.

An entirely different explanation, offered by Gieseler, is based on a passage in *Li chi* wherein it is said that in the house sacrifice was made to the Lord of the Smokehole, but abroad to the Lord of the Soil. Here tutelary gods are thought of as male. Gieseler's suggestion is that the *ts'ung* was originally a pottery tube which lined the smokehole of the house. It thus became the special symbol of the Lord of the Smokehole; later it was appropriated for ritual worship to the Lord of the Soil. From this point, according to Gieseler, it came into association with the cosmic deity Earth (Ti), whom he also considered as male. One can only say it is a far cry from a tutelary to a cosmic deity, and that a ritual connexion between the Lord of the Soil and the deity Earth is scarcely thinkable.

Bernhard Karlgren, whose views are bound to command respect, says that *ts'ung* were originally containers for ancestral tablets. He envisages first a tall hollow cylinder, and then, to prevent this from rolling, or for convenience while being stored, he imagines four stone slabs or corner prisms bound together with it to give it a square outer section. The *ts'ung* we know are derived from these contraptions, he says, and the incised horizontal grooves are vestiges of notches cut in the original slabs to hold the thongs more firmly in place. We noticed the same sort of segmented edge, apparently serving a similar purpose, in the case of some jade *ko*.

Michel, as we saw, believes that *ts'ung* were originally sighting tubes used in combination with the *hsüan chi*. He believes that their connexion with Earth lay in the fact of their being astronomical instruments which were presumably adjusted to the terrestrial horizon.

So what, after all, are *ts'ung*? Are they wheel-naves, rectangles, vaginas, chimney pots, containers for ancestral tablets, or astronomical sighting tubes? Laufer's explanation of the jade's shape is obscure, showing only his aptitude for finding what he called 'a well-meditated symbolism' in such shapes. Those offered by Erkes and Gieseler are simply surmises resting on assumptions regarding the sex of the deity Earth and the basic connexion between the deity and the jade.

Karlgren's theory involves a long string of associations. In its primary role the *ts'ung* is a container of royal ancestral tablets – and Karlgren points out that the graph used in Chou times to write it was the same as that used for 'ancestral temple'. Again, referring to a variety called *tsŭ ts'ung* in *Chou li*, Karlgren says that the graph standing for *tsŭ* was originally the pictogram of a phallus, and this pictogram also carried the meaning 'royal ancestor'. Yet a third concept expressed by the phallus pictogram, Karlgren says, was that of the Earth God, Ti, under an alternative name, T'u. Thus the royal ancestral tablet-container, *ts'ung*, is associated in people's minds with the royal ancestor himself; the royal ancestor and the cosmic deity are also cognate ideas, since the same graph stands for both. The *ts'ung* therefore came to be used in ritual worship of Earth; but, partly because of its primary association with the family of the feudal overlord, it remained also a symbol of aristocratic authority.

Karlgren's smoothly argued theory has everything to commend it, except perhaps its intrinsic improbability. There is no evidence that the earliest *ts'ung* was of tall proportions, which is what the theory requires since the tablets themselves were tall; in fact there is some reason for supposing that its ultimate ancestor may have been a squat stone ring. Again, a container must be able to contain, and must necessarily be closed at one end; the *ts'ung*, on the other hand, is essentially a tube, open at both ends.

This tubularity of the *ts'ung* well fits it for use as a sighting tube. My comment, however, is that very few actual *ts'ung* could have been used as sighting tubes in combination with *hsüan chi* as we know them. The average size of a *hsüan chi* is about five inches. The distance from the eye at which such a disc should be held in order to cover the requisite area of sky is four inches, and this gives us the length of the *ts'ung*. A *ts'ung* such as that of plate 38, for instance, would have to be fitted with an unprecedentedly large *hsüan chi*, for it is nearly twenty inches long. The answer may be, of course, that these are late *ts'ung*, whose forms have proliferated away from the prototype; but, as I say, we really do not know what the prototype looked like. *pl. 38*

If, however, it looked anything like the neolithic jade ring of figure 10, then may we not reconsider the statement of *Ku yü t'u p'u*, that they were wheel-naves? Inserted into the hub of a wooden wheel, such a form would be well adapted to serve as an axle bearing, while the toughness of the stone would guarantee it a long life. It is interesting to note that a squat *ts'ung* found among the lovely burial jades recovered from the site of T'ai-p'ing-ch'ang in Szechwan, the upper date of which is given as 1500 BC by Chêng Tê-k'un, was actually described as a wheel-nave by one of its investigators.[25]

Decorative objects in jade

Most of these take the form of small carved plaques cut from slabs a few millimetres thick. In Hansford's opinion they were usually, if not invariably, cut with metal tools. A good many are perforated, and we can assume that they were sewn on to clothing as amulets or articles of jewellery; or fixed, as by nails, to other objects perhaps made of wood. *pls 41–49* *col. 10*

A brief study of neolithic material from Chinese sites, or from those in surrounding areas, will show us immediately that scarcely any representational art was attempted in prehistoric China. One of the greatest mysteries of Chinese archaeology, it seems to me, is the sudden and spontaneous outburst of animal representation that appears to have coincided with the first historical dynasty, the Shang. Animal designs are everywhere; and one can truly say that some of these figures, in sheer verve and vitality, have never been equalled anywhere else. The forms are usually stylized; but, if it is sometimes difficult to tell precisely what species of animal is portrayed, the impression created of a type – of what the late E. H. Minns called 'the pure idea' of a feline, bovine, fish, and so on – is instantaneous and unmistakable. Strict attention to diagnostic detail was evidently not uppermost in the designer's mind. He sought rather to interpret the essential, private *élan* of a whole class. More will be said in the next chapter about the question of animal representation in archaic Chinese art. We reproduce a group of these small decorative objects without further comment here.

pls 44–49

Until the excavations made by the Academia Sinica in 1934–5, sculpture in the round was hardly supposed to have existed in China before the Han dynasty. The extraordinary jade pieces reproduced on plates 41 and 42 are, to the best of my knowledge, unique. The first is supposed to have come from a Neolithic site south of T'ai-yüan in Shansi, and the Museum authorities at the William Rockhill Nelson Gallery of Art, Kansas City, to which it belongs, assign it to the second or third millennium BC.

pls 41, 42

This is sculpture in the round, and if it could be confidently assigned to the prehistoric period it would represent an astonishing *tour de force*; for carving would probably have been without metal tools. Even allowing that the date is more likely to be late in the second millennium, and therefore, probably contemporary with the Shang, the bird especially is still a superb imaginative essay; a condensation of the essential features of the bird, perhaps a pigeon, made without the least trace of effort in its execution or loss of vitality in the result. Anyone familiar with the work of Henry Moore or Brancusi, in which directness of expression is achieved by rigid elimination of non-essentials, must surely be impressed by the same quality manifest in this carving. Cutting away of the lower surface into a sort of lug suggests that it was at one time socketed into some other object, although it would be difficult to say exactly what.

pl. 41

TOOL TYPES

22 Axe, jade. From Kucha, Chinese Turkestan. Perhaps third millennium BC. Length: 6 in. Musée des Antiquités Nationales, Paris.

23 Axe, yellowish-green jade. From Hsin-hsien, Honan. Perhaps third millennium BC. Length: 5 in. Ostasiatiska Museet, Stockholm.

24 Celt-like instrument [p. 47], white jade with brown and yellow mottling. Chou dynasty (c. 800 BC). Length: 7 $^{13}/_{16}$ in. Nelson Gallery of Art, Kansas City.

Chisel, dark green translucent jade. From
e Pan-shan cemetery, Kansu. Middle Yang-
ao Culture (*c.* 2000 BC). Length: 3⁷/₈ in.
stasiatiska Museet, Stockholm.

Flat axe, heavily calcined ivory jade with
edian perforation, nine longitudinal grooves,
d indentations on the side edges. Perhaps
hang dynasty. The shape is that identified by
u Ta-ch'êng as of dance-axes, put in the
nds of performers of the *ta wu* dance in the
hou ancestral temple as described in *Li Chi*.
ength: 4³/₄ in. Art Institute of Chicago.

Adze, so-called *chên kuei,* dark brown jade
ith green mottling. Chou dynasty or earlier.
ength: 9³/₈ in. British Museum.

Chisel, black jade flecked with green, in-
sed with a crescent moon and a constellation
three stars. Probably Chou dynasty. Length:
⁷/₁₆ in. British Museum.

TOOL AND WEAPON TYPES

Knife, so-called *hu,* probably jade. Shang
nasty. Length: 11⁵/₈ in. Museum of Science,
uffalo.

Celt-like implement, brown-green jade,
ith incised demonic mask. Probably Chou
nasty. For a discussion of similar masks see
ge 157. Length: 7¹/₄ in. Freer Gallery of Art,
ashington.

Spearhead, pale green jade with bronze
ndle inlaid with turquoise. Shang dynasty.
ength: 7¹/₄ in. Fogg Museum of Art, Cam-
idge, Mass.

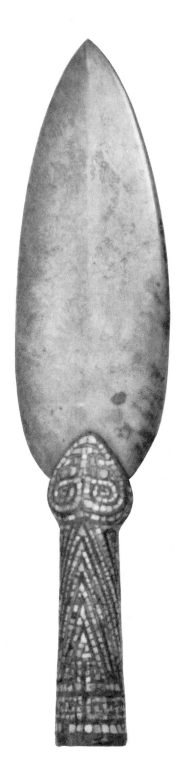

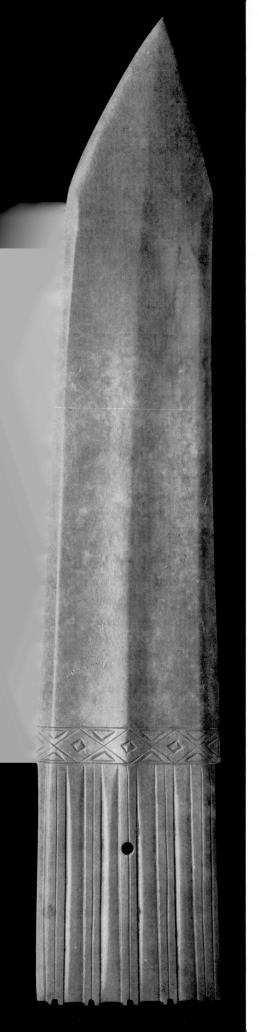

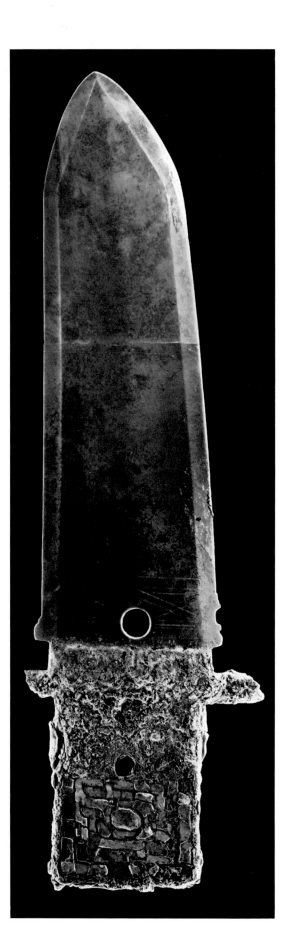

WEAPON TYPES

32 Dagger-axe, *ko,* white jade. Shang dyn.
Length: 17 13/16 in. Nelson Gallery of
Kansas City.

33 Dagger-axe, *ko,* dark blue-green jade
bronze handle inlaid with turquoise. Sh
dynasty. Length: 11 5/8 in. C. T. Loo, Fr
Caro Successor, New York.

THE PI

opposite

34 (centre) Perforated disc, *pi,* green jade
small dark spots. From the Pan-shan ceme
Kansu [see p. 56]. Middle Yang-shao Cul
(c. 2000 BC). Diameter: 5 7/8 in. Ostasiati
Museet, Stockholm.

35 (above) Perforated disc, *pi,* jade, with
cised ornamentation suggesting a *t'ao-t'ieh* fo
Chou dynasty (perhaps eighth century
Diameter: 9 5/8 in. Seattle Art Museum.

36 (below) Perforated disc, *pi,* light green j
shading to dark [see p. 56]. Probably C
dynasty. Diameter: 8 1/8 in. British Museum

ASTRONOMICAL JADES

37 Perforated disc, *hsüan chi,* greyish-white jade with corroded surface. Probably Shang dynasty. Diameter: 7 ³/₄ in. Francis Hopp Museum of Eastern Asiatic Arts, Budapest.

opposite page

38 Perforated tube, so-called *tsung,* dark-green and golden-brown jade. Probably Chou dynasty. Height: 19 ⁵/₈ in. British Museum.

39 (above) Perforated tube, so-called *tsung,* mottled greyish-black and dark green jade. Probably Chou dynasty. Height: 8 ¹/₈ in. British Museum.

40 (below) Perforated tube, so-called *tsung,* amber jade with brown splashes. Probably Chou dynasty. Height: 2 ⁵/₈ in. British Museum.

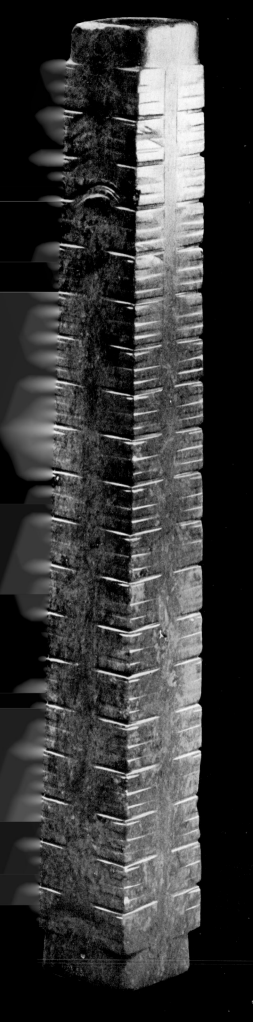
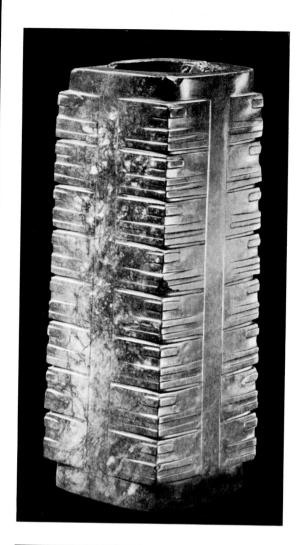

opposite page

41 Bird, green jade. Said to have been found in the vicinity of T'ai-yüan, Shansi. Probably second millennium BC [see p. 60]. Length: 5 ¹/₂ in. Nelson Gallery of Art, Kansas City.

42 Bovine figure, dark green and grey jade. Believed to be from An-yang, Honan. Second millennium BC. Length: 5 ¹/₄ in. Collection of Mrs Walter Sedgwick, London.

43 Bell-shaped pendant, light green jade, with conspicuous T-scores at the edges [see p. 99], the main field with confronted tiger heads in relief. Shang dynasty. Length: 4 in. Art Institute of Chicago.

44 Pendant, brownish-green jade, in the form of a flattened bird in profile. Shang or early Chou dynasty. In his discussion of this piece Alfred Salmony (1952) identifies the bird as a male of one of the native species of pheasant, which might qualify it as an ancestor of the Han Phoenix [see pp. 152–154]. Length: 3 ¹/₈ in. Art Institute of Chicago.

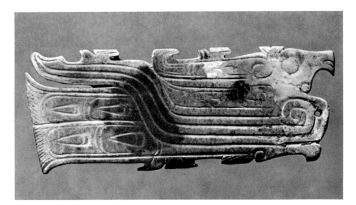

45 Pendant, ivory jade, in the shape of a bovine mask. Shang dynasty. Width: 2 ⁷/₈ in. Art Institute of Chicago.

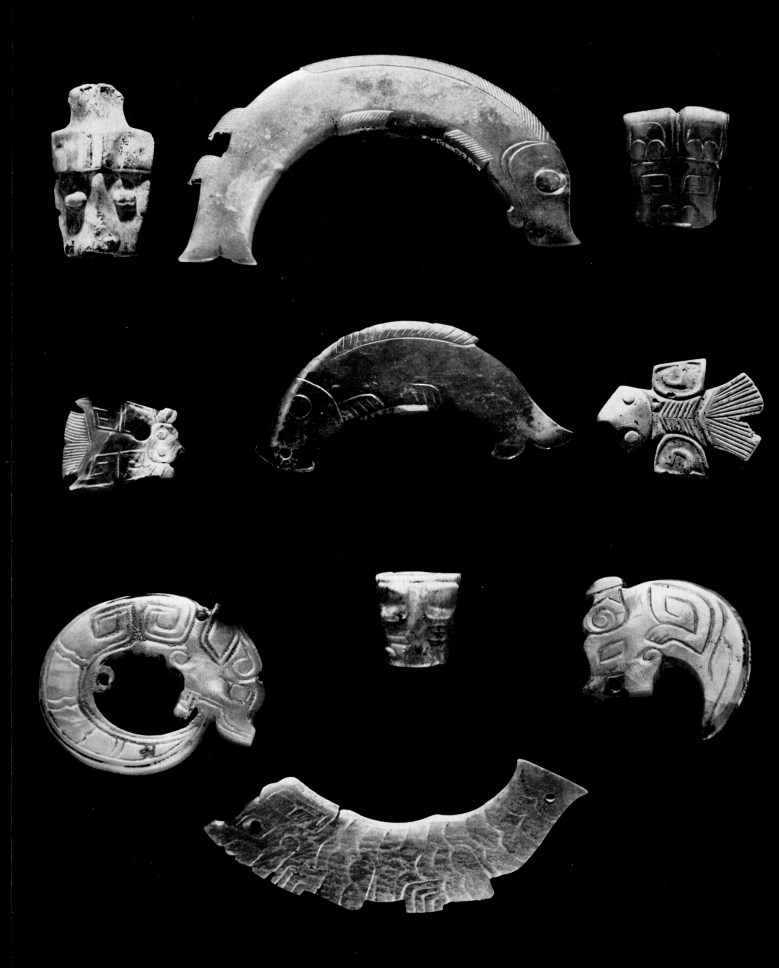

46 (left) Fish, bird and monster-mask
pendants and amulets, all probably Chou
dynasty. Length of longest fish: 5 ¹/₂ in.
C. T. Loo, Frank Caro Successor, New
York.

47 (right) Necklace of ten pieces, of
which four are large ornamental pendants, milky grey, light green and brown
jade, strung together by means of braided
gold wire. Late Chou dynasty, perhaps
fourth century BC. Said to have come
from Lo-yang, Honan. Length: 16 in.
Freer Gallery of Art, Washington.

48 Dragon ornament, jade. Late Chou dynasty (sixth to fourth centuries BC). Said to
have come from Chin-ts'un, Honan. Length:
5 in. Royal Ontario Museum, Toronto.

49 Pair of plaques or pendentives, white jade,
carved in the form of arched and convoluted
dragons. Late Chou dynasty, probably fourth
century BC. Length of each: 2 3/16 in. C. T. Loo
et Cie, Paris.

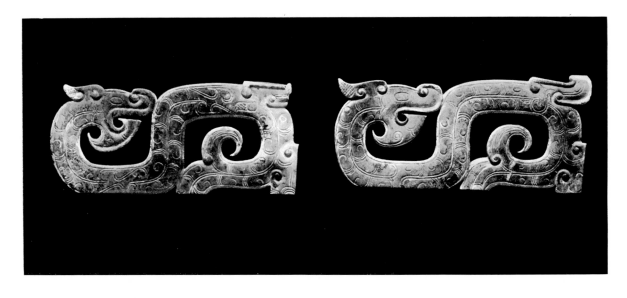

III BRONZE: SHANG AND CHOU DYNASTIES

The beginnings of the Bronze Age in China

In 1898 or thereabouts occurred an event that was to prove outstanding in the annals of Chinese archaeology. At the hamlet of Hsiao-t'un, some 2 miles north-west of the city of An-yang, which lies on the Peking–Hankow railway in northern Honan, were discovered thousands of inscribed bones and tortoise-shells. We are not sure how the attention of scholars was drawn to the find; but the story goes that some of the bones were sold by Peking druggists as that standard item of the old Chinese pharmacopoeia, 'dragon bones', and that the Grand Secretary Wang I-jung came across some of them being pounded up in his kitchen. It may have been he who recognized for the first time the archaic written characters we now know to be those of the Shang dynasty. Various scholars joined in the search for more bones, and for the place of origin. Despite a smoke-screen put up by dealers and other interested persons, the site was finally located some ten years later.[1]

Well over a hundred thousand inscribed fragments are now known, and as excavation at the site continues, still more of the writings are being found. Most are incised with some sort of stylus, but a very few are brushed; and they are generally rather short, rarely comprising more than a dozen or so characters. Thanks to the fact that the forms of these show likenesses to graphs inscribed on the bronzes of the following dynasty, the Chou, and thanks to a tradition of epigraphical studies that extends back in China at least two thousand years, most of the characters can be equated with modern forms and the contents of the inscriptions read.

Recent discoveries suggest that writing in Shang times may have been more widespread through society than was at first believed, for an inscription of sixteen characters on an ox scapula was found a few years ago on the site of a house thought to have been occupied by a commoner. But the vast majority of the inscriptions can properly be called part of the royal archives of the dynasty. They consist of questions put to the ancestors who acted as oracles for the ruling house, addressed through the agency of scribes–priests–diviners. The favourite bone was an ox scapula. Questions – and occasionally verdicts and verifications – were written on one surface; the diviner applied the point of a red-hot tool to a specially prepared lentoid cut on the other, and the verdict was read from the conformation of cracks that appeared on the front face. This was the distinctive technique of scapulimancy to which we have already referred [p. 21].

The An-yang finds proved what scarcely a Westerner had believed up to that time: that this dynasty, which is the second in traditional Chinese history-books [p. 17], really did exist. In 1929 the Academia Sinica began systematic excavation at An-yang. Not only did the dynasty exist, but it existed – or at least its aristocracy did – in conditions of almost unbelievable splendour. Foremost among the treasures recovered from An-yang are hundreds upon hundreds of finely-cast bronze vessels. Orthodox history gives 1766–1122 BC as the period occupied by the Shang dynasty, but there are good reasons for supposing that it actually began about 200 years, and ended about 100 years, later. There is a well-established tradition that the site at An-yang was occupied by the nineteenth Shang sovereign, P'an Kêng, 273 years before the end of the dynasty; or in the year 1300 BC on the basis of the revised chronology. Accordingly, we can safely say that the art of bronze-casting was fully fledged in China at least as early as 1300 BC.

*

When first writing this book, I had to report at this point that no trace of any bronze art antecedent to the late Shang period, as represented by An-yang, had yet been detected. So swift has been the stride of archaeological discovery in China during the last ten years, that the situation is now entirely altered. At Chêng-chou, on the south bank of the Yellow River about 100 miles south-south-west of An-yang, the early Shang capital of Ao has been definitely identified.[2] Ao is by tradition supposed to have been founded by the tenth Shang ruler, Chung Ting, perhaps about 1450 BC; and the massive remains of a rammed earth wall, up to sixty feet wide at its base and extending for more than a mile in either direction, probably mark the original urban limits. But the inhabited area around Chêng-chou was also extensive, with settlements scattered over a radius of 10 miles; and some of these belong to the Late Neolithic phase, and yield pottery of Lung-shan type [p. 31]. At Chêng-chou itself, the Shang culture seems to have passed through four stages, of which the first three antedate An-yang and lie between about 1500 and 1300 BC. The fourth dovetails with Hsiao-t'un 1, the earlier occupation at the An-yang site, so that between them Chêng-chou and An-yang provide an archaeological panorama that extends from the Late Neolithic to the end of the Shang. It is in the first three Shang stages at Chêng-chou that evidence of bronze has been found, representing the elusive formative phase of Chinese Bronze Age culture that archaeologists had sought for so long.

The Early Bronze Age in China still poses many problems. Apart from a few characters scratched on bones other than oracle bones at Chêng-chou, we still have no clue as to the origin of that vast, fantastic cultural edifice, the Chinese written language. Nor have we evidence which would allow us to decide whether a basic knowledge of bronze-casting permeated into China from the West. The Chêng-chou stage is not truly primitive, for the bronzes found here are complete vessels and not the simple tools cast in open moulds that mark the inception of the Bronze Age in the West. But the theory that an advanced bronze-casting technique was imported, permissible before the discoveries at Chêng-chou, is now at a discount. So is the notion that the Karasuk Culture of the Minousinsk region of south Siberia (c. 1200–800 BC) was the original donor. As far as China is concerned, the interest of Karasuk lies in a manifest connexion between its animal-style art and the naturalistic representation of animal forms found more rarely at An-yang, and in the possibility that it may have contributed some weapon-types to the north Chinese armoury during the last centuries of Shang rule.

The bronze vessels found at Chêng-chou, as also at Liu-li-ko near Hui-hsien some fifty miles to the north-north-east, are primitive versions of the An-yang masterpieces – more summarily executed, with a simpler decorative vocabulary, and fewer and less specialized shapes. They belong, however, to the same tradition, and there appears no reason why they should be distinguished stylistically from the corpus of later vessels belonging to the so-called First Phase.[3] I shall not, therefore, describe them as a separate group.

The period now under survey opens about 1500 BC, and ends with the fall of the Chou dynasty in 256 BC. Apart from the fact that much of what has been written on the early history and social and economic life of these times is conjectural, we cannot in any case do more here than indicate the general pattern of life in Bronze Age China. The period falls naturally into three phases. First, that of Shang overlordship, lasting from about 1500 to 1027 BC; second, that of Chou overlordship, lasting for the next two and a half centuries; third, a phase of diplomatic and active warfare between independent states paying only nominal allegiance to Chou rule, lasting about five centuries from the middle eighth to middle third centuries BC.

Over seventy Shang sites, all marked by the presence of the characteristic grey pottery [p. 29] but with no trace of bronze in most of them, have now been located in north China. They cover an area extending eastwards into Shantung and westwards as far as Shensi; to the south, Shang cultural remains have been found in the northern parts of Kiangsu and Anhwei, and to the north in Hopei. This distribution suggests an original centre somewhere in Shantung – where tradition locates at least one of its early capitals, Yen – or perhaps in the valley of the Huai river. The drift was towards the west and north-west. The Shang rulers changed capital frequently, perhaps under pressure of hostile tribes on their eastern marches, perhaps because of floods, and we may not suppose that they ever administered the whole area over which their sites have been located. The picture is rather that of a mobile city-state, bronze the hallmark of its culture, whose relations with the neolithic settlements beyond its walls were fluid, ill-defined, and impermanent. There was, however, some delegation of royal power to outlying areas towards the end of the Shang overlordship, marking the inception of a feudal order of society.

It is perhaps significant that the oldest Chinese bronze implements known are not tools, but weapons. Military superiority enabled the bronze-using city-dwellers to bring into subjection more and more of the surrounding stone-using peasantry, and thus the introduction of bronze was not so much economic in its effects as social; it served to confirm the ascendancy of a city-dwelling, military aristocracy. Reserves of the metal were conveniently stored in the form of sacrificial bronze vessels which could be readily melted down to make weapons as need arose. Thus the ritual bronzes with which we mainly deal in this chapter were far more than the material concomitants of a distinctive system of ancestor and family worship; they were also a formidable reserve stock of war material. And bronze continued to fight for the feudal nobility throughout the entire Bronze Age. While agricultural craft tools were still being made of stone right up to the coming of iron in the fifth century BC, and beyond, bronze brought no benefits to the peasantry, whose only contact with the metal could have been in time of war. They must have feared and detested it.

We know next to nothing of the classes of society in Shang times. The existence of a hunting and warrior nobility, who were also landowners and slave-owners, has to be taken for granted; for such a group is not mentioned in contemporary inscriptions. But this was probably not a feudal aristocracy in the strict sense, since there was no decentralization of feudal power to speak of, and the nobility continued to live in the town. There was also an official class, among whom the scribes–priests–diviners, *chên jên*, were most important; and, as Creel says, 'there is some reason for believing that they may originally have been rather humble servants of the royal household, whose position gradually increased in power and dignity'.[4] A whole area at the An-yang site was evidently occupied by an industrial proletariat of builders, monumental masons, potters, jade-carvers, bronze-smiths, silk operatives, and so forth.

Below the artisans was a fourth, indeterminate class of agricultural workers and personal servants. Some of these were undoubtedly slaves, captured on military expeditions; others may have been serfs on the suburban estates of the landowning nobility, and local peasantry.

The second part of the Bronze Age opens with the Chou conquest of the Shang. Such an event is a natural starting-point for latter-day myth-building and much of the Chou version of it shows signs of having been retrospectively concocted. But it seems certain that the Chou peoples came from the west, and followed the line of the Wei and Yellow river valleys in their march against the Shang; that they had known of the existence of the Shang for many generations; and that they recognized them to be the most advanced people living in the north China plain. The Chou were probably their tributaries and keepers of their western marches.

We have already seen how a sense of cultural inferiority may have prompted the Chou to invent the genealogy that established their right to rule north China [p. 17]. They claimed to be descended from the Hsia. But according to orthodox history the Shang genealogy also ran into the Hsia. Thus, however it came about, the Chou had managed to give themselves the air of being related to the Shang. Whether they were so in fact is open to question, although there are stories of Shang princesses being sent to the west as wives for their early rulers. In any case, there seems no doubt but that they valued Shang culture, and were anxious to preserve it. Indeed, within the bare limits of safety, such potentially subversive practices as sacrificial rites to the Shang royal ancestors, continued to be carried out under their patronage.

As far as concerns material culture, and particularly bronze-casting, there seems to have been no real break with tradition on the accession of the Chou. Styles changed, but only gradually; the technique deteriorated, but only after some time. Faced with evidence of this sort, we can reach but one conclusion about the Chou people and their racial origins. They were not barbarians; nor were they invaders of different race. They were Chinese, whose social organization and material culture were simply provincial versions of Shang China. When the Chou came into power there was no period of acclimatization to be got through. Shang legal and penal codes, ceremonies, sacrifices, and so forth, were readily understood, and quickly adopted, and the Chou settled down to administer the whole of China north of the Yangtze.

Taken all in all, it is perhaps remarkable that they held it together as long as they did. Their political conceptions, it is true, seem to have been much broader than those of their predecessors. But everything was against them. Their capital in the Wei river valley near modern Ch'ang-an was badly situated as a centre of government. It was ill-served with communications; and the country naturally broke up into cantons, separated by formidable topographical barriers, each of which had the makings of an independent state. The policy of granting fiefs to its military aristocracy also held the seeds of an excessive decentralization of Chou rule. Each feudal overlord was the civil and military head of his fief, with every opportunity of making himself independent of the central authority. The year 771 BC, when the Chou king moved his capital from the Wei river to Lo-yang in central Honan following attacks by the Jung barbarians, marks an end of effective Chou rule.

Throughout the third period – that of the so-called 'Spring and Autumn Annals' (722–481 BC) and 'Warring States' (481–221 BC) – the geographical field covered by 'Chinese' history was expanding. At the beginning of the Chou period fiefs were small, and there was a large number of them. Those on the periphery were 'warden' states – defensive outposts of the Chinese way of life set against the barbarian peoples who ringed it round. But the ultimate limits of possible Chinese advance had not been explored; and the first 300 years of Chou rule are marked by expansion and consolidation on the part of the border states, and by a series of barbarian wars. This encroachment, undertaken in the first place mainly for defensive reasons, was carried on in four key areas – in the south, the north-west, the north, and the north-east. It led to the rise of four great outlying powers: Ch'u in the south, Ch'in in the north-west, Chin in the north, and Ch'i in the north-east. So vast were the territories brought under the control of these four hegemonies that each individually probably came to control more effective power than the united efforts of the entire congeries of central states, the *chung kuo*, could command. The expansion of Ch'u throughout the Yangtze watershed, in particular, was a deliberate and successful piece of independent empire-building.

Each of the four big Powers in turn made its bid for supremacy. Ch'in's final victory was due partly to a strong natural defence system, partly to ease of west–east communication along the Wei and Yellow river valleys into the north China plain, and partly to the uncompromising realism with which its rulers carried out their plan to bring all China under one rule. The Ch'in Empire (221–206 BC) marks the end of feudal decentralization in China, and the beginning of bureaucratic administration and a central government; it also marks another stage in the age-old ebb and flow between Plateau and Plain.

When allowances for the special characteristics of each individual independent state have been made, the social organization of Chou times is seen to be roughly similar to that of the Shang overlordship. The basis of its economy remained an industrial and agricultural proletariat of artisans, peasants, and slaves. In a properly-run state, says Mencius, everybody should be able to eat meat and wear silk. Chou society, like that of the Shang, was all too clearly divided between a majority who ate millet, wore hemp clothes, and used stone implements and earthenware utensils, and a ruling minority of meat-eaters who wore silk and had bronze.

*

The ritual bronze vessels of ancient China are among the most exquisite objects in metal ever made. We now know of over 12,000 of them, and about a third are inscribed. But not only do the bronzes form a *corpus inscriptionum* of surpassing interest to the historian; by their very existence they bring to life the whole character of the period in a way that no historical account could ever do. The secular bronze art has not the same stature, and we shall have less to say about it here. We propose, therefore, to discuss the materials and techniques of bronze-casting; the functions of the ritual vessels; their classes; and the decorative styles they display. A study of inscriptions would take us too far into the fields of epigraphy and palaeography, and we shall do no more than mention their general nature.

Bronze alloys and casting techniques

The composition of Chinese bronze alloys from the Shang through the Han is remarkably inconstant; nor as a rule do the proportions of copper, tin, and lead in a given alloy bear any relation to the purpose of the object made from it. Frequent presence of a high lead content, as proved by many recent analyses, comes as a great surprise, violating as it does the canonical formulae found in classical Chinese texts which do not mention lead at all.

Lead is introduced into a bronze alloy, partly perhaps in order to lower the melting-point, but more especially to improve the flow of the metal and so enhance the delicacy of its casting. So in Mediterranean bronze statuary lead occurs in proportions varying between 1 and 11 per cent, and in south India in proportions as high as 25 per cent. We do not on the other hand expect to find it in alloys used for casting bronze weapons, yet Watson records the case of a Chinese spear-head, a sample from which contained 15 per cent lead and only a trace of tin.[5]

An analysis of metal from the bodies of eight bronze vessels thought to belong to the Chêng-chou period (1500–1300 BC) was recently published by Barbara Stephen.[6] In every case the percentage of lead was higher than that of tin. In one *chia* it was over four times as high; in another the amounts were 26.8 and 7.8 respectively. Two sets of analyses published by Li Chi in 1957 reveal proportions closer to the rough Western formula of nine parts copper, one part tin.[7] Thus of five *ko*, the respective proportions of copper, tin, and lead averaged 80, 11.5, and 6 per cent, while in the case of eight miscellaneous Shang examples the corresponding percentages averaged 86, 11.7, and 0.84 – even closer to the norm. Iron and zinc were present in infinitesimal amounts in these samples.

Several factors may have contributed to this variability of the bronze alloy. Possibly the formula varied from one foundry to another; perhaps high cost of tin encouraged use of lead; possibly formulae varied with supply of the constituent ores. In any case it is something for which we may well be grateful, because long burial in the alkaline soil of China has wrought most marvellous sea-changes in the colour and surface texture of the metal, each individual bronze assuming the patination appropriate to its particular metallic constitution and the conditions under which it was buried. This adventitious incrustation on the bronzes is, to modern eyes, the crowning glory of their otherwise immaculate and exquisite forms.

While flat objects such as weapons, tools and mirrors were undoubtedly cast with the aid of temporary two-piece moulds or 'flasks', it has generally been supposed in the West that the bronze vessels of ancient China were made exclusively by the *cire-perdue* or 'lost wax' process. This involved building up a wax model, or facsimile of the vessel to be cast, upon a fire-proof clay core or armature shaped to the containing space of the intended vessel. Decoration was either carved by hand upon the surface of the wax, or was impressed by means of negative dies. The wax model was then coated with a fine liquid clay slip containing a refractory, after which successive layers of coarser clay were applied until a substantial outer mould had been built up around the model. The whole assemblage was now secured by means of metal pins. On heating, the wax vacated the space between inner core and outer mould, into which molten bronze could now be poured. The channels through which the wax had escaped became inlets for the molten bronze (runners), and effluents for the escape of air (risers). The complete bronze-casting of course included castings of these, which had to be detached, and their scars tooled down, after the mould and core had been broken away.

The *cire-perdue* process is capable of yielding extremely fine castings. It also allows appurtenances such as handles and legs to be cast solid with the bowl of the vessel, and permits reproduction of openwork and undercut relief. The disadvantage is that once the outer mould has been formed on the wax model, it cannot subsequently be inspected for possible flaws, and the vessel must be cast come what may. Nor can the mould be used a second time. The process leaves few tangible traces; yet there is little doubt but that the ancient Chinese bronze-smith knew of it, and exploited it with unequalled virtuosity. It is also certain, in the light of new evidence, that many vessels were made by the alternative method of direct casting from composite moulds made up of several piece-moulds.

A number of fragments of composition material were recovered from the An-yang site, bearing negative patterns of typical bronze designs. Some of these fragments had smooth edges and were provided with keys by means of which they could be fitted together; in this way a complete mould could be built up around a clay or composition core, with a space left between representing the bronze vessel to be cast. Small particles of bronze were found in some of this negative relief, according to Karlbeck, so that direct casting from them was certainly attempted.[8] They could not have been used more than once for this purpose.

More recently, solid clay blocks of halves and sections of vessels have been found at An-yang, in some cases with relief decoration, or outline ink-drawing of relief decoration, already in place on their surfaces. These must have been models, or permanent positive matrices, from which negative piece-moulds were taken; the piece-moulds would later be assembled around a solid clay core, possibly with the intervention of a wax 'pad' to ensure uniformity of thickness in the space between.

In a recent study Watson has summarized the probable procedure through which the mould was prepared for casting. In the first stage an unornamented clay model was made – complete or in halves, as convenient. Next, elements in the high-relief decoration were applied in the form of previously moulded clay plaques. The whole was then baked to pottery hardness. After firing, the low-relief details were painted and then engraved on the background between the main motifs. The negative piece-moulds were then applied to the model, and taken off in appropriate sections; the joints between them were trued, and then they in their turn were fired. They were then assembled around the clay core. Taking into account the weight of the latter, it is assumed that casting was done with mould and core upside-down. The core, and the core of the hollow foot if the vessel was intended to have one, was centred by means of plugs of bronze or some combustible material. The sections were so arranged that the joints between them lay as far as possible along the vertical and horizontal boundaries of the vessel's décor; little tooling of the surface then needed doing, once the vessel had been cast.[9]

Present evidence suggests that bronze vessels of the Chêng-chou period were mostly cast direct from composite moulds, as described above.[10] Not until a late stage in the later occupation of the An-yang site (Hsiao-t'un 2) do we come across vessels whose forms seem to predicate the cire-perdue process. We may perhaps hazard the guess that the process appeared in China not earlier than the twelfth century BC, whether imported from the West or no there is as yet no means of telling.

The purpose of the ritual bronzes; inscriptions

Ritual bronzes were made for actual use at ancestral sacrifices. Ancestors are, of all cosmic beings, those to whom the Chinese have traditionally given pride of place. They were to be consulted about every important matter of domestic concern; their memory and achievements were to be perpetuated by constant ritual observance. But the living, too, would one day become ancestors. They therefore looked to posterity fitly to honour their name in turn.

Judging from their inscriptions, Shang vessels were made in honour of particular individual ancestors. A few graphs serve to record the ancestor's name, and less frequently that of the person who had the vessel cast. But early in the Chou period the inscriptions underwent a change of character. They became fuller; and we can now see how vital was the role that they, and the vessels that carried them, played in feudal Chinese society and religion. Not only do they record the name of the ancestor in whose honour the vessel was cast; they almost invariably name the donor, and, since his wish was to make his name illustrious to posterity, the precise circumstances that led to the casting. A suitable occasion would be that upon which the ruler – or feudal overlord – conferred upon the vassal a fief, gifts of clothing, or some other reward in recognition of valued service. The inscription might then contain the following sorts of information:

1. The date and place of the audience.
2. The officials present.

3. The edict of investiture.
4. The vassal's thanks.
5. The vassal's resolve to cast a vessel, or vessels, to mark the occasion.
6. The names of the ancestors on whose behalf the vessel was cast.

The inscription would end with pious hopes – sometimes for long life on the part of the donor; almost always with the wish that the vessel should be used by posterity. The formula 'may sons and grandsons for a myriad years cherish and use (this precious sacral vessel)' crops up over and over again.

I append a typical example of one of these fuller inscriptions. It is to be found on a vessel long known to Chinese scholars as the *Sung ting* because it was a *ting* [p. 86] made to the order of a certain Sung, on an occasion when the Chou king sent him to govern Chêng-chou. This was a satellite town located some 10 miles east of the eastern Chou capital of Lo-i (770–225 BC), but the occasion celebrated in the inscription seems to have been about a half century before the move from the western capital of Tsung-chou – here simply called Chou – in 771 BC. It runs:

'The 3rd year, 5th month, last quarter, *chia hsü* day; the King being at the Temple [of the former Kings] K'ang and Chao in the Chou capital. In the early morning the King arrived at the Great Room and took up his position. The Steward Hung assisted Sung in entering the Gate and taking his place in the middle of the Courtyard. The Lord of Yin received the King's Mandate. The King called upon the Recorder Kua Shêng to deliver the Decree in writing to Sung. The Royal Decree ran: "Sung, we order you to [go and] govern Chêng-chou. We bestow on you [the income of] 20 families, and the supervision and charge of the newly-established [town of Chêng-chou]. We permit you to use the amenities of the Royal Palace, and bestow upon you a black garment, embroidered silk, a red skirt, a scarlet [jade half-ring] *huang*, a banner hung with bells and a horse-bridle, for use in your capacity as an official." Sung prostrated himself, bowed his head, received the Decree Book, fastened it to his girdle, and so departed. In return he presented [a jade tablet] *chang* [and said]: "I, Sung, dare in reply to proclaim the great glory and unfailing munificence of the Son of Heaven [the King], wherewith I shall make precious sacrificial wine and food vessels for my august father, my respected paternal uncle, my august mother, my respected paternal aunt, thereby to show my filial piety and to solicit tranquillity of heart, piety, pure blessing, a steady salary and long life. May I, Sung, enjoy a myriad years and the bushy eyebrows of old age. May I be a faithful servant, and may the Son of Heaven enjoy an auspicious end. May my sons and grandsons cherish and use [these precious sacrificial vessels]."' [11]

Classes of ritual vessels

Sacrifice to ancestors involved the offering of food and wine. Naturally, therefore, vessels for cooking, containing and serving food, for pouring and drinking wine, and for mixing it with water, predominate among ritual bronze objects. There is also a small class of water utensils, and a number of miscellaneous objects associated with the sacrifice, such as tables, ladles, and bells. The total number of separately-named ritual objects, according to some classifications, is well over fifty. For description here I have selected twenty only. These classes, which I take to be the leading ones, are grouped below as food, wine, and water vessels.

Figure 11 shows that in reviewing certain classes we may expect to find continuous development in form, that is shape and decorative imposition, throughout the three stylistic phases

12 *Bronze ritual wine goblet,* ku, *the middle and lower zones filled with delicately wrought squared spirals and* t'ao⁄t'ieh *in low relief. From An⁄yang. First Phase (B style), Shang dynasty. Height: 10 in. Art Museum, University of Singapore.*

13 *The middle zone. Height:* 2 5/16 *in.*

14 *Detail of the foot. Height:* 2 3/8 *in.*

15 Bronze four-sided ritual wine vessel, ho
cast together with its cover. The legs are i
part hollow within, like those of li, their uppe
parts modelled as quasi-human masks. Th
vessel is heavily flanged. First Phase (A style,
Shang dynasty, one of a set of three found a
An-yang. The affinities between this remar
kable bronze and a type of Neolithic potter
ewer [pl. 18] are discussed on pages 30–3
and 92. See O. Sirén, 1924, pl. 19, for a
intermediate form in bronze. Height: 24 5/8 in
Kaichiro Nedzu Collection, Tokyo.

16 (above right) Bronze ritual water vesse
i, with handle modelled as a bovine anima
the neck-belt with a low-relief design of de
formed bird-figures, the body with horizonta
fluting. Second Phase, early Chou dynasty
perhaps 825 BC. This is the Ch'u Huan i
self-named in its inscription. See plates 6
68, and 86 and their captions. Length: 15 in
Collection of Mrs W. Sedgwick, London.

17 (below right) Bronze ritual food vesse
kuei, First Phase (B style), early Cho
dynasty. This is the K'ang Hou kuei. It wa
cast for a Marquis K'ang, as we learn from it
inscription, to commemorate a royal breve
charging him to administer the land of Me
following an abortive revolt on the part of th
heir of the last Shang ruler there, an even
which took place shortly after the Chou con
quest. The vessel may thus be dated to the en
of the eleventh century BC. See page 99
Height: 9 1/2 in. Collection of Captai
D. Malcolm, London.

18 Bronze ritual food vessel, tui, the bowl and its reversible cover being approximately identical in shape. Geometrical ornament in the Chin-ts'un style consisting of a turquoise inlay. Third Phase, late Chou dynasty, probably fifth century BC, found at Pao-chi, Shensi. Height: 15³/₄ in. Fogg Museum of Art, Cambridge, Mass.

19 Bronze ritual food vessel, kuei, with a corona in the form of spreading openwork tongues on the cover [cf. pls 62, 69 and 72]. The handles modelled as a pair of dragons in the act of devouring (or disgorging) a second pair which rear up boldly, as Sirén says, 'like the prows of galleons'. The body cast together with a massive stand, with an allover décor of inter-woven degenerated snake-dragons. Second Phase. The inscription on this kuei dates it to the period c. 580–534 BC. Height: 14 in. British Museum.

of vital achievement from the Shang down to the beginning of the Han in 206 BC. In other cases the entire history of the class lies within the confines of a single phase. The wine vessels, for example, disappear almost unanimously at the end of the tenth century; and with the single exception of the *chih* these truant forms never emerge, not even during the archaising Third Phase which saw the rebirth of so many First Phase decorative motifs. Drink, apparently, played a less conspicuous part in the social and ceremonial life of the Chou than it seems to have done in Shang times.

The table is also meant to introduce readers to the familiar appearances of typical members of the vessel-classes, all of which will be found reproduced with minor variations in the accompanying plates. A synoptic illustration such as this leaves much unsaid, and could prove a source of misunderstanding. Take for instance the *ting*. The typical First Phase *ting* shown *pls 54, 56* in the table is not the form we encounter during the Second and Third Phases. Nor is it precisely that of *ting* found in the earlier part of the Shang period as represented at Chêng- *pl. 58* chou and Liu-li-ko. Still less does it resemble that of the Neolithic pottery *ting* from which it undoubtedly ultimately descends. In the Neolithic hinterland the forms of pottery vessels are more fluid, less solidified. A pot on three legs suggests now the *ting*, now the *li*, now the *chia*. It would be wrong to assume that the differentiated classes of bronze vessels to which these names are given descend by orthogenesis from equally differentiated Neolithic pottery prototypes.

Another sort of ambiguity invests the nomenclature of the bronze vessel-classes. There are those whose names are recorded, at least occasionally, in the inscriptions they bear; and these include *li, ting, hsien, kuei, hu, lei, ho, p'an, chien*, and *i*. These classes, in other words, name themselves and enjoy the legitimate status conferred by a patronymic, even though their formal appearances may reveal the lineaments of a mixed ancestry. In other examples exactly the reverse is the case. The vessel called *fang-i*, for example, enjoys excellent status as a formal class. *pl. 74* It is entirely *sui generis*, and cannot possibly be confused with any other vessel-class; moreover its form is invariable. Its name, on the other hand, enjoys no status whatsoever, since it merely means 'rectangular sacrificial vessel', and is a recent convention. The same is true of the classes now christened *tui* and *kuang*. *col. 18, pl. 84*

In other cases, vessels received their names in the intermediate past, from the antiquarians of the Sung dynasty (AD 960–1279) who ransacked Chinese literature in an attempt to identify the anonymous bronzes then coming to hand as a result of the collecting mania that swept the Sung aristocracy. It is probably no coincidence that the majority of these were vessels of the wine category that had disappeared shortly after the advent of the Chou. Thus the Sung scholars identified the classes *tou, yu, chüeh, chia, tsun, chih*, and *ku* on the strength of references in the Classics, in the *Shuo wên* scriptionary [p. 42], and various exegetical books. In almost every case these identifications have withstood the test of time.

Information conveyed in figure 11 will not be recapitulated in the brief notes that now follow.

Li are cauldrons mounted on three hollow legs, the containing space of the bowl being con- LI tinuous with that of the legs, so that cooking food is brought into close contact with the heat *pls 51, 53, 55* of the fire. Neolithic pottery *li* are found throughout the Plain as far west as western Honan, but do not reach into Kansu until late in the Bronze Age. *col. 5*

The form of *li* assimilated into bronze during the First Phase was in general use in Honan at the opening of the historical period. Made of the characteristic coarse grey pottery of the day, they are tall and stately vessels mounted on three well-spaced legs. Sometimes these legs are shaped like breasts, being deeply cleft and flowing smoothly into the body of the vessel;

	FOOD						WATER		
	COOKER			CONTAINER			CEREMONIAL ABLUTIONS		
NAME OF CLASS	*li*	*ting*	*hsien*	*kuei*	*tou*	*tui*	*p'an*	*chien*	*i*
FAMILIAR APPEARANCE									
WHETHER SELF-NAMED	yes	yes	yes	yes	no	no	yes	yes	yes
ANCIENT GRAPH AND MODERN EQUIVALENT	鬲	鼎	甗	簋	豆	敦	盤	監	匜
PHASE PRESENT	1 2 3	1 2 3	1 2 3	1 2 3	- 2 3	- - 3	1 2 3	- - 3	- 2 -
NEOLITHIC FORM									

11 Table of bronze types and their antecedents. The graphs are all in forms which appear on the bronzes themselves

sometimes they are stubby, splayed, and less smoothly articulated with the body. This is the variety found in the early Shang levels at Chêng-chou, where it is duplicated in bronze.

Li may or may not have a single vertical carrying-handle mounted at the side between shoulder and mouthrim. In the bronze version this handle is replaced by a pair of 'ears' mounted upon the mouthrim; the latter is often flattened and everted in both pottery and bronze forms.

During the Second Phase a new type of *li* appears. The bowl is much shallower, so that the legs stand farther apart and are connected in a long flat curve or arch. A pottery version from Hsiao-t'un approximates to this.

Third Phase *li* are often provided with covers which can be reversed for use as accessory vessels.

TING
pls 50, 52, 54, 56–58
pl. 16

fig. 12

The *ting* tripod is essentially a bowl mounted on three solid legs. Pottery prototypes are conspicuous in the Lung-shan and Yang-shao Cultures, the ancestry being at least as venerable as that of the *li*. At Yang-shao-ts'un and at Hou-kang 3 [p. 29] the vessel is a rounded bowl on three solid legs which are made separately and luted onto the body. This approaches nearest to the typical First Phase bronze vessel.

The Lung-shan variety is of squat proportions, with a flat base and with three well-spaced solid legs of conical form. Here is a pot closely similar to the ancestral pottery *chia* [p. 91], and also to the *li* saving only that its legs are solid. *Ting*, *li*, and *chia* are in this tradition closely

86

WINE										
CONTAINER					GOBLET				SERVER	
tsun	*yu*	*hu*	*lei*	*fang-i*	*chia*	*chüeh*	*chih*	*ku*	*ho*	*kuang*
no	no	yes	yes	no	no	no	no	no	yes	no
1 — —	1 — —	1 2 3	1 2 3	1 — —	1 — —	1 — —	1 — —	1 — 3	1 2 3	1 — —

except for *chia* which is in oracle-bone script

related vessels. So at Chêng-chou bronze *ting* have a deep bowl-shaped body which sags below into three bulbular depressions, one over each leg; the vessel would be identical with *li* from the same site, were its legs hollow. This indeterminate form, which survives into the An-yang part of the First Phase (1300–1027 BC), is what Karlgren calls *li-ting* in recognition of its hybrid ancestry. He claims, however, that the décor of late First Phase *li-ting* is not indeterminate, but is discreet and absolutely distinctive to the vessel-type. For this reason he would add *li-ting* to the repertoire of bronze vessels as a separate vessel-class. *pl. 58*

Following its début in bronze, the form of the *ting* shows much modulation. In the First Phase a rectangular version co-exists with the usual bowl-shaped variety; sometimes it has a cover. In the Second Phase the body becomes shallower, and 'ears' no longer rise from the mouthrim, but are mounted on the body, whence they curve outward and upward. Legs become thin and attenuated, and splay out at the junction with the body and at the foot so that they look rather like the legs of Chippendale chairs. An even greater variety of form is found in the Third Phase. The square type reappears, sometimes provided with a spout, opposite which is a single handle. As a rule, late *ting* are covered, and the cover has three equidistant projections – sometimes small animals modelled in the round, sometimes ring handles – whereby the cover when turned over can be used as an accessory dish. *pl. 59* *pl. 54* *pl. 57*

Vessels of this distinctive class may be described as steamers. The form is composite, the lower portion of the vessel being shaped like a *li*, into the mouth of which fits a deep, bowl-shaped HSIEN vessel. In bronze specimens the two portions may be cast separately or, more usually, as one. The idea underlying the *hsien* is that food placed in the upper portion of the vessel is cooked by steam heat coming from the lower. Accordingly the bottom of the upper part of the vessel is perforated in pottery examples; in bronze specimens a grille is hinged on to the brim of the lower part, or to the base of the upper.

Pottery specimens directly forecasting the shape of bronze *hsien* have been found in the first three Shang levels at Chêng-chou (1500–1300 BC). Moreover Andersson has produced what might be called the archetype of all *hsien*, illustrating the manner in which the composite vessel came about. At the site of Pu-chao-chai near Yang-shao-ts'un, contemporary with Hsiao-t'un I, he found a pot of grey ware, the bottom of which was perforated and covered with 'fur' on the inside; nearby lay a *li* of the same ware which had a single ridge running round the inside of the mouth, such as would have served to support an upper vessel.

pl. 13 He proceeded to reconstruct a prehistoric *hsien*.

The bronze form is fairly stable. At the beginning of the Second Phase a four-legged variety with square section occurs, the two components being cast separate; 'ears' may be mounted on the upper portion, the lower portion, or both. Yetts records the inscription on one *hsien* saying that the vessel was 'for use while campaigning, while travelling, wherewith to make soup from rice and millet' – proof that bronze vessels were not always used solely for ceremonial purposes.[12]

KUEI The form of this bronze vessel, stripped of accessory features, is unmistakably derived from
pls 61, 62; col. 17, 19 a pottery prototype. Such vessels, containers of cereals used as food for ritual and ordinary
pl. 19 purposes, were called *tui* by the Sung cataloguers. But Jung Kêng has shown that this was because they mistook the graph found on the bronzes for an archaic form of *tui*, instead of deciphering it as *chiu*, the old equivalent of a modern form pronounced *kuei*, or rather 'guei'.

Variant First Phase shapes are numerous. The starting-point is a round, rather shallow bowl mounted on a wide, shallow, and slightly spreading ring foot. The bowl may have no handles at all, or two laterally-placed vertical handles, or four; or else the handles may be L-shaped 'ears' mounted below the mouthrim, as in Second Phase *ting*, in which case the vessel is sometimes designated as *yü* in its inscription.

pl. 61 Special care was devoted to the design of the handles. The upper part is normally an animal mask, and from the underside of the lower part hangs a pendant that sometimes seems to simulate the tail, feet, or claws of a bird. Sometimes, on four-handled *kuei*, these downward projections are continued so as to form legs by which the vessel is raised aloft.

All known *kuei* seem at one time to have had covers, and these could usually be reversed
pl. 62 to act as extra dishes. Second Phase *kuei* are often mounted on a massive square stand cast together with the rest of the vessel; but *kuei* shapes are curiously unpredictable, and sometimes three rather puny-looking legs are found instead. An odd example in the Brundage collection has a clapper-bell fixed on the inside of the hollow stand.

TOU Pottery ancestors of these food-containers have been recovered in large numbers from the
pl. 60 Lung-shan site at Ch'êng-tzŭ-yai and also from Yang-shao and other sites in the region of
col. 3, pl. 20 the Plain. The pottery version is shaped like a cake-stand, and comprises a shallow dish mounted on a tall, hollow, and often perforated flared foot.

It is strange that this basic shape should not have become regularly established as a bronze vessel-class during the First Phase. Apart from a few pieces of doubtful date, to which Watson draws attention [13], no bronze *tou* seems to be earlier than the beginning of the Second Phase, and by far the majority of them are found in the Third. Third Phase examples resembling the pottery prototype are not unknown, as, for example, one excavated in 1955 from the tomb of a marquis of Ts'ai state dating from the beginning of the fourth century BC. But most of them take a somewhat different form, that of a bowl mounted on a tall flared foot and surmounted with a domed cover which could be reversed to act as an independent vessel. The cover is usually fitted with a single flared projection, so duplicating the form of the *tou* itself, or else with three equidistant ring-handles or small, naturalistically modelled animals.

The Neolithic pottery vessel, we may note, continued to be made in Korea until as late as the fifth century AD, its form essentially unchanged from that of its Lung-shan and Yang-shao ancestors.

The vessel now conventionally called *tui* occurs only in the Third Phase. Like an Easter egg, it is divisible into two more or less identical halves, each having curious projections by which it can be stood upright. When put together, the two halves sometimes make a perfect sphere.

Êrh ya has this to say of the *tui*: 'Although the *tui* is a container like the *fu* and *kuei*, it differs in being completely round, top and bottom, inside and outside.' [14]

TUI
col. 18

This class, etymologically speaking, is not a class at all. The oracle-bone version of the modern character for *tsun* shows a narrow, bottle-shaped vessel, with pointed base, tall neck, and a somewhat flared narrow mouth, held aloft by a pair of hands. Such amphorae, known as *p'ing*, are commonly found at sites of the Middle Yang-shao Culture in Honan, and were presumably used for carrying water over the difficult *loess* terrain. The form of the oracle-bone character suggests that *p'ing* may have been used in ritual worship. They were not translated into bronze, however, and in the Bronze Age context the character for *tsun* simply means 'sacrificial wine vessel'. It occurs on countless bronzes, very often in the expression *pao tsun i* or *pao tsun ting* meaning 'precious sacrificial wine and food vessels' – as in the inscription on the Sung *ting* [p. 80].

Since the Sung dynasty the name *tsun* has been applied to a variety of squat and thickened bronze *ku* [p. 92] too large to have been used as a goblet. This application, entirely without warrant, is today so firmly established that there seems little point in disputing it. On the other hand the Classics frequently make mention of vessels called *hsi tsun*, *hu tsun*, or *hsiang tsun*, meaning thereby bronze sacrificial wine vessels cast in the form of sacrificial animals, tigers, and elephants respectively. These vessels are readily identified, and were so identified by the Sung antiquarians.

The menagerie grouped under the heading *hsi tsun*, 'sacrificial wine vessel in the shape of a sacrificial animal', is known to include owl, ram, hare, tapir, ox, horse, and rhinoceros, among others. All are modelled with tremendous verve; with this group we are in fact concerned with bronze derivatives of the Shang tradition of limestone sculptures [p. 173], conceived and executed *en ronde bosse*.

Both the squat *ku*-shaped *tsun* and the animal *tsun* appear only late in the First Phase, let us say the eleventh and tenth centuries BC, and do not survive beyond it.

TSUN
pls 63, 66

Like vessels of the last class, *yu* are known only from a late stage of the First Phase, and have no pottery ancestors. The form of the oracle-bone character implies an asymmetrical proto-

YU
pls 64, 65

type made of some perishable material – Watson suggests a leather bottle or wine-skin, Yetts a gourd perhaps provided with handles of bamboo plaitted strips. The rhomboid pattern on the handle of the *yu* shown in plate 64, he says, is a memory of this type of handle.

As frequent references to them in the Classics testify, *yu* – whether bronze or otherwise – were used for carrying offerings or presents of black millet wine. An inscription on a famous Second Phase bronze, the Mao Kung *ting*, speaks of the gift of 'a *yu* of black millet wine' to a high official in anticipation of loyal service to be rendered by him to the house of Chou. The date of the *ting*, about 800 BC, makes it probable that the *yu* referred to was not of bronze. The inscription on a *yu* said to have come from An-yang indicates that it was a 'sacral vessel for travelling' – further evidence, perhaps, in support of the identification.

It was the Sung cataloguers who first suggested that some *yu* might be bronze vessels of the type we show. The form, that of a covered bucket with a swing-handle, is in fact admirably adapted for transporting liquids, and there is no doubt at all that the Sung scholars were right. The typical bronze *yu* is a substantial, handsome vessel with low-slung belly and sloping shoulders, so that it discloses a shape-relationship with *hu* [see below]. In its earlier version the carrying handle is set across the long diameter of the vessel's oval section; in later examples, from the very end of the First Phase, it is set in line with the long diameter. This is a less practical arrangement for carrying purposes but on the other hand the important design on the two main faces of the vessel need not now be interrupted.

pl. 65   There is a variant cast in zoomorphic form which I shall mention again shortly [p. 97].

HU
pls 67–72

No convincing pottery prototype has been claimed for this vessel, though Chêng Tê-k'un illustrates a Lung-shan black pottery jar from Liang-chu which he calls a *hu*; it is perhaps a contemporary pottery imitation of a bronze vessel-form. The *hu* is in any case essentially a pot. Its tall, graceful shape is of a sort that a potter would take natural delight in throwing, as is witnessed by a range of fine glazed pottery imitation *hu* made in Han times, when the bronze vessel-class was still flourishing.

Hu are among the largest bronze vessels. Their proportions vary somewhat, but the basic features – low-slung belly, sloping shoulders, tall neck, and a slightly flared and rather narrow mouth – are more or less invariable. All these features are shown by the oracle-bone graph with which the modern character *hu* is equated; it also shows a pair of laterally mounted loop-handles, and a cover or stopper surmounted with a conical lid-knob.

Hu are normally provided with means of suspension. Sometimes these are tubular 'ears' mounted at the sides below the mouthrim, sometimes loop-handles cast solid with the vessel in the same position, sometimes free-hanging ring-handles suspended in their turn from small loop-handles. Chains or cords were passed through 'ears', loop-handles, or ring-handles, and the *hu* could then be carried around like a *yu*. Indeed, a tall covered vessel of the First Phase, much resembling it, is often called a *yu*. One so labelled is in the Minneapolis Institute of Arts. Yet the outline drawing of this piece might have served as a model for the oracle-bone graph equated with *hu*. Typologically, in fact, the tall so-called *yu* is not a bucket so much as a stoppered bottle; it is an intermediate vessel-form, but perhaps it is more of a *hu* than a *yu*.

LEI
pl. 73

Lei are large bowls or vases which the ritual texts say were used for holding either wine or water. Their distinguishing feature, in contrast to such vessels as *yu*, *hu*, and *chih*, is that they have high, broad, keel-shaped shoulders with a body gradually narrowing below, giving them a tough, workaday appearance quite unlike the gentle and inert form of, say, the *hu*. Pottery versions of *lei* are found in the three early Shang levels at Chêng-chou; a particularly

famous *lei*, made of the characteristic kaolinic white stoneware of An-yang, is now in the *pl. 12*
Freer Gallery.

The Shang bronze *lei* is often square in section, with a cover similar to the 'roof-lid' of the
fang-i. In later periods the vessel tends to become wider and squatter in its proportions, while
retaining the same tense, high shoulder. *Lei* are usually provided with two or four integrally
cast loop-handles mounted on the shoulder, often with free ring-handles depending from
them.

These alleged wine-containers are quite distinctive as to shape, obviously modelling an archi-   FANG-I
tectural form. The cover suggests a high-pitched and fully hipped roof, while the body is   *pl. 74*
square or rectangular, leans slightly outwards, and is differentiated from a base which might
be regarded as an imitation of the pounded earth platform on which all important buildings
from the Shang period onwards were elevated.

It is clear that the pottery prototypes of these vessels have to be sought among pots of the *li-ting*   CHIA
type, the typical splayed and bayonet-shaped legs being vestiges of the hollow conical sup-   *pls 75–77*
ports of the latter. The earliest bronze *chia*, those from Chêng-chou, are flat-bottomed, with   *fig. 12*
the body pinched in to form an explicit waist above the shallow belly zone, and then flaring   *pl. 75*
out gradually towards the wide mouthrim. On the latter stand two curious capped pillars.
A side-handle is usually mounted in the same vertical plane as one of the legs.

Chia are associated in the Classics with wine, and they are usually classed as goblets, but
what we call *chia* would seem to be inconveniently shaped for drinking purposes, and far
too large. There is little doubt but that the vessel was used for heating wine over a charcoal fire,
and that the capped pillars, as Yetts first suggested, were devices by which it could be removed from the fire with the aid of a pair of tongs.

12 Prehistoric pottery *li-ting* from
Pu-chao-chai, Honan province. In this
vessel the forms of *li, ting* and *chia* are all
implicit. The bronze form of *chia* shown
in plate 76 could well be a descendant

The First Phase *chia* is a lovely vessel, arresting in its appearance, a perfect adaptation to
metal of a pottery type, yet so stark and rigorous in its form, we almost feel it must have been
conceived in metal from the start. A square version exists alongside the round.

The *chüeh* is a wine goblet shaped like an inverted helmet mounted on three tall, lance-shaped   CHÜEH
legs. The mouth projects forward into a long, trough-like spout, and backward into a broad,   *pls 78–79*
rapidly tapering tail. Two capped pillars, like those of *chia*, stand on opposite sides of the
mouthrim near where the latter extends into the spout. A small side-handle lies in the same
vertical plane as one of the legs, and at right-angles to the line of the mouth and its extensions.
The spout is to its left. On the wall of the bowl within the handle an inscription of one or
two characters may sometimes be found.   *pl. 79*

As with the *chia*, we have here a vessel of breath-taking originality, clean and beautifully
balanced, inconceivable in any medium other than a metal casting. One searches the military
vocabulary for words to describe its resolute, uncompromising air, and perhaps expressions
like 'helmet' or 'lance-like', used above, really choose themselves.

Dr Li Chi once arranged a series of Neolithic pottery vessels in such a way as to demonstrate
an evolution of form leading up to that of the *chüeh*. A pot from Chêng-chou certainly seems   *fig. 11*
to approach to an ultimate limit of plastic elaboration possible in clay, and its form does
strongly resemble that of the simpler types of bronze *chüeh* recovered from the same site. We
must also bear in mind a probable family relationship between the *chüeh* and the *chia*, whose
origin in the pottery *li-ting* seems to be firmly established. It is, however, intrinsically unlikely
that a pottery shape should have evolved *sui generis* as far as the stage represented by the Chêng-

chou pottery *chüeh*, but much more likely that such a vessel is itself an imitation of an already existing bronze form. In short, the hypothesis of a pottery prototype for the bronze *chüeh* cannot be accepted unreservedly.

The alternative theory, advanced by Kuo Pao-chün, is that the *chüeh* was once a vessel of ox horn. To make it stand upright, two bamboo legs were tied to it to make, with the tip of the horn, a three-point base. The capped pillars, on this theory, are vestiges of these two legs projecting above the level of the mouthrim.

The Chêng-chou bronze *chüeh* is a thin-walled vessel with a flat bottom and tiny capped pillars; sometimes there is only one of these – which does not help Kuo Pao-chün's theory. An intermediate form with slightly rounded base and fully developed capped pillars is known from An-yang, and presumably belongs to the earlier period of occupation (Hsiao-t'un I). It leads directly towards the apotheosis of the bronze *chüeh*, the most evocative of all Chinese bronze forms, as accomplished in the later period of occupation at An-yang.

pl. 79

CHIH   *Chih* may be described as small *hu* lacking handles; sometimes covered (and always meant to be); sometimes round in section, but typically oval; and with a mouth rather wider and more flared, in proportion, than that of the *hu*. No obvious pottery prototype exists. At its best the *chih* is a most graceful, easy, sophisticated sort of vessel, strong yet feminine in the elegance and sweetness of its line.

The class went out of fashion at the end of the First Phase, but was revived during the Third Phase, which took an archaizing trend.

KU   Mystery surrounds the origin of this very lovely and distinctive class of bronze. A tall vessel
pls 80, 82; col. 12   of *tou* type, found in the black pottery of Lung-shan and the grey of Hsiao-t'un, is thought by Andersson and Chêng Tê-k'un to be its predecessor. But Kuo Pao-chün said that it originated in a vessel made of horn. His imaginary reconstruction shows two trumpet-shaped pieces of animal horn interlocked at their narrower ends and bound together at that point, the middle of the resulting vessel, by a collar of similar material. Corresponding to these three horn sections would be, if Kuo is right, the three main horizontal zones of the bronze version.

An inexplicable feature of many *ku* is a small cruciform perforation, which may be repeated four times, set in a plain recessed field just below the waist of the vessel. On an early Shang bronze from Liu-li-ko this field is also ornamented with three horizontal ribs. Now a squat
pl. 81   ivory beaker found at Chêng-chou has just such a plain field towards its base, relieved with two horizontal ribs and with a single cruciform perforation. The beaker, assuming it does not imitate a bronze *ku*, thus qualifies as its possible ancestor; and Kuo Pao-chün may not have been wide of the mark in supposing that the prototype of the bronze was made of animal horn.

HO   *Ho* may be simply described as vessels in the shape of tea-pots or kettles; they were probably
pl. 83, col. 15   used for mixing wine with water or cordials. We have already mentioned a Ch'i-chia-p'ing
pl. 18   pitcher of grey ware whose form is reminiscent of that of the sumptuous bronze *ho* from the Nezu collection [p. 30]. Ch'i-chia-p'ing, as was noticed, is probably partly contemporary with the late Shang, so that the shape of the pot may well be derived from that of the bronze. It will be observed that the domed lid is in each case an integral part of the vessel.

The bronze form varies a good deal; but *ho* are usually mounted on three or four short legs, and the body may then have something of the shape of *li* or *ting*.

These are bronzes shaped like sauce-boats, for which no pottery prototype can be adduced. KUANG AND I
They are put together here because the Sung cataloguers made no distinction between them, pls 84, 85; col. 16
and it is not certain that any exists, despite the fact that *kuang* are reckoned to have been used
for mixing wine and water, *i* as ewers. The word *kuang* was only recently applied by Wang
Kuo-wei to vessels of the First Phase, some of which have a vertical partition running across
the shorter axis, such as might have been an adaptation for the purpose of mixing liquids.
Wang's identification depends on a passage in *Shih ching*, 'Book of Odes', in which mention
is made of a lover drawing water from the *chin lei*, 'bronze *lei*', and drinking it out of the
ssŭ kuang. The word *ssŭ* can mean 'bovine'; so Wang assumed that it referred in this context
to the ox-head which adorns the covers of some, though not all, so-called *kuang*. The question
is, could such singular vessels conceivably have been used as drinking goblets?

The word qualifying *lei* in the *Shih ching* quotation is *chin*, 'bronze'; so that we might by
parallelism expect *ssŭ* also to refer to the material of the vessel out of which the lover drank.
One of the meanings of *ssŭ* is 'horn'. If the *ssŭ kuang* was a drinking-horn it is obvious that fig. 47b
the bronze sauce-boat is no such vessel, and that *kuang* is a misnomer as applied to it. No
bronze *kuang* is self-named.

Bronze *kuang* are covered, whereas *i* normally are not. Yetts has, however, drawn attention
to a covered vessel the style of which accords with a Second Phase attribution, and which is
named *i* in its inscription; so that the two types of vessel cannot be differentiated by the fact
that some have covers. Watson says that a gap of at least two centuries intervenes between the
disappearance of the *kuang* and the appearance of the *i*; and he therefore concludes that the
two vessels do not belong to the same lineage. This may well be so as far as concerns their
function. The fourth-century BC *Tso chuan* speaks of the *i* as a vessel used for washing the
hands, and it was probably associated with the *p'an* in ceremonial ablutions. It seems equally
probable to me that the form of the First Phase *kuang* suggested to later bronze-designers that
of the Second and Third Phases *i*.

The vessels show much variation in shape. The covered ones have cover and upper parts
of the body modelled in the shape of zoomorphs. In later examples the cover usually disappears, but the spout is still enclosed above by an animal mask, and the body is supported
on four legs. At a still later stage the spout is open above, and the legs may then be replaced
by a hollow, spreading base; from which, in still later examples, legs again begin to appear.
Finally, by the fourth century BC, versions are found having neither legs nor base; and in
these a free-hanging ring-handle takes the place of the vertically hung fixed loop-handle at
the back.

Chêng Tê-k'un illustrates pottery prototypes for these shallow bowls or basins made in the P'AN
red paste of Yang-shao, the black of Lung-shan, and the grey of Hsiao-t'un. The bronze pl. 86
version is nevertheless rarely found during the First Phase, though there are some that seem fig. 11
to date from the very end of the Shang dynasty. They were used together with *i* for washing
the hands or perhaps the ceremonial vessels during the ancestral sacrifice. Most are circular,
but there is a rare oval variety. Most have a shallow, wide, and spreading base, from which
three puny legs resembling those found on some Second Phase *kuei* may arise. Handles are
usually up-turned 'ears' mounted below the mouthrim, but these are sometimes replaced by
ring-handles freely hanging from animal masks. The flat inner surface of *p'an* makes them
suitable for long inscriptions, among which is one having no fewer than 357 characters – a
document comparable in length with, say, one of the chapters of the *Shu ching*, 'Book of
History'.

This is typically a large bowl, with mouth elevated on a prominent recessed collar, and with two or four side-handles cast with the vessel, from which ring-handles may be freely suspended. The *chien* was made only in the Third Phase, and no Neolithic pottery prototype can be cited.

The graph for *chien* found inscribed on some specimens shows a person bending over a bowl, apparently contemplating his reflection in the water. Whether written with or without the 'metal' determinative, this character can mean 'to examine, inspect'; but with the determinative it may also mean the vessel *chien*, as well as a type of mirror. Perhaps this bowl served vicariously as a mirror therefore, but references in pre-Han texts testify that it was normally used for displaying or storing foods, and was sometimes filled with ice for this purpose. *Chien* are among the very largest bronze vessels made. One in the Cernuschi Museum is no less than 40 inches across the mouth.

The styles of the ritual bronzes

The ritual bronzes of ancient China do not by any means display a single decorative style. Style is an elusive quality – nowhere more so than in Chinese bronze art – and it is always easier, and generally sufficient, to sense the difference between two pieces rather than say precisely where it lies. Only when decorative elements are dissected out do we find that a prescriptive basis – what Karlgren calls a 'grammar' – really does exist for these general impressions of difference. Motifs found on some bronzes are altogether absent from others, or appear in stylized or degenerate form; on yet others, later in date, they may reappear in subtly different guise. Shapes, too, undergo the same apparent evolution.

A detailed interpretation of the historical development of bronze art in China is the business of a bronze specialist, and the reader will not expect it from me. Most scholars agree that, for the purpose of classifying the bronzes, the whole classical period can be divided into three chronological phases – the First, Second and Third Phases inaugurated by Yetts in 1936.[15] Yetts, who died before the Chêng-chou discoveries were announced, intentionally left the boundaries of his three phases vague; for with the criteria at his disposal it was rarely possible to date a bronze with a probable margin of error of less than a few decades. Controlled excavation of many sites yielding bronzes has in the last decade already refined and clarified our notions regarding the dating of a bronze, and it is now usually possible to specify the century in which a given vessel was made.

The stylistic phases, and the rough dates to which they may be assigned, are as follows:
1. First Phase: 1500–950 BC
2. Second Phase: 950–550 BC
3. Third Phase: 550–250 BC

The Swedish scholar Bernhard Karlgren has devoted nearly thirty years to a remarkable series of studies on Chinese bronzes[16], wherein his method has been to isolate a given motif and then to analyse its distribution at various periods and among the various vessel-classes. His conclusion is that this distribution is not haphazard, but obeys certain prescriptive rules. Thus he is able to isolate 38 style criteria which are distinctive of his Archaic Period, corresponding to the First Phase, not one of which appears in the Middle Chou period, corresponding to the Second Phase.

In recent years Karlgren has concentrated on the art of the First Phase, revealing the existence of a dichotomy between what he calls Primary and Secondary Styles within this Phase. Motifs marshalled into his A group are found only on vessels in the Primary Style; those in his B group are exclusively associated with vessels in the Secondary Style; those in his C group are distributed indifferently between vessels in either style. His latest discovery is that the occurrence of motifs *within the Style* is also regulated. To take an example, the cicada, which belongs to the A group and hence is found only on vessels in the Primary Style, occurs abundantly on *ting* but never on *yu* or *kuei*. The B-group compound lozenge with central protruding spike, contrariwise, is common on Secondary Style *ting* and *kuei*, yet never occurs on *yu* of the same group. A vessel that broke the rules governing these stylistic conventions would stick out like a sore thumb, in Karlgren's view, and would immediately invite suspicion as to its genuineness.

pl. 82

pl. 52

There can be no denying the validity of these painstaking analyses of the elements that go to fashion the style of a period. In the rich confusion of bronze-vessel décor they disclose conventional patterns or constellations characteristic, perhaps, of the particular schools in which the designers worked, and of the particular types of vessel they were called upon to model. Only we cannot as yet give a precise meaning to this conventional symbology; or say why the cicada, for example, should refuse to be featured on *kuei* or *yu*.

Karlgren held the view that this conformity to pattern implied an earlier period free from conventional restrictions in bronze décor design, and a greater variety of shapes, motifs, and constellation of motifs, etc. The contrary seems actually to have been the case, for the decoration on the Chêng-chou and Liu-li-ko bronzes is as conventionalized as that of vessels from An-yang; and the variety of shapes and motifs is meagre, and does not correspond at all to Karlgren's picture of a period of 'a freer high bronze art, with a whole array of vessel-types, décor motifs, and ornamental constellations not yet bound by fixed conventional rules'.

*

Our first reaction to the art of the ritual bronzes may well be that we are coming into contact with something thoroughly unfamiliar, not to say hostile. The shapes of the vessels, and the strangely potent beings they advertise, convey the impression of a spirit that is almost barbaric, and we perhaps have to remind ourselves that they are, after all, highly civilized works of art. But the more prolonged our examination of structure and content, the less acute does this feeling of strangeness and hostility become. We find that we are acquiring a new and first-rate aesthetic experience.

The forms portrayed on the bronzes undoubtedly had some symbolic import, but of what nature we cannot say. All sorts of explanations of the better-known motifs have been given by both Western and Chinese critics; but, as with the interpretation of early jades, these explanations rarely convince and are often entirely fanciful. The commonest motifs are zoomorphs; animals are portrayed, but again it is not always easy to say just what sort of animals. They are usually very highly stylized.

But two sorts of stylization are possible. Animals portrayed in the steppe art of the northern nomads, for instance, are vividly alive no matter how contorted may be the attitudes in which, owing to technical limitations, they have been posed. It is an art characterized by what E. H. Minns called 'style instinct with life'. Even when basic forms are tampered with, so that deer antlers turn into heads of birds, fishes' tails unaccountably become rams' heads, small beasts parade on the limb joints, and so forth, the impression of actuality remains. The animal forms of the bronzes are not stylized in this sense only; they have become, as it were, abstract or heraldic. This is especially true of the mysterious class known as 'dragons'. Just as much liberty is taken with their forms as we find in nomad art. Several heads share a single body, several bodies merge into a single head, composite animals appear, tails turn just as inconsequently into birds' heads on Chinese bronzes as they do on Scythian plaques. But often it is from disintegrated or decomposed bodies that these secondary forms arise, bodies composed of nothing but a mass of meaningless spirals out of which peers only a pair of glaucous and protrusive eyes.

pl. 65 That is not to say that Chinese bronze designers were incapable of modelling real animals. On the contrary they frequently did so with astonishing finesse, careless of the conceptual constraints that affected their plastic treatment of the human face and form. Some secular *pl. 89* bronzes of the late First Phase, particularly the ibex and horse heads forming finials of chariot-poles or pommels of knives, are admirable examples of this buoyant art, which is displayed *pl. 66* also in the modelling of animal *tsun*. It reappears after centuries in the delicate little herbi-*pl. 57* vores that graze on the covers of Third Phase *ting* and *tou*. Was it something the Chinese learnt from the nomads, or was it innate in their artistic genius? The same freedom of ap-proach, the same apparent insight into the inner life of the subject, is seen again two thousand years later in the work of the Sung *animalier* and flower-and-bird painter [see pp. 315–322]. When it came to designing the sacrificial vessels, however, the impulse to model naturalistic-ally was held back in order to depict another kind of reality – the psychological reality of the monsters who were the intermediaries between the worshipper and the ancestral spirits.

Animal forms, however stylized, are set against a background of geometrical shapes among which the spiral is ubiquitous. In bronzes of the First Phase, and to some extent of the Third, designers seem to have been impelled by *horror vacui* to load every square inch of surface with this magic combination of zoomorphs and spirals. Human and plant forms do from time to time venture into this formidable arena, but they are interlopers. The obsession with animals is inescapable. We are dealing with an iconography.

THE FIRST PHASE Style criteria named by Karlgren for the period covered by the First Phase number thirty-eight. A Chinese bronze can confidently be dated between the thirteenth and tenth centuries BC or earlier, if it displays some of these elements and none of those introduced in later Phases. They may be divided into two groups, of which the first comprises vessel-types or parts of vessels and the second decorative motifs. The vessel-types are: rectangular *ting*, *li-ting*, *yu*, *ku*, *pls 58, 59, 64, 65, 74–84* *chüeh*, *chia*, *kuang*, and *fang i*. According to this notion, therefore, the vessels shown on plates 58, 59, 64, 65 and 74–84 must necessarily all belong to the First Phase. Parts of vessels include cylinder legs, legs of *ting* modelled in animal form, lid-knobs as opposed to discs, and vertical segmented flanges.

Decorative motifs divide into those portraying animals, or parts of animals, and those that are purely geometrical. The animal forms are multitudinous, and one doubts whether any analysis of them can ever reach completion, although that is what Karlgren seems to be aim-ing at. The most important will be discussed below.

T'AO-T'IEH. No motif in Chinese art has invited more speculation as to its meaning than this. In its fully developed form it is a device in which two confronting zoomorphs in profile form the left and right sides of an animal mask seen in full face; the *t'ao-t'ieh* from the bronze *pl. 50, fig. 13* of plate 50 has been isolated and redrawn as figure 13 to make apparent what is meant. There is a difference of opinion as to how it originated; whether the confrontation of two animals or animal heads seen in profile first suggested the idea of a frontal mask, that is, or whether an original mask acquired, by a fanciful proliferation of its form, a *double entendre* in the shape of two confronting animals seen in side view. The latter belong to the species of one-legged dragon called *k'uei* [p. 98]; and as this creature does not occur on any of the Chêng-chou

96

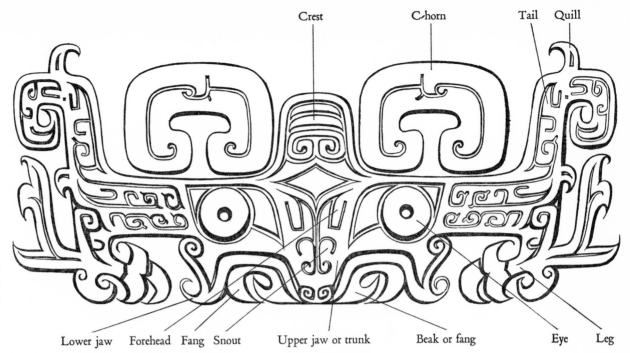

Crest   C-horn   Tail   Quill

13 *T'ao-t'ieh mask
from the First Phase
ting* of plate 50

Lower jaw   Forehead   Fang   Snout   Upper jaw or trunk   Beak or fang   Eye   Leg

bronzes, whereas the *t'ao-t'ieh* does, the second explanation must presumably be the correct one. An elementary sort of *t'ao-t'ieh* is scratched on the side of a red pottery bowl from the Neolithic site of Shih-chia-ho in Hupeh; it is perhaps the earliest known example of the   *pl. 11*
motif in Chinese art, but its appearance is cryptic and suggests nothing of the form of a possible ancestor.

The idea of a connexion between the *t'ao-t'ieh* and similar forms in the art of Mycenae, Persia, India, and Amerindia has often been mooted and is of course extremely attractive, but it should be resisted as far as possible. On Chinese bronzes the mask may in one sense represent the sacrificial animal; in another, as Watson supposes, it may symbolize 'an appalling tigerlike monster intended to avert evil'.[17]

Chinese accounts as to the meaning of *t'ao-t'ieh* are conflicting. A passage in *Tso chuan* [p. 53] speaks of noxious spirits at large in the hills and wastes, and tells how these were depicted on the Nine Cauldrons of the legendary Yü the Great, to give people a fair idea of what they looked like. By the third century AD the commentator Kuo P'o is identifying the *t'ao-t'ieh* with one of these. But a passage in *Lü shih ch'un ch'iu*, attributed to the third-century BC writer Lü Pu-wei, runs: 'On Chou vessels there was put a *t'ao-t'ieh* with a head, but no body. He is eating a man and (thinks he) is going to swallow him; but already his (the *t'ao-t'ieh*'s) body is destroyed. The object of the design was to warn people that the hour of disaster was at hand.' One can easily see the allegorical possibilities of such a theme. According to Dr Waley, whose translation of the passage is given above[18], a warning against the acquisitive State is intended; but this of course is late Chou moralizing. In fact, certain early vessels of the *yu* class *are* modelled in the shape of an animal apparently in the act of eating a man.   *pl. 65*
But this is not the *t'ao-t'ieh* we know; and, as Yetts points out, there is no sign in such portrayals that the animal's body is in any way deficient. On the other hand, *t'ao-t'ieh* portrayals – although they do not indeed show a man being devoured – do exhibit various stages in reduction of the bodies of the confronting animals, as will presently be explained. Perhaps that was what Lü Pu-wei had in mind when he made his curious observation about the destruction of the *t'ao-t'ieh*'s body. By Sung times the cataloguers had seized on the idea supposed by Waley

97

to be a warning against territorial greed, and reinterpreted it as an injunction against lust and gluttony.

Karlgren analyses the *t'ao-t'ieh* motif into six different types. But for our purpose only two need be mentioned. In the first of these, parts of the body, such as jaws, snout, horns, legs, *fig. 13* and tails, however summarily treated and scattered, can yet be seen as distinct, accentuated elements raised above the spiral background. The mask of figure 13 is a good example of this class. In the second, the animal forms are indistinct, or what Karlgren calls 'dissolved'. They *pl. 79* are there, but they need finding. Often only the eyes, as we said, betray their presence among the maze of spirals that form their bodies.

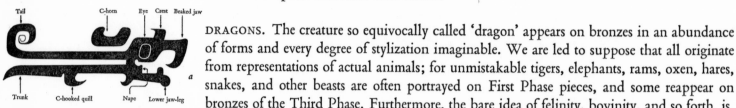

DRAGONS. The creature so equivocally called 'dragon' appears on bronzes in an abundance of forms and every degree of stylization imaginable. We are led to suppose that all originate from representations of actual animals; for unmistakable tigers, elephants, rams, oxen, hares, snakes, and other beasts are often portrayed on First Phase pieces, and some reappear on bronzes of the Third Phase. Furthermore, the bare idea of felinity, bovinity, and so forth, is, as has been noted, nearly always present even when diagnostic detail is lacking. Indeed, it often creates its own disturbing impression of actuality.

Within these ill-defined limits, the bronze designer, and especially the Shang designer, evidently felt free to vary the anatomy of the dragon as imagination prompted. From an artistic point of view, the result is that mechanical repetition is avoided; and in this feature of the design, subordination to a main plan goes hand in hand with what seems to be a delightfully easy and personal treatment of the theme.

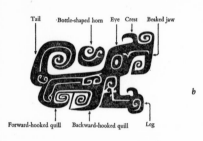

14 *K'uei* dragons:
a from a First Phase square *ting;*
b from the First Phase *yu* of plate 54

The *t'ao-t'ieh* mask of figure 13 serves to illustrate points of anatomy of most dragons. As here, we can usually recognize a jaw, or jaws, armed with what Karlgren calls beak, but which might equally be thought of as tusk or fang; a snout; forehead; crest; horn; eye; body; tail; and leg. Many variations are to be found. In one, the head is lowered so that front jaw and snout have the appearance of a sort of trunk; in this variety both jaws are present and the mouth is open. When two such forms combine to make a *t'ao-t'ieh*, as they do in figure 13, the two foreheads in combination go to make a hooked shield. In a second type the head is *fig. 14b* erect and beaked upper jaw and crest are very conspicuous. But what has happened to the lower jaw? It has apparently coalesced with the front leg. Note that the *t'ao-t'ieh* itself, regarded as a mask seen in frontal view, has an upper jaw only; very rarely indeed are both jaws present.

Other anatomical points are referred to in figure 14. Of horns alone Karlgren counts six varieties; those illustrated here – the 'C-horn' and the 'bottle-shaped horn' – are isolated from the body, but others are properly attached to it. 'C-horns' predominate; those of figures 13 *fig. 14a* and 14a, it will be noticed, are downturned and upturned respectively.

Bodily excrescences also include those Karlgren calls 'quill' and 'curl', thirteen varieties in all. As well as these, a tail usually rises erect from the dorsal surface of the body. If the body is split horizontally the upper member may be thought of as a wing. There may be one or two visible legs, presumably representing two or four legs as seen in profile. One-legged animals are spoken of in several pre-Han texts as *k'uei lung*, 'k'uei dragons', and this was therefore the name given by the Sung cataloguers to the bronze variety having one *visible* leg. *K'uei* were in some way connected with rain-making.

These are but cursory remarks on a creature whose 'grammar', as recorded on the bronzes, Karlgren has been at great pains to analyse. The question is how far 'grammatical' laws were actually obeyed in the designing of dragons. To some considerable extent, no doubt; but, I am quite sure, *not* down to the finer points of detail. In these, it seems to me, the sensibility

98

of the designer had full play. Mechanical adherence to a copy-book pattern was not demanded, any more than it is expected in a spoken or written language. Hence it would be asking too much to expect exact iconographic laws to emerge from analysis of every twist and turn the unpredictable bronze 'dragon' takes.

BLADES. The upper part of the *ku* of plate 82 and the legs of the *ting* of plate 50 are orna- *pls 82, 50* mented with what Karlgren calls 'rising blades' and 'hanging blades'. Furthermore, the bodies of several First Phase vessel-types, especially of *ting*, are decorated with rather similar triangular forms. Some of these quite obviously portray an insect – the cicada – in more or less stylized form; others, according to Karlgren, do not.[19] In others the cicada pattern is limited to the apex, the rest of the blade being occupied with an elongated *t'ao-t'ieh*.

*

We need mention only one other animal form distinctive of the First Phase. This is what Karlgren calls the 'free animal's head', which may be characterized as a decorative element *col. 17* that does not form part of a leg or handle, yet which *is* treated plastically. It may take the form of a *t'ao-t'ieh* or resemble more obviously the head of an ox, ram, hare, or other quad-ruped.

The remaining motifs – those not deriving from animal forms – may be more briefly men-tioned. The spiral appears in a variety of forms, and is the most important single motif after the *t'ao-t'ieh* and dragon. It is the device called by the Sung cataloguers *lei wên* or 'thunder *pl. 67* pattern' – a designation evidently based on a chance resemblance it bears to the archaic form of the character *lei* for 'thunder'. Other geometrical devices are lozenges – often worked up into a large overall pattern – interlocked T's, vertical ribs, spiral bands, and what Karlgren calls 'T-scores' on the above-mentioned segmented flanges. Two elements found together on *pl. 73* the *kuei* of colour plate 17 may perhaps originate ultimately from some plant form. One is the *col. 17* 'round eddy' or 'whorl circle', called by the Chinese *yüan wo*, and this motif goes back to the *pl. 76* Chêng-chou bronzes; the other, called 'square with crescents' by Karlgren, is named *ling hua* or 'flower of the water-chestnut' by the Chinese.

It might now be helpful to submit two of the vessels here illustrated to brief description, citing in brackets those elements adduced by Karlgren as being distinctive of the First Phase.

Plate 50. *Ting.* Of deep bowl-shape on three cylinder legs (K. 8) with vertical upright *pl. 50* 'ears' rising from the mouthrim. The body divided into six zones by vertical segmented flanges (K. 13) showing T-scores (K. 37). Each zone occupied by a *k'uei* dragon confronting its fellow in the next zone so as to form a single *t'ao-t'ieh* mask (K. 15). The dragons of the trunked variety (K. 19), the foreheads combining to form the upper part of the face, the trunks to form the lower part of the nose and nostrils. The horns C-shaped, the opening of the C facing downwards. The bodies decorated with spirals (K. 30). The background com-posed of squared spirals (K. 29). The legs of the vessel with hanging blades.

Colour plate 17. *Kuei.* Of flattened bowl-shape, mounted on a wide and somewhat spread- *col. 17* ing hollow base. Two vertical flanged loop-handles at the sides, representing tusked animals with upright horns above, and with vestiges of parts of birds below. The body divided into three horizontal registers. The upper and lower decorated with *ling hua* (K. 38) and *yüan wo* (K. 35) with two free animals' heads (K. 14) on the upper register. The middle register with vertical ribs (K. 36).

It must be obvious from the foregoing descriptions that we have here two vessels in every way typical of the First Phase.

The existence of two styles within the First Phase was shown by Karlgren in his 'New studies on Chinese bronzes', published in 1937. While he thought that the Secondary Style in general came later than the Primary Style, he believed also that the two may have lived side by side for a century or so at An-yang, and that the Secondary Style might have been the product of a rival school of casters, perhaps working for some branch of the nobility more recently come into power.

I have already said something about the manner in which decorative motifs are distributed between the two Styles [pp. 94–95] and do not intend to discuss it further. The visual effect of segregating groups of motifs in this way, however, is evident when one compares the two *pl. 50, col. 17* vessels described above, the *ting* being in Primary Style, the *kuei* in Secondary.

Karlgren has drawn attention to the fact that what he calls a 'uni-décor' characterizes the Primary Style. No part of the vessel's surface is left empty of symbolic forms. As Karlgren puts it when speaking of the 'dragon', 'its accumulation was evidently meant to load the sacral vessel with a great dragon force, an enormous magical power'. But in bronzes of Secondary Style one is aware of a new feeling at work. It is seen in the tendency to dispose decoration in horizontal registers, thus making possible the sort of rhythmic contrast displayed by the *kuei* of colour plate 17. Obviously a different effect is being sought. Something of the menace and potency of the *ting* has evaporated by the time we reach the *kuei*. With the former it is the content that rivets our attention. With the latter this pressure is released, and one gets the feeling that the Secondary Style bronze caster, too, may have been less psychologically confined. The *kuei*, to use a loose phrase, is more of an essay in pure aesthetics; whereas the significance of the *ting* lies rather in its content than its style.

The novel situation brought about by the Chou conquest of the Shang in 1027 BC is reflected in the diversified forms of bronze vessels cast during the following century, a period to which some would apply the label 'transitional'. Certain vessels known to have come from the Chou region assume mannered and extravagant forms quite unlike those made within the Shang domain, and presumably represent vestiges of an independant Chou idiom that had been developing within the main tradition possibly for generations before the conquest. Yet these vessels fall stylistically within the confines of the First Phase. There was no sudden break in style coincident with the arrival of the Chou.

By about 950 BC the forms of the bronzes had become more homogeneous, and a new and highly individual style arose. It is characterized in part by the exodus of almost all the wine *pl. 85, col. 16* vessels and the advent of one or two new vessel-classes. These include the *i* ewer, a rectangular *kuei* with rounded corners called *hsü*, and a rectangular shallow dish with conforming cover, *fu*. Absence of vessels like *chüeh*, *chia*, *yu*, and *kuang*, with their luxuriating shapes in itself lends an air of composure to the Phase. The prevailing mood is well defined by the modulated *pl. 54* form of the *ting* with its shallow, flattened bowl mounted on three cabriole legs; a complacent shape which at its best is no more than elegant, at its worst supine, banal, and visually uninteresting.

In keeping with these moderating trends, the décor too undergoes a quiet revolution and virtually frees itself from iconographic content. Zoomorphs are in eclipse. Apart from animal *pl. 68* handles, often topped by a pair of fanciful horns shaped like snail shells, they are hardly ever found on Second Phase bronzes. True, the principal decorative element is often a narrow horizontal low-relief band of deformed figures that trace their descent from a late First Phase bird motif; but these are remarkably self-effacing. Second Phase designers, in short, seem to have been aiming at an even more openly decorative treatment of surface than that essayed in the First Phase Secondary Style, and at a final rejection of the bodeful monsters of the Primary Style in favour of abstract motifs that may have seemed in better taste. The Second Phase is in fact memorable for vessel-shapes of an almost ceramic purity, and for simple and coherent decorative schemes that fit them to perfection; this notwithstanding a certain deterioration in technical standards.

A group of bronzes excavated in 1954 from a small grave at P'u-tu-ts'un near Ch'ang-an in Shensi province serves to mark the inauguration of the Phase. The vessels are dated by an inscription on a *ho* in which mention is made of the Chou king Mu (reigned 947–928 BC). *pl. 83* Their sobriety of form contrasts visually with the exuberance of the First Phase montage, but the bird-figures disposed as a horizontal band below the mouthrim are still faintly recognizable for what they once were.

A second group of vessels, linked together by their inscriptions, contains the *kuei* of plate 61 and two others very like it, and the Sung *ting* whose inscription was translated on *pl. 61* page 80. It includes a *hu* which is twin to that of plate 68 and an *i* in similar style to that *pl. 68* in the Sedgwick collection. Their inscriptions do not name a Chou ruler, but merely record *col. 16* that the events leading up to their casting took place in his third year. Kuo Mo-jo took him to be King Mu; but stylistic considerations – the total deformation of the bird-figures within the horizontal zones, for example – call for a date about a century later, either during the reign of Li Wang (857–828 BC) or of his successor Hsüan Wang (827–781 BC).

These handsome vessels model the new and distinctive Second Phase repertoire with telling effect. We see on the *kuei* and *i* the deformed-bird band in place beneath the mouthrim, while *pl. 61, col. 16* the rest of the body is covered with finely-cast horizontal fluting. Yetts suggested that this latter might have been an innovation from the Near East, and drew attention to similar fluting on a gold jug and silver rhyton in the British Museum, from Achaemenid Persia and dating from the fifth century BC. The motif could equally well have been assimilated from a ceramic tradition, though as far as I know pots so decorated did not exist in China at this time.

The flared base of the *kuei*, between the animal masks over the clawed feet that serve as its legs, is decorated with a fish-scale pattern seen also in the same position on the *p'an* of plate 86. *pl. 86* Figure 15 shows the motif as it appears on a well-known *ting* which long formed the chief treasure of the Buddhist monastery on Silver Island in the Yangtze river; here it is repeated in three alternating rows occupying the main decorative zone on the sides of the vessel.

15 Imbricated ornament from the Second Phase 'Silver Island' *ting*

The Sung *ting* exhibits yet another typical Second Phase motif, namely the continuous wave band or meander with faulted sides, called by the Chinese *pan yün*, 'undulating cloud'. This beautifully executed motif, often doubled and with a bold chiselled effect, well exemplifies the new freedom enjoyed by the Second Phase designer, and begins a morphological sequence that ends in the intricate traceries of interwoven dragon-forms illuminating the surfaces of bronzes of the Third Phase. The *hu* in the Art Institute of Chicago features the same motif *pl. 68* on the neck zone, while below it is translated into the frantic convolutions of snakes that writhe over the surface. Its relationship with the *hu* in the above-mentioned Sung set dates it to about 800 BC.

*

In 1923 some hundreds of bronze vessels, now widely dispersed, were recovered from a cemetery at Hsin-chêng in central Honan; they may be dated to a period of two hundred years between the middle eighth and the middle sixth centuries BC. The gradual elaboration of the Hsin-chêng style is best illustrated by the transformation of the wave bands of which we spoke above. At an early stage they develop heads ambiguously resembling those of the old-time dragons and those of birds, but on the whole more dragon-like. At the same time, as though engaged in some frothy fluvial sport, the animals begin to intertwine, each junction between their ribbon-like bodies being marked by a supernumerary eye. Later they become compacted, squared-off, reduced, abbreviated, in a word, packaged; so that they lose – not for the first time in Chinese bronze art – all resemblance to real animals and become standard pattern-units capable of being impressed mechanically by means of dies on the surface of the wax model, as in fact they were.

pls 69, 87, 88   There are no chronological milestones to record the rate of this metamorphosis. Possibly its later stages were compressed into a few decades at the very end of the Phase. We may then think of it as a bridge passage, of quickening tempo, leading from the languid and easy-paced art of the Second Phase to the brisk, pulsating, and thematically rich Third Phase, which opens with something of a fanfare around the year 550 BC.

THE THIRD PHASE   The Third Phase falls mainly within the period known to Chinese history as *Chan Kuo*, which we call 'The Warring States' (481–221 BC). At this time all pretence of feudal loyalty to the Chou was cynically dropped, and the great hegemons embarked on aggressive courses of action that were to lead to the extermination of all of them, Ch'in alone excepted [p. 77].

In a time of political fragmentation we naturally expect to find regional variants within the framework of a common national style, and this was the case with Third Phase bronze art. As things now stand, it seems vaguely possible to distinguish a northern and a southern variant, separated, though not sundered, by the line of the Yellow River. Bronzes recovered at *pls 55, 56, 57*   the village site of Li-yü in the far north of Shansi typify the northern idiom, often called the 'Li-yü style'. One might conceive of an axis connecting Li-yü with the site of Chia-ko-chuang near T'ang-shan in eastern Hopei, nearly 300 miles to the east, whence many Third Phase *pl. 85*   bronzes were excavated in 1953; this we might call the Chao-Yen inter-state axis. Again, there seems to have been free exchange of workshop ideas between Honan, as represented by *pls 62, 69, 72, 87*   Hsin-chêng, and Shou-hsien 300 miles away to the south-east in Anhui; and here we might speak of an axis connecting the states of Chêng and Wu. A third axis, materializing later in the Phase, seems to connect Ch'ang-sha in Hunan in the old territory of Ch'u state, with *pl. 91, col. 18*   Chin-ts'un on the site of the late Chou capital near Lo-yang in Honan, 500 miles to the north.

In formulating these three somewhat unreal divisions, which however appear far less unreal when we are confronted with the vessels themselves, we must bear in mind how little is known of the factors governing the diffusion of local styles from one part of the country to another.[20] Every local variant was in some degree a synthesis to which each contributed, while all of them were subject to exotic influences which today are largely illegible. The influence of nomad art, particularly, is manifest throughout the Phase and in all its regional sectors.

The Third Phase may be described as hybrid in origin, eclectic in taste, and synthetic in style. Looking outwards, it freely absorbed foreign elements; inwards, it refurbished some of the old First Phase motifs that Second Phase designers had discarded. In retaining much of the art of the Second Phase it showed its conservatism, but it was progressive in its capacity to generate new design-elements through the interplay of the various influences to which it was exposed.

pls 55, 56, 57   On turning to Li-yü we find a mature, sophisticated, and easily identifiable style. The basic element in the design is a squared-off pattern-unit consisting of interweaving flat bands in which the interlaced dragons of the Hsin-chêng series can be dimly discerned. The pattern-

102

unit is repeated in horizontal zones round the perimeter of the vessel, and was evidently imposed on the wax model by means of a die; the zones are separated by fillets imitating plaited or twisted cords. The bodies of the dragons are sometimes plain, and set against a background of spirals; sometimes they are themselves covered with a filigree of spirals attached to incomplete triangles. All these narrow couloirs are commonly filled with a black inlay reminiscent, in its appearance, of that found on some First Phase bronzes. *pl. 52*

Naturalistic animals and birds, mounted on the reversible covers of the circular *ting*, *li*, and *tou* so favoured by Li-yü designers, may be an acquisition from the animal art of the northern *pl. 57* nomads, transmitted through the Ordos. The 'turned animal head' often borne by these beasts has also been claimed as an original feature of nomad art, while the pear-shaped cells on their bodies, meaningless and vestigial in the Chinese rendering, are found over the whole province of the animal-style in the steppes, translated into several different media, and serving originally as cloisons to hold inlays of turquoise, enamel, and other materials.

16 Cow with turned head on the cover of a Third Phase *ting*

Thus the Third Phase penchant for inlaying, which grew stronger in course of time, may *pls 31, 33* have been aroused either through contact with the nomads, or as a result of renewed acquaintance with Shang bronze art, in which inlaying of semi-precious stones, turquoise, malachite, or lapis, was often used with brilliant results; and this sort of ambiguity is typical of the Phase.

The Li-yü bronzes seem to have been cast between about 550 and 500 BC. To the same period may also be assigned those from T'ang-shan. They include a majestic *i* ewer, and a *pl. 85* *tui* whose décor is much in the Li-yü manner though somewhat mechanically realized. Outstanding is a *hu* in the pear shape that was to become the permanent form of the vessel during the Third Phase and on through the Han. The body of the *hu* is divided into twelve panels formed by raised double ribs imitating the plaited cords of a carrying cradle – such a device as might have been used by a nomad to carry a water-flask made of gourd, leather, or even pottery, in safety from one encampment to another.

This *hu* is possibly the oldest known example – and certainly the only one reported from a closed find – of a type of vessel generally known as 'hunting *hu*' because it is decorated *pls 70, 88* with scenes of the chase. The theme is not conspicuously Chinese, for it depicts people quite seriously engaged in hunting for their daily meat, with animal-faced shamans acting out some sympathetic rite to attract the game within bowshot, and not the aristocratic pastime one would expect in the luxury-filled context of Third Phase bronze art. Some of the later 'hunting *hu*' show us indeed the gentler world of a Chinese country estate – target practice on the lawn, gathering mulberry leaves for silkworms, striking at a chime of bronze bells. But the hunting theme always takes priority; and bearing this in mind, as also the naïve pictorial convention with which it is expressed (at least in the case of the T'ang-shan and some other *hu*) we shall probably conclude that it originally came from over the northern border of Yen state, and was a concept of the tribal peoples who hunted the forests of south Manchuria.

Passing now to the southern zone, the region of Karlgren's 'Huai style'[21], we encounter a corpus of vessels, all of them *hu*, so closely related in their forms that they can be assumed contemporary. They include four from Hsin-chêng; one from the tomb of a Marquis of Ts'ai state, found at Shou-hsien in what was once Wu state; and the *hu* in the Cull collection, *pls 72, 69* which was also probably cast in Wu. All six vessels have a pair of serpentine dragons to serve as handles, climbing in suspended animation up the neck towards the mouthrim, and looking backwards over their shoulders as they climb. The Cull *hu*, that from Shou-hsien, and two of the Hsin-chêng quartet, have in common a corona made up of double or single flared petals, sometimes in openwork; the device is found on covers of Second Phase *kuei*, *col. 19* but seems to be distinctive of the Third Phase when it appears on *hu*. Two of the Hsin-chêng *hu* so closely resemble the vessel that once belonged to the Marquis of Ts'ai that it is a question whether they are not all products of the same workshop, despite the distance separating them.

Now the Cull *hu* can be dated to a year shortly after 482 BC, when the event occurred that occasioned its casting. Moreover, the Ts'ai *hu* must have been cast a few years on either side of 493 BC, when the Marquis or his predecessor left his little country to seek refuge in Wu. So we can safely say that the style shown by all these vessels was flourishing by the beginning of the fifth century BC, and probably began to form itself at least half a century earlier.

pl. 69 The fine Cull *hu* epitomizes in its form the absorptive character of Third Phase bronze art. So the petals of the corona display a revived First Phase *t'ao-t'ieh*, seen also on the next-to-lowest register on the body. The registers are filled with strap-like interlaced dragon-forms in the Li-yü manner, and are similarly divided by fillets imitating plaited cords. The broad bodies of the dragons are filled with spirals joined to triangles, as at Li-yü. They are further enriched by the incrustation of a new element, variously called 'comma-shaped hook' or 'hook and volute', and comprising a tiny raised stud terminating a delicate and sharply-carved hook-form. Here is a distinctively Third Phase motif, used with enlivening effect. In *pl. 87* a later development, the little commas come to lie at all angles on the surface which they cover, giving a distinct impression of life, and with an odd resemblance to germinating wheat seedlings – which is how the Chinese in fact describe them. An equally enriching effect is wrought by granulations occupying narrow bands on the bodies of *t'ao-t'ieh* and dragons.

It will be observed that the upper margin of the topmost register on this *hu* takes the form of a Second Phase wave band with faulted sides.

*

pls 91, 104 The latest development in Third Phase bronze art, which took place in the fourth and third *col. 18* centuries BC, is known to us largely as a result of the despoliation of one great tomb at Chin-ts'un in Honan in 1936, and subsequent systematic excavation of hundreds of graves in the suburbs of Ch'ang-sha in Hunan, the old Ch'u state. By this time a new graphic invention, lacquering, was becoming popular and was beginning to influence the character of decorative schemes applied to bronze. So, while the aim of the designer is still primarily to please the eye, he abandons the bright coruscations of surface so typical of the earlier part of the Phase, and employs flat geometrical patterns, often relieved with inlays of gold, silver, or copper, more rarely of turquoise, malachite, and glass. The design is often symmetrical about a diagonal axis; interlacing scrolls terminate in spirals, while often a broad inlaid band runs beside a narrow, opening out together into a common broader panel or cartouche. There is in this system a remarkable resemblance to Celtic art.

A second type of décor is based on the invincible dragon, a curvilinear beast equipped *pls 102, 103* with the head of a bird of prey commonly found on mirrors and other small objects of bronze. This, like so many of the motifs we have been discussing, stands at the head of a long metamorphosis, out of which it emerges as the 'cloud-scroll' of Han times, where we shall encounter it shortly [pp. 147–148].

50 Bronze *ting*, ornamented with three pairs of confronted *k'uei* dragons, each pair forming a prominent *t'ao-t'ieh* mask (one visible this side), all on a ground of squared spirals. First Phase (A style), Shang dynasty. For a fuller description see page 99 and figure 13. Height: 9¼ in. Collection of Mr and Mrs F. Brodie Lodge, England.

51 Bronze *li*, with neck-belt of dissolved dragonlike *t'ao-t'ieh*. First Phase (B style), *c.* 1000 BC. Inscribed *shih ch'in*, 'Scribe Ch'in'. Height: 7 1/2 in. Ostasiatiska Museet, Stockholm.

53 Bronze *li*, the neck-belt of fish-scale pattern [see p. 101]. Second Phase, Chou dynasty (*c.* eighth century BC). One of a group of five *li* bearing the same inscription, translated by Karlgren as: 'Po-fu has made for the Lady Chi of Pi [near Ch'ang-an] this fine *li*; may for myriad years sons and grandsons forever treasure and use it and sacrifice [with it].' Height: 4 7/16 in. Ostasiatiska Museet, Stockholm.

52 Bronze *ting*, with neck-belt of deformed dragons, the body with compound lozenges each containing a 'spike'. First Phase (B style). Shang dynasty, probably from An-yang. Height: 7 3/4 in. Collection of Dr Felix Guggenheim, California.

54 Shallow bronze *ting*, mounted on cabriole legs, and with bands of highly degenerated *k'uei* dragons. Second Phase, Chou dynasty (*c.* eighth century BC). Height: 11 3/4 in. National Museum, Peking.

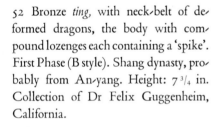

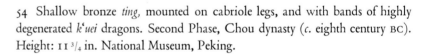

55 Bronze *li*, with reversible cover. Third Phase (Li-yü style),
Chou dynasty (sixth or fifth century BC). Height with cover: 9 ¹/₄ in.
The M. H. de Young Museum, San Francisco.

56 and 57 (below left) Bronze *ting*, with cover, decorated all over
with belts of interlocked dragons, their bodies filled with 'hook and
volute' motif. The cover shows three naturalistically modelled cows
with heads turned to one side, the so-called 'turned animal-head'
motif [see figure 16]. Third Phase (Li-yü style), Chou dynasty,
sixth or fifth century BC. Height: 7 ³/₄ in. British Museum.

58 (below) Bronze *ting*, or *li-ting* [see p. 87], on three stubby pointed
legs, with two vertical loop handles on the heavily flanged mouthrim; the body ornamented with a neck band of three raised ribs, the
belly with a double chevron band. First Phase, early Shang dynasty
and similar to others excavated at Chêng-chou and Hui-hsien.
Height: 19 ¹⁵/₁₆ in. Royal Ontario Museum, Toronto.

59 (above) Rectangular bronze, *fang ting,* with two upright handles modelled as dragons with bottle-shaped horns. The neck-belts occupied with pairs of confronted *k'uei* dragons. The rest of the body filled with rows of prominent bosses and a panel of vertical ribs on all four sides, and heavily flanged at the corners and down the middle of each side. The upper parts of the legs cast in the form of animals' heads with horns *en ronde bosse* and heavy hooked flanges between them. First Phase (B style), early Chou dynasty, end of eleventh century BC. Its inscription relates this vessel to King Ch'êng (*c.* 1024–1005 BC). Height: 11 in. Nelson Gallery of Art, Kansas City.

60 (below) Bronze *tou,* on flared base and with reversible cover shaped like the body, the décor consisting of belts of scroll-like dragons treated in linear fashion and inlaid in gold. Third Phase, late Chou dynasty. Height: 5 15/16 in. Freer Gallery of Art, Washington.

opposite page

61 (above) Bronze *kuei* on three small feet and with reversible cover; the upper parts of the handles modelled in the form of monsters; neck-belt of deformed bird-figures; the main body with horizontal flutings; the foot-belt with fish-scale pattern. Second Phase, Chou dynasty. This important vessel is related through its inscription to the Sung *ting,* whose inscription I have translated on page 80. Identical or highly similar inscriptions are borne by two other *kuei* also closely related to the *hu* of plate 68 and an *i* equally closely related to that of colour plate 16. Thus we may expect the vessels featured in these three plates to have stylistic features in common (as also the *p'an* of plate 86). The inscription names the third year of a king; on stylistic grounds the vessel may be ascribed to the second half of the ninth century BC, and the king should therefore be Hsüan Wang and the date 825 BC. Height: 12 in. Nelson Gallery of Art, Kansas City.

62 (right) Bronze *kuei,* with reversible cover, the handle (or foot) of which is in the form of an open flower chalice of five petals. The body is cast solid with a massive rectangular stand. Third Phase, from the tomb of a Marquis of Ts'ai state, excavated near Shou-hsien, Anhwei. The vessel can be dated on the evidence of its inscription to about 493–447 BC. Height: 14 1/8 in. Institute of Archaeology of the Academy of Sciences, Peking.

63 Four-sided bronze *tsun,* the upper part of the neck with rising blades, the neck-belt with confronted *k'uei* dragons, the shoulder with free animal's head, the centre field with confronted crested birds, the foot-belt with confronted *k'uei* dragons, all motifs on a ground of squared spirals. Flanges with T-scores at the corners and down the middle of each side. First Phase (A style), early Chou dynasty. Height: 13 ¹/₂ in. Freer Gallery of Art, Washington.

64 Bronze *yu,* with swing handle and cover, the neck-belt ornamented with *k'uei* dragons, the centre field with confronting *k'uei* dragons forming a prominent *t'ao-t'ieh* mask on each side, the foot-belt with *k'uei* dragons of variant type, all on a ground of squared spirals. First Phase (A style), late Shang dynasty. Height: 10 ³/₄ in. Cull Collection, Wales.

RITUAL WINE VESSELS

65 Bronze *yu,* in the form of an ogre apparently devouring a boy. First Phase (A style), Shang dynasty. For a discussion of this motif see page 97. Height: 12 3/4 in. Sumitomo Museum, Kyoto.

66 Bronze *tsun* or *hsiang tsun,* in the form of an elephant. First Phase (A style), Shang dynasty. This is the Camondo *tsun.* For a discussion of *hsiang tsun* see page 89. Length: 38 in. Musée Guimet, Paris.

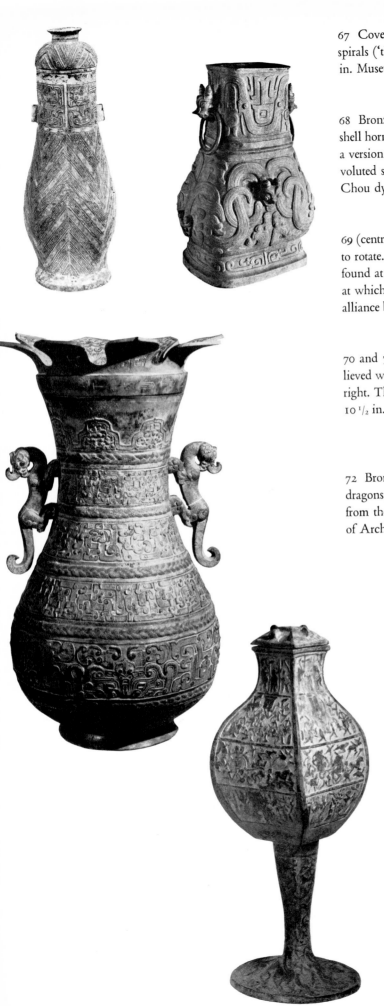

67 Covered bronze *hu,* with chevron bands of alternating fine and coarse squared spirals ('thunder pattern'). First Phase (B style), early Chou dynasty. Height: 12 ¹/₂ in. Museum of Fine Arts, Boston.

68 Bronze *hu.* The handles hang from fully modelled dragons' heads with snail-shell horns; neck-belt contains within a faulted wave pattern (*pan yün*) (on this side) a version of the prehistoric 'wild sheep's horns' motif [see pl. 9]; centre field of convoluted snake-dragons surrounding heads like those of the handles. Second Phase, Chou dynasty [see pl. 61 and p. 100]. Height: 20 ¹/₁₆ in. Art Institute of Chicago.

69 (centre left) Bronze *hu,* one of a pair. The corona, a petalled flower, can be made to rotate. Third Phase (Hsin-chêng style), early fifth century BC, said to have been found at Hui-hsien [see pl. 87]. This is the Huang Ch'ih *hu,* named after the place at which a conference mentioned in its inscription was held in 482 BC, to form an alliance between Wu and Chin [see p. 104]. Height: 19 in. Cull Collection, Wales.

70 and 71 (below) Four-sided bronze *hu* with cover, mounted on a tall foot; relieved with ceremonial, domestic and hunting scenes, one of which is shown on the right. Third Phase ('hunting *hu*' style), late fifth or early fourth century BC. Height: 10 ¹/₂ in. M. H. de Young Museum, San Francisco.

opposite page

72 Bronze *hu* with openwork corona, side-handles modelled as a pair of feline dragons; raised on four animal supports. Third Phase, fourth or fifth century BC, from the same tomb as the *kuei* of plate 62 [see p. 103]. Height: 31 ¹⁵/₁₆ in. Institute of Archaeology of the Academy of Sciences, Peking.

73 (right) Four-sided bronze *lei* with lid, in vague semblance of a building; the lid with a disjointed *t'ao-t'ieh*; the neck-belt with confronted birds; freely modelled bovine heads appear on a ground of confronting *k'uei* dragons on the shoulder and on hanging blades in the centre field. At the corners and down the middles of the sides are flanges with T-scores. First Phase (A style), late Shang dynasty. Height: 21 in. Nelson Gallery of Art, Kansas City.

74 (below right) Bronze *fang i*, perhaps a model of a house or granary, the knob reproducing the roof-form of the lid, the latter with *t'ao-t'ieh* mask upside-down in relation to the body and the centre field's mask, the neck-belt with confronted, the foot-belt with opposed *k'uei* dragons; the whole heavily flanged. First Phase, Shang dynasty. Height: 11 1/2 in. Fogg Museum of Art, Cambridge, Mass.

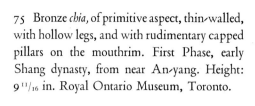

75 Bronze *chia,* of primitive aspect, thin-walled, with hollow legs, and with rudimentary capped pillars on the mouthrim. First Phase, early Shang dynasty, from near An-yang. Height: 9 ¹¹/₁₆ in. Royal Ontario Museum, Toronto.

76 Bronze *chia,* the neck-belt with confronting *k'uei* dragons forming *t'ao-t'ieh* masks, the belly with whorl circles (*yüan wo*). First Phase, early Shang dynasty. The waisted body is believed to be a characteristic of the early Shang dynasty [see pls 75 and 78]. Height: 9 ⁷/₈ in. British Museum.

opposite pa

77 Bronze *chia,* the neck-belt with confronted *k'uei* dragons, the centre field with a disjointed *t'ao-t'ieh* mask, the pillar capitals with whorl circles (*yüan wo*). First Phase (A style), Shang dynasty, found at An-yang. Height: 8 ¹³/₁₆ in. Hakuzuru Art Museum, Kobe.

78 (below left) Bronze *chüeh,* with flat base and waisted body, bearing a décor character-istic of the First Phase. Early Shang dynasty, from Hui-hsien, Honan. Height to top of capped pillars: 7 ⁷/₈ in. Royal Ontario Museum, Toronto.

79 (below right) Bronze *chüeh,* the body orna-mented with dissolved *t'ao-t'ieh* in low relief, but with prominent eyes; the character *tsê,* 'book bundle', in intaglio inside the loop of the handle. First Phase (B style), Shang dynasty, probably from An-yang. Height: 8 in. Collec-tion of F. G. Macalpine, England.

80 Bronze *ku,* of primitive appearance, simil to another recently excavated at Hui-hsien ar belonging to the Chêng-chou period. Fi Phase, early Shang dynasty. Compare th shape with the fully metamorphosed *ku* of pla 82 and also a possible prototype in plate 8 Height: 11 ³/₁₆ in. British Museum.

81 Ivory beaker excavated at Erh-li-kar Chêng-chou, Honan. Early Shang dynast This beaker has the horizontal ribs of plates and 58 and the enigmatical cruciform perfor tion of plate 80. Institute of Archaeology of t Academy of Sciences, Peking.

82 Bronze *ku,* the upper section with risi blades (cicada), the middle and lower with d jointed *t'ao-t'ieh* masks, all on a ground squared spirals. First Phase (A style), Sha dynasty, probably from An-yang. Height: 13 i City Art Museum, St Louis.

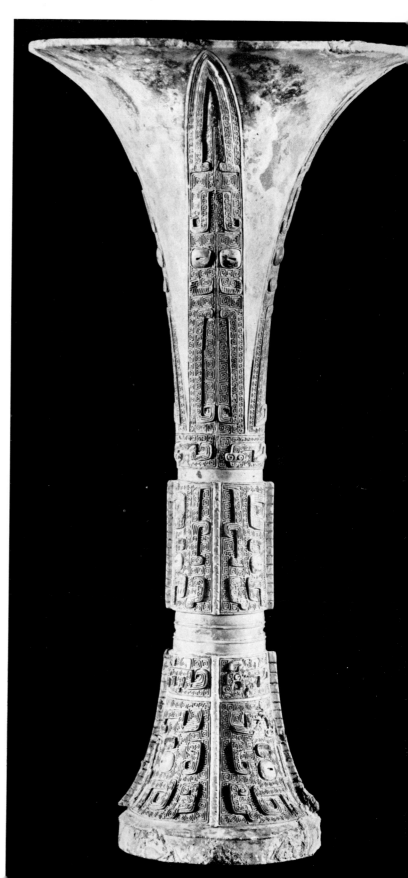

83 Bronze *ho,* its cover joined to its side-handle by a one-link chain; neck-belt with low relief band of deformed bird-figures, body with double chevron band and shaped like a *li.* Second Phase, third quarter of the tenth century BC. Excavated at P'u-tu-ts'un, Shensi. The inscription names King Mu, who reigned *c.*947–928 BC. Height: 10.9 in. Shensi Province Cultural Properties Commission.

84 (left centre) Bronze *kuang,* with cover, in the form of an owl and a winged feline monster. First Phase (A style), late Shang. Height: 9 1/2 in. Fogg Museum of Art, Cambridge, Mass.

85 (below left) Bronze *i,* of unusual theriomorphic form, the body mounted on three cabriole legs, the centre field filled with fish-scale pattern. Third Phase, perhaps end of sixth century BC, excavated from a tomb near T'ang-shan, Hopei. Height: 6 1/4 in. National Museum, Peking.

opposite page

86 (above) Bronze *p'an,* the foot-belt with fish-scale pattern, the neck-belt a low relief band of deformed bird-figures, the handles two S-shaped dragons with feline horns, the vessel supported on three human figures. Second Phase, late ninth century BC [see the related pls 61 and col. 16]. Diameter: 16 1/2 in. M. H. de Young Museum, San Francisco.

87 (centre) Bronze *chien,* with four vertical side-handles, two with linked rings; three belts of interlacing dragons, their bodies filled with the 'hook and volute' motif, are separated by fillets of plaited cord pattern. Third Phase (Hsin-chêng style), early fifth century BC, said to have come from Hui-hsien, Honan. This is named the Chih Chün Tzü *chien* by its inscription, which also states that it belonged to a Prince of Chin, a state featuring in the inscription on the *hu* of plate 69 the style of which resembles that of this *chien.* Diameter: 20 3/8 in. Freer Gallery of Art, Washington.

88 (below) Bronze *chien,* with four vertical loop handles bearing *t'ao-t'ieh* escutcheons and with linked rings; the inside rim with a procession of geese in *repoussé* style. The neck-belt, centre field, and foot-belt of hunting scenes separated by fillets of 'hook and volute' motif. Third Phase, late fifth or early sixth century BC. The quality of the casting suggests Hsin-chêng workmanship, but the engraving may have been done in Hopei where the 'hunting *hu*' [see pl. 70] style seems to have first set foot in China. Diameter: 24 3/16 in. Freer Gallery of Art, Washington.

89 Chariot pole finial in the form of an ibex. Early Chou dynasty, about 1000 BC. Length from muzzle to ear-tip: 2⁵/₈ in. Academy of Arts, Honolulu.

90 Tiger in the form of a loop handle probably originally belonging to a bronze bell of the class called *ch'un*. Third Phase, late Chou or early Han dynasty. Length 8³/₈ in. Collection of Dr F. Guggenheim, California.

91 (above) Chariot pole finial in the form of a dragon's head; the head plated with gold foil, the teeth and the whites of the eyes with silver foil, the pupils made of glass; the tongue, and perhaps the ears, cast separately. Third Phase (Chin-ts'un style), late Chou dynasty, very probably from Chin-ts'un, Honan. Length: 10¹/₁₆ in. Freer Gallery of Art, Washington.

92 Gold openwork dagger handle fashioned as a clot of interlocking dragons. Third Phase, fourth century BC. Length: 4 3/8 in. British Museum.

93 Coffin handle in the form of a *t'ao-t'ieh* mask with ring, handle hanging freely from the snout. Third Phase, fifth–fourth centuries BC, perhaps from Ku-wei-ts'un, Hui-hsien, Honan. Height: 6 1/4 in. British Museum.

IV LACQUER AND SILK: HAN DYNASTY

Discovery of undoubted Chinese lacquers and silks of the Han period (205 BC to AD 220) at site after site from Korea to the Near East alone might invite speculation about the Han Empire and its range of contacts. But thanks to the tradition of history-writing founded by Ssǔ-ma Ch'ien's *Shih chi*, 'Historical Records'[1], and to painstaking surveys of almost every aspect of social, economic, political, and military history in the first great dynastic chronicle, *Ch'ien han shu*, 'History of the Former Han Dynasty'[2], and its successor, *Hou han shu*, 'History of the Latter Han Dynasty'[3], we need ask of archaeology little more than corroboration of what we already know. In fact it does much more for us. The practice of burying with the dead not only their personal belongings, but also pottery models of every conceivable article of domestic use (*ming ch'i*), has provided us with a means of reconstructing Han daily life in fine detail. Material remains help to round out the picture of a fully documented phase of Chinese history.

That these various sources of information should be available is perhaps no accident. There is an air of urbanity about the period; an accent on corporeal values and worldly well-being that seems to go together with the bureaucratic belief in record-making for its own sake. In spite of its ups and downs, of internal rebellions, and a threat to its very existence from no-mads in the north during its first hundred years or so, one can scarcely bring oneself to think of the Han period in dramatic terms. The outlook on life of colonial officers and their women-folk in Korea, for instance, seems to have been no less self-contained and complacent than that of colonial administrators at all times, the world over. The inventory of chattels found in their graves reads like the catalogue of a departmental store: lacquered occasional tables with dishes, trays, bowls, spoons, and ladles; hats, leather shoes, fragments of silks and wool-len clothes, and chests for clothes; seals of office and writing-brushes; belt-hooks, jewellery, combs, hairpins, and mirrors; cosmetic outfits comprising nests of lacquered boxes holding pomades, face-powders, powder brushes, rouge, and mascara; even a divination set for for-tune-telling. A civilized and self-conscious period, evidently. Yet, despite its grandeur, per-haps a trifle dull.

Lacquer and silk are, by general consent, luxury commodities. They are also highly suit-able for export, being both light and strong; and each had reached a peak of technical and artistic excellence by Han times. Small wonder, then, that they quickly found their way on to foreign markets when, at the beginning of the first century BC, China began for the first time to participate directly in world trade. Han lacquer and silk, in fact, serve to illustrate the theme of Chinese political expansion which we shall go on to discuss in a moment.

But in another and less obvious way lacquer and silk form a link by which we can connect material culture with the social and economic life of the times. For they served to satisfy a new demand from the home market. Both were costly, and both lent themselves to large-scale manufacture and standardization of quality. Precisely such ready-made symbols of wealth and class-solidarity are in demand whenever a large ruling class is found. Such a class now existed.

The unification of China and the widening of her political frontiers had brought into being a vast new administration of civil and military officials. Furthermore, unstable economic conditions following the eclipse of the feudal nobility had caused a redistribution of wealth into the hands of industrialists, urban financiers and land-holders. These now became large-scale manufacturers. Consumer goods and raw materials produced under their direction – cereals, textiles, salt, iron, and so forth – were marketed by a new merchant class who kept the whole *bourgeoisie* and Court nobility supplied with luxury articles while regulating the price of basic commodities to their own advantage. There were, as a matter of fact, imperial lacquer and silk-weaving factories; but production and sale were never government monopolies, and it seems reasonable to suppose that by far the bulk of such wares was manufactured and sold privately.

The political and military background of the Han Empire

For a hundred years after the defeat of Chou state by Ch'in in 256 BC, China struggled for political unity, and to preserve the new idea of an imperial and centralized government against the disintegrative forces of the old feudal order. A few years after the death of the First Ch'in Emperor, Ch'in Shih Huang Ti, in 210 BC, the Ch'in dynasty was liquidated by a makeshift alliance between a disaffected aristocrat, Hsiang Yü, and a peasant revolutionary leader, Liu Pang; the latter became the first emperor of the Han dynasty in 202 BC. After half a century of precarious Han rule, a crisis came and was safely passed in 154 BC when a rebellion involving seven vassal princes was decisively crushed and the new dynasty was finally freed from internal threat to its security.

Beyond the Great Wall, meanwhile, the horse-riding nomads of the steppes had banded themselves together under the leadership of a Turkish tribe, the Hsiung-nu. These were the ancestors of the Huns who later appeared in Europe, and for convenience we shall henceforward refer to them by this more familiar name. Relations between the Huns and the Chinese, though always negative, seem to have been fairly close; and it has been suggested that the new Hun ruler, the Shan Yü, was an equivalent of the Chinese Emperor in the eyes of his followers, and that the consolidation of the Hun power was in a way an emulative response to the unification of China under the Ch'in.

From the beginning of Han times, as we read in the Imperial Annals, the Huns were a thorn in the Chinese flesh, annually intruding over the border, and terrorizing the country far and wide. In a futile attempt to placate them, the early Han emperors sent Chinese princesses as wives to their rulers, as well as expensive gifts of manufactured goods, mainly silks. This supine policy changed drastically when Emperor Wu came to the throne in 140 BC. A planned military campaign, undertaken between 133 and 119 BC and led by two of China's most daring generals, carried the battle into Hun territory and so crippled its power that China was scarcely bothered by nomad aggression for 300 years to come. The success of this campaign promoted the opening up of Central Asia by Chinese expeditionary forces, paving the way for diplomatic and commercial intercourse with the West.

The Western Regions: the drive of the Ta Yüeh-chih

In 165 BC a nomadic tribe, the Yüeh-chih, had been badly beaten by the Huns in western Kansu, and the main horde, the Ta Yüeh-chih, had fled westward across the steppes. After much tribulation they eventually reached the fertile middle basin of the Jaxartes river (Syr Darya). This was the independent kingdom of Sogdiana (Ch. K'ang Chu), formerly a satrapy of Alexander's but long since separated from the main Seleucid Greek Empire by a powerful new neighbour, Parthia (Ch. An Hsi). Weakened by wars against the Parthian Mithridates I, the Sogdians were no match for the nomads, who proceeded to occupy the whole region between the Jaxartes and Oxus rivers by about 130 BC.

Two years later the Ta Yüeh-chih took possession of another Macedonian kingdom, Bactria (Ch. Ta Hsia), with its capital at Bactra some 20 miles south of the Oxus. Consolidating their hold over Bactria, the horde now swept south-east, following the line of the Kabul river, past Begrām and Taxilā, and on into the Indus Valley. Thus were laid the foundations of a great new empire, the Kushān, that at its zenith at the end of the first century AD reached westwards to within a few hundred miles of the Roman frontier on the Euphrates, and eastwards across the Punjab to its capital at Mathurā in Uttar Pradesh. So it was that a nomad tribe from the other side of Asia – people who knew the Chinese and had traded with them as far back as the fourth century BC [p. 44] – came to lodge themselves solidly west of the Pamirs, on the borders of the civilized Western world.

The Western Regions: the quest for the Heavenly Horse

In 138 BC Emperor Wu sent an envoy, Chang Ch'ien, to seek out the Ta Yüeh-chih and negotiate an alliance with them against the Huns. In this the envoy failed; for when at last he reached the Ta Yüeh-chih, ten years later, he found them preoccupied with their plans for the conquest of Bactria. Chang returned to China in 126 BC, without a treaty, but with plenty to say about the various countries he had passed through – the 'Western Regions', as the Chinese came to call them.

The commercial implications of Chang's report do not seem to have been properly understood. This was natural enough, since although he was a shrewd observer, his information about Parthia and places further west, which he had not visited, was extremely vague. There seems to have been no notion of the tremendous potential market represented by the Western world. Instead, what struck Emperor Wu most was his emissary's talk about a horse of superior quality, the so-called 'heavenly horse', *t'ien ma*, bred around the headwaters of the Jaxartes, within the independent kingdom of Fergana (Ch. Ta Yüan). Thinking to procure some of this breed for use against the Huns, Emperor Wu sent a diplomatic mission to the Fergana capital. It was badly received; and when it reached the Fergana frontier on its return journey (106 BC) its members were callously murdered. In 102 BC Wu despatched a vast expedition, including some 60,000 fighting men, to undertake reprisals. The Fergana capital was besieged for forty days, after which the inhabitants obligingly beheaded their king and capitulated. A few dozen 'heavenly horses' were obtained.

Here, in the valley of the Upper Jaxartes, west of the Pamir divide, was the ultimate western limit of the Han Empire. In Central Asia, China was for the time undisputed master, and embassies to countries further west now passed freely at the rate of ten or more a year. Inside a generation Chinese military genius had created a new imperial power in Asia and had thereby shifted the whole balance of Asian politics. By crossing the Pamirs, Chinese armies had done what Alexander 200 years before had failed to do, and in the perspective of world history the result was immense. On the one hand, Chinese silk reached the markets of Rome, where it quickly became the leading item in the costly Oriental trade which, according to Hudson, 'was one of the major factors in the economic decline of the Roman world'4. On the other hand, as will be recounted in the next chapter, the countries of eastern Asia were invaded by missionaries of a new religion, Buddhism, as a result of contact with India through the Kushān Empire.

The Western Regions: the mission of Kan Ying

In AD 97 a Chinese ambassador called Kan Ying was sent westwards with instructions to proceed to a place called Ta Ch'in. By this time China was aware that more was to be had in the West than impractical alliances and horses with supernatural powers. Ta Ch'in, we now believe, was the Roman Empire, or at least its eastern province of Syria. Curiosity about Ta Ch'in probably meant that the Chinese were now intent on opening up direct trade with Rome through her Syrian outposts, thereby eliminating middleman profits.

Parthia, as map 2 clearly shows, was a profit-taking intermediary in the now expanding silk trade. The Chinese watched the silk as far as Parthia's frontiers, but of its subsequent fate they knew nothing; they understood only that there was a large consumer nation somewhere further west. The Parthians did nothing to enlighten them. Kan Ying was prevented from taking the direct overland route across Syria to the Levant. And when eventually he reached the Persian Gulf, and was ready to set sail for Ta Ch'in, he was gently dissuaded from making the voyage. In *very* favourable conditions, he was told, it could be done in two months, but mariners generally put three years provisions on board. 'There is something in the sea', they said, 'which is apt to make a man homesick, and several have thus lost their lives.' Fan Yeh, the author of the 'History of the Latter Han Dynasty', comments: 'When Kan Ying heard this, he stopped.'5 Writing more than 300 years later, Fan Yeh of course saw the situation far more clearly than had Kan Ying. Of Ta Ch'in he astutely observes: 'Their kings always desired to send embassies to China, but the An-hsi [Parthians] wished to carry on trade with them in Chinese silks, and it is for this reason that they were cut off from communication.'6

Nevertheless, despite the unsolved whereabouts of Ta Ch'in, and Parthia's uncommunicativeness, trade in Chinese commodities was pushed relentlessly forward. Map 2, which shows the distribution of Chinese silks and lacquers found in various parts of Asia, will serve as an index of its spread westward. Tun-huang in China; Lou-lan, Ying-p'an and Niya in Chinese Turkestan; Begrām in Afghānistān; Dura-Europos and Halebie-Zenobia in Mesopotamia; and Palmyra in Syria, are all places on or near the direct trade-route to Rome.

Chinese expansion in the South and East

During the first half of Emperor Wu's reign most of the independent kingdoms of south China were absorbed into the Han Empire, an important exception being Nan Yüeh in the far south, occupying present-day Kwangsi and Kwangtung provinces as well as Tongking and northern Annam in Indo-China. Nan Yüeh fell in 112 BC to the combined forces of six of Wu's generals, and the whole of China Proper came under Han rule. A rebellion broke out in the Indo-Chinese provinces in AD 40, but was put down by General Ma Yüan in the course of a brilliant campaign. Chinese settlers proceeded to populate the region, penetrating as far south as Thanh-hoa on the Chu river in northern Annam, where brick tombs of the Han period have been recently excavated, and fragments of silk and lacquer, as well as many other remains of Chinese occupation, brought to light.

In the north-east, diplomatic intrigue and the need to outflank the Huns in that quarter led the Chinese to annex the independent principality of Ch'ao Hsien, occupying south Manchuria and north Korea, in 108 BC. Of the four commanderies into which Ch'ao Hsien was now divided, the most important was Lo-lang with its capital about 4 miles south-west of Pyong-yang and on the south bank of the Ta-t'ung river. This rich site, including over 1,300 Han tombs, has been excavated by Japanese archaeologists, and some of the finest Han remains known to us unearthed, including a few silks and an abundant collection of lacquers of superb quality. More finds of Han lacquer have been made at Nan-shan-li and Ying-ch'êng-tzŭ on the Liaotung Peninsula, at Pei-cha-ch'êng near modern Kalgan in Inner Mongolia, and at Yang-kao in northern Shansi. These commanderies in the region of the Great Wall were Han military outposts set against the Huns, about whom a little more must now be said.

pl. 110, col. 26

pl. 99

The Northern Regions

Meanwhile the nomads stretched in a great arc across the steppe belt. West of the Urals, the tribes known to Roman historians as Setae, Sarmatae, Alani, Aorsi, and so on, were in contact with Greek colonies on the Black Sea, such as Panticapaeum on the Kertch Peninsula. From these centres articles of Greek manufacture were freely sold to the nomads, a fact which accounts for the presence of objects bearing Hellenistic decoration in so many Scythian and Sarmatian tombs. Indeed, the nomads' cultural range was considerable. The Aorsi, we know, traded with Babylonia and even India through Armenian and Median intermediaries. And to the south-east, in Sogdiana and Bactria, the Ta Yüeh-chih were now in close contact with the Hellenistic culture of the Middle East, with its inheritance of Greek, Iranian, and eastern Mediterranean styles and decorative motifs. Further east, the Huns, fleeing westward from the victorious Chinese, were beginning to appear in Hither Asia; and beyond them, extending over the Altai region and Outer Mongolia, were more Huns.

In 1924–5 a Russian expedition led by P.K. Koslóv explored a group of tumuli in the mountains of Noin-ula near Lake Baikal, some 70 miles north of Urga and 7 miles east of the Urga–Kyakhta road. Excavation revealed that these were tombs of horse-riding nomads, very probably Huns. Objects found included some imported from China, others from the West, and others of local manufacture; but this last group was by far the smallest. Chinese patterned silks were prominent. A Chinese lacquer dish bears a date corresponding to the year 2 BC, and the strong likelihood is that the tombs belong to the first century of our era.[7]

pls 97, 100, 114, 116, 117
fig. 31

Having tried to account in historical terms for the presence of Chinese lacquers and silks at sites in the Asiatic provinces shown on map 2 – namely, the Middle East, Siberia, Mongolia, Chinese Turkestan, Manchuria, China itself, Korea, and Tongking – we now propose to take up the separate stories of lacquer and silk in Han times. But decorative motifs are common to both, and will therefore be treated in a short end-section on their own.

*

There is no conclusive evidence to show that true lacquer-ware was made anywhere outside China in Han times. Indian, Burmese, and Ceylonese lacquer (Hind. *lakh*) derives from the gummy deposit on trees of an insect, *Tachardia lacca*, and is what we in the West call 'resin lac' or 'shellac'. When European craftsmen sought to imitate Far Eastern lacquer-ware in the sixteenth century and later, it was this substance that formed the base of their varnishes. But the properties of resin lac are quite different from, and generally speaking inferior to, those of true lacquer, which is the unadulterated natural juice of the lac tree (*Rhus verni-cifera*, Ch. *ch'i shu*), a native originally of China, today found also in Annam, Korea, and Japan. The discovery of this substance, and its exploitation as a protective and decorative envelope applied to articles made of wood and other materials, is something the world owes to China.

Composition and mode of preparation of lacquer

Trees, the average life of which is between fifteen and twenty years, are tapped in summer. They emit a grey, syrupy juice, the essential constituent of which, christened urushiol, after the Japanese *urushi*, 'lacquer', is a hydrocarbon with the chemical formula $C_{14}H_{18}O_2$; on exposure to oxygen, this substance spontaneously polymerizes – that is, it forms molecules of much higher molecular weight – and so behaves in a way as the earliest of all plastics known to man. Urushiol occupies 74 per cent of the volume of lacquer juice, the remainder being made up of 20 per cent water, 2 per cent albumen, and 4 per cent of a gum similar to gum arabic. After being strained several times through hemp cloth, lacquer juice is heated over a slow flame to remove excess moisture and is afterwards stored in air-tight vessels. It is then ready for use, with or without addition of colouring-agents.

Properties of lacquer

Lacquer is almost unbelievably resistant to water. A lacquer object may lie buried in moist earth, or be flooded with water, for years and perhaps centuries; yet, provided no mechanical injury is sustained whereby the wood or fabric underneath is exposed to the action of mois-ture, it will emerge as fresh and unimpaired as ever. Japanese archaeologists who excavated the Lo-lang tombs say that their solid wooden chambers, surrounded by hard clay soil, had acted as natural reservoirs, so that many of the tombs were heavily flooded. Yet they remark: 'lacquer objects have been wonderfully preserved in this constantly wet condition, though naturally they have changed their original positions as a result of drifting about in the water.'[8]
fig. 31   To this we may add that the Noin-ula *kurgan*, from which was recovered lacquer in superb condition, were so water-logged that pumps had to be used throughout the excavation; and that the Ch'ang-sha tombs, where a great find of late Chou lacquers was made some twenty years ago, were completely inundated by subsoil water.

By virtue of this and other qualities, such as high resistance to heat and acids, lacquer excels both as a protective envelope and as a vehicle for surface decoration. On their account it has always won the admiration of the West. As early as AD 1345 or thereabouts, the Arab Ibn Baṭuṭṭah visited Canton and particularly admired the brilliance and solidity of lacquers then being made for the markets of India and Persia. And lacquer was a leading export to western Europe during the seventeenth and eighteenth centuries. So the Jesuit missionary Le Comte, writing from Peking in 1685, pays it this tribute:

'Besides the brightness and lustre which is the property of varnish [from Fr. *vernis*, 'lac-quer'], it hath moreover a certain quality of preserving the wood upon which it is applied, especially as they do not mix any other matter with it. Worms do not easily breed in it, nay, and moisture scarce ever penetrates it, not so much as any Scent can fasten to it; if during meals there be any Grease or Portage spilt, if it be presently wiped with a wet Clout, one not only finds no remainders or signs of it, but does not so much as perceive the least smell.'

Uses of lacquer

Its known preservative and water-resisting qualities led to use of lacquer as a protective dope on a whole range of materials and manufactured objects in Han and earlier times. In the manufacture of vessels such as those illustrated on plates 98 and 105–110 it was applied to *pls 98, 105–110* wood alone, to wood covered with hemp cloth, and to hemp cloth alone. It was applied to the silk fabric of hats and the leather of shoes, in order to stiffen and waterproof these articles. Lacquered cushions of plaited bamboo were found at Lo-lang; and from the so-called 'Tomb of the Painted Basket', at the same site, a large collection of lacquered weapons of war and accessories, such as sword-sheaths and hafts, cross-bows, shields, and chariot-wheel spokes, came to light. As Mänchen-Helfen remarks, probably all war-gear was lacquered whenever possible, to protect it from rot and rust.⁹ Coffins at Noin-ula and Lo-lang were lacquered inside and out.

*

We have seen [p. 102] how curiously hybrid is the Third Phase bronze style. Some of its motifs, for instance, the twisted- and plaited-cord patterns that serve to divide horizontal *pls 55, 69, 87, 88* zones on the vessels, show how ready their makers were to imitate in bronze the forms and textures of other materials. Mänchen-Helfen thinks that metal inlays of the Third Phase rep- resent the vestiges of an earlier art of lacquer-painting or -stencilling on bronze; for inlay not only fills the narrow channels of spirals, T-forms, and so forth, where it is perfectly appro- priate, but also often occupies the broad, shallow areas forming the bodies of naturalistic birds, beasts, and humans in the hunting-scenes so typical of these inlaid bronzes. How were such spacious and freely-executed designs transferred to the bronze? Presumably by way of the wax model [p. 78]. They may have been drawn by hand, stencilled, or stamped on wax by means of dies; but whatever method was used, Mänchen-Helfen believes that the original design was painted with lacquer and a brush. Pre-Han texts speak of use of lacquer as a writing-material. Why should it not have been used for painting also?

But if the bronze art of the Third Phase is a complex containing motifs, styles, and tech- niques typical of art-forms other than bronze – such as painting in lacquer – it is no less the main channel through which all these features were later disseminated among the multi- tudinous art-forms of Han times. If therefore the inlaid bronzes of the Third Phase contain *pls 61, 104; col. 19* echoes of an earlier tradition of lacquer-painting, we have equally to recognize that the styles and motifs characteristic of these bronzes were in turn bequeathed to Han art generally, and made their appearance more or less indiscriminately in almost every medium – including lac- quer – in which it found expression.

Painting in lacquer: the ancestor of later Chinese pictorial art?

That lacquer was used abundantly in pre-Han China is a comparatively recent *fait acquis* provided by the Chin-ts'un, Ku-wei-ts'un, and Ch'ang-sha finds. These no more than hint at what may have been a superb art of painting in lacquer during the late Chou period. Fragments of a lacquered frieze on the wall of the Chin-ts'un tomb chamber [p. 104] reveal tantalizing glimpses of what W. C. White supposes was a design, freely drawn in lacquer, of dragons and phoenixes.[10] A lacquered wood casket (*lien*) from Ch'ang-sha is decorated with figures of men in long, graceful robes attending a banquet. Photographs of this painting in a Chinese publication entirely fail to do it justice, but the author may well be right when he says of it that 'no more important document in the early history of Chinese painting is known'.[11]

pls 105–109, col. 26

By Han times painting in lacquer on lacquer displays such suavity, such vitality and certitude, as to suggest that designers had long been familiar with the graphic qualities of the medium. We may well ask whether pictorial conventions thus established may not have had a profound effect on the subsequent course of Chinese painting. But whether or no one feels inclined to give priority to lacquer as the medium in which the pictorial genius of China first found expression, Han lacquers are unquestionably outstanding documents in its early development.

The technique of lacquering

PRIMING

Well before Han times it had become the practice to interpose a special priming between the lacquer layer and its wood support in order to prevent the former from the effects of exudation of moisture from the wood. The word *huan* is sometimes used in pre-Han texts with the same sense as *ch'i*, 'lacquer', but from Han citations it is clear that *huan* was really a priming substance of this sort. *Shuo wên* defines it as 'lacquer with ash [particularly bone ash], mixed and applied'. The mixture was presumably spread on the wood, allowed to dry, and then ground down to form a smooth and non-absorbent surface suitable for the application of lacquer alone. In other words, it was very much like a traditional European gesso applied to a wood panel. On a few Han lacquers, inscriptions state that they were thrice *wan* (= *huan*); and this must mean that the articles in question were coated three times with lacquer and ash before the craftsman was satisfied that the priming was complete.

The vast majority of Han lacquers, including most of those found outside the borders of China Proper, appear to have been constructed by some such means as this. By a more refined process, a layer of hemp cloth was glued to the surface of the wood base and was then primed to receive successive coats of lacquer; and here we have a technique closely similar to traditional European marouflage, in which canvas is glued to a wood support and then primed to receive painting in tempera and oils. In the final stage, reserved for the finest and costliest goods such as the cosmetic box of plate 98, lacquer was applied to an armature of hemp cloth alone, just as in European painting oil paint came to be applied to the primed surface of an unbacked canvas mounted on a stretcher [see p. 296].

pl. 98

From inscriptions on the vessels themselves, we know that the Chinese called these advanced techniques *chia chu*, 'lined with hemp cloth', or simply *chu*, 'on hemp cloth'; this does not necessarily imply that the wood support had been dispensed with in such cases. Thus an inscription on a vessel of AD 45 names the vessel as *mu chia pei*, 'a cup (*pei*) of wood (*mu*) lined (*chia*) [with hemp cloth and lacquered]'. The technique later came to be used for the manufacture of Buddhist images. The Japanese, who took it over from the Chinese, called it *kanshitsu*, 'dry lacquer'. If lacquer was applied to hemp cloth alone, they called it *dakkatsu-kanshitsu*; if modelled on a solid wood core lined with hemp cloth, it was *mokushiu-kanshitsu*.

pl. 140

Inscriptions, engraved on the vessels, often give names of workmen (*kung*) responsible for various stages of their manufacture. First comes the *su kung*. The original meaning of *su* is 'a

20 Gilt-bronze toilet box, lien, *the inside of its lid painted with a phoenix among cloud-scrolls. Han dynasty. Diameter of lid: 7 in. Victoria and Albert Museum.*

21 *Part of a polychrome silk with a repeat pattern of winged feline dragons and flying ducks in a landscape of cloud-scrolls, Chinese characters interspersed reading from right to left: 'Climb high places, clearly see Four Seas (i.e. the whole world)'. Later Han dynasty, from Lou-lan, Chinese Turkestan. The pattern-unit is repeated in the warp direction (vertically) every two inches. National Museum, New Delhi.*

22 (right) *Part of a polychrome silk with a repeat pattern of beasts, mostly feline, processing through a landscape of convoluted cloud-scrolls interspersed with Chinese characters: 'Patterned silk of Han-jên. May you be blessed with sons and grandsons without cease.' Later Han dynasty, from Lou-lan, Chinese Turkestan. The pattern-unit is repeated in the warp direction once every two inches. National Museum, New Delhi.*

below from left to right

23 *Part of a polychrome silk. Later Han dynasty, from Lou-lan, Chinese Turkestan. The checks measure 0.25 × 0.2 in., the stripes (from the top) 0.9, 1.6, 1.3, 1.4, and 1.5 in. National Museum, New Delhi.*

24 *Part of a polychrome silk, with a repeat pattern of horizontal meanders enclosing the characters for: 'May your posterity continue to adorn each generation.' Later Han dynasty, from Lou-lan, Chinese Turkestan. The pattern-unit is repeated in the warp direction (vertically) every 0.6 in. National Museum, New Delhi.*

25 *Part of a silk polychrome with an allover pattern-unit comprising an open zigzag lozenge joined to a highly stylized 'bird-dragon' [figure 24b]. Later Han dynasty, from Lou-lan, Chinese Turkestan. The pattern-unit is repeated in the warp direction every 1.9 in. in the weft every 5.2 in. National Museum, New Delhi.*

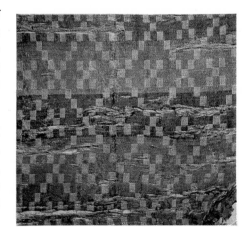
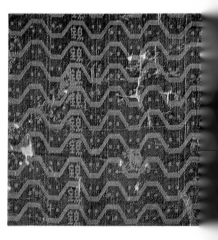

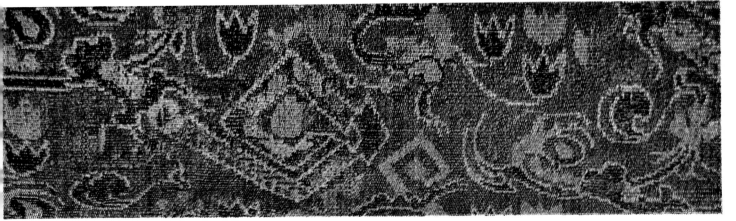

26 *Section of a round lacquer tray with a painting of Hsi Wang Mu, the Queen Mother of the West, and an attendant. Other parts of the tray feature a dragon, a tiger, and two pairs of galloping horses, all surrounding an inscription with a date corresponding to the year AD 69. Later Han dynasty, from the tomb of Wang Kuang, Lo-lang, Korea. Height of painting: 3 1/8 in. Keijo Museum, South Korea.*

plain cloth', but it quickly assumed the metaphorical sense of 'plain', 'white', or 'unembroidered', and so came to mean the ground to which ornament is applied. With this range of meanings for *su* it is difficult to decide exactly what task was allotted to the *su kung*. He may have had to prepare the plain ground priming, *huan*; or he may have been responsible for glueing the hemp cloth on to its wood support; or for building up a hemp-cloth armature if no wood support was used.

LAYERING

The priming completed, the lacquerer, or *hsiu kung*, now took over. Several successive thin coats of lacquer were applied, each being allowed to dry out before putting on the next. In Ming and Ch'ing lacquers, multiplication of lacquer layers is carried to extreme lengths, for frequently thirty or more are applied. But the process is also of considerable antiquity. We read in *Li chi* or 'Record of Rites', dating from Han times, that a coffin was prepared for the Chou feudal ruler as soon as he was enthroned. Each year throughout his life it was given a fresh coat of lacquer, after which it was allowed to dry and was then stored until the following year.[12] In this connexion a curious point must be noticed, one that perhaps links up with lacquer's most distinctive property: its resistance to water. To 'dry' effectively, lacquer needs a humid atmosphere, and a temperature of between 70° and 80° F. Accordingly, freshly-painted lacquer-ware was customarily placed in a damp pit or trench dug in the earth and called the 'shadow-house'; under these conditions it attained its greatest pitch of hardness and durability. And here again we have an instance of the extraordinary conservatism of Chinese industrial techniques. In *Shih chi*, Ssŭ-ma Ch'ien tells how the Second Ch'in Emperor wished to lacquer the walls of his capital. His dwarf approved the idea, saying that no robber could ever hope to scale such smooth surfaces; he asked only how the walls were to be got into the 'shadow-house', and the project was abandoned.[13]

The outermost layer of lacquer was of crucial importance, for upon its smoothness of texture depended the brilliance and lustre of the finished article. The workman who applied it was a specialist called in the inscriptions *shang kung*, or 'workman [who lacquers] the topmost [layer]'.

Classes of lacquer decoration

The article now passed into the hands of the *hua kung*, or painter, and others whose job was to decorate it; and here it will be convenient to cite briefly the main techniques of surface decoration displayed by Far Eastern lacquer-ware. It is traditionally divided into two main classes – painted lacquer (*hua ch'i*) and carved lacquer (*tiao ch'i*); but one might reserve a category for inlaid lacquer, both painted and carved, and for that in which relief decoration is worked up with a putty of lacquer, charcoal, lamp-black, and other substances. All these classes of decoration – and the lesser sorts into which both Chinese and Japanese connoisseurs customarily divide them – originated in China and have their roots in the range of technical processes available to Han lacquerers.

CARVING AND RELIEF MOULDING

Lacquer when hard can be cut, carved, or engraved with as much precision as can ivory. This type of work reached its climax in the eighteenth century with the *tours de force* of the imperial workshops of Peking, and there is little sign of it before Han times. An impressive Third Phase lacquer plaque in the Löw-Beer collection, featuring a *t'ao-t'ieh*, is stated by its owner to be made of carved lacquer alone, and we have also examples of Han lacquer engraving in which the design is cut through to a more lightly-coloured priming, or else is filled in with white or sometimes red pigment; the inscriptions themselves were cut in this way.

pl. 112
pl. 99

A character appearing in some Han lacquer inscriptions, naming the workman to whom lacquered articles were consigned after leaving the hands of the *hua kung*, has sometimes been read as *t'ung*, 'red' or 'to paint red'; whence the term *t'ung kung* is translated 'the decorator in red [lacquer]'. But it is now generally agreed that *t'ung* is really a variant of *tiao*, 'to engrave, to carve', and that the *tiao kung* was he whose most important job was to engrave the inscription and to make it harmonize pleasingly with the rest of the decoration.

PAINTING AND INLAYING

Black and red seem to have been the earliest lacquer pigments used in China, the former probably derived from iron sulphate or lamp-black, the latter from cinnabar. Black lacquer for the outside, red for inside, seems to have become conventional at least as early as the fourth century BC, especially for decorating coffins. Thus the outer shell of a coffin at Chin-ts'un was lacquered black outside, red inside; so were the coffins of Wang Hsü and his wife at Lo-lang. A lid belonging to Löw-Beer, bearing the date 4 BC, is lacquered black outside, red inside, as are almost all Han vessels from Chinese Turkestan, Lo-lang, Noin-ula, and elsewhere. Generally speaking, if the two colours are used together, red is applied on top of black, not vice versa. Probably there was a chemical component in the red that made it unsuitable for painting black lacquer over it.

By late Chou times a white derived from white lead, a light blue-grey and another shade of red had been added to the lacquerer's palette, as we know from lacquers reported to have come from Ku-wei-ts'un. Green from a chromium compound, yellows from cadmium and ochre, and blue, are all found on Han lacquers and may not have been known previously. In chapter 93 of *Ch'ien han shu* [p. 121] we read that the emperor's coffin was painted with vermilion inside, while the outer walls had representations of the green (*ch'ing*) dragon and white tiger, and of the sun and moon painted in gold and silver respectively. These latter pigments were certainly in vogue by the second century AD, for they are found on lacquer-ware from the 'Tomb of the Painted Basket' at Lo-lang, dating from that century.

Among the costliest and most beautiful painted lacquers of Han times were those ornamented with inlays of bronze, silver, gold, and tortoise-shell, with gilt-bronze handles and feet and other accessories in metal. The workman named after the *shang kung* is the *t'ung êrh k'ou huang t'u kung*, an expression rendered by Mänchen-Helfen as 'the bronze-handle gilder'. But I think we may assume that the work of this craftsman included all embellishments of the sort mentioned above. Some of these vessels must have been extravagant indeed. The cosmetic box of plate 98 has a quatrefoil device originally composed of silver plates inlaid on the lid, as well as inlaid silver figures of animals round the sides of both box and top of lid; and it is evidently an *objet de luxe*. Others may have been even more handsome.

pl. 98

Just as Pliny attacked the expensive tastes that were bankrupting contemporary Rome, so there were those who censured the Chinese fashion for luxury lacquer-ware. In *Ch'ien han shu*, Kung Yü is reported as having stated that over five million cash were being wasted annually on the lacquers of Shu and Kuang-han, the principal manufacturing centres for lacquer, which were in Szechwan province. He tells how he followed the Emperor on one occasion into the Empress's palace, and there saw richly-ornamented and painted lacquer dishes, and lacquer tables adorned with gold and silver. And as Roman historians approved the frugality of emperors who abstained from luxuries like Chinese silks, so, too, Fan Yeh in his *Hou han shu* praises Empress Têng, wife of Emperor Hsiao-ho (reigned AD 89–106), for renouncing the Szechwan lacquers with their gilt-bronze rims.

On the whole the lacquers found at Lo-lang and other Chinese outposts, even if made in Szechwan, scarcely seem to be the luxury wares the texts make so much of. Very rarely are they inlaid with gold or silver. Perhaps they reflect the less gaudy tastes of a later period. More probably they are simply cheaper versions of the *objets de luxe*. So the silver-inlaid quatrefoil of the cosmetic box has as its counterpart a quatrefoil painted in yellow and outlined in red lacquer on several Lo-lang boxes. Similarly, yellow lacquer used in the depiction of animals and birds – such as the duck flying through cloud scrolls on a Noin-ula fragment – was al-most certainly intended as substitute for a gold inlay.

*

We have dealt with six workmen whose functions are known to us from contemporary in-scriptions on lacquer. They are: the workman who prepared the priming; the lacquerer; the lacquerer of the outermost layer; the gilder; the painter; and the engraver. Two others are mentioned. One was the *ch'ing kung*, an expression usually translated as 'cleaner' (and per-haps 'polisher'); the other is the *tsao kung*, who may have been the foreman or the person res-ponsible for checking the finished article off its long production line. All these men must have been masters, since between them they were apparently responsible for the whole output of the factory. No doubt each had apprentices working under him, by whose labour output could be kept up; but the mere fact that their names were recorded on the finished article, as a means of showing with whom responsibility lay for each stage of its manufacture, proves that supervision must have been personal and strict all along the line. To some extent the master-craftsmen changed their jobs around; we can, in fact, follow the movements of indi-viduals from one department to another as their names crop up in successive inscriptions.

To round off this section on lacquer, I append an English version of the inscription in sixty-seven characters on the vessel shown on plate 110, bearing a date corresponding to   *pl. 110* AD 4. It runs:

The fourth year of the *yüan shih* reign-period (AD 4). Made at the western factory in Shu commandery. Imperial pattern (*tsao ch'êng yü*). A lacquered, carved, and painted wood cup (*pei*) with gilt-[bronze] 'ears' (handles). Capacity one *shêng*, 16 *yüeh*. Priming by I; lacquer-ing by Li; outer coat by Tang; gilding of the 'ears' by Ku; painting by Ting; [inscription] engraved by Fêng; cleaning [and polishing] by P'ing; passed by Tsung. Officer command-ing the Factory Guard, Chang; Manager, Liang; Deputy, Fêng; Assistant, Lung; Chief clerk, Pao.

*

Silk is perhaps China's greatest single contribution to world material culture. So overwhelm-ing was the impression made by this lovely textile when it was displayed for the first time in the Near East not later than the end of the first century AD, that no opulent society of antiquity could thereafter bear to be without it. In 'touch' – fineness, closeness, softness and suppleness – in lustre and brilliance of colour, and in the scale and complexity of its woven designs, Chin-ese silk far outmatched the heavy tapestry woollens and linens then being made in Syria. As the monk Dionysius Periegetes put it, writing in the third century AD: 'The Seres [the Silk People, the Chinese] make precious figured garments, resembling in colour the flowers of the field, and rivalling in fineness the work of spiders.'[14]

From its first appearance in the Western world, Chinese silk was recognized as a material strictly *hors concours*, inimitable, rare, elusive, greatly to be coveted; yet political conditions were such that a steady supply at fixed and reasonable rates could never be guaranteed. A tremendous incentive thus grew to unveil the well-kept secret of its origin and method of pro-duction. The story goes that during the reign of Justinian (*c*. AD 552), eggs of the Domestic Silkmoth, *Bombyx mori*, were successfully smuggled into the Byzantine Empire concealed in a hollow tube – according to the contemporary Procopius, by certain Indian monks who had lived for a long time in the country of the Seres, Serinda. Certain it is that from about the sixth century knowledge of sericulture and of silk textile technology slowly spread westwards to the shores of the Mediterranean, and the demand for imported Chinese silk cloth grew less insistent.

Reeled silk provides the finest natural textile thread known to man. So, where intensive sericulture is practised, there one may expect to find advanced methods of loom construction, complex weaving techniques, and high-quality textiles. And correspondingly, in societies depending mainly on short-staple fibres like flax, cotton, and wool, which make relatively inferior yarns, textile processes are likely to be less forward. That this is true as a general principle is implied by the textile historian Vivi Sylwan when she says: 'I, like others, arrived at the conclusion that the technical development in textiles, from relatively primitive methods towards the somewhat mechanized forms which preceded the more modern machine production, has taken place mainly in the silk workshops.' [15]

Unquestionably the presence of Chinese silks on local markets awoke the spirit of emulation among Western weavers. By the end of the third century AD the Han system of pattern-building begins to appear in certain Syrian weaves, and a little later in Egypto-Roman figured woollens and early Sassanid Persian silks woven with imported Chinese reeled silk thread. Silk fabrics, woven from Chinese thread, were being made in Byzantium soon after Constantine chose it as his capital in AD 324. The decorative influence most strongly at work was an Eastern one; few Hellenistic motifs are to be found.

*

Roman naturalists and historians like Pliny, groping blindly in an area they did not understand, supposed that raw silk was produced commercially in various parts of Western Asia; and this belief was shared by the Chinese themselves. A tendency can also be observed among some modern Western textile historians to deny to China the exclusive invention of sericulture, and of the advanced techniques required to weave reeled silk thread to best effect. It is barely possible that India was producing cloth woven from the spun silk of wild silkworms at this time, but there is no evidence at all that reeled silk was being manufactured anywhere in the world outside China. Moreover we find bountiful evidence of its presence in the Chinese economy at least a thousand years before the beginning of the Christian era, and the complexity of the weaves then being made testifies to the existence of looms and weaving techniques far in advance of anything to be found in the West.

The paramountcy of silk among the natural textile fibres lies mainly in its excellence as a warping thread. It is the warp that has to withstand the rigours of weaving, the repeated blows of the reed as it packs the weft threads together at the 'fell', the point at which the cloth is being woven. Absence of a strong, elastic warping thread of uniform tensile strength placed a restriction on the technical development of Western weaving during historical times, and explains the predominance of the weft in most early Western textiles. Not until the seventeenth century, for example, were English weavers able to produce a really satisfactory cotton yarn for warping, and the finest English cottons up to that time were woven with a linen warp. Many examples of such mixed or mustered fabrics were among the rags found at Palmyra, dating between AD 83 and 273; they include silk-linen, silk-wool, and linen-wool. In the first two groups the silk was always reeled Chinese silk, and was used only for the warp.

It is possible to take off the cocoon of the dead silkmoth chrysalis a continuous filament almost a mile long, of uniform diameter and unparalleled tensile strength and elasticity. The weaver naturally seeks to exploit these qualities. So he invents coupled rotary warp- and cloth-beams worked by a crank, so that once the warp has been set up, a piece of almost indefinite length can be woven, section by section, without ever taking it off the loom. If a draw-loom device is installed, whereby warps can be raised in selected combinations in a regular series of sheds, a patterned fabric of great complexity can be woven with patterns appearing in repeats in both directions of the cloth. The manipulation of the shuttles and of the reed provides sufficient work for one pair of hands, and the work of raising the two heddles required to weave plain cloth can best be transferred to treadles operated by the feet. The pulling of the drawcord bundles, which requires the services of a drawboy, can only be effected if the warp lies horizontally. From all these considerations we may deduce that the Chinese had invented a horizontal frame loom, with rotary warp- and cloth-beams, incorporating a semi-automatic reed, equipped with a device coming within the general category of a drawloom attachment, and with treadle-operated heddles for opening the two primary sheds, long before the need for such a loom arose in the West. Evidence provided by actual fabrics strongly suggests that this invention took place as early as Shang times.

Silk was allegedly given to China by a 'culture heroine', the legendary Empress Hsi Ling Shih, wife of the Yellow Emperor, who about the middle of the third millennium BC is supposed to have taught 'how to treat the cocoons and the silk in order to give the people clothes ...'.[16] Silk may in fact have been in use within a few centuries of that time, for a single cocoon of an unidentified silkworm was found at the Middle Yang-shao site of Hsi-yin-ts'un in Shansi (c. 2200–1700 BC). The cocoon had been cut, though whether by man or by the escaping moth is uncertain, so that we cannot tell whether silk taken from it, or from others like it, was reeled or spun.

The significance of the Shang silk weaves

Thanks to brilliant pioneer studies by Dr Sylwan[17] we have ample evidence of silks from Shang times. Textiles used for wrapping bronze objects buried with the dead sometimes get impregnated with corrosion products from the metal and become, as it were, fossilized, so that the structure of the weave can be made out under the microscope. Dr Sylwan has examined fragments of silk adhering to a bronze axe and a vessel of the *chih* class [p. 92], both of which can be assigned to the First Phase (1500–950 BC) on stylistic grounds.

Of the three fabrics thus investigated, the oldest known silks in the world, two proved to be cloths with tabby weave, in which each weft thread passes over one warp, under the next, over the next, and so on across the web. One of them showed roughly the same number of threads in each direction, the density being about 35 threads per centimetre. In the other cloth there were twice as many threads in the warp direction as in the weft, the count being 72 and 35 threads per centimetre respectively. According to some nomenclatures this weave would be called a 'warp rep'. The point of interest is that most of the Han silks, woven over a thousand years later, are also warp reps. Moreover the thread density is much the same; thus of 22 Han silks found at Palmyra, the average thread density was 68 and 35 for warp and weft respectively. In Shang times, then, we already discern that ascendancy of warp over weft in the weave which possession of a strong and reliable warping thread strongly encourages.

The third fabric investigated by Dr Sylwan was patterned in the loom. It is a wonderful weave, standing at the head of the long tradition of Chinese silk damask weaving, in which a design is made to appear in a self- or single-coloured fabric by causing certain warps to pass over two or more wefts instead of merely alternating with them. Such passages are called *pls 94, 95* 'warp floats', and the effect of massing them together is to block in a raised pattern of characteristic appearance on the front face of the cloth.

Analysis of the Shang weave, which has a repeat pattern of two concentric lozenges enclosed within longitudinal zigzag bands, reveals that no fewer than sixteen different combinations of warp threads had to be raised to weave it. Two of these combinations provided the two basic sheds required for weaving ordinary cloth, which would probably have been opened by a pair of treadle-operated heddles. The other fourteen had to have special provision made to raise them, in the form of fourteen drawcord bundles constituting a primitive sort of drawloom. In figure 17 we see that the weft thread marked 1 passes under warps 2, 4, 6, etc., but also under 15, 21, 27, 33, etc., and these odd warps have to be tied up together and raised by means of a drawcord bundle whenever weft throw 1 is repeated.

Dr Sylwan's observation, that the thread used for these Shang textiles was reeled silk of *Bombyx mori*, is of first-rate importance to textile historians since it gives a provisional *terminus ante quem* for the introduction of true sericulture in China.

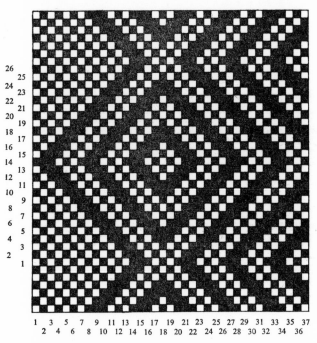

26
25
24
23
22
21
20
19
18
17
16
15
14
13
12
11
10
9
8
7
6
5
4
3
2
1

1 3 5 7 9 11 13 15 17 19 21 23 25 27 29 31 33 35 37
2 4 6 8 10 12 14 16 18 20 22 24 26 28 30 32 34 36

17 Reconstruction of pattern-units on a Shang 'twill' (warp runs up the page) after Sylwan

pls 97, 100, 114, 116, 117
col. 21–25 When, therefore, we contemplate the sumptuous Han patterned silks with their delicate and intricate designs so skilfully adapted to the capabilities and limitations of the material, we are looking at the direct descendants of a craft that stretches back to an extreme antiquity, one whose technical apparatus shows no sign of any fundamental change. To recapitulate, it comprises use of reeled silk thread, with all that this implies; use of a horizontal loom with drawloom attachment; ascendancy of warp over weft in the weave, with the warps producing the pattern. Even the optimum thread density and ratio seem to have been worked out and firmly adhered to – 70 threads per centimetre in the warp, half that number in the weft.

Chinese sericulture and silk technology

Very recently successful attempts have been made in China to rear silkworms on a diet of lettuce leaves; but the traditional food plant, at least of *Bombyx mori*, has always been the mulberry and nothing else. Two varieties of white mulberry, *Morus alba*, are commonly recognized in China. *Yeh sang* is the wild mulberry, a plant producing small and relatively few leaves, but with abundant fruit and of a hardy stock. *Lu sang*, the domestic or cultivated mulberry, produces few berries but much foliage. Silkworms fed on the former yield silk that is coarse and of inferior quality, so that the general practice in starting a plantation is to sow fruit of the hardy wild stock, and graft cuttings of the domestic variety when the saplings have grown a foot or so high.

The tree is allowed to grow for five years before its leaves are first fed to the caterpillars, attaining a height of about 6 feet each autumn and being cut back to 18 inches in the following spring. After the fifth year's growth the tree is kept at a standard height of six feet, being headed down to that height whenever necessary.

Feeding lasts about thirty days, and it is a matter for careful calculation how many silkworms can be brought to maturity with the quantity of leaves available. Approximately a ton of leaves is needed to rear an ounce or so of newly-hatched worms, yielding eventually about 12 lb. of silk (from which only about half can be reeled) from 130 to 140 lb. of cocoons. A fully-grown tree will produce 80 lb. of leaves in a season, so that some thirty trees are needed to produce 6 lb. of reeled silk.

About ten days before the mulberry breaks into leaf, in mid-April, eggs of the silkmoth are brought into the house from the place where they have been in cold storage, and are allowed to incubate at room temperature, or are placed in the clothing and warmed by body heat. The process of hatching should be complete for each batch of eggs in the course of 24 hours; and in this, as in every stage of sericulture, controlled environmental conditions help to ensure that the caterpillars in each batch are at a more or less identical stage of growth and are acting in unison. The newly-hatched caterpillars, now about a tenth of an inch long and no thicker than hairs, are carefully brushed into bamboo baskets and are fed with clean, fresh mulberry leaves chopped small. During the next 26 days the worms undergo a succession of four moults, feeding in between; after the last moult they feed much more voraciously and indiscriminately. In a few days they now consume something like twenty times their body weight of leaves, and get to be about 2 inches long. It is said that a mouthful of leaves fed to them at this stage will yield the equivalent weight of raw silk.

About 35 days after hatching, worms are ready to spin their cocoons. They stop feeding, take up a semi-erect posture, and are then transferred to straw trusses called 'silkworm hills', *ts'an shan*, some 60 or 70 worms to a truss. Spinning lasts 5 days, the silk being extruded in a continuous figure-of-eight pattern from the openings of two silk glands running the length of the body. As the two liquid threads emerge they are drawn together and are enclosed in a coating of gum, sericin, which binds them into a single filament. The filament rapidly hardens on exposure to air, but the gum in which it is embedded stays moist long enough to cause its loops to stick together as the cocoon is woven. When spinning is finished, the whitest and hardest cocoons are chosen for breeding purposes. Moths emerge from them after about 10 days, and are allowed to pair. The females lay their eggs on the same day, and these are collected and set aside to provide the next season's crop. The remaining cocoons are graded. Those intact will provide the reeled silk; those in any way damaged will be spun into refuse silk.

In traditional Chinese manuals of silk-farming, one notices how explicit are the instructions given for each stage in the life-history. All possible means are taken to bring the life-cycle fully under control. 'Silkworms', we are told, 'require to be equal in three things: the eggs should all be laid together, they must all be hatched together, and begin to spin together.' It also seems that silkworms are temperamental creatures, easily affected by adverse conditions such as noise and vibration: 'They cannot bear to be near where people pound in a mortar', the same authority tells us, 'neither do they like mourning, nor pregnant women.'[18] They also shun the smell of wine, of vinegar, smoke, musk, and oil. They refuse damp leaves, nor will they eat hot ones. It might appear from all this that successful rearing of a batch of silkworms is no simple matter; it *does* transpire that the outstanding quality of silk as a textile material, maintained throughout the whole of Chinese history, depended on a deep understanding of the need for uniformity at all stages of manufacture, and on an intimate knowledge, accumulated and handed down from time immemorial, of the problems peculiar to the craft of sericulture.

Reeling

Cocoons are put into very hot water which softens and partly dissolves the sericin that binds the filament loops together. While still immersed, the cocoons are stirred with a bamboo comb whose teeth catch up the end of each filament, the *maître brin*. On lifting the comb from the water, silk begins to unravel from all the cocoons, which bob up and down on the surface of the water as the filaments are lightly jerked. The operator now disengages from the batch a number of filaments varying according to the quality of the thread to be reeled, the finest thread being composed of six or seven filaments, coarser grades having as many as 25 or 30. These filaments are gently jerked up and down, so that several yards of silk are unravelled from the cocoons and are taken up by hand. This is surface floss, inferior filament of uneven denier, fit only to make refuse silk after spinning; it is broken off and set aside.

As soon as the operator is satisfied that the filaments are unravelling clean and smooth, he leads them to a treadle-operated reeling machine, through an eye, and on to the reel. As the filaments pass through the eye they are drawn together and agglutinated into a single thread. Before being run over the reel, the thread may be given a slight twist so as to rinse it of excess water and help dry it out. It was not the usual practice in China to 'throw' the silk; that is, to insert a strong twist in the thread throughout its length, amounting perhaps to 8 or 10 turns per inch. While throwing increases the tensile strength of the thread, it also robs silk of some of its lustre, and tends to bring out any unevenness in the thread, as well as adding to cost of production. Unthrown silk was normally quite strong enough to serve as a warp, particularly if the thread was largely ungummed, that is to say still protected by its envelope of sericin, as it usually was in traditional Chinese practice. At any rate all experts are agreed that Chinese silks of the Han period, wherever found, show no perceptible twist in the thread.

*

With the thread now winding steadily on to the reel – and perhaps several threads are being reeled simultaneously on a single machine – the cocoons gradually yield up their mile-long filaments. As each becomes exhausted and reduced to a paper-thin, transparent bladder (*pellette*), a new filament is skilfully grafted on to the end of the old. In this way great skeins of silk called 'books' can be reeled as a single continuous thread. Such skeins formed a leading item in the silk export trade to the West in Han times.

Han dyes and mordants

Han silks show a fairly complete colour-range, including a bright and solid crimson, brown, yellow-brown and beige, bronze-yellow and olive-green, a brilliant green, bright blue, dark blue and violet, white and black. In the present condition of the silks, reddish-brown is the dominating shade; but this must often bear witness to some lost colour which has changed character as the result of contact with chemical reagents in the soil. Russian analysts, using both the spectroscope and ultraviolet light, have been able to plot some of the original colours of these fugitive dyes, including the brilliant green mentioned above. A dull white often masks the presence of indigo blue which has been oxidized by such common reagents in the soil as nitric acid. It can be restored by reduction with hydrosulphide.[19]

Most if not all of the Han dyes were extracted from plants. And they were *adjective* dyes, in that they required mordants to bring out their colours and render them insoluble; as opposed to *substantive* dyes, which are applied direct and need no mordant. But the only dyes whose presence in Han silks has been definitely established are those produced by alizarine from the madder plant (*Rubia cordifolia*), which seems to have been used from time immemorial as a colouring-agent in China, and indigo from *Polygonum tinctorium*, the indigo plant of north China.

We do not, of course, know the exact state of Han dyeing science. Indigo requires no mordant, and is not susceptible to colour modification. But madder can be made to produce a wide range of hues depending on the nature of the soluble metal salt used as a mordant and its concentration in the vat. Mordanted with alum, madder gives a range of bright and very stable reds. With copper it could be used to produce a blue, though there is no evidence that this was done in Han China. With iron acetate it would yield black and a range of browns. I am not sure how the green was produced; theoretically it could be got by mordanting madder with oxidized iron. It is probable, then, that dyers relied largely on madder as the dyestuff and experimented intensively in the use of a range of mordants.

We should note that the patterns in the polychrome weaves are made by using threads of several different colours in the warp. Silk thread that has not been degummed cannot be satisfactorily dyed, since sericin absorbs dye freely, and its subsequent removal from the dyed thread would lead to loss or patchiness of colour in the final article. We may assume, therefore, that in this case the sericin was removed by 'boiling off' before the silk was dyed.

The Han silk weaves: the damasks

In the case of the Shang patterned silk discussed above [p. 138] the design is produced by warps that are floated over three wefts, under one, over three and so on; all the warps in the patterned area contribute to the design, so that all take the same $3:1:3$ course. But if warp A passes over wefts 1, 2, 3, etc., warp B will start its course by passing over wefts 2, 3, 4, warp C over wefts 3, 4, 5, so that the floats move diagonally across the web. Such a weave is a twill. One of the monochrome Han silks found at Lou-lan is also of this type. The design is an allover pattern of alternating squares, or checkerboard, each square being made up of eighty adjoining warps, all of which interlace with twenty-eight wefts through the pattern area and whose floats pass over three wefts and move diagonally.

It may very well be that the twill weave used for pattern-making paved the way for the typical Han damask, the structure of which is, however, rather different, as can be seen from figure 18. Here area A, including warps 1–8 and wefts 1–16, is the pattern area. From weft 17 onwards an ordinary ground weave is woven through area B by means of two ground-weave heddles. It will be seen that the warp floats *are* placed diagonally, but that the pattern floats, unlike the twills, alternate with ordinary ground-weave warps (nos 2, 4, 6, etc.) following an over-one, under-one course.

The pattern can only be read on the front face of the silk, where the warp floats are massed together. The pattern-warps in fact lie mainly on the front face, while the ground-weave

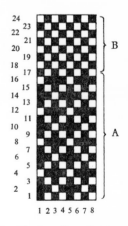

18 Part of the front face of a Han silk damask in diagrammatic form (warp runs up the page). As with figure 20, white squares represent passages of weft over warp on the front face of the material, black squares or rectangles, passages of warp over weft

warps have been carried to the back of the material, creating what is virtually a double or 'compound' fabric. Perhaps the ground-weave warps were introduced to give structural solidity to the weave in a way that pattern-warps alone, floated over three successive wefts, fail to do. But absence of a decipherable pattern on the reverse face was probably felt to be a disadvantage which, as we shall see, was overcome in the polychromes by a somewhat different and perhaps somewhat later system of weaving.

Inspection of figure 18 will show that only four different combinations of warp threads, or four different sheds, need be made to weave this small section of the material; wefts 1, 2, 4 and 18 pass through one or other of these four sheds, as do all the other wefts, and the design can be woven by entering the warp through four heddles, a perfectly practical number for weaving. But this will not suffice for allover pattern-units as complex as those shown in figure 19. This represents part of a typical Han damask from Lou-lan. It will be seen that the pattern, here comprising four complete units and part of a fifth, is bilaterally symmetrical about the mid-vertical axis, which represents a line of weft. From this point in the weave the pattern turns over, being woven with exactly the same sheds, but made in the reverse order. The vertical axis being along the width of the piece, we may assume that the complete double pattern was repeated over and over again through the length of the fabric; that is, in the warp direction.

Figure 20 shows part of the courses of the ten pattern-warps that build up the backward hind leg of the 'dragon' and part of the border an inch and a half from the bottom right-hand edge of figure 19; between the pattern-warps lie the ground-warps. The first pattern-warp is floated over wefts 6, 32, and 36; the second over wefts 4, 8, 30, and 34, and so on; each behaves in a different way. It follows that every other weft throw has to pass through an entirely different shed. In making the shed for weft 2, for instance, quite a different combination of warp-threads must be raised from that required for weft 4. In fact, for weaving this pattern, the number of different combinations of warp-threads will be half the number of weft throws, plus one for the ground weave represented by the alternate wefts 1, 3, 5, etc. In the fragment shown there are thirty-seven weft throws, of which eighteen (the even-numbered throws) require special sheds. The total number of sheds to be formed is therefore nineteen.

But, in fact, from the side of the design shown in figure 19 to the 'turn-over', there are eighty wefts. To weave this pattern, forty-one different sheds are therefore needed. It can be calculated that in the full width of the fabric there were probably some 1,500 pattern-warps, each entering into at least one combination, and usually many. So in setting up the warp for weaving, the operator would have to determine in the case of each pattern-warp the number of combinations of which it was a member, and for each combination ensure that it was correctly tied up with all the other threads, out of a possible 1,500, which entered that combination. Having done so he – or rather his drawboy, sitting at another part of the loom – had to pull the forty different bundles in correct sequence at the precise moment when ground-heddle 2, lifting warps 2, 4, 6, 8, etc., was being operated. On reaching the turn-over, the forty bundles had to be pulled in correct reverse sequence.

The scale and complexity of woven patterns of this type point unmistakably to use of a drawloom. Quite apart from the physical impossibility of picking a shed by hand through 3,000 different warps so closely set together, we have visible proof that these weaves were made mechanically. For when a mistake occurs, such as passage of a pattern-warp over one weft, over another, and under a third – instead of over all three – it is invariably repeated at cor-

19 Reconstruction of pattern-units on part of a Han silk damask from Lou-lan, drawn by R. J. Charleston. Lighter areas were reconstructed on the basis of the surviving pattern (darker areas). Warp runs across page

responding points in the design throughout the weave. But a mechanical arrangement of 41 treadle-operated heddles, needed to weave the fabric in question, would be even more absurd than would the fourteen required to weave the Shang twill. Once again we are forced back to some sort of drawloom.

It is not, of course, possible to say what was the actual arrangement of the drawcords. But it should be noted that despite its complexity such a system would not put production of patterned silks on a commercial scale out of the question. Setting up a warp for pattern-weaving is, of course, an almost superhuman business. But, once done, the great length of fabric that could be woven without interruption would quickly compensate for initial outlay. And, once the warp was set up, weaving of these superb silks would follow automatically, and would continue so for the whole piece. It may well have been the case that setting up a particular design was put in the hands of the same operative time and again; and that the weaver stuck to weaving it year after year, until pulling the drawcord bundles in proper sequence became second nature to him.

The Han silk weaves: the polychrome silks

Figure 21 shows part of the weave of a polychrome silk. In these, as we have said, the design can be read just as easily on the reverse as on the front face. Every warp-thread, in fact, is a pattern-thread, and the preselected design is set up with alternating warp-threads of two different colours. In our example, area A appears as a red patch, area B as blue. In area A, red

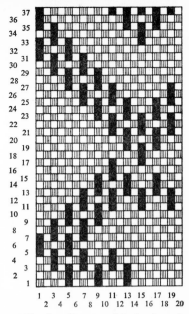

20 Weaving diagram of the backward hind leg of the dragon of figure 19 (warp runs up the page, and warp-floats are indicated in black)

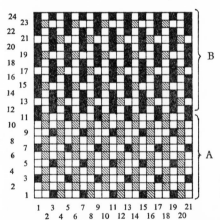

21 Part of the front face of a Han polychrome silk in diagrammatic form (warp runs up the page)

warps pass over three wefts, under the next, over the next three, etc., on the front face of the material. Meanwhile blue warps on either side of them are passing *under* three wefts, over one, under three, etc., so that the reverse face in area A appears blue. Between areas A and B the colour scheme changes. The red warp now goes to the back face; and in making this change it passes either *over two* wefts (in the cases of warps 2, 6, 10, etc.) or *under two* (warps 4, 8, 12, etc.). After weft throw 11, the red warps appear on the front face of the material only at every fourth weft throw, so that it is the back face that now appears red. The blue warps behave in exactly the reverse manner, coming up to the front face at weft throw 11, and thereafter predominating on that face, which appears blue. We have already given one reason why the polychromes may perhaps be regarded as more highly evolved than the damasks. Of special interest in this connexion is the modification in the polychromes whereby, in leading the warps to and from the front face of the material, they are made to pass over, or under, only two wefts. This allows for a more gradual transition from one part of the design to the next *pls 95, 100* than is possible in the case of the damasks. The result, as can be seen by comparing plates 95 and 100, is that while the damask designs are 'squared off' and do not allow for much elaboration of detail, the polychromes display much smoother edges to the patterns, and so favour the use of curvilinear design such as cloud scrolls.

The polychrome pattern-system is in fact more skilfully adapted for pattern weaving of all types of subject than is that of the damasks. So, perhaps, it is later. And this conclusion is also reached by Dr Sylwan, who points out that 'at least some of the patterns in these damask silks have their roots in an ornamental art older than Han'; she suggests that the damasks were no longer fashionable in metropolitan China in late Han times, but were very much to the taste of the Hellenistic countries of the Middle East, precisely on account of their more rectilinear style [p. 274]. This would perhaps account for the fact that Chinese patterned silks found at Palmyra were almost all of them damasks, whereas those found at places much nearer China, such as Noin-ula and Lou-lan, were nearly always polychromes.

The décor of Han lacquer and silk

Han decorative design, as featured in lacquer and silk, displays astonishing imaginative resource and a catholicity of subject-matter unparalleled elsewhere in Chinese applied art. The range of motifs is almost inexhaustible.

Designers drew not only on those handed down by devious paths to Third Phase bronze art [pp. 102–104], but also invented a whole set of new motifs, and borrowed and adapted everything that came their way from abroad. Yet, in spite of the variety of its sources, Han decorative design has great integrity. Naturalistic birds and animals consort with stylized versions of similar beings; foreign motifs are boldly planted in a purely Chinese *mise en scène*; rectilinear devices jostle alongside freely-executed forms with rounded contours, such as so-called 'cloud-scrolls' and spirals; but through it all runs a common spirit, a verve that speaks of thorough assimilation, and a curious grasp of what can perhaps best be described as the inner life of its subjects.

This art would make a rewarding study for the art historian. But no one so far has attempted systematically to trace its multitudinous origins, or to explain the significance of its motifs. Some are obviously decorative only. Others, equally clearly, are not. Fantasy and a sort of dread are present, echoes of a rich mythology that only occasionally shows itself. Fleetingly we come on familiar ground, to the world of Taoist fancy found in *Lieh tzŭ* and *Huai nan tzŭ*[20]; then the mist descends, as it was wont to do over the elusive Taoist Isles of the Blest in the Eastern Sea, and we are groping in a region of hostile presences, of beings that seem to belong to a more primitive, less codified set of ideas. And if the reader should think this far-fetched, let him turn to plate 108, showing the inside of a lacquer cup from the Ch'ang-sha find. This design seems to me dream-ridden. Would it be rash to claim a kinship between it and the work, say, of Paul Klee – one that involves not only style and presentation, but also perhaps its underlying psychological purport?

pl. 108

The popular beliefs of the Ch'u tribes who lived in the Ch'ang-sha region are preserved in poems belonging to the anthology called *Ch'u tzŭ*, that had a profound influence on the forms of Han poetry. Here is evidence of a cult of the dead, of spirit-journeys and shaman go-betweens; of a pattern of thought quite distinct, as Waley says, from that of magical Taoism.[21] Beyond doubt, exotic ideas and beliefs not only from Ch'u but also from the northern steppe-belt and elsewhere, helped to fashion the distinctive *Zeitgeist* of Han times, and permeated its art.

To qualify himself for the task of elucidating Han art, a scholar would have to be able to estimate the nature and strength of such outside cultural influences, and of their impact on the received native folk-lore as recorded in Han and pre-Han texts, until he had reached the point of being able to predict what elements in Han popular belief might, because of their compulsive appeal, force their way into decorative design. Bushell, Chavannes, and Laufer, among others, made successful attempts to do this in the case of episodes depicted on Han bas-reliefs [p. 173]. Some still resist identification; but the meaning of others is quite clear, and this is because they illustrate more or less familiar legends or historical events. Subjects favoured for portrayal on objects primarily of utility, such as lacquer-ware, silk, pottery, and mirrors, on the other hand, are not usually descriptive in this sense, and it is less easy to say what meaning should be read into them. In these circumstances we can do little more than indicate the general character of Han decorative design and trace the continuity in time, and from one material to another, of a few specially popular motifs.

Formal decorative motifs

Of abstract, geometrical, or non-representational motifs in Han art, the lozenge and its derivative, the zigzag band, are perhaps most common. The lozenge is naturally a basic element in decorative design throughout the world, appearing in its most rudimentary form on primitive pottery as a diaper pattern produced by incised cross-hatching. The Chinese seized on this element, and exploited it more thoroughly than did any other race of antiquity. It is one of the style criteria adduced by Karlgren for First Phase bronzes, and we see it again on the Shang silk of figure 17, where rows of lozenges are enclosed by simple zigzag bands; exactly the same combination occurs on the jade dagger-axe of plate 32, attributed to the Shang period. Discussing this piece [p. 55], we remarked that the motif was such as a jade-carver would instinctively choose, but it is no less well suited for reproduction as a textile motif, and perhaps that is what it first was. We illustrate a small series of variants taken from Han silks of various provenance and plate 116 shows another selection grouped together on a Noin-ula polychrome silk.

Its chief modification is that called 'lozenge with faulted angles' or 'zigzag lozenge', variants of which can also be seen in the illustrations. This form seems to be distinctive to China, and the question is how it originated. One obvious answer is that it developed from three adjacent lozenges linked or merged together, the one in the middle being somewhat larger than the two supporting it. Turned over on their sides, and placed end to end, these triple lozenges would appear as in figure 23 a. In the next stage, represented by figure 23 c, the motif may be read either as a series of contiguous lozenges with faulted angles, or as a pair of opposed compound zigzag bands. Compound zigzag bands clearly reveal themselves when the motif is divided into two halves along the mid-horizontal axis, the two bilaterally symmetrical halves being slightly separated, as in figure 23 d.

The compound zigzag band is not of course destined to reach full maturity on round objects such as mirrors, but comes into its own when a continuous linear border is called for, as in the damasks of figures 19 and 23 b and d. Once again we have to recognize a motif highly suited to the technical conditions of silk-weaving.

One variety of the zigzag lozenge is the 'open zigzag lozenge'; and here we have an outstanding example of the conservation of decorative design over centuries. On the polychrome silk from Lou-lan this motif can hardly be older than the first century AD. Yet it is to all intents and purposes the same form as appears on a large number of Shou-hsien mirrors

22 Simple and zigzag lozenges on Chinese silks; *a* polychrome silk, Lou-lan; *b* silk damask, Palmyra; *c* polychrome silk, Noin-ula; *d* polychrome silk, Kertch Peninsula; *e* polychrome silk, Lou-lan; *f* silk gauze, Noin-ula. (Not to scale)

23 Possible evolution of the zigzag band: *a* linked lozenges on a polychrome silk, Lo-lang; *b* continuous zigzag lozenges on a silk damask, Palmyra; *c* zigzag bands on a pre-Han mirror-back; *d* zigzag bands on a silk damask, Palmyra (not to scale). See plates 95 and 96

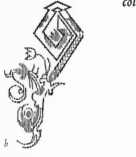

a

b

24 The open zigzag lozenge: *a* on a Han mirror-back; *b* on a polychrome silk, Lou-lan (col. 25)

col. 52

pl. 96
pl. 102

pls 62, 69, 72;
col. 18

pl. 102
pl. 103

fig. 25a

pl. 67

pls 105–109

pl. 109

pl. 107

belonging to the third century BC, part of one of which is shown in figure 24a. The resemblance is not limited to the lozenge: it extends to the curvilinear form with which it is merged, the 'cloud scroll' which we shall discuss presently.

The inlaid silver quatrefoil of the lacquer toilet box has already been mentioned, as also have later imitations in lacquer painting from Lo-lang [p. 134]. It, too, is a favourite Han motif, and goes to show the Chinese origin of the important Palmyra damask of figure 23 b. It is also common on pre-Han mirrors of Karlgren's type C dating from the third century BC, but its pedigree is actually far older. It appears, for instance, on the mirror of plate 102, Karlgren's type A, which is not later than the sixth–fifth centuries BC. It is in fact a stylized flower, and Gyllensvärd has recently illustrated its relationship to the floral coronas found on so many Third Phase *hu*, as well as some *kuei*, and he says that the prototype of them all is the lotus.[22]

Last among Han formal decorative motifs is the so-called 'cloud scroll'. In broadest definition, this is a convoluted and curvilinear ribbon which encloses other more representational elements within its loops, thus binding them into an integrated design. Curves are deep, with strongly-marked changes of direction. Moreover, at various points along the curves, and especially at their apexes and where they change direction, excrescences of one sort or another are almost always to be found. In these lies a clue to the probable origin of all Han cloud scrolls. For the excrescences are vestiges of living tissue, and the cloud scrolls themselves are highly stylized and attenuated remnants of actual animals. In this sense the cloud scroll is not strictly 'formal' at all. We use the word only to stress its prevailingly decorative function in Han times.

The early history of this residual motif may be read in a series of Third Phase bronze mirrors, Ch'ang-sha lacquers, and miscellaneous objects. On the mirror-back of plate 102 we see four symmetrically disposed dragons having birds' heads. The three creatures on the mirror of plate 103 (fourth–third centuries BC) have distinctly birdlike forms resembling ostriches; while of the pair on a flat bronze ring damascened in gold and silver, dating from the same period, each has a head bearing wattles and a long curvilinear crest.

To all these creatures Karlgren gives the name 'bird-dragon'. They are invariably disposed with formal radial symmetry and create a strongly decorative effect. They also contrive to give an impression, by no means always agreeable, of sustaining a robust and highly individual life of their own. It is impossible to be more precise about them. They are creatures born of the high-flying imagination of the Third Phase bronze designer, and we may not examine too closely what natural order they represent. Their ancestors are somewhere to be found among the confronted crested birds and dragons of First Phase art, from which they descend through endless transformations elaborated in the bronze design of subsequent centuries.

From these chimerical yet still recognizably *organic* creatures, we pass to far less coherent figures displayed on the Ch'ang-sha lacquers. There is no general agreement as to the date of these pieces, but second-century BC mirrors found in some of the Ch'ang-sha tombs are perhaps contemporary with many. On the toilet box of plate 109 the 'bird-dragon' appears as a long, straggling, filamentous thread four times repeated, in two shades of vermilion lacquer. Figure 25 b shows one of the blue elements extracted from the décor of a similar box, in the Löw-Beer collection.[23] In both schemas the figures are symmetrically disposed, and consist of filaments that broaden at intervals into curious hooked or swallow-tailed cartouches barely suggestive of parts of birds; in figure 25 b those at the extremities may be meant for heads, while that in the middle suggests a feathered thigh, with lower leg-bone directed forward and terminating in a toed foot represented by a tightly curled spiral. The lid of another box displays three scrolled threads like tendrils radiating from the centre of the design and broaden-

146

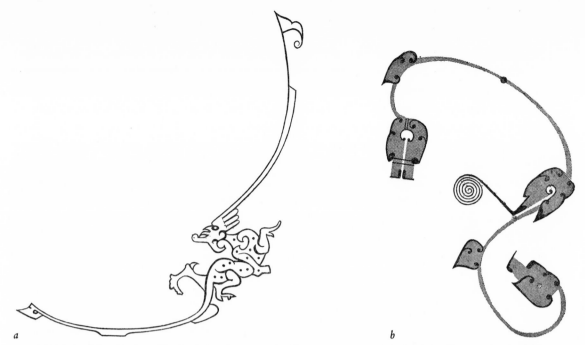

25 Evolution of the cloud-scroll: *a* bird-dragon on an inlaid bronze ring in the Woods Bliss collection; *b* part of the blue element on a lacquer box in the Löw-Beer collection

ing here and there into vague protoplasmic patches. The outermost curve of each element, however, terminates in a fairly naturalistic portrayal of a swiftly running bird, with plump body, slender neck, and narrow head with a short creat rising from the back and beginning to curl forward over the top.

On the lacquer cup of plate 108 the main field is made up of two straggling figures, squared *pl. 108* off into what are roughly H-forms and lying in reversed symmetry about the long axis of the cup. The left-hand uprights of the H-forms, lying along the short axis, terminate in birds' heads in opposition in the centre of the composition. A hooked beak and a prominent eye may be distinguished, and a crest projecting backwards and terminating some way behind in a forward-facing tightly rolled spiral. The other upright blossoms above into a quite indecipherable abstraction, while sitting at one end of the bar of the H is an impressive rectangular cartouche that represents perhaps another bird, perhaps a mask in the general category of *t'ao-t'ieh*.

At this stage the convoluted 'bird-dragon' has lost almost all semblance of reality. The motif has been translated into a new medium, and capriciously converted into a linear system enclosing crude and even slightly comic graphs, reminiscent, as I have said, of the dream images of Expressionist art. We should notice, nevertheless, that the two figures on the cup of plate 108 are still discreet and discontinuous, and are cardinal features of the design. As if *pl. 108* to lead the eye to discover their cryptic theriomorphic content, a perfectly decipherable 'bird-dragon' is placed at either end of the cup. Note its hooked beak, conspicuous eye, and short backwardly directed crest which ends as a tightly rolled spiral.

*

The evolution of the Han cloud-scroll proceeds from such presentments to a version found on bronze mirrors of Karlgren's type F, which belong firmly to the Han period and to the se- *pl. 101* cond century BC. The linear figures are now no longer distinct, but come together to form a continuous band having the appearance of a mountain chain, a landscape peopled with fantastic trees, animals, and humans. Perhaps the mountainous scenery of the Taoist Isles of the

Blest is depicted, and the beings are Taoist Immortals, *hsien jên*, and their weird familiars. Taoist the subject certainly is; but the setting may be China herself. Her Sacred Mountains, and especially Mount T'ai in Shantung, were known to be no less the abodes of Immortals than was the island paradise in the Eastern Sea, as inscriptions on these self-same mirrors testify. One, translated by Karlgren, runs: 'If you ascend the T'ai-shan you will see the divine men ... they yoke the Hornless Dragon to their chariot; they mount the floating clouds ...' Another goes: 'If you ascend the Hua-shan [in Shensi], you will see the immortals [*hsien jên*]'. And a third: 'If you ascend the Hua-shan, the phoenixes will assemble [round you]; you will see the divine men; may you be preserved forever; may your longevity be of ten thousand years.'[24]

The search for longevity, if not immortality, was an obsession of the early Han aristocracy, and was carried on by means of expeditions into the Eastern Sea and to the high places on earth where the *hsien jên* were known to live and where they garnered the life-giving essences [pp. 159–160]. The inscription on a polychrome silk from Noin-ula conveys a wish for long *pl. 100* life rendered by Yetts as: 'May this confer fresh spiritual vitality, so that longevity may be extended over a myriad years.' The silk depicts a winged immortal astride a winged horse at 'flying gallop', while in his hands he holds what is probably a gourd from which issues a cloud of vapour (*yün ch'i*) symbolic of his power to free soul from body. Further to the left is another winged quadruped, which I am tempted to identify as that fabulous animal of good omen, the Heavenly Deer (*t'ien lu*). The meandering scrolls that interweave across this silk thus represent a Taoist mountain paradise, as they do on the F-type mirrors. But the only clue to their parentage lies in the little spiral excrescences – called by Karlgren 'Han curl borders' – that rise in groups of three from the sides of the scroll, and the thickened tops of the mountains, which are all that now remain of the *disjecta membra* of the pre-Han 'bird-dragon'.

fig. 26 An inlaid tube in the Imperial Academy, Tokyo, features a similar Taoist landscape; and here the excrescences are topped with little upright strokes massed together, perhaps a means *pl. 99* of indicating grass. Exactly the same device is used in the mountain landscape of plate 99, a lacquer table top, in which a Heavenly Deer is sporting. The fine Han bas-relief, of which *fig. 29* a rubbing is reproduced as figure 29, depicts winged Immortals riding the backs of winged dragons; but we are now air-borne, and have 'mounted the floating clouds', for the meandering scroll with its abundant spiral excrescences surely suggests a cloud rather than a rock for-*pl. 98* mation. On this, as on the toilet box of plate 98, which also depicts a Taoist paradise, it is at last proper to speak of Han 'cloud scrolls'; and the excrescences, following Löw-Beer, may be called 'cloud-tips'.[25]

pl. 110 Lo-lang lacquer-ware of the first century AD shows the cloud-scroll in a state of partial or complete decomposition. Scrolls disintegrate and disappear, while 'cloud-tips' are progressively elaborated until they form a virtually independent decorative device having the appearance of flames. The beautiful animals so exquisitely posed within the scrolls in their turn now suffer attack; and in the last stage of decay they can be told apart from 'cloud-tips', spirals, and remains of scrolls only by the fact that they are painted yellow, while the shattered scroll and its derivatives are painted red.

Life-forms

Within a short space one cannot possibly hope to present pictures of *all* the beasts and monsters encountered in what Charleston calls the 'Jabberwocky' of Han art.[26] Those we propose to discuss are the ones appearing on lacquers and silks here illustrated. Outstanding among

148

26 Part of a landscape inlaid in gold on a bronze tube of the Han dynasty in the Imperial Academy, Tokyo, showing a 'Parthian shot', the horse in the conventional 'flying gallop', and a naturalistic tiger

them are animals belonging to two groups of four called Ssŭ Shên and Ssŭ Ling, involving five animals of which three appear in the magnificent silk of figure 19.

That human social order corresponds to a universal cosmic order seems to have been a belief innate in the Chinese over most of their history. So the first-century AD cynic Wang Ch'ung says: 'The destiny of the State is connected with the stars. Just as their constellations (*hsiu*) are propitious or unpropitious, the State is happy or unhappy. As the stars revolve and wander, men rise and fall.' [27]

Scarcely a class of observed phenomena failed to find its place in the system of fancied correspondences that grew up in Han times. North, East, South, and West, the Four Quadrants into which the vault of Heaven was divided, surrounded the circumpolar Central Palace of the supreme ruler T'ai-i[28], just as upon Earth the Four Directions of terrestrial space (*t'ien hsia*, 'Under Heaven') surrounded the palace of the emperor. They corresponded also with the Four Seasons – Winter, Spring, Summer, and Autumn respectively; and the Four Cardinal Points corresponded with the seasonal solstices and equinoxes. Presiding over them were the above-mentioned Ssŭ Shên or Four Supernatural Beings, Tortoise, Dragon, Phoenix, and Tiger respectively; and these in turn symbolized the four classes into which animals were divided in Han times – shell-covered, scaly, feathered, and hairy creatures – and were brought into association with the Four Elements, Water, Wood, Fire, and Metal, and the Four Colours, Black, Green, Red, and White.

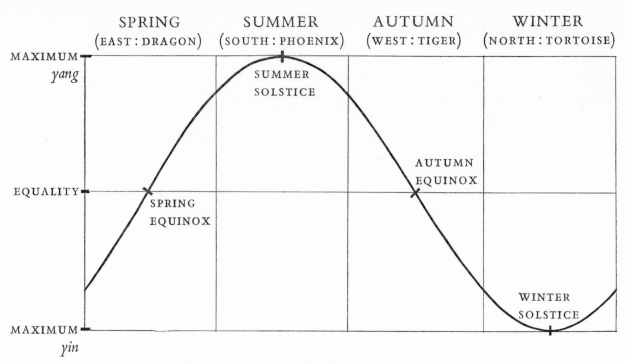

SPRING (EAST : DRAGON)   SUMMER (SOUTH : PHOENIX)   AUTUMN (WEST : TIGER)   WINTER (NORTH : TORTOISE)

MAXIMUM *yang*

EQUALITY

MAXIMUM *yin*

SUMMER SOLSTICE

AUTUMN EQUINOX

SPRING EQUINOX

WINTER SOLSTICE

27   The alternation of *yin* and *yang* throughout the Chinese solar year

If this cosmogony was arbitrary, the causal theory of two antithetical but complementary forces working it is a rudimentary scientific hypothesis analogous to modern theories of wave-motion. Indeed, their interaction can best be explained by means of a graph. Associated with the name of the fourth-century BC scholar Tsou Yen, the dualistic concept of *yin* and *yang* explains all celestial and terrestrial revolutions as alternating phases of ascendancy and declen-sion of these two forces. The essence of *yin* is shade; light is the essence of *yang*. *Yin* also mani-fests itself in other qualities usually put on the minus side, such as moisture, cold, weakness, femaleness, and so forth; while *yang* incorporates their opposites – dryness, warmth, strength, maleness. At the spring equinox (as our graph shows) *yang* and *yin*, day and night, are equal. Thereafter the days lengthen and *yang* begins to wax, reaching its apogee at the summer sol-stice. Then with the shortening days it begins to wane, until the autumn equinox is reached and day and night, *yang* and *yin*, are once more equal and opposite. Now *yin* comes to the fore. It waxes throughout the autumn, until at midwinter's night it has reached its maximum strength – if such a word can be applied to *yin*. It then begins to wane, and on its downward path reaches parity with *yang* at the spring equinox of the following year.

The Ssŭ Shên were inevitably drawn into this solar cycle. 'At the spring equinox', says *Shuo wên*, 'the Dragon ascends to the sky; at the autumn equinox it enters the abyss.' The meaning becomes clear when we learn that the Dragon, *lung*, was a constellation and so was subject to the inexorable counterpoint of *yin* and *yang*. It comprised stars in our Scorpio and Boötes. Its leading horn was our Arcturus (α Boötis). When Arcturus became visible above the eastern horizon at sunset, it was the eve of the spring equinox. As night deepened Arc-turus rose in the sky, bringing in its wake a second horn (α Virginis), a heart (α Scorpionis), and a tail corresponding to the tail of Scorpio; and for twelve hours the Dragon ruled the night sky. Each following night Arcturus rose and set a little earlier, until by the time of the autumn equinox it had reversed its position in the heavens relative to the sun, and was rising

150

as the sun rose, setting as it set. And when it grew dark enough to observe the constellation, they saw that its horn had already plunged below the horizon. The Dragon was entering the abyss.

Meanwhile on the other side of the horizon the Tiger, represented by Orion, was steadily climbing the sky. The antithesis between Dragon and Tiger, and the qualities they represented, was thus in some way connected with the behaviour of the two great antithetical constellations which appear to chase each other endlessly across the heavens, through the nights, seasons, and years. The similarity between the Chinese saurian dragon (*lung*) and the Greek conception of Scorpio as a tailed reptile, as well as between the Tiger, the personification of War in Chinese eyes, and the Greek supreme hunter Orion, may indicate a Hellenistic influence on early Chinese astronomical notions.

Just as Spring marked the beginning of the year (*li ch'un*) and a period of ascendancy of *yang* under the beneficial influence of the Dragon, so daybreak marked a similar beginning, a similar ascendancy of *yang*. In accordance with their notions of cosmic correspondences, the Han Chinese naturally associated the East Quadrant with Spring, since it was in the east that the sun rose at daybreak. The Dragon presided over both.

*

The Ssŭ Shên appear for the first time as a formal category on certain Han mirrors of the well-known TLV type, made in the Loyang region during the period 100 BC to AD 100. Other Han objects that display it include walls of tomb chambers, sides of coffins, sides of memorial pillars (*ch'üeh*), lacquer-ware, bricks and tiles, domestic or ritual vessels, and in all probability silks, and date preponderantly from the first century AD or later. Then may have been the culmination of the cult. The category Ssŭ Ling (Four Efficacious Beings), in which the *ch'i-lin* or Unicorn replaces the Tiger, seems to have been a later development, and is rarely encountered in Han art, as a set at least [p. 156].

With the coming of Buddhism both groups gradually lost ground until about the sixth century, when the Ssŭ Shên had a brief new lease of life. Thenceforward they quickly disintegrated. The Tortoise [p. 155] became separately incorporated in new cults, while individual portrayals of the others seem to have had little more than emblematic meaning from the T'ang period onwards.[29]

Monster as the Han Dragon undoubtedly is, it is a good deal more palpable than its predecessor on the bronzes. That featured as figure 28 is drawn from a rubbing taken from one side of a stone sarcophagus found at Lu-shan, just over the western border of Szechwan, in Si-kang. The coffin is dated AD 212.[30] The exceptionally handsome creature has the top of his head turned towards us, so that it is not easy to make out facial details, which are usually best seen in profile. Notice, however, the scaled and serpentine body, long arched neck, pectoral wings, dorsal crest with three spines, feline legs and clawed feet, and long sinuous tail. Two horns like those of antelope sprout from the forehead. The upper lip is fleshy and the gaping mouth holds what appears to be a ribbon.

The winged Dragon on a lacquered table top from Ch'ang-sha has much the same anatomy in spite of his vaguely *folâtre* appearance. Mouth has a wide gape and fleshy upper and nether lips, snout is large and somewhat upturned, and a massive forehead rises almost vertically and bears two sweeping, backwardly projecting horns. The sprightly pair on the bas-relief of figure 29 much resemble him, especially in the treatment of the mouth with open gape. He on the damask from Lou-lan is a close relative. The legs are markedly feline, and the fore-paw is uplifted in

THE DRAGON

28 Dragon on a Han stone sarcophagus dated AD 212, found at Lu-shan, Sikang

pl. 118

fig. 29

fig. 19

151

a gesture that has been claimed for western Asia, but that is well established in China before Han times.[31] The body is long, the tail long and convoluted. Unpatterned patches on the body represent scales; a single wing appears in profile, and the neck is long and arched. The muzzle shows a prominent upturned snout, gaping jaws, and a beard or barbel depending from the nether lip. Other points are generic.

col. 21, pl. 95   The Dragons on the polychrome silk from Lou-lan and the Palmyra damask show a somewhat different aspect, since they are in three-quarter view. But this type is also well attested in Han art; and once again we note long, serpentine body; convoluted tail; feline legs with padded claws; wing; arched neck; horns; massive forehead; and mouth with wide gape – and equipped with powerful canine teeth.

29 Han dynasty Taoist paradise from a bas-relief, with winged immortals (*hsien jen* or *yü jen*) and winged dragons amid cloud-scrolls, as featured in *Chin shih so*

30 Han dynasty bas-relief showing part of the constellation Ursa Major the form of a chariot in which sits an officer of the Great Bear's court; phoenix or bird-dragon on his left and a feline dragon on his right abo him; from *Chin shih so*

THE PHOENIX   The words used in Han texts and inscriptions on mirrors to name members of the Ssŭ Shên are binomes whose first character indicates the appropriate colour of each animal. *Ch'ing lung* is the Green Dragon; *pai hu*, the White Tiger; *shên wu*, Sombre or Black Warrior, is an unexplained designation for the Tortoise; and *chu niao* (or sometimes *chu chüeh*) is the Red Bird. This last presided over the South Quadrant, corresponding to Summer. Referring to this creature [p. 150] we gave it the name of Phoenix, as is customary; but in fact 'Phoenix' is the conventional translation, not of *chu niao*, but of the classical Chinese term *fêng huang* denoting a mythological bird. Is *chu niao* then the same as *fêng huang*? And may the term 'Phoenix' be aptly applied to either?

Fire, for evident reasons, is made to correspond to Summer in the Chinese cosmogony. There is thus an implied connexion, as well as the obvious one of colour, between Fire and the Red Bird. I do not need to emphasize the intimate relationship that exists in Western mythology between Fire and the Phoenix, which every year cremates itself, and out of whose ashes a new Phoenix springs. The suggestion made by de Saussure that the Western legend is based on some sort of acquaintance with the *fêng huang* of China cannot be summarily dismissed.[32]

To understand the close connexion between the *fêng huang* and Fire, it must first be explained that in China the stars on the celestial equator are divided into 28 Stellar Mansions called *hsiu*, seven of which lie in each of the Four Quadrants. Also that the stars are again divided into twelve groups corresponding to Jupiter's twelve-year cycle; each of the Four Quadrants contains three of these duodenary groups.

Now of the three duodenary groups in the South Quadrant, the abode of the Scarlet Bird, that in the middle is called 'quail's heart', or literally 'quail's fire' (*shun huo*), while the asterisms comprising the eastern group constitute 'quail's head', and the western 'quail's tail'. One Shên Kua, writing in the eleventh century AD, comments: '... the Scarlet Bird of the Astronomers is a symbol based on the quail. Therefore they called the seven "mansions" (*hsiu*) of the Scarlet Bird in the Southern Quadrant by the names "head", "fire" (= "heart") and "tail" of the quail.' Now the fourth-century BC Taoist Ho-kuan Tzŭ tells us: 'The phoenix (*fêng huang*) is the bird of the "quail's heart"; it is the essence of the principle *yang*.'[33] Thus at a single stroke we have the probable equation *fêng huang* = quail = *chu niao* – in an astronomical context at least. The *fêng huang* is the same as the Scarlet Bird, the ruler of the South Quadrant, the essence of *yang*, whose Element is Fire. The name 'Phoenix' may be suitably applied to either creature.

A complete concordance of factors congregated in the South Quadrant would include light, heat, fire, the summer season, and the colour red, all aspects of *yang*. This is obvious to dwellers in northern latitudes, for whom the sun shines hottest and brightest at noon on Midsummer's Day, when it reaches its highest altitude and is due south on the meridian. Summer migrants suddenly arrive from the south, and return south with the coming of Autumn. Such birds are the proverbial portents of Summer, and would be particularly suited as symbols of the South Quadrant. The quail is such a migrant. Its physical attributes could be made to strengthen the symbology by an ingenious rationalization. So Shên Kua, pointing to the fact that one species of quail is red, says that the quail alighting on a tree is as Fire lighting on Wood, Wood being the Element of Spring, Fire of Summer.

It is thus likely enough that the quail was the symbol on which the Scarlet Bird was based, as Shên Kuo said. In giving it cosmic status, however, its designers seem to have improved its anatomy at various points, and the result is a sort of ornithological mosaic of parts taken from various sorts of birds. 'No one knows the species of the Scarlet Bird', Shên Kua observed while on the subject, and even today its identification is hotly disputed. The naturalist Sowerby, for instance, believed that it took its form from that of the domestic rooster, whereas Lo Chen-yü opined that the prototype was the eagle. Sir Aurel Stein described the birds featured on the Lou-lan silk of figure 19 as cranes, whereas Andrews said they were peacocks.

An early version is that seen on the Noin-ula cup of 2 BC, with which those on the cup of AD 4 may be closely compared. The body is shallow and boat-shaped, the neck long and arched. The pointed tail is continued in a long, thin, and soaring tail-plume which appears

31 Phoenix on a Han lacquer bowl dated 2 BC, found at Noin-ula

fig. 19
fig. 31
pl. 110

to curl forward in a tight spiral; and at the back of the head is a crest formed of three parallel curving lines, of which the uppermost is also scrolled forward. From the dorsal surface of the body rises a third scroll, in all probability meant for a wing-plume. The legs are long and slender, one being raised in front of the breast with its lower leg-bone prolonged, as Charleston observes, 'in an impossible curve and terminating in an arrangement of three toes reminiscent of an old-fashioned fruit-fork'.[34] In respect of all these features resemblance to the 'bird-dragons' of the Ch'ang-sha lacquer cup is striking.

pl. 108

pl. 185 The earliest known example of a Chinese painting in ink on silk, recovered in 1949 from a fourth–third-century BC tomb at Ch'ang-sha, features a somewhat similar Phoenix. The animal has a shallow body, erect wing, scrolled wing-plume, and a triangular tail from which arises a long, filamentous tail-plume scrolled forward. On one of the long slender legs a sharp spur can plainly be seen above the heel. This of course suggests one of the Phasianidae, a family of Gallinae which includes Peafowl, Silver Pheasant, Red Jungle-Fowl (from which the domestic rooster descends), Greek Partridge, Red Spur-Fowl, and Quail, every one of which is a southerner in relation to north China, and so might qualify in Chinese eyes as the ruler of the South Quadrant.

pl. 116 Without question, however, the most striking point of the Han Phoenix is its superb tail, which more than any other single feature has made the word *fêng* synonymous with elegance and sexual beauty. Occasionally this is abnormally long, and trails the ground as do those of *pl. 115* some pheasants. On west China bas-reliefs of the early third century AD the tail-plumes, usually three in number, sweep up and over in a graceful curve echoing that of the head-crest. Sometimes they bear a distal knob, and so look rather like bullrushes; on other specimens they show a terminal 'eye', and then the reference to a peacock in his pride seems unmistakable.

Examination of one portrayal after another of the creature Phoenix leaves us with the overwhelming impression of a large gallinaceous bird, exotic to China; a handsome stranger with swaggering crest and nodding plumes, yet with the powerful flight and some of the physical features of cranes, whose brief summer visits were hailed with joy and wonder in the localities where it condescended to alight; and whose appearance, seen but fleetingly, could be represented only in the most flattering and sumptuous bodily array.

In conclusion, we should perhaps say that the binome *fêng huang* reflects the belief that Phoenixes were bisexual birds, needing no mate in order to reproduce, their male parts incorporated in *fêng*, their female in *huang*. Where in Han art we find two Phoenixes confronted, and especially where one carries a crest and the other does not, we may assume that the artist intends them for cock and hen, being unable to visualize the anomaly of a bisexual *pl. 115* form. The pair strutting on the roof-tree in the bas-relief of plate 115 illustrates this convention, the male being on the left. In the case of the silks it would be impossible, because of the utilization of the 'turn-over' in weaving them, to show the signs of sexual differentiation.

TIGER AND TORTOISE The *yin* animals, Tiger and Tortoise, call for no more than brief mention here. As represented *fig. 26* in Han art the Tiger is a realistic-looking animal with long and sinewy body, feline legs and claws, and a long wavy tail. In recognition of his supernatural status he is usually featured with a pair of wings.

His cosmological situation is also plain to see. The West Quadrant came to symbolize Autumn because of cosmic correspondence between day and year, the fall of the year being equivalent to sunset just as Spring corresponded to sunrise. The Tiger symbolized Autumn in much the same way as did the Dragon Spring. *Shuo wên* observes of the Tiger: 'He is the king of mountain animals'; and the contemporary Wang Ch'ung comments as follows: 'Tigers emerge at a certain time just as dragons appear at their appointed season. The *yin* creatures come out in winter, the *yang* reptiles in summer.'[35] In the autumn the tiger comes down from the forests of the western highlands to ravage the plain, and with his coming the constellations of the West Quadrant rise in the night sky.

According to a venerable Chinese convention the Tortoise is female only, and we must therefore call the creature 'she'. The belief arose, Yetts supposes, 'from the anatomical fact that, the genitals of the tortoise being hidden in a sort of cloaca, there is no visible organ to mark the sex'.[36] Thus the idea grew that the Tortoise could be fecundated only by another animal, the Snake. Han and later portrayals of the Ssǔ Shên – and perhaps of the Ssǔ Ling – *fig. 32* show Tortoise and Snake coupled in a sexual embrace; and the same convention is observed *pl. 101* when, from T'ang times onwards, the Tortoise became a deity of latter-day Taoism.

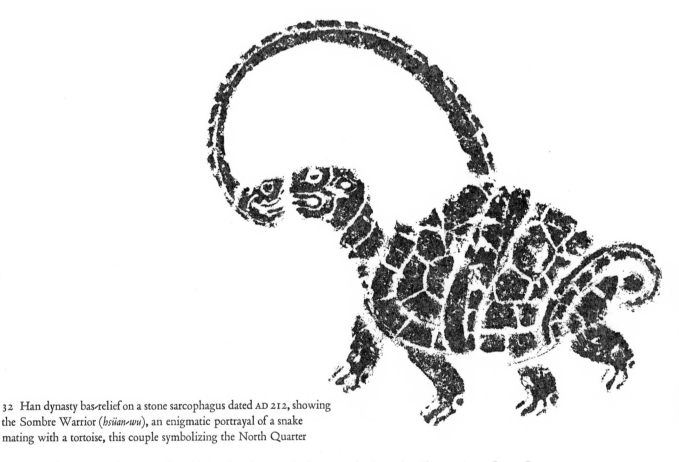

32 Han dynasty bas-relief on a stone sarcophagus dated AD 212, showing the Sombre Warrior (*hsüan-wu*), an enigmatic portrayal of a snake mating with a tortoise, this couple symbolizing the North Quarter

Use of tortoise plastrons for divination by oracle-bone technique in Shang times [p. 73] may explain why supernatural powers were attributed to the Tortoise very early in Chinese history, and account for legends in which she emerges from the waters of the Yellow River bearing magical writings on her back. Her association with the North is self-evident. Dark of hue, cold-blooded, slow-moving, and secretive of habit, frequenting low-lying and watery places, she is the very essence of *yin*. Her withdrawal from public affairs with the coming of winter symbolized the slacker rhythms of human life in that dark season, return of the men from the fields, and the time of women's work inside the tightly-shuttered homesteads of north China; just as did the emergence of the Dragon from his winter sleep, the season of re-birth and release from the dominion of *yin*.

155

33 Unicorn from a Han bas-relief, as featured in *Chin shih so*

fig. 19

The *ch'i lin*, or Unicorn, is one of the Objects of Good Omen (*hsiang jui*), appearance of which was in Han times considered to be an auspicious sign indicating the birth of a virtuous ruler or a period of peaceful rule. The Ssŭ Ling seems to have been a group of this sort, for we read in *K'ung ts'ung tzŭ* that 'when benefits shall be distributed over mankind by a Son of Heaven and universal peace shall obtain through him unicorns [(*ch'i*) *lin*], phoenixes [*fêng (huang)*], tortoises [*kuei*] or dragons [*lung*] are the harbingers of it'.[37] A Unicorn is supposed to have appeared at the time of Confucius's birth.

The Han dictionary *Erh ya* says of the Unicorn that it has the body of an antelope, the tail of an ox, and a single horn; while *Shuo wên* remarks: 'The *ch'i lin* is an animal possessed of human-heartedness (*jên*). It has the body of a horse, the tail of an ox, and a horn [with a tip of] flesh.' A *ch'i lin* featured among the Objects of Good Omen from the Shantung bas-reliefs, rubbings of which were reproduced in *Chin shih so* [p. 55], is very much like a horse indeed, except for its cloven hoofs and the single club-shaped and backward pointing horn. It has a horse's robust neck, barrel chest, and rounded hindquarters. I am inclined to think that the model for this portrayal, and perhaps for other Han representations of *ch'i lin*, was the indige-nous horse of the northern steppes and of ancient China, *Equus prjevalskii*. In particular, the tail bears a switch of long hair rising from its distal end and not from the root – an unusual and characteristic feature of this horse. *Equus prjevalskii* was of course well known to Han artists; a fine sculpture of one is mentioned in the next chapter [p. 173].

Our animal featured on the Lou-lan damask of figure 19, it must be confessed, only vaguely resembles this horse. The forehead, for instance, is of the sort which commentators speak of when they say that the *ch'i lin*'s forehead is that of a wolf; and the tail shows no distal crop of hairs. But in its stocky build, massive neck, barrel chest, rounded hindquarters, and short legs the resemblance is a good deal more apparent. As for the horn, we cannot of course be certain that a single one was intended, since even if there were two, only one would be seen in profile; moreover, post-Han portrayals of the beast frequently show it with two horns. But, as Charleston says, representations of real animals with a single horn are not foreign to pre-Han art. One of these is the rhinoceros, and the suggestion has been made that *ch'i lin* inherit their single horns from this beast. On the other hand an upright mane is a peculiar feature of the steppe horse, one always emphasized in bronze inscription graphs standing for *ma*, 'horse'; I think we must therefore consider a possibility that the single horn of *ch'i lin* is simply a highly stylized rendering of the mane of *Equus prjevalskii*.

DUCK AND CARP

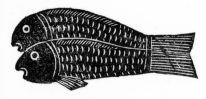

34 Two fish (carp) joined bodily together and labelled *pi mu yü*, 'fish sharing eyes', from a Han bas-relief as featured in *Chin shih so*

Among the Objects of Good Omen depicted in *Chin shih so* are two somewhat enigmatic symbols, *pi i niao*, 'birds sharing wings', and *pi mu yü*, 'fish sharing eyes'. The portrayals show that in each case a pair of animals joined together like Siamese twins is meant – the birds with one pair of wings between them, the fish with one pair of eyes. They also reveal that the birds are a species of duck, the Mandarin Teal, and the fish some sort of carp, the fish *par excellence* of ancient China.

Duck and carp are among the most familiar denizens of the countryside, and of the larders, of north China, and for this reason alone must have recommended themselves as subjects for portrayal by the nature-loving Han designers. But their known habits also fit them as symbols of domestic happiness, and in particular of conjugal fidelity. Both go in pairs. Paired carp symbo-lize sexual union, while the tremendous reproductive powers of this fish help to associate it in po-pular imagination with abundant human progeny. The prodigality of its spawn sets a standard for human prosperity, a symbolism enhanced by the fact that the characters for 'fish' and 'super-abundance' are pronounced as homophones (*yü*). So close is conjugal attachment between male and female Mandarin Teal that this bird is called *yüan yang*, the first character designating the drake, the second the hen. It is popularly supposed that male and female remain faithful to each other for life, and that they pine away and die if forcibly separated. Such ideas fully account for the happy invention of 'birds sharing wings' and 'fish sharing eyes' as Objects of Good Omen in Han folk-lore, and for presence of these creatures, united in flesh and blood, in Han art.

The polychrome silk from Lou-lan bears a repeat design of a single flying duck. Clearly *col. 21* this is not the *pi i niao* motif, but its presence on a silk carrying a good-luck message strongly argues that the symbolism of conjugal felicity was in its designer's mind. Similarly, the gold carp that swim in pairs, one fish above the other, in the quiet waters of the lovely blue-green *pl. 117* silk from Noin-ula are not physically united, yet one can hardly doubt but that the same hope for domestic happiness is here expressed.

A good deal could be written about the Han *t'ao-t'ieh* and its derivation from that found on T'AO-T'IEH the ritual bronzes. But we are nearing the end of a long and somewhat discursive chapter, and a detailed discussion of the motif, coming at this point, would do little to enliven it.

The essential mask confronts us, bilaterally symmetrical around the weft axis, on the border of the damask shown in figure 19. We may sense its emblematic or talismanic purpose, and *fig. 19* see in imagination another identical mask on the opposite side of this now fragmentary silk. The cryptic dragons in profile, forming left and right sides of a completely assembled *t'ao-* *pl. 50* *t'ieh* as seen on First Phase bronzes, have altogether vanished. We are looking at a mask in full face and nothing more.

The individual features that compose this particular presentment may be met in one form or another at all periods of Chinese bronze art back to the First Phase. They include a crest of upright hairs (or feathers) on the forehead; scrolled forms at the side of the head, meant either for horns or ears; a pair of doubly curved plumes (or horns) arising from the cheek; other plumes springing from the upper arm; large eyes; broad nose, terminating above in heavy eyebrows and below in flared nostrils; open jaws, with what may be meant for teeth set in the upper; and fore-limbs with three claws, or possibly four. There is no need to postulate, as some have done, a Western origin for this ensemble.

Yet what does apparently reveal a Western influence, in the mask of figure 19, is the peculiar bowed and akimbo attitude of the fore-limbs or arms. It is as though the creature were holding something across its face. Charleston has drawn attention to the similarity between this detail and that found on a bronze pendentive from north China comprising mask and ring. The mask is in full face, with shoulders hunched, arms akimbo, and hands clutching the ring on either side of the face. Derivation from a Greek Gorgon is strongly suggested, and becomes certain when we take into account the amazing little bronze belt-hook of plate 113, a presentment of Chih Yü, the Han Chinese God of War.[38]

Now a variety of *t'ao-t'ieh* in the form of a ring-handle, wherein the ring is cast separately and passes freely through an 'eye' made by the monster's projecting nose, is a familiar ingredient in Third Phase bronze art. Such ring-handles are attached to the sides of late Chou *pl. 93* ritual vessels, burial furniture, etc.; and applied clay imitations, whose function is decorative only, are commonplaces not to say clichés of Han pottery. But much closer to the version on our silk, and on the pendentive, is a now well-documented group of Han *t'ao-t'ieh* from the west China bas-reliefs. The monster is again shown with arms akimbo, and hands clasping *fig. 35b* a ring which merges with the jaws as it does in the mask of figure 35a. This form of *t'ao-t'ieh* is almost invariably associated with portrayals of auspicious animals on the west China bas-reliefs, and undoubtedly carried some talismanic meaning now lost.

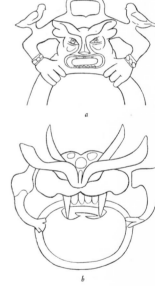

35 *T'ao-t'ieh* masks: *a* in the form of a Han bronze pendentive; *b* from a Han bas-relief

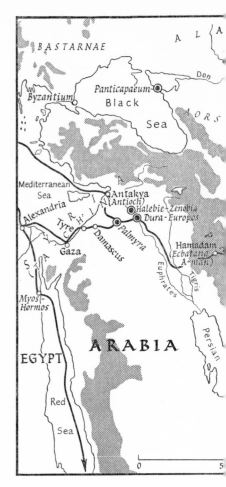

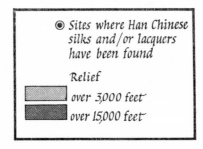

Map 2 The Silk Routes

THE 'PARTHIAN SHOT'   This name is given to a motif wherein a mounted archer, riding a horse at 'flying gallop', shoots backwards at a target in his rear. There has been much discussion as to its origin, which Gallois considers to be ultimately Phoenician, passing thence to Mycenae, to Greece, thence perhaps to Greek colonies on the Black Sea, and thence via Sarmatian and Scythian art to China.[39] It also makes its appearance on Parthian and Bactrian coins and, later, on Sassanian silverware.

pl. 88   I do not know of evidence to show that the 'Parthian shot' entered Chinese art before Han times. The scene repeated four times on the inlaid bronze *chien* of plate 88, in which an archer riding in a chariot shoots backwards at a bear, does not strictly qualify. The earliest known Chinese portrayal of the complete motif may therefore be on the inlaid bronze tube *fig. 26*   in the Imperial Academy, Tokyo, perhaps dating from the beginning of our era, where a mounted archer shoots backwards at a tiger. It also occurs on the Shantung bas-reliefs, dating from the first century AD[40], and on the decorative shoulder bands of a long series of Han *pl. 98*   lead-glazed pottery wine vases.[41] On our cosmetic box of plate 98 the archer shoots forwards at a fabulous beast confronting him.

THE TREE OF LIFE   It was, I believe, Pfister who first suggested that a tree occupying the middle of the motif *pl. 114*   portrayed on a Noin-ula polychrome silk is derived from the ancient Mesopotamian Tree of Life.[42] He notes a broad resemblance between it and another, embroidered on a silk damask

158

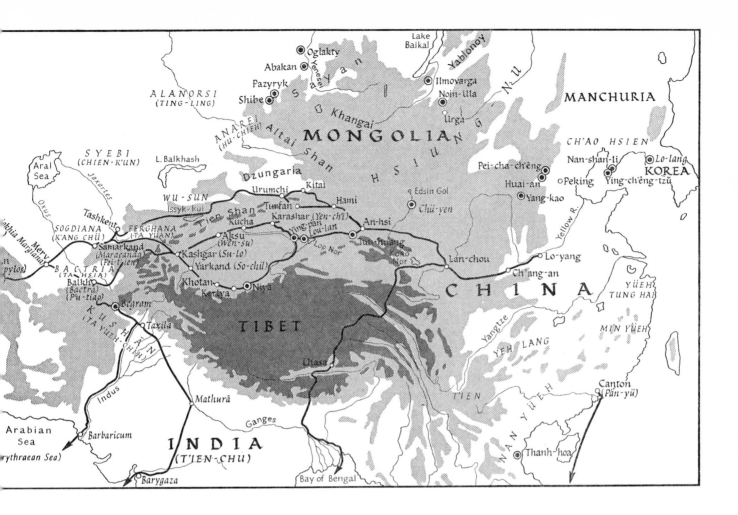

from Palmyra, the branches of which are similarly disposed in three symmetrical pairs and bear slender and upright cone-shaped objects at their tips; from the top of the main stem arises a cluster of three more cones. He compared both versions with a tree featured on the Shantung bas-reliefs, having two symmetrical pairs of branches from each of which hangs a large, shapeless sort of fruit.

The notion of a Tree of Life, growing in a paradise inaccessible to ordinary mortals, and bearing fruit capable of rejuvenating, reanimating, or prolonging life when eaten, is part of the stock of world myth. Sometimes associated with a Well or Fountain of Life-giving Water, and varying in species according to its geographical setting, it crops up in Egyptian, Sumerian, Babylonian, Phoenician, Greek, Islamic, Siberian, Japanese, Polynesian, Norse, and Gaelic folk-lore, and no doubt in that of many other cultures as well.

First mention of the Chinese and Japanese paradise, the Isles of the Blest in the Eastern Sea, may be in the book called *Lieh tzǔ* [p. 144]. Its description is gradually elaborated throughout the Han period. Its immortal inhabitants float weightlessly in the air from island to island. All its animals are pure white. Its terraces and palaces are of gold and jade. Gay-plumaged birds fly through its groves, whose trees are laden with pearls and gems. Its flowers are sweetly perfumed, and they who eat its fruit are assured of youth and long life. Enormous rocks of jade exude a sweet water like wine, conferring longevity; and the *ling chih*, 'fungus of immortality', is cultivated and harvested by the Immortals as ordinary people grow rice. Immortals, beasts, and birds, all feed on this fungus, and the birds sometimes carry it abroad in their beaks. Ssŭ-ma Ch'ien recounts that during the reign of the First Ch'in Emperor [p. 122] birds looking like crows or ravens appeared in China carrying *ling chih*. When they dropped the fungus on the faces of dead soldiers these sprang again to life.

Chinese accounts of the Isles of the Blest do not specifically mention a single Tree of Life and in depicting what I believe to be this tree – and this paradise – on the Noin-ula silk, the designer is making a more or less literal translation of the conventional Western Asiatic presentment. The motif travelled widely. Like the myth behind it, it is known in almost every ancient culture of the Old World, including Assyria and Babylonia, Palestine, Egypt, Mycenae, and India. The Arabs carried it to Spain, Sicily, and western Europe, while under Byzantine auspices it reached Russia and Italy.

All versions have the same heraldic air – a highly stylized, geometrical tree flanked by two figures. At Mohenjo-dāro, these are bulls; at Suza, lions; on Sumerian seals, mountains; on Sassanian silks, ducks or the Holy Ibis; from Assyria, figures with eagles' heads; from Cyprus, goats eating; from Crete, snakes; from a seventh-century AD relief at Venice, stylized trees; from a twelfth-century Sicilian textile, peacocks. And so on. In medieval Europe, the tree becomes the Tree of Knowledge, and the figures Adam and Eve.

pl. 114 Assuming the tree in the middle of our silk to be the Tree of Life, we thus expect to find figures flanking it on either side. They are birds, standing back to back, and apparently pecking at the plants that form the lateral limits of the motif. The birds stand on rocks conventionally treated as a number of more or less rectangular blocks, irregularly superimposed on each other. The plants, as may be confirmed by reference to other examples of Han art in which they appear, are the giant life-giving fungi, *ling-chih*, and the birds the paradisial creatures who feed upon it. We indubitably have, in this rocky landscape, a cameo of the Chinese Isles of the Blest, admirably adapted from the Western Asiatic motif of the Tree of Life.[43]

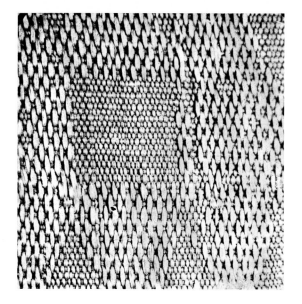

94 Part of a silk damask magnified by about five times actual size to show the warp-float effect discussed on page 138. From Palmyra, Syria. Han dynasty. Damascus Museum.

95 (above right) Part of a beige silk damask woven with a repeat pattern of continuous zigzag bands forming rows of zigzag lozenges; within each lozenge of the lower row, a pair of confronted feline dragons, regardant. Later Han dynasty, from Palmyra, Syria. Size of fragment shown: about $2^{1}/_{4} \times 2$ in. Damascus Museum.

96 Bronze mirror-back (Type C) with parts of four fluted continuous zigzag bands forming rows of lozenges; in each lozenge a central stylized four-petalled flower on a ground strewn with 'comma' pattern and with radiating striated bands. Late Chou dynasty, third century BC, from Shou-hsien, Anhwei. Diameter: $8^{1}/_{2}$ in. British Museum.

THE CLOUD-SCROLL AND TAOIST PARADISE LANDSCAPE

97 Three fragments of plain silk taffeta sewn together, and embroidered in chainstitch with a pattern of cloud-scrolls displaying 'cloud tips' and 'Han curl borders' [see p. 148]. Han dynasty from Noin-ula, Northern Mongolia. Hermitage Museum, Leningrad.

98 Covered toilet box, *lien,* ornamented in shades of yellow and red lacquer on a greenish-red ground, once black, the top and sides of the lid with cartouches inlaid in silver (on this side featuring a 'Parthian shot'). Han dynasty, from Hai-chou, Kiangsu. Height with lid: 4 in. British Museum.

99 Part of a table-top in black lacquer etched through to a white priming, and depicting a Heavenly Deer, *t'ien lu,* in a stylized Taoist landscape [see figure 26]. Han dynasty, first or second century AD, from Yang-kao near Ta-t'ung, Shansi. Kyoto University.

100 Part of a silk polychrome woven with a repeat pattern in greenish-brown outlined with gold on a purple ground, and depicting Taoist Immortals and their familiars flying through a mountain landscape interspersed with Chinese characters. Han dynasty, from Noin-ula, Northern Mongolia [see p. 148]. Size of fragment shown: 3×8 in. Hermitage Museum, Leningrad.

101 Bronze mirror-back (Type F) with relief casting depicting a conventionalized Taoist mountain landscape peopled with five groups of Immortals, four times repeated. Han dynasty, second century BC, perhaps from Shou-hsien, Anhwei. Among the groups are an Immortal riding a feline dragon, or tiger, and another playing a flute in the presence of two listeners. The central knob represents a tortoise in the embrace of a snake [see p. 155]. Diameter: 7 1/4 in. Freer Gallery of Art, Washington.

102 Bronze mirror-back (Type A) with four 'bird-dragons' in low relief encircling a four-petalled flower. Late Chou dynasty, sixth or fifth century BC. Diameter: 4 ¹/₂ in. Stoclet Collection, Brussels.

opposite page

103 Bronze mirror-back (Type D) with three flying 'bird-dragons' encircling the central perforated knob by means of which the mirror is suspended. Late Chou dynasty, third century BC. Diameter: 6 ³/₁₀ in. Museum of Fine Arts, Boston.

105 Inside cover of a three-section toilet box, *lien,* lacquer on wood. The centre medallion is ornamented with three fantastic 'bird-dragons' in blue embellished with 'Han curl borders' and illuminated by terminal 'cloud tips' in red. Late Chou dynasty, from Ch'ang-sha, Hunan. Overall diameter: 11 ³/₄ in. Collection of F. Löw-Beer, New York.

106 (below left) Interior of a wine cup, *yü shang,* decorated with a pair of highly attenuated 'bird-dragons' in red lacquer on a black ground. Late Chou dynasty, third century BC, from the region of Ch'ang-sha, Hunan. Length: 6 ¹¹/₁₆ in. Nelson Gallery of Art, Kansas City.

104 Bronze mirror-back, damascened in gold and silver. A pair of highly conventionalized 'bird-dragons', a single 'bird-dragon', and a horseman in combat with a tiger (all inlaid in silver) alternate with three convoluted geometrical scrolls terminating in stylized animals' limbs (all inlaid in gold). Late Chou dynasty, fourth or third century BC, from Chin-ts'un, Honan. Diameter: 6 ⁷/₈ in. Hoso-kawa Collection, Tokyo.

107 (below right) Lid of a toilet box, *lien,* ornamented with three fantastic 'bird-dragons' in two shades of red lacquer on a black ground. Late Chou dynasty, third century BC, from the region of Ch'ang-sha, Hunan. For a discussion see pages 146 to 147. Diameter: 8 ¹/₄ in. Nelson Gallery of Art, Kansas City.

108 Interior of a large wine cup, *yü shang,* decorated with conventionalized and quasi-naturalistic 'bird-dragons' in two shades
of red lacquer on a black lacquer ground. Late Chou dynasty,
third century BC, from the region of Ch'ang-sha, Hunan. For a
discussion of this piece see page 147. Length: 9 3/4 in. Nelson
Gallery of Art, Kansas City.

109 (right) Lid of a toilet box, *lien,* ornamented with fragmentary 'bird-dragons' in two shades of vermilion lacquer on a deep chocolate ground. Late Chou dynasty, third century BC, from the region of Ch'ang-sha, Hunan. Part shown: $7 \times 4^{2}/_{3}$ in., total diameter: $10^{1}/_{4}$ in. Collection of Dr Paul Singer, New Jersey.

110 (below) Exterior of a large wine cup, *yü shang,* in vermilion and brownish-red lacquer on a black ground. Han dynasty, dated AD 4, from Lo-lang, Korea. For a translation of the band of characters inscribed just above the footrim see page 135. Length: 10 in. British Museum.

**THE SSŬ SHEN
(ANIMALS OF THE
FOUR QUARTERS)**

111 Bronze mirror-back, of TLV type; a central perforated knob on a quatrefoil ground, outside which is a rectangular field containing 12 studs alternating with the graphs for the Twelve Earthly Branches (that for North at the top). In the main field between 8 more studs and the TLV figures are animals in linear relief, including those of the Four Quarters [see pp. 150–151]. The following may be detected: Sombre Warrior (between NW and N); *ch'i-lin* (N–NE); dragon (NE–E); a pair of phoenixes (SE–SW); a pair of tigers (SW–NW). Han dynasty, from the region of Lo-yang, Honan. Diameter: 7 1/8 in. Collection of the late Mrs B. Z. Seligman, London.

112 Carved lacquer plaque, perhaps decoration for a sword pommel, with quasi·human mask over a highly stylized *t'ao·t'ieh* composed of C·shaped bands terminating in commas and ornamented with oblique parallel striations and herring·bone pattern. Late Chou dynasty, fourth century BC or earlier. The closest stylistic affinities of this piece are with Third Phase bronze mirrors of Karlgren's category B. These are dated to the fifth to sixth centuries BC, but the plaque is possibly not so old. Diameter 1 5/8 in. Collection of F. Löw·Beer, New York.

113 Belt hook, *tai kou*, in the form of Ch'ih Yu, the Han God of War; bronze, formerly gilt and inlaid with turquoise. Later Han dynasty. Length: 6 1/2 in. Freer Gallery of Art, Washington.

PHOENIXES AND TREE OF LIFE

opposite pag

114 Part of a silk polychrome woven with a repeat pattern showing the Tree of Life in a Taoist landscape, the selvedge at the top. Han dynasty, from Noin-ula, Northern Mongolia. For an explanation of this motif see page 160. Remaining width: 15 in. Hermitage Museum, Leningrad.

115 Detail of a limestone slab carved in low relief and depicting the mythical visit of the Chou King Mu to the Queen Mother of the West, Hsi Wang Mu. On the roof-tree are two strutting phoenixes, cock to the left, hen to the right, and between them a magician controlling their movements. Later Han dynasty, *c.* AD 114, from a funerary chapel said to have stood in Ching-ping-hsien, Shantung. Height: 31 1/4 in. Metropolitan Museum, New York.

116 Part of a silk polychrome woven with a repeat pattern in red and sand colour on a blackish-brown ground, showing simple and zigzag lozenges in various combinations, with paired phoenixes in feet-to-feet opposition, the selvedge to the right. Han dynasty, from Noin-ula, Northern Mongolia. The pattern-un is repeated on the warp axis about every 6 in. There are 114 threads per centimetre in the warp, 26 in the weft. Width of fragment shown: *c.* 12 in. Hermitage Museum, Leningrad.

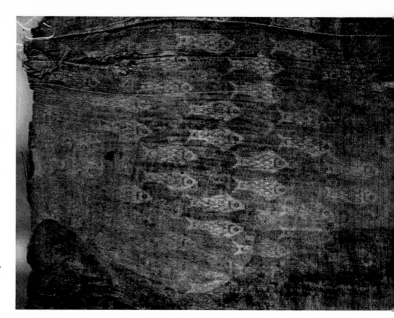

117 Part of a silk polychrome woven with a repeat pattern of paired fishes in gold on a blue-green ground [see p. 157]. Han dynasty, from Noin-ula, Northern Mongolia. Size of fragment shown: *c.* 2 1/2 × 3 1/2 in. Hermitage Museum, Leningrad.

118 Part of a table-top painted in red and black lacquers and featuring a long-tailed dragon. Han dynasty, first century AD, from Lo-lang, Korea. Length of entire table: *c.* 26 3/4 in. Length of this motif: *c.* 5.9 in. Fogg Museum of Art, Cambridge, Mass.

V SCULPTURE: SIX DYNASTIES AND EARLY T'ANG

Pre-Buddhist sculpture in China

Until the coming of Buddhism at the beginning of our era China had no consistent tradition of figure-sculpture and, as far as we know, little enough of any other. Two fairly recent discoveries make us modify the old view that sculpture was unknown before Han times. First are some marbles excavated at An-yang in 1934–5. They are impressive pieces, superbly executed and immaculately finished, measuring up to a yard or so in their greater dimensions. But the tradition to which they belong is that of bronze art. Favoured subjects are quasi-natural beasts and birds that remind us of animal *tsun*, while surface-treatment echoes conventions of First Phase bronze décor. The art seems to have disappeared after Shang times.

A second discovery worth reporting is that of wooden sculptures, some of which show signs of having been lacquered, in the Ch'ang-sha tombs [p. 126]. Men and women are portrayed, their features summarily rendered with bold linear cuts; others, better described as anthropomorphic, are grotesquely adorned with real deer's horns and long, protruding tongues. It is likely that these latter are effigies of shamans, *wu*, whose amiable job it was to escort the dead in their spirit-journeyings, while the former were simply *ming ch'i* – burial furniture of a type similar to the pottery figures of attendants accompanying the dead man, so common in Han tombs. Recent discovery of figures somewhat similar to the shaman effigies at Hsin-yang in southern Honan suggests that the associated cult was not entirely foreign to metropolitan China in the fourth–third centuries BC, but its relations to the magical Taoism of Han times, and of its monstrous carvings to the iconography of Han funerary sculpture, remain undisclosed[1] [p. 144].

Sculptures of Han times – I omit here the above-mentioned ceramic statuary – fall into two groups, bas-reliefs and figures carved in the round. The former served to illustrate scenes from Taoist mythology and passages of Chinese history, real or imagined, and lined the death-chambers of Han nobility. Since personages depicted on these slabs are placed in a contemporary setting, they help to shed light on the details of Han daily life. They are, of course, simply translations into stone of a pictorial art in some less enduring medium, and their connexion with Buddhist figure-sculpture is slight; although certain decorative elements of this purely native Chinese glyptic art do reappear among accessory motifs of Buddhist votive steles. *pl. 129*

We also have a very few examples of figures carved in the round from Han times. Best known is the portrayal of a horse of steppe type trampling down a nomad, which stands at the burial mound of the Han cavalry general Ho Ch'ü-ping in the valley of the Wei river in Shensi. Unkind words have been said about this group. To my mind, judging only from photographs, it is a most effective piece of secular monumental sculpture, having the odd vitality one associates with the Former Han period, to which it undoubtedly belongs. Other Han animal sculptures are known both at this site and elsewhere; but again, little stylistic or iconographic connexion with Buddhist art is apparent.

173

General characteristics of Buddhist sculpture in China

Chinese Buddhist sculpture can hardly be called an exemplary art. It does, admittedly, display an austereness and sincerity befitting its iconic function, especially conspicuous during the early period with which we propose to deal. And this, tempered by what Dr Cohn calls 'a visionary sweetness' of the features, lends it peculiar charm to Western eyes. But the symbolic content is confined almost entirely to the mask. Herein lies a real difference between Chinese and other great sculptural traditions. In both Greek and Indian sculpture the body, no less than the mask, helped to express certain mental and psychic qualities or conditions. For the Greeks, beautiful or noble physical form was the counterpart of ideal character, intellect, and personality, such as they ascribed to their gods. The distinctive individuality of each was matched to a corresponding portrait type. A naturalistic treatment was employed to illustrate these differences. The gown, for instance, gives the impression of an actual garment clothing a living wearer. It is a mode of expression one might call idealized realism.

Cult-images of early Indian Buddhism present a somewhat different case. The body is expressive, but not of an ideal ethical or intellectual type. Instead, it symbolizes the highly concentrated mystical state called *dhyāna*, in which mind and body are simultaneously implicated. The word is usually translated as 'meditation', but the practice by which *dhyāna* is attained involves putting the body into postures it would not normally assume, and the outcome is not a state of mind only. 'Every stage of it', says Chanda, 'also permeates the whole body.'[2] We find several representations of a male god in *dhyāna* on seals of the Indus civilization (*c.* 2500–1700 BC), and such images are habitual to early Buddhist and Jain sculpture. The rigidity of the pose places limitations on the sculptor, forcing him away from a naturalistic treatment, while use of conventional signs such as the *uṣṇīṣa*, or top-knot, carries him a stage further away from pure realism. With such a cult-image, in which the internal relations between various parts of the body assist at a technical demonstration, nothing must be allowed to come between the worshipper and its essential nudity. Clothing is a hindrance; and Indian sculptors either discard it altogether, or mould it closely to the body as a sort of second skin.

In Chinese Buddhist sculpture, on the other hand, the body usually plays a subordinate role. It expresses neither natural posture nor the rigidity, the muscular tension, of trance. Its organic relation with the head is not always easy to accept. Sometimes the head is disproportionately large, and the body suffers a diminution – not of the sort we find, say, in Negro sculpture, which apparently results from a need to gain greater plastic effect than the human body normally offers, but rather due, one feels, to sheer failure to grasp its plastic and symbolic possibilities. Summary treatment of the body is often linked with an unconvincing rendering of drapery. It neither follows the natural rhythms of movement, nor does it reveal the underlying form. The gown is still recognizably a garment, but its folds are rendered schematically and there is a tendency for parts of it to develop into independent decorative motifs. This is especially evident in the treatment of its lower hem during the first part of the period we are to discuss.[3]

pl. 126

A second limitation of Chinese Buddhist sculpture – one that we find in that of Greece and Europe, and to a lesser extent India, but from which Negro sculpture is entirely free – is that its frontal aspect dominates all others; or, as Fry says when speaking of the European tradition, 'it approaches plasticity from the point of view of bas-relief'.[4] Indeed, this is a more constant feature of Chinese sculpture than of any of the other traditions I have named. Images in cave-shrines are obvious examples of objects meant to be looked at from the front only. The same is true of those adorning the niches of votive steles; while the stele itself is not conceived of *en ronde bosse*, but is simply a two- or four-sided bas-relief. Free-standing images are comparatively rare, but even in these plastic feeling is not always strong. Few examples stand the test of being viewed from the sides, let alone the back, and if the reader will turn to plates *pls 142–144* 142–144 he will be able to see to what extent visual interest is concentrated in the frontal view.

Because of this reluctance to render form in three dimensions, we seldom find convincing accounts of complicated bodily movement or posture such as Indian sculptors delighted to attempt. Towards the end of its evolution, Chinese Buddhist sculpture did partly free itself from this inhibition, and in T'ang and later times much looser and more subtle postures may *pl. 139* be met with. The sculptures have depth, and interest is not confined to the frontal plane alone. Yet even now the plastic formula is incomplete. The back is no more than a flat slab.

One is forced to conclude that the special qualities inherent in sculpture as an art-form are but poorly represented in that of China. The Chinese themselves appear never to have rated their sculpture very highly. Few names of individual sculptors have been preserved, and next to nothing of their work; most of the others were what we would call monumental masons, and the sensibility they express is not personal, but is a common quality of race and age. We are dealing with a 'primitive' art.

*

So much having been said by way of criticism, the reader may be wondering why he should concern himself with Chinese Buddhist sculpture at all. The answer is, of course, that universal criteria of the sort we have mentioned do not in the least control our private capacity to enjoy a given piece of sculpture. There is no such thing as a canon of aesthetics valid for all sculptural traditions, or even for traditions standing in close historical relation, like those of India and China, and whose basic motivations might appear to be the same. Chinese Buddhist sculpture was the property of a great religious faith. Its formal appearance was meant to generate or express the religious emotions peculiar to early Chinese Buddhism, emotions to which we have no direct personal access. Seen in this light, negative descriptive generalizations concerning it no longer mean anything. For example, the Chinese sculptor's apparently negative attitude towards the plastic and sensuous qualities of the symbolic human form may have been the outcome of his positive preoccupation with the treatment of its drapery. Commenting on this, Sullivan remarks: 'The body seems about to disappear altogether under a cascade of drapery that no longer defines the figure beneath but ... in its expression of a state of spiritual ecstasy seems to deny the body's very existence.'[5] Such analyses, whether right or wrong, knock us off our academic perches, unsettle our preconceptions, and may help us to gain new and unexpected insights into an unfamiliar field of experience.

As is the case with Indian sculpture, a large proportion of the prodigious output of Chinese Buddhist statuary is commonplace, is void of life, serves its religious purpose and says no more. Yet in this stony waste we from time to time encounter pieces so freely and wilfully conceived, and so brilliantly executed, that they altogether transcend our critical formulas and rank as works of high art. It is on their account that we value the tradition of Chinese Buddhist sculpture. And on account, too, of countless thousands of lesser pieces – the sculptures of the cave-shrines, the gilt-bronze statuettes, and so forth – which do not pretend to be high art, but which have an unaffected charm and vigour and a happy air about them. This was a popular, journeyman art. Considerations of time and cost are often betrayed in the summary workmanship of these small votive pieces, and the repetitive nature of the work tends, as I have said, to obliterate personal sensibility. Yet it retains distinction and even majesty, owing no doubt to its simple and direct mode of expression, unmarred by overtones of sentimentality or the falsely dramatic.

175

The period under discussion

Buddhist sculpture began to be made soon after the beginning of our era in China. It has gone on being made ever since. Buddhism came to China from India, and the evolution of Chinese Buddhist sculpture has from time to time been affected by contact with Indian models. We can trace three main impulses of this sort, corresponding to the three chief stylistic phases into which Dr Sirén classifies Chinese Buddhist sculpture:

1. The Archaic Period. From about AD 400 to 550.
2. The Transitional Period. From about AD 550 to 618.
3. The Period of Maturity. From the beginning of the T'ang dynasty in AD 618 until about AD 700.

Exception might be taken to the use of words such as 'archaic' and 'mature' to distinguish between styles, and I prefer the less equivocal classification into numbered phases employed by Professor Yetts. Apart from the fact that descriptive labels are avoided, this system is much the same as Sirén's except that Yetts brings his Third Phase to an end in AD 844, the year of the third great persecution of Buddhism. A fourth phase contains sculpture made between that time and the present day. It is one marked by steady loss of artistic integrity, and we omit it altogether here.

Against this stylistic background we propose to fit our account of Chinese Buddhist sculpture from the fourth century AD and to the beginning of the eighth. It includes the whole of the First Phase, covering the rule of the Northern Wei (AD 385–535), Eastern Wei (AD 534–50), and Western Wei (AD 535–57) in north China; the whole of the Second Phase, including the Northern Ch'i (AD 550–77), Northern Chou (AD 557–80), and Sui (AD 580–618) in north China; and the first eighty or so years of the Third Phase and of the T'ang dynasty (AD 618–906). We shall bring it to an end in AD 700, or thereabouts, mainly because of restrictions involved in our method of treatment as discussed in the Introduction [p. 14], but also because by the end of the seventh century AD the main stylistic and iconographic conventions had already been formulated. I think it would be generally agreed that the greatest masterpieces, and probably the bulk, of Chinese Buddhist sculpture in stone had already been produced before that date. Sirén, for example, speaks of new styles and techniques which ushered in the period of 'maturity' and 'which became manifest during the second quarter of the seventh century (reaching their full development about the middle of the century)'.[6]

Again, return of pilgrims armed with texts and images from India has always been the signal for outbreaks of devotional zeal in China. In AD 645 the pilgrim Hsüan-tsang arrived back in China after having spent sixteen years travelling in India and the Buddhist kingdoms of Central Asia. Hsüan-tsang, the story goes, brought home seven statues of Buddha to serve as models for Chinese sculptors. An immediate, though short-lived, spate of image-making now occurred in China, as inscriptions at the Lung-mên cave-shrines clearly attest. These shrines are only a few miles away from Lo-yang in Honan, a sort of secondary capital during most of the T'ang period, and their contents may therefore be taken as reflecting the state of Buddhist sculpture, and of the religion, while the caves were being cut. Of a total of III dated dedicatory inscriptions for the entire T'ang period, no fewer than fifty-three cover the fifteen years immediately following Hsüan-tsang's return. The middle of the seventh century AD was evidently a climax in the history of Chinese Buddhist sculpture.

Sculpture was not, of course, the only art-form flourishing during the period now under review. But little else of its material culture, except pottery, is known to have survived. From meagre evidence we can tell that both painting and architecture were passing through active

pls 146, 149–151

176

phases of development. Yet so abundant are sculptural remains in stone, so vigorous is the artistic tradition they manifest and – as inscriptions testify – so closely are they linked with the religious aspirations of people of all classes, that we are probably not mistaken in regarding Buddhist sculpture as the outstanding art-form of the early medieval period in China.

This chapter is concerned with two main topics: the subjects and styles of the sculptures. But if these are to be made intelligible, we must first touch on a number of cognate themes. They are, firstly, political conditions in China from the end of the Han period to the middle of the seventh century; secondly, the beginnings of Buddhism and of Buddhist sculpture in China; thirdly, the early history of Buddhist sculpture in India and countries between it and China; and lastly, the development of Buddhist doctrine and its influence on the choice of motifs for portrayal.

Political history of China from AD 220 to 700

For a detailed account of this period may I refer readers to chapters 7 and 8 of Eberhard's *A History of China*. Here we shall review only its main features. Until AD 580 the political pattern is, to say the least, confused. One petty dynasty follows another in quick and dismal succession, dates overlap maddeningly, and the pattern of states, kingdoms, and empires on the map is kaleidoscopic. Apart from struggles between native dynasts, serious inroads were made by nomads from the north. In fact, no fewer than four foreign powers controlled north China during this time. But from AD 580 to the end of the period, China enjoyed national unity of a sort, and peace, after a fashion.

Out of the confusion one salient fact emerges. The south now becomes an area of colonial development, and soon acquires political and cultural independence. Already during the last hundred years of Han rule more and more people had been moving south of the Yangtze to escape the unrest round the Throne, where rival cliques headed on the one hand by Court eunuchs and on the other by Confucianist ministers contended for the right to control the succession. Real power lay in the hands of provincial generals, who alone were capable of putting down intermittent peasant revolts, such as that of the Yellow Turbans which began in AD 184. By about AD 150 the country was already divided into three blocks, each controlled by military factions. War-lords got into the habit of reinforcing their armies with foreign man-power, and the most powerful general in the north, Ts'ao Ts'ao, had actually settled a number of Hun tribes in Shansi between AD 180 and 200 in return for armed help. It was the thin end of the wedge. From this time forward northern Shansi became a base, although not the only one, for nomad aggression in north China.

Between AD 220 and 265 China was split into three kingdoms. While Wei in the north and Shu in the west fought each other to a standstill, the southern state of Wu enjoyed comparative tranquillity and became a haven for refugees from the north. Indian Buddhist missionaries freely entered the great port of Nan-hai on the site of modern Canton, and the religion made important gains in Wu throughout the century.

In the north, Wei was followed in AD 265 by Western Chin, a dynasty founded by one of the Ssŭ-ma's, a collateral branch of the family of the Han historian Ssŭ-ma Ch'ien. It proved to be short-lived. The Huns moved south from their base at Tai, the modern Ta-t'ung in northern Shansi just south of the Wall, captured Lo-yang (AD 311) and Ch'ang-an (312) in quick succession, and founded their dynasty, the Former Chao, in AD 316. A second Hun dynasty, the Later Chao, succeeded it in 329.

CHINA DISMEMBERED
(AD 220–385)

177

map 3

North China was now beset on all sides by various mutually hostile confederations of nomads disposed in four main groups – Tibetans in the north-west, Hsien-pi in the north-east, Huns in the centre and, treading hard on their heels in the north, the Tabghach Turks whom the Chinese called T'o-pa. Unlike the Hsiung-nu of Former Han times, who had abominated the Chinese way of life, these latter-day Huns passively allowed themselves to become sinicized, and in the process lost their taste for fighting. In AD 352 the Later Chao were overwhelmed simultaneously by a Hsien-pi tribe called Mu-yung in the east and the Tibetans under their great leader Fu Chien in the west; the latter founded the Former Chin dynasty in the same year.

By AD 384 north China was again in terrible turmoil. Out of the ruck there now emerged the T'o-pa, based on the old Hun stronghold at Tai, who had gathered over a hundred Hun and Hsien-pi tribes beneath their banner. The dynasty they founded in AD 385 proved to be far more enduring than any of its predecessors. It was to become the first great patron dynasty of Buddhist sculpture in China.

The ready espousal of Buddhism by untutored nomads is not without significance. 'On this clean slate', says René Grousset, 'Buddhism could write its message without difficulty.'[7] And indeed primary possession of the new and dynamic religion, heterodox and foreign as they were foreign, must have been of tremendous psychological help to the nomads as they strove to reach a cultural parity with the bland and sophisticated Chinese.

THE T'O-PA DYNASTIES: NORTHERN WEI (AD 385–535) EASTERN WEI (AD 534–50) WESTERN WEI (AD 535–57)

From the outset the new dynasty, called Northern Wei, began to adopt Chinese manners and modes. Long contact with Chinese settlers who had sought refuge under their regime in the north had given them a taste for civilized life. Thus, when they became masters of north China, they established at Tai an imperial court modelled strictly on Chinese lines. More and more Chinese officials found employment at this northern capital, which had been renamed P'ing-ch'êng in AD 376. As they extended their conquest eastwards, the Northern Wei found the task of governing far-distant territories and millions of Chinese peasants altogether beyond them. Administration could not be put in the hands of tribal chiefs, whose loyalties were uncertain, and regional government was left, willy-nilly, to local Chinese gentry.

Thus, from quite early on, both central and provincial government were largely in Chinese hands. By the middle of the fifth century, Chinese at Court were beginning to press for removal of the capital to a more central site. Campaigns against the southern Liu Sung dynasty [p. 180] gave the Northern Wei control of north China down to the Yangtze, and in AD 494 they were able to transfer the capital to Lo-yang. The Buddhist cave-temples at nearby Lung-mên were begun soon afterwards.

This policy of sinicization was to be the downfall of the Northern Wei. Outlying T'o-pa tribes went into revolt about AD 530, invested the whole of Shansi, captured the capital, and massacred its inhabitants. By the time the dust had settled, in AD 534, the Chinese had taken themselves off to their eastern stronghold, together with a puppet Emperor whom they installed as the first ruler of the Eastern Wei dynasty (AD 534–50), with his capital at Yeh. The T'o-pa had moved westward with another figure-head, whom they placed on the throne of the Western Wei dynasty (AD 353–557) with its capital at Ch'ang-an in Shensi.

THE NORTHERN CH'I DYNASTY (AD 550–77); THE NORTHERN CHOU DYNASTY (AD 557–80)

Political and racial rivalries in north China now set in the old familiar pattern – the Chinese in the east, upon the Plain; and various foreign remnants, T'o-pa, Hsien-pi, and Huns, with a very few Chinese, on the Plateau in the west. The two puerile dynasties, Eastern and West-

ern Wei, were followed by the no less impotent Northern Ch'i and Northern Chou, respectively, in the same regions.

There is little to be said in favour of the Northern Ch'i dynasty, whose rulers, remarks *pls 130–132*
Eberhard, 'were thoroughly repulsive figures, with no positive achievements of any sort to their
credit'. And yet some of the loveliest of all Buddhist sculpture was produced under its patronage. Perhaps this was because it was the true inheritor of the cultural traditions of the
Northern Wei, grown up under Chinese guidance, and because nearly all the old centres of
north Chinese Buddhism lay within its territory.[8] For whatever reason, Northern Ch'i sculpture has an air of refinement and sophistication that contrasts sharply with the rather primitive
work done under the Northern Chou, as far as we can tell from the few surviving pieces *pls 133, 134*
assignable to that dynasty.[9]

For about four years after the downfall of the Northern Ch'i in AD 577, the Northern Chou
controlled all north China. Then a new Chinese ruling family, the Yang, came into prominence through marriage alliances with influential Northern Chou leaders. For, as Eberhard
clearly shows, the Northern Chou had been deteriorating in much the same fashion as had
the Northern Wei, except that in its case sinicization was involuntary. Cut off from their
life-giving nomadic roots by more than two hundred years of settled livelihood, the T'o-pa
and their like had no choice but to lose their identity among the ever-present Chinese. In
AD 581 a scion of the Yang family called Yang Chien managed to make himself Emperor of
a new dynasty, the Sui, after killing off members of the Northern Chou imperial house. With
the Sui, China was once more united under Chinese rule.

Kansu lies directly across the main route to Central Asia and India. Control of the Kansu THE KANSU STATES
map 3
Corridor was therefore always a paramount Chinese interest; and in the period under discussion, much energy was spent by both northern and southern dynasties in endeavouring to
secure this. Buddhist enterprise was now flourishing everywhere from Kansu to the Pamirs;
and the tiny and more or less autonomous oasis kingdoms that spanned the route all gained
great economic benefits in consequence. In Kansu, a rather anomalous Chinese kingdom,
the Former Liang, had somehow managed to survive while Huns, Tibetans, Hsien-pi, and
T'o-pa in turn were crowding into north China. Between AD 313 and 376 this little realm
had grown in strength. Like the south-eastern kingdom of Wu a hundred years earlier, it became a place of refuge for many native Chinese, attracted by its good and peaceful administration. Within its borders the first great Buddhist architectural enterprise in China Proper, the
cave-temples at Tun-huang, was begun in AD 366.

In AD 439 the Northern Wei gained control of the whole corridor as far west as Tun-huang,
where a Hun dynasty, the Later Liang, had been in possession since AD 397. The Wei drove
them from the district, and evacuated 39,000 Tun-huang families to their capital at P'ing-
ch'êng. This event is of some importance because sculptors were among the persons moved.
Work on the second great group of Chinese cave-temples, at Yün-kang not far from the
Wei capital, had begun as early as AD 414; but not until the middle of the century was any
real progress made, no doubt with the help of craftsmen from Tun-huang. *pl. 120*

From AD 439 to the end of our period the political history of Kansu is of no particular
interest, since it always lay within the jurisdiction of the dynasty controlling the Plateau; that
is to say, of the Northern Wei, Western Wei, Northern Chou, Sui, and T'ang.

There were five southern dynasties: Eastern Chin (AD 317–419); Liu Sung (AD 420–78); THE SOUTH
Southern Ch'i (AD 479–501); Liang (AD 502–56); and Ch'ên (AD 557–88). They were

remarkably undistinguished. 'Nothing happened at court', says Eberhard, speaking of that of the Liu Sung, 'but drinking, licentiousness, and continual murders.' Succeeding rulers seem to have behaved no better; although the fact that average expectation of rule was less than eight years could have afforded them little encouragement to reform themselves. Only one is at all well known outside China, namely Emperor Wu, first ruler of the Liang dynasty (reigned AD 502–50). He became an enthusiastic Buddhist, and retired to a monastery some years after reaching the throne, no doubt in the hope of atoning for misdemeanours committed in getting there. It was he who officially welcomed to China the Indian Bodhidharma, reputed founder of the Ch'an Buddhist sect in that country. He was eventually given the complimentary rank of Bodhisattva [p. 190], in which guise he is occasionally portrayed in later Buddhist sculpture.[10]

THE SUI DYNASTY (AD 589–618)
THE T'ANG DYNASTY (AD 618–906)

The military, political, and social history of the long and culturally renowned T'ang dynasty is dealt with in a general way in chapter six. Here we are concerned only with the Sui and the first four reigns of the T'ang, a period of about a hundred years during which Buddhism prospered as never before or since.

Yang Chien [p. 179] had declared himself Emperor in AD 581, but the Sui dynasty did not officially begin until eight years later, by which time the last southern dynasty, the Ch'ên, had been disposed of and all China brought under one rule. It was a period of national reconstruction on a grand scale. Ch'ang-an, capital during the reign of Yang Chien (Emperor Wên, reigned AD 589–605), and Lo-yang, capital during the reign of his son (Emperor Yang, reigned AD 605–18), were extensively laid out and rebuilt. New fortifications were put up along the line of the Great Wall; and vast canal works were completed by which Ch'ang-an, Lo-yang, and the lower Yangtze region were linked by water. All this led to social unrest, and hastened the fall of the dynasty, but helped to put its successor on a solid footing. For the greatness of the T'ang dynasty rested largely on administrative reforms and public works which had been begun during this short transitional period, much as did that of the Han upon Ch'in statecraft.

The Sui emperors were great patrons of Buddhism. Emperor Wên, in particular, seems to have had a positive hankering for the elegance and grandeur with which Buddhism and its works could ennoble daily life. He introduced laws protecting Buddhist property. And we are told that he ordered the construction of nearly 4,000 temples; old images to the number of a million and a half were to be repaired, and over 100,000 new ones made of materials such as gold, ivory, bronze, sandalwood, lacquer, and stone.[11] This imperial patronage is reflected by the large number of known sculptures bearing Sui dynasty dates, and by a perceptible development in their style and execution.

pls 135–137

In AD 615 north China was invaded by new tribal oppressors, the T'u-chüeh, better known to us as Turks. This was the beginning of the end of the Sui dynasty. One of the ablest of the Chinese commanders, Li Shih-min, founded the T'ang dynasty three years later, placing his father Li Yüan upon the throne. The first T'ang emperor was hostile to Buddhism, and in fact not a single known piece of Buddhist sculpture can be dated to his nine years' reign. But with the accession of Li Shih-min as Emperor T'ai-tsung (AD 627–50), the pendulum swung again in favour of Buddhism. It was the period of Hsüan-tsang's travels, and of a great spate of image making at Lung-mên. On his return, Hsüan-tsang installed himself at Ch'ang-an and set to work translating Indian Buddhist scriptures. Others joined him, and for the next hundred years or so Ch'ang-an became a great centre of Buddhist scholarship, visited by pilgrims from Japan, Korea, and other countries of Far Eastern

Buddhism. Texts were translated into Chinese, and thence into Uighur Turk, Tibetan, Korean, and Japanese.

Patronage of Buddhism was continued by the third T'ang ruler, Kao-tsung (AD 650–83), and by his successor, Empress Wu (AD 684–705). This extraordinary person, daughter of a provincial governor, had been a concubine of Emperor T'ai-tsung at the age of fourteen. Following brief retirement to a Buddhist monastery upon his death, she became in turn Kao-tsung's concubine and Empress, after murdering her own daughter by the Emperor and causing the rightful Empress's hands and feet to be cut off. When Kao-tsung died in AD 683 – probably poisoned by his consort – she manœuvred one of her sons on to the throne and thenceforth ran the country as she chose. In AD 689 she openly proclaimed herself 'Emperor', changed the name of the dynasty to Chou, drastically altered the calendar, and introduced a dozen or so new characters into the written language. In the meantime she carried on an intrigue with a disreputable Buddhist monk for whom she built a temple, and whom she eventually had murdered.

The Empress strongly favoured Buddhism. In AD 672, for example, we find her giving 20,000 strings of cash towards making a colossal image of Amitābha Buddha at Lung-mên. *pls 149–150* Vast sums were now spent in endowing Buddhist temples, and more images were made than at any other time during the T'ang period. They were not always approved of. The famous Buddhist priest Tao-hsüan complained that the sculptors made them indistinguishable from dancing-girls 'so that every court wanton imagined that she looked like a Bodhisattva'.[12] Empress Wu, who seemed to be aiming at becoming religious as well as secular head of the empire, certainly believed that she herself was one. By dexterous interpolations in one of the scriptures she managed to pose as a reincarnation of the Bodhisattva and Future Buddha Maitreya [p. 191].[13] And it is interesting, although almost certainly coincidence, that about this time the forms of Bodhisattvas in sculpture, hitherto represented as male, begin to wear *pl. 145* a decidedly feminine air. There was a strong element of truth in Tao-hsüan's assertion.

The beginnings of Buddhism and of Buddhist sculpture in China

We have now to go back on our tracks to notice a few early literary references to Buddhism in China, and to the making of Buddhist images in the period before the first known dated examples. These records, when combined with information yielded by yet earlier surviving Indian images, are invaluable in helping us to trace the stages by which style and iconography in Chinese Buddhist sculpture grew away from their roots in native India. They have been ably summarized by Yetts.[14]

The first reliable known reference to Buddhism in Chinese literature is found in a fifth-century AD text called *Wei lüeh*; it records that an ambassador from the Ta Yüeh-chih [p. 123] was giving oral instruction on the tenets of Buddhism to a Chinese official in China in 2 BC. In the light of present knowledge it seems most improbable that any image of Buddha was made in China at this time. Indeed, we have no reason to suppose that such a thing was then to be found anywhere in the Buddhist world, India included. All evidence indicates the first century AD as the earliest possible date for the first Indian Buddha image; and making allowance for time taken to reach China, one could scarcely expect to find it in that country before, say, the beginning of the second century AD.

The oldest reliable reference to actual Buddha images in China relates to the year AD 166, when an anti-Buddhist memorial, the first of many of its kind, was delivered to the Throne by an astrologer named Hsiang Ch'iai. He criticizes its preoccupation with mystical religions, and mentions statues of Taoist personages – the mythical Huang Ti and the quasi-historical Lao Tzŭ – and also of Buddha. Maspero has shown that by the end of the second century AD a Buddhist community was flourishing at Lo-yang. It seems that the first Chinese Buddhist monk, the translator Yen Fou-t'iao, was ordained there in AD 180.

In the Three Kingdoms period (AD 220–65) Lo-yang continued to be a centre of Buddhist activity. The first set of monastic rules (Sanscrit *vinaya*) was issued there by an Indian named Dharmakala (Ch. Fa-shih) some time towards the middle of the century; and we are also told that he made a Buddha image 'as glorious and heroically beautiful as if it had been (really) the adamantine (body) under the twin trees [the *sala* trees under which Buddha attended *nirvāṇa*]' [15]; and that various relics of Buddha as well as images and *sūtras* from the West were deposited in the Fa-yün Temple which he built at Lo-yang.

About this time the South first heard of Buddhism. A foreign priest called K'ang Sêng-hui, whose ancestors had evidently been Sogdians living in India, and whose father had come to the port of Chiao-chih at the head of the Gulf of Tongking as a trader, 'was anxious to propagate the religion in the South and to set up icons and temples there on a grand scale'.[16] He accordingly set out overland for the Wu capital of Chien-yeh and arrived there in AD 247. He later founded the first Buddhist temple in south China.

During the third century Buddhism spread triumphantly to every corner of China. Its progress is well documented, not only in dynastic histories, but also in special works on Buddhism. Such texts often speak of early Buddhist images, either imported or manufactured in China, but usually not in terms that allow us to visualize them in the absence of surviving examples. China, as well as India, was enjoying its first bout of unrestricted iconolatry. People wanted to know what the Buddha and his satellites looked like, and the early images were doubtless claimed to be actual portraits or at least faithful copies of actual portraits.

One of these portraits, or portrait-types, is worth a little attention because chance survivals have given us some idea of what it may have looked like. It is a figure of Śākyamuni, the historic Buddha, and it is generally called the 'Udayāna image'. The story is that Śākyamuni, having gone to preach to his mother in the Tuśita Heaven, the abode of the Future Buddha Maitreya, had been so long away that Udayāna, King of Kauśāmbī, despaired of his ever coming back to earth. He accordingly sent 32 craftsmen, with sandalwood for making an image, to the disciple Maudgalyāyana and begged him to transport them to the Tuśita Heaven. This the disciple did. When the portrait was finished it was installed in the Jetavana Monastery at Śrāvastī; where, so the story ran, it is still to be seen. Kauśāmbī, I should add, is in south-central Uttar Pradesh, and Śrāvastī is 150 miles to the north-east near the Nepal border. These geographical locations suggest that the original image from which the legend sprang was of native Indian type, and was made in the style of Mathurā in Uttar Pradesh [p. 183], no doubt during late Kushān or early Gupta times; that is, in the third or fourth century AD.

This image was to become the most famous icon of Far Eastern Buddhism. It would be tedious to retrace its reported wanderings across Asia, or to disentangle the truth from the many conflicting reports concerning its whereabouts at any given time, or to separate the true image from a number of rival claimants. According to one transmission, the image flew of its own accord from India to Kucha in Chinese Turkestan, whence the famous translator Kumārajīva bore it off to China in AD 405. A few years later it was taken to Ch'ang-sha in south China, then to Chiang-tu, and at length to K'ai-fêng in Honan. In AD 985 the Japanese priest Chōnen was at K'ai-fêng and caused a copy of the image to be made; this is fact, not legend, for Chōnen took the copy home to Japan, and it is to be seen to this day in the

Seiryō Temple at Kyōtō. A few years ago a cavity at the back of the image was opened. Manuscripts were extracted, including one bearing Chōnen's own handprint, that entirely confirmed the tradition of the image's origin.[17]

Our notions of what the 'Udayāna image' may have looked like are based mainly on the Seiryō copy. The K'ai-fêng image on which it was based is lost. It was transferred to Peking and placed in the Sandalwood Temple there, but disappeared in 1900 during the Boxer Rising.

fig. 39d

The 'Udayāna' reports, emanating from different sources and relating to several different pieces of sculpture, have in common a mere name and an unsubstantial legend. What they serve to show is the zeal with which early Chinese Buddhists sought to acquire authentic images direct from India. Chinese sculptors could and did take their models from the *ateliers* of the oasis monasteries that stretched across Chinese Turkestan; and the First Phase of Buddhist sculpture in China is the end-product, with something added, of a long stylistic evolution that began in the schools of north-west India some time in the first century AD. It is a lovely, endearing style, but there is no reason to suppose that ordinary lay donors placed any great value on its aesthetic qualities.

To the believer the efficacy of an icon is measured by the closeness of its historical connexion with the Being it represents; in this respect the local product and its Central Asiatic prototype were palpably inferior. Faced with a *pukka* Indian image, newly arrived from the Holy Land of the Faith, they could feel they were in the very presence of the Lord of the World, receiving the precious balm of his True Law (*saddharma*) from his own lips; and, by causing such an image to be copied, they could accumulate unbounded merit both for themselves and their dependents.

The effect of importing single images direct from India was, of course, to infuse new life periodically into Chinese Buddhist sculpture as a whole. Gupta art [p. 198] is one of the most satisfying embodiments of religious feeling the world has ever seen. By the middle sixth century AD Chinese sculpture was being directly affected by it. One of the statues brought by Hsüan-tsang to China in AD 645, an alleged copy of the 'Udayāna' image which he says he saw at Kauśāmbī, was almost certainly a Gupta original. Whether or no we accept reasons for linking an early T'ang torso of Śākyamuni in the Victoria and Albert Museum with the 'Udayāna' type, there can be no doubt that it was closely inspired by a Gupta model [p. 203]. Willy-nilly, therefore, direct contact with India forced Chinese sculptors to work out new problems of stylistic synthesis, and led to the creation of the Second and Third Phases. In my opinion these problems were satisfactorily solved and native Indian influences on Chinese sculpture proved entirely beneficial. This, then, was the effective outcome of Chinese obsession with the 'Udayāna' image.

pls 142–144

Indian origins of the Buddha image

The earliest known image of Buddha, found at Kauśāmbī, bears a dedicatory inscription of the second year of the Kushān king Kanishka, and two similar standing images from Sārnāth and Sāheth-Māheth (Śrāvasti) are dated to his third year. Kanishka's dates are in dispute. According to one view the beginning of his reign coincides with the Śaka era of AD 78, but the majority of modern scholars place it within the second quarter of the second century AD. The three images mentioned above are typical products of the Mathurā school, and show plain stylistic connexions with a group of monumental figures of local tutelary deities, *yakshas*, datable to the second–first centuries BC.

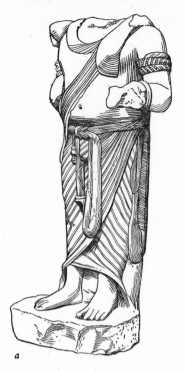

36 Two standing images: *a* a *yaksha* from Patna in the India Museum, Calcutta; *b* a Buddha from Mathurā in the Musée Guimet, Paris

THE STANDING BUDDHA

One such *yaksha* figure, found at Patna, is compared in figure 36 with a standing Buddha image almost identical in appearance to that dedicated in Kanishka's third year. It will be seen that *yaksha* and Buddha belong to the same fraternity. Both are healthy endomorphs, inclined to corpulence, with fleshy breasts and deep navels. Both stand in strict frontal pose, the weight evenly distributed between the two feet. Both figures wear a heavy under-garment (*antaravāsaka*) tied at the waist by a girdle whose lappets hang down between the legs or on to the right thigh. The Buddha wears a diaphanous outer garment (*sangāṭhi*) which is draped over the left shoulder and crosses the chest diagonally to the other side; in the *yaksha* figure a scarf is similarly draped across the chest from the left shoulder. In both images, as far as can be told, the right arm is uplifted and the left lowered to the hip. The Buddha clutches a fold of his outer garment in his left hand; several of the *yaksha* figures are shown with the left hand clutching a purse in the same position.

In portraying the standing Buddha, then, Mathurā sculptors turned to the *yaksha* as their model. It is perfectly clear that both were ultimately based on the popular conception of what a king should look like. Compare, for instance, the Mathurā standing Buddha of figure 36 b with a sixth-century AD description of auspicious signs, or *lakshaṇa*, by which a Great Man (*mahāpurusha*) or Universal King (*cakravartin*) may be recognized: 'Kings have rounded legs ... and excellent thighs similar to an elephant's trunk, and fleshy, equal knees. Kings have elevated middle part of the belly. Kings and happy men have thick, fleshy and low nipples ... One whose neck is marked with three folds like shells is a king.'[18] Buddha, we may recall, was born the son of a king. According to his sooth-sayers he might have been a Universal Monarch; instead he chose to become a great teacher (*siddhi*). So public opinion was not really wrong in ascribing to him kingly attributes.

LAKSHAṆA

Among the aforesaid *lakshaṇa* may be mentioned the incised circle or concavity between the eyebrows (*ūrṇā*) and the elongated ear-lobe, both of which are almost invariable features of Buddha images. The exact meaning of the former is uncertain, though a circle of hairs, as described in the *lakshaṇa* lists, may perpetuate the belief that thick eyebrows, continuous over

37 Development of the Buddha's head-dress: *a* 'karpadin' type on the Kaṭrā Buddha; *b* Gandhāra type; *c* Gandhāra type as modified at Mathurā; *d* 'native Indian' type; *e–h* the corresponding Chinese versions

the root of the nose, were signs of great wisdom such as was credited to a *mahāpurusha*. The lengthened ear-lobes were an obvious token of kingly rank, weighed down by the burden of heavily jewelled ear-rings.

The meaning of a third symbol, the cranial bump called *ushṇīsha*, is more obscure. If it is an abnormality, it may be what Münsterberg calls a 'supermind'.[19] It may be more rationally explained as the vestige of a top knot of hair. In early *lakshaṇa* lists the word *ushṇīsha* simply means 'turban'; so plainly there is a connexion between the turban, symbol of royalty, and the Buddha's cranial bump. Buddha, we know, wore a turban when he was a prince, and there are Indian sculptures showing people worshipping it.

A famous seated Buddha found at Kaṭrā near Mathurā, probably contemporary with, or even a little earlier than the standing Buddhas described above, has the hair tied in a snail-shell top knot called a *karpada*. Buddha images of the early Gandhāra school [see below] simi-larly show the hair piled high on the top of the head as a chignon, and encircled by a fillet. Such coiffures, according to Sir John Marshall[20], were the indoor dress of aristocrats, as they are today of the Sikhs, who put up their long hair into a bun on the top of the head before draping the turban.

figs 37a and b

It is probable, therefore, that the cranial bump is the result of a deformation of the Gandhā-ran type of chignon, or of the coiled top knot or *karpada* of the Mathurā image. Perhaps the conversion to a cranial bump was brought about deliberately, for the presence of the *karpada* must have been bewildering to those who knew that Śākyamuni shaved off his hair on becoming an ascetic.

Let us now turn to the seated image. This has features in common with the standing type, and the question which was first used for portraying Buddha remains open. But the seated image, unlike the standing, is essentially that of a being in *dhyāna* or *yoga* posture; and the image in *dhyāna*, as we have noticed [p. 174], is much older in Indian art than the beginnings of either Jain or Buddhist iconography. It has none of the popular appeal of the ruler-type of *yaksha* from which the standing Buddha descends; we are here at the opposite pole of Indian

THE SEATED BUDDHA

38 Three seated images in *dhyāna: a* Jain *āyāgapaṭṭa; b* seated Buddha from Mathurā in west Uttar Pradesh; *c* seated Buddha from Sārnāth in east Uttar Pradesh

religious experience, that of personal physical and psychological discipline as a means of emancipation from cosmic laws. Images in *yoga* posture, especially in the seated pose usually called *dhyāna-āsana*[21], portray not kings or gods with kingly attributes, but ascetics and those who have gained Enlightenment by following the path of asceticism.

A Jain votive slab (*āyāgapaṭṭa*) from the Kankāli mound at Mathurā, dating from about the beginning of the Christian era, shows us this generic image of the Yogi, *dhyānayogi*, in
fig. 38a   quintessential form: nude, expressionless, shorn of all emotive content. Such an image, we may well believe, provided the model for the creation of the seated Buddha. A Buddha image also
fig. 38b   from Mathurā in the Boston Museum of Fine Arts has features derived from it, combined with others adopted from the early standing Buddhas. Thus an upper garment is draped over the left shoulder, leaving the right shoulder bare, in precisely the convention found on the stand-
fig. 36b   ing Buddha of figure 36 b; and the arms and hands are not in orthodox *dhyāna* position, but make the habitual gestures of the early *yaksha* and standing Buddha images. Yet in its posture, and in the proportions and general shape of the torso, its derivation from the nude Jain seated image is plain to see. The latter has a long history at Mathurā, extending right through the Kushān period. We cannot doubt but that its existence helped to pave the way for the
figs 38c, 39b   ineffably beautiful seated and standing Buddhas of the Gupta period, such as we find at Sārnāth.

Mathurā and Gandhāra

While the Mathurā school was at its zenith, a new sculptural style was being developed in the kingdom of Gandhāra, in the Peshāwar and Rāwalpindi districts of West Pakistan. Centuries earlier the Macedonian Greek invasion of north-west India under Alexander had

186

39 Four standing Buddha images: *a* Gandhāra type; *b* Mathurā type from Sārnāth; *c* Gandhāra type as modified by Mathurā; *d* 'Udayāna' image in the Seiryō Temple, Kyōtō, Japan

brought in its wake a taste for Hellenistic art, exemplified by the splendid coins struck during the reigns of such Greco-Bactrian rulers of the Punjab as Demetrius and Eucratides. A second much later Hellenistic influence may be traced to Alexandria, and is represented by a large number of imported or imitation Mediterranean statues and statuettes in bronze, gold, stucco and other materials, excavated at Begrām and Taxilā [p. 123] and datable to the first and second centuries AD.

At a date which is still very much a subject of controversy, sculptors in the Gandhāra region began to produce images of Śākyamuni Buddha in this provincial Roman style, commonly called Greco-Buddhist. They used as their model the idealized Apollo, with clean-cut features, simpering expression, and an uncanonical mass of wavy hair; they clad him in a mantle naturalistically treated after the fashion of a Greek *himation*, the deeply undercut folds *fig. 39a* of which effectively hid the contours of the body beneath. It is impossible to say, on evidence at present available, whether Gandhāra deserves the credit for the invention of the Buddha image; the direct evolution of the Mathurā type of standing Buddha from very much earlier native Indian *yaksha* models might lead to the conclusion that it does not.

Probably towards the end of the second century AD the Buddhist art of Mathurā began to be influenced by this new and distinctly un-Indian style. The outcome was a quite novel type of Mathurā image, in which nominal adherence to the Gandhāra formula was observed, while allowing the true spirit of Mathurā art to shine through. In Gandhāra the mantle covered both shoulders and the whole body. It was meant to look like an actual garment. According to Madame Lohuizen-de Leeuw it did not even represent the same material as that depicted on the early Mathurā images; for the former was wool, the latter a Benares muslin of the utmost delicacy, Kāśī tissue.[22] In executing images based on Gandhāran originals, Mathurā sculptors still treated the gown as though it were made of this lighter material. It

187

40 Image of the goddess Hārītī found at Skārah Ḍherī

was effectively reduced to a succession of soft and rounded relief ridges, representing folds falling symmetrically from both shoulders and enclosing the body, as Rowland says, 'as though nude in a mesh of cords'. The volumes that emerge are those of the body, not of the gown. Nipples, navel, pudenda, the inner planes of arms and thighs – features that a heavy gown would obscure – are distinctly suggested; and the lappets of the girdle beneath the gown are plainly visible, as though the latter were transparent.

The new synthetic style quickly took root, and began to filter back into Gandhāra, passing thence to Central Asia and China. The standard type of seated and standing Buddha images of the Far East thus stem more or less directly from this hybrid presentment, originating at Mathurā in the second century AD.

The spread of the Mathurā image

Sculptures in the unmistakable mottled pink Sikri sandstone used by Mathurā sculptors have been found as far east as Bodh-Gayā and Patna in Bihar, and west as far as Taxilā; two of the earliest pieces, as we saw [p. 183], come from Kauśāmbī and Śrāvastī, the very places associated with the legend of the making of Udayāna's statue [p. 182]. Clearly, then, Mathurā was in a position to influence style and iconography wherever Buddhist sculpture was being made, and in due course its presence begins to make itself felt in late Gandhāran art.

By the third–fourth centuries AD Gandhāran Buddhist sculpture had spread far into Afghānistān from its original centre in the upper Indus valley. In this latest phase, called by Sir John Marshall 'Indo-Afghan', the Mathurā idiom is very conspicuous. In many of the seated images the right shoulder is bare, after the Mathurā manner, and the gown is treated as though made of far lighter material than that of earlier Gandhāra sculptures. Its folds tend to be treated as though they were merely a series of padded ridges forming a schematic pattern on the surface of the body, and not concealing its contours; and this, too, is typical of late Mathurā style. A number of other features, including the late manner of rendering the hair in the form of conventional 'peppercorn' curls and the position of the hands known as *dharmacakra* [p. 203], have also entered Gandhāran art via Mathurā.

fig. 39b and c
fig. 37d
fig. 38c

fig. 40

A bizarre image of the goddess Hārītī found at Skārah Ḍherī bears a date corresponding to AD 270, or AD 342 according to another interpretation [23], and is therefore late in the tradition. Here the conventions of Gandhāra and Mathurā seem to have got thoroughly out of hand, although the Mathurā spirit is still plain to see. The mantle is nothing but a tight pattern of meaningless channels, and the modelling is appallingly summary judged by the assured standards of Hellenistic art. Yet the image has a vitality rare in Gandhāran sculpture. The mask, with its boldly-cut eyebrow ridges and wedge-shaped nose, is no longer the emasculated portrait of some Greek youth. It is a bare 'concept-symbol', as Fry would put it, expressionless, betraying nothing of any interior psychological state; and it foreshadows that of images such as the fifth-century Yün-kang colossus of plate 120.

pl. 120

Various stages in the later treatment of the Mathurā-type Buddha image can be traced in sculptures at Buddhist sites along the land route between Afghānistān and the Chinese cave-shrines of Shansi and Kansu. At the Rawak *vihāra*, Khotan, and at Kharashahr on the northern edge of the Tarim basin in Chinese Turkestan, the gown is rendered in artificial manner, the folds falling in almost vertical ridges on the thighs, while between the legs they form an apparently separate series of crescentic pleats. In the same locality seated Buddha images are found in which the bare right shoulder of the early Mathurā manner is covered with a fold of the mantle. In a region of climatic extremes, this may reflect a reluctance to bare the torso, even that of a graven image. At any rate the feature was copied in early Chinese Buddhist sculpture, and appears on the above-mentioned colossus of Yün-kang. *pl. 120*

From these indecisive Central Asiatic treatments, the final step taken by the Mathurā standing and seated Buddha image in its transformation to the Chinese type is a short one. The First Phase Maitreya of plate 121, now in the Metropolitan Museum, New York, bears *pl. 121* a date corresponding to AD 477.[24] Let us briefly run over the lineage of this superb end-product of a long stylistic evolution. It originates from the earliest type of standing Buddha images, probably made at Mathurā during the first century AD, based upon *yaksha* models. In common with these, it stands with feet well spaced, weight borne equally by each; right hand is raised, left outstretched at the level of the waist; the head carries a top knot; the volumes of the gown are not allowed to obscure those of the body. It next reflects the Hellenistic influence of Gandhāra. The top knot is hidden under a high chignon; the gown covers the whole body and is hung from the shoulders. But it is treated in the style evolved by late Mathurā sculptors working from Gandhāran models, for its folds are reduced to schematized ridges. Lastly, it shows the impress of late Gandhāran art and of the schools of Central Asia; the mask is of the abstract type we saw on the Hāritī image of Skārah Ḍherī, and the mantle-folds follow the system elaborated at such centres as Kharashahr and Rawak, falling in vertical lines down the thighs, and between them, where they hang more loosely, being broken up into lunulate pleats.

One might think it well-nigh impossible that an image embodying such varied stylistic influences could have any vitality or authenticity left. Yet the Chinese sculptor has given it a new lease of life. We may have here a legacy of the 'Udayāna' tradition that stemmed from Kumārajīva's alleged image brought from Kucha [p. 182].

Mahāyāna Buddhism and its impact on Buddhist art

Up to this point we have spoken only of the image of Buddha, and of those non-Buddhist Beings whose portrayal seems to have played a primary part in fashioning it. Now we must say something about doctrinal developments by which the historical Buddha, Śākyamuni, became a personal God and an object of worship, and by which other personages, the Bodhisattvas, found their way into the scriptures (*sutras*) and were in their turn worshipped, and of whom images were also made. These developments belong to the history of the northern Buddhist church, the Mahāyāna or 'Great Vehicle'.

The germ of the doctrinal split into Mahāyāna and Hinayāna (the 'Small Vehicle', according to the Mahāyānists) can be traced back to the Second Buddhist Council held at Vaiśālī about a century after the *nirvāṇa* of Buddha in 544 BC, when the monastic community (*saṅgha*) broke into two dissentient groups of sects, the Mahāsāṅghika and the Sthaviravāda (Theravāda). Their subsequent history is extremely complex; but broadly speaking the Theravāda held, or claimed to hold, the orthodox and original doctrine, while the Mahāsāṅghikas were in the role of dissenters and radicals. While the concept of a personal God is not entirely lacking in Theravāda, it was the Mahāsāṅghika that actively propagated the idea of a supramundane and omniscient Buddha and saviour, and thus paved the way for the fully-fledged theistic Buddhalogy of the Mahāyāna system in the first century AD.

The core of the difference between Mahāyāna and Hinayāna Buddhism can be found in the development of the concept of the Bodhisattva in the former. The primitive faith taught that the path to salvation must be sought by the individual alone, as Buddha had sought it, giving no help to others and receiving none in return. Having found the path, the seeker was now a perfected being (*arhat*), next door to a Buddha; but to lay worshippers all this was incomprehensible. Even to become an ordinary monk (*bhikshu*) was too difficult for most of them. What chance had they of attaining to Buddhahood?

The Mahāyānists now proclaimed that Buddhahood was a practical goal for everyone. Help in bringing its seeds to flower came from the Bodhisattvas, beings who had attained to Enlightenment, ripe for Buddhahood, but who were deliberately delaying its onset in order to help ordinary mortals along the same path. In elaborating the Bodhisattva doctrine during the first and second centuries AD, Mahāyānism made itself a religion of universal appeal, authoritarian and ultramontane.

Where did the Bodhisattvas come from? Many, no doubt, were invented. But others seem to have been gods of alien faiths, requisitioned by Buddhism as it broadened its geographical range. An identification has been proposed, for instance, between the Bodhisattva Maitreya, the Vedic Sun Mitra, and the Iranian Sun God, Mithras.

At the same time the conception of Śākyamuni alters. He has not passed forever from human ken. Indeed, the historic Buddha is now only the earthly shadow, the *avatār*, of an absolute and unvarying principle, a Buddha of infinite duration eternally dwelling on the Vulture Peak, whence his messages carry to mankind. Nor is he alone. Infinite myriads of Buddhas have preceded him into Buddhahood, and all now dwell in their respective Paradises, surrounded by multitudes of worshippers. The present dispensation, a *kalpa* containing inconceivable aeons of years, has seen seven earthly Buddhas of whom Śākyamuni was the last, and is presently to welcome an eighth. This is to be Maitreya. And the final phase

pl. 122

of the present *kalpa*, in the course of which Maitreya is to descend from the Tuṣita Heaven to undergo his last human incarnation, was reckoned to begin a thousand years after the death of Śākyamuni. The advent of Maitreya was expected daily by Chinese Buddhists after the millennial year, AD 433. It is not surprising, therefore, to find that during the fifth and sixth centuries his popularity out-rivals even that of Śākyamuni in China, as is witnessed by the great number of images dedicated to him; or that a favourite vow of Buddhist devotees was to be reborn in the Tuṣita Heaven, thence to descend to earth in his company.

All these elaborations of Buddhist cosmology find expression in the most widely-read Mahāyāna *sūtra* of all, the *Saddharma-puṇḍarīka*, or 'Lotus of the True Law' (Ch. *Miao fa lien hua*

pl. 126

ching), perhaps first written in the second century AD. Here Śākyamuni preaches the message of salvation, the Mahāyāna, on the Vulture Peak, and illustrates by parables its superiority over all other means to salvation. He forecasts the coming Buddhahood of a great many attendant persons. He performs a miracle, restoring to life an ancient and altogether extinct Buddha called Prabhūtaratna, who voices his approval of Śākyamuni's discourse. Together they sit enthroned in Prabhūtaratna's burial mound (*stūpa*), magically suspended in the sky, while infinite multitudes of Buddhas congregate from the ten directions of space to pay them worship. Towards the end of the *sūtra* the Bodhisattva Avalokiteśvara (Ch. Kuan-yin) is introduced, and his hymn of saving grace is sung. Another Bodhisattva, Samantabhadra (Ch. Pu-hsien), then charges himself with the task of protecting all who shall preach the Law after the *nirvāṇa* of Śākyamuni.

As its English translator remarks[25], the Lotus *sūtra* has the character of a dramatic performance; and as the various Buddhas and Bodhisattvas make their appearance, one after the other, we get the feeling that they are being officially presented for the first time. Its influence on the Chinese popular religion and its iconography was profound. Motifs such as that of the 'Thousand Buddhas' – those for whom Śākyamuni foretold Buddhahood in the course of his sermon –, Śākyamuni and Prabhūtaratna sitting together in the *stūpa*, and Śākyamuni's

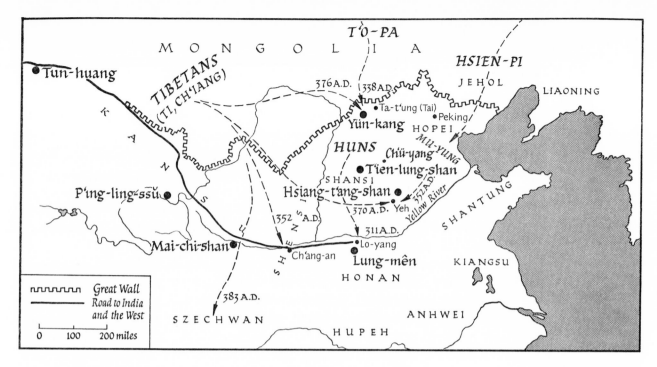

Map 3 Buddhist cave-shrines and the movement of nomadic tribes into North China

Paradise, are all directly inspired by this text; and incidentally, are original creations of Chinese Buddhist sculpture.

Provided only the mind of the devotee is set on good works, 'Lotus' assures, Enlightenment now becomes virtually automatic. It therefore repeatedly prescribes for lay believers the practice of dedicating sacred images. This was what they wanted to be told. Mahāyāna Buddhism, at this level, was not difficult for the ordinary man to grasp, even when it offered nothing more tangible than Enlightenment; and it was soon to promise even more attractive rewards. They accordingly set about making images.

Śākyamuni, Maitreya, Amitābha, Avalokiteśvara

The early and continued popularity of Śākyamuni as a subject of Chinese Buddhist sculpture needs no particular explanation, since he had the prestige of being the Founder of the Faith and since his image had long been established in the art of Mathurā and Gandhāra. Publication of texts such as the Lotus *sūtra*, in which he is the central figure, must have done much to ensure the multiplication of his image in every part of the Buddhist world.

Nor is the Chinese cult of Maitreya [p. 190] difficult to understand. The first translation of the *sūtra* foretelling his approaching Buddhahood, *Maitreya-vyākarana* (Ch. *Fo shuo mi lo hsia shêng ching*) was made as early as AD 303 by one Dharmaraksha, and it was followed about AD 400 by an extremely popular version done by Kumārajīva [p. 182]. Among the earliest known dated Chinese Buddha images, those of Maitreya preponderate. Wegner records no less than eighty-five named examples of Northern Wei date[26], and Chavannes identifies thirty-seven from Lung-mên inscriptions covering that period.[27] After Northern Wei times, numbers begin to fall off, perhaps because of disappointment caused by his failure

191

to appear on earth, but more probably because another Buddha, Amitābha, has come into the limelight. Yet the Maitreya cult by no means disappeared; we have seen [p. 181] how the T'ang Empress Wu tried to pass herself off as an incarnation of the Buddha as late as AD 690.

Amitābha Buddha is the third member of the great trinity. His origin is obscure, possibly Iranian, and his cult-image is unknown in the early Indian schools and does not seem to have originated there. A miniature figure appearing in the head-dress of Avalokiteśvara [p. 190], as featured at fifth–seventh centuries AD Deccanese cave-shrines, such as Nāsik, Aurangabad and Ajaṇṭā, may be presumed to be that of Amitābha. Apart from this we meet him only in the late and highly synthetic context of the Tantric worship of *Dhyāni* Buddhas, and then by no means frequently. His real following seems always to have been in the Far East.

Amitābha is mentioned in 'Lotus' as a Buddha presiding over the Western Paradise called Sukhakara (Sukhāvati). Not much is said, and perhaps his personality is here only just beginning to make itself felt in Buddhist dogma. Fuller descriptions of his Paradise are found in the Greater and Lesser Sukhāvati *sūtras* [28], both translated for the first time into Chinese during the third century AD. It seems a delectable place, with its gardens, rivers, palaces, pavilions, jewel-bearing trees, flowers, and fruits; with swans, curlews, and peacocks performing every night a concert 'each uttering his own note', and with the blessed company of souls reborn into it, who by happy inspiration are said to rise from the calyces of lotus flowers. Here is a final concession to popular taste. The idea of Enlightenment, of Buddhahood and of *nirvāṇa*, was all very well for a saint. But it was cold comfort for lay believers. Whereas prospect of a more or less indefinite period of felicity in a Paradise was one to fire the imagination and rouse the senses. The Amitābha cult in China comes nearer to worship in our sense than any other branch of Chinese Buddhism.

pl. 132

In the fifth century, worship of Amitābha was much encouraged by the translation of the 'Meditation on Amitāyus' (Amitābha) *sūtra*, in which Śākyamuni discloses means whereby an ordinary layman may by meditation have a foretaste of the paradisal bliss. From this time donors constantly voice the wish to be reborn in the Western Paradise. The earliest known to me dates from the year AD 518 when a donor at Lung-mên, in dedicating a statue to Amitābha, hopes 'that her husband may be reborn in the Western Regions'.[29] The number of dedications to Amitābha now rapidly increases, and a century or so later he has become by far and away the most popular personage in Chinese Buddhism.

A fourth personage, the Bodhisattva Avalokiteśvara [p. 190], has always found favour among lay worshippers. His popularity during the Northern Wei period is only exceeded by that of Śākyamuni and Maitreya, if we rely on the evidence of dedicatory inscriptions, and is second only to that of Amitābha in T'ang times. Over the period of image-making with which we are here concerned, Avalokiteśvara is in fact the most popular Buddhist personage after Amitābha; but if we include later periods not surveyed here, we shall not hesitate to say that more images of Avalokiteśvara have been made in China – and indeed throughout the Far East generally – than of any other single personage of Buddhism.

The iconography of Chinese Buddhist sculpture

BUDDHAS

Dealing with the creation of the Buddha image at Mathurā, we saw how the standing image may be derived from that of the *yaksha*, which in turn is modelled on the representation of an earthly monarch; how the seated image probably took shape from earlier images in *dhyāna*, and specifically from the nude seated image of Jain art; and how certain features of Buddha images, the cranial bump, lengthened ear-lobes and *ūrṇā*, are renderings of *lakshaṇa*, conventional auspicious signs whereby a Great Man or Universal Monarch could be recognized. Moreover, we noticed that the costume of a Buddha comprises an under-garment (*antaravāsaka*) tied at the waist with a girdle, and an outer garment or mantle (*sanghāṭi*), which is either draped across the left shoulder only, or hangs from both. No other clothing is normally worn. The head is unadorned and uncovered; and the hands hold no attributes.

These features are common to all Buddhas, and by virtue of them, or some of them, Buddhas can be clearly differentiated from the beings whose spiritual condition most resembles theirs, namely the Bodhisattvas. For Bodhisattvas, although portrayed in a variety of seated and standing poses, are never in Chinese sculpture shown in the posture of meditation, *dhyāna*. Of the *lakshaṇa*, they commonly carry lengthened ear-lobes, but rarely *ūrṇā* and never a cranial bump. They are usually nude down to the girdle, but their torsos are loaded with jewellery in rich abundance [p. 198]. And the head-dress is always an elaborate coiffure with a diadem in which the miniature effigy of a Buddha or other attributes may appear. Further, they very often carry objects in their hands which are supposed to be means of identifying them.

Some of the first Śākyamuni Buddha images made at Mathurā are called Bodhisattvas in their inscriptions, but this is presumably only in deference to an age-old prejudice against representing the Buddha's person, broken down with the coming of the Mahāyāna doctrine and the figural schools of north-west India. Except for these, the only Bodhisattva that can be identified with any conviction, whether at Mathurā or Gandhāra, is the Buddhist Messiah, the Bodhisattva Maitreya. He is usually shown standing – a manly, moustached, and magnificently frilled and furbelowed figure, wearing as a rule a highly self-satisfied expression, and in general looking like a popular idol of the modern Indian screen. He holds in his left hand the ambrosia flask, *amṛta kalaśa*, which contains the nectar of immortality.

Less definite is the identification of two satellites, standing at the proper right and left of the seated Buddha, as Avalokiteśvara and Maitreya. On the reliquary casket recovered from King Kanishka's *stūpa* at Peshāwar, executed in early Gandhāra style, they are certainly Indra and Brahmā, as they are in several Mathurā trinities including the fragment shown in figure 38 b. *fig. 38b* This flagrant exaltation of the new god over those of the *ancien régime*, using iconographic means, can be traced backward to the early native Indian schools (examples from which show the two Hindu gods worshipping the empty seat on which Buddha gained Enlightenment) and forward into Gupta and Pāla times. But as Mahāyānism wins its victory in the north-west the Bodhisattvas Avalokiteśvara and Maitreya take their rightful places as the chief acolytes, standing on the proper right and left sides of the Buddha; the former has the lotus, the latter the ambrosia flask. Several reliefs depict Brahmā and Indra as well, sandwiched in between Buddha and Bodhisattvas, barely managing to get into the picture, so to speak.

*

The iconography of Mathurā and Gandhāra, like that of the earlier Indian schools of Sānchī and Bhārhut, is rich in illustrations of the life of Buddha and his former lives (*jātaka* stories), but is deficient in specifically Mahāyāna themes. To all intents and purposes Śākyamuni, Maitreya, and Avalokiteśvara are the only Mahāyāna deities portrayed in Indian art up to the medieval period. The essence of Mahāyānism is the multiplication of its gods[30]; but this process is not taken as far in India, or in the intervening countries of northern Buddhism, as it is in China. The culminating personality, and the most popular cult-image, is always that of Śākyamuni. Until we get to the Far East. As Mahāyānist texts found their way to China and Japan a demand arose for images of beings never before portrayed in India. The iconographic range of Chinese Buddhist sculpture between the fifth and eighth centuries AD is thus preceptibly wider than that of its Indian parent. How were the new subjects worked up?

Scriptures are not text-books of iconography, yet in effect they constitute a sort of vade mecum for the sculptor, both by suggesting to him new themes for representation and, sometimes, by indicating the right way to portray them. 'We examined the scriptures and investigated literary sources in arranging the figures and depicting the scenes', runs part of an inscription on a stele dated AD 776 found at Tun-huang.[31] And Waley stresses this role of *sūtras* when he says: 'As regards iconography, then, it is to the texts and not to an oral tradition that the Buddhist turns. Very instructive in this respect is the *Higashi-yama Ōrai*, a correspondence between a [Japanese] Buddhist abbot and his parishioners written early in the twelfth century. By intending donors he is again and again consulted concerning the proper methods of representing the various Paradises and divinities. In each case he replies by citing a text.'[32]

One can well imagine how the illiterate audiences listening with childlike wonder to readings of the first Mahāyāna *sūtras* must have longed for graphic illustrations of what they heard, and can understand the obsessional hold that motifs such as the 'Thousand Buddhas', and Śākyamuni and Prabhūtaratna in the *stūpa*, taken from the Lotus *sūtra* came to exercise over the minds of patrons and artists alike. Similarly the Amitābha *sūtras* [p. 192] provided iconographic material for countless representations of that Buddha's Western Paradise, in which a *pl. 132* charming and diagnostic detail is often the presence of naked infant souls emerging from lotus blooms to be reborn in his company.

Another *sūtra* highly popular in China during the fifth and sixth centuries AD was *Vimalīkīrti-nirdeśa* (Ch. *Wei mo ch'ieh so shuo ching*), or 'Vimalīkīrti's Discourse on Emancipation'. This lively and even satirical essay is clearly meant to appeal to the wealthy patrons of the Faith. It tells how the rich man, Vimalīkīrti, credited with miraculous powers of wisdom, is lying on his sick-bed wondering whether Śākyamuni will send to enquire after his health. Reading his thought, Śākyamuni sends Mañjuśrī (Ch. Wên-shu), the Bodhisattva of Wisdom, and the two begin a memorable disputation.

The venerable disciple Śāriputra (Ch. Shih-lo), who is made to feature as the Aunt Sally of the proceedings, feeds Vimalīkīrti with a stream of puerile observations, to which the rich man replies by performing various relevant feats of magic, of allegorical import. Thus he conjures up a Heavenly Maiden scattering flowers, 32,000 Lion Thrones (for his audience to sit upon, Vimalīkīrti having previously cleared his house of all furniture in order to speak on Emptiness), and a Bodhisattva with a bowl of perfumed rice out of which the whole company is fed, including 84,000 wealthy men of the district who have been attracted by its fragrance. The scene at Vimalīkīrti's house, where these unwonted events are taking place, is *pl. 128* repeated endlessly in the cave-shrines and upon the votive steles of the sixth century AD – significantly in proximity to portraits of the rich donors whose prestige the story of Vimalīkīrti was undoubtedly intended to endorse.

Extended themes such as these present no great problems of identification. It is when we come to examine portrayals of individual Buddhas and Bodhisattvas that the trouble starts. In spite of all the spadework that has been done on the subject of Chinese Buddhist iconography – by Chavannes, Sirén, Tokiwa and Sekino, Nagahiro, and Mizuno, to mention but a few[33] there is still no sure path through the maze of iconographic alternatives we face when we begin our attempt to run one of these personages to earth. Conscientious efforts to be guided by the scriptures, such as I have mentioned above, were undoubtedly exceptions to a general rule; and it may well be that sculptors kept no more than two models in their *ateliers*, one for Buddhas, the other for Bodhisattvas, and that a purchaser who wished to dedicate an image of a particular Buddha or Bodhisattva would be supplied from stock with one of the appropriate type, space being left for a suitable inscription to be added after purchase. If this was indeed the practice it perhaps explains a discrepancy, often noticed by the student of Chinese Buddhism, between the orthodox manner of portraying the being named in the inscription and the actual image that meets the eye; this is frustrating, for we naturally expect that the various beings whose iconography we are trying to establish will remain true to their own identities, and not go lending their names to others who according to the rules should not resemble them at all. It is disappointing to find that iconographic conventions we had imagined as fixed are still fluid and imprecise, and that a limit is often reached beyond which we cannot proceed with the identification in hand. The worshipper, who after all paid for the statue to be made, was presumably incompetent to estimate the degree of its divergence from an iconographic ideal. One thing is certain. If he understood it to represent Maitreya, he used it to worship Maitreya.

I shall now attempt to prescribe a set of very general iconographic rules, of limited application and based on empirical observation such as would quickly be gained by any student in the course of an elementary survey of the field. To these I shall add an iconographic table, *table 3* the ambiguousness of which will doubtless become clear as soon as they are consulted, but which more or less summarize the iconographic information set out at greater length in the first edition of this book.

So, provided the reader has learnt to distinguish between a Buddha image and that of a Bodhisattva [p. 193], he can perhaps advance from that base with the aid of the following five rules:

1. A Buddha seated in *dhyāna-āsana*, and in *dharmacakra* or *bhūmisparśa mudrā*, may normally be identified as Śākyamuni. If in *dhyāna-āsana* and *dhyāna* or *abhaya* and *vara mudrā*, however, the Buddha may be either Śākyamuni or Amitābha; he will not in any case be Maitreya.
2. A Buddha seated in *bhadrasana* is Maitreya, whatever his *mudrā* may be.
3. A Bodhisattva seated in *bhadrasana*, or much more frequently in a similar posture but with ankles crossed, is also Maitreya, whether his hands are in *dharmacakra* or *abhaya* and *vara mudrā*.
4. A Bodhisattva with a miniature Amitābha Buddha (whether seated or standing) in his head-dress, is Avalokiteśvara. A Bodhisattva seated in the posture of 'royal ease' (*mahārājalila*) is normally Avalokiteśvara; so is one holding in one hand a lotus bud or flower on a long or short stalk, or a fly-whisk, or a 'willow-branch', while in the other he holds a water-pot, flask, or bottle.
5. A Bodhisattva mounted on an elephant is Samantabhadra [p. 190]; one mounted on a lion is Mañjuśrī [p. 194].

If, at this stage, he is still in doubt – it may be he is confronted with an image of a Buddha in *dhyāna mudrā* and *āsana* – the table [p. 204] will enable him to make his identification *table 3* perhaps more precise. Thus, for instance, seven Buddhas in the halo would point to Śākyamuni, five to Amitābha.

pl. 119

Known Chinese Buddhist sculptures of the fifth to eighth centuries fall into four main typo-logical groups. Earliest are small gilt-bronze votive statuettes[34] popular during the whole pe-riod under survey and later. Evidently they answered a need for cheap, standard domestic cult-images; yet they are conspicuously free from the shoddy workmanship, summary design, and sentimental treatment that often spoil such merchandise. Indeed, although seldom on a large scale, they include some of the noblest pieces of Chinese sculpture we know; and throughout the whole period they sensitively reflect prevailing stylistic trends.

pls 121, 124, 125, 136, 137

Next, and coming rather later, are large rectangular votive steles. This form, according to Sirén, arose from the inscribed memorial slab of Han and later periods which, he says, was 'originally made to be raised at both sides of the tombs of prominent men, at the time of their burial'.[35] Two such slabs, each with a single perforation near the top, could be used to sup-port a pole between them, whereby the coffin was lowered into the grave. Unornamented in

pl. 129

Han times, they later acquired a pair of intertwined dragons disposed over their rounded tops; and this decorative element persisted when the slabs were taken over by Buddhists and trans-

pls 126–129, 132

formed into votive steles.

A third class includes the sculptures of the cave-shrines, by far the fullest and most impres-sive corpus of surviving material. Although a dozen or so of these sites are known today, they are mostly in ruinous condition and only a few need be mentioned here.

pls 145, 148
pls 120, 122, 123
pls 131, 141

They are Tun-huang at the north-west end of the Kansu corridor, and the newly-dis-covered caves at P'ing-ling-ssŭ and Mai-chi-shan at the south-east end of the corridor, all three sites being almost plumb in line; Yün-kang in northern Shansi; Lung-mên in Honan; T'ien-lung-shan in central Shansi; and Hsiang-t'ang-shan in Hopei. The earliest, Tun-huang, is also the most western; and in fact the Chinese cave-shrines are simply the eastern termination of a series that begins in the rock-cut Buddhist monasteries of India,

map 3

and continues across Afghānistān and Central Asia into China.

In none of the above-mentioned classes of sculpture is the subject conceived *en ronde bosse*. Images were almost invariably set against some sort of background, and all had to be looked at more or less from the front. But about Sui times free-standing stone sculptures begin to appear, planned on the sort of scale and given the same individual treatment we associate with the works of European master-sculptors. These may be thought of as constituting a fourth typological group. They are, however, few and far between. One of the leading pro-

pls 135, 139, 142

duction-centres for them was Ch'ü-yang near Ting-chou in northern Honan, where a fine-grain micaceous marble was to be had.

THE FIRST PHASE
(*c.* AD 400–550)
pls 119–128

The First Phase is by no means stylistically one. There were a grand style and a lesser style, as well as several provincial schools and, as one would expect, a number of pieces that lead into the transitional Second Phase. Yet all convey the same impression of a feverish energy and high nervous tension. It is hard to say what impulse drove their makers so hard. But several writers have commented on what seems to be an emotional kinship between this Phase and early medieval Christian sculpture. I mention the comparison only because it may help us to recognize a definite quality pervading all First Phase sculpture, its primitiveness. The word 'archaic' is, as I have suggested, misleading. But when we look at the Lung-mên

pl. 122

caves with their row upon row of curiously animated occupants like that of plate 122 – bodies long and angular, waists slender, shoulders sloping, necks exaggeratedly tall and supporting long, narrow heads that look like heavy flowers swaying on thin stems – we cannot help feeling that a communal emotion is being discharged, that a whole *Volksgeist* is expressed and not merely the verve and sensibility of the individual artist.

The grand style need scarcely detain us, for we have already dealt with it and its stylistic antecedents [pp. 188–189]. It is well exemplified by the Śākyamuni of plate 120 and the Maitreya of plate 121. These were major works, and their makers seem to have held closely to the Mathurā recipe in designing them, no doubt taking it for the *sans pareil* of authenticity. Typical of the style is a somewhat mechanical and abstract modelling of the mask, broad forehead, a wedge-shaped nose with semicircular eyebrow-ridges springing from its root, a small mouth with corners turned up in an 'archaic' smile; and a convention by which mantle-folds are rendered as raised double ridges, so that the gown appears padded [p. 187]. No attempt is made to give the mask the characteristics of an ordinary human face. It offers no clue to racial identity, mental disposition, psychological state, or emotional mood, as does that of classical European sculpture. Yet, as Rowland says of it: 'The very absence of the qualities that make for what we call naturalistic representation raise the idol beyond and above the classical standard, whereby the gods are made anthropomorphic to accommodate the limitations of the worshipper in imagining the object of devotion.'[36]

The lesser style is more personal. A happier illustration could hardly be found than the gracious little study of a celestial musician (*gandharva*) from Lung-mên, shown on plate 123. Apart from the air of friendly intimacy it radiates, the piece manifests an objective interest in decorative composition for its own sake, in the beauty of its formal layout. This cool detachment underlies all the impassioned lyricism of the First Phase, whose sculptors sought not only to satisfy the bare requirement for mass-produced cult-images, but also to create miniature essays in tectonic design. With minor pieces such as the *gandharva* we are as far away from the hieratic immobility of the grand style as is possible to imagine; far nearer, I think, to the purely Chinese spirit present in, say, bronze and lacquer décor.

This does not mean that the lesser style was altogether free from clichés and mannerisms: the conditions under which it was made neither called for nor encouraged individual treatment. Images had to be produced quickly, cheaply, and in enormous numbers. What the lesser style *does* consistently display is that genius for creating dynamic tensions, by the interplay of related parts inside a compositional framework, so typical of Chinese art. Within such formal limits sculptors experimented freely with decorative detailing, nowhere to better effect than in the sides and lower edge of the gown, which falls like an evening skirt over the throne in a cascade of pleats ending in stiff, pointed 'swallow-tail' projections, elaborated beyond reason and with the most brilliant effect. We are reminded – as so often in Chinese decorative design – of suddenly-arrested movement; perhaps of a great bird's wing still arched and vibrating from its recent flight.

Like that of the grand style, the mask of the lesser style is of abstract type. Its proportions vary from a preternaturally long and narrow shape to one that is almost square; but all exhibit the same facial features. The 'archaic' smile is here more pronounced than in the case of the large hieratic pieces, and the mouth is small. Eyes are reduced to elongated slits. High, arched eyebrow-ridges spring from the root of the nose, and are emphasized by incised lines. Earlobes, of course, are conventionally lengthened; and the chin is frequently pointed. This is a slight, evasive sort of beauty. And it creates the impression of a pristine innocence, of a childlike purity that permeates the whole of First Phase Chinese Buddhist sculpture.

One other feature is to all intents and purposes distinctive of the First Phase. This is the large leaf-shaped aureole or nimbus that forms a backing to seated and standing images of both Buddhas and Bodhisattvas. It is almost always present, and where it is not I think we

pls 120, 121

pl. 123

pls 124–126

pls 122, 123

pl. 120

197

pl. 125

can assume it originally was. Bronze examples are adorned with an outer zone of flame-ornament, partly cast and partly engraved, within which is a circular halo backing the head. Corresponding versions in stone are incised and/or carved in relief, or the aureole may take the form of a painted background for a stone image.

THE SECOND PHASE
(*c.* AD 550–618)
pls 129–137

Although occupying only some seventy years between the fall of the Eastern and Western Wei dynasties and the beginning of T'ang, the Second Phase marks a real advance in the history of Chinese Buddhist sculpture. First Phase styles rapidly became demoded; and the original Mathurā formula that had groped its way across Afghānistān and Central Asia to China, and that formed the starting-point for all First Phase treatments, lost ground. But the Mathurā formula had also travelled east to the great centres of Buddhism in central and east-ern India. And there it had flowered into a new native Indian art, Gupta. The gravely beau-tiful standing and seated sandstone Buddhas of Sārnāth belonging to the fifth century AD are, as we have seen, stylistically related to nude Jain images of the late Mathurā school [p. 186]. Though clothed, these Buddhas were given an appearance of nudity by reducing the gown to a few incised lines, so leaving the eye free to explore every significant passage of the underlying form[37]. The Buddha image was thus successfully transfigured to accord with age-old Indian conceptions of the naked body as an expressive symbol.

figs 38, 39b

Having once divested the body, Gupta sculptors proceeded to fetter it again with every conceivable article of accessory ornament. Canonically, a Buddha may not be personally adorned; but he is given a delicately carved circular halo bounded by a beaded border, within which is a luxuriant plant-trail, and within which again is a lotus rosette backing his head. Bodhisattvas, entitled to princely regalia, positively drip with jewellery – high and ornate dia-dems, necklaces and girdles both hung with pendants, armlets, bracelets and wristlets, ear-rings, jewelled chains, and a long scarf hung from the shoulders and looped through a large ring at the mid-riff. But their bodies remain essentially nude; and the *tribhanga* posture in which they stand [p. 203], a legacy from earlier Indian schools represented by Sānchī, Bhārhut, and Bodh-Gayā, contributes to the impression of a purely physical *élan*.

fig. 38c

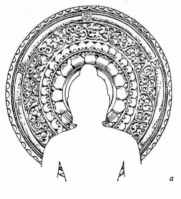

41 Two circular halos: *a* from a standing Buddha image found at Sārnāth, India; *b* from a seated Chinese Buddha image, probably of the Sung period, but repro-ducing the style of the Second Phase

The new style was now absorbed into Second Phase Chinese Buddhist sculpture, but not in its entirety. Decorative motifs were accepted without question. The carved floral halo, for instance, is faithfully imitated in sculptures of the Northern Ch'i dynasty, as comparison be-tween Indian and Chinese examples makes clear. In other and more fundamental respects, the Second Phase clung for a time to First Phase conventions, and succumbed only gradu-ally to the influence of the new Indian school.

In reducing the gown to a system of incised lines, Indian sculptors reaffirmed the supremacy of the nude body with its inherent plastic values. Chinese sculptors knew of no such tradi-tion; and the gown, however subordinated to the body of its wearer, is always an appreciable entity in First Phase sculpture. Indeed, the very way in which its folds are schematized, in accordance with the Mathurā formula, tended in Chinese hands to diminish the plasticity of the image itself; for it encouraged sculptors to work the folds into an independent decora-tive pattern, such as is best deployed upon a flat surface. This irresistible instinct for pattern-making effectively prevented First Phase sculptors from ever emancipating their work from its original condition of relief-carving meant to be seen from front view only. The tendency in Second Phase sculpture was to deprive the gown of its decorative interest, with a resulting gain in plasticity.

In its treatment of mask and of bodily movement, a step towards Indian standards taken by Second Phase sculpture was a step nearer realism. For whatever symbolic meaning earlier

Indian sculpture possessed, it was superficially a naturalistic art in respect of these features. Under Gupta inspiration, the mask in Second Phase sculpture no longer retains its earlier abstract quality; features and expression begin to resemble those of actual faces. Such characterization is of course only relative. A hieratic mask must never be allowed to look too human; and Chinese sculptors of the Second and Third Phases distinguished in treatment between the abstracted other-worldliness of Buddhas and Bodhisattvas, and the portrait-realism of lesser beings. Yet, compared with that of the First Phase, the Second Phase mask is fuller and more rounded, the 'archaic' smile less evident, and the execution of eyebrows, eyes, nose, and lips less perfunctory. At the same time images begin, ever so slightly it is true, to stir to life.

As a rule all we can discern is a slight movement away from absolute rigidity of pose, a slackening in tension of one leg so that the body tilts somewhat at the hips, again in the opposite direction at the waist, and again in the first direction at the shoulders. This is the *tribhanga* posture of which Indian sculptors made so much; but never is it so pronounced, so aggressively *déhanchée*, as we find it in Indian treatments of the sixth century or, for that matter, in their Chinese counterparts of the seventh. *pls 133, 134*

All these tendencies are conveniently illustrated by the white sandstone cave-sculptures of T'ien-lung-shan, a few miles south-west of T'ai-yüan in Shansi. This master-work was begun soon after the founding of the Northern Ch'i dynasty, and was continued into the T'ang and beyond. A particularly strong Indian impulse, it seems, was being directed towards T'ien-lung-shan – indeed, Sirén suggests that Indian sculptors may have worked there – and its contents represent the *avant-garde* of Chinese Buddhist sculpture during much of the Second and Third Phases. *pls 131, 141*

Plate 131 shows one of the oldest parts of T'ien-lung-shan, the west wall of Cave 3 dating from AD 560. A simple and orderly arrangement is adopted in this and other early caves at the site – a trinity of which Śākyamuni Buddha is central figure on the north wall, an Amitābha trinity on the east, and a Maitreya trinity, shown here, on the west. There are some accessory figures in very low relief, and walls and ceiling were once brightly painted, yet the contrast between this sober layout and the unplanned profusion of First Phase sculpture at Yün-kang and Lung-mên leaps to the eye. Moreover, the carving of the main images, judged by First Phase standards, is in surprisingly high relief. The treatment of the gown is still linear, but its folds are far more deeply undercut; they still project in winglike lobes from the sides and lower hem of the skirt, but their whole appearance is softer and more rounded, and the emotional tension drops in consequence. *pl. 131*

Sculptures in Caves 10 and 16 at T'ien-lung-shan are rather later, and are more directly modelled on Indian prototypes, than are those of Caves 1, 2, and 3. Indeed, the critical swing in favour of Gupta conventions probably occurred sometime between the making of these two groups. For in this second group there is no reference at all to the First Phase linear convention. The stark Gupta formula – body a rounded and monumental mass, gown a series of light incisions upon its surface – is peremptorily commandeered. A large Śākyamuni seated in *dhyāna*, right hand in *abhaya* and left in *vara*, in Cave 16, resembles seated Buddhas of the fifth and sixth centuries AD from Sārnāth closely enough to persuade us that its maker, whether Chinese or Indian, worked directly from a Gupta model.

Here, for a moment, Chinese and Indian traditions seem to meet. But towards the end of the Second Phase the former again begins to diverge. Sui pieces at T'ien-lung-shan are of inferior quality and in poor condition; and the best-known examples of late Second Phase work come from various sites in Hopei and Shantung.

42 Image of Śākyamuni in Cave 16, T'ien-lung-shan, Shansi. Second Phase

The school of Ch'ü-yang in south Hopei [p. 202], working in the local white micaceous marble, begins to be prominent towards the end of the Northern Ch'i. Like the sculptures of Caves 10 and 16 at T'ien-lung-shan, Ch'ü-yang work has a monumental massivity – from which the lightly etched mantle-folds in no way detract – but the mass has grown stylized and abstract. We now contemplate not so much the surface brilliance of carved drapery, or the evocative beauty of an underlying body, as a certain type of abstract volume for its own sake. The favoured shape is ovoid, and the plastic mass grows in volume from the feet and culminates in the weighty, rounded shoulders. Sirén observes that this movement is directly contrary to that preferred by First Phase and early Second Phase sculptors, in which the mass grows downwards from a small head and narrow, sloping shoulders, to culminate in the pea-cock magnificence of the skirt.

pl. 135   Pride of place among these images must be given to the colossal standing Amitābha of plate 135, now in the British Museum. Mantle-folds, we observe, are reduced to lightest possible relief, and the wavelike band at the lower hem is all that is left of the multitudinous pointed lobes so distinctive of First Phase treatments. A Second Phase characteristic is presence of three horizontal creases on the neck, a common feature of the Kushān and Gupta Buddha image; and a mannerism seemingly confined to the Sui period is the double-curved eyelid.

Among its minor features, the Second Phase exhibits great wealth of floral and other ac-cessory ornament on halos, above niches, above doorway arches, as decorative bands on steles, *pl. 132*   and on carved or incised lunettes and balustrades. Nearly all this art is exotic. The lotus, as rosette or as plant-trail, in which it seems to be crossed with the Western acanthus, comes *pls 129, 136*   ultimately from India, as do various types of *bodhi*-tree, *apsaras* bearing garlands, *yakshas* hold-ing up censers, and grotesque masks supporting *stūpas*. Of Iranian and Hellenistic ancestry is the vine-trail [p. 276]; and an oval jewel enclosed in a beaded border, distinctive of the Phase, is Sassanid Persian. All this decoration, and especially plant-trail and lotus rosette, is carved with great care and precision; something of its quality can be gauged from the Vimalakīrti *pl. 128*   scene shown on plate 128.

pl. 131   The atmospheric, vaguely Baroque, effect of layouts such as the Maitreya group of plate 131 is reproduced in the forms of elaborately carved and pierced stone lunettes, balustrades, and steles, distinctive of the Phase. The steles are especially interesting. Twin *bodhi*-trees stand erect, forming the sides of a massive aureole, and project upwards a luxuriant canopy of leaves. *fig. 43*   Against this backcloth are pinned flying *apsaras* bearing jewelled garlands. Often the *stūpa* of Śākyamuni and Prabhūtaratna [p. 190], held aloft by a *yaksha* and festooned with garlands, closes the design above. Through irregular perforations of varying size, light falls on to the forms of the main personages seated or standing in their formal group beneath the trees. The scene has a vivid, theatrical quality; and the figures, like persons in a tableau, create an im-pression of actuality, the direct outcome of that feeling for three-dimensional space which was the greatest single acquisition of the Second Phase.

THE THIRD PHASE   By the end of the Second Phase, Chinese sculpture had deviated quite perceptibly from the
(AD 618–*c.* 700)   stylistic standards of Gupta art. Images such as the Amitābha colossus of plate 135 have little
pls 138–151   in common with contemporary Indian work, despite direct descent from Gupta-inspired
fig. 42   models such as the Northern Ch'i Buddha of figure 42. During the Third Phase a decided reaction in favour of Indian standards set in. This renaissance does not coincide with the chronological limits of the T'ang dynasty (AD 618–906). A concourse of recorded events beginning with the return of Hsüan-ts'ang to China in AD 645 [p. 180], and terminating with the building of the Ch'i-pao Terrace of the K'uang-chai Temple at the capital, Ch'ang-

an, under Empress Wu (AD 684–705), helps us to fix the period of vital achievement in the second half of the seventh century. By the beginning of the eighth, the creative stream is running dry. There is no new infusion of style or subject-matter; modelling becomes clumsy, workmanship inferior. We therefore close our account of Chinese sculpture at this point.

The Phase is marked by unprecedented interest in the human form. Chinese sculpture now surrenders, momentarily but completely, to the seductions of the mature Gupta style. Free-standing images of the Bodhisattvas and of Brahmanical gods such as Vishnu, as well as the figural sculptures and murals in rock-cut temples such as Ajaṇṭā and Nāsik, dating from about the sixth century AD, became models for the entire world of Buddhist art in the succeeding centuries. T'ang sculptors carry a stage further the trends already manifest in Second Phase style – naturalistic treatment of mask, reduction of gown to a tracery of lines so that it forms a *draperie mouillée* over the naked body beneath, and modelling of figures in the round and as though in movement.

43 Stone stele showing Maitreya Bodhisattva in the Tuśita Heaven. Second Phase

44 Two Bodhisattva torsos: *a* from Sāñchī, India; *b* from Lung-yen-shan, Paoting, Hopei (plate 139)

pl. 139

pl. 138
pl. 139

pl. 145

pl. 148

pl. 146

pl. 141

pl. 142

The highest refinements of Third Phase style are best exhibited by Bodhisattva images. That illustrated in figure 44, reported to have come from a temple at Lung-yen-shan near Pao-ting, Hopei, has been recommended as 'perhaps the finest example of Buddhist sculpture in existence'.[38] It stands in a pronounced *hanche* posture. The weight rests upon the right leg, which is somewhat advanced, while the left, a little behind, is slightly flexed and poised on the ball of the foot as if about to step forward. This movement swings the left hip outwards so that the trunk inclines at an angle to the legs, the right shoulder rising to restore the balance; were head and neck present their axis would again be parallel to that of the legs. Modelling is naturalistic, skilfully suggesting the texture of firm and supple flesh, while well-developed chest, narrow waist, and broad hips give the image an almost feminine air. In figure 44 I have set it beside an Indian Gupta Bodhisattva image, perhaps of Maitreya, to show how closely together the two national styles now ran. The Indian piece is conceivably a little later than the Chinese; but this does not matter for our purpose, which is to provide an ocular demonstration of the successful hybridization of the lovely late Gupta formula in Chinese sculpture of the second half of the seventh century AD.

The images originally installed on the Ch'i-pao Terrace at Ch'ang-an [p. 200], transferred thence to the Pao-ch'ing Temple in the same city, and thence to various Japanese and American collections, are clearly the work of a local *atelier* and must all have been done at about the same time. They consist of Buddha trinities, and single images of the Eleven-headed Avalokiteśvara which resemble in their style a free-standing statue of the same divinity dated AD 691. A characteristic specimen is shown on plate 138. Comparison between it and the Lung-yen-shan Bodhisattva is instructive. For the former would appear to be a deliberately 'sinified' version of the latter. Note a close similarity in treatment of the lower garment below the girdle and a broad resemblance in detailing of necklet and scarf upon the chest. Yet what a world of difference in style and execution. The modelling of the Lung-yen-shan Bodhisattva is free and naturalistic. That of the Ch'ang-an image has become strictly methodized; the roll of flesh forced up by pressure of the girdle, for example, is quite clearly rendered according to a formula. Moreover, graceful and infinitely dignified as this image appears, it has lapsed into a rooted Chinese immobility of posture. There is only the barest suggestion of *tribhanga*. The foot of the slightly flexed left leg is advanced a mere inch or so, while the comparative slimness of the hips corrects what Chinese sculptors may have felt to be an unduly profane feature of Indian prototypes.

Here, then, is what appears to be the cursory re-styling of an exotic formula, done to conform with national aesthetic standards and by no means the first of its kind. If this is so, the Lung-yen-shan Bodhisattva may be awarded an earlier date than those from Ch'ang-an. The recently rediscovered cave-shrines at P'ing-ling-ssŭ in southern Kansu help to confirm this view. Of the lovely sculptures in site at these caves none is more revealing than the Amitābha group shown on plate 145; the image third from the left, strictly Avalokiteśvara, has all the vernal freshness and animation of pose displayed by the Lung-yen-shan piece. Note the emphatic *tribhanga* in which the divinity stands, a pose even more uncompromisingly adopted by the Avalokiteśvara of plate 148, also from P'ing-ling-ssŭ.

Presence of the Guardian King Vaiśravana at the far end of this *tableau* immediately relates it to the colossal Amitābha group at Lung-mên, carved between AD 672 and 675. I am therefore inclined to place the P'ing-ling-ssŭ images, as well as that from Lung-yen-shan and the T'ien-lung-shan Bodhisattva of plate 141 in the eighth decade of the century.[39]

Provenance and material both identify the Lung-yen-shan Bodhisattva as a product of the Ch'ü-yang school. The fine headless torso of plate 142 was found in the immediate vicinity of this place, 17 miles north-west of Ting-chou. It, too, is made of the local white micaceous marble. We have here an image standing in some stylistic relationship to the Seiryō copy of the alleged 'Udayāna' portrait of Śākyamuni discussed above [pp. 182–183], as is apparent when we examine the treatment of the mantle-folds in the two cases. The distinctive arrange- ment of the folds on the *back* of the image also resembles that found on a series of wooden figures in Japanese temples, dating from AD 800 to 1300, which in other respects conform to the 'Udayāna' type.[40] We saw that one of the statues brought by Hsüan-ts'ang from India in AD 645 was claimed as a true copy of the 'Udayāna' image seen by him at Kauśāmbī, and that the latter was in all probability a Gupta piece of no great antiquity. It may very well be, therefore, that the Ch'ü-yang image was based on some such prototype, and was made not long after the pilgrim's return to China.

pl. 143, fig. 39d
pl. 144

The fact that it was found in the precincts of a temple dating only from the eleventh cen- tury has led some to propose a Sung date for the Ch'ü-yang image. To my mind it has none of the overtones of an archaistic piece, while the verve and spontaneity of its workmanship would hardly have been possible before the opening of the Third Phase. Perhaps the closest Chinese parallel is an image of Maitreya in Cave 4 at Lung-mên, bearing a date correspond- ing to AD 648. In short, the Ch'ü-yang statue has good claim to be accepted as an early image in the true line of descent of the Far Eastern 'Udayāna' portrayal – a rare masterpiece dating from the last great burst of creative achievement in the history of Chinese sculpture.

Positions of the hands (mudrā) and of the legs (āsana)

MUDRĀ

1. *Bhūmisparśa:* 'Earth-touching'. Right arm pendent, hand turned palm inwards and point- ing downwards as though touching the ground.
2. *Abhaya:* 'Freedom from fear'. Right arm flexed, hand shoulder-high, palm turned out- wards and pointing downwards.
3. *Vara:* 'Giving'. Left arm pendent, hand turned palm outwards and pointing downwards.
4. *Dharmacakra:* 'Preaching'. Arms flexed, hands held before breast. Tip of thumb and of one finger of one hand touch one finger of the other.
5. *Vitarka:* 'Discussion'. One arm flexed, hand held before breast, palm outwards. Tip of thumb touches that of one other finger.
6. *Añjali:* 'Adoration'. Arms flexed, hands held before breast, palms together, fingers point- ing upwards.
7. *Dhyāna:* 'Meditation'. Many variants. In all arms are flexed, hands lie on lap, one on top of the other or with fingers interlocked.

ĀSANA

A. *Seated*

1. *Dhyāna (Padma, Paryanka):* 'Meditation', 'Lotus', etc. Legs flexed and interlocked, feet resting on opposite thighs, soles upwards.
2. *Bhadra:* Sometimes called 'European'. Both legs pendent, separate, or with ankles crossed.
3. *Lalitā:* One leg pendent, other flexed in a horizontal position, its foot resting on opposite thigh.
4. *Mahārājalila (Ardha-paryanka):* 'Royal ease'. Both legs flexed, one vertical, other horizontal, feet touching.

B. *Standing*

5. *Kayotsarga:* Feet symmetrically placed, weight equally balanced between them.
6. *Tribhaṅga:* 'Thrice bent'. Weight rests on one leg. Other knee is bent, foot slightly ad- vanced. Thus the line of the hips is oblique, and that of the shoulders slopes in the oppo- site direction.

BUDDHAS						
	ŚĀKYAMUNI (*Ch. Shih-chia*)		MAITREYA (*Ch. Mi-lo*)		AMITĀBHA (*Ch. O-mi-t'o*)	
	standing	*seated*	*standing*	*seated*	*standing*	*seated*
ĀSANA	kayotsarga	dhyāna	kayotsarga	bhadra (rarely with ankles crossed)	kayotsarga	dhyāna
MUDRĀ	abhaya and vara (or left hand holding gown) vitarka	abhaya and vara dhyāna, dharmacakra, vitarka, bhūmisparśa	abhaya and vara (or left hand free)	abhaya and vara (or left hand free)	abhaya and vara	abhaya and vara
SUPPORT	lotus pedestal	lotus throne lion throne diamond throne	lotus pedestal	lotus throne lion throne	lotus pedestal	lotus throne
ATTRIBUTES	alms-bowl rarely	nil	alms-bowl and/or ambrosia flask in some early examples		nil	nil
HALO (aureole or niche)	Seven Buddhas of the Past		Seven Buddhas of the Past		Five Dhyāni Buddhas	
ATTENDANTS AND ASSOCIATED COMPLEX	usually appears as a single cult-image ⟨optional in scenes portraying the preaching of the Lotus Sūtra are:⟩	2 Bodhisattvas (usually Maitreya and Avalokiteśvara, sometimes Mañjuśrī and Samantabhadra); 2 disciples (Ānanda and Kāśyapa); 2 lay monks; 2 guardians; dwarf yaksha supporting censer; Mañjuśrī and Vimalikīrti; *ad lib.*	usually appears as a single cult-image	2 Bodhisattvas either standing or seated in 'meditating' pose (*ssŭ wei*)	usually appears as a single cult-image ⟨optional in Paradise scenes are:⟩	2 Bodhisattvas (Mahāsthāmaprāpta and Avalokiteśvara) 2 disciples; 2 lay monks; 2 guardians; 2 lokopālas; dwarf yaksha supporting censer; reborn souls emerging from lotus calyxes

BODHISATTVAS					
	MAITREYA (*Ch. Mi-lo*)			AVALOKITEŚVARA (*Ch. Kuan-yin*)	
	standing	*seated*	*seated*	*standing*	*seated*
ĀSANA	kayotsarga tribhanga	lalitā	crossed ankles (rarely bhadra)	kayotsarga tribhanga	lalitā, dhyāna, mahārājali (typical of Fourth Phase wood sculpture)
MUDRĀ	añjali	'meditating' pose (*ssŭ wei*)	abhaya and vara dharmacakra	abhaya and vara, vitarka and vara; in trinities: añjali otherwise unorthodox	dhyāna; in trinities: añjali otherwise unorthodox
SUPPORT	lotus pedestal	jewel throne with lion supporters	feet may be upheld by Earth Goddess or 2 dwarf yakshas; lion supporters	lotus pedestal	lotus throne
ATTRIBUTES	in some early examples while the right hand is in abhaya mudrā the left hand holds a flask or fold of dhoti in trinities, often the same attributes are carried as Avalokiteśvara: flask in one hand, lotus bud or fly-whisk in the other		Dhyāni Buddha often appears in head-dress	lotus, fly-whisk, willow-branch, or purselike object in upheld hand; water-flask (kuṇḍikā) or bottle in lowered hand; Dhyāni Buddha in head-dress; Tantric forms	Dhyāni Buddha in head-dress
HALO (aureole or niche)	Seven Buddhas of the Past			Seven Buddhas of the Past or Five Dhyāni Buddhas	
ATTENDANTS AND ASSOCIATED COMPLEX	in trinities, or larger groups, usually stands on left of Śākyamuni	2 standing Bodhisattvas; 2 guardians; yaksha supporting a censer; flying apsaras bearing garland; grotesque mask supporting stūpa; bodhi-tree; *ad lib.* (Maitreya gaining Enlightenment under the bodhi-tree)	2 'meditating' Bodhisattvas (up to AD 510); 2 standing Bodhisattvas (after AD 510); 2 kneeling monks in añjali mudrā (after AD 510); 2 guardians (after AD 510); lay figures worshipping a censer; *ad lib.* (rarely Maitreya as a Buddha) (Maitreya in the Tuśita Heaven)	usually appears as a single cult-image one of the two Bodhisattvas in Śākyamuni and Amitābha trinities	

119 Gilt-bronze votive statuette of Śā-kyamuni Buddha. First Phase, dated AD 338. By far the earliest dated Buddha image yet found in China, it shows Śākyamuni sitting in *dhyāna mudrā* and *āsana*. With its Apollo-like mask, and the folds of its gown methodized after the Mathurā manner, this image must be regarded as a provincial, that is a Chinese, version of a late Gandhāra prototype. For a particularly close parallel see O. Sirén (1925, plate 238a) and H. Münsterberg (1956, plate 1). Height: 15½ in. M. H. de Young Museum, San Francisco.

120 Colossal red sandstone image of a Buddha with an attendant Buddha. First Phase, Northern Wei dynasty, reign of Hsiao Wên-ti (AD 471–499). *In situ* at Cave 22, the Yün-kang Caves, Shensi. The Buddha sits in *dhyāna āsana* and *mudrā,* and is probably Śākyamuni. His attendant is perhaps Maitreya. Note the similarity of the latter to that of plate 121. Height: *c.*540 in.

121 Gilt-bronze votive statuette of Maitreya Buddha. First Phase, Northern Wei dynasty, dated AD 477. The Buddha is Maitreya, his hands more or less in *abhaya* and *vara.* This is the most important of thirty-five known dated bronze statuettes made between AD 390 and 500. Height: 55¼ in. Metropolitan Museum, New York.

FIRST PHASE: THE LESSER STYLE

122 Grey limestone image of Maitreya Bodhisattva. First Phase, Northern Wei dynasty, early sixth century AD. From the Lung-mên Caves, Honan. Maitreya Bodhisattva is sitting in the Tuśita Heaven awaiting the moment of his final incarnation on Earth, and his coming Buddhahood. A perfect example of the lesser First Phase style. Height: 21 1/4 in. Rietberg-Museum, Zurich.

123 Grey limestone image of a celestial musician (*gandharva*). First Phase, Northern Wei dynasty, early sixth century AD. Probably from the Lung-mên Caves, Honan. Height: 25 1/4 in. Victoria and Albert Museum.

FIRST PHASE:
LINEAR ELABORATION OF MANTLE-FOLDS

124 Gilt-bronze votive statuette of Śākyamuni Bud-dha. First Phase, Northern Wei dynasty, early sixth century AD. Found in Hopei. One of an early group of bronze statuettes showing the Buddha on a lotus pedestal, hands in *abhaya* and *vara*. Height with pedestal: *c.* 12 in. Metropolitan Museum, New York.

125 Gilt-bronze votive statuette of Maitreya Buddha. First Phase, Eastern Wei dynasty, dated AD 536. The Buddha stands in *abhaya* and *vara mudrā* and is backed with a leaf-shaped aureole of exquisite workmanship. Height: 24 in. University of Pennsylvania Museum, Philadelphia.

126 Grey limestone votive stele. First Phase, Eastern Wei dynasty, dated AD 536. From Honan. The scene is the Preaching of the Lotus *sūtra*. Śākya-muni is seated in *dhyāna āsana* on the Lion Throne, hands in *abhaya* and *vara*. He is attended on his proper right by Kāśyapa, Avalokiteśvara in *añjali,* and a guardian (*dvārapāla*), and on his left by Ananda, Maitreya in *añjali,* and a guardian. Remaining height: 40 ³/₅ in. Rietberg-Museum, Zurich.

127 and 128 Stone memorial stele (the Trübner stele). First Phase,
Eastern Wei dynasty, dated AD 543. Found in the Tsung-ning ssǔ,
Honan. The top register (half of it now broken off) features a niche
containing Śākyamuni preaching the Lotus *sūtra* on the Vulture Peak
[see pl. 126].

The middle register (in detail on the right) represents the meeting of
Vimalikīrti with Mañjuśrī described on page 194. To the left on a
lotus throne (*padmāsana*), beneath an enriched canopy, sits Mañjuśrī.
He wears the princely costume of a Bodhisattva and his head is adorned
with a circular halo. His right hand is in *abhaya* and in his left he holds
the *t'an-p'ing,* or wand of discussion. He is attended by some thirty
persons. Towards the centre appears the dignified figure of Śāriputra,
engaged in dispute with the Heavenly Maiden, who stands on the
other side of a pair of Gingko trees. The bearded Vimalikīrti sits in a
decorated house on the right, with fourteen attendants. He wears a
heavily padded gown and holds his attribute, a fan, in his left hand.
Above the house can be seen a Bodhisattva bearing one of the thirty-
two thousand lion thrones; and to the left and right above the Gingko
trees are other flying Bodhisattvas with bowls of food. Beneath the
panel two lines of donors in separate niches are shown, each accompanied by an attendant bearing an umbrella, and named in an adjacent
cartouche. Remaining height of stele with base: 156 in., width: 44 in.
Metropolitan Museum, New York.

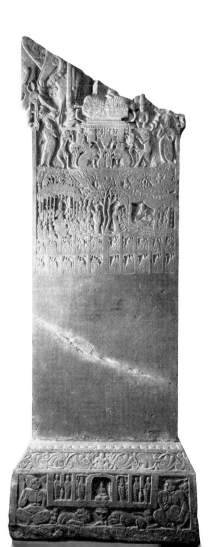

129 (left) Stone votive stele of the Yen family, dated AD 557. The central figure is probably Śākyamuni Buddha, although his posture is not. At his sides are Ananda and Kāśyapa, then the two traditional Indian monks (*bhikshus*) with conical coiled head-dresses, and then two indefinable Bodhisattvas. Below the throne are high-stemmed lotus flowers and guardian figures and lions surrounding an incense burner supported by a *yaksha*. Above the central group is a Vimalikīrti scene [see pl. 128]. At the top are the traditional pair of interlacing dragons, here on a monumental scale, draped around a niche containing Maitreya. Height: 59 in. Rietberg Museum, Zurich.

130 (centre) Dark grey limestone image of Avalokiteśvara. Second Phase, Northern Ch'i dynasty (AD 550–577). A standing miniature Amitābha Buddha appears in the head-dress. Height: 61 in. Victoria Gallery of Art, Melbourne.

131 (above) Sandstone image of Maitreya Buddha attended by two Bodhisattvas. Second Phase, Northern Ch'i dynasty (AD 550–577). *In situ* on west wall of Cave 3, the T'ien-lung-shan Caves, Shansi. The Buddha sits in *bhadrāsana*, the posture distinctive of Maitreya Buddha in Chinese Buddhist sculpture. The attendant Bodhisattvas are probably meant for Śākyamuni and Maitreya himself. This is one of three similar trinities occupying Cave 3.

132 Grey limestone slab. Second Phase, Northern Ch'i dynasty, c. AD 570–585. From south Hsian-t'ang-shan near Ching-tê, Hopei. The slab features the Paradise of Amitābha. Before the main Buddha is a lotus tank with infant souls being reborn as Buddhas from lotus calices.

To left and right are Mahāsthāmaprāpta and Avalokiteśvara. Back
stage, left and right, are two-storeyed pavilions with what appear to be
curved roofs [see pp. 390*ff.*]. Height: 131 3/4 in. Freer Gallery of Art,
Washington.

133 (far left) Stone image of Avalokiteśvara. Second
Phase, Northern Chou dynasty (AD 557–580). From
Ch'ang-an, Shensi. The Bodhisattva holds in the
upraised left hand a cluster of lotus buds. A small
seated image of Amitābha Buddha appears in the
head-dress. Height: 98 ½ in. Museum of Fine Arts,
Boston.

134 (centre) Grey limestone image of a Bodhisattva.
Second Phase, Northern Chou dynasty (AD 557–580).
This image, almost certainly of Avalokiteśvara, is ex-
ceptional among Northern Chou pieces for the re-
straint and sensitivity of its modelling. Height: 37 in.
Victoria and Albert Museum.

135 (right) Colossal white micaceous marble image
of a standing Amitābha Buddha. Second Phase, Sui
dynasty, dated AD 585. Found at Hsiang-pei near
Ting-chou, Hopei. The Buddha stands in *abhaya* and
vara. This sculpture is a product of the nearby Ch'ü-
yang *ateliers*. See page 200. Height: 216 in. British
Museum.

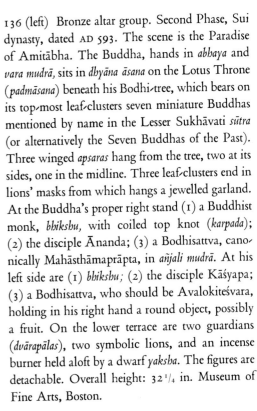

136 (left) Bronze altar group. Second Phase, Sui dynasty, dated AD 593. The scene is the Paradise of Amitābha. The Buddha, hands in *abhaya* and *vara mudrā*, sits in *dhyāna āsana* on the Lotus Throne (*padmāsana*) beneath his Bodhi-tree, which bears on its top-most leaf-clusters seven miniature Buddhas mentioned by name in the Lesser Sukhāvatī *sūtra* (or alternatively the Seven Buddhas of the Past). Three winged *apsaras* hang from the tree, two at its sides, one in the midline. Three leaf-clusters end in lions' masks from which hangs a jewelled garland. At the Buddha's proper right stand (1) a Buddhist monk, *bhikshu*, with coiled top knot (*karpada*); (2) the disciple Ānanda; (3) a Bodhisattva, cano-nically Mahāsthāmaprāpta, in *añjali mudrā*. At his left side are (1) *bhikshu;* (2) the disciple Kāśyapa; (3) a Bodhisattva, who should be Avalokiteśvara, holding in his right hand a round object, possibly a fruit. On the lower terrace are two guardians (*dvārapālas*), two symbolic lions, and an incense burner held aloft by a dwarf *yaksha*. The figures are detachable. Overall height: 32¼ in. Museum of Fine Arts, Boston.

137 (below) Gilt-bronze votive statuette of the Bodhisattva Avalokiteśvara. Second Phase, Sui dynasty (AD 589–618). In his left hand the Bo-dhisattva holds a fly-whisk (*chauri*), in his right an *amṛta kalaśa* or ambrosia flask. See figure 55 c. Height: 22.9 in. Stoclet Collection, Brussels.

138 (below) Stone image of the Eleven-Headed Avalokiteśvara Samantamukha, 'All-Sided One'. Third Phase,
T'ang dynasty, *c.* AD 690. From the Ch'i-pao Terrace,
Sian, Shensi. Ten heads appear in the head-dress. The
Bodhisattva stands in slight *tribhanga,* left hand holding
a lotus bud; other attributes are indecipherable. Height:
30 ⁵/₈ in. Freer Gallery of Art, Washington.

139 (right) Headless white micaceous marble statue of a
Bodhisattva. Third Phase, T'ang dynasty, *c.* AD 670.
From Lung-yen-shan, Pao-ting, Hopei. A superb example of the Ch'ü-yang school. See pages 201–202 and
figure 44 b. Height: 73 in.

140 Image of a Buddha, dry lacquer on wood with traces of lacquer paint. Third Phase, T'ang dynasty, early seventh century AD. From the Tai-ssŭ Temple, Chêng-ting-fu, Hopei. The Buddha sits in *dhyāna mudrā* and *āsana* and is probably Amitābha. Height: 38 in. Metropolitan Museum, New York.

141 (right) Sandstone image of a Bodhisattva. Third Phase, T'ang dynasty, end of seventh century AD. From the T'ien-lung-shan Caves, Shansi. The Bodhisattva stands in slight *tribhaṇga*. It is not possible to determine his identity. His high chignon seems to be broken off. Height: 27 ¹/₂ in. Royal Ontario Museum, Toronto.

142, 143 and 144 Side, front and back views of a white micaceous marble image of a standing Buddha. Third Phase, T'ang dynasty, *c.* AD 670. From the Hsiu-tê Pagoda near Ch'ü-yang, Ting-chou, Hopei. The Buddha is probably Śākyamuni. Its possible relationship with the Udayāna image of Śākyamuni is discussed on pages 202–203. It is a typical product of the Ch'ü-yang school. Height: 57 in. Victoria and Albert Museum.

opposite page

145 Red sandstone image of a Buddha accompanied by two Bodhisattvas and two Guardian Kings (loko-palas) of which only one can be seen. Third Phase, T'ang dynasty, about AD 670. *In situ* in Niche 51, the P'ing-ling-ssŭ Caves, Lesser Chi-shih Hills, Yung-ching county, Kansu. The Buddha is probably Ami-tābha, and the Bodhisattva on his left, standing in extreme *tribhaṇga* [*cf.* pl. 148], is then Avalokiteśvara. The Guardian King at the far end, upheld by a dwarf *yaksha,* is Vaiśravana, the ruler of the North and of the *yakshas.* The attribute held in his right hand is probably a *stūpa* [*cf.* pls 146 and 147].

146 (above left) The north wall of the Fêng-hsien grotto [see pls 149 and 150] showing an attendant *dvārapāla* (guardian) at the right and at the left the Guardian King of the North, Vaiśravana [*cf.* pls 145 and 147], standing on a dwarf *yaksha* and holding a model *stūpa* in his left hand.

147 (above right) Tomb-figure in the form of Vaiś-ravana (To-wên), the Guardian King of the North; off-white earthenware splashed with green and amber glazes. From a tomb at Han-shên-chai, Sian, Shensi. T'ang dynasty, *c.* AD 650.

148 Stone image of the Bodhisattva Avalokiteśvara. Third Phase, T'ang dynasty, *c.* AD 670. *In situ* in Niche 50 at the P'ing-ling-ssŭ Caves, Lesser Chi-shih Hills, Yung-ching county, Kansu. The Bodhisattva stands in marked *tribhaṇga,* holding in the left hand a lotus bud on a stalk, in the right an ascetic's water-flask. See figure 55 a. Notice the skirt (*dhoti*) closely moulded to the body.

149 and 150 Colossal grey limestone image of Ami-tābha Buddha (in detail on the opposite page) in *dhyāna āsana* and *mudrā,* on the rear wall of the Fêng-hsien grotto at the Lung-mên Caves, Honan. Third Phase, T'ang dynasty, AD 672–675. The Buddha is accompanied by two standing *bhikshus* (monks) and two Bodhisattvas (one only of each shown here). The Bodhisattvas are presumably Avalokiteśvara and Ma-hāsthāmaprāpta. An inscription on the plinth records that the T'ang dynasty Empress Wu in AD 672 gave twenty thousand strings of cash from the cosmetics fund towards the cost of the image. It was finished three years later. Height: *c.* 600 in.

151 Grey limestone head of a colossal Buddha, with traces of paint‑
ing and gilding. Third Phase, T'ang dynasty, *c.* AD 650–700. Prob‑
ably from the Lung‑mên Caves, Honan. The hair is rendered ac‑
cording to the 'peppercorn curl' convention. The *ūrṇā* is of darker
stone fitted into the forehead. Height: 24 in. Rietberg‑Museum,
Zurich.

VI POTTERY: THE T'ANG AND FIVE DYNASTIES

The speciality of Chinese pottery

A nation's pottery is one of the hallmarks of its culture. We all know that the historical advance from savagery to what has been called 'Neolithic barbarism' coincided with a change from nomadic to settled economy, consequent on the discovery of agriculture. Among other acquisitions made at this stage, pottery is outstanding; and the main pottery traditions of Eurasia naturally stem from the four great river valleys – Nile, Tigris-Euphrates, Indus, and Yellow River – where were the earliest agricultural settlements. Successful creation of a pottery tradition, indeed, depends on a complex of factors which obtained only among the river-valley agriculturalists. First, pottery-making is necessarily a sedentary occupation; the potter has to stay in one place while he takes the pot through the successive stages of its manufacture. Second, settled living conditions promote the growth of pottery industries, while nomadic life retards it; since pots, being fragile, are comparatively useless to the nomad but make practical utensils in the hands of the householder. Third, the alluvial plains of the great rivers provide superabundance of highly plastic secondary clays, from which simple pots can most readily be made.

Other factors help to build up a rich and stable pottery tradition. One is what Gordon Childe calls 'multiplication of wants in an advanced society'. Pots are now needed to serve a wide range of domestic requirements, and their manufacture becomes the full-time occupation of a specialist. Lastly settled livelihood brings with it leisure, and with leisure a growing taste for things pleasing to live with as well as serviceable. The potter is now a craftsman, and gains an important voice in the community. He can demand from it the economic security he needs to explore his technical resources, and produce better and better-looking pots.

These conditions have, of course, existed at various times all over the world. But in no region have they been more fully or continuously fulfilled than in the great alluvial plains of China, where settled life has been lived steadily for over 4,000 years, and where shortage of other materials suitable for making pots has been offset by great wealth of all types of clay. As a result, China has led the rest of the world in respect of the technical and artistic excellence of her pottery during most of that time.

Among early inventions, that of the potter's wheel was crucial; for it allowed him to throw, in the space of a minute or two and with pleasing symmetry, a vessel that might have taken an hour to build up by hand alone. In western Asia the wheel was in general use by the beginning of the third millennium BC, whereas we have no evidence of its use in China until about a thousand years later. Again, a great advance is made with the discovery of glaze, by which a porous pottery body is rendered impermeable to liquids. Glazes maturing at low temperatures were used in the Near East as early as the fourth millennium BC and nothing at all comparable in antiquity comes out of China. Her ceramic record begins about the middle of the third millennium BC with the manufacture of the exquisite although tech-nically fairly straightforward wares discussed in chapter one. At the very outset the Chinese seems to have been a natural potter; during ensuing centuries his insights into the nature and potentiality of his materials led him to discover the complex secret of vitrification, and by about 1500 BC the ancestors of the high-fired porcellanous stonewares and porcelains of T'ang and Sung times were already born [p. 256].

As we shall see by and by, it was in making these high-fired vitrified wares that the Chin-ese potter so outshone all others. From at least as early as the ninth century AD the rest of the world regarded them with awe and wonderment, and their commercial distribution was vast [p. 255]. They were credited with miraculous powers. Those that reached Europe during our Middle Ages were lovingly cradled in costly Gothic silver-gilt mountings. And again, when western European Powers began to trade direct with the Far East in the sixteenth and seven-teenth centuries, these were the goods that were above everything else most eagerly sought. Western alchemists gave up their attempts to transmute base metals into gold, and instead sought to discover the secret of the translucency, brilliance, and hardness of the wares they came to call 'porcelain'.

One can fairly say that from the time of Dwight at Fulham and Böttcher at Meissen, around the end of the seventeenth century, the main stream of European ceramic art flowed in a chan-nel previously moulded by Chinese potters. The influence was almost entirely one-sided. Dur-ing the eighteenth century, it is true, enormous overseas demand for Chinese wares did have a marginal effect on the native tradition, and produced the bastard art that the late Dr Cohn aptly called by a bastard name, the *europoiserie*. But this was slight and short-lived compared with the overriding dominion that Chinese potters exercised over European ceramics; so that not only bodies and glazes, but shapes and decoration as well, were made to resemble Chinese models as closely as possible. Only recently has Europe shown any sign of recover-ing her earlier ceramic genius, and even today many studio potters and industrial designers still seem unable to break away from the authoritarian standards of Chinese pottery.

But the technical expertise of the Chinese potter only partly accounts for the fascination we find in his wares. At the risk of seeming obvious, may I say that the beauty of a pot resides in its form – and by form I mean not only its basic shape, but the sum of all its manifest aesthetic properties. While the form taken by a given pot necessarily depends on the technical processes involved in its manufacture, the thought that underlies its very creation is the service it is designed to perform. Fitness for purpose is the fundamental requisite in a pot, and is also, according to Plato's proposition, a measure of its beauty. If a bowl, or a tea-pot, or for that matter a drain-pipe, does not conform to a certain basic design it will not be serviceable; but beyond that, I question whether most of us would find such a pot ever really pleasing to the eye, no matter how much care may have been spent in embellishing its appearance. In a very fundamental way, the pleasure we get from a pot springs from our intuitive awareness of its suitability as a vessel. The best pots insistently remind us, as we contemplate them, of the use for which they are intended; and if we seek to handle them, it is perhaps in response to their silent demand to be put to this use, even though they may spend most of their time in a show-case. The tactile appeal of Chinese pottery is particularly strong.

It is of course true that qualities other than bare functional efficiency influence our feelings about the beauty of a pot. It is no less surprising how much pottery which otherwise presents an air of sensibility and good taste fails to pass this basic test. *All* other qualities, it seems to me, naturally follow the first intelligent appraisal on the part of the potter of the service his pot is to perform. Although Chinese pottery shapes are varied and full of subtlety, the ultimate intention of fitness for purpose is seldom lost sight of. Only late in the tradition do we find here and there pots masquerading as objects made of other materials, or pointlessly fanciful in design. Lesser ceramic traditions more frequently employ such disguises and distractions, and indeed the urge to conceal the functional aspect of a manufactured article by every means, or to present it as a whimsical imitation of another, is not confined to potters in particular, but seems to be a sporadic aberration of the whole race of industrial designers.

*

The fullest definition of a vessel's form would include its decoration too. We see today a reaction in favour of decoration in the applied arts, due partly no doubt to the insistence with which so many functionalist designers proclaimed that *mere* utility is synonymous with beauty. That is of course nonsense. A plain earthenware tea-pot is satisfying because it has been honestly designed and with purposeful intent. It is not a work of art. There is a world of difference between articles made as simply and as cheaply as possible, in order to meet a bare minimum specification, and those in which aesthetic ends are consciously sought. But again, decoration must never be allowed to become an end in itself. Since it is an integral part of form its character must be determined by basic shape, and so ultimately by function. When a pot becomes a mere vehicle for some sort of surface display it falls away from the standard we seek in a work of art.

Much of the painted pottery of European antiquity can be condemned as ceramic rubbish on this score. In Attic black- and red-figure ware, for example, surface decoration attracts our interest away from the underlying shapes of the pots, and does so even when its role is decorative and not iconographic. By the sixth century BC the Greek pot has become little more than a support on which mythological and historical episodes, or scenes from daily life, are depicted. No wonder shapes tend to take on a stereotyped and mechanical character – to efface themselves so to speak. True, these vessels may never have been intended for actual use. This does not alter the fact that in them the basic ceramic values have been destroyed; to my mind, therefore, they are bad pots.

In his *Art and Industry* Sir Herbert Read makes a useful distinction between what he calls 'rational' and 'intuitive' art, and illustrates this by comparing an Attic piece with a Chinese vase of the Sung period. 'Both are without decoration', he says, 'and both depend for their appeal on form alone [that is basic design or shape]. The Greek vase is based on exact measurements, and its proportions are regular ... the Chinese vase does not obey such rules.' We apparently have a real difference in mental climate here. Greek pottery aspired to the standards of modern 'machine art'. The tendency is evident both in shapes and surface decoration. For shape seems to have been rigidly determined by an external pattern; and surface by the criterion of 'shop finish' that Roger Fry found so distasteful when it makes its appearance in art, since it necessarily eliminates all trace of the workings of individual sensibility. Indeed, someone has said that the Greeks deliberately ignored glazing techniques used by earlier Near Eastern potters, and with which they were perfectly familiar, simply because the heavy glazes led to irregularities of surface which could be avoided by using other sorts of finish.

Standards such as this seem to me thoroughly unsound. Clay has a life of its own. As it rises and falls on the wheel, its changing dynamics remind one irresistibly of the impetuous growth-movements of young living things. Indeed, I can think of nothing that conveys so exactly the same impression of plastic resolution, of automaticity and inner purpose, as the first twenty-four hours in the life of a fertilized egg, filmed under the microscope, which with neat and definite orientations, invaginations and extrusions, expansions and contractions, rapidly organizes itself into individuality from an undifferentiated ball of living matter. One almost always gets the same impression when looking at Chinese pottery, even though actual movement has been arrested. Not so with Greek. Much of it looks as though it had never been alive, as though it had been cast and afterwards turned on the lathe following the methods of modern mass-production.

Without continuing the comparison, we may summarize by saying that the genius of the Chinese potter lies in a natural and direct approach to his materials, in willing participation in what Honey calls 'the act of collaboration between the craftsman and a mass of wet clay'. The upshot is that Chinese pottery as a whole creates the impression of tremendous artistic integrity. It is an exemplary art. And if we may indent the qualities on which its distinction depends, they are:

1. The pot is designed primarily with an eye to its function as a vessel, and no labour is spent in trying to disguise that function by distorting its shape.

2. Although every technical device known to pottery is fully exploited, no desperate effort is made to get rid of imperfections arising from natural limitations in method or material.

3. Decoration harmonizes with shape. Form, in other words, is an indivisible unity.

Chinese ceramic materials and techniques

The physics and chemistry of pottery manufacture are difficult topics to take up, difficult to understand, and almost impossible to generalize about. Whether we seek help from treatises written by ceramic technologists, or from the empirical records of studio potters, we are likely to be quite baffled by what we read. On the one hand we are led into a world of forbidding abstractions – of lattice structures, ions, colloids, eutectics, and so forth – while on the other we may get drawn into a judicious debate on the relative effects of wood ash of apple or pear upon the distinctive appearance of glazes in which they are compounded. The gap between theoretical and practical approaches seems unbridgeable; and a simple and at the same time scientifically unexceptionable account of the behaviour of ceramic materials in the process of pottery manufacture has not to my knowledge been written, and perhaps in the nature of things never will be.

The classical Chinese potter was a traditional empiricist. Had he ever thought of compiling a handbook for the use of aspiring apprentices, we may be sure he would have confined himself to practical procedures, with perhaps some litanies and rituals for ensuring their success, but certainly with no attempt at any rational explanation or detailed analysis of phenomena observed. Although the tradition was rich, and ever-expanding, it was at heart conservative. The fact that standard types of ware were being produced over hundreds and indeed thousands of years, shows that practical procedures in those sections of the industry devoted to their manufacture were rigidly controlled; there was no other way to make these pots.

col. 35, 36
pls 157, 159 If therefore we select the high-fired, dense, resonant, partly translucent green-tinted celadons and the high-fired, dense, resonant and translucent white porcelains of Hsing type as representing a climax in the Chinese tradition, we may then simply direct our enquiry into ceramic materials and techniques towards an understanding of the way in which these essentially stable types of ware were created. Practically every other aspect of the tradition gets covered in the course of such an enquiry.

232

27 Tomb-figure with winged feline body and grotesque
human head; of fine off-white earthenware splashed with
green, yellowish-brown and colourless glaze. T'ang
dynasty. Height: 13 in. Art Museum, University of
Singapore.

28 *Globular jar with body pushed into a six-sided form and standing on a tall, hollow foot; of stoneware with a tem-moku-type glaze. T'ang dynasty. Height: 4 $^1/_8$ in. Cunliffe Collection, England.*

29 *Jar of greyish-white earthenware largely covered with a lustrous mono-chrome prussian blue glaze. T'ang dy-nasty. Height: 7 $^1/_8$ in. Collection of Marchese G. Litta-Modignani, Capalbio.*

30 (right) *Covered jar of fine buff earthenware largely decorated with green, blue and yellow glaze colours all covered by a translucent and colourless glaze. T'ang dynasty. Height: 10 $^1/_8$ in. British Museum.*

31 Ovoid two-handled jar of grey stoneware partly covered with a cloudy brownish-black temmoku-*type glaze applied in two stages. T'ang dynasty. Height: 7 ³/₈ in. Art Museum, University of Singapore.*

Clays used in pottery manufacture are of two types, primary and secondary. Primary clays are those found in close association with the parent rock from which they were decomposed, whereas secondary clays lie at some distance from the parent rock, whence they have been carried away usually by the action of water. Primary clays are mainly free from mineral impurities (except such as are present in the parent rock) and their particle-size is comparatively large; secondary clays are inextricably contaminated with many incidental mineral and even organic impurities, and their particle-size is comparatively small. In effect this means that a primary clay will be white in colour and will fire white, but will be relatively difficult to work; whereas a secondary clay will be highly plastic and workable because of its small particle-size, but will not as a rule be white nor will it burn pure white. For the production of white ware a white-burning primary clay is clearly essential. The name 'china clay' or *kaolin* is commonly given to a group of chemically allied primary clays having this desirable property. Kaolin derives its name from a locality in the pottery district of Ching-tê-chên in Kiangsi, where it occurs in particularly large deposits. Confusion is liable to arise because the word is applied not only to the raw material but also to its basic chemical constituent, otherwise called kaolinite or pure clay substance. But the latter is present in *all* clays, whether primary or secondary, and whether white-burning or no. Kaolin *is* clay, and all clays contain kaolin in the sense that they all contain pure clay substance. I shall for convenience continue to refer to kaolin in this sense.

Kaolin is composed of alumina, silica, and water roughly in the percentages 40, 46, 14, and is therefore technically a hydrated aluminium-silicate. It is formed by the breakdown of molecules of a closely-related mineral called feldspar, which in company with quartz and mica makes up the substance of the gneiss and granite rocks that cover most of the world's land surface. By far the commonest variety of feldspar is orthoclase or potash spar, $K_2O \cdot Al_2O_3 \cdot 6SiO_2$; and the geologists' view of the formation of kaolin is that on exposure to the action of water and carbon-dioxide potash spar loses its potash, and four molecules of its silica, but gains two molecules of water, and so acquires the theoretical composition of kaolin, namely $Al_2O_3 \cdot 2SiO_2 \cdot 2H_2O$. So far, so good.

Now we well know that for a lump of clay to take durable and permanent form – or a hollow vessel, provisionally fashioned from such a lump – it has to be hardened and densified by firing. If ordinary clay is heated to about 550° C, or somewhat below the red heat of a bonfire, this permanent change will come about. The water chemically combined in the kaolin molecule is expelled, and an aluminium-silicate called metakaolin is formed, $Al_2O_3 \cdot 2SiO_2$. Ware so fired is known as terracotta or unglazed earthenware. Made of red-burning clays, this is the pottery of antiquity and of primitive communities all over the world; in inducing the irreversible changes accompanying its manufacture the primitive potter shows himself, as Anna Shepard puts it, as one of the world's first chemical engineers.[1]

If we continue to heat our sample, a series of thermal reactions takes place in the course of which more silica is expelled from the aluminium-silicate molecule. The final product of this decomposition is an amorphous substance called mullite, $3Al_2O_3 \cdot 2SiO_2$, which begins to form at temperatures between about 900 and 1050° C. In the same temperature range also the free silica in the sample begins to soften and fuse, and then very gradually over a temperature rise of another 300 degrees turns into a viscous, glassy melt in which all other molten substances go into solution. This is vitrification, the physical transformation of clay substance into porcelain.

Throughout the long vitrification interval mullite remains refractory, and indeed crystallizes out in the form of long needle-shaped crystals within the melt. Crystallization of mullite is complete at about 1310° C, and thereafter no change occurs in this highly refractory compound until about 1830° C, at which temperature it dissociates into corundum (Al_2O_3) and liquid silica. We are not concerned with such an extreme heat. The firing range of porcelain, over which it becomes completely vitrified, lies roughly between 1300 and 1400° C; and over this range mullite remains crystalline and stable while the rest of the body has become one homogeneous, amorphous, and increasingly fluid glassy melt. Thus it is by virtue of the presence of mullite alone that the pot resists complete collapse at the high temperature needed to ensure complete vitrification of a porcelain body. Rightly did the Chinese call kaolin the 'bones' of porcelain.

Hence there are two morphological phases to the matured porcelain body: a highly refractory and amorphous silica glass, which is actually an extremely viscous supercooled liquid, and a disordered felted mass of crystals of the even more refractory mullite scattered through the glass matrix. In a normal porcelain body the glassy phase comprises about two-thirds of the body weight, while if only two parts of lime are added to the batch its contribution can amount to 94 per cent. Such a body is almost completely non-porous.

The amount of silica released by the dissociating kaolin molecules is not in itself sufficient to ensure satisfactory vitrification in a porcelain or stoneware body, and in practice extra silica in the form of quartz has to be introduced to the amount of perhaps 25 per cent by weight. Another practical problem has to be faced. Pure silica is extremely refractory, with a softening point at 1728° C, a temperature far higher than can ever be reached by any traditional type of kiln. How then is it possible to induce the free silica in the porcelain body to soften and fuse at a temperature 700 degrees or so lower, as stated above? It is done by a flux. Certain compounds act as fluxing agents towards other compounds when heated together in a certain proportion (the eutectic, of which I wrote so disparagingly on page 232), lowering the minimum temperature at which these will melt.

Feldspar acts as such a flux towards silica. When feldspar is added to the composition of a pottery body it lowers the softening point of the quartz, as well as of the silica liberated by the kaolin in its molecular transformations, to about 1000° C. Once the softening reaction has set in, it continues until complete vitrification has taken place, this consummation depending as much on the total amount of heat absorbed as on the maximum temperature reached, as also on the precise chemical constitution of the body and several other contingent factors. The percentage of feldspar in the classical porcelain composition is 25.

Lastly, since the kaolin, feldspar and quartz mixture is relatively non-plastic, difficult to work, or 'short', normal Western practice is to add to it a proportion of a highly plastic and fairly white-burning secondary clay such as a ball-clay, thereby increasing its plasticity. We cannot say whether the Chinese did this. We hear of Chinese potters 'souring' their raw materials – leaving them exposed to all types of weather – for as long as a hundred years, thus effectively reducing their particle-size. It may be that by so doing they were able to dispense with ball-clay and confine their body formula to the quintessential trio – kaolin, feldspar, quartz.

*

It is technically possible and often necessary to induce vitrification at temperatures much lower than those indicated above, by employing other natural fluxes such as lead, lime, wood ash, or calcined bones. Indeed almost any impurity present in a pottery body will act as a glass-forming flux at low temperatures. For this very reason such impurities must not be allowed to enter into the composition of the stoneware or porcelain body. The ultimate ceramic quality is hardness, and hardness can be achieved only through high-temperature vitrification. When a porcelain body is properly vitrified its hardness may reach 8 on Mohs' scale, so that it is harder than jade, while even the surface of its glaze will be harder than steel. Early attempts made by European potters to achieve whiteness and translucency, which were for historical reasons the two qualities associated in the European mind with Chinese porcelain, usually succeeded only at the expense of such primary virtues as hardness, denseness, mechanical strength, and resistance to sudden temperature change. A case in point is that of English bone china.

What set the Chinese on the road to discovering and mastering the secrets of high-temperature vitrification? My own guess is that the answer lies in the peculiar construction of the traditional Chinese kiln, which is of the 'bank' or 'climbing' variety.

We are to imagine a stepped tunnel, or a graduated series of interconnected brick chambers, half-buried in the slope of a hill and extending upwards for perhaps a distance of 50 yards. Such a kiln, with chambers some 12 feet high, would provide setting space for thousands of pots, and was no doubt originally owned and used communally. The occasion of its firing would be a local event, not to be undertaken lightly, but fraught with anxiety and suspense. After several days spent in cleaning and mending kiln shelves and supports, in placing the 'green' or unfired pots, and in gathering wood for fuel, the fire in the firebox below would be duly lit, and for several more days cautiously tended while the wares dried out. Then the rate of firing would be smartly increased. The steady advance of kiln heat towards the brilliant white glare of the porcelain range would be watched in admiration, while at night the flares of flame and the swirl of smokes issuing from blowholes on the sides of the kiln would make it appear like a huge captive dragon, writhing and bellowing as though suffering a sort of paroxysm.[2] As the monster slowly cooled, and as the still hot wares were being extracted from its body, it must have seemed to its attendants as if some familiar miracle had taken place, an upheaval as great as childbirth.

As the hot gases pass upwards through the successive chambers of a bank kiln they yield up much of their heat, so that the temperature in the topmost chamber is much lower than in that nearest the firebox. The steepness of such a temperature gradient can perhaps be guaged by the behaviour of a 3-chamber bank kiln built for Bernard Leach by the Japanese potter Matsubayashi. When the temperature in the chamber next the firebox reached the region of 1300° C, Leach notes, that in the middle chamber was about 1000° C, that in the upper chamber no more than 700° C.[3] In this kiln then, and at peak firing temperature, the upper chamber was hot enough for firing soft earthenwares, the middle chamber for refractory earthenwares, and the chamber nearest the firebox for refractory porcelains and stonewares, this being the hottest part of the kiln.

The firing of such a kiln being highly laborious, protracted, and costly, the potter must strive to utilize every inch of kiln space for setting his wares. What the Chinese potter had to do was to find a pottery body capable of withstanding the consuming heat generated in the hottest part of his kiln. So he may have been led to discover white and translucent porcelain. For the essence of porcelain is kaolin; and kaolin, as we have seen, is the one ingredient in a pottery body whose molecule, when heated within the firing temperature of hard porcelain, liberates a substance (mullite) capable of remaining solid when all else has gone into a liquid melt.

Glaze

Earthenwares fired at temperatures much below the porcelain vitrification range are relatively soft and porous, and if they are to be made impermeable to liquids they must be glazed. I have mentioned that lead acts towards silica as a flux; when lead and silica are combined in the eutectic proportion, the softening point can be depressed to as low as 750° C. If they are heated together for some time at this temperature, then on cooling we have a homogeneous, non-crystalline material which is in fact crude glass, but which a potter would call a 'frit'. For purposes of glazing, frit is ground into powder and is then transferred to the unfired earthenware surface in the form of a thin film, either by dipping the pot into water in which the glaze materials are held in suspension, or else by pouring, spraying or brushing. On firing, this granular film vitrifies completely between about 600 and 800° C, forming a smooth and homogeneous skin of impermeable glaze on the surface of the body.

Lead-silicate glazes first appear in China in Han times. Considering the long history of glasses and earthenware glazes in the Near and Middle East, and the absence of such a tradition in China, it seems likely that Chinese lead-silicate glazes were originally fritted, and that the frit was the *liu li* or crude glass which we are told was a leading export from the Roman Orient to China at that time. Later they may have been compounded raw in China simply by grinding together lead ore (galena), sand, and limestone, or else were fritted locally in the manner described above.

Technical difficulties were encountered in applying lead-silicate glazes in Chinese pottery. When molten, such glazes are very fluid and it is difficult to prevent them forming undesirable drops or adhesions. Further, the high alkali content of a traditional lead-silicate glaze raises its expansion coefficient. On cooling it strains to shrink more than the underlying body, and so shatters itself into a mosaic of irregular fragments separated by hair-cracks, the well-known crazing or crackle. Crackle is not necessarily a blemish, and may come to be valued for its own sake. It opens up a path, however, through which moisture may penetrate deep into the glaze, where it combines with free alkalis to form crystalline products that split the glaze into a series of very thin concentric sheets, which appear iridescent, and which sooner or later flake away. T'ang earthenware glazes are much more stable than those of Han – they are after all several centuries younger – but none are particularly good ceramic fits.[4]

Very different is the case of the feldspathic glazes of porcelain and stoneware. The bodies of these wares being dense and virtually non-porous, glaze is not required to render the vessels impermeable to liquids. It does, however, improve the mechanical strength of the pot, as well as its resistance to sudden heat changes; and, being easy to clean, it renders food-vessels more hygienic in use. Being rich in fluxes it readily takes into solution some of the silica in the body of the ware during vitrification, and so becomes intimately united with it by way of an imperceptible 'transition layer'. Being composed of much the same materials as the body, its thermal behaviour is almost identical. As a result it is far more stable than earthenware, and is to all intents and purposes indestructible. It is highly resistant to acids, which explains why porcelain or stoneware fragments that have lain in the soil a thousand years or more come out looking as fresh and sharp as though they had been fractured only yesterday. Lastly, a feldspathic glaze adds marvellous new qualities to the plastic form – qualities of surface texture, depth and muted colour that gladden the senses and harmonize the mind.

Since a stoneware or porcelain glaze has to withstand kiln temperatures up to about 1350° C it must be tolerably refractory, otherwise it will run off the pot and may even volatilize. It must, on the other hand, be fairly fluid so as to flow into a thin coating when the body substance is merely soft and viscous. Its vitrification range must therefore be somewhat lower, and somewhat narrower, than that of the body. It will mature at temperatures between about 1250 and 1285° C, and on cooling its surface will become so hard that steel will not scratch it.

Over and over again one is struck by the natural kinship between the various elements used in the making of Chinese porcelain and stoneware, and the inevitable way in which they assemble together to determine the vessel's inherent form. Assuming that wood was always used as kiln fuel, then it may be averred that the earliest stoneware glaze was an ash glaze caused by the fluxing of wood ash accidentally blown on to the hot pottery surfaces by the fierce draught through the kiln. Once the phenomenon had been traced, the Chinese potter could always avail himself of a substantial supply of raw glaze material in the form of ashes left over from the previous firing. Provided he consistently used the same sort of wood as fuel, he could standardize his glazing procedure and control its results. We know that in Ming times Chinese potters burnt lime in layers alternating with fern and brushwood and after repeated calcination used the product as the flux with which they softened their glazes.

In practice feldspathic glazes are compounded of about 50 per cent feldspar, 20 per cent silica in the form of calcined flint, and some 30 per cent of fluxes which may be lime, or wood ash, or both. Since all the compounds present in wood ash – silica, potash, magnesia, alumina, phosphorus, soda, metallic oxides, etc. – are easily available in raw form, we must rule out the possibility of any mysterious alchemy in the power of wood ash *per se*. It is the number and variety of the compounds, and the varied combinations and proportions in which they occur, that gives to each ash glaze a slight but by no means salient individuality. Studio potters often spend long hours compounding ash glazes and trying their effects, and some are known to guard their precious formulae with a miser's care. There is perhaps an element of self-deception in all this.

The colour of a glaze

The subject of this chapter being T'ang pottery, what I shall say about glaze-colour will be with an eye on the repertory of colours developed by the T'ang potter. Colour in a glass or glaze results from the presence of metallic oxides. These may be artifically introduced; yet one or two are usually already present, even though only in minute traces. The exact spectral hue, the value, and the brightness (chroma) of a glaze-colour, by which it may be classified on the Munsell colour standard, as well as such qualities as lustre, surface texture, and opacity, depend upon a complex of factors including the atmospheric conditions in the kiln, the duration and rate of firing, the maximum temperature attained, the acidity or alkalinity of the glaze, the nature of the metallic oxide, its purity and its concentration – not least of all the potter's horoscope.

The kiln atmosphere is said to be oxidizing when the fire is consuming as much oxygen as it needs; it is reducing when not enough oxygen is available, and carbon-monoxide fills the kiln. Carbon-monoxide seeks to convert itself into carbon-dioxide by robbing the metallic oxides of some of their oxygen, so 'reducing' them. Both kiln atmospheres induce their own special colour effects, and Chinese potters quickly learnt how either might be produced at will at any stage in the firing operation.

Iron is the most common metallic impurity in clay, and its presence in the fired body always declares itself. If the kiln atmosphere is oxidizing, then iron is present in the form of its higher oxide (ferric oxide), and the body of an earthenware matures the rust-red of terracotta. Let the atmosphere be reducing and the lower oxide (ferrous oxide) is formed; the fired body is now grey or black. The colouring effects of oxidation and reduction on pottery bodies rich in iron are most typically displayed by primitive earthenwares: for instance those of the Lung-shan and Yang-shao traditions of China, the former being black, the latter red.

col. 4, 2

If the iron content of a pottery body is small, then the effect of oxidation or reduction will be correspondingly slight. This is the case with the T'ang earthenwares, which are fairly white-burning and which seem always to have been fired under oxidizing conditions; the body matures not rust-red but a warm and delicate shade of buff or cream. Comparative absence of iron in T'ang earthenware bodies suggests that the T'ang potter used either a high-grade kaolin containing between a quarter and three-quarters of one per cent iron, or else a white-burning secondary clay such as a ball clay, whose chemical composition would not necessarily differ greatly from that of a kaolin. Taking into account the large particle-size of such T'ang earthenware bodies as have been analysed, as well as the presence of mica fibres and quartz grains in them, one may conclude that kaolin was the main if not exclusive con-stituent. Kaolin had in fact been used as far back as Shang times for manufacturing a splendid *pl. 12* refractory white earthenware with carved surface-design somewhat resembling that of con-temporary bronzes; this was fired at about 1,000° C, and my impression is that most of the T'ang white earthenwares were fired around that temperature too.

When iron enters into the composition of a lead-silicate glaze fired in oxidizing conditions it matures as a bright and aggressive amber, or else some related hue such as golden-brown, caramel, chestnut, or tan. The colour appears either as a monochrome or in polychrome com-bination with the colours produced by copper and cobalt [see below]. The colours may be kept discrete, or they may be painted or dripped on to the body so that they intermingle some-*col. 32, 37, 38* what on firing.

col. 30 Copper, added to the composition of a lead-silicate glaze in the form of its higher oxide (cupric oxide), matures in an oxidizing atmosphere as a luminous leaf green, in high alkalinity tending towards blue-green. Copper may occur as a monochrome, or it may be combined with iron or cobalt, or with both, in the manner described above. When a glaze containing copper is painted, splashed, dripped or otherwise allowed to play together on the *col. 42* surface of the pot with one containing ferric iron, the so-called 'egg and spinach' colour-combination results – an effect extremely popular in T'ang times and one widely copied outside China.

Cobalt, first imported into China from the Middle East in T'ang times, came later to provide the blue of what is probably the most celebrated glaze in ceramic history, Chinese 'blue and white' with its countless non-Chinese imitations. When cobalt oxide is added to a lead-silicate glaze and fired in oxidizing conditions, it matures as a frail cornflower blue or *col. 29* as a brilliant prussian blue in concentrations up to about half of one per cent in an alkaline solution, or as a reddish-brown in higher concentrations with acidity. Again it may either occur as a monochrome or combine with iron and copper in the various ways indicated above. Full exploitation of the three colouring oxides, iron, copper, cobalt, with exemplary *col. 30* fructification of colour, can be seen in the beautiful covered jar of colour plate 30.

In order to improve the complexion of earthenware bodies containing small amounts of iron, it was customary to apply a thin slip of white-burning kaolinic clay; this was then over-laid with a colourless lead-silicate glaze often with a somewhat yellowish cast, or else with the green, blue, and amber glazes discussed above.

Bodies were also manipulated in various ways by combining white-, red-, or black-burn-ing clays during the process of wedging, when the clay is softened, homogenized, and freed from lumps or air pockets. This was in imitation of the 'agate glass' and *mille fiori* glassware first made in Alexandria and later in Rome at about the beginning of our era, in themselves imitations of variegated semi-precious stones. Since the marbling is actually in the clay, it can be traced on both outer and inner surfaces, beneath the transparent straw-coloured glaze with which these pots were usually finished. The effect was also obtained by combing slips of different colours, as in the case of the superb ewer of plate 174.

pl. 174

On turning to the glaze-colours of high-fired glazes, we again remark the ubiquitous presence of iron as a mineral impurity. If the potter is aiming at a pure white porcelain he certainly cannot risk introducing wood ash into the glaze, for this is bound to contain small amounts of iron. He must limit his glaze ingredients to feldspar, flint, and lime. Even so, he can hardly avoid contamination of the glaze by absorption of minute amounts of iron from the body. If the ware is oxidized, a warm cream flush like that seen on Sung *ting* ware results; if reduced, the ware displays a cool greenish or bluish tint, exemplified by the Sung *ying-ch'ing* or 'misty blue' range. The less adulteration of a kaolin body by iron-contaminated secondary clay, therefore, the whiter the porcelain will be.

In the case of the non-white stonewares, on the other hand, iron is an absolute godsend. It enabled Chinese potters working in the Yüeh and celadon tradition [pp. 255–263] to reproduce the delicate tints of nephrite with wonderful fidelity, while in respect of other inherent qualities these stonewares fully equalled and even outmatched true jade. It is a question whether the potter deliberately set out to imitate jade; certainly the connexion between the two substances was extremely close in peoples' minds. The muted greens of the Yüeh and celadon range, still, silent, permanent-looking, combine with the weighty stoneware bodies they so perfectly suit, to form what is probably the most noble ceramic product the world has ever seen.

col. 33, 35, 36

The amount of iron a glaze can hold without supersaturation depends on its acidity or alkalinity. With the addition of up to 10 per cent iron in acid solutions, the iron crystallizes out on reduction and appears black. If the glaze is partly neutralized by addition of alkalis, some of the iron goes back into solution, and on firing matures as a shade of brown. The lustrous blue-black Sung *temmoku* is an example of a supersaturated iron glaze, while the mottled, veined, or figured effects exhibited among this range of wares, the so-called *tessha*, *kaki*, 'oil spot', etc., result from partial reabsorption of iron by local application of alkaline solutions, often by means of the finger or brush.[5] It is easy to imagine how the earliest *temmokus* might have originated in the home of a Yüeh or celadon tradition, where the colour effect is normally produced by adding up to about 3 per cent iron oxide to the glaze, and we have at least one case of an early Yüeh factory producing *temmoku* side by side with the standard product [p. 256]. Existence of *temmoku* in T'ang times is now a recognized fact; a fine example is the black-glazed 'spittoon' of plate 183.

col. 28, 31, 40

pl. 183

Stonewares such as that of colour plate 40 raise a question as to the use of copper in T'ang high-fired stoneware glazes. The behaviour of copper under reduction is peculiar and usually temperamental. We may however say that reduction of copper from cupric oxide to pure metallic copper in colloidal solution takes place very readily, and that the colour effect yielded by colloidal copper varies according to the size of its particles. The scattering of light produced by large particles of colloidal copper gives an effect similar to the blue of the sky, and for the same reason. We may surmise, therefore, that the stonewares in question were fired in a reducing atmosphere, that the black or dark brown ground-glaze is a *temmoku* produced by supersaturation and crystallization of iron, and that the blue splashes are due to the presence of copper reduced to its colloidal state.

col. 40

If oxygen is let into the kiln during the closing stages of cooling, let us say for the last hour or so, it attacks the copper particles and breaks them down into a more finely divided state. A spectacular transformation occurs; the copper now appears red, the elusive copper red that some studio potters regard as a sort of ultimate state, a *nirvāṇa*, and that even the Chinese were by no means always able to achieve. Perhaps the purest copper reds were produced during the Hsüan-tê period of Ming times; certainly there is no evidence that the effect was known or sought during the T'ang period.[6]

T'ang pottery: the political background

In chapter five we summarized the political history of T'ang China down to about the year AD 700, and saw how during that time the great capital city of Ch'ang-an became a world centre for international Buddhist scholarship [p. 180]. It is this cosmopolitanism that I intend to stress in continuing the historical summary down to the end of the T'ang and through the Five Dynasties, for it is this which explains the extraordinary variety displayed by the forms of contemporary pottery.

During its first hundred years the T'ang dynasty engaged in a programme of military conquest up to the 'optimum' frontiers of the Chinese empire, in a way very similar to that of the Han. Mongolia, Chinese Turkestan, and Korea were in turn firmly incorporated. Despite initial resistance from the Western Turks, China extended her political influence into Russian Turkestan and Transoxiana, and began to appoint the rulers of Tashkent, while Gilgit, Kashmir, Kabul and Balkh were also administered by the Chinese viceroy resident at Kucha in Chinese Turkestan. China was thus the paramount power from the Yellow Sea to the borders of Persia and India, and her stock stood supremely high in the eyes of the rest of the world.

In 638 the last actual Sassanid Persian ruler, Yezdegird III, turned to China for help against the Arab onslaught in Mesopotamia. None was forthcoming; but for decades hence a steady stream of western Asiatic refugees passed eastwards, permeating Chinese Turkestan with Sassanian material culture and bringing all sorts of new knowledge to China herself. Thus the forms of T'ang pottery are profoundly influenced by those of Sassanian metalwork. Yezdegird died in 651. His son, Peroz III, took refuge in Tocharistan (the region of modern Balkh) and again appealed to China for help. It was refused on grounds of distance, but Emperor Kao-tsung recognized Peroz as 'governor' of Persia, with his seat at Chi-ling (probably Zaranj in Sijistan, eastern Persia) in 661. Here he was attacked by the Arabs and forced to flee once again to Tocharistan and, in 674, to China.

In 640 the Indian Emperor, Harsha, sent an envoy to China. Agents of Buddhism now passed freely between the two countries, and we find its influence in the forms of T'ang pottery bowls and bottles copied probably from representations of Indian vessels in Buddhist painting and sculpture.

The Greek Emperor Theodosius is also supposed to have sent an embassy to the Chinese court in 640; and indeed 'embassies' of one sort or another arrived regularly from the West from this time on until the middle of the following century. Most, no doubt, were trade missions. But some brought new religions. And a very few may have been genuinely diplomatic. The Arabs now extended their great sea-trade network to include south China ports, and to their chroniclers we owe several accurate accounts of the country and her products, including porcelain made during the ninth century [p. 251].

One can scarcely rate too high the invigorating effect of this influx of foreigners on the Chinese creative spirit and intellectual grasp. They came from every quarter of the known world. In cities like Ch'ang-an and Hangchow, whole districts were set aside for their living quarters. The foreign population of Canton alone must have been well over 120,000, for we learn from an Arab source that that number lost their lives when the city was fired by the

32 Jar with four ring-handles; off-white earthenware covered with a white slip and painted in blue and tan glaze colours, all overlaid with a transparent and colourless glaze. T'ang dynasty. Height: 6 5/16 in. Seattle Art Museum.

33 *Five-lobed bowl of Yüeh stoneware covered with a heavy translucent glaze. T'ang dynasty. Diameter: 7 ¹/₂ in. Victoria and Albert Museum.*

34 *Four-lobed shallow dish, the lobes foliate in profile; of olive-green 'Yo' stoneware, the glaze stained with a reddish discolouration due to burial. From Ch'ang-sha, Hunan province. T'ang dynasty. Diameter: 5 ⁷/₈ in. Art Museum, University of Singapore.*

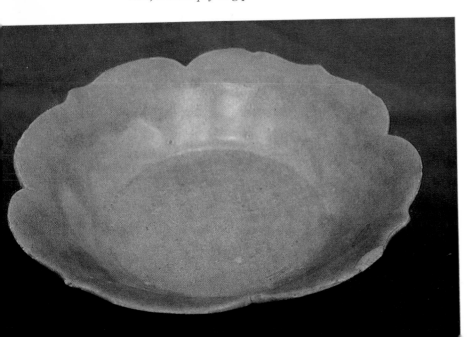

opposite page

35 *Five-lobed deep bowl of Yüeh stoneware covered with a grey-green glaze. T'ang dynasty. Diameter: 5 in. Cunliffe Collection, England.*

36 *Twelve-lobed bowl with fluted sides; of fine translucent Lung-ch'üan porcelain with green glaze. Sung dynasty. Height: 3 ³/₄ in. Collection of Mrs A. Clark, England.*

37 Dish on a prominent circular foot; of off-white earthenware decorated with a quatrefoil motif in green and amber glazes over a white slip. AD 700–800. Diameter: 18 in. Hose-kawa Collection, Tokyo.

38 Offering dish on three small feet, with incised centre medallion; of fine buff earthenware decorated with tan and dark glazes on a white slip. T'ang dynasty. Diameter: 11.3 in. British Museum.

rebel Huang Ch'ao in 879. Greeks, Syrians, Persians, Arabs, and Indians, as well as people from outlandish regions like Siberia and the jungles of south-east Asia, found homes and livelihood in China; and Koreans and Japanese helped to complete this varied assemblage on Chinese soil. Half a dozen new religions were introduced, and all gained some sort of hold. And in pottery, the shapes and motifs of Iranian, Mesopotamian and Syrian vessels were becoming as well known in China as they were in Byzantium, Alexandria, and Lombard Italy.

Meanwhile China was prospering. In particular, the great rift between North and South was now mended. Officials travelled freely over the entire country, and life at the big centres on the Yangtze and south of it was not different in quality from that at Ch'ang-an and Lo-yang. The population, made up mainly of peasants, landed gentry, State officials, soldiers, and the monks and nuns of Buddhism and other religions, stood at forty millions – over two million of them in the metropolitan district of Ch'ang-an. Buddhism, now thoroughly assimilated, helped in many ways to bring about this national unity, despite set-backs such as the Great Persecution of AD 844 [p. 176].

Then, with dramatic suddenness, the whole polity collapsed. In 745 a new Turkish power, the Uighurs, reconquered Mongolia. At about the same time the Ch'i-tan Mongols further east, in Manchuria, began to build up the strength that eventually allowed them to annex north China in 947.[7] In 751 they defeated the Chinese general An Lu-shan west of the Liao river in Jehol. In the same year an alliance of Central Asiatic tribes under the 'Black Cloth' Arabs commanded by Ziyad ben Salih, met and annihilated a Chinese army of perhaps 50,000 men on the banks of the Talas river, near modern Aulie Ata; this being one of the greatest battles in Chinese history. In 758 Korea seceded.

In 755 the famous An Lu-shan rebellion broke out. We cannot deal with its causes, but its effects on the internal regime were catastrophic. Ch'ang-an changed hands several times, and the Emperor sought refuge in Szechwan. It was on this trek to Szechwan, an epic in its way no less stirring than the Long March of the Red Army in the reverse direction, that the notorious Imperial favourite Yang Kuei-fei was butchered by the soldiery and her hair ornaments scattered in the dust, as Li Po relates in his imperishable poem nostalgic for the former glories of the T'ang Court. From this time we may date the final eclipse of the north-west. Although the Plateau has often been a springboard for movements aimed against eastern and central China, it has never since contained the seat of Government. The centre of gravity shifted east and south; and the north-west became, politically and economically, a hinterland. Ch'ang-an was not allowed to recover from its first shock. It was sacked again, this time by Tibetans, in 763; again, in 881, by the rebels of Huang Ch'ao's party; and again, by another rebel, in 904. T'ang emperors were now able to rule only with the help of various foreign powers such as the Turkish Uighurs and Sha-t'o; the remainder of the dynasty was devoted to a dispute, energetically conducted, as to who should found the next.

The rapid deterioration in T'ang home affairs may perhaps be traced back to a reform in AD 624 in which the old administration whereby government of prefectures was shared between a civil chief and a military prefect was changed to one in which the military authority had absolute control of a much larger unit approximating in size to a province. This person was put in charge of taxation.

For a long time the new system worked. Taxes *in specie* and commodities flowed into the capital. But steady oppression of the peasants in the form of crippling taxes and forced recruitment went on the whole time, and did not pass unnoticed. Poets such as Tu Fu and Po Chü-i did something to bring these malpractices to public notice; but nothing could be done to put a stop to them. The central government needed the support of the militarists, who alone could muster the huge armies required to defend the realm. And since armies cost money to maintain, military governors gradually stopped remitting taxes to Court. After the An Lu-shan rebellion they made themselves virtually independent war-lords by arrogating the right to hand on their posts to their sons. This move was of course fiercely challenged by the Court; and this, in turn, led to a fresh series of rebellions.

*

The period of fifty-four years following the downfall of the T'ang is known as the Five Dynasties (AD 906-60). Military governors turning automatically into independent war-lords; increased domination of the Turkish Sha-t'o in the north-west; steady advance of the Ch'i-tan Mongols into north China: these are the main political features of the time. North and South were divided. The South broke up into ten small kingdoms with native Chinese rulers, among them Later Shu in Szechwan and Yüeh in Chekiang. These states were not on particularly friendly terms with each other, but common commercial interests and constant threat of invasion from the North kept their wrangles within moderation, and gave to the South a remarkable cultural consistency during this period. Tea, printing and publishing in Szechwan, and the porcelain industry of Chekiang [pp. 255-262], were some of the economic and cultural factors helping to bring about the ascendancy that the South now began to gain.

In the North the capital moved eastwards, to K'ai-fêng. Five short dynasties, Liang, T'ang, Chin, Han, Chou, all dubbed *hou* or 'Later', now followed hard on each other's heels. Rivalries between their founders paved the way for Ch'i-tan infiltration, and in the end the dynasts were no more than puppets of the Mongol power. So for instance the Ch'i-tan helped to found the Later Chin dynasty (AD 936-47), but the price they exacted for this help was nothern Shansi including Ta-t'ung, and northern Hopei including Peking [p. 289]; and Peking, which now for the first time begins to be important, remained in Mongol hands until the beginning of the Ming dynasty in AD 1368.

In AD 960 the Sung dynasty was founded by general Chao K'uang-yin, one of many military adventurers who throve during this confused half century. For a moment China was reunited. But there was nothing settled about the situation. On the contrary the nomads were once again on the march; and for hundreds of years after the end of the T'ang, successive invaders moved into the North China Plain, sinified themselves, and were then in turn ejected by others lined up behind them in Mongolia and Manchuria.

T'ang pottery: why T'ang[8]

About no aspect of Chinese art have Western ideas changed faster than about pottery. Until the present century Europe was aware of little more than the contemporary products of the East, mainly because these were all the Chinese needed or cared to export. A historical review of Chinese pottery made late in the last century would of course have included Ming wares, as well as the brilliant polychromes of the eighteenth century and their offspring. But, from an aesthetic point of view, Chinese pottery was valued in Europe more for what it could contribute to the development of the last great historical phase of European decorative design, the Rococo, than for any intrinsic appeal it was felt to possess. Among the *cognoscenti*, 'Ming' was the password they murmured, and of any earlier phase of Chinese ceramic history they knew not a thing.

Arrival of pre-Ming Chinese pottery in Europe was probably as much a result of the Boxer Rising as of anything.[9] Western taste changed almost overnight and it became fashionable to regard the Sung as the classical phase of Chinese ceramics, although Han and T'ang tomb-figures and glazed earthenwares were beginning to be known and admired. Then, in two expeditions between 1910 and 1913, the Germans Sarre and Herzfeld discovered at the site of Samarra on the Tigris sherds of undoubted Chinese origin that caused a second and quite unexpected shift in the historical perspective. Samarra, a capital of one of the later Abbasid Moslem caliphs, had been founded in AD 838 and abandoned forty-five years later, after which it soon fell into complete decay. During that time Chinese and Arab empires marched together, and presence of Chinese pottery at Samarra need in no way perplex us. The crux of the discovery lay in the fact that some sherds were of a white translucent porcelain; and that others with green glaze, while not actually porcelain in the European definition, were at least high-fired and feldspathic, and closely resembled the wares long known to the West as Celadons. In AD 851 an unknown Arab author had recorded in his book, *The Story of India and China*, some observations evidently made by a merchant at Canton, one Suliman, to the effect that the Chinese there had 'pottery of excellent quality, of which bowls are made as fine as glass drinking cups: the sparkle of water can be seen through it, although it is pottery'.[10] These words were now called to mind, as were contemporary Chinese descriptions of tea-bowls resembling silver or snow, ice or jade. It seemed that yet another and even more formative period in the history of Chinese ceramics was being opened up.

Probably Sung wares still command greater admiration among collectors than any other. And with good reason. Their expressive beauty of shape, the gravity of their deep and peaceful glazes, their finely-restrained decoration, and the consummate and effortless manner of their making, all mark them out as the most sheerly lovely pots the world has ever seen. If we venture to put T'ang pottery alongside them, that is because T'ang wares can claim qualities all their own; a different order of beauty, but one no less compelling.

pls 160, 180; col. 36

*

The T'ang period has always been eulogized by the Chinese as their 'Golden Age'. It has been nominated 'the greatest period of creative art in China', and, I think more aptly, 'the most virile period of Chinese art'. It is above all the art of pottery that gives us a measure of this achievement. The great names of T'ang painting are really only names today. Contemporary architecture in the grand manner has vanished, save only in the great Buddhist foundations of Japan; while the art of Buddhist sculpture in China, declining with the religion, had by mid-dynasty nothing new to say. The evidence of T'ang pottery, on the other hand, is tangible and wholly affirmatory. Whether we seek it from the pot-sherds found at Samarra, and subsequently at the sites of the factories where the pots were made, and those of trade entrepôts and terminals all over southern Asia, or whether from the superabundance of lovely pots distributed among museums and private collections in various parts of the world, all evidence reveals a technical and artistic advance mounting to a climax unique in the history of Chinese ceramics. All pottery is articulate; but these pots speak to us explicitly of the T'ang artistic genius, its confident vitality, its gaiety, its power of acquisition and assimilation. Small wonder that in recent years an intense topical interest has focussed on T'ang pottery. The work of an art-historian is usually an index of contemporary taste in his particular field – at least this seems always to have been so in the case of Chinese ceramics. The topicality of T'ang pottery, then, is one of the reasons why I have chosen it to represent the T'ang period in this book.

The significance of form

Early in this chapter we defined the form of a pot as the sum of all its manifest aesthetic properties. We do not therefore mean simply its style, still less its actual shape and decoration, but a complex of factors that includes, as well as these, the materials of its body and glaze and the techniques of its potting and firing, all of which naturally influence the final form of the pot. Just as an individual pot has a unique form, so a ceramic tradition speaks its own form-language, and over the years and centuries this language changes, usually very gradually, sometimes quite abruptly. There is thus a perceptible difference between typical T'ang and typical Sung pottery-form, and the view has been held that this was not a gradual change, but abrupt.[11]

When we come to examine the formal differences between T'ang and Sung pottery, the first thing we are likely to notice is that the brilliant array of glazed earthenwares so characteristic of the T'ang period is completely missing from the Sung repertoire, our immediate impression being that a Sung gallery is a quieter and cooler place than one in which T'ang wares are being exhibited. It may well be that this disappearance of a whole ceramic range was deliberate; not of course officially ordained, but a decree of fashion, a 'new look', the outward symbol of something new in the air. Still it was a loss, an amputation of part of the received tradition; and it is this loss that gives us today the impression of a cataclysmic change in pottery-form on passing from T'ang to Sung.

Discarding the earthenwares, then, the Sung potter proceeded to work on the basis of the T'ang stoneware tradition, which was all that was left to him. No startling change in pottery-form took place; and a pot that some might claim positively as T'ang, others as Five Dynasties, yet others as Sung, may more fittingly be labelled simply as 'tenth century AD' if we are not to go beyond the bounds of present knowledge.

Gradually however the Sung came to assume its own ceramic personality, and in the event we have quite a clear mental picture of what is typically T'ang and typically Sung. To describe this difference in the language of the affections (even as we speak of the mouth, neck, shoulder, belly, and foot of a pot), we might say that the T'ang form is lively and robust, its shapes full and swelling, its decoration bold and assertive; whereas Sung form is, as Honey says, 'quieter and more contemplative'.[12] Figure 45 shows a series of typical pots from each period, which will perhaps help to convey what might be called the *bravura* of the one and the *recueillement* of the other.

On coming to examine differences in shape, as opposed to form, we find that these can be defined much more precisely. Thus the T'ang profile tends to divide up into distinct horizontal zones. Changes in direction are sudden. The line made by the foot-rim contrasts sharply with the curve of the body above it, shoulder and neck are no less distinctly articulated, and so are neck and mouthrim. By comparison, the Sung profile is a continuous one. The foot, belly, shoulder, neck, and mouth all tend to merge into a single modulated curve. Put another way, the typical T'ang shape is what Bachhofer calls a 'multiform co-ordinated unity', whereas the Sung is a 'perfect and indivisible unity'.[13] Sung shapes, one might say, reveal the workings of a conscious aestheticism that is missing from those of T'ang times. They leave behind the prosaic world of their predecessors; but in doing so they sometimes move away from the ceramic standard of fitness for purpose. The result can be seen in the foot of a particular type of tea-bowl. This, although a logical starting-point for the flat, conical body, is often contracted to a mere button. The bowl looks, and actually is, very unstable.

The essential practicality and strength of T'ang shape, by contrast, are well shown in the ewer of plate 173. It is a typical early T'ang earthenware. The body, a pale buff material which

T'ANG

pl. 164

45 a   T'ang vessel-shapes for comparison with 45 b

252

though low-fired is evidently kaolinic, is partly dressed with a white slip over which lies a thin lead-silicate glaze with a slightly yellowish tinge due to presence of ferric iron. This is an admirable colour harmony, but one quite naturally arrived at, here set off by a simple spiral pattern of punch-marks beneath the glaze. But the most striking thing about this pot is its shape. It rises sturdily from a strongly-planted, flat-bottomed base, swells over the shoulders, and curves cleanly in to a suitably wide and slightly flared neck. The curve is echoed by the two loop-handles and the carrying-handle, while the short, stubby spout is well placed and properly shaped for its purpose. Good workmanship is in every line of this piece, and yet the shape is not only practical, but quite compellingly interesting. In particular, the long double curve of the body is graceful and full of subtlety.

pl. 173

Contrasting elements, displayed by T'ang shapes, are no less observable in their decoration. As far as can be told from its stonewares, decoration played a subdued role in the Sung tradition. Whereas T'ang pottery, and especially T'ang earthenware, presents bold designs often rendered in vivid colours which were applied as strongly contrasted patches. As with shape, unity is brought about by combining distinct, although structurally interdependent, parts to form an organic whole. Hence a preference for formal symmetrical motifs such as the rosette. And just as the rosette gets its internal equilibrium from the thrust and counter-thrust of its components, so it in turn contrasts visually with the background against which it is defined.

col. 37
pl. 184

The 'butter-pat' type of applied mould, a device greatly favoured by T'ang potters, gets its effect in much the same sort of way. In these respects, indeed, T'ang pottery may be said to approach the condition of 'rational' art more nearly than does any other Chinese ware although, since mechanical accuracy is not what is aimed at, T'ang pottery never presents the inorganic, dead, even inimical appearance of a machine-made product. It does disclose, nevertheless, a feeling for order – carrying with it the idea of contrast – that is missing from Sung decorative design, in which the decoration is conceived as an overall unit, its shape curvilinear and asymmetrical, and its execution calligraphic and free.

pl. 167

The T'ang factories: literary notices

Until ceramicists and their agents began on-the-spot inspection of kiln-sites some thirty years ago, our knowledge of the T'ang pottery factories was drawn entirely from Chinese writings. Among these, two were specifically concerned with pottery manufacture, namely *T'ao shuo* ('Dissertation on Pottery') and *Ching-tê-chên t'ao lu* ('An Account of the Pottery of Ching-tê-chên'), the former dating from 1774, the latter from 1815.[14]

Each commences with an account of the Imperial factories at Ching-tê-chên as they existed in the eighteenth century, and then rambles on into a waste of expository matter gathered from dozens of primary sources and embodied in the text in the form of quotations. Pitfalls await those who seek to follow these texts – verbal ambiguities in the original Chinese, errors in their European translations, discrepancies between their respective versions of quoted material; but above all they are unsatisfactory because of their compilers' failure to think in pottery terms, to see the pottery traditions as an integrated whole in the way a potter would, and because of their preoccupation with some classes of ware to the exclusion of others and their interest in the extraneous rather than the intrinsic qualities of a pot. Indeed these Chinese scholars seem to have been no less lacking in ceramic sensibility than the Western fetishists of 'Kang-he' and 'Keen-lung' who began to assemble their weird collections just about a hundred years ago.

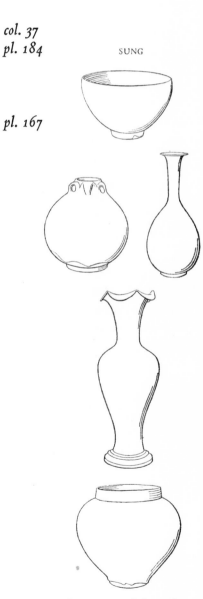

SUNG

45b Sung vessel-shapes for comparison with 45a

253

Notices of T'ang factories found in these texts are mostly taken from a work called *Ch'a ching* or 'Tea Classic', which exists in a separate version and is said to have been written in the eighth century AD by one Lu Yü. The author is concerned only with porcelains, and only with those porcelains which he considers suitable for making tea-bowls – a question of the colour of the glaze and the particular tint it imparted to the tea. If this standard seems somewhat artificial, what are we to make of a report in *T'ao shuo* concerning the 'musical cups' that came into vogue during T'ang times and which were arranged in groups of twelve, and later eight, so as to constitute a musical scale? 'Cups were chosen of close texture and pure sound', says *T'ao shuo*, 'not like those for drinking tea or helping wine, but by testing the good or bad fabric of each by actual manipulation.'[15] Cups by deviation become musical instruments; and flowery allusions to porcelain 'of the nature of' silver, ice, snow, or jade, take us even further away from reality into a private world of collectors' and connoisseurs' gush, and lead towards the dreadful potters' purgatory where pottery masquerades as bronze or basalt, and a tea-pot for fun disguises itself as a log of wood or even the family four-seater.

Under the heading '[Tea]Bowls', *Ch'a ching* has the following entry: 'The best [tea]bowls are those of Yüeh-chou. Then comes Ting-chou[16], then Wu-chou[17], then Yo-chou, and lastly Shou-chou and Hung-chou. Some people regard Hsing-chou as superior to Yüeh-chou, but this is undoubtedly wrong. Hsing porcelain (*tz'ŭ*) is like silver, while Yüeh porcelain is like jade – the first respect in which Hsing is not as good as Yüeh. And whereas Hsing porcelain is like snow, that of Yüeh is like ice – the second respect in which Hsing is not as good as Yüeh. Hsing porcelain is white, so that the colour of the tea is red, but Yüeh porcelain is green (*ch'ing*), and the colour of the tea is also green (*lü*) – a third respect in which Hsing does not come up to Yüeh.' Lu Yü goes on to observe that Yüeh bowls were straight-sided, did not flare outwards at the mouth, and had narrow, splayed footrims. They held half a pint or less. Yüeh was green in colour, as was Yo; whereas Hsing was white, Shou yellow, and Hung brown. Only Yüeh and Yo were really fit for drinking tea out of, the colour of the others giving an undesirable tint to the brew.

One other T'ang notice is worth quoting at this point. It occurs in a small work on music called *Yo fu tsa lu*, allegedly written at the end of the tenth century AD by a certain Tuan An-chieh, and runs: 'In the first year of the Ta-chung period of the T'ang dynasty [AD 847], one of the officers appointed to compose the music was Kuo Tao-yüan, Governor of Ta-hsing-hsien [the modern Peking]. He was skilled in the art of playing upon musical cups, and used twelve cups of Yüeh-chou and Hsing-chou porcelain, the tones of which surpassed those of the hanging musical stones of jade.'[18]

From these notices we gather that two wares, the green Yüeh and the white Hsing, were esteemed above all others during T'ang times. What appears to be a further reference to them occurs in the writings of the Arab Tha'alibi, who died in AD 1038. Of Chinese pottery he says: '... And the best of it is the apricot-coloured (*mishmishi*), thin, clear, ringing strongly; next to this comes the cream-coloured (*zabadi*) of the same kind.' Kahle, from whose paper I quote the above extract[19], thinks that the apricot in question may have been *mishmishi shami*, the Damascus apricot, which has a grey-green skin. It appears, then, that Tha'alibi too considered a green-coloured and a white porcelain to be pre-eminent among T'ang ceramics.

We see that there was some disagreement as to the relative merits of Yüeh and Hsing, and as to what qualities in them should be esteemed. At least two distinct sorts of T'ang stoneware have in any case now been plausibly linked with the Yüeh and Hsing factories and we shall proceed to a brief description of each.

In full autumn wind and dew the kilns of Yüeh open;
And a thousand peaks are despoiled of their halcyon-green.
LU KUEI-MÊNG (ninth century AD)

Yüeh is the old name for what is now Chekiang province on the eastern seaboard of China, and Yüeh _yao_ (Yüeh ware) that of a classical Chinese porcelain celebrated in the writings of Chinese poets, topographers, and antiquarians from as far back as the eighth century AD. After long centuries of steady production, historical circumstances caused the decline of the Yüeh factories towards the end of the tenth century, leaving behind only a name and an accumulating legend. Within the last generation the combined efforts of scholars, fieldworkers, dealers, and collectors, in China and abroad, have rescued Yüeh from a thousand years of oblivion, and it is now seen to occupy the very heart of the tradition of high-fired stoneware manufacture in China.

The excavations at Samarra [p. 251] marked the opening of this phase of rediscovery, since they yielded fragments of a green-glazed stoneware of T'ang date, not conflicting with the description of Yüeh found in _Ch'a ching_ [p. 254]. Sherds of the same ware were soon reported from other sites outside China, for example from ninth- and tenth-century strata at Suza, from the rubbish heaps of Fostat (Old Cairo), and from Brāhmanābād in West Pakistan, a city destroyed by flood about AD 1020.

Today the sites of ancient ports, market towns, and capital cities in almost every country of south and east Asia, as well as east Africa and even more remote places, have yielded up examples of Yüeh and other contemporary Chinese wares, sometimes in enormous quantities, and we thus get a picture of the exclusive products of a particular locality in China coming to the forefront of world trade in the ninth–tenth centuries AD, much as did the lacquers of Szechwan at the beginning of the Christian era. I have appended a select bibliography in which reports of these finds have been listed, country by country, for those who would care to follow more fully the story of the peaceful penetration of this most beautiful ware.[20]

With tangible evidence now to hand to show that a high-fired stoneware of ultimate ceramic quality was being manufactured in China in T'ang times, a search began to find the location of the Yüeh factories. Sung records transmitted through _T'ao shuo_ and _T'ao lu_ stated that the so-called 'secret-colour ware', _pi sê yao_, was made in the Yü-yao district of Chekiang some 40 miles east of Shao-hsing, the old capital of the Princes of Yüeh (AD 907–78) for whose exclusive use the ware was reserved. If this _pi sê yao_ was Yüeh _yao_, or a special variety of Yüeh, then the Yüeh factories must surely be looked for in the Yü-yao district. Now the sixteenth-century local district guide mentions that during T'ang and Sung times the _pi sê yao_ of Yü-yao was made at a factory on the shore of a lake, the Shang-lin-hu, about ten miles north of the district town. With all this in mind, the Japanese scholar Manzō Nakao delegated his fellow-countryman Mantarō Kaida to visit the spot; it was thus Kaida, in 1930, who first stumbled on the waste of stoneware sherds and kiln debris lying disregarded on the pinewood slopes above the Shang-lin lake, this being the primary centre for the production of _pi sê yao_, the quintessential Yüeh ware.

It remained for J.M. Plumer to show a close similarity between the Shang-lin-hu sherds and those found at Samarra, proving that the latter were of Chinese manufacture, originated in Chekiang province, and were to be identified as Yüeh ware of the T'ang period.[21]

Shortly after the discovery of Shang-lin-hu, other Yüeh kiln-sites began to be reported, some of them belonging to periods obviously far older than the T'ang. Tê-ch'ing, a place 25 miles north of Hangchow, was discovered in October 1930 by a third Japanese, Tsuneo

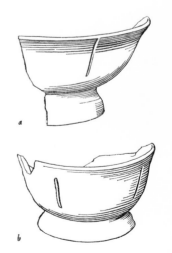

46 Fragments of foliate bowls; _a_ from Samarra; _b_ from Shang-lin-hu

pl. 170

Yonaiyama; the site has been assigned to the period including the Han and Six Dynasties. Among typical Yüeh fragments were spouts in the shape of chickens' heads, such as adorned a well-known type of ewer. Some sherds exhibited an opaque black glaze of the type the Japanese call *temmoku* [p. 243], particularly *korai temmoku*, which until that time had usually been associated with the Sung period and which was totally unexpected in a context so very much earlier.

Chiu-yen, a site about midway between Shao-hsing and Hangchow, was discovered in July 1936 by yet another Japanese, Yuzo Matsumara; its wares, too, are generally regarded as extending back to a much earlier period than that represented by Shang-lin-hu – undoubtedly as far back as the first century BC, and quite possibly to the late Chou period – while on the other hand scarcely reaching forward into the T'ang. Though obviously related to the later Yüeh of Shang-lin-hu in their material and method of manufacture, Chiu-yen wares present a quite different appearance, the potting being somewhat rough and ready, and the shapes robust. In modelling vessels in the forms of animals the Chiu-yen potter exploits a rich vein of fantasy, yet keeps always in mind the sturdy, workaday purpose the pot is meant to serve.

The assiduous Japanese, who, like the English, are privately quite crazy about what the latter with fond disparagement call 'pots' (just as they call their wives 'old thing'), sealed their achievement in Chekiang in 1944 when Shigehiro Yoneda investigated an important kiln-site at Yü-wang-miao, two miles west of Shao-hsing. Yü-wang-miao seems to have been contemporary with Shang-lin-hu, for the sherds from the two places are remarkably alike, and there is disagreement as to which of the two produced the finer ware.[22] Confronted with pots or sherds not actually found *in situ*, it would hardly be possible to say from which of the two sites they came.

Shortly after World War 2 the Chinese took up the work of exploration from the Japanese. In 1954 they discovered a Yüeh factory, closely similar in its *œuvre* to that of Chiu-yen, at the village of Shang-tung about 30 miles south of Hangchow, and another at Wang-chia-lü a few miles south of Chiu-yen itself; and a few years ago added to the list eight Yüeh kilns of Shang-lin-hu type found about 9 miles south of Huang-yen in central Chekiang. This constellation of Yüeh sites is shown on map 4, T'ang pottery site numbers 4–8.

*

How far back in history does the production of Yüeh *yao* extend? That is a difficult question to answer. Considered purely from the technical point of view – the *matière* of the body and the techniques used to make the pot – we have in Yüeh the culmination of a tradition that can be traced back to the early part of the Shang period, which of course gives China absolute priority for the manufacture and commercial production of high-fired feldspathic stonewares. Shang pots recently found at Chêng-chou (*c.* 1500–1300 BC) are large, with very sharp corner-points at the neck and a high, keel-shaped shoulder. The body is high-fired and feldspathic, and is decorated with cord or mat impressions, or S-shaped figures, all finished with a high-fired yellowish-green glaze. This is evenly applied to the outer and inner surfaces of the vessel, so that there is in this case no question of a natural glaze deposit such as would be caused by wood-ash falling on the surface while being fired [see p. 241].

Of the same high ceramic quality are pot-sherds found by Dr Li Chi at An-yang, some years before World War 2, lying in undisturbed strata containing oracle bones. The yellowish-green glaze was applied by a brush, and was confined to a band encircling the shoulders of the vessels. The peak firing-temperature must have been around 1,300° C, since at that temperature the body of a test piece changed colour and became harder.

39 Bowl in the shape of an Indian Buddhist patra or alms-bowl, with applied relief medallions; of stoneware with a blue-black temmoku-type glaze, the medallions touched with brown and green. T'ang dynasty. Height: 6³/₄ in. Nelson Gallery of Art, Kansas City.

40 *Bottle with globular body and small bulbous neck; of stoneware with a dark olive* temmoku-*type glaze relieved with cloudy bluish-white splashes. T'ang dynasty. Height: 8 in. Collection of Mrs A. Clark, England.*

41 *Pilgrim flask with moulded decoration featuring a vintaging scene of Hellenistic type; of stoneware encrusted with a heavy olive-brown glaze. Tʻang dynasty. Height: 8³/₈ in. Victoria and Albert Museum.*

42 *Amphora vase with paired handles in the form of dragons; of fine buff earthenware partly covered with green, yellowish-brown and colourless 'egg and spinach' glazes. T'ang dynasty. Height: 12 1/4 in. Art Museum, University of Singapore.*

43 *Ewer with pinched trefoil mouth, in the form of an oinochoe; of off-white earthenware covered with a white slip and decorated with green, blue and amber glazes. T'ang dynasty. Height: 13 3/4 in. Tenri Museum, Nara.*

Probably closer to a purist's definition of Yüeh are vessels taken in 1954 from the P'u-tu-ts'un tomb dating from the late tenth century BC [see p. 101], among which is one des-cribed as a stemmed dish (tou) with bluish-green glaze. Even more important from the stand-point of ceramic history was the excavation in March 1959 of a tomb near T'un-ch'i in south Anhwei, well within the old Yüeh region, from which over 70 pieces of glazed stoneware were recovered. The shapes (as was to remain the case for at least a thousand years to come) rather slavishly imitate those of contemporary bronzes such as the favourite tou, the hu, p'an, and tsun, and the vessels may be regarded as ersatz bronzes. The colour of the glaze is either a dirty brown or green, sombre tints that suggest the patination of old bronze, which is what the potter may have had in mind. The brown was applied with the brush, the green ap-parently by dipping in the glaze. Discovery of similar stonewares is reported from Loyang in southern Honan, and Tan-tu in south Kiangsu.[23]

Next in the series of high-fired stonewares of Yüeh type come some early Yüeh pots col-lected by the late Sir Herbert Ingram, which are now in the Ashmolean Museum, Oxford. The decorative features displayed by these pots, particularly a diapered band at the shoulder, suggest a Chiu-yen provenance, whereas their forms decidedly resemble those of bronzes of perhaps the third century BC. We know that such bronze forms as hu, lien, etc., continued to be expressed in pottery long after they had ceased to be made in metal, which makes it almost impossible to date them accurately; they fit somewhere into the period 200 BC to AD 200. Karlbeck, who submitted them to a careful examination, was first inclined to view them as having been made at Chiu-yen itself, but later broadened his view and admitted than they may have been made elsewhere in the Yüeh region.[24]

In 1924 C. W. Bishop excavated a number of pots of Yüeh type from a grave at Hsin-yang in Honan dated to the year AD 99. The excavators reported that on first seeing these pots they took them for Sung stonewares of the well-known celadon range. Certainly they are in the Yüeh tradition which eventually produced the celadons, but how far they really do resemble the celadons is another question, so subjective are people's impressions of pot-tery. The Japanese ceramicist Koyama has noted a resemblance between this group and the products of Tê-ch'ing, and at one time actually attributed them to this factory.

In 1953 a group of vessels of Chiu-yen type was discovered in the tomb of a general called Chou Chu, who died in battle in the year AD 279, at a place called Chou-mu-tun in the I-hsing district of Kiangsu bordering on northern Chekiang. These are perhaps the earliest pieces of indubitable Yüeh for whose manufacture we can award a terminal date. Incense-burners predominate; the technique is advanced, and the ceramic form delightful. I-hsing was destined to become an important pottery centre in later centuries, and it may well be that a Yüeh kiln was located here. Otherwise the ware could easily have come up from Chekiang, I-hsing being under a hundred miles from Chiu-yen, and about fifty from Tê-ch'ing.

map 4
pl. 154

*

Several of those who visited Shang-lin-hu were lucky enough to pick up sherds and wasters of Yüeh ware with a 4-character inscription recording their dates, incised beneath the glaze within the footrim. The remarkable fact is that most of these inscriptions, as well as others on complete bowls in Western and Japanese collections, refer to the date AD 978. Probably these pieces are to be associated with an actual historical event, for it was in 978 that the Princes of Yüeh finally capitulated to the growing Sung power. On March 24th the Sung Emperor T'ai-tsung received in audience the last Yüeh Prince, Ch'ien Su, and accepted from him an enormous gift of no fewer than 50,000 pieces of porcelain. They were undoubtedly of the finest quality, and it is very probable that all of them were dated in honour of the occasion; indeed perhaps it may not be too wild a speculation to surmise that the few whole pots known to bear the date in question are survivors from the original tribute, and that the sherds and wasters picked up at Shang-lin-hu were rejects from this vast firing – which possibly was one of the last. For early in the eleventh century a new factory to the south began production of the famous Lung-ch'üan celadon, which can be thought of as the direct descendant of Shang-lin-hu ware, even though it came to develop special characteristics of its own. Production of celadons at Lung-ch'üan continued until well into Ming times, and indeed has never entirely ceased. The factory is today receiving government assistance; the seven remaining old-time operators have successfully relayed the ancient techniques to a new generation, and production has become semi-mechanized. No attempt at originality of design is being attempted – perhaps it is too early for that – the pots being simply copies of the forms that became conventional for this type of ware as early as the Sung.[25] Thus the stoneware tradition, in which Yüeh was centrally situated, leaves a continuous record throughout the whole known period of Chinese history.

col. 36 is shown in the left margin next to this paragraph.

*

The Yüeh body is hard, grey, and feldspathic. The glaze does not as a rule amalgamate with the body, but lies like a transparent cuticle on its surface, broken sherds showing no transition layer. The ware is always fired under reducing conditions. Small amounts of reduced iron in the body and glaze impart a characteristic range of shades including a warm brown, olive-brown, grey-green, and a celadonlike sea-green. Exposed portions of the body are re-oxidized during cooling, when air is let into the kiln, and 'flash' to a warm rust-red.

col. 41, 33, 35 is shown in the left margin next to this paragraph.

The shapes of Yüeh vessels are not very varied. Apart from a few familiar lines such as chicken-spouted ewers, two-section vases, covered toilet boxes, and writers' brush-pots, the vast majority of the pieces are bowls, as *Ch'a ching* says. Top-quality bowls are rather deep, their sides being fairly straight and often divided into five lobes. The inside bottom is usually marked off by means of two closely parallel incised circles enclosing an arabesque design of masterly draughtsmanship. On the best pieces this is drawn freehand by incising or engraving on the leather-hard body; but rouletting with a wheel, combing, carving, or moulding may also be employed, either separately or in combination with line engraving. Floral motifs such as lotus and tree peony are popular, but there are also dragons, phoenixes, fish, parakeets, and other creatures in a rich repertoire. The vase of plate 164 gives some idea of the quality of the work.

pls 170, 164 and *col. 33, 35* are shown in the left margin next to this paragraph; *pl. 164* is shown lower.

Top-quality Yüeh bowls have footrims which are deep, slightly splayed, and conical in cross-section, the base within the footrim being invariably glazed. The bowls were fired separately, not one inside the other, and for this purpose they were made to stand either on a circular sandy ring or else on five separate clay spurs set on the base within the footrim (see the Yo *yao* bowl of plate 158 which was fired by the same technique). On removal from the kiln, the broken ends of the spurs were ground down so that only the scars remained. Except for these scars, the entire inner and outer surfaces of the bowl were covered with glaze.

pl. 158 is shown in the left margin next to this paragraph.

Coarser wares were fired otherwise. One method was to support the bowl in the kiln with the aid of a ring of spurs on which the underside of the footrim rested. After firing, spurs and footrim would be neatly ground down until the surface was perfectly smooth and free from glaze. By another technique the bowls were fired in stacks, each bowl nestling inside the one beneath, but separated from it by a ring of spurs placed so as to support the upper bowl upon its footrim. On removal from the kiln, the bowls had to be broken apart and the spur marks ground down, both on the inside bottom and on the footrim of each, until only the scars remained. A more carelessly finished variety had its footrim spurs ground down, but those inside the bowl left standing. The bodies of all these coarser types are heavy and rather crudely potted, and were probably designed to withstand the rigours of shipment. On the whole the best Yüeh lines did not go for export.

Hsing

The second of the two great T'ang stonewares, Hsing *yao*, falls within the European defini- *pls 157, 159, 161, 182*
tion of porcelain by virtue of its whiteness and translucency; it is also hard and resonant, and often highly lustrous. The body is kaolinic and white-burning, but the potters seem usually to have added a coating of white slip for extra measure. The glaze is glossy and dead white, except for where it runs in drops with a slightly bluish tinge, and is moderately full of bub-bles. The shapes as we know them are less varied than those of Yüeh. Bowls, presumably tea-bowls, predominate; but there are smaller bowls describable as saucers, and larger bowls or basins presumably not intended for holding tea.

The Hsing potters practised certain conventions which, although in no single case ex-clusive to this factory, do in the aggregate combine to give a highly personal character to the ware. One is the rolled lip, presumably meant to strengthen the mouthrim and prevent it sagging at peak firing temperature; another is a fluted band on a mouthrim which is itself *pls 157, 159*
slightly contracted inwards, an attractive feature found on several of the bowls; yet another is division of the body into five lobes – though this characteristic is shared by Yüeh and Yo *yao*.

While hesitating to describe this beautiful ware as 'utility', the fact remains that potters did not trouble greatly about surface finish, at least on the outside of the bowl. Wreathing-marks left by the turning tool are visible below the level of the glaze and under it; as seen in profile, the body turns in to meet the outer edge of the footrim along a horizontal line made by a single summary cut of the turning tool. The elaborate firing devices used by the Yüeh potter are missing in the case of Hsing. The footrim is typically very wide and shallow, so that the base within it is reduced to a mere recessed button. Neither footrim nor base is as a rule glazed.

It was the late Gustaf Lindberg who in 1957 first proposed to identify the ware described above as Hsing *yao*[26], though as long ago as 1925 Sarre had mentioned Hsing-chou in con-nexion with the white Chinese sherds found at Samarra.[27] Similar sherds from Brāhmanābād are in the British Museum, while the present writer has also picked up quantities of them, together with Yüeh, from the deserted site of the medieval seaport of Mahatittha in northern Ceylon. Wherever Yüeh went, Hsing kept company. Just as they are bracketed together in the critical mind of Lu Yü, so too we find them together in the deserts to which the trade products of T'ang China once found their way.

The Hsing kiln-sites have not been located at the time of writing. Hsing-chou is the mod-ern Hsing-tai some fifty miles north of Tz'ŭ-chou in southern Hopei – itself a primary pro-duction centre during Sung times. A hundred miles to the north-east of Hsing-tai lies Ting-chou, near where the famous white Ting porcelain was produced, also in Sung times. About twenty-five miles north-east of Hsing-tai is Chü-lu, a city overwhelmed by flood in AD 1108, from the ruins of which large quantities of household stonewares have been recovered, some with a white and minutely crackled glaze, some with a sumptuous blue-black *temmoku*-type glaze. Hsing-chou evidently lay in the very heart of a pottery country.

From information supplied by *T'ao shuo* we can probably get a more exact bearing on the Hsing kiln-sites. It quotes the late eighth-century *T'ang kuo shih p'u* as saying that 'the white porcelain cups of Nui-ch'iu ... were distributed among high and low alike throughout the empire', and it adds that this Nui-ch'iu lay within the administration of Chü-lu district (*hsien*) in Hsing county (*chou*). *T'ao shuo* draws the natural conclusion that Nui-ch'iu ware was that known to Lu Yü and more generally as Hsing *yao*, and we may well agree. Yüeh-chou and Ting-chou both gave their names as county towns to wares made many miles distant, and the same no doubt applied in the case of Hsing-chou. The Hsing kiln-sites, there-fore, should be looked for in the vicinity of Chü-lu, at a place now or formerly known as Nui-ch'iu.

pls 160, 180 Apparently production at Hsing-chou came to a halt at the beginning of the Sung period to be succeeded by a new Imperial factory at Ting-chou, just as Lung-ch'üan succeeded Shang-lin-hu.[28]

Other T'ang factories

It seems probable that one other classical T'ang pottery has now been identified, the green-glazed stoneware of Yo-chou, modern Yo-yang in north-east Hunan. Shortly after World War 2 small quantities of a ware shipped from China under the name Yo *yao* began to arrive *pl. 158* in the West. Bodies ranged from a heavy, coarse earthenware to a superb stoneware fully equal to the best of Yüeh. Judging by the shapes of the pots, Yo *yao* had a long production history extending perhaps as far back as the Han.

Yo stonewares have in common a dark-grey body and an olive-green glaze with finely-meshed crackle. Nearly all of them are heavily stained with a red earth which is most notice-able in the crackle, on the comparatively glazeless mouthrim, and on unglazed parts of the body. The fact is significant, for it suggests that they were all dug up in the same part of the *col. 34* country, and indeed they are said to have been recovered from graves in the Ch'ang-sha region of Hunan, some 85 miles south of Yo-yang.[29]

Yo kiln-sites have not yet been located, and the ware remains something of a mystery. It may have been exported in small quantities together with Yüeh and Hsing.[30]

*

A T'ang kiln-site at Ch'iung-lai in western Szechwan in the far west of China has been known since 1936. The place is about 20 miles south of the town of Ta-yi which is itself about 60 miles west of the provincial capital, Chêng-tu. Involuntarily we think of the words of the T'ang poet Tu Fu, who was living in Chêng-tu in AD 756, in addressing his superior Wei Ch'u: 'The porcelain from the Ta-yi kilns is light and yet strong. It gives out a low jade note when struck, and is famed throughout the city. Your Excellency has white bowls surpassing hoar-frost and snow. Pray be gracious and send some to my poor mat-shed.'[31]

Ch'iung-lai may not, of course, have been the main production centre for Ta-yi ware, yet the pots recovered from the site must have been very close to those Tu Fu was hankering after. Perhaps he was a little over-complimentary. For charming as they are, these pieces are really only provincial interpretations of the classical T'ang forms (though there is an original line of slipware pleasingly painted with slight brush-strokes suggesting a floral motif); they are discussed and fully illustrated in a recent book by Chêng Tê-k'un, one of their earliest explorers. Most interesting among the finds, perhaps, are some moulds used to impress the interiors of oval four-lobed bowls.[32]

To pass from the gallery of Han ceramics into that of the T'ang is like leaving the dim and august twilight of a Royal Academy Exhibition of the 1910's to enter the warm sunshine of a contemporary show of post-Impressionist painting. Han pottery is very fine, but somewhat gloomy in tone, too academic, too confined in its forms by close proximity to the great bronze-vessel tradition. The majesty of the bronzes assures distinction to their poor relations in Han pottery; the Han ceramic genius exercises itself in much exquisite modulation of basic shape within the formal limits of the two classes most favoured for reproduction, *hu* and *lei*, and ex-plores no further. The rich and sombre glazes, too, are aesthetically appropriate to the weighty mass of the vessels, accentuating the impression of metal, but are too limited in their appeal to be of lasting interest or to stimulate the Han potter into inventing new lines on which they could be tried. He was happier and far more creative when escaping from the tyrannical pre-sence of the bronze tradition into the childlike world he prepared for the dead, modelling funerary wares in the form of well-heads or granaries, miniature models of cooking-stoves, farm-yards, pigsties, farm animals, paddy-fields, ponds, or river boats; or deftly working up his clay into the delightful images of tomb servants, musicians, acrobats, or dancers.

pls 147, 152, 153, 250

The four centuries that make a bridge between Han and T'ang are still somewhat of a dark age in the history of Chinese ceramics. One thing is clear; memories of the great bronze-vessel tradition and the society it represented were fast receding. There were no regrets, no afterthoughts. Nostalgia for the past, that so often over the centuries invaded the Chinese artistic consciousness and dictated its choice of themes, is nowhere apparent. A gap widens, presently to be filled with an influx of ceramic forms from abroad, caused partly through the agency of nomad invaders, partly as a result of Buddhist missionary enterprise, and scarcely at all by trade. By Northern Ch'i times western Asiatic vessel-types begin to appear in the Chinese repertory, their surfaces often heavily encrusted with *appliqué* decoration of exotic de-sign. The new forms are as yet only crudely assimilated into the native tradition.

It is at this point that we reach the hall of T'ang pottery. The photographs and text figures that adorn this chapter well illustrate the astonishing variety of shapes, sizes, bodies, glazes, colours, textures, that greets us as we enter. A few are refinements of native Chinese forms inherited from the Six Dynasties and earlier periods, but the vast majority are such as had never before been seen in China. Classical antiquity lay well and truly buried, and would not be disinterred until the advent of the Sung with its obsessional interest in the ritual and ceremonial of the China of Confucius, its distaste for anything new from abroad – the limited *Weltanschauung* that seems to accompany one of the two cyclical phases of Chinese history. A rhyton illustrated by the scholarly compilers of *Chin shih so* (1822) is confidently identified by them as an ox-headed drinking horn of the Chou dynasty, *Chou ssŭ kuang*, but is clearly either a Parthian original like that of figure 47a, or else a loving T'ang copy of one. An almost identical vessel is featured in the 1752 edition of the compendium of bronzes in the Imperial Sung dynasty collection called *Hsüan-ho po ku t'u lu*, and described as an animal-shaped sacrificial wine vessel of the Han period, *Han hsi tsun* [see pp. 89 and 93]. Such a vessel could have been made in the T'ang period; in succeeding ages no antiquarian would in his wildest dreams have imagined its true ancestry. The T'ang was too busy for antiquarian pur-suits; and when tracing the ancestries of T'ang pottery shapes and decorative motifs we can afford to ignore China's own antiquity as a possible source.

The great majority of T'ang vessel-types originated, then, abroad. The curious thing is that despite their exoticism, extreme in some cases, the moment they get translated into Chinese

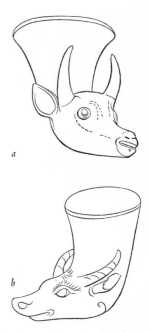

47 *Rhytons: a* Parthian glazed earthenware *rhyton; b* vessel featured in *Chin shih so* (1822) as a 'Chou dynasty *ssŭ kuang*'

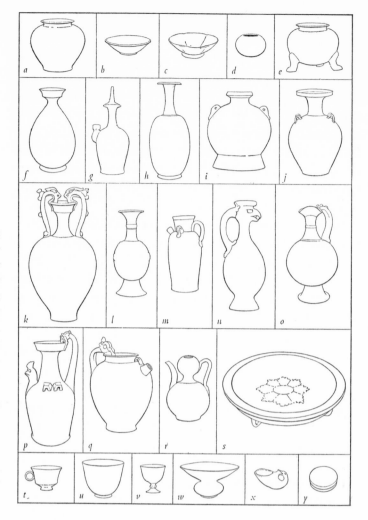

48 T'ang pottery shapes: *a* jar;
b plain bowl; *c* lobed bowl; *d* alms-
bowl; *e* bowl on three feet; *f* short-
necked bottle; *g* kuṇḍikā; *h* long-
necked bottle; *i* pilgrim bottle;
j two-section vase; *k* amphora;
l three-section vase; *m* plain ewer;
n bird-headed ewer; *o* oinochoe;
p chicken-spouted ewer; *q* jar ewer;
r double-gourd ewer; *s* offering dish;
t handled cup; *u* beaker; *v* stem-cup;
w 'spittoon'; *x* rhyton; *y* covered box

49 *a* T'ang glazed earthenware jar;
b Seine-Rhine Roman glass bowl
(early second century AD) found at
Colchester, England

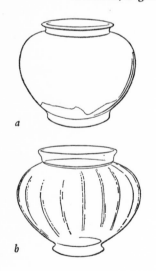

pottery they are all transformed and acquire the unmistakable T'ang ceramic family likeness. Their very diversity seems to have challenged the T'ang potter to create out of them a new, distinctive unity; just so, human migrants and refugees from many different parts of the world willy-nilly build a new nation in a new land, and find a common language. From India came *pātra, kuṇḍikā, amṛta kalaśa*; from the Greek world came *amphora, rhyton, oinochoe*; from Syria the stem-cup, perhaps also one form of bottle, decorative or utilitarian form-compo-nents such as dragon-handles and neck ribs; from Persia came the pilgrim bottle, the spittoon, a part at least of the bird-headed ewer, possibly the four-lobed bowl decorated with fish, and many decorative motifs.

*

For present purposes I do not think a detailed account of the T'ang vessel-types will be ne-cessary. I have accordingly made a selection from among the range of vessel-types drawn in outline in figure 48, dealing summarily with most, and discussing at rather greater length those that for one reason or another appear to me of greater interest from the art-historical point of view.

JARS
pl. 156, col. 28–32
fig. 49

The typical T'ang jar, with its high shoulder and fulsome curves, is a highly individual ves-sel-type rather unlike anything we know from earlier periods, and the possibility is that it is an imported form, perhaps originally taken from the Syrio-Roman tradition.[33]

266

In this category we include plain bowls, bowls with rolled mouthrim, and bowls with the body marked off into five lobes.

The five-lobed bowl appears not to have been made before T'ang times – nor perhaps subsequently, since Sung bowls seem to have always had six lobes, sometimes more. The lobes are marked by means of nicks at intervals along the mouthrim, by vertical indentations down the sides of the body (the lobes then pushed slightly into bulges), or by narrow vertical trails of slip down the inside surface. In confining this form solely to the stonewares with their pearly translucent glazes the T'ang potter was perhaps bent on reproducing in clay the fresh limpid beauty of the lotus flower; if so, he often well succeeds. The shape is indigenous, and no foreign prototype need be contemplated.

These bowls are typically decorated on the inside bottom with a moulded design of a fish or fishes among water-weeds. The type occurs in contemporary Chinese silverware together with three other classes of small domestic vessel (the miniature stem-cup, the handled cup, and the spittoon), and in view of the fact that the craft of the silversmith in China was virtually a creation of refugee Sassanian craftsmen we should perhaps on *a priori* grounds seek for the ancestors of all four classes in Persian metalware. In the case of the four-lobed bowl with fish design the issue is made rather more complicated because of the existence of an oval lugged bowl or cup in the Han lacquer tradition, sometimes reproduced in pottery, as also of shallow earthenware and stoneware bowls or basins of the same period featuring a pair of fish incised on the inside bottom in much the same position as in the T'ang four-lobed bowls.

Turning to possible Western prototypes for the latter, we have in figure 50b what H. C. Gallois considered to be its ultimate ancestor in the shape of a charming little bronze cup found near Cologne together with late Roman remains dating from before the fifth century AD. On the strength of it Gallois argued that 'a four-lobed receptacle derived from the pure oval was invented in the West and travelled to China where it found great favour in T'ang times'.[34] It may be thought that a single example is not sufficient evidence on which to base a theory.

In this particular variety of four-lobed bowl it will be seen that the mouldings are vertical, and carry down to the foot. In another category, that especially associated with Sassanian metalware, the mouldings as seen from above are longitudinal and do not necessarily dip down as low as the footrim. Thus the side-lobes take the form of cup-shaped vesicles from which other smaller vesicles may be 'budded off', so presenting the unusual appearance of the bowl of figure 51a, in which we can actually count *eight* lobes.[35] In this case the inside bottom is marked with the outline of a fish in solder, suggesting that a small *appliqué* fish, probably in gold, had at one time been fastened there. It was on the strength of this bowl that Gallois argued the Western origin of the fish motif.

Several silver bowls similar to this bowl, though not with the fish motif, have been found in south Russia, and have generally been regarded as Sassanian in origin. However a similar eight-lobed silver bowl in the Victoria and Albert Museum having two fishes engraved on the inside bottom, one at each end, is quite definitely T'ang Chinese, as is the four-lobed silver bowl of plate 163. There is thus, it seems to me, a possibility that *all* these silver bowls are of Chinese origin; and so long as this doubt exists it would probably be unwise to say definitely that the form of the Chinese pottery four-lobed bowl with fish design is derived from a Sassanian metal ancestor.

Indian Buddhist mendicants when they arrived in China carried with them only three articles other than their clothing which their law allowed them to possess – the *khakkhara* or

OVAL FOUR-LOBED BOWLS
pls 161–163

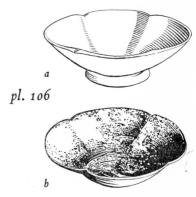

pl. 106

50 Four-lobed bowls: *a* T'ang Hsing *yao* porcelain bowl; *b* Roman bronze bowl from Cologne, Germany

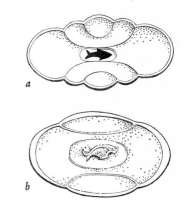

51 Lobed fish-bowls: *a* Sassanian silver dish from Koulagyche, Perm, USSR; *b* T'ang glazed earthenware bowl

BOWLS IMITATING INDIAN BUDDHIST BEGGING-BOWLS

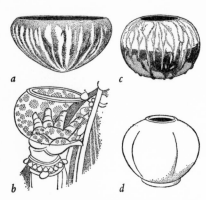

52 Alms-bowls: *a* T'ang glazed earthenware alms-bowl in the Shōsō-in Treasury, Nara, Japan; *b* glass (?) alms-bowl featured in a painted banner from Tun-huang; *c* T'ang glazed earthenware alms-bowl; *d* T'ang Yüeh *yao* porcelain water pot

fig. 52 a

SHORT-NECKED BOTTLES

col. 41

staff, the *kuṇḍikā* or water-bottle, and the *pātra* (Ch. *po-to-lo*) or begging-bowl. This last was of special sanctity because of legends woven round Śākyamuni Buddha's own begging-bowl, and the vessel passed automatically as a vessel-type into the repertory of the T'ang potter. The original Indian vessel, as depicted in Buddhist wall-paintings and on temple banners found in Chinese Turkestan, is a flattened globular bowl with a small and sometimes slightly in-vaginated mouth, and of course with no foot. A form of *pātra* in use in India today is simply half a coconut shell, which may have supplied the original model for the pottery type.

The Chinese imitated the Indian unglazed earthenware *pātra* both in earthenware and stoneware, throwing these handsome shapes a little carelessly and covering the stoneware specimens with thick and unctuous glazes of *temmoku* type. They also made a much more sophisticated stoneware vessel based on it, which served apparently as a writer's brushpot. Speaking of porcelain waterpots used at the writing table, the eighteenth-century *Chang wu chih* mentions globular bowls (*wêng*) 'with small mouth shaped like Buddhist alms-bowls, and others with spherical ribbed body'.[37] Evidently this refers to vessels shaped like figure 52 d, which is of Yüeh *yao*.

A variant type of *pātra*, a glazed earthenware bowl with wide mouth and shallow body gently falling away below to a pointed bottom, is known to us from a group of twenty-five in the Imperial Shōsō-in at Nara, Japan, founded in AD 756 by the widow of the Nara Emperor Shōmu as a repository of his personal treasures; these are almost certainly part of the original foundation. A Chinese pottery bowl of essentially similar form was found by von le Coq at Kysyl in Chinese Turkestan during the course of his archaeological reconnais-sances there in 1905–6.[38]

No such form exists in the pre-T'ang tradition, and the T'ang version may perhaps derive from a Sassanian silver form such as the bottle of figure 53 a. The late Antique heavily *repoussé* decoration of vintaging scenes found on these Persian bottles does not occur on their Chinese counterparts as far as I know, but such scenes are perfectly at home on other members of the T'ang range, especially the pilgrim bottle.

53 Short-necked bottles: *a* silver-gilt bottle, part of the Oxus Treasure, Mazanderan, Persia; *b* T'ang glazed earthenware bottle

54 Reconstruction of an Indian pottery *kuṇḍikā;* fragments from fifth–sixth centuries AD

268

The three varieties of tall-necked bottle have no Chinese ancestors, and again we must look abroad. The first variety is the *kuṇḍikā* (Ch. *chün-ch'ih-ka*), or Buddhist monk's drinking bottle. The vessel was so designed that the *bhikshu* could drink without his lips coming into contact with the defiling clay, an Indian notion. It was filled with water through the L-shaped funnel which we would call a spout, and the monk inverted it to drink out of the nipple luted on to the vessel's mouthrim, holding it a short distance away from his lips.

The Indian *kuṇḍikā* is known to us from countless broken fragments recovered at the sites of ancient Buddhist monasteries dating from as far back as the third century BC, and is featured on many bas-relief sculptures contemporary with the T'ang. The Chinese devotee I-ching has left an exact description of the vessel as he saw it in use during his travels in India between AD 673 and 689[39], as reconstructed in figure 54.

The Chinese pottery version is copied from the Indian original unchanged in its essentials. In the hands of the T'ang potter it becomes a tall and graceful form, reproduced not only in stoneware but also in copper and bronze, and the type was often beautifully rendered in celadon during the Kōryō period in Korea (AD 936–1392). One might perhaps add that the Indian *kuṇḍikā* passed also into south-east Asia, and that in Ming times the Chinese studied and captured the local market for these vessels, supplying Malaya and Indonesia with their favourite models in Ming china for a period of some three hundred years.[40]

The second and third varieties of tall-necked bottle are also connected with Buddhism, but are the attributes of gods, not men. As found in Indian sculpture, particularly that of the Gandhāra school [p. 186], they are diagnostic of images of the Bodhisattva Maitreya, and they are to be identified as *amṛta kalaśa* or ambrosia bottles (Ch. *pao p'ing*). Ananda Coomaraswamy notes that they are appropriate to any deity in his capacity as an immortal, since they hold the water of life which is capable of raising the dead when sprinkled over the corpse.[41] Figure 55 c–f shows how ordinary T'ang earthenwares were evidently based on this Buddhist form. It will be seen that the centre field is invariably a decorative band, the lotus palmette evidently being especially favoured.

The second variant is a plain bottle which according to Prodan passed from Alexandria through Gandhāra into Northern Wei China.[42] I am not myself convinced about the origins of this vessel. It did, however, certainly reach China under the auspices of Buddhism, and is often to be seen as an attribute of Chinese figures of Bodhisattvas of the T'ang period. Emerging into pottery it becomes one of the most satisfying of T'ang pottery shapes.

This class, which is of western Asiatic origin, owes its name to the fact that small replicas were brought by pilgrims from the shrines of Christian saints, especially in the eastern Mediterranean between about the third and seventh centuries AD, filled with holy water or with oil from the sanctuary lamps. It is essentially a domestic carrying-flask for water, such as might have been in use among travellers in the deserts of western Asia. Taking into account the intense curiosity with which the T'ang Chinese scrutinized the stream of foreigners entering their country along the Silk Road, together with their pack animals and every item of their costume and equipment, its assimilation into the T'ang pottery range was probably quite inevitable. At the same time it is doubtful whether Chinese pottery pilgrim bottles were ever actually used for long-distance journeys, considering their weight and small holding-capacity. According to Gallois they were funerary wares, meant as equipment for the spirit-journeys of the dead.

The Chinese pottery version was probably cast in the form of two separate roundels of clay which were then impressed with moulded relief decoration by means of dies; afterwards they

TALL-NECKED BOTTLES
pls 165, 168

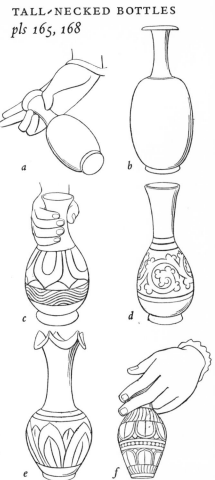

55 Tall-necked bottles: *a* from a T'ang sandstone Bodhisattva at P'ing-ling-ssŭ (plate 146); *b* of T'ang glazed earthenware (plate 168); *c* from a Sui gilt-bronze Bodhisattva; *d* of T'ang glazed earthenware with vine scroll; *e* of T'ang glazed earthenware with lotus band and foliate mouth; *f amṛta kalaśa* from a fragment of Gandhāran sculpture

PILGRIM BOTTLES
col. 41

56 Pilgrim bottles: *a* glazed earthenware bottle from Deve-Hüyük; *b* T'ang glazed earthenware bottle

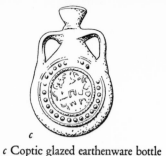

c Coptic glazed earthenware bottle

AMPHORA VASES
pls 164, 166
col. 42

would be luted together with the addition of ring handles and a neck. The heavily-moulded T'ang pilgrim bottle usually features Hellenistic subjects analogous to those on the Syrian pieces which Gray believes may have been their ancestors.[43] The flat foot is of course a Chinese modification, clearly showing that the original purpose had in such cases been supplanted. It does not occur on western Asiatic examples, which were specifically designed for carrying purposes, their handles being specially offset to this end.

The vase shown in figure 58 a, now in the Buffalo Museum of Science, probably dates from the Sui dynasty. The standard T'ang amphora could easily have arisen from such a vessel merely by substituting for the loop-handles on its shoulders the serpent- or dragon-handles climbing to the mouthrim which are constant features of T'ang amphorae. Again the modifying influence is western Asiatic. A Syrian glass vessel such as that of figure 58 b, for instance, might well have suggested the idea of dragon-handles, as also that of the ribbed neck.

One means by which Western glassmakers added decorative interest to their handles was by fringing them with a pincered glass overtrail. The handle shown in figure 57 a is on a jug made in the Seine-Rhine glassfield dating from the third century AD, now in the Colchester Museum. Several similar examples are known. An upstanding row of crests – so suggestive, as Thorpe remarks, of a coxcomb – is the usual form taken by these overtrails, and I think there can be but little doubt that they were known to Chinese potters through Syrian models, and helped to determine the particular form taken by T'ang serpent- or dragon-handles.

The basic form of the Sui amphora, with minor modifications, is that of the Han pottery *hu*, or at least of one variety of *hu* often decorated with a belt of hunting scenes round the shoulder. Especially diagnostic is the bowed neck and the little cup-shaped mouth perched on top of it, both taken direct from the Han pattern-book. The cup-shaped mouth is one of those design elements, of which I shall speak in a moment, that ramify through the T'ang pottery tradition and are not restricted to a particular class; it can be seen on the amphora of plate 166, and again on the short-necked bottle of figure 53 b.

The elegant form of the T'ang two-section vase of plate 164 is easily derivable from vessels such as the Sui amphora, and no foreign prototype need be sought for vessels of this class.

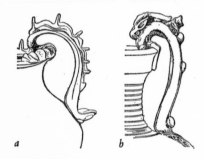

57 *a* handle on Seine-Rhine Roman glass jug; *b* handle on T'ang pottery amphora

58 Amphora vases: *a* Sui white pottery amphora; *b* Syrian glass amphora

59 Bird-headed ewers: *a* T'ang glazed earthenware ewer; *b* Sassanian parcel-gilt ewer from Pavlovka, Kharkov, USSR

Figure 59 a shows a typical specimen of a rather stereotyped T'ang pottery form seen also in plate 169. Nothing exactly like it is known in the earlier Chinese tradition, and we have only to confront it with one of a well-known series of Sassanian metal ewers recovered from sites in south Russia, to satisfy ourselves as to its true parentage. There is an overall resemblance in form. But specifically, the bodies of both vessels are laterally compressed so that they are oval in section and well fitted to receive on their sides the two relief medallions (moulded by means of a pair of dies in the Chinese example) which are so characteristic of the class. The motif displayed by the Chinese pot, a personage riding a lion, is found repeatedly on Sassanian silver plates. The ewer of plate 169, on the other hand, exhibits on one side a dancing phoenix and on the other a 'Parthian shot'; these did not come in with the Sassanian metal form, but have been adapted from the Han repertoire [pp. 152 and 158].

The T'ang bird-headed ewer provides a neat example of the filtration of a motif from one culture to another. The hinged metal cap on the Sassanian example is certainly not meant to represent a bird's head, yet does in some indefinable way suggest one. The T'ang potter probably needed little encouragement to make it into one, simply by grafting on a bird's head already well established in the Chinese tradition, such as can be seen crowning a splendid ewer in the Royal Ontario Museum. There can be little doubt but that this is a Chiuyen piece [see p. 256], and therefore unlikely to have been influenced by the Sassanian influx of T'ang times.[44]

It is of course true that a sea-route linked the Mediterranean and the ports of south China well before the T'ang dynasty, on the basis of which it might still be possible to claim a western origin for the bird-head motif, even though the transmission may have taken place several centuries earlier. That is the view adopted by H. C. Gallois in an important paper.[45] In support of his case he cites a blue-glazed earthenware fragment in the form of the head of a bird of prey which he himself found at Cairo. As in the Chinese examples now under review, the mouth is closed, and liquids were poured in and out through an aperture on the top of the head, which seems at one time to have been provided with a funnel. The Cairene fragment Gallois dates to between 100 BC and AD 100. He cites the still earlier example of a Greek jug with bird-head from Aegina.

Gallois was led to investigate the origin of the bird-head motif when he came across a glazed earthenware fragment in the Cairo Museum of Arabic Art which bore a striking likeness to the bird-head crowning a famous Chinese ewer, probably of the tenth century AD, now in the British Museum. He considered that the fragment dated from about the eleventh century AD and belonged to a Cairene ewer imitating a T'ang original – 'an ersatz production which the history of pottery has taught us not to be astonished at'. Moreover, the bird-head crops up again on Islamic metal and pottery ewers of the twelfth and thirteenth centuries.

Taking into account the absence of the bird-head motif among known Sassanian metal ewers, and accepting the view that its ultimate origin is indeed Western, then we seem to have a case of a motif travelling from the Mediterranean to China, there becoming involved in the Chinese elaboration of a Sassanian metal ewer, and after the lapse of several centuries returning to the West in this new composite form. The story, if true, is a strange one; but, as Gallois says, exactly what we might expect considering the incredible amount of borrowing that went on over the centuries between the leading ceramic traditions of the Old World.

The T'ang *oinochoe* is simply a three-section vase such as that shown in plate 167, with the addition of a single dragon-handle and with a pinched-up trefoil mouth instead of a plain

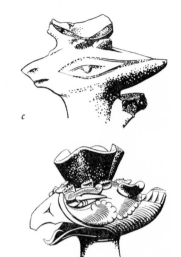

c neck of Egyptian glazed earthenware ewer; *d* mouth and neck of T'ang white porcelain bird-headed ewer

fig. 59 c and d

OINOCHOE
col. 43

one. These last two features bespeak the distant influence of the Greek *oinochoe* perhaps transmitted by means of some Syrian glass intermediary. Thus the single rib on the neck may be a vestige of the overtrail commonly found on the necks of Syrian glass vessels.

60 *Oinochoe: a* Greek pottery jug; *b* Syrian glass ewer; *c* T'ang glazed earthenware ewer

HANDLED CUPS
pls 175, 176

pl. 176

The handled cup, the most familiar article of domestic crockery in the West, the hardest worked member of the busy little band of social workers presided over by the tea-pot, is scarcely known at all in China. It makes its appearance there in T'ang times, but its presence is overshadowed by a much more splendid version in silver, from which it was perhaps copied. It apparently disappears again before the Sung. What it was used for is by no means evident; certainly not for drinking tea.

The T'ang silver cup is no doubt based on a Sassanian model, but this in turn was preceded by a similar form in Syrian glass of the third century AD, itself preceded by earlier forms such as the Luristan bronze cup of perhaps the seventh century BC. Characteristic of the entire range is a sharp corner point or flange almost at the bottom of the cup, beyond which the body turns in sharply to the foot.

61 Cups with handles: *a* bronze cup from Luristan, Persia; *b* Syrian glass cup; *c* gold and silver cup from Malaya Perestchepina, Poltava, USSR; *d* T'ang parcel-gilt cup; *e* T'ang glazed earthenware cup

STEM-CUPS
pls 178–180

pl. 178

Figure 62 shows a series of stem-cups from widely differing provenances; sufficient, I hope, to demonstrate convincingly the Western origin of the lovely T'ang pottery stem-cup. As with the handled cup, a Sassanian metal form probably supplied the immediate model for the T'ang stem-cup; and, like the handled cup, the metal form was reproduced with beautiful effect in T'ang silverware.

Figure 62 calls for no particular comment, but I would draw the reader's attention to 62 c, *fig. 62* a little masterpiece from Syria which has been in the Shōsō-in Treasury [p. 268] since AD 756, and was once owned by the Emperor Shōmu. The goblet is of blue Syrian glass and it rests in a 'calyx' of gold supported on a silver base; apparently at one time all the metalwork was of silver, and it would be a fair guess that this is in any case of T'ang Chinese origin, and represents a repair following the breaking of the original glass stem.

62 Stem-cups: *a* silver stem-cup, the Antioch Chalice; *b* glass, gold and silver stem-cup in the Shōsō-in Treasury, Nara, Japan, perhaps Syrian; *c* bronze and silver *niello* stem-cup, the Tassilo Cup; *d* Sassanian silver stem-cup, part of the Poltava Treasure; *e* T'ang silver stem-cup; *f* T'ang white porcelain stem-cup (plate 179)

To call such distinguished looking vessels as those on plates 181–183 'spittoons' must seem SPITTOONS
pls 181–183 absurd, not to say slanderous, and my own belief is that wares of such quality had some other use in T'ang China. It has been suggested that they may have held flowers. How lovely a single white lotus would look floating in the lustrous black bowl of the *temmoku* piece, or a *pl. 183* pink lotus cupped in the white luminosity of the Hsing, the reader can well imagine. *pl. 182*

Yet whatever purpose these bowls may have served in China, their ancestor was beyond doubt a western Asiatic vessel which was a spittoon. In figures 63 a and b we have two ob-vious models, both of glass, the one Sassanian, the other perhaps Syrian. Even closer to the T'ang type, however, is the metal spittoon of figure 63 c, representing a vessel that can be bought in any bazaar in India for a rupee or so, made of tin, aluminium, or brass; a form introduced into India from Persia, doubtless, at the time of the Muslim invasions.

*

Out of these divers vessel-shapes and decorative motifs, and many more besides, the T'ang potter created his tradition. Its homogeneity is increased by deliberate redistribution of certain formal elements that entered the tradition through a single vessel-type. No doubt this distribu-tion obeys certain rules, so that a diligent student might be able to discover a 'grammar' of T'ang pottery form similar to that elucidated by Karlgren for the ancient bronzes, though of course on a much slighter scale. Certain vessel-shapes also travel from one class to another, an excellent example being that of the jar. It appears in its most simple form in colour plate 29; or, with cover added, in colour plate 30; or, with two ring handles, in colour plate 31.

But now let us observe how the jar begins to make its presence visible among vessel-classes of quite different typological origins. The bowl on three splayed legs in the form of animals' *pl. 155*

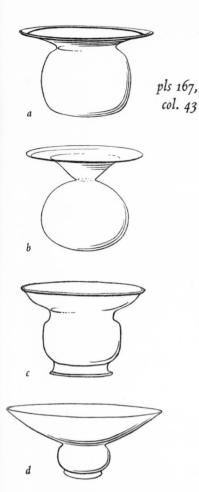

pls 167, col. 43

63 'Spittoons': *a* Sassanian glass spittoon; *b* glass spittoon in the Shōsō-in Treasury, Nara, Japan, perhaps Syrian or Persian; *c* modern Indian aluminium spittoon; *d* T'ang 'Yo' *yao* 'spittoon', perhaps used as a flower holder

pls 161, 162, 184, 169

col. 41

feet really traces its descent from a cylindrical pottery jar made in Han times. The T'ang potter leaves the legs unaltered, but converts the cylindrical body into the form of his well-understood jar. Remove spout and dragon-handle from the ewer of plate 171, and what do we have left but a T'ang jar? We may also recognize it occupying the middle section of the three-section vase and *oinochoe*. In the case of the Hsing *yao* spittoon of plate 182, it will be seen that the upper part of this vessel is simply a straight-sided bowl essentially similar to such typical Hsing bowls as that of plate 159, save for the perforation at its base.

Use of certain specific forms as standard design elements which can penetrate into any part of the repertory, endows T'ang pottery with great internal coherence and a profoundly organic character. Using the illustrations provided here, as well as in other portfolios of T'ang pottery[46], the reader may if he cares discover other examples of the deployment of these standard units.

T'ang decoration

Decorative motifs on T'ang pots fall into the same two categories as are found in Han art – the formal, geometrical or abstract, and the naturalistic or representational. Although this dichotomy is nothing new in Chinese decorative design – indeed it can be traced back as far as First Phase bronze art – it corresponds also to a division of styles in the Western world contemporary with T'ang. Sassanian art, which contributed so much to the pattern-book of Chinese ornament, both during the T'ang period and before, has its roots in Assyria and Babylonia and shows a preference for formal, geometric, and symmetrical designs. But this art had from time to time assimilated Hellenistic motifs that featured plant-forms, birds, animals, and human beings rendered in a naturalistic and representational style. Although such motifs were rapidly translated into the antinaturalistic idiom of Iranian art, the latter was always hybrid in point of subject-matter. Further west, in Syria, the palaces built by the early Umayyad caliphs – for instance the Mschatta dating from the eighth century AD – show in their decorative detailing the powerful hand of Hellenism, in subject-matter and to some extent in style. Yet even here a pronounced anti-Hellenistic tendency is at work, emanating from Persia and Byzantium. Umayyad art, no less than Sassanian, is the child of utterly dissimilar parents. Indeed, from whatever part of the Western world T'ang designers took inspiration, whether from Iran, Syria, Byzantium, or even Egypt, decorative motifs and styles belonged to one or other of these two great categories – the geometrical and abstract, corresponding roughly to the Iranian circle, and the naturalistic and representational one of Hellenism.

In what follows we propose to deal only with the formal elements in T'ang pottery decoration. Naturalistic motifs such as fishes, flying game-birds, phoenixes, and backward shooting archers, have already been described under the heading of Han decorative design [pp. 152–157]. Others, such as flying *apsaras* and the lotus, came in with Buddhism. Yet others such as Dionysian scenes are Hellenistic in their inspiration, but possibly with some Indian or central Asiatic modification. These motifs are competently rendered; but the T'ang potter did not waste his invention on them, and in consequence they hold relatively little interest for us, whether aesthetic or historical.

Formal elements in T'ang decoration

First in importance is undoubtedly the medallion or rosette which forms the centre-piece of so many T'ang polychrome offering dishes. Figure 64a shows this motif on the back of an enamelled bronze mirror in the Shōsō-in Treasury at Nara; it is compared with the centre-piece of a T'ang dish formerly in Marquis Hosokawa's collection. Here is a western Asiatic, ultimately Assyrian, motif which might be regarded as a conventionalized flower or floral diagram. On inspection, however, its structure as seen on the mirror and dish appears rather more complicated; for the 'petals' are actually composed of the leaves of adjoining cloven- or half-palmettes arranged in a ring. The design can thus be read in two ways.

The symmetry of this type of medallion is strictly radial, and its visual effect static. In this respect it contrasts with another type of medallion, also western Asiatic in origin, in which the symmetry is spiral and the visual effect dynamic. Figure 64c shows it as it appears on a silver dish, evidently Sassanian, found in south Russia and now in the Hermitage Museum, Leningrad[47]; below it is the centre medallion of another T'ang dish, from the Takeuchi Collection in Japan. At this point we may also refer to the dishes shown in plate 184 and colour plate 38.

Common as is the first of these two variants in T'ang pottery, it is the second that seems more at home on Chinese soil. The abstract patterns of Han and pre-Han decorative design are characterized by a feeling for spiral symmetry seen, for example, in the 'round eddy' and the squared spiral of bronze décor, as well as in more elaborate patterns like that displayed by the lacquer box of plate 107.

On the silver bowl from Lysiewa, also Sassanian, the two motifs are combined. The outer zone consists of eight cloven palmettes, the split inner leaves of which bend backwards to meet the inner leaves of adjoining palmettes at their tips, so making an outline precisely similar to that of a well-known group of T'ang eight-foil bronze mirrors. In this part of the design the symmetry is radial. Within the centre field, on the other hand, the design moves spirally. Bunches of foliage, suggesting a conventionalized acanthus scroll, enclose a heraldic-looking bird – compare the flying goose or duck of the Chinese version on colour plate 38 – and the whole motif has a decided swing.[48]

While on the subject of the medallion, one might say a few words about the technique used by T'ang potters for making it. The design was incised deeply on the 'leather-hard' surface of the dish. Thus were formed compartments, separated by a pattern of 'ditches', upon which glazes of contrasting colours were laid. Such a method could be regarded merely as an expedient to prevent the glazes from running together. But it also gives an effect somewhat similar to that of *cloisonné* enamelling, developed in the Byzantine Empire from Roman times onwards.

Did T'ang China know of Western enamels, and is this earthenware technique a conscious attempt to imitate them? There is disagreement as to where the Shōsō-in enamelled bronze mirror was made. True *cloisonné*, as far as we know, was not produced in China until Yüan times (AD 1277–1368) and it seems highly improbable that the Japanese could have had it centuries earlier. Thus a Japanese claim that this mirror was made in Japan seems over-bold. The Shōsō-in mirror at least tells us that Western enamelling was known to the East by the T'ang period; the fact may also be significant that use of glazes of several different colours upon one pot is not known before T'ang times. On balance, therefore, we may perhaps conclude that the T'ang 'ditch' technique does owe its origin to Chinese familiarity with Western enamelling.

Another feature of these large T'ang dishes is the stippled ground, usually reserved in white against a single-coloured glaze, that customarily surrounds the centre-piece. This is perhaps related to the pattern of raised dots or 'seeded ground' seen on many T'ang pilgrim bottles and other vessels in which moulded relief design is employed. All may originally have been

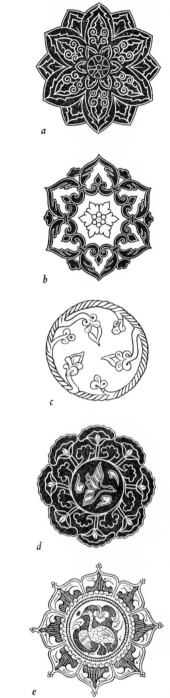

64 Rosettes: *a* back of an enamelled mirror in the Shōsō-in Treasury, Nara, Japan; *b* centre medallion of a T'ang glazed earthenware offering dish; *c* centre medallion of a Sassanian silver dish from Kaigorodskoie, Viatka, USSR; *d* centre medallion of a T'ang glazed earthenware offering dish; *e* centre medallion of a Sassanian silver bowl from Lysiewa, Perm, USSR

fig. 56b
fig. 64e

65 Seine-Rhine Roman glass bottle
with neck spiral and merrythoughts

col. 38

fig. 53a
col. 41

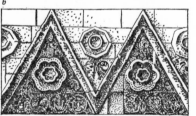

66 Chevrons and rosettes: *a* on the
T'ang glazed earthenware jar of
colour plate 30; *b* on the Mschatta
façade, Syria

imitations of the patterns of punched-in circles commonly found on Sassanian silverware, such for example as form the ground for the centre field of figure 64e. And here is another motif that may have reappeared in the West after having made the journey to China and back. According to Lane the ground pattern of raised dots on certain types of Islamic earthenware is copied from Chinese pottery then being imported into the Middle East.[49]

The main compositional element of centre medallions is, as we said, the palmette or open flower. In fact one great department of historical Western ornament is based on a continuous sessile stem which at intervals gives off alternately open and closed plant-forms. The theme is of great antiquity. It can be traced back both to Egypt and Assyria. It is stylized in a number of ways – as anthemion, lotus and bud, bud and fir-cone, egg and tongue, etc. – but all have in common a tight, budlike member alternating with an open, flowerlike form, regularly repeated. On the medallion of figure 64b the lesser element is represented as a single bud-shaped compartment enclosed between adjoining half-palmettes. In that of figure 64d it is more prominent, somewhat resembling the 'cloud-scrolls' within the centre field; here the larger elements, corresponding to the palmettes of figure 64b, have the aspect of lotus leaves on stalks. The similarity of this system to that shown on the dish from Kaigorodskoie needs no comment; clearly they have a common origin. Alternate open and closed plant-forms connected by sessile stems appear in T'ang pottery not only as closed medallions, but also as ornamental bands.[50] And the palmette itself appears repeatedly as a decorative motif, either singly or as a repeat pattern.

Another great class of formal design is based, ultimately, on the vine-trail. In Hellenistic art this is rendered naturalistically. It is scarcely more stylized on the silver bottle from the Oxus Treasure, and in this more or less realistic form it makes its appearance on T'ang pilgrim bottles. It is still a recognizable grape-vine. In Western Asia the motif passes through many stages of formalization and degeneration from Sassanian times onwards. On the Mschatta façade, for example, it is seen at one time as a single trail with regular loops enclosing realistic bunches of grapes, leaves, and tendrils, and at another as a double trail forming a row of circles or ovals and enclosing highly formalized versions of leaves, grapes, and tendrils. It is this orientalized version that makes its appearance in eighth-century European art. In T'ang China, too, the motif rapidly becomes stylized, and is often broken up into discontinuous elements – as in the 'sea-horse and grape' bronze mirrors. In other cases it degenerates completely and functions simply as a decorative scroll, its true nature betrayed only by the withered little tendrils that escape here and there from its loops as seen in figure 55d.

Also traceable to western Asia is the chevron band. It makes its appearance on glass vessels, both from Syria and from the Seine-Rhine glassfield, and in all cases in the same position as on the T'ang jar. Of a bottle dating from the eighth century AD found in Kent, Thorpe says that it 'seems to be reposing in a flower of six petals or in the gentle squeeze of a star fish' – an observation that might well have been made of the T'ang piece.[51] The six-fold symmetry of the latter's chevron band is echoed by the six-petalled rosette that has usually been described as 'plum blossom' and that forms an all-over pattern reserved against the apple-green glaze. When we compare this combination of chevron band and rosette with the motif as it appears on the contemporary Mschatta façade, we receive direct confirmation of the powerful influence Syrian art was exerting on ceramic decorative design during the T'ang period in China.

PRE-T'ANG POTTERY FIGURES AND VESSEL

152 Tomb-figure in the form of a musician playing a lute; of unglazed earthenware. From railway excavations at Hsin-tsao-hsiang, Mien-yang, Szechwan. Later Han dynasty.

153 (above right) Tomb-figure in the form of a *danseuse;* of unglazed earthenware. From railway excavations at Hsin-tsao-hsiang, Mien-yang, Szechwan. Later Han dynasty.

154 Incense burner surmounted with the figure of a cock; light grey stoneware with translucent brownish-yellow glaze. Early Yüeh ware (before AD 279). From a tomb at Chou-mu-tan, I-hsing, Kiangsu.

JARS

155 (above left) Globular jar on three paw feet; buff earthenware with green, blue and amber three-colour glaze. T'ang dynasty. Height: *c.* 3 in. Cunliffe Collection, England.

156 (below left) Ovoid two-handled jar; grey stoneware, partly covered with a dark brown glaze of *temmoku*-type relieved with diagonal flows of lighter brown. T'ang dynasty. Height: *c.* 10 in. Collection of the late Dato Loke Wan Tho, Singapore.

BOWLS

157 (above) Bowl with pie-crust mouthrim; lustrous white Hsing porcelain. T'ang dynasty. Diameter: 4 ³/₄ in. Lindberg Collection, Sweden.

opposite page

158 (above left) Deep bowl with five nicks on the mouthrim and five corresponding indentations on the sides; five spur-marks on the base. 'Yo' stoneware with minutely crackled olive-green glaze stained by burial in ferruginous earth. T'ang dynasty. Diameter: 6 ³/₈ in. Cunliffe Collection, England.

159 (above right) Deep conical bowl; white Hsing porcelain. T'ang dynasty. Diameter: 7 ¹/₂ in. Lindberg Collection, Sweden.

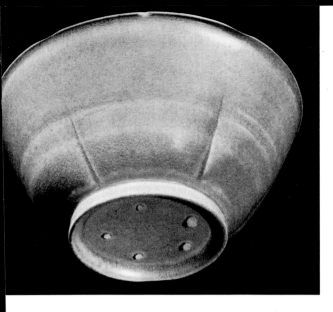

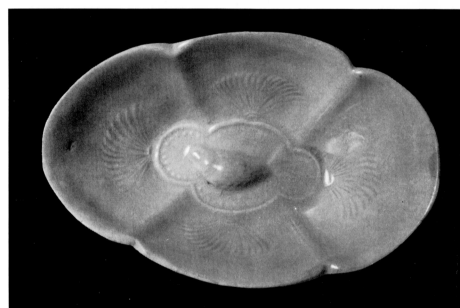

160 (centre left) Eight-lobed bowl; incised white Ting porcelain. Sung dynasty. Diameter: 8 ¹¹/₁₆ in. Collection of Mrs A. Clark, England.

161 (centre right) Four-lobed oval bowl with moulded design of fish and water weeds [cf. pl. 162]; lustrous white Hsing porcelain. T'ang dynasty. Length: 5 in. Museum of Science, Buffalo.

162 and 163 (right) Inside and side view of a four-lobed foliate dish on a flared foot; beaten silver. The inside engraved with a design of fish and water weeds [cf. pl. 161] bordered by four flying ducks. T'ang dynasty. Collection of Dr C. Kempe, Sweden.

VASES AND BOTTLES

164 (above left) Two-section vase, the body finely incised with a lotus design; Yüeh stoneware with lustrous grey-green glaze. T'ang or Five Dynasties. Height: 11 ½ in. City Art Gallery, Bristol.

165 (above) Bottle, its shape derived from the Indian Buddhist *kuṇḍikā* or mendicant's water-flask; stoneware covered with a cloudy blue-grey glaze relieved with *flambé* strawberry patches. T'ang dynasty. Height: 11 in. Victoria and Albert Museum.

166 (left) Amphora vase with paired handles in the form of dragons; off-white earthenware dipped in a colourless glaze covering the upper part of the body. T'ang dynasty. Height with handles: 18 ⅛ in. Staatliches Museum für Völkerkunde, Munich.

167 Three-section vase, the centre section with applied relief medallions; fine greyish earthenware with green and amber glaze
colours painted on the medallions, all covered with a transparent
colourless glaze. Height: 9 ³/₈ in. Collection of Mrs A. Clark,
England.

168 Bottle, its shape derived from the Indian
Buddhist *amṛta kalaśa* or ambrosia flask; off-
white earthenware dipped in a transparent
colourless glaze. Height: 10 ¹/₂ in. Victoria and
Albert Museum.

EWERS

from left to right

169 Bird-headed ewer, this side bearing an embossed medallion depicting a dancing phoenix (the other, invisible, side shows a 'Parthian shot'); off-white earthenware with a colourless glaze over a white slip. T'ang dynasty. Height: 13 ³/₄ in. Museum of Science, Buffalo.

170 Chicken-spouted ewer; early Yüeh ware with olive-green glaze. T'ang dynasty or earlier. Height 13 ¹/₁₆ in. Musée Guimet, Paris.

171 Ewer with handle in the form of a climbing dragon; greyish-white stoneware with a matt black glaze of *temmoku*-type largely covering the body. T'ang dynasty. Height: 10.9 in. British Museum.

172 (right) Ewer of light grey stoneware covered with a matt brownish-black glaze of *temmoku*-type. T'ang dynasty. Height: *c.* 12 in. Collection of the late Dato Loke Wan Tho, Singapore.

173 Ewer of pale buff earthenware with straw-coloured glaze over a white slip. See pages 252–253. T'ang dynasty. Height: 8½ in. Art Gallery and Museum, Glasgow.

174 Globular ewer; off-white earthenware, the body marbled with red and black slips in imitation of Western 'agate glass' and covered with a creamish glaze. T'ang dynasty. Height: 4.6 in. Collection of Mrs A. Clark, England.

CUPS

175 Handled cup of off-white earthenware covered with a minutely crackled creamish glaze. T'ang dynasty. Height: 1⁷/₈ in. Collection of C. S. Wilkinson, London.

176 Miniature handled cup of beaten silver engraved with palmette scrolls and floral arabesques on a punched-in seeded ground. T'ang dynasty. Height: 1³/₄ in. Collection of Dr C. Kempe, Sweden.

177 Beaker of fine buff earthenware, largely covered with a translucent glaze. T'ang dynasty. Height: 3¹/₂ in. Victoria and Albert Museum.

STEM-CUPS

178 (right) Miniature stem-cup of gilt-bronze engraved with hunting scenes. T'ang dynasty. Height: 1 ¹³/₁₆ in. Collection of Dr C. Kempe, Sweden.

179 (right centre) Stem-cup of fine white translucent porcelain, perhaps Hsing ware. T'ang dynasty. Height: 3 in. Collection of the late Mrs S.G. Seligman, London.

180 (far right) Stem-cup of white Ting porcelain with ribbed foot and metalled rim. Sung dynasty. Height: 3 ³/₈ in. Collection of Mrs A. Clark, England.

'SPITTOONS'

181 (far left) 'Spittoon' of beaten silver with an engraved design of a blossoming spray of three flowers and five leaves. T'ang dynasty. Height: 4 1/4 in. Collection of Dr C. Kempe, Sweden.

182 (left centre) 'Spittoon' of greyish stoneware covered with a near-black *temmoku*-type glaze. A date brushed on the base corresponds to AD 841. Height: 4 3/8 in. Ingram Collection, England.

183 (left) 'Spittoon' of white Hsing porcelain covered with a cream-coloured glaze. T'ang dynasty. Height: 4 1/2 in. Royal Ontario Museum, Toronto.

184 Offering dish mounted on three small feet and with an incised centre medallion; off-white earthenware coated with a white slip, painted in green, blue and amber glaze colours, and covered with a transparent colourless glaze. T'ang dynasty. Diameter: 11 1/2 in. Lindberg Collection, Sweden.

VII PAINTING AND CALLIGRAPHY: SUNG AND YÜAN DYNASTIES

The political and social background

For nearly four hundred years after the fall of the T'ang dynasty, as after that of the Han, north China lay at the mercy of the northern nomads. But whereas during the earlier period the Chinese had managed to keep a cultural initiative in the north – witness, for example, the great creative burst of Buddhist sculpture there during the sixth century AD – they now abandoned it to its fate. By AD 936 the northern frontier was to all intents and purposes no longer the Great Wall but the Yellow River, and after AD 1126 not the Yellow River, but the Yangtze. The activating Chinese spirit, which so long had leavened the cultural squalor of her invaders, seemed at last to have spent itself in the interminable task. The Sung is a time of withdrawal and self-examination.

Meanwhile the Chinese civilization delivered over to the invaders did not wholly disintegrate under their rule. We shall, for instance, see in the next chapter how native architectural traditions were kept alive by successive nomad dynasties in the north, a phase that may be said to have culminated with the founding of Kublai Khan's new capital at Peking in AD 1267. Even so, the pro-Mongol Marco Polo reserved his highest praise for the city built a hundred years earlier by the Southern Sung at Hangchow, south of the Yangtze. North China did not so much lapse into barbarism during the long phase leading to the Ming restoration in AD 1368 as fail, understandably enough, to keep pace with the rapid cultural advances made in the Augustan south.

At the beginning of the Five Dynasties the dynastic capital was shifted from Ch'ang-an to K'ai-feng in central Honan; so it continued on the accession of the first Sung emperor, T'ai-tsŭ (reigned AD 960–76). Meanwhile the Ch'i-tan [p. 249] rapidly extended their influence through Hopei, Shantung, northern Shansi, and northern Honan. In AD 936 they made Peking their southern capital and took the dynastic name of Liao. In AD 947 they advanced south as far as K'ai-fêng, on which occasion they sacked the city and then voluntarily retreated. But from the founding of the Sung dynasty right down to the break-up of their kingdom in AD 1125, the Liao seem to have had no aggressive intentions towards their neighbours to the south. Following attacks made on them by the second Sung emperor, T'ai-tsung, in AD 979 and 986, they once more demonstrated their strength by advancing to the Yellow River; but again they voluntarily retreated to Peking after signing a peace treaty with the Sung in AD 1004.

During the reign of Emperor T'ai-tsŭ the Sung campaigned successfully in south China. Canton fell in AD 971, and Nanking four years later. The Sung annexed far more than the territories of these polished southern dynasties; they gathered up the fine flower of their Court life and transplanted it to K'ai-fêng. At the beginning of the second millennium the capital was perhaps the most prosperous and enlightened city in the world.

For a hundred years the political situation was remarkably stable. It would have been well with the Sung if they had allowed it to remain so. In the event, the young Emperor Hui-tsung (1082–1135), a dilettante, could not be restrained from trying his hand in State affairs. Determined to recapture from the peaceable Liao the lands they had now occupied for nearly two centuries, the Emperor conceived the idea of a military alliance with a vastly less desirable Power, the half-savage Ju-chên Tunguses of Manchuria. Thus encouraged, the Ju-chên came down from the north and attacked the Liao in AD 1114. A year later they adopted the dynastic name of Chin, and in AD 1122 occupied the Liao capital of Peking.

Between Sung in the south and oncoming Chin in the north, the Liao kingdom was annihilated. But in effect all that had been done was to clear a way for the Chin to take its place. By 1126 the new aggressor was on the banks of the Yellow River; K'ai-fêng was be-sieged, and late in the same year it capitulated and was sacked. Emperor Hui-tsung was deported to Manchuria, where he died in 1135.

The Sung moved south, and for a month or two had their headquarters at Nanking. But the Chin immediately followed up their success with an attack on that city, and then launched a campaign throughout the south as far as Ning-po (1129–30). The harassed Sung were not allowed to settle down until 1132, when they at last made a capital at Hangchow, under the name Lin-an. Six years later a peace treaty was signed ceding to the Chin all ter-ritories as far south as the Huai river; and in 1165 the two Powers signed a treaty defining mutual rights. As with Sung and Liao, friendly terms were now gradually being established between the Chinese and their conquerors. Both were becoming aware of a much more for-midable force than either gathering in the north – the Mongols of Genghiz Khan.

The great Mongol began his assault on China in 1209, when he overran a small Tangut kingdom called Hsi Hsia in the north-west marches. A year later he vainly tried to cross the Great Wall opposite Peking, in the face of fanatical Chin resistance. For two years he was held at the Wall; but then he stormed it, descended into Hopei, Shansi, and Shantung, blockaded Peking, and captured it in May 1215. The capital was looted for a month.

In 1219 Genghiz left the Far East for Persia and did not return until the winter of 1224–5. Once again he stopped to deal with the Hsi Hsia, during which campaign he died, in August 1227. He was succeeded by his son Ogotai (reigned 1229–41). A long struggle against the still unconquered Chin now ensued, and it was not until May 1233 that K'ai-fêng was finally taken. Ogotai was prevailed on not to destroy it.

In 1236 two Mongol armies crossed the Yellow River and laid waste Hupei and Szechwan. Perhaps their generals judged that the time was not ripe for a *coup de grâce*, the densely populated and deeply intersected countryside of central China being in any case quite unsuitable for the sort of military operation they had been used to. At all events, they retreated. Ogotai's second suc-cessor, Mangu (reigned 1251–9), together with Mangu's brother, Kublai, who was then gover-nor of Honan, launched a new attack in 1258; but this too petered out a year later when Mangu died and Kublai had to go to war with his youngest brother to settle the right of succession.

In 1273, with Kublai firmly on the throne, the final assault began. In that year the twin cities of Hsiang-yang and Fan-ch'êng on the Hsiang river in Hupei were reduced after a siege that had lasted five years, and the Mongol armies were free to move on Hangchow. The Southern Sung capital fell in February 1276 shortly after Marco Polo's arrival in China. In 1280 the last Sung ruler was killed; and for the first time in history a foreigner was master of the whole of China proper. Kublai took for his dynasty the name of Yüan.

The conquest, which had taken seventy years to achieve, lasted a bare century. It was a miserable century for China. Despite recent attempts made to whitewash the Yüan administration, and especially that of Kublai Khan, the truth seems to be that during this century the peasant class – that is to say, the Chinese nation – was well on the way to being wiped out. From an estimated hundred millions in 1125, it had by 1329 been reduced to forty-five millions; and of that number seven and a half millions were officially reported starving. The solidly entrenched Chinese gentry, the Buddhist Church, the army of occupation, the non-Chinese officials employed by the Mongols, and the Mongols themselves, had between them appropriated almost all the cultivated land. Those peasants who were not tenant-farmers, remitting to their landlords something like fifty per cent of their annual produce, were directed into forced labour on these estates – that is, into serfdom. Against such a background, the paper statutes that give an air of enlightenment to this bloody régime seem no more than the cheapest of catchpenny schemes.

Popular revolutionary uprisings, at first directed indiscriminately against all oppressors of the people, whether Mongol or Chinese, began as early as 1325. Rebellion became general throughout east China in 1351, when the Yellow River breached its dykes and the Government attempted to force a large body of peasantry into labour service to repair them. Two years later the liberator Chun Yüan-chang began to direct the human flood into anti-dynastic channels, and so shattered what up to then had been a virtual coalition of Chinese gentry and Mongol overlords. The latter, debilitated by the excesses of Court life, and with their empire breaking up behind them, were in no physical or psychological condition to deal with revolt on a national scale. Nanking was liberated in 1356; twelve years later Peking itself fell, and the last few Mongols straggled belatedly back to their old homeland. The long period of foreign aggression and internal *coups d'état* was at an end, and China was once more firmly united under a native house, the Ming.

*

Intellectual and artistic life during the Sung and Yüan dynasties was concentrated in the capitals and provincial cities. The intelligentsia lived on their government salaries – whether as members of national academies or no – on their inherited wealth, or on the private patronage of the gentry. At a time when several new picture-categories were coming into prominence, comparative absence of documentary painting having a social theme – what we would call genre – is a measure of the extent to which artists were divorced from popular life. What little there is of it portrays the leisurely distractions of the Court, the gentry, and the intelligentsia themselves, and shows us next to nothing of the condition of the people. Had genre painting then appeared upon the scene, it would doubtless have taken its place beside the poems of Tu Fu of the T'ang dynasty – and to some extent those of the Sung poet Su Shih – as an expression of truly Confucian indignation at the social injustices of the day. But Chinese painting was already speaking the language of symbolic, not of natural truth, and the framework to which its symbols related was not that of human experience exclusively. To have added to this hidebound tradition a popular imagery like Courbet's, or to have swept it from within with the satirical fire of a Goya, would have needed not only a revolutionary pictorial genius, but one with human-heartedness – *jên* – large enough to compel him to seek out and share the miseries of the people. There was none such forthcoming.

It must be admitted that Sung painting shows no symptom of the frustration that its limited social context might have engendered. The very immunity from political pressure enjoyed by the painter probably encouraged him to concentrate on purely pictorial problems, to adopt that art-for-art's-sake attitude, which in Europe arose only when the painter had despaired of ever finding loyal and intelligent patronage for his work. We do not mean to imply that painting fulfilled no social function whatever; nor do we forget the role of religious painting. But the philosophical and cosmological ideas, to which the leading picture categories of landscape, flowers and birds, and bamboos gave necessary expression, were circulating among a cultural *élite* insulated equally from the world outside China's frontiers and from other social worlds within. Painting reflected an exquisite parochialism, one for-

col. 51 ever typified by the nice but little more than decorative personality of the Emperor Hui-tsung.

In Yüan times this ivory-tower position was rudely shaken by the advent of the Mongols, and Chinese painting faced an ideological crisis. Few painters cared to have anything to do with their new rulers or with Government; those who did, found themselves handling themes that recalled the wider Asiatic horizons of the T'ang. Paintings of nomad life, and especially of horses, were now in great demand. Painters like Chao Mêng-fu and Jên Jên-fa were eager to acknowledge their indebtedness to the great T'ang *animaliers*, though not with perfect reason; for they invested their own work with a degree of naturalism acceptable, no doubt, to Mongol taste, but nowhere to be found in ancestral Chinese pictorial art.

Elsewhere, the main stream of Chinese painting flowed on more or less undeflected, and gathering strength from its own sources, as its exponents delved with positively Pre-Raphaelite zeal into the pattern-book of early Sung painting. Thus emerged *wên jên hua*, the manner of

pls 223–226 painting of the absentee *wên jên* of whom Ni Tsan, Huang Kung-wang and Wang Mêng were typical. In this nostalgic atmosphere traditional landscape, flowers and birds, and bamboos reached a peak of aesthetic refinement. In the images of storm-tossed bamboos by

pls 200, 205, 206 Li K'an, Ku An, and Wu Chên we may perhaps see, as Dr Cohn observes, an allusion to China suffering under the lash of the invader, and in the plum blossom of Tsou Fu-lei and Wang Mien, the flower of spring, 'an emblem of the longed-for native-born ruler'.[1] But if so, these were no more than masonic signs, expressing rather the private hopes of the gentry class than the public discontent that finally set the country free.

The materials of Chinese calligraphy and painting

In 1949, while excavation at tombs in the Ch'ang-sha region dating from the fourth or third century BC was under way, a welcome and totally unexpected discovery was made. This was no less than an actual example of painting on prepared silk, in ink, and with the brush.[2] It depicts in lively and polished style the figure of a young woman, perhaps an enchantress, accompanied by a phoenix and a one-legged dragon whose movements she

pl. 185 appears to be controlling.

By many centuries the oldest of its class, this miraculously preserved fragment reveals the antiquity of that simple and irreducible trinity on which the classical Chinese painter built his achievement – the ink in which his pictorial statement was made, the brush with which it was conveyed, the primed silk which received and recorded it. The Ch'ang-sha painting does not so much illustrate the antiquity of these three components *individually*, for which plenty of independent evidence exists as we shall see, as tell us that by the third or perhaps fourth century BC they had already entered into the harmonious combination that we have specifically in mind when we think of Chinese painting, a dramatic extension of its known history which a generation ago few students of Chinese art would have dared to foresee.

THE HAIR WRITING BRUSH   An old Chinese tradition allows the invention of the hair writing brush to a general of Ch'in state called Mêng T'ien, who lived towards the end of the third century BC.[3] The overwhelming weight of evidence is that it was in use long before that time, and at least as early as the late Shang period. We have seen that some form of brush was used in painting the designs on Yang-shao pottery. We know also of a few rare examples of brushed inscriptions on Shang oracle bones. Again, the forms of characters cast as inscriptions on bronze vessels of the same period show modulation of line and curvilinear shapes, indicating that some form of hair brush was used for writing the original drafts that served as their models. Moreover a bronze graph clearly shows a writing brush with partly-dried hairs outspread.

The oldest actual specimen of a hair writing brush, mounted in a bamboo holder, was recovered in 1954 from a fourth-third century BC tomb at Ch'ang-sha. Quantities of narrow bamboo slips used as writing tablets have also been excavated at various sites during the past few years, including a batch bearing a total of 1,500 characters brushed in ink which was found in a fourth-century BC tomb in Hsin-yang-hsien, Honan, along with knives used for cutting and trimming the slips. Sets of slips, each bearing a single vertical line of characters, were threaded together top and bottom concertina-wise to form book-bundles which were the ancestors of both scroll and codex in China.[4] Such a bundle is represented in the oracle-bone graph shown in figure 67a; another version of this graph may be glimpsed on the body of the *chüeh* of plate 79, beneath the handle of the vessel.

A great variety of animal fibres has at one time or another been used for making Chinese hair brushes. During the Han period rabbit was reputedly most popular. The Six Dynasties' painter Hsiao Tzŭ-yün apparently used a brush with a core of human baby's hair, but rabbit continued to be the favourite choice. Ou-yang T'ung of the T'ang adopted one with a core of fox fringed with rabbit, while Chêng Kuang-wên favoured a stiff variety made of fox and deer and called 'hen's claws'. All these brushes had short tips, and it was not until late in T'ang times that the long soft tip made of sheep's wool was introduced by Liu Kung-ch'üan. Hu Kuei of the Five Dynasties used a wolf-hair brush, fit instrument for a nomad Mongol. Su Shih and Huang T'ing-chien of Sung times used brushes with a core of mouse-whisker fringed with sheep wool made by the renowned Chu-ko family of Szechwan.

Today sheep and goat remain favourite for bold work, rabbit for more delicate. But the fibres of sable, wolf, fox, deer and hare, and the bristle of hog, are also widely used. After plucking and washing in lime-water to remove oil, the fibres are tied in a bundle, care being taken to grade them so as to form a fine and pliable point when moist. The bundle is then glued into the hollow socket of a wooden holder, bamboo or reed being obvious choices for this purpose. Brushes are made in eight to ten sizes, though in practice the artist rarely uses more than five.

67 Writing: *a* oracle-bone graph apparently showing wooden writing slips joined together by a cord, and equated with the modern character for *tsê*, 'book bundle'; *b* oracle-bone graph showing a hand holding an open writing brush and equated with *c*, the modern character *yü*, 'writing instrument', and *d*, the modern character *pi*, 'writing brush'

pl. 187
pl. 201

INK By ink we mean here what the Chinese call *mo* and what the Romans knew as *atramentum*, namely a fluid suspension of black carbon particles in an aqueous solution containing glue. *Mo* must be distinguished from *ch'i*, in which the particles were held in suspension in liquid lacquer, the word *ch'i* meaning variously 'lacquer', 'black lacquer' and 'black', depending on its context. It is again different in essential nature from the late-Roman sepia, and from modern writing-inks which depend for their density and permanence on a chemical reaction between their iron and acid constituents.

Chinese ink is obviously of extreme antiquity. I do not think it would be very rash to suggest that the paints used on the Yang-shao pots are basically glue-bound carbon inks or distempers; and the brushed Shang oracle bones point to its use as a writing medium – though certainly not very extensive – a thousand or so years later. The evidence of late Chou bamboo slips brushed in ink has already been cited; a manuscript in ink on plain white silk, or perhaps a scribe's copy of an author's holograph, has also been found in a Ch'ang-sha tomb.[5]

While ch'i continued to be used for inscribing and painting on lacquerware, mo would have been found more suitable as a writing medium for silk, and later paper, owing to its lighter consistency. We may also perhaps surmise that silk had not long been in use as a writing surface by the fourth century BC; that disciple of Confucius who wrote down a memorandum of one of his master's sayings on his sash may have been its true pioneer.

Carbon for making early sorts of mo came from a large variety of natural products. We hear of lamp-black obtained by burning an assortment of vegetable oils and fats, including lacquer; and the first professional ink-stick makers whose names have survived, Li Chao and his son Li T'ing-kuei of the Five Dynasties, are credited with having been the first to use chinawood oil, t'ung, for this purpose. There are also references to a substance called shên mo or 'stone-oil ink'. Professor Wang Chi-chên believes that while in some cases this was a preparation made from coal or graphite, in others it could only have been a derivative of petroleum.[6] The eleventh-century Shên Kua speaks of experiments successfully made to obtain lamp-black for ink by burning the 'stone-oil' (shên) of Fu-chou and Yen-chou (Yenan) in Shensi, a locality that is today known to be rich in oil deposits.

The soot of several woods has also been used in making ink. Pine soot is by tradition given pride of place among these, as yielding a blacker and more lustrous ink than any de-rived from the true lamp-blacks. But whatever the source of lamp-black for ink-making, subsequent manufacture follows a similar routine. The carbon deposit is brushed into pot-tery jars, and liquid glue – the best of which for this purpose comes from donkey hides – is added by pouring through a sieve. The amounts of carbon and liquid glue are kept at a ratio of about two to one. The mix is now heated for a few hours, after which it is thoroughly pounded; musk and camphor are added to neutralize the smell of the glue, and the plastic mass can then easily be moulded into cakes, balls, and sticks and left to harden. When used for writing or painting, the solid ink is ground in water upon the abrasive surface of a bronze, stone, or pottery ink-slab.

For upwards of a thousand years the ink-stick, often elaborately ornamented with gilt or lacquer designs, has been the most popular form of commercial mo. Such sticks were both durable and economical in use. The Sung scholar Hsü Hsün is said to have owned one made by Li T'ing-kuei which was as thin as a chop-stick and less than a foot long, yet which he and his brother used for over ten years, writing at the rate of some five hundred characters a day. No ink-stick was considered mature until it was at least a few years old, and really ancient pedigreed sticks commanded fantastic prices. Thus by the time of Hui-tsung, Li T'ing-kuei's sticks were reputedly worth their weight in gold. They must by then have become extremely hard, for specimens could be immersed in water for several months without dissolving, and we are asked to believe that their edges were sharp enough to cut wood.

An ingrained antiquarianism prompted Chinese collectors to hoard old ink-sticks, and so ensured survival of many types of mo long after they had disappeared from the market. Sung ink made from a mixture of pine soot and chinawood oil lamp-black was by com-mon consent the finest ink ever made in China. This esteem, and the fact that a good deal of Sung ink was still available during Ming and Ch'ing times, led many latter-day callig-raphers and painters to use it – among them Tung Ch'i-ch'ang, Fu Shan, and Wu Wei. Here is one instance of the special difficulties that are liable to be met with when we attempt to date Chinese paintings on the strength of the materials that went into their making.

Paper is another of the tremendous empirical inventions first made in China. All evidence suggests that it originated there in Han times – six centuries before we hear of its use by the Arabs, and more than a thousand years before it appeared in Europe – the tradition being that in AD 105 an officer of the Imperial Guard named Ts'ai Lun offered it to the Throne as a cheap substitute for silk. That it was so regarded from the outset is suggested by the fact that it was named *chih*, the character for which seems previously to have denoted a type of writing silk or perhaps a sort of near paper made from wild or refuse silk. Ts'ai's paper is said to have been made out of linen waste, old rags, fishing-nets, and bark of trees. It was therefore an almost pure rag paper; it was probably not sized in any way, so that it was of the sort we would call 'water-leaf' and the Chinese 'unripened'.

Within a generation the new material was everywhere replacing silk for writing purposes, by virtue both of its comparative cheapness and of its excellence as a writing surface. So a certain Ts'ai Yüan, who died thirty-seven years after the supposed date of its invention, is recorded as having sent to a friend the copy on ten paper scrolls of a collection of philosophical writings, with apologies for being unable to afford silk. The oldest known surviving paper is one recovered from the Edsin-gol region not far from Kharakhoto by Bergman in 1931. With it were wooden slips, the latest of which is dated to the year AD 98. The paper need not of course necessarily be as old as the slip; all the same, the date AD 105 for the invention of paper must be regarded as arbitrary.[7]

Many specimens of Chinese paper dating from the first ten centuries of our era have been found at sites in Chinese Turkestan; and the famous Tun-huang library provides us with an abundance of others made between the early fifth and early eleventh centuries AD. The characteristics of selected samples have been well described by R. H. Clapperton in his book on the history of paper-making.[8] Here let us remark only that all of them are 'laid'; that is to say, the fibres were lifted out of the vat in which they had been steeped, by means of a flat tray, or 'mould', consisting of fine bamboo strips set parallel and very close together and connected lengthwise by means of others set considerably farther apart. When the sheet was taken off the mould and dried, it was found to bear the impress of these strips in the form of horizontal 'laid lines' and vertical 'chain lines' visible as a faint pattern in the paper. This method of manufacture was standard throughout Europe and Asia until 1750, when Baskerville invented the woven wire mould; indeed, the whole technology of Chinese paper-making was adopted and rigorously practised by the rest of the world during all this time.

By Sung times numerous proprietary brands of paper were circulating in China, many with fancy names and distinctive trade-marks. The best were customarily set aside for use long after the date of their manufacture, as were ink-sticks, and even if they could be positively identified we should hardly be in a better position to date paintings done on them. Most celebrated was a brand called Ch'êng Hsin T'ang, 'Mind-clarifying Hall', which was originally made from pulp of young bamboo for the last ruler of the Southern T'ang dynasty, Li Hou-chu (reigned 959–75). It was already rare by the late eleventh century, at which time calligraphers and painters competed to get hold of even the smallest piece of it. A picture attributed to Emperor Hui-tsung, entitled *An Autumn Evening by a Lake*, is thought by Chinese authorities to be done on Ch'êng Hsin T'ang. And Sir Percival David, who reported this fact at the time of the International Exhibition of Chinese Art held in London in the winter of 1935–6, comments that the paper is covered with a barely visible embossed pattern of lotuses, and that the painting shows signs of retouching – perhaps evidence that the paper itself was of exceptional value.[9] Another specimen, bearing a poem by the Sung calligrapher Huang T'ing-chien, has an allover design of melon vines.[10]

While for certain sorts of writing Chinese calligraphers have always preferred to work with a coarse sheep-hair brush and unsized paper, by which to give an impression of the dexterity and speed of the strokes, the normal practice was to use sized papers made by adding a sizing agent to the liquid 'stuff' in the vat. The paper was thereby hardened and protected against the inroads of moisture, while employment of similar agents as tempera for inks and pig-ments brought about a sympathy between medium and surface, and a consequent durability, rarely to be found in European painting.

Of these agents glue was by far the most common, although we hear of early papers primed with gypsum, and others loaded with wheat-flour or rice-meal which gave a strong and very white surface. A European writer of 1781 speaks of alum in connexion with sizing Chinese papers. This is an interesting example of a traditional paper-maker's practice [11], the alum serving to harden the actual sizing agent, hide glue, when added in a proportion of about five per cent. Similar mixtures were also used for priming Chinese painting silk. No injurious chemical agent was employed for bleaching papers. Sheets were bleached naturally by exposure to sun, air, and wind. After drying they were calendered on a board by means of a polishing stone such as agate, a technique in use today in such regions as Kashmir, where traditional Chinese methods still survive.

SILK   We have already explored the early history of silk in China, and need only reaffirm that this material was in common use as a surface for writing or painting at least as early as the third century BC. Nor is there a great deal to say about varieties of artists' silk made during the period of famous names. We are told of certain minor differences between the weaves of silks used at various times, but these are hardly reliable criteria on which to date a given painting. As with ink and paper, artists habitually made use of ancient material; thus we have in *Ming shih lu*, or 'Veritable Records of the Ming Dynasty', a list of Ming paintings done on Sung silk in the collection of the Ch'ien-lung Emperor.

Rather more detailed information is available concerning traditional methods of priming silk for writing and painting. Up to the end of the sixth century, so the seventeenth-century *Chieh tzŭ yüan hua chüan* or 'Mustard Seed Garden Painting Manual' tells us, unprimed silk alone was used.[12] The standard T'ang artists' silk, *sêng chüan*, was primed by immersion in a hot glucose solution, after which chalk or starch was beaten into its surface until it was smooth enough to reflect light. This method, which is said to have been invented by the painter Wu Tao-tzŭ (*c.* AD 700–60), apparently went out of fashion at the end of the Five Dynasties period. Another variety of T'ang painting-silk called *lien chüan* seems to have been unprimed; instead it was beetled on a polished stone slab until the interstices of the web were filled in and the silk presented a uniformly smooth surface. *Lien chüan* is said to have been first used by Chou Fang (*fl.* AD 780–816) in his portrayals of Court life.

Primings of glue mixed with alum came into use after the Five Dynasties period and very quickly became general. The proportions of glue to alum varied somewhat according to the season of the year; in winter they were as ten to three, in summer as seven to three. *Chieh tzŭ yüan* tells how the liquid solution was applied in three coats by means of a flat brush called *p'ai pi*, the wash being worked from left to right across the width until a smooth surface had been achieved. Needless to say, artists attended personally to the priming of their silks, which they obviously regarded as a matter for the utmost concern and pride; when the priming was completed, says *Chieh tzŭ yüan*, and the silk appeared as clean as snow and as pure as river water, 'one could be happy in contemplating it alone'. One is bound, too, to notice how the loving care devoted to these processes matches that of early European tempera and oil painters

44 *Scenes from the life of the Buddha; a silk banner from Tun-huang. T'ang dynasty. In the top scene Śākyamuni is bidding farewell to Chandaka, his groom. In the middle scene two gods or devas appear before Śākyamuni, one of them armed with a razor with which to shave off his hair; in the foreground kneel the five companions who according to Buddhist legend accompanied the Buddha during the period leading up to his Enlightenment. The third scene depicts Śākyamuni alone beginning the life of austerity. 22 × 7 3/4 in. British Museum.*

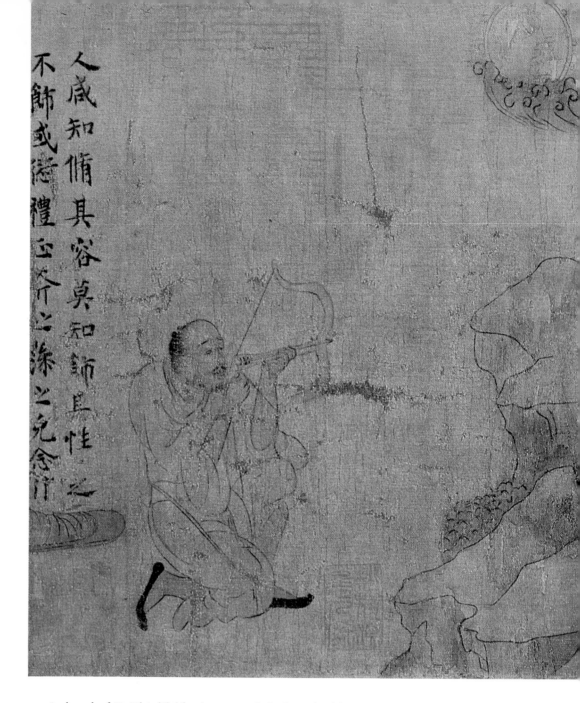

人咸知脩其容莫知飾其性性之不飾或愆德禮正斧斧之淨之兒念符

45 *In the style of Ku Kʻai-chih (fourth century* AD), *landscape detail from* Admonitions of the Imperial Instructress *in ink and colour on silk. The moral of the text accompanying this scene is the emptiness of achievement and the inevitable fall from the pinnacle of success. It is not clear how the scene exemplifies this. The kneeling figure seems to be aiming for the tiger on the right-hand side of the mountain. See page 330. Height: 9³/₄ in., length of complete scroll: 137¹/₂ in. British Museum.*

46 *In the manner of Chʻên Chü-chung (beginning of the thirteenth century), one of four album leaves entitled* Wen Chi's Return, *in ink and colour on silk. Lady Wen-chi was captured by the Huns* c. AD 150. *She was abducted into Mongolia where she lived for some twelve years married to a Hun chief and bearing him two children. When at last she was ransomed she no longer wished to leave her nomad home and her desolate parting from her husband and children and the poignancy of her return to civilization were the themes of many paintings [see pl. 221]. Height: 9.8 × 22 in. Museum of Fine Arts, Boston.*

月滿則虧崇猶摯拳洚駛機
隆而不殺物興盛而不衰日中則昃

47 *Avalokiteśvara* (Kuan-yin), *painting on silk. From Tun-huang and dated* AD *910. A nun by the name of Yen Hui is shown on the left, holding a censer. On the right is an Im-perial 'probationary chamberlain' named Chang Yu-ch'eng. The donor of the painting wished to commemorate these two persons by means of it, as is stated in the dedicatory inscriptions. 30×19¹/₄ in. British Museum.*

in preparing their panel or canvas surfaces. In European techniques the surface was invariably sized with a light glue before laying on the gesso; after which, as Cennini says, it was rubbed and polished with iron rods until it looked like ivory.[13]

Whereas in the European tradition the picture is built up by means of colour alone, the form of a Chinese picture almost invariably results from a combination of colour with line, or from line alone. Colour itself is thus not a primary means of construction in Chinese painting. Other differences between the two traditions lie in the way in which the colour is applied, as we shall presently see. Here we propose to offer a few remarks on the nature and preparation of Chinese artists' colours, and to modify one or two commonly held notions concerning them. It is *not* true, for instance, that the only pigments known to the traditional Chinese painter were mineral in origin. Some were certainly vegetable. Other colours of vegetable origin were not pigments in the strict sense at all, but were water-soluble dyestuffs. Again, pigments were *not* mixed with water alone, as is sometimes stated. Had they been, the particles would not have cohered nor would they have attached themselves properly to the ground. A pure and very fine glue was therefore added as a binder, usually after the ground-up pigment had been mixed with water; so that Chinese artists' colours were similar in kind to Chinese ink, and to size-bound pigments widely used in Europe before the coming of oil-bound paints. They were what we would technically call 'distempers'.

Most of the colours used by Chinese painters seem to have been known to the colourmen of European antiquity and the Middle Ages, as well as to the mural painters of Ajanta. Six other than white lead are prominent – a blue derived from azurite, a green from malachite, a yellow from orpiment, a vermilion from cinnabar, carbon black, and metallic gold; to these may be added the earth pigments. In the Chinese and European traditions size, gum, and even wax and honey have at one time or another been used to temper them.[14] They were generally applied unblended with other pigments – although one colour might be laid over another in the actual painting – and in both traditions they have proved to be remarkably permanent.

Chieh tzŭ yüan supplies much information respecting the nature of artists' colours, and detailed recipes for their manufacture. The range was quite extensive. Among the yellows, for instance, we find Pheasant Yellow (*hsiung huang*), Stone Yellow (*shih huang*), and Rattan Yellow (*t'êng huang*). *Hsiung huang* was prepared from the gum exuded by *Celosia cristata*, a plant of the Amaranthus family known to us as Cockscomb and to the French as Crête-de-Coq. The plant seems to have had similar associations for the Chinese too, since *Chieh tzŭ yüan* tells us that only the finest and most transparent *ch'i kuan huang* or 'cockscomb yellow', referring to the gum, should be used in preparing *hsiung huang*. *T'êng huang*, or Rattan Yellow, might as easily be called Gamboge since it comes from Cambodia, the country from which European gamboge gets its name. It is not clear whether the two colours are identical in origin; European gamboge is a gum-resin derived from the Gamboge Tree, *Garcinia morella* or *Gambogia gutta*; *t'êng huang* is also a gum-resin, but Petrucci says that it is the exudation of the fruit of *Calamus draco*, the Calamus Palm.[15] Stone Yellow is hydrated peroxide of mercury, or orpiment.

In the range of reds a painter could choose from among Vermilion (*chu sha*), Coral Dust Red (*shan hu mo*), Carmine (*yen shih*), and Red Ochre (*chê shih*). The native deposits of sulphide of mercury or cinnabar, the source of Chinese Vermilion, are among the purest in the world and the Chinese pigment is justly famous for exceptional beauty and permanence. Of the other reds perhaps the most interesting is Carmine, which *Chieh tzŭ yüan* says stains the hand. We may therefore assume it was an organic dyestuff, in all probability carthamine from *Carthamus tinctorius*, the Saf-flower. When *Chieh tzŭ yüan* was written, the best variety was coming from Fukien; it was marketed as a cosmetic rouge, being put up into small discs or balls of cottonwool which made handy powder-puffs. For use by the painter, *Chieh tzŭ yüan* recommends soaking the cottonwool balls in hot water to extract the dye, then making the solution more concentrated by evaporating in a water-bath.

Blue pigments included Stone Blue (*shih ch'ing*), identical with the Azzura della Magna known in Europe since the earliest times. The mineral in question, azurite, is basic carbonate of copper. A blue of vegetable origin was Indigo Blue (*tien hua*), from time immemorial used as a textile dyestuff [p. 140]; in north China it was extracted chiefly from *Polygonum tinctorium*, whereas in Kwangsi, Kwangtung, and Fukien, *Indigofera tinctoria* was the source of supply. Use of lime as a 'filler', to brighten the dye and reduce its cost, accords with a principle still employed in the production of modern pigment dyestuffs in the West.

Apart from the three primary pigment colours, Chinese painters made much use of a green called Stone Green (*shih lü*) prepared from powdered malachite, the basic copper carbonate which, with azurite, is formed by the action of air, water, and carbon dioxide on primary copper sulphides. For white, and as an opacifier, they had Flake White (white lead, or basic lead carbonate) which they called *ch'ien fên* or 'lead powder', but which was often dumped in the company of other white powders such as rice meal and calcined oyster-shell used as distempers, face powders, and so on, all going by the name of *fu fên*. They had a liquid gold size called *ju chin*, Milk Gold, and they had a glossy black called *yen mei* or Soot Black, which was simply a pure carbon variety of Chinese ink [pp. 293-294].

This seventeenth-century catalogue of Chinese artists' colours may be supplemented by two partial analyses of actual pigments from the mural paintings at Tun-huang. R. J. Gettens reported the presence of azurite (*shih ch'ing*), malachite (*shih lü*), vermilion (*chu sha*), and red and white lead, as might be expected. But he also records several pigments of organic origin including a yellow presumed to be gamboge (*t'êng huang*), indigo (*tien hua*), the saf-flower red (*yen chih*), and carbon black (*yen mei*); and these are perhaps unexpected, since it is often asserted that animal and vegetable pigments cannot be successfully used in mural painting.[16] Noël Heaton mentions azurite, malachite, metallic gold (*ju chin*), yellow from orpiment (*shih huang*), carbon black, and a red iron oxide perhaps the same as *chê shih*. He also speaks of a brown derived from a bituminous earth such as enters into the composition of Van Dyke Brown. We await confirmation of these findings, as well as a thorough chemical analysis of the perhaps narrower range of pigments used by the conventional painter on silk or paper.

The methods of Chinese calligraphy and painting

Having taken stock of the surfaces, primings, media and pigments used in traditional Chinese painting and calligraphy, we now reach the point at which the artist picks up his brush and proceeds to record the visual image uppermost in his mind. His way of doing this differs from any of the pictorial methods that have at one time or another been applied in Western painting, and particularly from those of painters in oil on canvas. Differences in method are partly due to use of different materials, and to this extent can be explained, as we shall try to do, while constant practice of a particular method will gradually affect the whole character of a pictorial tradition. Other observable differences between Chinese and Western painting result from cultural differences between very different types of society. We spot them instan-taneously, and value their existence since they afford us a novel view of life. But we do not as a rule attempt to explain them, since they seem to lack a rationale; in order to discover one, a profound analysis of the parent society, its structure and inner motivations, would have to be made. Preoccupation with certain sorts of subject-matter, avoidance of others, conventional ways of representing space, natural forms, facial features, drapery – these are among the charac-teristic clauses of a pictorial code which becomes the academic norm for a particular society. How unconsciously faithful a painter is to his own tradition, how difficult it is for him to speak in an exotic pictorial language, can be seen in the comical efforts of eighteenth-century European pottery-painters essaying the Chinese style, and of their Chinese counterparts exe-cuting commissioned European themes.

*

Now the materials used in Western oil-painting are such as to encourage the artist to work step by step recording with his brush a series of visual awarenesses, or percepts, of objects actually within his field of vision. The very nature of his materials is such as to enable him to work as deliberately as he pleases, to alter and delete throughout each phase of an oil-painting's transformation, blocking-in, laying-in of dead colour, and bringing the picture together. He need start out with no conception of the finished picture other than that in-articulately proposed by the subject before him, whether a landscape, a still-life, a nude, or someone sitting for a portrait. His temptation is to record the continuous series of percepts that constitute his complete visual exploration of his subject. The percept thus comes to exercise a sort of tyranny over the artist's expression, blocking his imaginative flow, leading him away from subjective or idealized statements towards a literal realism.

The nature of the traditional Chinese artist's materials, on the other hand, discouraged him from painting *seriatim* from percepts, or from the immediately ensuing primary memory image or after-image. There was to begin with no question of modifying his work as he went along. What he once committed to the picture surface could never be undone. Brush-strokes in black-ink monochrome or colour on silk or paper can be erased only with the utmost difficulty, and in practice the artist was given no sanction to do this. Moreover, al-though the picture surface was sized it was by no means non-absorbent, so that brush-strokes had to be laid lightly and rapidly if they were not to spread. The nature of his materials thus exacted of the artist a great certitude and speed of execution; it demanded that he should record without hesitation an image already fully and precisely formed in his mind's eye. He could not, and did not, work from an external model.

Chinese calligraphers and painters presistently remind their pupils of the need for master-ing the double technique of projecting and recording mental visual images, which they ex-press in the words *i tsai pi hsien*, 'the idea precedes the brush'. A single example must suffice here [but see also p. 329]. Speaking of the way to paint bamboos, the Sung scholar Su Shih says:[17] 'To paint the bamboo, one must have it entirely within one. Grasp the brush, look intently [at the paper], then visualize what you are going to paint. Follow your vision quickly, lift your brush and pursue directly that which you see, as a falcon dives on the springing hare – the least slackening and it will escape you.' The question is, what *did* the painter see?

Among the various mental images recognized by conventional psychology – the primary memory image, the secondary memory image, the eidetic image, the imagination image, the hallucination – differences are of quality and degree. All of them are of course based on pas visual experience, but how closely a given image resembles any *particular* past visual experience, how vivid, detailed, stable, colour-saturated it is – these factors vary according to the nature of the image and the sort of person who is projecting it.

In the first edition of this book I put forward the view that Chinese calligraphers and painters may have enjoyed the use of the eidetic faculty, by means of which a percept appears automatically in full detail after the original act of perception has ceased. It has been estimated that about half of all school-children possess the faculty, and that it is retained and used at least occasionally by about one adult out of every ten. The eidetic image has of course no objective existence, and the subject knows this, yet it is none the less seen. It is detailed, stable, vivid, and colour-saturated. It is not necessarily a complete and faithful copy of the original percept, but may show characteristic modifications depending on the 'aesthetic reaction' of the subject. The image may be successfully projected long after the original act of perception has taken place[18], and the ability to project it can be educated.

In the case of Chinese calligraphers and painters, the eidetic faculty would have been exercised from a very early age in the process of memorizing and learning to reproduce the forms of the written characters, the classical elements in the scholar's education. A written character is an abstract pattern of strokes, conveying no visual meaning whatsoever, and the ability to project at will a detailed image of its unique form would be of enormous help to a child whose task was to master how to write it.[19] Habitual use of the eidetic faculty as an aid in learning to write Chinese characters in childhood would be the best possible guarantee of its survival, in adult literates, as a permanent psychological disposition.

In putting this forward as a substantial possibility, I do not mean to suggest that the mental images from which Chinese painters worked were exclusively or even normally eidetic. Secondary mental images, which are awarenesses apprehended long after the original act of perception, may be no less vivid, detailed, and stable, though they are not pseudo-perceptual and are likely to be strongly affected by awarenesses of other similar percepts previously experienced, as by the aesthetic reaction of the percipient. What is abundantly clear from the writings of Chinese painters is that the images, whether eidetic or no, were very powerfully visualized and could be produced only as the outcome of some form of sustained attention or preliminary psychological 'set'. The doors of perception open only when the ordinary activities of the mind have been inhibited, and an abnormal disposition deliberately promoted.

pl. 211   In his *Lin ch'üan kao chih*, 'The Great Message of Forests and Streams', the eleventh-century landscapist Kuo Hsi says: 'In painting any view ... the artist must concentrate his powers in order to unify the work. Otherwise it will not bear the peculiar imprint of his soul. His whole soul must attend the completion of the task, otherwise his energies will be dulled ... If a painter forces himself to work when he feels lazy his productions will be weak and spiritless, without decision. This is because he cannot concentrate.' A simple preparatory ritual might no less help to promote psychic conditions favourable for projection of clear, detailed, and steady mental visual images. Kuo Hsi's son recounts how his father 'would seat himself at a clean table, by a bright window, burning incense to right and left. He would choose the finest brushes, the most exquisite ink; wash his hands, and clean the ink-stone, as though he were expecting a visitor of rank. He waited till his mind was calm and undisturbed, and then began.'[20] Other painters found that for them inspiration came most readily when under the influence of drink, others when listening to music, but all agree in stressing the need for some sort of special psychological preparation before commencing to work. Its effect was undoubtedly to empty the mind of irrelevant preoccupations, while heightening its faculty for visualization. For the image must be wooed; it behaves, as H. H. Price says, almost as if it had a will of its own.

*

More important than the question of the nature of these images is that of their content, for this is what largely gives Chinese painting its distinctive character. All mental visual images tend to preserve salient features only, to be interfered with or reinforced by others of their class, to mould themselves in accordance with the aesthetic reaction of the subject, and to contain conceptual elements not present in the original percept. We very well know with what devotion Chinese painters went about the task of furnishing a store of memory images of their favourite motifs. Huang Kung-wang in the Fu-chun mountains of Kiangsi, Wang *pls 223, 226* Mêng at Mount T'ai in Shantung – painters like these developed a passion for their motifs no less obsessional than was Cézanne's for Mont-St-Victoire. Flower-and-bird painters observed and committed to memory the characteristic movements and appearances of living things so attentively that they lost awareness of the world outside that bright circle. When in his studio the painter cleared the channels of his visual imagination, all these related images sought release through them, and finally burst forth in a single, definitive image, which partook somewhat of all of them and which was yet unique and characteristic of its creator. It was indeed the expression of his oneness with the world of non-human reality and values.

That such a discipline must lead to a mode of aesthetic expression altogether different from European naturalism must, I think, be obvious. On looking at a Chinese painting, what perhaps strikes us most forcibly is the fact that, although its delineation is as vivid and sure as though the painter had stood in the presence of his motif, there is never any question of actual portraiture. If the motif is a bird or some other living creature, we behold not a specified individual but an image that somehow seems to contain a reference to every specimen of that particular kind that ever was; if a mountain landscape, the picture is never mere topo-graphy. The surface attributes, which, by their inconstancy, make of every percept relating to that particular mountain a unique and unrepeatable experience, have been shed, disclosing the bony structure on which they are all based and upon which we lovingly construct, in imagination, an ideal image of some beloved object that shall correspond to our conception of its essential truth. Such images Francis Galton called 'generic'.

A written character, too, is the record of a generic image based upon every percept of that character previously borne in the mind of the calligrapher. Indeed the written character may be regarded as the classic example of a non-specific image, since it can never be said to possess *pl. 204* specific material being, as does a mountain or a bird. The calligrapher generates it afresh out of his visual imagination. But even were he to copy it from a written model the principle would still hold good; for that model would itself be the record of an earlier generic image in the mind of the person who created it.

All these findings about the methods of Chinese calligraphy and painting may be summed up in the words of Victoria Contag, who says that the artist 'selects and collects perception data first and then *he creates* image-forms to which he adjusts his inborn qualities'.[21] So was fashioned in China a precise and compelling world of pictorial abstractions, that 'second reality' of which the philosopher Hsün Tzŭ spoke as long ago as the fourth century BC and which has been the domain of Chinese calligraphers and painters ever since.

If the danger to the Western artist was undue attachment to the real world of specified particulars, his Chinese counterpart was no less in danger of being submerged in this world of generic images. For the artistic genius of the old masters brought into being a pattern-book

305

of pictorial abstractions to which the lesser artist could turn when his own inspiration flagged. Copying from old masters, begun as a training in pictorial technique, often ended in technical expertise no less empty of true visionary experience than that of the Western artist who recorded in literal terms only what was before his eyes. During the long derivative phase of Ming and Ch'ing painting these pictorial schemas were used over and over again, until they degenerated into the most threadbare of clichés. Leaning thus heavily on the visual imaginations of their predecessors, latter-day painters lost the precious faculty of projecting mental visual images *sui generis*, which was their real inheritance from the past. Rare was the painter who could declare with Shih-t'ao (*fl. c.* 1660–1710): 'I am always myself and must naturally be present [in my work]. The beards and eyebrows of the old masters cannot grow on my face. The lungs and bowels [thoughts and feelings] of the old masters cannot be transferred into my stomach [mind].'[22]

*

Although what we have so far said of the painter's method is true of picture-making generally in China, exceptions to the rule can always be found. When speaking of painting from memory images, for instance, we might have mentioned that some painters, especially landscapists, did make working sketches of their subjects *sur le motif*. A dictum of Huang Kung-wang's is often quoted in this connexion: 'The painter should always carry with him some brushes in a bag, then when he comes across startling trees in a beautiful landscape, he should at once make drawings of them so as to preserve their natural idea [characteristics].'[23] But there seems no reason to suppose that such sketches were ever used to paint from directly. They served rather as *aides-mémoire*, to consolidate in the painter's memory awarenesses of characteristic or unusual percepts destined to become part of the stock from which mental visual images would later take their origin.

In a different category come draft sketches, *fên pên*, which fulfilled the same purpose as the preliminary studies made by European landscapists like Claude Lorraine, Constable, and Turner. And just as we value these studies for their vitality and structural simplicity, so Chinese collectors valued *fên pên*. Hsia Wên-yen says in his *T'u hui pao chien* (1365): 'The masters of antiquity called their drafts *fên pên* (studies); many of them have been preserved by former generations as precious things, because their spontaneous and sketchy character is wonderfully natural.'[24]

Again, although Chinese pictures were normally painted *au premier coup*, in one continuous process, Yüan painters seem often to have built up their landscapes in three stages of composition. First the main structure was laid down in pale grey ink outline. Darker elements were then added, which often partly covered the brushwork of the previous stage. Finally the darkest lights were laid. According to Soper this was the process that Ming and Ch'ing critics had in mind when they spoke of *p'o mo*, or 'broken ink'. The term is a puzzling one and has caused a good deal of controversy and misunderstanding. I personally share Soper's opinion, that in Sung times *p'o mo* referred to the technique of graded ink washes [p. 318], and that its meaning subsequently changed.[25]

Lastly, the nature of the Chinese painter's materials was such as to make corrections while working almost impossible; but when he had a large composition on hand, the painter might very well make a rough preliminary sketch in charcoal to guide him through the later stages of its construction. This *esquisse* was then fixed with light ink and a fine brush, a process which the Chinese called *hsiao lo pi*, or 'small touching with the brush', and which corresponded to the first stage of *p'o mo* composition described above. We first hear of *hsiao lo pi* in Jao Tzŭ-jan's *Hui-tsung shih êrh chi* (late thirteenth century) closely matching Cennini's description of the same process in European painting several centuries later.[26]

The painting finished, the painter allowed it to dry in air, or hurried it forward by blotting with powdered chalk, which was afterwards brushed off with a fine fur duster. When dry, the painting was turned over on its face, moistened with a light gum, and backed with several layers of thin backing paper. These in turn were pasted on to a larger mount, which often had elaborately woven brocade borders. In the case of hanging scrolls, called *chou*, these borders served much the same purpose as the frame of a European picture, definite propor- tions being maintained between the widths of upper, lower, and side margins. For horizontal scrolls, *chüan*, the borders obviously did not fulfil this function, since the whole picture surface was not intended to be displayed simultaneously. Whether hanging scroll or hand scroll, its mount was usually weighted by means of cylindrical end-pieces of wood, which also served as rollers and which were often adorned with finials made of precious materials. Hand- scrolls would be tied with tapes, labelled on the outside for easy reference, and stored away until required for perusal: hanging scrolls were naturally hung. *col. 52*

As well as *chou* and *chüan*, there were two minor Chinese picture formats. *Tou fang* were small paintings, more or less square in format, which were mounted on the leaves of ex- pensively got up albums, *ts'ê*. *Shan*, which had rounded corners, were used for covering the structures of fans. *pl. 205*
pl. 222

Calligraphy: written characters

From materials and methods we pass naturally to subject-matter. The oldest and most preg- nant subject for the Chinese brush is the written character, the semantic unit on the basis of which – like our word – all written meaning is built up. The Western student, whether of Chinese art or letters, is hardly likely to be on terms of more than uneasy familiarity with the Chinese written character, and will certainly try to avoid making any sort of generaliza- tion as to what it actually is; even more reluctant must he be to explain what aesthetic quali- ties attach to calligraphy practised as a fine art (*shu fa*), for this is a matter on which a Westerner cannot be expected to speak with assurance. Under the circumstances it will perhaps be best to confine our account largely to a description of the evolution of the script in historical times, and, as regards the aesthetics of calligraphy, to refer readers to the writings of Chinese authorities on the subject, such as are mentioned below. *pls 201, 203, 204*

Identical materials and methods used in Chinese writing and painting sufficiently account for a family likeness between them, and when both are the work of the same artist this bond is strengthened by the factor of personal style. Looking at pictures such as the landscape by Mi Fei, or Wu Chên's bamboo study, we can hardly fail to appreciate that inscription and painting were done under one and the same creative impulse – with what the Chinese would call *ch'i mo pu tuan*, 'no break in flow of spirit'. But we might also feel that pictorial and written elements in some way assist each other in bringing out the meaning of the whole – that in some measure they are speaking the same language. That is essentially so. Of course it often happens that the actual content of the inscription helps to clarify the theme of the painting; yet the two may be said to be related in another and far less obvious sense. For a written character, like the subject of a painting, is a fixed and indissoluble concept-symbol. It awakens in the mind of the reader the concept he has learnt to associate with it; and it does this not, as in the case of Indo-European words, by making speech-sounds visible, but by the direct impact of its formal structure on the brain which perceives and discriminates it. *pls 213, 202*

Moreover, however arbitrary the formal structure may now appear to be, nevertheless in origin and intrinsically it is a graphic image or sign representing some quality, state, or relation in the world of sensory perception, or else a combination of such images or signs.[27]

In calling the Chinese written character 'fixed and indissoluble', we mean that its form is not capable of being converted into any specific grammatical category or part of speech by temporary modification, as is our stem-word. Addition or subtraction of formal elements would simply destroy the characteristics by which the reader has learnt to distinguish it from all the other characters that he knows; it would change or more probably altogether lose its identity. But in saying that its composition is fixed, we do not mean that its superficial appearance, its physiognomy, has remained unaltered. On the contrary, the appearances of all existing characters are the result of gradual stylization over many centuries, while from time to time they have been radically re-shaped in the mould of various historical styles of script. The process was virtually complete by Han times, so that a person able to read modern Chinese script would have little difficulty with original Han writings. A Shang inscription, on the other hand, would make no sense to such a person, because he would be unable without special knowledge to decipher the graphs and thereby equate them with their modern equivalents. The latter are only the former grown to full maturity; yet so changed is their appearance that even simple pictograms can now rarely be recognized for what they really are. In their continuous transformation from explicit pictures or signs into abstract patterns of strokes, the symbols of Chinese calligraphy contrast markedly with those of Chinese painting. For the trend towards abstraction in treating the subject-matter of Chinese painting is cyclical; over and over again it reverts to a pristine realism. Calligraphy, we might say, is the main stem of Chinese graphic symbolism. Painting is its deciduous foliage, and, if for that reason only, it is subsidiary in its nature.

*

68 Great curly script (*ta chüan*): an ink squeeze taken from the Stone Drums

The forms of the graphs current in Shang writing seem to have been more or less standard, though different recording techniques led to a perceptible difference in calligraphic quality, or *ductus*, between inscriptions on oracle bones (*chia ku wên*) and those on bronzes (*chin wên*). During the latter part of the Chou period, however, radically different ways of writing evolved among the contending states, leading to forms of characters which cannot be deciphered even today, and when an integrated administration again emerged under the First Ch'in Emperor (ruled 221–10 BC) the need for a script reform became apparent. The model on which the new script was based was one called *ta chüan*, Large Curly Script, which tradition has always associated with the inscriptions on a set of stone drums discovered as long ago as the seventh century AD and still preserved in Peking. *Ta chüan*, as modified by the First Ch'in Emperor's prime minister Li Ssŭ and two of his colleagues, became *hsiao chüan* or Small Curly Script.

The stone drums are now known to have belonged to the fourth-century BC Duke Mo of Ch'in, and the forms of the characters inscribed on them are like those of the Shang and early Chou tradition. The standardization under the Ch'in seems therefore to have adhered fairly closely to Shang and early Chou formulations, and the modern epigraphist Lo Chên-yü goes so far as to say that between 30 and 40 per cent of Shang oracle-bone graphs known to him approximate very closely to the equivalent *hsiao chüan* forms used as entry characters in the first Chinese epigraphical dictionary or scriptionary, *Shuo wên chieh tzŭ* [p. 42].

Shuo wên was compiled about a hundred years after the Ch'in reform, at a time when scholarly contact with the more ancient forms of writing had been lost. Its author, Hsü

Shên, succeeded in salvaging over eleven hundred specimens of these obsolete forms which he called *ku wên*, 'ancient graphs'. In his preamble he explains that they were invented by Ts'ang Chieh, minister of the legendary Emperor Huang Ti [p. 41], who noted the tracks made by birds in the sand and used them as models for fashioning the script. Perhaps these *ku wên* really did appear as meaningless as bird tracks to Han scholars, though we today can easily see their close formal symmetry to modern Chinese; there is a story that in the year 150 BC a wall at Confucius's old home at Ch'ü-fu collapsed revealing hidden copies of Confucian classics written in characters so long obsolete that scholars found it impossible to decipher them, ineptly comparing their forms, so Hsü Shên says, to tadpoles.

fig. 69

The 'modern script' or *chin shu*, in which the text of *Shuo wên* was originally written, was that properly known as *li shu* or 'clerical writing'. Allegedly an invention of another Ch'in dynasty minister, Ch'êng Miao, *li shu* was a simplified *hsiao chüan* made in order to expedite the vast amount of minor clerical work occasioned by the Ch'in conquest.[28] The original list of three thousand words in *hsiao chüan*, said to have been compiled by Li Ssŭ himself, was reputedly copied in *li shu* at the beginning of Han times; and *li shu* became the standard Han script. Surviving specimens are inscribed on wooden slips from Chinese Turkestan, Mongolia, and the Tun-huang *limes*, on Han funerary slabs and memorial tablets (*pei*), and on the lacquers, silks and bas-reliefs which we have already discussed. In Later Han times it blossomed into a very lovely variety called *pa fên*, Eight-tenths Script.

fig. 69d

pls 191; col. 21, 22, 24

To all intents and purposes Chinese script was by this time finalized in the form we know today. Henceforward there are no major changes in style. Subsequent developments are, in fact, no more than calligraphic excursions from the well-founded base of Han *li shu*. Out of *li shu* emerged the three modern modes of Chinese calligraphy – *k'ai shu*, *hsing shu*, and *ts'ao shu*. Just how they did so is a much-disputed question. According to traditional Chinese authority each originated as a separate script variant in Han times, and each is supposed to have developed more or less independently thereafter. The odd thing is that the abbreviated forms, *hsing* and *ts'ao*, are by some scholars given longer pedigrees than *k'ai*.

However that may be, there is no mistaking the stylistic similarities between *li shu* and *k'ai shu*, Official Writing, otherwise known as *chên shu* or Regular Writing. *K'ai* is a formal hand, analogous to our print script, and in due course it provided the model upon which printed characters were based. It was already fully fledged by the beginning of the fifth century AD, as is proved by a superb Buddhist *vinaya* MS. dating from AD 400 recovered from Tun-huang, which is written with the brush, in ink, and on paper. Classic examples of *k'ai shu* are also preserved for us in the form of countless inscriptions in Buddhist cave-shrines of the late fifth and early sixth centuries AD, and on Buddhist steles of the same period.

Other inscribed stones reputedly perpetuate the *k'ai shu* of Chung Yu (AD 151–230)[29], who is credited with having made improvements on the original *k'ai shu* said to have been launched by Wang Tzŭ-chung (AD 126–68), and also of Wang Hsi-chih (AD 321–79), most celebrated of Chinese calligraphers and supposed author of a second important modification in the style. But inscriptions in this category were engraved in imitation of original MSS., called *t'ieh*, that sometimes ante-dated them by many centuries. As documents they are evidently far less trustworthy than those engraved on *pei*, which were copies made direct from contemporary originals done mainly by anonymous calligraphers.

Hsing shu, Moving Writing, supposedly invented by the Later Han dynasty calligrapher Liu Tê-shêng, may be described as a semi-cursive form of *k'ai*. The boundary between the two styles is in any case extremely vague. Thus Driscoll and Toda in their book on Chinese calligraphy reproduce rubbings of two T'ang stones featuring a famous *t'ieh* entitled *Lan*

69 Styles of script: A sentence of classical Chinese composed of the four characters *wan pang hsien ning*, meaning 'the multitudinous nations have laid down their arms', and written in *a* oracle-bone script (*chia ku wen*); *b* bronze script (*chin wen*); *c* small curly script (*hsiao chüan*); *d* clerical writing (*li shu*); *e* official writing (*k'ai shu*); *f* moving writing (*hsing shu*); *g* grass writing (*ts'ao shu*)

t'ing hsü, alleged to have been written originally by Wang Hsi-chih, and generally regarded as a classic example of *hsing*.[30] But to an inexpert eye the forms of the characters differ scarcely at all from those that appear on another stone allegedly perpetuating a *t'ieh* by Wang – the *Huang ting chin* – a rubbing of which is reproduced by Chiang Yee as an example of *k'ai*.[31] The likelihood is, of course, that none of these stones faithfully preserves Wang's authentic style. Another possibility is that the term *hsing*, as used in ancient times, referred to a different style from the one we now recognize; the poem by Mi Fei is typical of the latter.

pl. 203
fig. 69g

Lastly, *ts'ao shu*, or Grass Writing. The origins of this highly abbreviated and often well-nigh illegible style are more perplexing than any: tradition tells of three separate *ts'ao* styles in Han times. *Li ts'ao*, a direct offspring from *li*, is said to have been invented by the Former Han calligrapher Shih Yü. *Chang ts'ao*, also directly descended from *li*, may owe its name to the fact that it was first authorized during the reign of Emperor Chang (reigned AD 76–88); its invention is ascribed to a calligrapher named Chang Pê-ying. The third style, *chin ts'ao*, is considered to have been a hybrid derived from the other two and introduced by Ts'ui Yüan (*fl.* AD 89–105).[32] According to tradition *li ts'ao* and *chang ts'ao* fell into disuse at the end of the Three Kingdoms [p. 177], while *chin ts'ao* survived to become the true pro-genitor of all subsequent *ts'ao shu*. It was apparently the most cursive of the three, its char-

pls 201, 204

acters being joined together in a manner typical of much *ts'ao* writing done since.

Thus far tradition. We may perhaps wonder whether the Chinese passion for attributing cultural inventions to named personages may not have effectively obscured the real historical origins of the three modern modes of Chinese calligraphy, and whether there is not an *a priori* case for assuming that modern *k'ai* arose from *li*, *hsing* from *k'ai*, and *ts'ao* from *hsing*. In calling them 'modern', let us add, we must bear in mind that they were probably estab-lished not less than fifteen hundred years ago.

We must also observe that, as far as can be told, no style of Chinese writing has been entirely abandoned even though it may have fallen into disuse for centuries at a time. Thus *chüan shu* continued to be used during the Han period, but gradually fell out of favour during the following centuries, to be revived again only in the nineteenth century. Precautions were at various times taken to preserve earlier or variant styles; so a *pei* dating from the period of the Three Kingdoms (AD 220–65) bears an inscription repeated line by line in Ch'in dynasty *chüan shu*, a variant *chüan shu* of Wei kingdom, and Wei kingdom *li shu* respectively.[33] By Sung and Yüan times *k'ai*, *hsing*, and *ts'ao* were the current scripts, while *li shu* and *chüan shu* had by then become 'art-forms' practised by calligraphers with antiquarian leanings who acquired special reputations for that type of work. The ninth-century Chang Yen-yüan, for example, excelled in *li shu* and *pa fên*; Hsü Hsüan of the tenth century was expert in Han dynasty *chüan shu*; and so on. The situation has remained unaltered to this day. During the nineteenth century, excavation of Han and Northern Wei inscribed steles led to a great revival of interest in epigraphy, which was again encouraged by comprehensive publication of Chou and Shang bronze inscriptions (*chin wên*) and by discovery of the Shang oracle-bone inscriptions (*chia ku wên*) at the end of the century.

But for ordinary purposes, and as a vehicle for the highest achievements in calligraphy practised as a fine art, *k'ai*, *hsing*, and *ts'ao* are entirely sufficient. From an aesthetic point of view no distinction is made between them; while as regards their forms, the three styles merge imperceptibly into each other. Thus it is not always possible to decide into which class a particular piece of writing falls. The *hsing* of one calligrapher may have something of the formality of *k'ai*; that of another may lean towards the freer type of expression characteristic of *ts'ao*. Indeed, the particular properties of each should ideally leaven those of the other

two '... *ts'ao* exclusive of *chên* [*i.e. k'ai*] lacks caution and sobriety', says the T'ang calligrapher Sun Kuo-t'ing, '*chên* [*i.e. k'ai*] devoid of *ts'ao* becomes too stiff for personal use'.[34]

*

As I said at the outset, I do not feel competent to embark on a discussion of Chinese
calligraphy as an art-form. Among the very few attempts to interpret its aesthetics for the
benefit of Western readers are an article by Lin Yutang[35] and a full-length book by Chiang
Yee.[36] Yet many of the issues they raise strike me as highly speculative; nor can one feel
confident that their method of treatment would be approved of by Chinese calligraphers
generally, nor that they have entirely resisted the temptation to over-emphasize those aspects
of the art that are likely to be most meaningful to a Westerner. For example, we are familiar
with the notion that handwriting gives a clue to the personality of the writer, and would
probably agree that the free styles of Chinese calligraphy offer just as much scope in this
direction as does European cursive handwriting. But when Chiang Yee undertakes to describe not only the character traits but even the physical appearance of some of the calligraphers whose writings he reproduces, one is bound to wonder what traditional sanction
there is for this sort of thing, or what it has to do with the appreciation of calligraphy as a
fine art. Similarly his views, and those of Lin Yutang, concerning the influence of calligraphic form on those of other Chinese art-forms must, I think, be treated with great caution
[p. 391]. On the other hand, his exposition of the various brush-strokes and of the compositional principles of Chinese characters, based on traditional Chinese writings, seems to me
entirely sound. An admittedly tentative essay by Driscoll and Toda[37] is also based on authentic Chinese source material.

Before leaving the subject of *shu fa*, I may perhaps touch on certain matters which, from a
reading of these books, appear to me to be relevant to an appreciation of its aesthetic qualities.
It is, for instance, helpful to consider the difference between Chinese and Western calligraphy.
Revival of the craft of formal penmanship in the West during the last fifty years has given
currency to the idea that Western calligraphy is an art-form *sui generis*. In this connexion we
should note that the basic units out of which Western writing is composed, the letters of the
alphabet, are phonetic symbols and as such are simple in form, strictly limited in number,
and relatively unchanging in appearance. Words are no more than linear combinations of
these continually recurring basic elements; it follows that words cannot hold any inherent
visual interest, since their forms are determined not by principles of structural design, but by
the amount and nature of the phonetic material they have to carry. Each Chinese character,
on the other hand, is organized within the boundaries of a square, and is conceived of and
executed as an organic whole. Notwithstanding, therefore, that the elements out of which it
is composed – the brush-strokes – must make an intellectually intelligible pattern, and notwithstanding that certain combinations of brush-strokes do recur from one character to
another, each separate character in the amazingly rich Chinese vocabulary in fact constitutes a fresh problem in structural dynamics, an 'adventure of movement' whose successful
resolution is a triumph of artistic management. And this, I maintain, is not a difference in
degree, but an absolute difference in kind.

This leads on to a second consideration, as to whether the meaning of the characters enters
at all into the practice of calligraphy as a fine art. In the case of the formal hand, *k'ai shu*,
the characters are rarely if ever recognizable images of the objects, states, or relations they
represent, even when they are intrinsically simple pictograms; and no such possibility need
be contemplated. But the cursives, especially *ts'ao*, afford great scope for formal elaboration

on the part of the calligrapher; so that a latent tendency to think of characters as actual images might influence him, consciously or unconsciously, to manœuvre their forms accordingly. It would then follow that knowledge of the meaning of a character, or of a piece of writing, might add to an appreciation of its formal beauty on the part of a beholder. Chinese experts generally deny that this is so; the well-written character is an essay in abstract design, and no other factor enters into one's response to its dynamics. The fact that the majority of the Chinese nation has hitherto been kept illiterate, they point out, has done nothing to prevent a nation-wide love and appreciation of calligraphic art.

Yet so visually stimulating are the forms of Chinese characters, so rich in life movement, that one finds oneself constantly scrutinizing them for contained images, as one might the ink-blots on a set of Rorschach cards. Looking at the upper right-hand character of figure 70, for example, I am impelled to see in it a bird of prey hovering, its talons outstretched, over some small animal victim. Knowing that this character means something like 'sudden' or 'menacing', I can hardly relinquish the thought that some such image was in the mind of Su Shih when he wrote it. The form of the top left-hand character, which means 'lightning', is equally suggestive.

We must not be beguiled by such fancied correspondences between form and meaning. It may nevertheless be helpful, as part of an education in the structural dynamics of Chinese characters, to allow the imagination to seek out resemblances between their forms and those of unrelated natural objects generally; for the Chinese insist that an animistic principle is at work in calligraphic composition, that the creative impulse which generates the movement and posture, the rhythm and organic cohesion of the Chinese character, is inspired directly by the forms of nature. In his book Chiang Yee happily shows a series of characters along-side the natural forms they suggest to him.[38]

From these general considerations we pass to specific questions of artistic technique – the nature of the brush-stroke and the various forms it takes; the organization of brush-strokes into visually satisfying patterns in the formation of individual characters; and the organization of individual characters into whole pieces of writing. The excellence of a piece of calligraphy is determined ultimately by the quality of the individual brush-strokes. The habit of thinking in numerical categories has led traditional Chinese scholarship to seek to decide how many different kinds of stroke make up the complete repertory for the calligrapher. A classification based on the eight strokes of the character yung, 'eternity', has been ascribed variously to Ts'ai Yung and Wang Hsi-chih, and is undoubtedly of great antiquity, but it has been steadily amplified by later commentators, such as the Ch'ing dynasty scholar Li Fu-kuang who enumerates thirty-two strokes in his Yung tzǔ pa fa. Chiang Yee describes and illustrates sixty different strokes or combinations of strokes; but, as he admits, this is a selection only. Their real value, presumably, is as models by means of which the practising calligrapher can gain experience of characteristic movements of the brush, and the muscular control needed to execute them. His basic brush technique achieved, he has unlimited opportunity for developing a personal style; for this will depend not only on his particular manner of hand-ling the brush, but also on the type of brush he chooses, whether it is full of ink or partially dry, whether his ink is dense or weak, and so on.

The actual movement made by the brush in executing the stroke, the path described by the tip of the brush on the paper, and the question as to what constitutes a good brush-stroke, and what a bad, seem to me too technical for discussion here. What is perhaps worth men-tioning is the fact that in Chinese eyes the good brush-stroke is essentially irregular, and this irregularity lies not only in the inevitable modulation of line and texture brought about by

70 Grass writing (ts'ao shu): an ink squeeze taken from a t'ieh allegedly by Su Shih

71 The modern character yung, 'eternity', and its component brush-strokes

varying degrees of pressure of the brush tip, but can be seen also in the relative massivity or slenderness of individual strokes, in the curves described by their axes, and in the direction in which they fall onto the paper; horizontals and verticals, for instance, rarely lie in a strict horizontal or vertical plane. The brush-stroke, in fact, should imitate the dynamic asymmetry of the forms of nature. In all these respects it contrasts with the disciplined stroke in Western formal penmanship, made by the edged pen, wherein the writing tool itself determines the character of the lettering, and produces predictable gradations in the quality and direction of movement of the strokes.

The principle of dynamic asymmetry also applies to the organization of individual characters. Here again the Chinese have been apt to lay down prescriptive rules, and in *Ta tzŭ chieh kou pa shih ssŭ fa*, 'Eighty-four Laws in the Construction of Large Characters', the Ming calligrapher Li Shun undertook a comprehensive exposition of principles of construction. Bearing in mind the fact that each Chinese character is an *unicum*, this sort of analysis can obviously never be complete. It does, however, serve to illustrate the conception of the character as an organic whole, whose parts are not arbitrarily juxtaposed but are integrated into a system of internal tensions and exchanges of energy, like those of a living being.

Sometimes our attention is drawn to the dominant stroke, which functions as a sort of backbone to give structural integrity to the character as a whole. In another group of characters, those in which the 'roof' radical appears above, we see how this element serves to integrate the cluster of strokes lying under its protection – as Chiang Yee observes, 'like the members of a family sheltered by one roof'. In other cases, like *hsin*, 'heart', and *hsiao*, 'small', the character comprises a very few strokes, separately brushed, and is in obvious danger of disintegrating visually; it must be organized according to the principle of 'implied connexion', the spaces between the strokes being filled with what Chiang Yee calls 'invisible muscles' that knit them together. In other instances what gives the character poise and stability is a massive horizontal stroke at its base; in yet others it is held together by a central vertical which acts like a stake, pinning it to the ground. But perhaps the most illuminating examples are those characters composed of identical left and right halves. In forming these the calligrapher must avoid the lifelessness that would result from strict bilateral symmetry and frontal presentation. One half, usually the left, is therefore made smaller than the other, and it is no fancy to say that as a result energy seems to flow from the larger to the smaller, with a consequent gain in vitality, while visual interest is maintained by presenting them not in rigid frontality, but in slightly twisted and differing postures. But in truth the principles of formal composition are, as we said, endless; and in practice every good calligrapher, while recognizing their general truth, modifies them according to the special nature of each character he has to write. They are discussed and illustrated by Driscoll and Toda at some length, and by Chiang Yee at greater, and I shall say no more about them now.

There remains the question of the organization of individual characters into whole pieces of writing. Here indications are vaguer, and perhaps it would be true to say that the placing and spacing of individual characters relative to each other is largely a matter of personal sensibility, and is not different in kind from the spacing of letters and arrangement of words in Western formal penmanship. On the other hand, it is a universal rule that characters composed of many strokes, which therefore appear dense, are allowed to occupy more space than those composed of few. Here again the analogy based on life and its relationships is not lacking. 'To describe this happy sequence of large and small characters', says Chiang Yee, 'we use the simile of the Chinese family. We say that it is like proud grandparents reviewing long lines of offspring ... We live in very large families, several generations residing in different parts of the same house; sometimes as many as thirty or forty persons are sheltered by one roof. And precedence and respect are always given to elders, for we reverence age and like to ponder the long human tradition which our family system maintains. Hence there is about characters arranged in a sequence that can be fitly likened to a fine family, an intimate relationship, a "family likeness", and an ordered dignity.'

Painting: the picture categories

A good idea of the subject-matter of Sung and Yüan painting can be got from *Hsüan-ho hua p'u*, the anonymous grand catalogue of Emperor Hui-tsung's collection, the preface of which is dated AD 1120.[39] *Hsüan-ho hua p'u* classifies paintings into the following ten groups: (1) Taoist and Buddhist, *tao shih*; (2) Human affairs, *jên wu*; (3) Palaces and other buildings, *kung shih*; (4) Foreign tribes, *fan tsü*; (5) Dragons and fishes, *lung yü*; (6) Landscapes, *shan shui*; (7) Animals, *ch'u shou*; (8) Flowers and birds, *hua niao*; (9) Ink bamboos, *mo chu*; (10) Vegetables and fruits, *su kuo*.

The order in which these picture categories appear is meaningful. It is an order of moral priority, the official view of painting ever being that it either serves a didactic purpose or is worthless if not subversive. Thus religious art, including portrayals of gods, stands at the head of the list, and is followed by a group of paintings including portraits of legendary heroes. Groups 3 and 4 also relate to men, while group 5 includes that fountain-head of moral virtue, the dragon. But the didactic value of the remaining categories is less apparent, and for this reason they occupy the lower half of the list. 'When one sees pictures of the Three Kings and of the Five Emperors, one cannot help assuming an attitude of respect and veneration', is a remark attributed to the poet Ts'ao Chih (AD 192–232), who goes on to say: '... by this we realize that painting serves us as a moral guide.'[40]

For the same reason it almost inevitably happens that the order of priority roughly repeats the historical order in which the picture categories come into being. Tradition tells of pre-Han paintings portraying ancient culture-heroes, of Han paintings of dragons and celebrated personages, and of the morally elevating themes of Ku K'ai-chih in the fourth century AD [p. 330]. The few remaining fragments of pre-Sung painting tend to bear out literary tradition as to the early popularity of religious paintings; for in spite of what later art-historians have said about the prominence of T'ang landscape, almost everything that has actually survived can be classed as Buddhist or Confucianist in content. There is also sufficient evidence to indicate a thriving tradition of animal painting in T'ang times, as well as of architectural painting. But as for other categories – landscapes *per se*, flowers and birds, bamboos, and vegetables and fruits – for all we know of T'ang or earlier examples of these, they may scarcely have existed at all.

By the time of *Hsüan-ho hua p'u*, however, the situation had radically changed. The order of priority for the classes listed in that book certainly did not correspond to their actual order of popularity among collectors of the day. Of some 6,400 paintings entered in the catalogue, nearly half belonged to the eighth group, that of flowers and birds. Taoist and Buddhist subjects were represented by rather fewer than half the number of flower-and-bird paintings, and landscape came only a little way behind, far ahead of the remaining categories.

Moreover we must remember that this collection was a repository not unlike one of the great national collections of the West today. Many of its paintings had been handed down from father to son for generations, and probably no more represented the actual taste of the day than does, say, the opulent Franks collection of Chinese porcelain in the Victoria and

Albert Museum. Less public collections often give a far better impression of contemporary taste, as doubtless was the case in China towards the end of the eleventh century AD. Flower-and-bird painting and landscape were in all probability even more popular forms of picture-making than their tally in *Hsüan-ho hua p'u* suggests. They were unquestionably the two greatest pictorial achievements of the Sung period, and they will be given due precedence in the account that follows. In fact I propose to ignore all the other categories, except ink bamboo, and so conform with what were very obviously the artistic preferences of the age.

Contemporary Sung comment helps to show which way the wind was blowing. Lip service was still paid to the older and less fashionable didactic classes; but the landscapist Mi Fei, who does so in his *Hua shih*, is quite obviously far more taken up with landscape – and particularly, let us remark, with landscape in a style recognizably like his own. All other *pl. 213* classes he contemptuously dismisses. 'The study of Buddhist paintings implies some moral advice; they are of a superior kind. Then follow landscapes, which possess inexhaustible delights, particularly when they have haze, clouds, and mist effects; they are beautiful. Then come pictures of flowers and grass. As to pictures of men and women, birds and animals, they are for the amusement of officials and do not belong to the class of pure art treasures.'[41]

A remark of Kuo Jo-hsü's is no less revealing: '... in comparison with the past', he says, 'modern times have fallen behind in many respects, but also have made further progress in others. If one is speaking of Buddhist and Taoist subjects, secular figures, gentlewomen, or cattle and horses, then the modern do not come up to the ancient. If one is speaking of landscapes, woods and rocks, flowers and bamboo, or birds and fishes, then the ancient does not come up to the modern.'[42] Kuo does not go so far as to say that the reason why contemporary didactic painting could claim no great exponents, whereas landscape and flower-and-bird painting attracted many, was because the former was no longer in demand while the latter was all the rage. Had he done so he would have placed himself in the embarrassing position of seeming either to question the rightness of traditional values or to reprove the taste of his own day.

The category of Chinese painting called *hua niao*, 'flowers and birds', is to some extent FLOWER-AND-BIRD cognate with European still-life painting in subject-matter, yet spiritually the two have little PAINTING or nothing in common. One thinks rather of Dürer's finely-drawn studies of wild life, *pls 192–196; col. 48, 50–52* permeated with his intense visual curiosity; and of Picasso's inspired illustrations to Buffon's *Natural History*, wherein this master shows an intuitive sympathy with his subjects scarcely less profound than that of the greatest Chinese painters in the *genre*. But these are rare exceptions. Generally speaking, animals and plants are for Europeans nothing more than physical presences altogether devoid of any deeper psychological implication. Except in a human context they have little evocative power as pictorial symbols, and consequently in depicting them no more is sought than external verisimilitude.

Asiatic peoples, on the other hand, have always invested natural life with a profound *mystique*; in China especially, this trait long outlived the primitive stage of human culture in which it is normally so powerful a factor, and by Sung times had found expression in a completely sophisticated form of picture-making. As a result, the tradition of Sung Chinese flower-and-bird painting made itself felt throughout Asia. In Japan it had important off-shoots in the work of such fourteenth- and fifteenth-century masters as Tesshū, Ogouri Sōtan, Nōami, Shūkō, Sesshū, and Sesson, while its workings can easily be seen in Iranian painting of the Timurid dynasty covering the same period. From Persia it came ultimately to affect the art of Mogul India.

Among the Chinese themselves, flower-and-bird painting is a major form of pictorial expression, which for upwards of a thousand years has exercised their aesthetic imagination to an extent comparable with, say, our European nude. The thousand-year-old tradition, we might add, is being devotedly upheld in the art schools of modern China. In this connexion Professor Chang Jên-hsia writes: 'There are no restrictions as to style, the only principle being to emphasize the significant and the beautiful, discarding everything that is superfluous or unnecessary.'[43]

'To emphasize the significant ...' Fundamental to Sung thought, as expressed in the neo-Confucianist cosmogony of the school of Chu Hsi (1130–1200), was the notion that to all sentient lives, and indeed to all things, events, and relationships, attached a governing principle, *li*, which was distinctive of the class to which each belonged.[44] Though there might be more classes of *li* than classes of things, the number was yet fixed and irreducible and amounted to the T'ai Chi, or 'Supreme Point of Perfection', often equated with the Tao of the Taoists. Corresponding to this formal cause of each existence was its material cause, *ch'i*, which seems to have been envisaged as a highly tenuous substance, or vital gas, that by cohesion and compaction in various patterns produced the events and things of each distinct category; if *li* gave them inherent natures, *ch'i* invested them with their material forms. According to the neo-Confucianists, perfecting one's knowledge (*chih chih*) meant awakening to the fact that one had T'ai Chi within oneself, that one existed in each and every object, event, and relationship in the external world and that each was part of oneself. It meant reaching out to all the *li* in the universe from the foothold of the *li* one knew; and to know *li* one had to 'investigate things' (*ko wu*). This was Li Hsüeh, the School of the Study of the Li.

The precise nature of the technique for doing this was never formulated; but in so far as Li Hsüeh involved attaining the general by way of the particular it may be said to have been inductive in principle. Equally, since the aim was self-cultivation and not scientific knowledge, its propositions were formal ones calling for no experimental verification. It could not therefore be made the basis of a scientific methodology. Moreover its critics in the later Hsin Hsüeh, School of the Study of the Mind, denied even that it was the true path to Sagehood. A studied approach to external phenomena was uncalled for, they said. The Sage was truly at one with Heaven, Earth, and all things, but his recognition of this fact depended only on the workings of his intuition and not on 'investigating things'. The Ming philosopher Wang Yang-ming put matters to the acid test. In the language of Li Hsüeh adherents, he 'went out to' the bamboos in his garden and began to 'ransack their natures'. After several days spent in the task he had to admit defeat. He had totally failed to fathom the *li* of the bamboos. With gentle irony Wang remarked that all he had managed to do was make himself ill.

But we should not allow this sort of demonstration, aimed at exposing the deterministic nature of Chu Hsi's cosmogony, to shake our faith in objective contemplation as an aid to altogether other modalities of psychic experience. The feeling a Chinese flower-and-bird painting gives us – that its author is somehow *en rapport* with the rational mode of being of a particular plant or animal species, that is to say its *li* – should at least persuade us of their efficacy when applied to pictorial ends. Whether or not he sought perfect knowledge in Li Hsüeh terms, the flower-and-bird painter at any rate strove so to fit himself by protracted observation and deepening insight as to identify himself with his subject, eliminate subjective and objective distinctions, and eventually capture and transmit something of that characteristic mode of being. Probably, as Rowland suggests, the much-disputed phrase *ch'i yün*, usually translated in some such way as 'rhythmic vitality', is simply an expression of this ultimate objective.[45] Practice of such disciplines, coupled with complete mastery over their materials which we may take for granted, fully explains the uncanny knack of seeming to step through an imperceptible barrier into the looking-glass world of their subjects, demonstrated over and over again by Sung and Yüan masters of *hua niao*.

Clearly if Nature's lower creation shares T'ai Chi impartially with her highest, every living thing has didactic significance for mankind and so qualifies as a pictorial symbol. The 'flower-and-bird' *genre* cannot therefore be strictly limited in scope; its subjects include not only flowers and birds, but all the *ch'ien wu*, the 'thousand living things'. We find studies of small mammals, flying insects, shellfish, fresh-water creatures, and aquatic plants, all entered under the heading *hua niao*; Ch'ien Hsüan's *Squirrel on a Peach Bough*, for instance, *pl. 195* is thus in every sense except the most literal a true flower-and-bird painting. On the other hand, the larger mammals are given a picture category of their own; and so is the bamboo, with its rather special technical relationship to calligraphy. Yet through them all runs the *pls 200–204* same unmistakable thread, the identification of Self with Not-Self which was the keystone of neo-Confucianism, the 'infeeling' of the painter with the natural world.

Not until the tenth century AD did flower-and-bird painting begin to emerge as a picture category in its own right. Its exponents dominated the academies of the Five Dynasties and Northern Sung; and it was apparently in their work rather than in landscape that the main divergences in pictorial style and composition grew up. Indeed so strong was the influence of flower-and-bird painting on other picture categories, notably landscape, that a study of its development provides the best possible introduction to the history of Chinese painting as a whole during the three centuries now under review. For this purpose we shall consider what is known of the work of four leading flower-and-bird painters – Huang Ch'üan, Hsü Hsi, the Emperor Hui-tsung, and Ch'ien Hsüan.

The first, Huang Ch'üan, was a *tai chao*, a 'Painter-in-Attendance', at the Shu court in Szechwan during the Five Dynasties period, subsequently taking office under the Sung and receiving the post of Assistant Secretary to the Department of Imperial Instruction. His two sons, Huang Chü-ts'ai and Huang Chü-pao, both held important positions in the Sung Academy under its founder T'ai-tsŭ.[46] Both perpetuated their father's manner of painting, which thus passed direct to the head of the Sung Academy tradition and became established as the first Academy style. There is general agreement that it consisted of firm and delicate boundary lines filled with flat washes of colour, a technique defined by the Chinese term *kou li t'ien ts'ui*.

We can only speculate as to the type of composition favoured by Huang Ch'üan, for nothing remains that can be proved to be his work. A hand scroll in the collection of Mrs Ada Moore, New York, entitled *Assembly of Birds on a Willow Bank*, has been ascribed to him; and perhaps this attribution is as acceptable as any other. *Assembly of Birds* certainly gives the impression of perpetuating a late tenth- or early eleventh-century AD composition; in this respect it clearly resembles such well-authenticated works as the recently-discovered frescoes by an unknown master at the tomb of the Liao Emperor Shên-tsung at Lin-tung in Inner Mongolia, painted shortly after 1031.[47]

Assembly of Birds can best be described in Rowland's words – a habitat group with a painted backcloth. For despite the beauty of its execution, it is as airless as a showcase in some provincial museum of natural history, in which someone has attempted to provide, for its palpably moribund occupants, a realistic setting of seashore, marsh, or tropical savannah. The scroll shows a lack of structural organization.[48] In this respect it is scarcely more than a procession of unrelated incidents, and in general is far less pictorially satisfying than the flower-and-bird paintings ascribed to Emperor Hui-tsung, or even to Hsü Hsi and his immediate followers.

The second flower-and-bird painter now under discussion is Hsü Hsi. Whether any originals by this master survive today is a very debatable question, one that has been in-

col. 48

vestigated in a primary article by Rowland concerning paintings attributed to Hsü now in Japan.[49] But there can be no denying his historical significance in the eyes of posterity, who regarded him as the pioneer of a new style. His innovations in composition were probably no less significant.

Hsü Hsi was a contemporary of Huang Ch'üan working in the Southern T'ang court at Nanking. But he was always clearly distinguished from Huang in the writings of Chinese critics on account of a sort of rustic vigour which they called *yeh i*, 'crude'. One says: 'The Huangs' flower paintings show a marvellous handling of colours. Their brush-work is extremely fresh and finely detailed; the ink lines are almost invisible, [the work] being com-pleted by the use of light coloured washes alone. [Their sort of painting] is spoken of as "sketching from life" (*hsieh shêng*). Hsü Hsi [on the other hand] would use ink and brush to draw in a very broad way, add a summary colouring – and that would be all. [With him] spiritual quality is pre-eminent, and one has a special sense of life-motion. [Huang] Ch'üan disliked his methods, called his work coarse and ugly, and rejected it as being without style (*pu ju ko*).'[50]

What were these unorthodox methods that the Academician, true to his type, regarded with such disfavour? It is by no means certain that the famous *mei ku*, the 'boneless' or 'line-suppressed' style, originated with Hsü Hsi or whether, as is usually supposed, with his son or grandson Hsü Chung-ssǔ. But we have a fair idea as to what it looked like. *Chieh tzǔ yüan* describes it thus: 'For flowers painted in *hsieh shêng* contours are dispensed with. One uses only white mixed with either opaque or clear colours. You must have the idea [in your head] before beginning to paint. These flowers are different from those painted by the con-tour method (*kou li*). The branches and the leaves must all be made by means of colour. We call this "boneless painting" ...'[51]

What most strikes us about the paintings ascribed to Hsü the Elder in the Chion-in, Hōryūji, and Inouye collections in Japan is the way by which graduated washes of colour are cleverly used both to suggest local tone and to model relief form. The petals of the lotus flowers common to all of them are rendered with fine outlines filled with exquisitely mod-

col. 48

ulated washes of crimson paint, while the forms of the duckweed leaves in the Hōryūji pain-ting are built up by means of umber washes alone.

Undoubtedly a new and liberating style had been added to the technical repertory of Chinese painting by the middle of the eleventh century. Yet we cannot definitely say that the *mei ku* style involved total abandonment of line, or even deposed it from its primary place. While discussing a *mei ku* painting, the late eleventh-century critic Kuo Jo-hsü notes that it bore an inscription by the famous calligrapher Ts'ai Chün-kuo (1012–67) who traced the style back to Hsü Chung-ssǔ; Kuo comments that the innovation may have resulted from 'some fit of enthusiasm' on Hsü's part, and that he did not necessarily subsequently 'eschew brush and ink [*i.e.* outline] entirely'.[52] Modern critics are in fact agreed that *mei ku* was a combination of ink outline and graded colour washes, and that from the Hsü family it passed to Chao Ch'ang, who in turn transmitted it to the great flower-and-bird painters of the twelfth and thirteenth centuries. It developed into what has been called the second Academy style.

In respect of composition, the group of paintings in Japan attributed to Hsü shows a marked advance from the archaic type of composition associated with the name of Huang Ch'üan. The field of vision is narrowed. That reluctance to cut short nature's rambling procession, which we seem to sense in compositions like *Assembly of Birds*, and perhaps also in early landscapes such as *Festival for Evoking Rain*, has been overcome by an act of will   *pl. 207* aimed at extracting from natural disorder the order and meaning of a concept-symbol, a recognizable 'thing'. If not a single object, at least a self-contained group of objects is here brought into focus and made to dominate the composition. The handful of lotus flowers that are the theme for all these paintings make up an intelligible whole. To safeguard this unity, the convention of the 'cut branch' is adopted where appropriate; the living threads which would draw us away from what the painter wants us to see, are ruthlessly slashed by the picture frame. Chao Ch'ang is traditionally regarded as the inventor of the 'cut branch'; we may at least conjecture that it originated fairly early in the tradition first launched by Hsü Hsi and his successors.

Another characteristic of these compositions, one that seems inescapable in all classical phases of Chinese art, is that of balanced asymmetry. The lotus stalks are all disposed on one side, and so leave a *coulisse* on the other, down which the beholder's eye naturally travels into the depth of the scene. This device, as Rowland remarks, has its counterpart in a convention of Chinese landscape painting that also seems to have originated in the eleventh century, one   *pl. 207* that may well have developed from it. An open corridor representing a river valley is left on one side of the picture, while the other is occupied by a mountain massif. Again the effect is to lead the eye into deep space, to invite it to begin circumambulating the mountain mass rather in the way it tends to do in some of Cézanne's landscapes. We shall shortly see how balanced asymmetry reached its climax in the work of Hui-tsung and that of Southern Sung landscapists like Ma Yüan and Hsia Kuei.

By the end of the eleventh century the new style and manner of composition were finding their way into the Sung Academy tradition as typified by the work of the third great flower-and-bird painter now under discussion, Emperor Hui-tsung (1082–1135). In a brilliant essay in style analysis Benjamin Rowland has examined and upheld the credentials of a series of four paintings traditionally attributed to Hui-tsung[53], one of which is reproduced here as colour plate 51. While there is really no such thing as proof positive of an attribu-   *col. 51* tion in the case of an early Chinese painting (and especially, we may feel, when the painter to whom the work is credited happens to be an emperor), we can at least agree that these four paintings are by the same hand, and do most probably faithfully reproduce the Emperor's personal style and manner of composition. They thus illustrate the position established by flower-and-bird painting at the beginning of the twelfth century, and the question is, what common characteristics of style and composition do they manifest?

Hui-tsung stood firmly in the middle of the Academy tradition; we are told that he took lessons from the famous painter of bamboos Wu Yüan-yü (second half of eleventh century), and also from Wu's tutor, Ts'ui Po (active *c.* 1069–77). Probably, as Yonezawa suggests, these painters adopted the second Academy style, in which fine outlines were combined with graded colour washes.[54] To what extent this was based on the *mei ku* style, if not entirely, we have no means of determining. If we take the view that outline played little or no part in the *mei ku* painting of Hsü's school, we shall naturally regard the fully fledged second Academy style as descended no less from the *kou li t'ien ts'ui* style of the Huangs [p. 317]. However that may be, a combination of outlines and graded colour washes seems to be characteristic of Hui-tsung's work. In *Quail and Narcissus*, outline is used for describing   *col. 51* such details as the beak and legs of the bird, and the leaves, leaf-veins, and petals of the flower. In contrast, the individual feathers of the plumage are not defined by outlines, but by a marginal lightening of tone where one feather overlaps the next; and this treatment closely *col. 48* corresponds to that of the individual lotus petals in pictures like the Hōryūji *Lotus Pond with Birds*, attributed to Hsü Hsi. There graduated washes are used to model relief, while in the Hui-tsung they serve merely to mark off one feather from another; the effect is different, but the technique is the same.

In respect of composition the paintings attributed to Hui-tsung mark an important advance. A single object is now discriminated from its surroundings, and with an intensity that is positively theatrical. Almost all suggestion of background, of local setting, is eliminated in *Quail and Narcissus*; in other paintings ascribed to Hui-tsung the subject stands out with an unearthly radiance, like a building floodlit against a night sky. But in securing this effect, all sense of actuality has been dispelled. We are left with a flat decorative pattern, a coloured shape like a cardboard cut-out, a cypher 'suspended' as one modern Western critic puts it, 'in the stillness of no time'.

In *Quail and Narcissus* the principle of balanced asymmetry is used in such a way as to rivet our attention on the subject. As if to emphasize its isolation, the painter imprisons it in a small area of the picture surface bounded by a sharp diagonal that runs across one corner. *pl. 219* It was the regularity with which the landscapist Ma Yüan employed this convention a hundred years later that earned for him the nickname 'One-corner Ma'. Although the term might seem to be no more than a literal description of pictures of this sort, it perhaps has a somewhat deeper meaning. Confucius once told his disciples that on lifting one corner of his argument he expected them to be able to 'come back to him with the other three' – making use of a metaphor which, according to Rowland, may have been taken from the laying out of rice plots. So, says Rowland, the expression 'one corner' used with reference to these paintings may have helped to put the beholder in mind of his own 'necessary response in mentally filling in the empty portions of a picture'. But whether the painter intended by its means to leave gaps into which the beholder might project his own mental images or whether, as I think more likely, simply to accentuate his subject by involving it in a dramatic interplay of full and empty spaces, the strong diagonal steadily grew to be a regular feature of Chinese painting during the twelfth century. If not its actual creator, Hui-tsung may rightly be regarded as one of its earliest practitioners.

Style and composition are conjoint means by which an artist expresses his aesthetic sensibility. Neither in Hui-tsung's paintings nor in those attributed to Hsü Hsi is the quest for lifelikeness uppermost; their decorative effect is therefore all the more pronounced. But the works attributed to Hsü Hsi are stamped with an artistic maturity, a painterliness and a feeling for organic structure, that Hui-tsung's paintings seem on the whole to lack. Were it not for the Emperor's undoubted influence on the subsequent course of Academy painting, exerted by virtue of his position, his artistic personality could I think be dismissed as negligible. But, as it expresses itself in his paintings, it is still quite a real one. Perhaps with better reason than in the case of *Assembly of Birds*, we are tempted to apply the label 'enumerative' to this painstakingly literal delineation of parts, and to see its author as typical of the corresponding psychological type, that called 'extraverted thinking' by Jung. It is not one that tends to produce outstanding masters.

One hundred and fifty years lie between Hui-tsung and the last of our four masters, Ch'ien Hsüan, during the course of which many flower-and-bird painters achieved fame. Among these may perhaps be mentioned Li An-chung, who painted in the second Academy style, but who seems to have used somewhat stronger outlines than are found in the work of his predecessors; there were also Li Ti, Mao Sung, Mao I, and Li Sung, all of whom took the second Academy style as their starting point and modified it exiguously to suit their individual temperaments. But no major stylistic change occurred until the coming of the Buddhist priest-painter Mu Ch'i sometime in the thirteenth century.

We reproduce as plate 196 one of two superb flower-and-bird studies attributed to Mu *pl. 196* Ch'i, whom some consider to have been the greatest master of Sung times.[55] Like its cele-brated companion-piece *Persimmons*, *Peonies* is rendered in ink monochrome alone, and in a *col. 52* very free and impressionistic manner, with individual brush-strokes combining to fix the artist's glowing vision in a pictorial form of astonishing power. Yet however revolutionary may have been Mu Ch'i's application of the ink monochrome technique to flower-and-bird painting, it had already shown its paces in other genres, notably that of bamboos [p. 322]. Nor did his influence perceptibly alter the subsequent course of Chinese flower-and-bird painting, which remained almost exclusively a product of the Academic tradition at least until quite recently. From an art-historical point of view the case of his contemporary, Ch'ien Hsuan, is far more pertinent.

Despite his undoubted talent Ch'ien Hsüan was a conservative and even reactionary spirit. Taking Chao Ch'ang as his model, he seems to have set out deliberately to restore what he took to be the manner of Northern Sung flower-and-bird painting. Practically speaking his style may be called *mei ku*. Descriptive outlines do appear, but he depends mainly on ink-washes and individual brush-strokes whereby to define his forms; as does Mu Ch'i. But his effect is not impressionistic. On the contrary his attention to detail, as can be seen from the scroll featuring flying insects in the Detroit Institute of Arts, is as scrupulous and minute as *col. 50* in the paintings attributed to Hui-tsung, and produces a far more realistic effect. In com-position, too, we find a number of superficial resemblances to the work of the Emperor. Thus he consistently upholds the convention of the 'cut branch', and his animals are simi-larly silhouetted against an empty background. Notice, too, in *Squirrel on a Peach Bough*, *pl. 195* how his branch traces an interesting pattern across the picture surface, just as do the deco-rative perches in some of Hui-tsung's most characteristic studies of birds. *col. 51*

His intention was to revive the past. But a painter cannot escape from his own historical context; and there is a very real difference between the warmth and animation of Ch'ien Hsüan's subjects and the chill artefacts of the Emperor's literal mind. They are incredibly alive. We must of course distinguish between the lifelikeness that faithfully records the clear-ness of a painter's own vision, and photographic naturalism which seeks only to reproduce actual appearances. Ch'ien Hsüan's studies are not portraits of particular animals and plants; his images are still generic. But, as H.H. Price points out, such images are not in fact general on account of any intrinsic content which they may have, but are in that respect no less 'full-blooded and fully specified particulars' than are the specified particulars in actuality to which they bear a general resemblance.[56] The scene created by Ch'ien Hsüan is real and palpable to our senses, despite the fact – and indeed perhaps for the very reason – that it exists on a different plane of reality from any similar scene in the world of appearances.

In striking this new note of pictorial realism Ch'ien Hsüan shows himself unavoidably in tune with the spirit of his times, the spirit which he personally found so antipathetic. Thus when he frames his subject against an empty background he is apparently following the lead given by Hui-tsung. But whereas the Emperor uses the empty spaces in order to produce dynamic tensions in the picture-plane, Ch'ien Hsüan instinctively creates an effect of depth by filling them with light. And with light of a particular quality. The insects in the Detroit *col. 50* scroll are bathed in what is unmistakably the wan light of autumn, that presses up against their bodies and floods the miasmal air in which they live.

If saturating light creates an illusion of three-dimensional space, the depiction of movement, as Friedländer reminds us, helps to strengthen this illusion by implying the existence of space through which such movement can take place. In recording the motions of his subject the painter naturally chooses one which it could not possibly hold for any length of time, and in doing so reinforces the 'illusion of life with which art has been and is concerned.'[57] Hui-tsung's creatures are rooted in an immobility from which we cannot imagine they could ever be freed, for we can scarcely credit them with any power of voluntary movement. How differently does Ch'ien Hsüan's squirrel strike us. Vibrant with life, the only moving thing in a world of stillness, he is about to step forward along a frail and perilous causeway. And this sensation of muscular tension is communicated to us. We want to participate imaginatively in his enterprise; we project our emotions, by empathy, into his being. It is this *participation mystique* which, as I have said, brings such extraordinary distinction to Sung and Yüan flower-and-bird painting as a whole, and invests it with a spirituality unique of its kind in the annals of world art history.

pl. 195

INK BAMBOO
pls 197–200, 202, 205, 206
In *Hsüan-ho hua p'u* (1120) paintings of bamboo are entered under the heading *mo chu*, or 'ink bamboo'. This term does not only mean bamboo painting done solely in monochrome ink; it also implies that brush and ink are used in a recognizably calligraphic way, and not merely to build up forms by describing boundary lines. Paintings of bamboo done by means of outline (*kou li*) were not admitted as a separate category in Chinese painting; nor, theoretically at least, can they be classified under *mo chu* [but see p. 323].

We have added ink bamboo to the categories of Sung and Yüan painting partly because of its intrinsic importance as a genre, and partly because what we can tell of its early history helps to verify our findings on the contemporary evolution of other picture categories, especially flower-and-bird. Furthermore it asserts, as no other picture category does, the underlying relations between painting and calligraphy. It is, I believe, perfectly proper to stress the kinship between Chinese calligraphy and *all* forms of Chinese painting, if only because identical materials are used for both, and both exact the same sort of muscular and nervous control in handling the brush. At the same time those who seek to set them apart can justly claim that outlines as used in Chinese painting are no more calligraphic than those of European drawing, since they are not modulated nor are they conceived of as having finite thickness; nor for that matter is the technique of colour- or ink-washes a calligraphic one. With ink bamboo, on the other hand, the relationship to calligraphy is far more intimate, for it extends from materials to brush techniques and eventually involves fundamentally similar aesthetic aims.

pls 200–204
A piece of bamboo has objective existence as a percept before it has been painted, whereas a written character has none. But their images as they exist in the mind of the artist are alike in this respect – that each is a symbol made up of a definite and limited number of distinct parts. If the symbol is to be propagated, these parts must be transferred intact to the picture surface. And if it is to make sense as a symbol, the proper relationship between its parts must be preserved. The whole is in fact greater than the sum of its parts; for in the form of the written character we read meaning, and in that of the bamboo we read life.

In both calligraphy and ink bamboo, each significant part is recorded by means of a single brush-stroke. With the bamboo, these significant parts are its macroscopic organs – leaves, nodes, and segments of stem. And just as an extra stroke on the part of a calligrapher falsifies the character he has written, so a strict economy of brush-strokes must be practised in *mo chu* painting. For not only does each brush-stroke define a particular macroscopic part – for purposes of representation it *is* that part. Since the number of parts in a given piece of bamboo is limited, the number of brush-strokes required to register them must necessarily be limited also. It follows that the aesthetic qualities of bamboo painting closely resemble those on account of which a well-written character is appreciated. They reside in the manner of execution of each individual brush-stroke, in the way these are organized into a significant pattern, and in the economy with which they are deployed.

When was this bridge between calligraphy and painting first built? Traditional genea-logies of bamboo painting trace the origins of *mo chu* back either to Wu Tao-tzŭ (AD 700–760), or to Lady Li of the Five Dynasties, who is supposed to have traced over the shadows of bamboos cast by the moon shining on the windows of her house. But, as in the case of flower-and-bird painting, we must judge from what has survived in more concrete form. There is in fact no reason for supposing that bamboo painting did not take much the same course as that of flowers and birds. That is, its first exponents worked with a *kou li* technique, using ink outlines sometimes filled with colour.

The oldest surviving Chinese paintings of bamboo are probably those that appear on scrolls featuring the Bodhisattva Kuan-yin [p. 192] recovered from the Tun-huang library, *col. 47* one of which bears a date corresponding to AD 910. The author of a recent article on bamboo painting, Wang Shih-hsiang, says of an example in the Musée Guimet, Paris, that its style must be considered a provincial version of that current in metropolitan *ateliers* early in the tenth century AD; and he suggests that bamboo painting got a foothold by being introduced as a supplementary iconographic theme in Chinese religious painting, just as did landscape in the European tradition.[58] In the Guimet scroll the leaves are painted in pure ink mono-chrome, the stalks in outline only.

A painting now in Japan entitled *Bamboo and Insects*, although obviously a thirteenth-century paraphrase, shows this same combination of stalks (and a few leaves) painted in out-line and leaves in ink monochrome.[59] It is interesting to note that *Bamboo and Insects* is tra-ditionally ascribed to Chao Ch'ang (*fl.* AD 1000); we have seen that Chao inherited the *mei ku* tradition of Hsü Hsi's school [p. 318], and that paintings in this style were composed partly of forms registered by outlines and partly of those built up by means of colour-washes alone. The attribution to Chao Ch'ang is thus consistent, stylistically at least, with what can be deduced of the nature of his work from literary sources. It tends to support the view that during the first half of the eleventh century ink bamboo and flower-and-bird painting followed parallel stylistic paths.

Other painters of bamboo who worked either wholly or partly in outlines were Li P'o (*fl.* AD 907–23), Huang Ch'üan [p. 317], Ts'ui Po (*fl.* AD 1069–77), and his pupil Wu Yüan-yü (second half of eleventh century AD). There is no evidence that any of these worked in pure ink monochrome, and the reason why paintings by Li P'o are entered under the heading *mo chu* in *Hsüan-ho hua p'u* is simply that there was no other category into which they could be conveniently fitted. The ascendancy of *mo chu* probably dates from the second half of the century. So Huang T'ing-chien (1050–1110), quoted with approval by Li K'an in his famous *Chu p'u hsiang lu*, 'Comprehensive Record of Bamboo', non-committally says: 'Ink bamboo started in recent times but we cannot trace its origins. ...'[60]

The man who by tradition is supposed to have done more than any other to give *mo chu* the status of an independent genre was Wên T'ung (active *c.* AD 1049, died AD 1079), whose work has stood as a model for aspiring bamboo-painters ever since. A painting in *pl. 197* what was the Palace Museum is considered by Wang Shih-hsiang to be of all surviving bamboo studies the one best qualified to bear his name. Essential features of all later *mo chu* are displayed in it. First, a marked economy in thematic material. A single branch sweeps across the picture surface from the upper border in the form of an S-curve – a shape subsequently attempted by many bamboo-painters, and which we have also encountered in the flower-and-bird paintings of Hui-tsung and Ch'ien Hsüan [p. 321]. Wang points out how much more difficult it is to achieve a satisfactory composition out of a single spray of bamboo than out of a whole clump. Indeed, Wên T'ung seems to be making a regular parade of his virtuosity; thus the individual segments of his stem are pronouncedly curved, witnessing to a technique so difficult for any except a master that the sixteenth-century critic Kao Sung accounts curvature of stem sections a positive fault.

The brush-stroke, as we have said, is all-important. That called *chung fêng*, in which the point of the brush holds to the middle of the stroke throughout its length, is habitually used in depicting the leaves, shaping them into sharp and beautifully poised forms which the Chinese call *hsien li*. *Chung fêng* is one of the standard strokes in calligraphy, and its constant presence in *mo chu* painting is a reminder of the inherent sameness of the two art-forms.

Finally, the painting attributed to Wên T'ung is conspicuously free from superfluous brush-strokes. For while the placing of each stroke upon the picture surface undoubtedly helps to create dynamic tension between painted and unpainted areas, its real purpose is to add its indispensable fraction to the organic whole, to the image of the plant portrayed. This was a standard that later painters usually failed to maintain, and the Ch'ing critic Chang *pls 202, 205* Kêng delivers judgment accordingly, taking as his paragon a painter two of whose bamboo paintings we here illustrate, Wu Chên. 'I have seen an ink bamboo painting by Mei Tao-jên (Wu Chên)', he says, '... Only at the base and the protruding tips of the branches are there, in places, one or two brush-strokes to obtain the proper effect; there are never empty dots and flips of the brush, made to fill in. ... Therefore when I consider modern painters who ... use a lot of delicate and empty brush-strokes to tie it all together, I think how conventional they are! In trying to avoid evenness, they don't realize they fall into the error of fragmentation. Ink bamboo developed from outline bamboo. The outline bamboo of T'ang and Sung had long leaves which overlap one another without delicate bits that serve only to fill in. From this I conclude that the use of empty strokes in dots and flips is a great error of bamboo painting in ink.'[61]

From the time of Wên T'ung until the onset of the Yüan period no really great master of *mo chu* emerged. Su Shih's high reputation is scarcely confirmed by the few paintings traditionally attributed to him, and Wang Shih-hsiang may very well be right in surmising *pl. 201* that he owes it largely to his undoubted skill as poet and calligrapher. But if the twelfth century was a period of comparative inactivity, the thirteenth and fourteenth witnessed a huge output of bamboo paintings, with the names of over fifty painters of the genre recorded for posterity. As happened with flower-and-bird painting and landscape, these painters wholly repudiated the hated century of Sung Academy professionalism and turned for inspiration to the great masters of the Northern Sung.

The four outstanding Yüan bamboo-painters were Li K'an, Ku An, Wu Chên, and Ni Tsan, and of these Li K'an is generally reckoned to have been the greatest. We are told that he devoted years of his life to studying the bamboo in all its aspects, travelling far and wide in south China and even into Annam so as to see its various species growing under natural conditions. He made the same close examination of the old masters, and in particular of Wên T'ung, whom he finally chose to be his guide. A painting attributed to Li in the

48 *In the manner of Hsü Hsi (died before* AD *975),* Lotus Pond with Birds, *one of a pair of paintings on silk mounted as a folding screen. See pages 318–319. The Tōindō, Hōryūji, Nara.*

49 In the style of Tung Yüan (fl. 947–970), Clear Day in the
Valley, *painting in ink and light colour on paper, probably not executed
before the Southern Sung period [see pl. 207]. 14³/₄ × 59³/₈ in. Museum
of Fine Arts, Boston.*

50 Ch'ien Hsüan (c.1235–1290), Early Autumn, *in ink and colour on paper. See pages 321–322 and plate 195.* $47^{1}/_{2} \times 19^{1}/_{4}$ *in. Detroit Institute of Arts.*

51 *Hui-tsung (1082–1135),* Quail and Narcissus, *in ink and colour on paper. The faint outline of a sloping bank serves to establish the 'one corner' organization of the picture surface and tends to isolate the subject and rivet our attention to it. See page 320.* 10⁵/₈ × 16¹/₂ *in. Nagatake Asano, Odawara, Japan.*

52 *Mu Ch'i (fl. 1200–1255),* Persimmons, *in ink on paper. See page 321 and plate 196.* 14¹/₈ × 15 *in. Daitokuji, Kyoto.*

Nelson Gallery of Art, Kansas City, is a true botanical description of two different species *pl. 200* of the plant arranged in two separate clumps. But faithful as they are to nature, these studies are far more than mere botanical illustrations. They are not portraits of particular plants. They are still the records of mental visual images, and are realistic to precisely the same degree as are the flower-and-bird paintings of Li K'an's near contemporary Ch'ien Hsüan *pl. 195* [p. 321]. What Li himself observes in his *Chu p'u hsiang lu* fully accords with the supposition that his bamboo studies, like so much other Chinese painting, were based on generic images forged and projected in the mind of the artist in an intensity of mental effort; he is here adding his own comments on Su Shih's essay, part of which we have already quoted [p. 303]: 'The painter must thus accumulate his power [faculties] until he arrives at the stage where he can rely on himself and possess the bamboo completely in his mind. At this stage he can move the brush and follow the model he sees before him [in his mind's eye]. If not prepared in this way he will grasp the brush in vain and gaze at the thing in front of him without being able to represent it.'[62]

We mentioned earlier the popularity of pictures of bamboo blown by the wind as emblems of resistance to the gale of Mongol conquest. Ku An (*fl.* 1350) is perhaps the best-*pl. 206* known painter of these. By his time Li K'an's manual of instruction for bamboo-painters, with its model illustrations of typical compositions, was already circulating. Still later the patterns and forms of leaves and other plant parts were to become so conventionalized, by means of such models, as to leave no room for freedom of expression on the part of painters who followed them; and bamboo painting all too frequently became a mechanical operation. There is a bare hint of what was to happen in Ku An's work. His leaves are arranged in conventional groups of four, some of them looking strangely like long-legged birds seen end-on in flight. Those bent by the opposing wind take the standard form known as *ting fêng*; those that stream with the wind are rendered according to the convention *shun fêng*.

Although Ku An's images are neither stereotyped nor banal, the artist seems unwilling to disclose his artistic personality and what little does emerge is of a precise and somewhat prosaic nature. The paintings of Wu Chên and Ni Tsan, on the contrary, emphatically proclaim poetic spirits. Both artists were out-and-out individualists, even eccentrics, and the differences in their respective styles are plain to see; but they are at one in refusing to wear the blinkers of a dreary academicism, in the violence with which they reject the canon of orthodox forms and patterns.

In an age of political oppression, rebellion against authority can take many forms. It is a healthy indication that at such a time two painters should be found absorbed in what appears to be a personal war against conformity in art, against the pattern-book, and in support of the role of the inimitable mental visual image, the source of all pictorial inspiration.

We shall say a little more about Wu Chên's bamboo studies when taking note of plate 202. *pl. 202* Those of Ni Tsan give the impression of a summary and indeed careless execution, which is *pl. 243* corroborated by his own estimate of his work. So apparently indifferent was he to a conventionally successful outcome that he deliberately used worn-out brushes, and generally speaking seems to have taken every possible step to make his paintings unappealing to contemporary taste. 'I, Chung, always like my bamboo paintings', he says. 'My bamboo is painted just to serve as an outlet for the inspiration within my breast. Why should I bother to compare whether it is like [bamboo] or not, whether the leaves are dense or sparse, the branches bent or straight. At times I smear about for a long while and when someone sees my picture he may well call it hemp or he may call it reeds. I certainly couldn't argue to convince him it is bamboo!'[63] Ni is here using the inconsequential and irrelevant language of the Ch'an [Jap. Zen] master. The bamboo, we might say, is for him the *Dharma*-Body of the Buddha.

Yet perhaps he protests too much. So totally does he reject the criterion of external verisimilitude, it is true, that his bamboos begin to take on almost the character of abstract symbols; those that appear in a painting of his now in the National Museum, Peking, have a dreamlike quality, a quietude and simplicity that lifts them altogether out of the real world. But they are still recognizable bamboos. Ni was an original genius, certainly, but not quite the nihilist he pretends to be. He infused the tradition of ink bamboo painting with the idea of a heterodox informality, and gave form to this idea. Thus he did for ink bamboo what Wang Hsi-chih is reputed to have done for calligraphy. For if the regular and meticulous forms of Ku An's bamboos correspond to orthodox *li shu*, those of Wu Chên and Ni Tsan are pictorial equivalents of the wayward and personal style, *ts'ao shu* [p. 310].

LANDSCAPE
pls 207–226; col. 44, 45, 49

The germs of Chinese landscape, *shan shui* or 'mountains and streams', are to be found as accessory elements in the pictorial motifs of Han and even pre-Han art [pp. 103 and 147]. A long period of gestation followed, and it was not until the tenth century AD that landscape as a picture category in its own right began to reach full formulation. From that time onwards it became the leading form of pictorial expression in China.

Just as happened in the development of European painting, Chinese landscape had to overcome certain psychological tendencies apparent in primitive picture-making generally before it emerged as a distinctive form. One of these was a disposition to scale everything to the dimensions of a human module, and to represent different human beings of a size commensurate with their importance as symbols in accordance with a 'spiritual table of precedence'. In the scroll *Admonitions of the Imperial Instructress* in the British Museum, considered by some to be a T'ang or perhaps Sung copy of an original by the fourth-century AD master Ku K'ai-chih and admittedly preserving a very early mode of pictorial composition, a kneel-

col. 45

ing huntsman is in one passage shown shooting with a bow at animals placed on a hillside scarcely larger than himself.[64] Man and mountain are both depicted in a naturalistic manner. But the 'faulty' scaling indicates a stage of development wherein the facts of objective reality are less pressing than the urge to establish a strictly human order of values. And this urge must eventually be brought under control by the painter; for while linear distortion may be both permissible and necessary as an aid to landscape composition, the form it takes cannot for that very reason be decided by the factor of human interest alone.

'Over-emphasis of meaningful parts', as Sir Herbert Read calls it, persists in some degree at all later stages in the history of Chinese landscape. Indeed it cannot properly be thought of as faulty scaling at all. The distortion that in primitive art serves primarily to indicate relations between man and his surroundings as they are felt to be, may in more sophisticated compositions continue to be used intentionally, both in order to emphasize objects of psychological interest and to safeguard the essential character of pictorial art as two-dimensional form. The two purposes are in fact complementary; for, as Sir Kenneth Clark says, the less a picture creates the illusion of actuality, the more it tends to interest the eye as decorative pattern. With precisely the same twin objectives in view, outstanding European artists have from time to time felt impelled to resort to similar means, despite the prevailing naturalism of the European pictorial tradition.[65]

Another problem for which conventional solutions may be found is that of representing depth on the flat picture surface. We shall presently describe in some detail the several conventions of linear perspective followed in Sung and Yüan landscape; but here we must notice that these stem from a range of elementary devices employed in pre-Sung graphic art, not in order to create an illusion of depth, but simply as a means of registering its existence and the relative positions of objects placed in depth. Seen from above, the individual features of a natural landscape all stand separate, like place-names on a map. The landscapist there-fore often adopts the simple expedient of the bird's-eye view to represent them; more distant objects are set higher on the picture surface than nearer, so that the horizon mounts to the top edge of the picture, or even beyond it. But as the observer comes nearer to the ground his angle of vision narrows, so that distant objects may appear to be partly masked by nearer. And this also suggests a convenient means of representing depth – the so-called 'imbricated' method by which objects are depicted overlapping one another. But whatever the viewpoint adopted, *every object is invariably drawn as though viewed from the same angle*, which would not be the case in an actual scene, assuming the position of the observer to be fixed. This rule applies to Chinese landscape long after it has emerged from its formative phase; the observer's position is *not* assumed to be fixed.

Less frequent expedients for representing depth are diagonals arbitrarily drawn to suggest recession, and reduction in size of distant objects. But whatever the device used in these early schemas, it is never allowed to rob the picture of its essential quality as a flat decorative design. It is a means of symbolizing depth, not of deceiving us into supposing that depth is actually there.

But what really delayed the emancipation of an art of landscape, in China as in Europe, was the fact that natural scenery has no finite form or functional organization. A horse, a tree, a human being, any separate entity, is readily discriminated from its surroundings in the act of perception by virtue of its finite form. But the nature of a stretch of countryside is such that it cannot be so discriminated; as Friedländer says, 'The "thing" is finite, but to landscape belongs infinity'.[66] And whereas a finite thing can be made to serve as a pictorial concept-symbol by defining its image within a descriptive boundary line, a landscape cannot be so symbolized. The only limits that can be found for it are those arbitrarily fixed by the picture-frame; consequently it cannot be used as a primary concept-symbol.[67]

Not until society endows nature herself with significant meaning will the painter seek to give organic structure to the disorder of natural scenery, to find for it pictorial 'boundaries by agreement'. As nature loses her terrors, as bit by bit man begins to identify her rhythms with his, to project his feelings into her appearances, so he gradually learns to tolerate a pictorial concept-symbol that can never be defined by virtue of any finite form which it has. But a transitional stage is helpful, perhaps even necessary. The early history of European landscape provides a curious instance of this point. Nature herself is boundless, and is bitterly hostile to intruding human life. Amid her desolation man seeks to provide for himself places of refuge and spiritual comfort; moreover such enclosures have finite form, and that finite form relates to a human module. The enclosed garden, *hortus conclusus*, thus presents itself as a suitable intermediate pictorial symbol; its boundary walls can be located wholly or partly within the picture surface, while beyond them one may be offered a glimpse of the wilderness into which man must presently make his way. In the Paradise Garden of the fourteenth and fifteenth centuries, the *mise en scène* for medieval enactments of sacred and profane love, poetic imagination happily invents the means of bridging the gap between the boundless amplitude of nature and the tight configuration of the finite thing.

The word 'paradise' is Persian in origin; and the new icon, and many of the ideas as-sociated with it, may very well have reached Europe from the Near East at the time of the Crusades. We must therefore keep in mind the exciting possibility of an ultimate Far Eastern influence for these charming Paradise scenes, indirectly transmitted by means of Persian miniature painting. Persian inspiration is for example detected by Sir Kenneth Clark in the *Madonna in a Rose Garden* by Stefano da Zervio in the Castello at Verona.

A corresponding stage in the history of Chinese landscape is missing. But a threadbare literary tradition perhaps testifies to its former existence. Thus Chang Yen-yüan in his *Li tai ming hua chi*, speaking of fourth-century AD landscape, observes: '... sometimes the figures are larger than the mountains. The views are generally enclosed by trees and stones which stand in a circle on the ground. They look like rows of lifted arms with outstretched fingers.' The enclosures of which Chang speaks in these somewhat gruesome terms might be compared to the settings in the calendar of the *Très Riches Heures du Duc de Berry*, in which greensward is hedged around by thick-growing and no less forbidding trees.[68] Again, the tradition which relates certain existing stone engravings and pictorial paraphrases to an alleged scroll painting by the T'ang painter Wang Wei entitled *Wang ch'uan t'u*, 'Picture of the Wang Enclosure', specifies that the theme of the original was the artist's estate. And this is corroborated by the extant panorama, part of which is occupied by a walled enclosure. Here, then, is an indication that in China, too, the metamorphosis of pure landscape may have taken place by way of representation of gardens or park scenery.

Ideas connecting man and nature are innate in Chinese thought, but not until Sung times did they crystallize into a devotional cult that could be made to fit indifferently into Confucianist, Taoist, or Buddhist contexts. But whatever philosophical implications the cult of nature may have had, its chief votaries belonged to the urban bureaucracy, and its emotional basis was the sense of spiritual claustrophobia that brought into being the Chinese town garden about the same time [p. 378]. An intimate, indeed tenderly lyrical relationship with nature was sought. The landscapist Kuo Hsi never tires of telling how the harassed official turns to nature with a childlike delight, and finds therein an unfailing respite from worldly trammels.

Sir Kenneth Clark points out that this same escapist attitude on the part of town-dwellers also largely nurtured the growth of pure landscape in European painting. Petrarch, who he says was probably the first European to express it, sometimes does so in language that might have been used by Kuo Hsi himself: 'Would that you could know with what joy I wander free and alone among the mountains, forests, and streams', he writes to a friend. But for the fourteenth-century Italian, surrender to nature is still sinful indulgence, and in a chastened mood he upbraids himself for having forgotten that nothing is wonderful but the human soul; he thankfully adds: 'Then, in truth, I was satisfied that I had seen enough of the mountain. ...'[69] In Petrarch's mind man still looms the larger, whereas for Kuo Hsi, nature is the very embodiment of spiritual truth and joy, and landscape painting an effective substitute for it. 'Having no access to the natural landscapes', he writes, 'the lover of forest and stream, the friend of mist and haze, enjoys them only in his dreams. How delightful then to have a landscape painted by a skilled hand!'[70] Clearly conditions for the transmutation of nature from an amorphous abstraction into a highly charged pictorial concept-symbol are hereby established.

The earliest European landscapes to express the pagan joy in natural scenery, which Petrarch so much dreaded, are those sometimes incorporated into Flemish and Florentine religious paintings of the fifteenth century. Dedicated to celebrating the beauties of the earth, they belong to what Sir Kenneth Clark calls 'the landscape of fact'. So perhaps do the earliest pure landscapes of China. The fresh vision of the wide world presented in such paintings as the landscape in Pollaiuolo's *Martyrdom of St Sebastian* (1475), where from a high vantage point the eye ranges the whole expanse of the Arno valley, has its counterpart in such a landscape as *Festival for Evoking Rain*, attributed to Tung Yüan. After this first meeting the two traditions part company. Materials and methods differ too greatly for there ever to be more than an occasional hint of a common aesthetic aim, while opportunities for cross-fertilization seem to have been entirely lacking until the eighteenth century.

pl. 207

It is perhaps in the *œuvre* of the painters of 'ideal landscape' – those that include among their number Giorgione, Titian, Claude Lorraine, Nicholas Poussin, J.R. Cozens, and Samuel Palmer – that European landscape most often approaches Chinese in spirit. For all these painters landscape had a spiritual significance far deeper than could ever attach to what Fuseli called the 'tame delineation of a given spot', or to the landscape of nineteenth-century Impressionism. Ideal landscape was exemplary landscape, typical, and not merely descriptive of an actual scene, and tinged with the painter's own poetic imagination; and it served, *inter alia*, to give semblance to the dream of a Golden Age. In so far as it drew its inspiration directly from literary sources, ideal landscape can properly be described as Virgilian or Arcadian; and in a more general sense as idyllic, poetic, or heroic.

We must not take the comparison too far. For, if I am right, the retrospective or nostalgic mood that so often supervenes in European ideal landscape is missing from Chinese; nor does the didactic value of Chinese landscape derive from any inherent literary content. It is uninhabited by legendary shades. Nevertheless the concept of landscape as transcending time and place and as possessed of more than human stature, the notion that it should partake of the sublime as music and poetry do, and that its language is essentially poetic as that of poetry is pictorial – all these ideas are also to be found in Chinese writings on landscape painting. Parts of Kuo Hsi's essay have a Wordsworthian uplift, and indeed read like Wordsworth; and when Kuo remarks that as a landscapist his guiding principle has ever been the ancient saying 'poetry is a picture without form, and painting is a poem with form', we connect the sentiment infallibly with that which lay behind the noble and aspiring tradition of European ideal landscape, *ut pictura poesis*.

PERSPECTIVE IN CHINESE LANDSCAPE

In all traditions of landscape art a stage comes when the problem of systematically reducing three-dimensional space to the two dimensions of the picture plane has to be faced. For not until a way is found of making depth and space intelligible to a beholder by pictorial means does landscape become pure landscape; although, needless to say, systems aimed at creating an illusion of physical actuality, at *trompe-l'œil*, are not the only possible ones. A meaning may be grasped imaginatively; it need not always express itself in literal terms.

But whatever the compositional system, familiarity with it is bound to breed intolerance of others. Certainly the discomfort so often felt by Westerners when confronted for the first time with a Far Eastern painting, is partly due to unfamiliar conventions of linear perspective used in its construction. By linear perspective we mean a system of representing depth by drawing alone. It contrasts with aerial perspective, in which space is suggested by depicting the softening of forms, and lightening of tones or colour, of distant objects compared with near. Chinese painters have always been sensitive to the modifying effect of atmospheric space on form and colour in pictorial composition; and Chinese ink, which yields a complete tonal range from the palest silver-grey to a deep, velvety black, is ideally suited for translating into two dimensions the 'continuous plastic weft' of three-dimensional space. That Chinese landscapists, especially those of the late eleventh and twelfth centuries, were past masters in handling the subtle but eloquent language of aerial perspective, needs no better testimony than illustrations such as plates 211, 213, 220, and 225 provide. With treatments

pls 211, 213, 220, 225

like these the Westerner should feel thoroughly at home, for precisely the same felicitous effects of diffused light are captured for us in the landscapes of French Impressionism.

But linear perspective is quite another matter. We should first remark that *any* system intended to translate three-dimensional space on to a flat picture surface is bound to be something of a compromise, however closely it adheres to optical laws. This applies even to so-called 'scientific' perspective, the invention of Brunellesco and his followers in the fifteenth century, and a standard subject of art-school curriculum from that day to this. The *certezze* which these Florentines hoped to achieve by applying geometrical rules to pictorial composition is itself an illusion. However naturalistic a landscape is intended to be, its realization depends on factors that can only be determined empirically by the artist when he comes to paint it; scientific perspective, as Sir Kenneth Clark observes, cannot be made the basis for naturalism in painting. It is unnecessary to embark on a lengthy description of this familiar system. The essential requirement is that the eye position of the observer is assumed to be fixed, as indeed it is for all practical purposes when he views a real landscape, the view being in perfect perspective only when he stands directly opposite the point at which perpendicularly receding lines in its composition appear to converge on the horizon.

In one important respect scientific perspective is definitely inimical to the true nature of painting. Painting is mural decoration; a painting that creates a strong illusion of depth no longer decorates a wall, and indeed to all intents and purposes eliminates it at that point. 'Art which decorates surfaces', says Friedländer, 'observes, more or less at all stages of development, a discreet reserve as regards the phenomenon of perspective – from disinclination to pierce or destroy [the surface which it decorates] through arousing a strong spatial illusion.'[71] There have always been European painters alive to this danger. Critics, too, have protested against the perversion of a picture from its true nature by imposing upon it the function of a magic box. Gautier, for instance, required of pictures that they should 'hang on the walls like a veil of colour and not penetrate them'[72]; and more recently and even more emphatically André Lhote has said: 'The picture, regardless of the exigencies of the subject represented, *must remain faithful to its own structure, to its fundamental two dimensions.*'[73]

The painter who more than any other was responsible for inaugurating this new phase of European landscape is of course Cézanne. It is not perhaps true to say that Cézanne's reaction was against scientific perspective as such; his concern was rather to restore natural forms to their proper place as the primary elements out of which pictorial form must be built up, a position which the Impressionist obsession with appearances had seriously undermined. Still, scientific perspective was incompatible with his deeper aesthetic aims. He did not in fact seek to imitate nature, but to create what he called 'a harmony parallel with nature' – in other words, something very like Hsün Tzǔ's 'second reality' [p. 305]. He thus showed himself a true heir of the European tradition of ideal landscape. Gowing speaks of his 'nostalgia, as for a golden age', and of his *réalisation* in words implying that it involved something closely akin to the generic image upon which so much Chinese landscape and flower-and-bird painting is based. 'The substantial vision which Cézanne reached at forty', Gowing says, 'shows us nature as ... a source of nourishment, the source in fact of the real material for rebuilding its likeness in an ideal, unshakable form.'[74]

But it is not only in their architectural proportions, their 'unshakable' air, that we seem to detect a Cézannesque quality in such Chinese landscapes as Huang Kung-wang's *pl. 223* *Mountain Village*. In composing his 'harmony parallel to nature', Cézanne knowingly distorted physical forms; and in making his own compromise between the need for registering their positions in depth and the independent claims of pictorial design, he instinctively resorted to modes of perspective drawing which, long considered obsolete in Europe, had been permanently incorporated into the tradition of Chinese landscape. Let us glance at them once again in the light of his *œuvre*.[75]

Firstly, over-emphasis of meaningful parts is characteristic of certain phases of Cézanne's work. The emotionally pregnant Mont St Victoire is usually drawn larger than life – or as if seen at closer range than is suggested by the proportions of other parts of the composition; and so, for instance, are bridge and church in the water-colour sketch *The Road to Gardanne*. This type of distortion constantly recurs in Chinese landscape. Compare, for instance, the buildings that feature in the far distance of the landscape in *High Temples in Snowy Mountains*, *pl. 209* attributed to Hsü Tao-ning, and the boat shooting the rapids in Hsia Kuei's *Ten Thousand* *pl. 217* Li *of the Long River*.

Secondly, Cézanne sometimes suggests recession by means of large overlapping planes which lie more or less parallel to the plane of vision like scenic flats, those representing more distant parts being placed higher up the picture surface than those representing nearer; for this convention to be really serviceable, the landscape must feature rising ground with hills or mountains in the distance. In Cézanne's work the planes are rarely complete nor are they easily discriminated. But in much fifteenth- and early sixteenth-century European landscape, foreground, middle distance, and background are clearly defined by means of three such planes – exceptions being compositions for which a high viewpoint is adopted, such as the above-mentioned landscape by Pollaiuolo [p. 332].

In China this principle was known as *san tieh fa*, the 'law of the three sections'. While in early paintings like *High Temples in Snowy Mountains* its use probably speaks of a technical *pl. 209* difficulty experienced in registering continuous recession of space, as it does in Europe, it persists as a convention into later periods when landscapists had long since mastered the techniques of aerial perspective. One important corollary to the principle must be noticed; each plane is drawn as though seen from the same angle of vision. Buildings and other ob- jects in the middle distance and background, which should show a foreshortening propor- tional to their height above the horizon, are drawn just as though they were at ground level. There are, in fact, three separate horizons. The eye is free to jump, indeed must jump, from one level to the next.

Thirdly, separate objects are drawn as though the eye were free to vary the horizontal direction along which it looks into the depth of a picture. We have seen that in compositions based on scientific perspective, this direction is established perpendicular to the picture plane. In some of Cézanne's paintings, notably his still lifes, different elements are drawn as though seen each from its own independent horizontal angle of vision; and, in his landscapes, build- ings are often shown with side- and end-walls more or less in the same plane.[76] This type of distortion is of course intended to fulfil a specific purpose of pictorial organization. It in- dicates neither an inability to draw nor a primitive urge to set forth what the mind knows about a thing rather than what the eye sees. And, as we gather from the way buildings are drawn in Huang Kung-wang's *Mountain Village*, it is an unexceptionable feature of tra- *pl. 223* ditional Chinese landscape.

Lastly there is vertical tilting of the plane of recession into the picture plane – a device analogous to the primitive convention of the bird's-eye view. The effect is as though the beholder were looking down on the scene from a height proportional to the height of the horizon as drawn on the picture plane. But whereas were he actually looking down on such a scene, his vertical angle of vision would vary according to the position in depth of each separate object perceived, in the pictorial convention all objects are drawn as though

335

seen from the same angle; they are not foreshortened in proportion to their relative positions in depth. In other words, each requires to be looked at from a different eye position. As a convention of primitive landscape, the bird's-eye view may have been suggested by early experiments in map-making. In Cézanne's work such a landscape as *Provençal Mas near Gardanne* provides its modern equivalent.

These devices are not of course used systematically by Cézanne, nor are they the only resources he has for registering depth on the picture plane. Neither are they strictly systematized in Chinese landscape. They can nevertheless all be condensed into a single principle of composition that marks them off sharply from the rigid system of scientific perspective. *The eye position is not thought of as fixed.* Were it the painter's aim to afford the illusion of an actual scene, he would necessarily have to establish a fixed eye position from which it must be viewed; but since he aims only to create a two-dimensional harmony 'parallel to nature', he is under no obligation to do this. By disregarding the inexorable geometry that decides how objects shall appear to the beholder when seen in their respective positions in space, the painter is free to distort their appearances so as to achieve a different sort of unity – the structural unity of a surface pattern. It is as a pattern that the beholder is meant to see it. His mind registers its contents one after another, as component features of an ideal landscape, while his eye is set free to resolve them into the basic ingredients of a unified pictorial design.

The Chinese equivalent for our term 'linear perspective' is *chin yüan*, or 'near and distant'; but the three categories into which *chin yüan* is divided do not so much define systems of perspective drawing as types of scenic view, each distinguished by the position of a main horizon from which the eye instinctively begins – although cannot complete – its exploration of the picture surface. Manuals of Chinese landscape painting illustrate typical examples of these schemas[77], with the aid of which any landscape can be assigned according to the Chinese classification; mountains are prominent in them all, as indeed they are in Chinese landscape generally.

Shen yüan, or 'deep distance', is explained by Kuo Hsi as that type of landscape in which the beholder is thought of as 'looking towards the back from the front' of the mountains. The corresponding illustration in *Chieh tzŭ yüan* shows that such compositions have a high horizon; the beholder is thought of as standing upon an eminence, from which he surveys a *pl. 207* range of countryside in something like bird's-eye view. The landscape attributed to Tung Yüan is typical of *shên yüan*; early European examples include the river scene featured in Jan van Eyck's Rollin Madonna altar-piece, *Charon's Boat* by Patinir, and the landscape in Pollaiuolo's *Martyrdom of St Sebastian*.

Kao yüan, or 'high distance', is described by Kuo Hsi as the type of landscape in which the beholder finds himself 'looking up to the top (of the mountain mass) from below'. The dominant horizon is therefore low, the eye being directed upwards through successively re*pl. 209* ceding heights represented by flat parallel planes, each with its own horizon. Hsü Tao-ning's *High Temples* is an excellent example of this type of convention. A good early European parallel is provided by the landscape panel from the St Leopold altar-piece by Rueland Frueauf the Younger (c. 1507) and there is a most remarkable compositional similarity between the Hsü Tao-ning and *St Jerome in a Rocky Landscape* in the National Gallery, London.

The third main type of *chin yüan* is called *p'ing yüan* or 'level distance'. *Chieh tzŭ yüan* defines this as the prospect when 'from the near parts [one is able to see] to the farthest parts'. As the corresponding illustration makes clear, this is the schema with which we in Europe are most familiar, the main horizon being located somewhat below the middle of the picture sur*pl. 211* face. A characteristic example is *Winter Woods*, attributed to Kuo Hsi.

336

PAINTINGS OF FIGURES AND ANIMALS

185 (below) *Woman with phoenix and dragon,* from Ch'ang-sha, fourth to third centuries BC. This is the first known painting on silk. The woman may be an enchantress or priestess [see p. 292].

186 (right) *Monk with a tiger,* tenth century AD. This expressive little picture in ink and colour on silk is in a class by itself among paintings recovered from the Tun-huang library [see p. 295 and *cf.* col. 44 and 47]. It shows a Chinese Buddhist monk crossing the wastes of Chinese Turkestan on his way home from India, heavily laden with sacred texts. There is disagreement as to whom it represents: some say the great Hsüan-tsang; others a Ch'an master called Dharmatrāta, who is the named subject of closely similar Tibetan portrayals dating from the eighteenth century. 31 1/2 × 20 3/4 in. Musée Guimet, Paris.

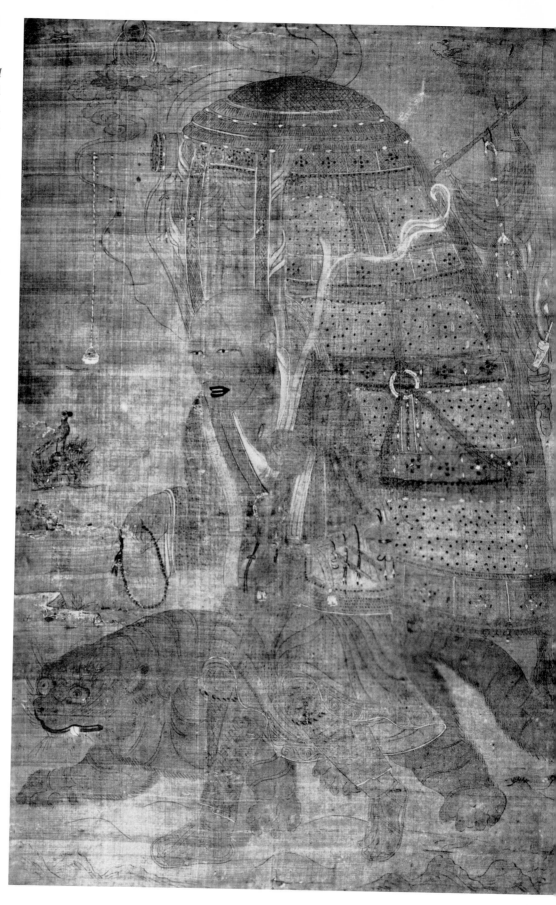

187 (left) Hu Kuei (*fl.* 923–935), *Mongol horseman,* a fa[n]
painting. Hu Kuei was a Ch'i-t'an Mongol who achieve[d]
fame as a painter of foreign tribes and horses. There is [a]
tenuous connexion, through the subject-matter of oth[er]
paintings attributed to him as well as that of some of the Tu[n]-
huang murals, between this painting and that of plate 18[6]
9 1/4 × 9 1/2 in. Museum of Fine Arts, Boston.

188 (above) Li Lung-mien (*c.* 1045–1106), part of th[e]
hand-scroll *The Five Horses,* dated 1086. In the accompany[-]
ing inscription the horse of this painting is named as Phoeni[x]
Head, and is described as a piebald, eight years old and fi[ve]
feet four inches in height. Li Lung-mien was an eclecti[c]
traditionalist with a preference for Confucianist themes b[ut]
a special aptitude for animal studies. His pen-name is take[n]
from the Lung-mien hills, Anhwei, to which he retired fro[m]
government office (his real name is Li Po-Shih). Heigh[t]
11 13/16 in., length of complete scroll: 72 in.

189 (far left) Liang K'ai (*c.*1140–1210), *Li T'ai-po Recitin[g]*
His Poems, in ink on paper. This painting and that of plat[e]
190 are in the style that belongs to the second part of Lian[g]
K'ai's life when he retired from the Sung Academy to be[-]
come a Ch'an (Jap. Zen) monk. It is a mixture of the ou[t]-
line style of Li Lung-mien [pl. 188], one of whose pupil[s]
was Liang's master, and the cursive calligraphic style of ink[-]
bamboo specialists, delivered impetuously and with breath[-]
taking economy. 31 1/8 × 11 13/16 in. National Museu[m]
Tokyo.

190 (left) Liang K'ai, *Ch'an Priest.* An alternative title [is]
Ink-splash Recluse. 19 1/4 × 10 7/8 in. National Palace Museu[m]
Taichung, Taiwan.

191 *The White Hare that Roams the Eastern Peak,* first century AD. This is one of a frieze of mural paintings of auspicious animals lining the lower parts of the walls of the south chamber of an elaborate brick tomb excavated in 1954 at Wang-tu, Hopei. The animals are named in accompanying inscriptions. The Eastern Peak is the sacred T'ai-shan in Shantung.

192 Unknown artist of the Sung dynasty, *Wild Flowers and Black Rabbit.* 14 3/4 × 16 1/2 in. National Palace Museum, Taichung, Taiwan.

193 Unknown artist of the Sung dynasty, *Mother Hen and Brood.* 16 1/2 × 13 in. National Palace Museum, Taichung, Taiwan.

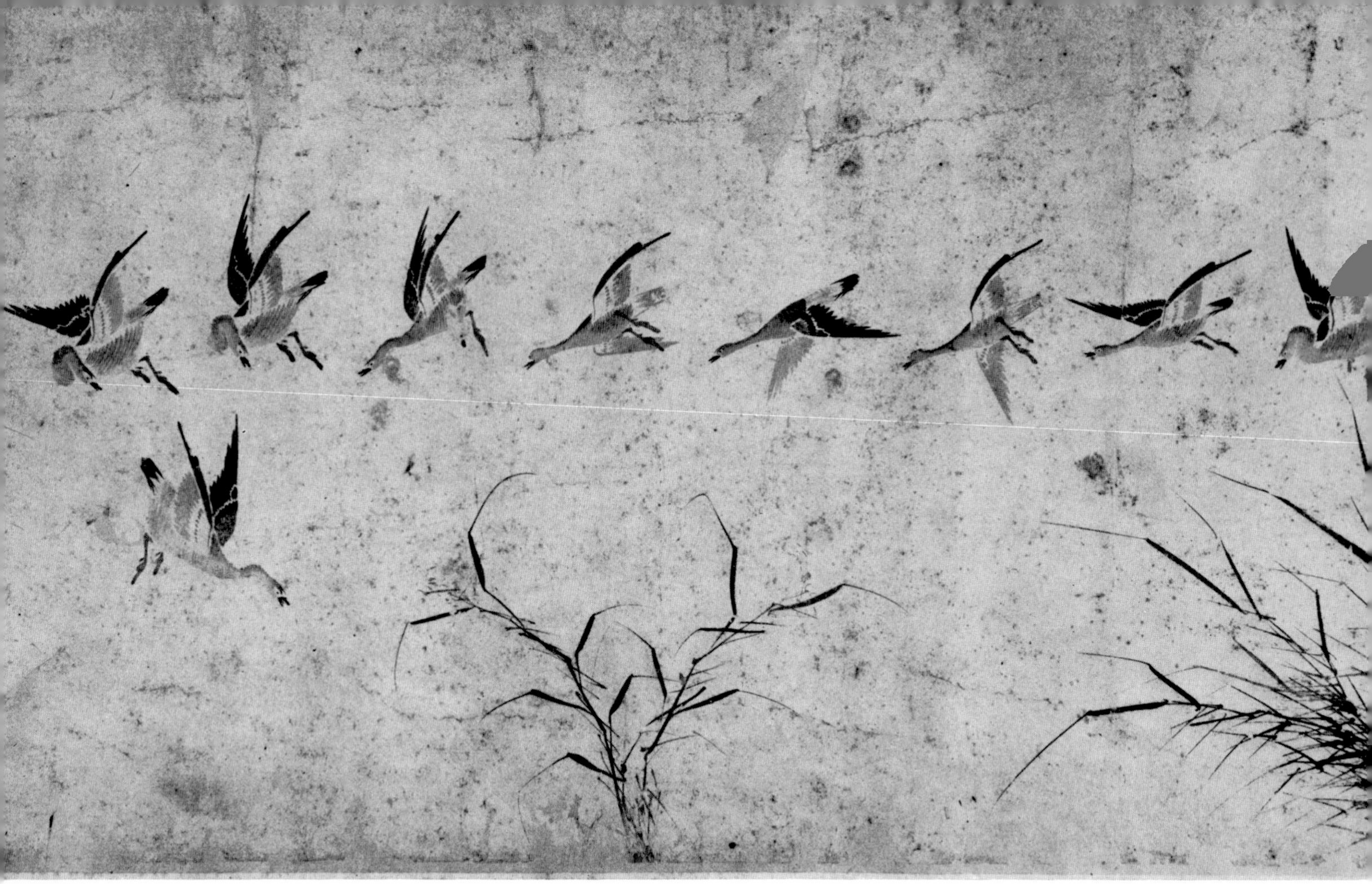

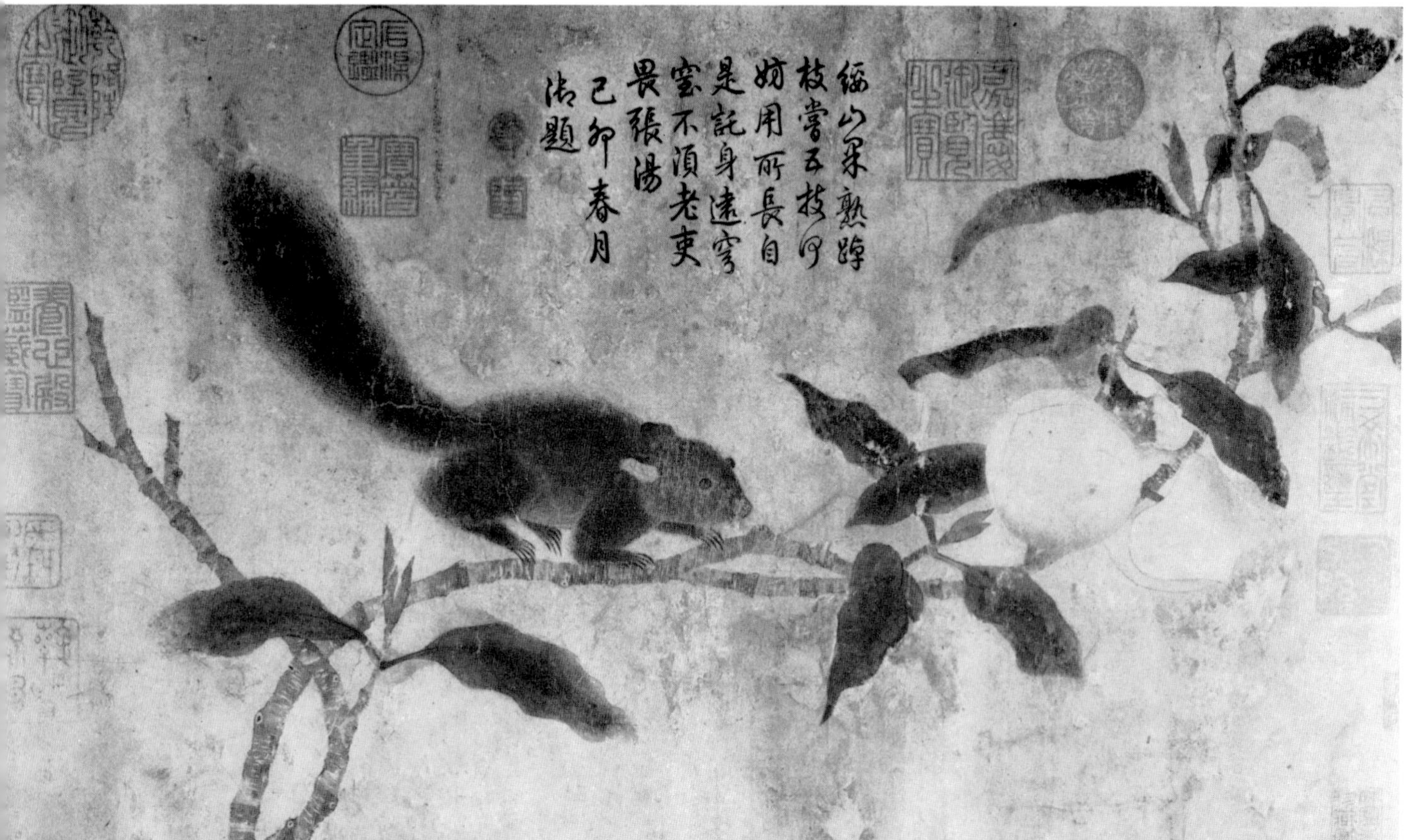
緣山果熟蹲
枝嘗五技何
妨用所長自
是託身遠穹
室不須老吏
畏張湯
己卯春月
洪題

FLOWER-AND-BIRD PAINTING

194 (above left) Attributed to Ma Fên, section of a scroll *The Hundred Geese* in ink on paper. Ma Fên came from Ho-chung in Shansi and lived in the first half of the twelfth century. He was the first of a famous line of Ma family painters. The painting is perhaps of the Southern Sung period. Height: 13³/₄ in., length of complete scroll: 183 in. Academy of Arts, Honolulu.

195 (left) Ch'ien Hsüan (*c.* 1235–1290), *Squirrel on a Peach Bough* in ink and colour on paper. The intrusive inscription is by the Ch'ien-lung Emperor. For a discussion of the painter and of this painting see pages 321–322. 10¹/₄ × 17¹/₄ in. National Palace Museum, Taichung, Taiwan.

196 (above) Mu Ch'i, *Peonies,* in ink on silk. Mu Ch'i came from Szechwan but lived a great part of his life in a temple near Hangchou as a monk. He was born early in the thirteenth century and is known to have been active in 1269. See p. 321 and col. 52. 14³/₈ × 15¹/₈ in. Daitokuji, Kyoto.

文同

K BAMBOO

(left) Wên T'ung (c. 1020–1079),
boo, hanging scroll in ink on silk [see
323–324]. Wên T'ung was a close
onal friend of Su Shih [pl. 201] and
deep bond that existed between them
is to have brought their respective
hic styles close together. 51 ¹³/₁₆ ×
₂ in. National Palace Museum, Tai-
ng, Taiwan.

(above) Wên T'ung, *Bamboo,* a
ble album-leaf in ink on paper.
₄ × 19 in. National Palace Museum,
chung, Taiwan.

(right) Attributed to Yang Wu-
ı, *Bamboo,* an album-leaf, in ink on
er. Yang Wu-chiu (Pu-chih) lived
Kiangsi during the first half of the
lfth century, and was known more
painter of plum-blossom. 12 ¹/₂ × 18
National Palace Museum, Taichung,
wan.

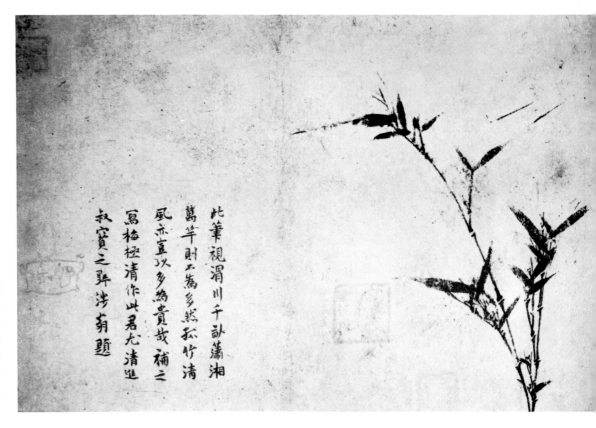

此筆視渭川千畝蕭湘
萬竿則不啻多矣然孤竹清
風亦豈以多為貴哉補之
寫梅極清作此君尤清
叔賓之雅涉菊題

INK BAMBOO
AND CALLIGRAPHY

200 (above) Li K'an (1245–1320), *Bamboo,* part
of a scroll, in ink on paper [see pp. 324 and 329]. Li
K'an, born near Peking, became a highly successful administrator, but is best known as the author
of the treatise on bamboos, *Chu p'u hsiang lu.* The
present scroll exists in two halves, one, in Peking,
bears the date 1307, the other, of which a detail
appears here, bears a colophon by Chao Mêng-fu
[see pl. 221] dated 1308. Height: 14 ³/₄ in., length
of complete scroll: 93 ¹/₂ in. Nelson Gallery of Art,
Kansas City.

201 Su Shih (1036–1101), *Cold Provisions Day;*
ink on paper. The poem was composed as well as
written [in *ts'ao shu,* see page 310] by Su Shih
(Su Tung-p'o), a universal genius who served as
an administrator and was also a poet, painter and
calligrapher of distinction. Preoccupied with problems of aesthetic expression, he stood, like Ruskin,
as the intellectual leader of an enthusiastic coterie
of outstanding talent that included such painters as
Li Lung-mien [pl. 188], Mi Fei [pls 203 and 213],
Wên T'ung [pls 197 and 198] and other remarkable men such as the reformist Premier Wang
An-shih (1019–1085). Su is the model of the Chinese scholar-gentleman-aesthete (*wên jên*).

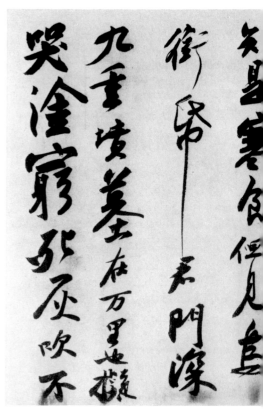

自我来黄州　已過三寒
食　年年欲惜春　去不
容惜　今年又苦雨　两月秋

蕭瑟　卧聞海棠花　泥污
燕支雪　闇中偷負
去　夜半真有力　何殊
病少年　病起頭已白

春江欲入户　雨勢来
不已　小屋如漁舟　濛濛
水雲裏　空庖煮寒菜
破竈燒濕葦

BAMBOO
AND CALLIGRAPHY

202 (left) Attributed to Wu Chên (1280–1354), *Bamboo shoots,* an album painting, in ink on silk. The painting bears the signature *Mei hua tao jên* or 'Plum-blossom Taoist', the *hao* name by which Wu Chên liked to be known. Wu Chên was born and spent most of his life in Chekiang, living as a typical *wên jên* avoiding service and public affairs under the Mongols. Several important landscapes are also attributed to him. This painting belongs to the second phase of his stylistic development when he had abandoned strict faithfulness to nature and conformity to the canons of Wên T'ung [pls 197 and 198]. See page 324. 8 3/4 × 8 1/2 in. British Museum.

203 (below) Mi Fei [see pl. 213], *Valedictory Poem,* in ink on paper; the poem composed as well as written by Mi Fei. The poem is written in *hsing shu* [see pp. 309–310]. Su Shih compared Mi Fei's brush to a sharp sword handled with consummate skill, and his characters do indeed show a remarkable dexterity and vitality, even aggressiveness, of brush-stroke. 12 5/8 × 25 1/2 in. National Palace Museum, Taichung, Taiwan.

204 (right) Hui-tsung [See col. 51], the last two characters (*hu* and *yeh*) of a long calligraphy scroll written in *ts'ao shu* [see p. 310]. National Museum, Peking.

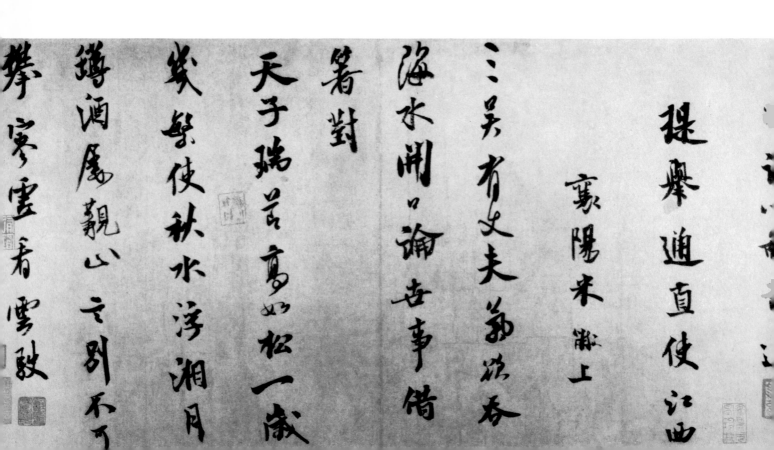

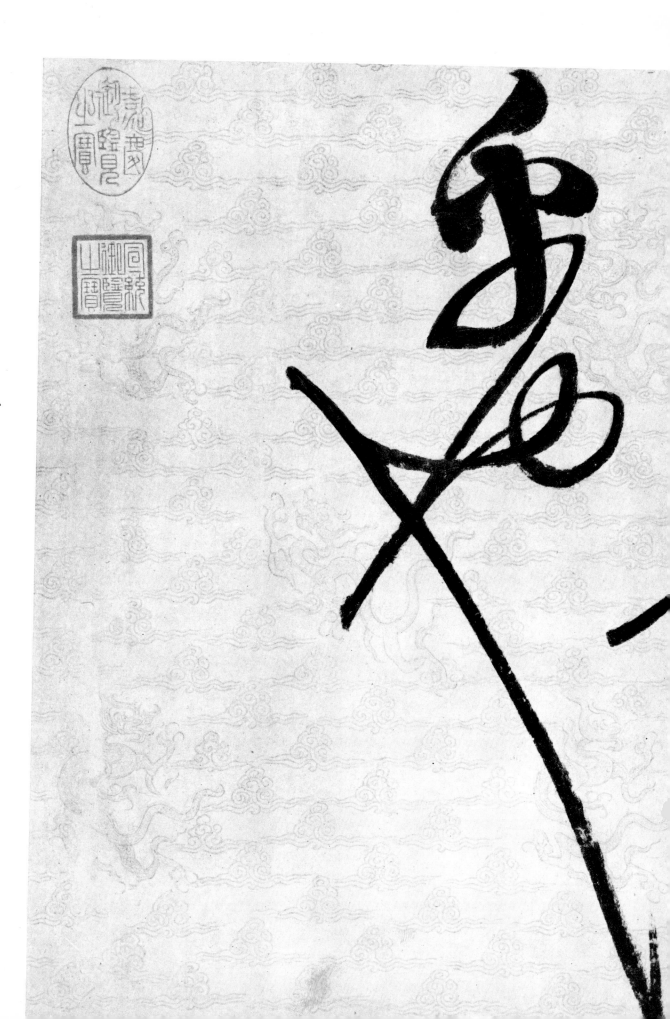

205 (left) Attributed to Wu Chên [see also pl. 202], *Bamboos in the Wind;* ink on paper. The poem and signature on the right are apparently written in *ts'ao shu* [see p. 310], in Wu Chên's hand. 30×21 3/8 in. Museum of Fine Arts, Boston.

206 Ku An (*fl.* 1350), *Bamboo in Wind;* ink on silk. For a discussion of the artist and his work see page 329. This type of painting was taken to symbolize Chinese stoicism in the face of Mongol tyranny [p. 292]. 48 3/8 × 20 7/8 in. National Palace Museum, Taichung, Taiwan.

LANDSCAPE PAINTING: NORTHERN SUNG

207 (left) Attributed to Tung Yüan (*fl.*947–970), *Festival for Evoking Rain;* ink and colour on silk. Tung Yüan was chief representative of the Yangtse school of painters, which also included Hsü Tao-ning [pl. 209], whose rugged landscapes contrast with the more gentle and recessive landscapes of the Yellow River school, of which Kuo Hsi [pl. 211] is a well-known exponent. The bird's-eye view taken here reminds one of the sort of painting Philip of Burgundy is said to have commissioned Jan van Eyck to do: 'half map, half landscape picture' [see pp. 332–333]. Tung Yüan's paintings, unlike those of his contemporaries, were in fact topographically true and based on sketches of real landscapes. Considerations of topography apart, the subject of this picture is somewhat obscure. The title literally means 'Dragon among the Villagers'; and the painting is usually taken to represent a rain-making ceremony at which the emperor ('Dragon') was present. The manner of painting the figures (to be seen low in the foreground) is similar to that in two other scrolls attributed to Tung Yüan showing scenes on the Hsiao and Hsiang rivers, fragments of which are in Peking and Shanghai. 61 ³/₄ × 63 ¹/₂ in. National Palace Museum, Taichung, Taiwan.

208 Attributed to Chü Jan (*fl. c.*960–980), *Seeking the Tao in the Autumn Mountains;* ink on silk. Chü Jan was a Buddhist monk, in Nanking and then in the K'ai-pao temple in K'ai-feng, the new capital, on the accession of the first Sung emperor in 960. 61 ¹/₂ × 30 ³/₈ in. National Palace Museum, Taichung, Taiwan.

209 (left) Attributed to Hsü Tao-ning (*fl.* 1030), *High Temples in Snowy Mountains;* ink on silk. A striking comparison can be drawn between this and a painting attributed to Patinir, *St Jerome in a Rocky Landscape,* in the National Gallery, London. Both are organized into three zones. In *St Jerome* a man and a dog go up a mountain towards the left of the picture in the middle zone, just as does the string of asses in *Snowy Mountains,* the zigzag path is a regular means of indicating recession in both traditions [see p. 335]. 65 1/4 × 34 3/4 in. Municipal Museum, Osaka.

210 (above) Attributed to Fan K'uan (*c.* 950–1030), *Sitting Alone by a Stream;* ink on silk, one of a group of large mountain landscapes. Fan K'uan was born in Hua-yüan, Shensi. 61 1/2 × 42 in. National Palace Museum, Taichung, Taiwan.

11 (above) Attributed to Kuo Hsi (c. 1020–1090), *Winter Woods;* ink on silk [see pp. 332–333]. The sense of recession and space in his paintings of Yellow River landscape contrasts with the landscapes of the Yangtse school [pls 207 and 209]. Pines in the foreground for establishing scale becomes a cliché in later Chinese landscapes. 60 1/4 × 39 in. National Palace Museum, Taichung, Taiwan.

12 (above right) Li T'ang (1049–1130), *Autumn Landscape;* ink on silk. Li T'ang was in Emperor Hui-tsung's Academy and became first director of Emperor Kao-tsung's (1127–1163). His work bridges the styles represented by Hsü Tao-ning [pl. 209] and by Kuo Hsi [pl. 211]. An innovation which was to become standard is the use of dry sweeping brush-strokes for the textures of rocks in the foreground [see pl. 217]. 42 × 17 1/8 in. Koto-in Temple, Kyoto. Japan.

13 (right) Mi Fei (1051–1107), *Landscape with Mountains;* ink on paper. Typically wên jên, Mi Fei held high government posts and was poet, calligrapher [see pl. 203], critic and eccentric [see p. 315]. 20 1/8 × 19 3/4 in. Fusetsu Nakamura, Tokyo.

SOUTHERN SUNG

214 Chiang Ts'an, part of the handscroll *Massed Verdure of Wooded Peaks;* ink and light colour on silk. Chiang Ts'an was active as a painter at about the beginning of the thirteenth century. Like Li T'ang he was a member of Emperor Hui-tsung's Academy of Painting (Hua Yüan), continuing to work under Emperor Kao-tsung after the flight of the Sung Court from K'ai-fêng to Hangchow in 1126. Like Li T'ang too, he was something of an archaising painter, his brushwork reminiscent of that of Chü Jan [pl. 208], and he helped to maintain the continuity of the Northern Sung landscape tradition. Height: 12 3/4 in., length of complete scroll: 116 1/2 in. Nelson Gallery of Art, Kansas City.

215 (above) Attributed to Hsia Kuei (*fl.* 1180–1230), the remaining four of *The Twelve River Views;* ink on silk: from right to left: 'Flying Geese over Distant Mountains', 'Returning to the Village in Mist from the Ferry', 'The Clear and Sonorous Air of the Fisherman's Flute', 'Boats Moored at Night in a Misty Bay'. Hsia Kuei lived at Hangchow. He was a member of the Academy during the reign of Emperor Ning-tsung (1195–1224). Like his contemporary Ma Yüan [pl. 219] he was profoundly influenced by Li T'ang [pl. 212] using for instance the same kind of brush-strokes to register the texture of rocks. Height: 11 in., length of scroll: 90 3/4 in. Nelson Gallery of Art, Kansas City.

216 (left) Detail of plate 215.

217 (right) Hsia Kuei, part of the handscroll *Ten Thousand Li of the Long River* (the Yangtse); ink on silk. See page 335. Height: 6 5/8 in., length of complete scroll: 422 in. National Palace Museum, Taichung, Taiwan.

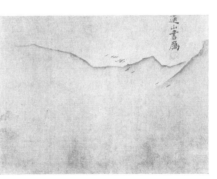

218 (left) Hsia Kuei [see pls 215–217], *A Cor[ner]* *of West Lake,* bearing an inscription by the Yü[an] dynasty artist Kuo Pi recommending it as Hsi[a's] masterpiece. 42 1/4 × 23 3/8 in. National Palace M[u]seum, Taichung, Taiwan.

219 (below) Attributed to Ma Yüan (*fl.* 119[9–] 1225), *The Hermit Fisherman.* Ma Yüan was a l[ater] scion of the famous line of Ma family painters [the] first of whom was Ma Fên [see pl. 194]. He ca[me] from Ho-chung in Shansi. For the years 119[0–] 1194 he was appointed *Tai-chao* of the Academ[y] of Painting. Like his contemporary Hsia Kuei [see pl. 215] he was influenced by Li T'ang [see [pl.] 212]. See page 320. 14 5/8 × 11 7/16 in. Nation[al] Palace Museum, Taichung, Taiwan.

opposite p[age]

220 Kao K'o-kung (1248–1310), *Mountain [in] Rain.* Of Central Asiatic origins, Kao was in g[o]vernment service under Kublai Khan, retiring [to] Hangchow in later life. Kao stands at the head [of] the amateur, the *wên jên,* revival, avoiding the idio[m] of the Southern Sung Academicians [pls 21[8–] 219]. He is said at first to have followed tent[h] century landscapists such as Tung Yüan [pl. 20[7] but in middle age of which this painting is pr[o]bably an example he modelled himself on Mi [Fei] [pl. 213], the *wên jên* ideal. Kao uses here a ve[ry] free style with broad splashes of ink particula[rly] appropriate to the moist and luminous atmosph[ere] of rain. 48 × 32 3/8 in. National Palace Museu[m], Taichung, Taiwan.

221 (left) Chao Mêng-fu (1254–1322), *Departure of Wên Chi from the Nomad Camp* [see col. 46]; ink on silk. Signed and dated 1301. Chao Mêng-fu was descended from the first Sung emperor but was called into service under the Mongols in 1286 and eventually became head of the Han-lin College. He was much criticized for collaborating with the enemy [see p. 292]. 51 1/16 × 35 13/16 in. National Palace Museum, Taichung, Taiwan.

222 (below) Attributed to Ma Ho-chih, *At Anchor on an Early Autumn Night;* ink and colour on silk. Like so many other famous painters of the twelfth and thirteenth centuries, including Hsia Kuei [pls 215 to 218], Ma Ho-chih came from Ch'ien-t'ang in Chekiang. He was active in the mid-twelfth century and is best known as the illustrator of a manuscript version of the *Shih ching* (Book of Odes), the manuscript being from the brush of Emperor Kao-tsung. 8 13/16 × 7 3/8 in. Formerly Collection of Masao Suzuki, Tokyo.

FOURTEENTH-CENTURY WÊN JÊN PAINTERS

223 (below) Huang Kung-wang (1269–1354), *Mountain Village;* ink on paper. An accompanying leaf bears a signed inscription saying that *Mountain Village* was painted by 'Completely Mad, the Taoist Huang Kung-wang' at Yün-chien [Chekiang] in 1342. With Kao K'o-kung [pl. 220], Wu Chên [pls 202 and 205], Ni Tsan [pls 224 and 225], and Wang Mêng [pl. 226] he is one of the great fourteenth-century *wên jên* landscapists taking as their models the Northern Sung landscape painters. In his work aerial perspective has virtually disappeared and surface texture is largely dispensed with, as are the diagonals and contrasting ink-tones that create the effect of recession. Cézanne's landscapes are brought to mind [see pp. 305 and 335], but the present painting's abstract qualities may tempt us to look closer to our own day; for instance, to *Landscape* by Mondrian which is similarly composed of short horizontals and verticals covering most of the picture surface and entirely unrelieved by intervening detail. 43 7/8 × 13 3/4 in. National Palace Museum, Taichung, Taiwan.

224 (below left) Ni Tsan (1301–1374), *Landscape;* ink on paper. Signed and dated 1362. Born of wealthy parents at Wu-hsi in Kiangsu, Ni Tsan did not start painting until his thirty-eighth year. In 1356 he left home and spent fifteen years travelling round the lakes and rivers of Kiangsu during which he met Wang Mêng [pl. 226]. 11 13/16 × 19 13/16 in. Freer Gallery of Art, Washington.

225 Ni Tsan, *The Jung-hsi Studio;* ink on paper. This is one of a group of pictures not so much of an identifiable place as variations on an ideal that seems to have been present in the painter's imagination [see also pl. 243]. 28 3/4 × 13 3/4 in. National Palace Museum, Taichung, Taiwan.

東山草堂

至正三年四月望日為
東山良友畫黃鶴山樵王蒙

雪霜兎象松下風草堂湧
崔宮主嚴東山良友知誰
是家石茶坐坐可同
己丑庚日尚尾

226 Wang Mêng (1310–1385), *Thatched Halls on Mount T'ai;* ink and colour on paper. Signed and dated 1344. Born in Chekiang, Wang Mêng spent most of his life in the T'ai district of Shantung. He is the last of the great fourteenth-century *wên jên* painters [pls 220 and 223–225]. He seems to have been genuinely fitted in temperament to interpret the spirit of eleventh-century Northern Sung landscapists [pls 207–210]. There is the same tendency to fill up the entire surface with brush-strokes – so much in contrast with Southern Sung landscapists [e.g. pl. 215]. The appropriate insistence on two-dimensional design makes the real break with Southern Sung landscape. It was achieved by Wang and his predecessor Huang Kung-wang [pl. 223] far more than by the other *wên jên* revivalists, Ni Tsan [pls 224, 225 and 243], Kao K'o-kung [pl. 220] and Wu Chên. 43 7/8 × 13 3/4 in. National Palace Museum, Taichung, Taiwan.

VIII ARCHITECTURE: HAN TO MING AND CH'ING DYNASTIES

In accordance with the scheme laid down for this book in its introduction [pp. 13–15], we should really be discussing Chinese architecture strictly in the historical context of Ming and Ch'ing times. For reasons that will appear later [p. 381] we propose to allow the sub-ject a broader and more general treatment. We shall divide it into two sections. In the first we shall view architecture as part of the physical framework of traditional Chinese life at its various levels of social organization, and with particular regard to the formal layout of towns and homesteads. In the second we shall describe such Chinese buildings as come within the general category of the hall (*tien*), and indicate how the materials and methods used in their construction account for the specific features they display. In this part, too, we shall give some account of a type of building never intended for living in, one that has always stirred the imagination of the West, the pagoda.

*

Architecture, it need hardly be said, is not only or even primarily the fashioning of individual buildings. Any system that 'encloses space on a scale sufficient for a human being to move in', as Dr Pevsner puts it, may be an essay in architecture. Enclosing secures privacy. It also defines a physical limit inside which people belong to one another as they do not belong to those who live outside. Seen in this light, there can be no theoretical upper limit to the scale and size of an architectural system, provided it encloses a functionally integrated human community.

As we very well know, the limit of social integration is reached where one community borders on another whose way of life differs markedly from its own. Inside a national society united by racial, linguistic, and political traits, differentiation between social communities is economic, and is based on division of labour. In traditional societies the world over, di-vision of labour runs deepest between town and country. When agricultural settlement reaches a certain density, the town automatically crystallizes out from the surrounding country-side as a community integrated by its non-agrarian livelihood; and the town is therefore the largest practical architectural enclosure that a traditional society can conceive of and build.

The walled town

The enclosing structure is, of course, the city-wall. This serves for defence in times of emer-gency, and not only for the townspeople, but also for farmers of the neighbourhood with whom they have reciprocal economic dealings. At the same time it defines the urban limit, and thereby fulfils a real sociological purpose. It is the concrete symbol of the functional

pls 227–229

differentiation into town and countryside in a traditional society. Moreover, the wall predicates a social equilibrium in which there is little growth or movement of population, since it encloses a limited area, and therefore a limited number of people. There can be no guarantee that functional differentiation and social equilibrium will be maintained indefinitely; but the wall will always uphold tradition and resist change. As we have seen, Chinese society reached a balance between rural and urban components at least as early as Shang times [p. 75]; it has kept it ever since.

pl. 227

In the north China plain, city-walls shut the towns off from the countryside, and give them a basic plan which they have retained for well over two thousand years, that of a square. Choice of the square was probably dictated by cosmological belief. Earth was thought of as square, and was worshipped by means of a square altar at sacrifices presided over by the ruler in his role of dynastic high-priest. We have already alluded to beliefs associating the ruler

pl. 229

with the deity Earth [p. 58], and by a natural extension of symbolism the royal precinct was also built square. But while magical symbolism could thus be made to account for the primary town plan, other factors may have been responsible for it in practice. In Europe, the 'open-field' system of subdividing agricultural land is said to have served as model for the grid street-pattern of early medieval towns, and in much the same way the Chinese 'well-field' (*ching t'ien*) may have given its form to the town-plan. By this system a rectangular area of land was divided into nine equal squares and allotted to eight families, each of which farmed one of the outlying plots, while the central plot was a joint undertaking whose yield went to the feudal overlord. We first hear of this scheme in the fourth-century BC *Mencius*, and it was doubtless more theoretical than actual. *Chou li*, the 'Chou Rituals' [see p. 45], rigorously applies the *ching-t'ien* system to the planning of the royal capital, but here again there was probably a gap between theory and practice, between the ritualist's *mandala* and the architect's final draft plan.[1]

Agrarian and administrative towns: the balance between rural and urban populations in China

Inside its wall the Chinese walled town is relatively flexible in structure. For one thing, the wall generally encloses a good deal more space than is actually required for housing. Large areas inside it have customarily been given over to market-gardening, or take the form of open courtyards inside administrative precincts or private homesteads. Thus small increases in population could be met without adding to the overall size or altering the shape of the town. Again, flexibility was secured by use of relatively small housing units of standard size. Extra accommodation was provided by multiplying the number of these units, not by increasing the extent or height of individual buildings. Lastly, the fabrics themselves were relatively impermanent. Use of wood is of course directly responsible for this. And one consequence of building in wood, apparently, was that the idea of the house as a long-term capital investment never took root in China as it did in the West. Whether this was so or not, the fact that most individual buildings in China were relatively short-lived, and were made over as occasion arose, did help to give flexibility to layouts in which they were used as constructional units.

The question of population changes is a critical one, as the history of the growth of Western towns convincingly shows. Sociologically, most traditional Chinese towns have been either market towns serving the needs of local farming communities, or administrative towns, the seats of the overlords. Of course the two types were never altogether distinct.

But the former, 'the nodal point in the net of the agricultural structure', as Gutkind describes it², represents the primitive township, grown naturally out of an agrarian background and enjoying immunity from sudden changes in population. Such spontaneous movements of population as have taken place in China have been from one part of the country to another, and not from country to town.

Siting of administrative towns, on the other hand, is dictated by military and political considerations. It has often been found necessary to shift the location of a capital half-way across China, and cases are on record where this has been accompanied by enforced resettlement of large numbers of people. Even when a district became a permanent administrative centre due to strategic position, foreign occupation or a dynastic change sometimes made demands upon the town itself with which it was altogether unable to cope. Extensive rebuilding, often on to an overlapping site, was then the answer. This task was often expedited by partial or complete destruction of the old capital by the invader, but seldom if ever was the new city built on exactly the same scale as the old. Usually it seems to have been planned from above, to a size determined by its new estimated population and importance.

Peking is the classic example of re-siting and re-scaling of an administrative town at intervals during the course of centuries; but the case of the old western capital, Ch'ang-an, is hardly less instructive. Its topographical advantages are not here our concern, nor will we bother with its history before Han times. Since then it has had three great changes of fortune, corresponding to three phases of rebuilding. The name Ch'ang-an first appears during the Former Han dynasty, when a new capital was built some miles south-east of the old Ch'in capital of Hsien-yang on the Wei river in Shensi, and abutting on the north-west edge of the present town. Between 194 and 188 BC large numbers of people were settled in Ch'ang-an. Its population in 192 BC is said to have numbered 146,000 persons, many of whom may have been those affected by a decree calling on all who lived within a 600 *li* (200 miles) radius to move into the new capital. Another enforced settlement seems to have occurred in 190 BC, when a further 145,000 are said to have been added to Ch'ang-an's population.

The city remained an administrative centre during the period of the Three Kingdoms and Six Dynasties [pp. 177–180]; but its importance steadily diminished until, in AD 581, the Sui began to rebuild it on a site adjacent to the south side of modern Ch'ang-an but extending further west and enclosing several times the present urban area. Ch'ang-an was the actual or nominal capital during the ensuing T'ang period; it then became a world metropolis numbering some two million people. We have already spoken of its decline, which may be said to have begun at the time of An Lu-shan's rebellion in AD 755 [p. 249]. The town was again rebuilt in Ming times, on a site occupied by the present city, and it has retained the same shape and roughly the same population ever since.³

Earth-shaking as such changes in the fortunes of great administrative centres like Ch'ang-an, Lo-yang, K'ai-fêng, and Peking no doubt were, we must remember that they were separated by long intervening centuries during which the gentler convulsions of city life were completely absorbed by their surrounding walls. There is nothing in China, whether in the history of its agrarian or administrative towns, to compare with the relentless march of urban development as we know it in the West.

Decentralization and the courtyard plan

Typically, the individual Chinese dwelling-house is divided into a number of standard units of floor-space, or bays, called *chien*. The walled homestead, in turn, consists of a number

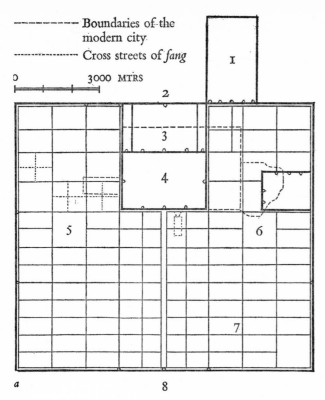
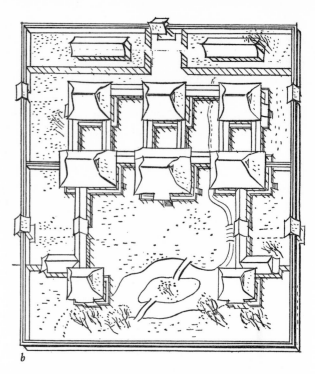

72 The courtyard plan: *a* the city of Ch'ang-an in T'ang times (618–906); *b* Japanese homestead of the Heian period (710–784). Key to *a*: 1, Ta-ming Kung; 2, An-li Gate; 3, T'ai-chi Palace; 4, Imperial City; 5, West market; 6, East market; 7, Wild Goose Pagoda (plate 251); 8, Ming-tê Gate

col. 46   of individual dwellings disposed round the sides of a central courtyard, or, if the size and im-portance of the family warrant, of a succession of courtyards. The town, similarly, is an aggre-
pl. 227   gation of private homesteads, while structurally and functionally it can also be regarded as one enormous homestead. The residence of the ruler lies on the main north–south axis, in the same relative position as that of the head of the private family. The relations between the ruler and his subjects were regulated; so were those subsisting between the head of the family and his dependants. It was thus perfectly natural that the plan of the family homestead, the courtyard plan, should have been adapted to the designing of the administrative town or city. Thus, for instance, the restored plan of a private Japanese homestead of the Heian period, based on a contemporary Chinese model, bears a real relationship to the plan of
fig. 72   the T'ang metropolis.

Functionally each community, whether individual household, clan homestead, or town, is largely autonomous and runs its own affairs. With this in mind, Gutkind draws an analogy between the whole architectural complex and 'the famous [Cantonese] ivory balls where likewise one fits into the other and yet each is a separate body that can revolve independently.'[4] But household, homestead, and town are by no means the only functional community units.
fig. 72a   Thus the town-plan of T'ang Ch'ang-an shows eastern and western districts, each with its own central market. Districts, in turn, are divided chequerboardwise into *fang*, rectangular blocks or quarters, each of which may comprise four smaller rectangles separated by narrow streets. A palace or an important office compound, says Sirén, might take up the whole of one *fang*, but ordinary residential homesteads normally occupied only a quarter of the area.[5]

In a word, decentralization is characteristic of the traditional Chinese town, just as it is of the private homestead; and the unity of Chinese architecture is thus revealed not only in its conservative methods of building construction, about which more will be said later, but also in the way successively smaller independent architectural units persistently repeat in microcosm the forms of the larger.

Subordination of important buildings

Decentralization in Chinese layouts is linked with another remarkable feature of Chinese town-planning – one, indeed, that goes to the very root of the difference between Western and Eastern architectural traditions. In the West a single building or group of buildings has tended, for ideological reasons, to dominate the rest of the town. Not only does it occupy a more prominent site than its neighbours, very often in the town-centre, but every expedient is used in designing it so as to make it the culminating emotional experience in the lives of the townspeople. Added height is of course one of these. But scale, proportion, and decorative enrichment all help to invest the great building with an overwhelming and unshakable authority. We can hardly wonder, therefore, that historians of Western architecture should manifest greater interest in the materials, methods of construction, forms, and styles of individual buildings, and less in larger architectural layouts.

In China, on the other hand, buildings that one might expect would dominate their neighbours physically do not do so. Indeed, nothing is so important as the walls. From outside the town, walls are all that can be seen of it; and on the inside the level lines of buildings with their low elevations stretch away to the skyline, where gate-houses stand like sentinels marking the city limits. The ideas of 'city-wall' and 'city' are, in fact, closely bound up, as use of the same word for each, *ch'êng*, sufficiently shows. There is no need to look beyond the walls, into the town, for buildings more imposing than they. As Gutkind puts it: 'they are its cathedral, as it were. ...'[6]

col. 57
pl. 228

The wall has its foundations deep in the agrarian soil of China and stands witness to a relationship between town and countryside promoted by mutual cultural and economic interest. But the residence of the ruler or his delegate proclaimed no such mutuality; the authority it represented was remote from the lives of the townspeople, whose loyalties were strictly localized and whose interests did not always tally with those of Government. A mutual indifference characterized its relationship with the town as a human community; and accordingly administrative precincts had the secluded character of private residences. They retired decently behind their courtyard walls, forever hidden from the sight of all but a few. Their walls need no explanation. But why, after all, a Westerner might wonder, was no advantage taken of site, or elevation exploited, so as to make visible the ultimate sovereignty of the State to the town and to the world?

There was no technical reason why not. It is perfectly true that most north Chinese towns stand on a flat area of plain; yet even where an eminence exists – such, for example, as the artificial mound called Prospect Hill in Peking – it seldom carries buildings of importance. It is also true that use of wood for structural purposes does tend to limit the height of buildings. But this is not enough to account for absence of structures, within the administrative precincts, whose psychological effect derives from height; other materials might have been used had height been a prime necessity. Chinese architects were perfectly capable of designing tall buildings – as is shown by the great pagodas of the Yangtze provinces, some of which are in the region of two hundred and fifty feet high. Again, platforms are integral elements in the elevations of Chinese buildings; and in some important edifices – ancestral temples, audience halls, and so forth – terraced platforms are very highly elaborated. Yet

pl. 240

pl. 229

terraced buildings do not really assert themselves over their neighbours, as the reader may verify by glancing at the aerial view of Peking on plate 229.

The seclusion, almost the self-effacement, of the imperial palaces hidden behind their enclosing wall probably had a political explanation, at which we have already hinted. Throughout China's long past, the idea of nationality remained nebulous. Indeed we may perhaps wonder how it could have been otherwise, taking into account the vast size of the country, and the absence of any inherent factor in the Far East corresponding to the competitive nationalism of Europe. Thus the Emperor did not, in Chinese eyes, serve to symbolize the Chinese people as a national comity; nor could he strictly speaking claim to represent any other body than the imperial clan of which he was the titular head. For official purposes the country was called by the name of the dynasty in power – as Ta Ming Kuo, Ta Ch'ing Kuo – but the Emperor's titles referred to the dynasty and not to the territory or nation. His duty was to safeguard the position and enhance the prestige of his particular family, just as was that of every other family head in China.

With few outstanding exceptions, then, Chinese buildings were not meant to foist dynastic or any other sort of authority on the world at large. As a result, no basic difference is discernible between the materials, methods of construction, forms, and styles of buildings designed as private residences, and those serving the State; no division into secular and religious styles; no qualitative distinction between 'architecture' and 'housing'.

South–north axiality

Division of the Chinese town into functionally independent units of different sizes does not lead to loss of internal coherence in plan. South–north axiality is the principle on which it hinges. Symbolism is implicit, for all important buildings, whether administrative or private, face south. The south–north axis is the celestial meridian writ small; and the Emperor's palace corresponds to the Pole Star (*pei ch'ên*), the circumpolar residence of T'ai-i [p. 150] from which he surveys the southerly world of men. The family elder is a petty ruler, and, like the dynastic ruler, he too turns his back on the north and faces south.

Symbolism apart, in a land so subject to threat of barbarian invasion and other hostile emanations from the north, this preference for looking in the opposite direction is understandable; the Chinese merely said that the north was the home of evil influences, and tried to keep something solid between them and it. The T'ang Imperial Palace, T'ai-chi Kung, lay in the shelter of Ch'ang-an's northern wall. Prospect Hill was built in Peking, we are told, to ward off evil influences from the Emperor's residence, a role specified by one of its titles, *Ta nei chih chên shan* or 'the Protecting Hill of the Great Within' [p. 375]. But whatever brought it into being, south–north axiality, together with the fact that the main entrance to a Chinese house is at the middle of a long side, not a short, determines the linear layout of main buildings straddled across the width of the enclosure one behind the other, with a succession of courtyards between. Lesser buildings line the sides of these.

pl. 235

pl. 227

As applied to the town-plan, south–north axiality results in the creation of a main processional way, a Via Sacra, running from south to north across the middle of the town and passing through the administrative precincts in doing so. This arrangement is age-old. The chief Imperial Palace of Hsien-yang [p. 363], built by the First Ch'in Emperor about 220 BC, lay on the north side of the Wei river. On the south side was an immense audience-hall.[7] And between them was a roofed two-storeyed gallery, spanning the river, said to have been 280 yards long and twelve wide. This south–north causeway might be compared

53 *The Great Wall at Pa-ta-ling, north of Peking [see map 3]. Originally pre-Han, reconstructed since the Ming dynasty.*

54 (left) Ceiling of T'ai-ho Tien (Hall of Supreme Harmony), the main hall of the San Ta Tien in the former Forbidden City, Peking; a Ming dynasty building rebuilt and further reconstructed in the seventeenth, eighteenth and nineteenth centuries. See plate 240 and page 377.

55 A p'ai-lou (memorial arch) on K'un-ming Lake, Summer Palace, Peking; a late Ch'ing dynasty construction. See plate 246.

56 Corner of a roof at the end of a covered walk in the Summer Palace, Peking, showing eaves construction and decoration; a twentieth-century reconstruction in traditional style. See plate 247.

57 The north-west corner of the wall of the former Forbidden City with watch-tower.

58 Chung-ho Tien (Hall of Middle Harmony) seen from the top of the plat-form on which stand the San Ta Tien, with T'ai-ho Tien in the foreground and Pao-ho Tien (Hall of Protecting Har-mony) in the background; a Ming building restored in 1627 and 1765. See page 377.

with the main avenue of T'ang Ch'ang/an, running from the Ming/tê Gate in the south *fig. 72a* wall to 'the An/li Gate in the north; with the main south–north axis of Hangchow, de/ scribed by Marco Polo as a street 'forty paces in width, and running in a direct line from one extremity of the city to the other'; with the main axis of modern Peking, five miles long; *pl. 229* and with those of Lo/yang, K'ai/fêng, Nanking, and many, many more ancient Chinese cities.

Individuality *vis/à/vis* the outside world is conferred on the town by its walls; internal organization is provided by its south–north 'spine'. Town/plans and aerial views enable us to register this fact at a glance, but to the actual inhabitants of such towns it could scarcely ever have been apparent. For unlike the Renaissance vista, no unbroken view along the processional way was afforded. And it was in any case interrupted by the presence on axis of the administrative enclosure. Even government officials and others who had access to the imperial precinct were by no means free to go as they chose. Some would be confined to the official sections, others to the domestic, and their points of entry to the way would be strictly regulated. Opening/up of the whole processional way to the general public is, of course, a very fundamental step to take; only very recently – to cite the case of Peking – has it become possible to walk across the city on its main south–north axis without having to break off at some point or other. For the processional way was not intended, any more than were the imperial palaces, to proclaim an ideological message to the townspeople. Inside the city/walls, in fact, there was very little to make them aware of the social organism to which they belonged; and the traditional Chinese town may have lacked conscious community feeling in consequence.[8] But this was of no more significance than that a cell should under/ stand its relation to the tissue, or a tissue to the organ, of which it is a part. The town *was* a biological organ, one tuned to respond to the life that lay outside it; unlike the Western town which turned its back on the pattern of rural life. In this symbiotic relationship the Chinese town participated involuntarily.

Without actually ever having crossed the processional way, one can hardly hope to estimate its psychological effect on those who had access to the whole or part of it. But comparisons might nevertheless be made between it and the approach to the Western town/centre along the open vista, as well as between it and other Chinese forms of aesthetic expression. The whole message of a traditional Western town can be read at a glance, whether the beholder sees it from without its walls, or stands at the head of a vista down which he has an uninterrupted view of its architectural climax. There is no need for him to change the axis of his viewpoint, although should he do so the prospect would remain essentially the same. By contrast, the impression given by a Chinese processional way was cumulative and not instantaneous; for the prospect, interrupted at intervals by gates and other buildings blocking its course, varied continuously as the beholder travelled along it. In his passage he experienced no visual climax and so no sense of anticlimax. Like a piece of music or a poem, the aesthetic effect corresponded to a complete series of physical impulses more or less regularly spaced in time.

The processional way thus embodies the same principle of linear displacement that we find in Chinese painting, where the beholder is not as a rule thought of as remaining in a fixed position but must pass, imaginatively, from point to point. Comparison is closest in the case of the landscape scroll, which the beholder unrolls section by section, so passing through a series of incidents which are the pictorial counterparts of the rhythmically/related *pl. 215* masses and spaces of the processional way. And the experience is complete only when the scroll has been perused from beginning to end. A Western landscape/painting, on the other hand, in which everything is seen at once and from a fixed standpoint, is directly comparable to the Western townscape in these respects.

Peking

pls 229–240; col. 54, 57, 58
Having discussed the general structure of the typical Chinese walled town, I should like to say something about Peking, that superb essay in co-ordinated town-planning which the architect W. Simpson once dismissed as 'an extended village of dirty streets and crumbling walls'.⁹ Peking is beyond doubt one of the loveliest cities in the world; and incidentally it embodies in its design all the principles of Chinese town-planning we have so far discussed. 'The truth is that Peking represents more fully than any other city at the present day', writes Yetts, 'the heritage of Chinese architectural achievement'. And Gutkind enthuses: 'Original conception and eventual reality are identical, fused together by an unsurpassable balance of rational thinking and spiritual clarity.'¹⁰

Peking, the present capital of China, occupies a site of no special advantage on the north China plain, looking it has been said rather like a flat box thrown to earth by a giant. Its general form, that of two adjoining rectangles, is shown in figure 73. The more northerly enclosure (the Northern City, Tartar City), is almost square, but its neighbour to the south (the Southern City, Chinese City), is much longer from west to east. The whole is enclosed within by imposing walls that separate Peking sharply from the surrounding countryside.

An administrative town of some sort has stood on or near the site now occupied by Peking for most of Chinese history. During the Chou period it was Ch'i, capital of Yen state. The town was destroyed by the First Ch'in Emperor, but was rebuilt under the Later Han at a site some distance south of old Ch'i. It was then called Yu. But not until AD 936 did Peking become of national significance, when the Ch'i-tan Tartars (Liao) made it their Southern Capital, Nan-ching [p. 250]. Fifty years later it was sacked again, and again rebuilt, its site being extended to the south-west. After the Chin conquest in AD 1122 [p. 290] the site was once again shifted, this time eastwards, so that it covered approximately the area on which the Southern City of modern Peking now stands. The imperial palace enclosure of the Northern Sung at K'ai-fêng, the Pien-ch'ing Kung, was carefully copied and much of its woodwork incorporated in the new Chin imperial residence, the city itself being called Chung-tu. In 1267 the Yüan Emperor Kublai Khan founded his capital of T'ai-tu on a site north of Chung-tu and more or less covering that of the present Northern City of Peking, but extending considerably further north.

The new Yüan city retained the age-old grid pattern. Marco Polo describes it thus: 'The whole plan of the city was regularly laid out line by line: and the streets in general are consequently so straight, that when a person ascends the wall over one of the gates, and looks right forward, he can see the gate opposite to him on the other side of the city. ... All the allotments of ground on which the habitations throughout the city were constructed are square, and exactly on a line with each other; each allotment being sufficiently spacious for handsome buildings, with corresponding courts and gardens. One of these was assigned to each head of a family; ... In this manner the whole interior of the city is disposed in squares, so as to resemble a chessboard, and planned out with a degree of precision and beauty impossible to describe. The wall of the city has twelve gates, three on each side of the square, and over each gate and compartment of the wall there is a handsome building.'¹¹

T'ai-tu plainly embodied many of the general and specific features of modern Peking. Thus the present Drum Tower in the northern part of the Northern City is, according to Cordier,

372

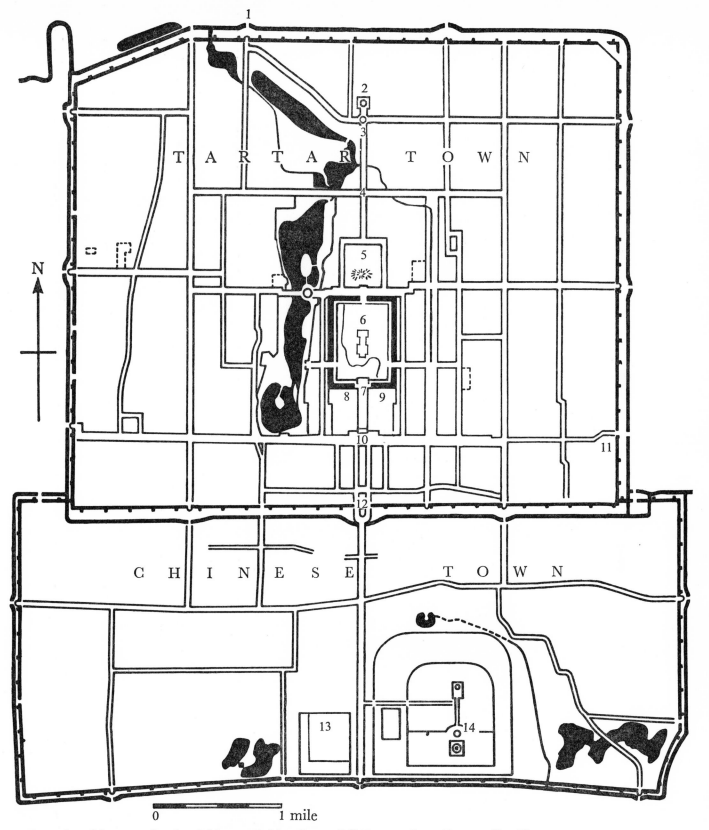

73 Town plan of the centre of modern Peking: 1, Tê-shêng Gate; 2, Bell Tower; 3, Drum Tower; 4, Hou Mên (Gate); 5, Prospect Hill; 6, San Ta Tien (plates 235, 240; col. 58); 7, Wu Mên (Gate); 8, Central Park; 9, Working People's Palace of Culture; 10, T'ien-an Mên Square; 11, Observatory; 12, Ch'ien Gate; 13, Temple of Agriculture; 14, Temple of Heaven (plates 230–233)

the same building as that recorded by Marco; while the nearby Bell Tower, though dating only from the nineteenth century and standing on a different site, can be assumed to perpetuate the architectural form of the building that sounded the curfew in Kublai Khan's Peking.[12]

In the heart of the Yüan city lay a complex of imperial residences and audience-halls, and it is fairly clear from what Marco says that their arrangement scarcely differed from what it is today. A square-walled precinct with sides a mile long corresponded to the present Imperial City. Within this enclosure was a second, much longer than it was broad. This was the Ta Nei, the Great Within, which we would call the Forbidden City. Its main edifice was the Khan's Great Palace, then called Ta-ming Tien, corresponding in all essentials to
pl. 240 the main palace hall of the present Forbidden City, the T'ai-ho Tien.

Marco describes in some detail the appearance of the palace buildings with their single storeys, and particularly remarks the terraces, marble stairs, parapets, and balustrades so typical of the later audience-halls of the Ming and Manchu emperors. He also mentions their
col. 54 brightly coloured roof-tiles, and the resplendent paintwork without and within, all gilt and silvered with paintings of dragons and other auspicious beasts. But his description is not explicit enough to allow us to draw up a detailed plan of the innermost palace enclosure; nevertheless, we may confidently say that it followed the general lines of the Chin imperial residence, itself based on the Sung Pien-ch'ing Kung, which in turn was based on the T'ang Ta-ming Kung and the Sui Kung Ch'êng. Moreover, its features were largely preserved in the Ming and Manchu layouts that followed the Yüan in Peking. And modern Peking still embodies this architectural tradition, now at least 1,500 years old.

At the beginning of Ming times Nanking was made the dynastic capital, but the Yung-lo Emperor restored Peking to that position on his accession in AD 1402. The Temple of
pls 230–233 Heaven was begun in the same year, and the walls of the Northern City thirteen years later. Rebuilding on the southern two-thirds of the Yüan layout, the Yung-lo Emperor was the founder of Peking as it now is. A great many existing buildings and most of the walls are either Yung-lo originals or replicas of them.

All through the Yüan and early Ming periods a large suburb had been growing outside the south wall of T'ai-tu and on the site of the old Chung-tu. In AD 1524 this suburban area was enclosed within earth walls, and in AD 1564 it was permanently incorporated with the Northern City by means of brick walls and gate-houses. In AD 1644 the invading Manchus allocated the whole area of the Northern City outside the imperial precincts for use of their bannermen, and the Chinese population began to shift to the Southern City. The terms 'Tartar' and 'Chinese', as applied to the northern and southern enclosures respectively, no doubt date from this period.

A good deal of rebuilding and restoration in Peking went on during the Shun-chih period (AD 1644–61), as it did also during the reigns of the K'ang-hsi and Ch'ien-lung Emperors, the last few Manchu reigns, and the Republic. It is going on actively today.
pl. 229
So much for the history of Peking. The aerial photograph of plate 229, as well as the
fig. 73 groundplan, will help to give us an idea of modern Peking. In the aerial view we are looking south. The large rectangle in the middle distance, the former Forbidden City, is the innermost core of the city – and indeed in imperial days of the empire and of the world, since it contained the private homestead of the reigning emperor and his family. The wide black frame surrounding the Forbidden City in the photograph is its moat, immediately inside which is its wall. The precinct is some thousand yards long and eight hundred wide.

South of the Forbidden City, and immediately beyond the smaller precincts that border it on its southern side [p. 375], runs the line of the south wall of the Imperial City, a rectangle enclosing the rectangle that is the Forbidden City. This area was not entirely closed to the general public in the days of the empire. Yet it, too, can be regarded as one vast homestead, where lived princes of the imperial blood and other nobles, as well as the countless officials whose dealings were with the Outer Court; that is, with the emperor in his official capacity as ruler. Prospect Hill [p. 366], the artificial height bounded by a rectangular wall in the foreground of our photograph, is well within the Imperial City. And so are the three lakes (San Hai) that together compose an informally planned pleasure-park, formerly called the Winter Palace, parts of the middle and southern of which can be seen on the right.

Some distance beyond the wall of the Imperial City is the line of yet another wall, interrupted by a massive gate-house, which marks the limit of the Northern City of Peking. South of it lies the Southern City, its prominent main axis leading direct to the south wall of the Southern City and of Peking itself. And to left of the axis at this far extremity and at the very top of the photograph, can just be made out the site of the Temple of Heaven on the left, while on the right is that of the Temple of Agriculture.

This lovely diagram of rectangles is given organic unity by the south–north spine that stretches across the city as far as the eye can see. Its integrating effect is so obvious from the photograph that we shall say no more about it, but would ask the reader to notice only that it is duplicated by other south–north axes to east and west; and in miniature by the spec- tacular Temple of Heaven layout, which lies just off the main axis in the southern part of the city, and which is shown in the aerial photograph reproduced as plate 230. I know of *pl. 230* nothing in European architecture capable of producing the same impression of abstract beauty, of a peculiarly concentrated, almost nervous, tension. We are looking north. In the foreground is the Altar of Heaven, a three-tiered circular marble terrace enclosed by a double *pl. 233* wall, the outer of which is square, the inner circular. The Altar of Heaven has been called 'the most sacred of all Chinese religious buildings'. Here, at dawn on the winter solstice, the emperor paid homage to Heaven, his only superior, and sacrifice of a bullock was made.

At the other end of this extraordinary long-bar magnet can be seen a similar but smaller three-tiered terrace, surmounted by a triple-roofed hall, the actual so-called 'Temple of Heaven'. This terrace, too, is an altar – the Ch'i-ku T'an, or Altar where Prayer for Grain *pl. 231* is Offered – although in fact sacrifice was made not upon the altar but in the hall. The whole layout is beautifully treed, and encloses approximately the same area as the Forbidden City.[13]

*

We have remarked that the processional way could have had very little meaning for private residents in Chinese administrative towns. But upon those who sought audience with the Son of Heaven in Peking, its impact must have been overwhelming. Suppose such a person, say a Western envoy – who in Chinese eyes would have been a tributary – ap- proached the city from the south. From the moment he crossed the outer moat he would have been forced into a sort of automatic dance, its rhythm set by the changing masses and spaces of each successive stage over which he made his way. First, a semicircular counterscarp surmounted by a massive gate-tower. Immediately beyond it, the south wall *fig. 73* of the Southern City with a second gate-tower, followed by a long and uninterrupted avenue leading straight across the Southern City to its north wall. Another counterscarp and gate-tower; and then the north wall was crossed at Ch'ien Mên with its five gateways. An open space, beyond which lay another gate, Chung Hua Mên, after which the way continued due north into what is today the enormous T'ien-an Mên Square, the impressive setting for public celebrations under the present Government. On the far side of the square it crossed the lower or 'outer' course of the Chin Shui Ho, River of Golden Water, by way of five parallel bridges with carved marble parapets. And again there was a wall, and ahead a gate-house with five vaulted openings beneath, T'ien-an Mên, or Gate of Heaven's Peace.

Passing through T'ien-an Mên, the visitor now entered the Imperial City and a long enclosure blocked at its northern end by Tuan Mên; beyond lay a second and yet longer enclosure with side-gates through which he perhaps caught glimpses of the courtyards and buildings of the Temple of Tutelary Gods, She-chi Miao, on the left, and on the right T'ai Miao, the Supreme Temple of the imperial ancestors.[14] At the back of the empty

pl. 234

stage on which he now stood was the enormous Wu Mên, Noon Gate, its two projecting wings surmounted by pavilions, set in yet another wall running west to east across his line of vision. Where, he must have wondered, was he being led?

One can well imagine the growing bewilderment and disquiet of such a person as he passed through one blank wall and beneath one brooding gate-house after another, to find beyond it only a featureless avenue leading to yet another wall and gate. Reality was softening into a dream. His mind, so long attentive to a distant goal somewhere ahead in this labyrinth of straight lines, so long expecting a climax that never seemed to come, must at last have refused to record and memorize the minor differences in scale, proportion, and decorative detail of the buildings that were the only landmarks of his progress. As he pressed forward into a world of emptiness and of deadening silence, dream must have intensified into a nightmare of *déjà vu*. Whatever self-possession he may have had at the outset must long since have drained away when, crossing Wu Mên, he finally entered the precinct of the Forbidden City. As William Empson has remarked in conversation, the Forbidden City was a bio-logical device for ruling the world. And, however ineffectually it may have regulated its own internal affairs, there can be little doubt of its capacity to reduce outsiders to a state of sup-plicatory awe.

pl. 234

Wu Mên, the Sublime Porte of old Peking, has been described by Sirén as 'the most fortresslike and monumental of all the buildings within the Palace City'.[15] Basically a Ming structure, it was rebuilt in 1647 and reconstructed or repaired in 1801. Its main hall and the four pavilions surmounting each end of its bastionlike wings are all double-roofed and connected by roofed galleries. Wu Mên was always far more than a gate-house; in the days of the empire many of its rooms were occupied by government offices. Together with the buildings that line its forecourt, it today houses the Historical Museum of Peking. It is crossed by three vaulted openings in the wall beneath it.

Beyond Wu Mên lies the first courtyard of the Forbidden City – and specifically of its Outer Court, Wai Ch'ao, wherein State business was transacted. Across this vast quadrangle

pls 238, 239

sweeps the upper course of the River of Golden Water, spanned, as were its lower reaches, by five marble bridges. The very water here flows through a marble conduit, itself surmounted by carved balustrades; and the effect of all this low-flung decorative detailing in dazzling white stone, harmonizing with the low elevations of buildings on either side of the court, but contrasting with the massivity of those on the axial line, and contrasting, too, with the muted reds and yellows of walls and roof-tiles, and with the brilliance of scarlet-painted columns and of gold, green, blue, and white beams and brackets above them, must be spectacular indeed. Here were halted, before dawn on 2 September 1656, members of the Dutch 'embassy' led by Peter de Goyer and Jacob de Kayser. They were joined by tri-butaries from the Mogul emperor of India, others from the Dalai Lama at Lhasa, yet others from a Mongolian state near the Great Wall. At the sound of a bell, all advanced to cross the last barrier separating them from the august presence of the Son of Heaven – T'ai-ho Mên, the Gate of Supreme Harmony.

T'ai-ho Mên, like Wu Mên, is a double-roofed open hall – it can scarcely be called a *pls 239, 237, 236* gate-house – standing on a terrace faced with marble and gained by means of three central flights of marble steps, with other single flights at each side. The imperial way, paved with marble slabs, runs direct from Wu Mên across the courtyard, over the middle bridge, and up the middle flight of the triple staircase. But this middle flight is actually a marble glacis richly carved with dragons in bas-relief, and flanked by narrow steps on either side; up it the emperor was carried in his chair, on occasions when he approached his audience-halls from the south – as he would do after visiting the Ancestral Temple or that of the Tutelary Gods [p. 376] or the altars at the Temple of Heaven. T'ai-ho Mên was originally a Ming building, reconstructed in AD 1645 and again at the end of the last century; in line with it on either side are smaller gate-houses, through which passed the processions of civil and military officials who accompanied the emperor.

North of T'ai-ho Mên is yet another courtyard giving direct access to the first imperial audience- or throne-hall. It is an enclosure some two hundred yards long which, says Sirén, 'seems still longer, because of the absolute bareness of the court that lies between, and the monotonously uniform, low buildings on both sides'.[16] The imperial way runs straight across it to the Hall of Supreme Harmony, T'ai-ho Tien. Built in 1627 under the Mings, *pl. 240; col. 54* and largely rebuilt on its original lines twice later in the seventeenth century and again in 1765 and under the Republic, T'ai-ho Tien is a double-roofed structure standing at the southern end of a huge plateau of terracing, the Dragon Pavement, which carries also the two halls directly north of it – the three forming a complex called San Ta Tien, the Three *pl. 235* Great Halls. Like T'ai-ho Mên, T'ai-ho Tien is approached by means of a triple marble staircase, but terrace and staircase are stepped inwards at three levels, and the surrounding carved balcony is repeated three times. In the hall itself, rites connected with New Year's Day, the winter solstice, and the emperor's birthday were normally celebrated. It was the most august building of the Outer Court. In a symbolical sense, at least, it was the seat of government of the reigning dynasty; and during the days of the 1911 Republic there was some talk, which came to nothing, of converting it into a Parliament House.

At T'ai-ho Tien official progresses normally terminated. Behind it, the Dragon Pave-ment narrows to accommodate a much smaller building, square in plan and with a single roof hipped to the top on all four sides, called Chung-ho Tien, or Hall of Middle Harmony. *col. 58* It, too, was originally a Ming building which was restored in 1627 and 1765, and Sirén says it retains its Ming character better than does T'ai-ho Tien. Though not an audience-hall, Chung-ho Tien was nevertheless used by the emperor in his official role; he here in-spected the agricultural implements and seeds for the coming year, and prepared himself for ceremonies to be enacted in T'ai-ho Tien. Behind Chung-ho Tien is the third hall in this group united by a common terrace, the Pao-ho Tien, Hall of Protecting Harmony. Smaller than T'ai-ho Tien, its general appearance and plan are similar, although its main roof is only half-hipped, and its front elevation is less impressive since it is masked by Chung-ho Tien. Pao-ho Tien is a late Ming building, repaired in the eighteenth century. In it the emperor received, among other persons, those scholars who had won top academic honours, and who were therefore destined for the highest administrative posts.

I have brought the reader up to the wall of the labyrinthine Inner Court, or Nei Ch'ao, representing the penetralia of the Forbidden City into which no person not a member of the imperial family or its personal staff was allowed to trespass. Architecturally this private precinct is in a sense an anticlimax, lacking the spaciousness, the calculated dynamism and the tension of the processional way. Some impression of its appearance can perhaps be got *pl. 229* from the aerial view, its main features being a reproduction at small scale of the Three Great Halls of the Outer Court, and a landscaped garden of the type I am going to describe.

At this point, therefore, I propose to break off my description of what is perhaps the most exemplary architectural city ever built. For Peking, it seems to me, is China in epitome. In its orderly layout it reflects the profoundest intellectual qualities of the Chinese themselves, which make for balanced relations between individual and family, family and State, human order and cosmic order. A static conception; but none more conducive to harmonious living, to a proper adjustment of individual and communal rights, has ever yet been invented.[17]

Rus in urbe: informal layouts

pls 241–247 We cannot leave the subject of Chinese town- and homestead-planning without at least mentioning the informal pleasure-park or garden, that calculated contrast to the formal geometry of the courtyard plan. Landscape-gardening is as integral a feature of the Chinese architectural genius as it is of the English, and a far older one. England's own contribution to the Rococo, the hybrid affair known throughout Europe at the end of the eighteenth century as 'le jardin anglo-chinois', owes its being to the architect William Chambers, who presented it, with a flourish of self-advertisement, in his *Plans, Elevations, Sections, and Perspective Views of the Gardens and Buildings at Kew in Surry, etc.*, published in 1763. The Kew pagoda dates from the previous year.

Chambers had been to China as a youth, and had written a glowing account of oriental gardening. Yet, despite his enthusiasm and drive, and despite the fashionable craze for *lachinage* that had hit Western Europe, one doubts whether 'le jardin anglo-chinois' would have taken root as it did had not the ground already been prepared. Throughout the first half of the century England was reacting against the dictatorship of France in matters artistic with a violence born partly of political animus, and was feeling its way back to more truly national standards of taste. Landscape-gardeners like Bridgeman, Kent, and Lancelot Brown had already begun to deliver the English garden from subjection to Palladian standards applied to layout, and the lifeless symmetry that went with them, and to restore to it something of its pristine charm.

The revelation of the Chinese romantic attitude towards Nature, as exemplified in Chinese landscape-garden design, gave added impetus to the movement, for it was felt that herein the English shared their taste with the most civilized nation on earth.

A single comparison serves to show how closely the views of the two nations agreed, apparently, concerning the subjective feelings engendered by Nature. It relates to that highly-charged symbol, the rock. Lin Yutang, voicing sentiments traditional among Chinese of the scholar class, says: 'The basic idea is that rocks are enormous, strong, and suggest eternity. ... Above all, from the artistic point of view they have grandeur, majesty, ruggedness, and quaintness. There is the further sentiment of *wei*, which means "dangerous" but is really untranslatable. A tall cliff that rises abruptly three hundred feet above the ground is always fascinating to look at because of its suggestion of "danger".'[18] The eighteenth-century English mandarin, T. Whatley, wrote: '... if the rocks are only high, they are but stupendous, not majestic; breadth is equally essential to their greatness ... the terrors of a scene in nature are like those of a dramatic representation; they give an alarm; but the sensations are agreeable, so long as they are kept to such as are allied only to terror. ...'[19]

Failing to meet Nature face to face, as they imagined they would like to do, the town-dwelling Chinese intelligentsia created her image on a smaller scale in their private demesnes – and, indeed, appreciated the practical advantage of doing so; for, as the seventeenth-century author of *Yüan yeh*, 'Garden Notes', sensibly says: '... If one can find stillness in the midst of the city toil, why then should one forgo such an easily accessible spot and seek a more distant one?'[20] Thus, while domestic and official cares still surround you, your window can become a magic casement looking through which you 'seem to face a rocky hillside, alive with rugged beauty'.[21]

pl. 244

In planning the Chinese garden, then, great ingenuity was exercised whereby to manage every inch of land into a series of dramatically contrasted scenic effects resembling those staged by Nature herself on a grander scale. Unable to rival Nature's dimensions, the landscape-gardener could at least see to it that such effects should follow thick and fast, the ingredient of surprise forever present and the emotions quickened, from time to time, with an agreeable sense of something like danger, *wei*.

Since Nature displays neither order nor symmetry – in macrocosm, at least – a studied irregularity in plan prevailed. There was usually no single focus of interest. Paths wandered. Walls followed natural contours, did not cut ruthlessly across them, as would have happened in a formal and symmetrical scheme. Moving water expressed the capriciousness of Nature; still pools mirrored her depths. Bridges were built zigzag. It was the fancy to say that this was to prevent devils, who travel only in straight lines, from pursuing people along them; actually it was to give a fresh visual interest to every few yards of the promenade. Rockeries were made the medium of an elaborate cult. The rocks, hauled from the bottoms of lakes, were often perforated or modelled by the waves of ancient seas, and had strange and suggestive shapes. Even in the seventeenth century up to two hundred measures of rice would be paid for a genuine fine specimen dredged from the bottom of Lake T'ai in Kiangsu. Such rocks have long since been almost unobtainable.

pl. 241

Gnarled creepers lay like sleeping dragons. Old trees, especially the pine, were transplanted at great expense. Quick-growing bamboo and banana were arranged in clumps. Flowers like the chrysanthemum, lotus, blossoming plum, and peony, chosen for their symbolic associations, grew close-guarded or at random, according to their nature, while covered galleries (*lang*) led from one arbour to another, and from pavilion to pavilion.

pl. 245

pl. 247

These were the gardens of the mandarinate. But at every level of Chinese urban life, the same love of Nature continually seeks expression as part of the art and artifice of living. House and garden are but aspects of the same cultural whole, *yüan chia*, 'garden home', so that no dividing line can be drawn between indoors and outdoors. We have chosen for illustration part of the Liu Yüan at Suchow. This city in Kiangsu had become celebrated for its gardens at least as early as Mongol times, when the landscapist Ni Tsan painted another of its gardens as one of his last and best authenticated works, the Shih-tzŭ Lin, Lion Grove, a garden that exists to this day.

pl. 245

pls 243, 242

But it was in Ming times that the gardens of Suchow gained their greatest fame. Liu Yüan – which originally meant 'the Liu family garden', but which, when a different character for *liu* was substituted following a change of ownership, came to mean something like 'lingering garden' – was designed in the sixteenth century and seems not to have greatly altered in character since. Sirén's appraisal of this place, which he visited in 1935, is intelligent and imaginative. After remarking the 'white-washed façades of the buildings divided by windows and doorways with ornamental gratings', so conspicuous in our photograph, he goes on to say that this facing gives as it were a 'continuous background to successive pictorial sections that stand out against them in more or less the same way as paintings on white paper. From whatever point one views this garden, one sees the water in the foreground and the white walls in the background'.[22] And elsewhere he says: 'Not only the leaning trees, but also the pavilions on the little islands, the bridges and the galleries on the banks are all doubled and lifted up – or sunk? – in an intangible dream-world; an atmosphere of playing shadows and reflected light.'[23]

On a grander scale are the pleasure-parks of the great imperial cities. The entire district around the vast West Lake, on whose eastern shore lies the old Sung capital of Hangchow, is wonderfully laid out with residences, temples, and magnificent gardens breaking the lake-line while the mast of the lofty Pao-shu Pagoda seems to break the sky. With the lake skil-fully managed into lagoons and islands crowned with pavilions and linked by long cause-ways to the mainland, and with pleasure-craft of every sort dotting the water, this unique panorama vividly calls to mind Marco Polo's famous description of it as it was 700 years ago.

pls 246, 247; col. 55, 56 West of Peking, the country between the town and the Western Hills was similarly im-proved by the Ch'ing emperors in building the Imperial Summer Palaces, the earlier of which was sacked by Allied forces in 1860. And the Winter Palace, with its festoon of lakes on the west side of the Imperial City of Peking, is a perfect foil for the humourless rigidity of the palace buildings and the processional way.[24]

We can perhaps best end this section on landscape architecture by quoting the words of the eighteenth-century Jesuit Attiret, whose description of the old Imperial Summer Palace, Yüan Ming Yüan, reveals an enthusiasm no less whole-hearted than Chambers', despite whatever predilection he must have felt, as a Frenchman, for formal symmetry. It well sum-marizes the compositional principles and design-elements we have been discussing:

'They go from one of the Valleys to another, not by formal strait Walks as in *Europe*, but by various Turnings and Windings, adorn'd on the Sides with little Pavilions and charming grottos: and each of these Valleys is diversify'd from all the rest, both by their manner of laying out the Ground, and in the Structure and Disposition of its Buildings.

'All the Risings and Hills are sprinkled with Trees; and particularly with Flowering-trees, which are here very common. The Sides of the Canals, or lesser Streams, are not faced (as they are with us), with smooth Stone, and in a strait Line; but look rude and rustic, with different Pieces of Rock, some of which jut out, and others recede inwards; and are placed with so much Art that you would take it to be the Work of Nature.'[25]

Wood as a building material

The oldest building of any size now standing in China is said to be a brick pagoda some 100 feet high at the Sung-yüeh Temple on the sacred mountain of Sung Shan in Honan; pl. 252 its date is AD 523. Use of brick or stone for monuments of this type, and for constructions in which strength and permanence are prime necessities, such as defensive walls, tombs, and bridges, has favoured survival of early examples of these. But for buildings capable of being lived in, the structural framework has usually been of wood. Few such buildings can be found in China dating from much before Ming times. Absence of great architectural monuments dating from antiquity in China serves to throw its archaeology into an un-familiar and seemingly minor key. When we think of historical cultures in other parts of the world, it is usually their building achievements that we have uppermost in our minds; their architectural remains provide us with a yardstick, so to speak, by which to measure their other dimensions. Yet almost all we know of the architecture of pre-Han China is mere

380

literary hearsay. People used to believe, and many still do, that the architectural work by which China is best known to the outside world – the Great Wall – dates directly from the Ch'in Empire of the late third century BC. This is inaccurate. If the core of the wall does in some places comprise Han, Ch'in, and even earlier materials, the stone retaining-walls and brick openings that give it its distinctive appearance in the region north-west of Peking are almost certainly no older than the early part of the Ming period. Yet the half-truth is un- *col. 53* critically accepted as the whole; and the Great Wall continues to get a disproportionate amount of attention from Westerners, who, as it seems to me, feel an unconscious need for something tangible in China to set beside the Egyptian pyramids, Mesopotamian *ziggurats*, Greek and Indian temples, and so forth, by means of which they are accustomed to visualize the shape of the most distant past.

What has endured of ancient Chinese architecture is rather its fundamental constructional principles and aesthetic aims. Provided these life-giving germs were safeguarded and given physical embodiment generation by generation, permanence of individual buildings was of lesser moment; it could not in any case be guaranteed, and seems not to have been particu- larly sought after. Relative impermanence of individual buildings, then, is the first and most obvious outcome of reliance on wood as the building material *par excellence*.

Consistent use of a single building material in China inevitably led to highly standardized methods of construction, and so to an absolute unity of architectural form. The second outcome of use of wood, therefore, is that Chinese architecture does not display the variety of historical styles with which we are so familiar in the West, and the architect was not required to produce original designs. Once the scale and size of a building project had been decided in accordance with sumptuary legislation depending on the rank of the client, choice of site, selection and preparation of materials, and erection of the building would follow more or less automatically. Regulation fixed the timber scantling and the number of bays and roof-trusses allowable for a particular building. An unwritten tradition determined methods of construction, and provided models for prefabrication of structural and decorative elements by carpenters and joiners.

The traditional Chinese architect, then, was more in the nature of a highly-skilled master builder, competent to supervise the construction of a building down to its smallest detail, but kept close to design and specification under the watchful eye of a building-contractor; in consequence his name is usually lost in the anonymity of a guild craft. Significantly, the only surviving classical Chinese treatise on architecture, *Ying tsao fa shih*, is primarily a builder's *vade mecum*. It gives detailed instructions for works in timbers of various sizes, for decorative wood-carving, exterior roofing, and so on, together with plans, sections, and detail diagrams for use of carpenters, joiners, monumental masons, and decorators. *Ying tsao fa shih* is an invaluable repository of technical data but it is neither a scholarly treatise on principles of construction or historical style, nor an original contribution to the theory of architectural design.

The architect in modern China is far closer to his Western counterpart, in having access to a wide range of new materials and a multiplicity of styles brought to his notice through contact with the West. He nevertheless inherits an instinctive conservatism, and a feeling for architectural integrity that is bound to check any inclination he might otherwise have to acquire the individualist standpoint of the Western architect. The problem of forging a new national style for China is a crucial one, and one that Chinese architects and art historians are acutely aware of. But we may reasonably expect that, the choice once made, it will be carried through consistently and China spared the grim experience of bogus and derivative architecture, erupted from any and every historical period and culture, and rendered more often than not in materials wildly unsuited to its multitudinous forms [see pp. 406–408].

The hall (tien): pillar and beam construction

The particular use to which wood is put in traditional Chinese building practice follows logically from its characteristics as a building material, and accounts for many distinctive features of the Chinese hall. The Chinese have, of course, always been firm believers in walls as defensive ramparts. They enclosed their homesteads, their towns, and even their homeland within some of the most massive fortifications ever built. But the very concept of an ensemble of dwelling-houses as a finite habitation unit enclosed inside a common protecting wall, does away with the need for defensive walls as part of the house itself. All that is then required of a house-wall is that it should hold off the weather. Accordingly it becomes a mere in-filling, a non-weight-bearing screen, a 'curtain-wall'. It may be constructed of the flimsiest materials imaginable, or of the first that come to hand, and is neither required to give rigidity to the structural framework nor to help in supporting the roof.

The earliest and still most favoured use for steel or reinforced concrete in modern Western building practice is as a structural framework for screen-walls which are themselves primarily partitioning and decorative in function. That is precisely the mode of construction used in Chinese practice, and the coincidence has not escaped notice by contemporary Chinese architects. The Nanking Museum building, for instance, would at first glance seem to be an orthodox wood-frame construction; actually its skeleton is reinforced concrete. Here is yet another case where China can gracefully accept a modern international building technique and modify it to suit her own architectural climate. Use of wood as a structural framework, says Liang Ssŭ-ch'êng, 'provides an excellent foundation for the adaptation of modern materials and techniques to the characteristic features of Chinese architecture'.[26]

fig. 74

fig. 75

The structural framework for the walls comprises upright wooden pillars, and longitudinal and transverse wooden beams lying in the planes of the walls. This type of construction is essentially that of the immemorial 'post-and-lintel' principle, except that the beams do not as a rule rest by dead weight on top of the pillars – as do those of Stonehenge, for instance – but are tenoned into or through their upper ends; capitals can therefore be dispensed with. The minimum number of pillars is of course four, one being placed at each corner; but in the case of large halls it is necessary to multiply them, especially along the long sides of the building, into regular colonnades tied together by the longitudinal beams, which thus have the appearance of architraves.

The depth of the hall is limited by the length of beams that span its vault. For this reason, extension of a Chinese building is usually longitudinal and not transverse. But if additional depth is desired, it can be secured by multiplying the longitudinal colonnades. Large halls often have two longitudinal rows of pillars within, so dividing the interior into three bays of depth. And very often there is an additional colonnade outside, forming an open portico in front, if not all the way round. These extra colonnades are all tied to the wall pillars by means of transverse tie-beams.[27]

In putting up a building, the platform on which it is to rest is constructed first. At an early stage, represented by Shang foundations excavated at An-yang, platforms were made of rammed earth held to shape during construction by wood shuttering, which was afterwards removed. These platforms, made somewhat larger than the buildings they supported, are today so hard that they resound when struck. Later platforms were faced with stone or brick, and by Han times had acquired elaborate wooden balustrades, with vertical posts and horizontal hand-rails forming bays filled with geometrical fret-patterns in carved wood. Still later, evidently after contact with Buddhist India, wood construction was imitated in stone or marble. The platform was then often terraced and given an elaborately moulded base incorporating various pseudo-Classical elements.

The main wood framework was next erected, its pillars being allowed to rest freely on mechanically independent footings sunk into the platform. Shang footings took the form of large ovoid boulders, sometimes capped by dome-shaped bronze discs. In recent dynasties the commonest form has been a rectangular stone block cut slightly larger than the diameter of the pillar, its upper surface in the form of a circular boss with flat top, its sides curving gracefully out to floor-level so that the load is spread without interfering with passage over the ground.

Had the pillars been sunk direct into the ground they would no doubt have been liable to rot at ground-level. Nevertheless it is also possible that the distinctive type of pillar-footing adopted in China may originally have been intended to counteract the effect of shifting sub-soil, and especially of ground-shock in an earthquake area. Neither Chinese nor Japanese architects seem to have thought of a building as inexorably rooted mechanically to the ground. In the case of the older wooden pagodas, for example, the central shaft is not firmly *pl. 253* tied to the main structure, but stands more or less free, so that small movements made by it will not spread to the rest of the building. Ground movement caused by earthquakes is lateral; clearly if a building can slide freely on stone bearings, if only very slightly, it will withstand earth-tremors better than a mechanically tied structure would do.

The roof-truss

The screen-wall being incapable of bearing heavy loads, roof-supports must be carried by the heads of the pillars. Transverse wooden beams, spanning the nave of the hall, are tenoned into or through the upper parts of each facing pair of pillars in the same way and usually at the same level as are the tie-beams comprising the false architrave. Chinese buildings are thus vaulted according to the pillar-and-beam principle. Two other types of vaulting – the cantilevered or corbelled arch and the true arch – are rarely used for roofing halls in China. Both are, however, typical of masonry constructions such as gate-openings and tombs, and the principles of both are applied in Chinese bridge-building, as we shall see.

Were no superstructure added to the main trusses, the roof would, of course, remain flat. Further modification in shape is usually decided by climate. In China, with its heavy seasonal rainfall in summer, roofs are invariably high-pitched in order to provide a run-off for rain-water. To secure a steep roof-slope, the long axis of the roof at the ridge-beam must be raised well above the level at the eaves by means of an internal arrangement of beams forming the roof-truss. The Chinese method of under-roof construction differs fundamentally from that used in the West, and results in a pronounced difference of architectural form.

The Western roof-truss, which supports the main purlins, and above them the common rafters and tiles, is a mechanically rigid isosceles triangle whose base is the transverse beam and whose sides are two sloping struts running from ridge-beam to eaves. The sides of the triangle are straight and the typical Western roof, seen in side elevation, has thus the outline of an inverted V.

The Chinese roof-truss, as can be seen from figure 75, is a somewhat more elaborate *fig. 75* system. Each main transverse beam carries a pair of queen-posts or spacing-blocks placed at

74 and 75 Section through a traditional dwelling-house (*wu*) showing columns, tie-beams, queen-posts, purlins and rafters (from *Ying tsao fa shih*); and the roof-truss itself

about the quarter span, and these in turn support a shorter transverse beam above. Into this may be socketed a second pair of queen-posts, also placed some distance in and also supporting a transverse beam. In this way the roof-truss rises as a series of steps, until the required height is reached at the head of a king-post standing immediately below the ridge-beam and supporting it. The main purlins (seen in section in figure 75) are lodged on the upper surfaces of each step immediately above the queen-posts, and figure 75 clearly shows that the depth and height of the steps may be so regulated that the line passing over their edges from ridge-beam to eaves is not straight, but curved concavely. Clearly such a system is suited either for constructing a curved roof or for supporting a sag. If in other words Chinese builders had at any time wished to create a curved roof, this is precisely the sort of substructure one would expect them to have invented. It would have been equally effective had they wished only to perpetuate an already existing sag, such as might have been brought about in the first instance by the dead weight of roofing material resting on a small roof with no internal supports. The point should be kept in mind, since it perhaps bears on the question of the origin of the curved Chinese roof [pp. 390–393].

The eaves and their supports

Deeply overhanging eaves are typical of Chinese buildings. They were not always, perhaps; but once the form was introduced, its advantages for a country as far south as China must soon have been recognized. South latitude and monsoon climate mean very hot summers, with the sun reaching a high altitude, and in most parts of the country a high seasonal rainfall. Overhanging eaves help to carry rainwater well away from the flimsy fabric underneath, and to give shelter from the sun when it is high in the sky and at its hottest – a prime consideration in China, where by tradition all buildings face south. Chinese roofing materials being very heavy, this overhang requires special support. Over the centuries an elaborate mechanical system of staying the eaves by means of brackets has come into being. Its evolution is the one real example of continuous historical change in the forms of Chinese buildings; but it is change inside a single, monolithic style, comparable to those in the column and capital design of Greek and Roman temple architecture, to each of which is designated a separate architectural order.

In briefly summarizing this system we must first define a few elementary terms. The word 'bracket' or 'bracket-arm' (Ch. *hua* or *hua kung*) will be used to name the basic component of a bracket-system, with its cardinal function of providing an independent point of support at its free end. The term 'bracket-complex' (Ch. *p'u cho*) will signify a cluster of bracket-arms with their accessory members all springing from a single pillar axis, such as we see in figures 76 and 79 to 81. The effective outward reach of a single bracket-arm will be called a 'step' (Ch. *t'iao*), and the vertical distance through which each member lifts its load will be called a 'tier'. When we speak of a 'two-step, three-tier' bracket-complex, we mean one which extends outwards in two stages, and carries its load upwards through three.[28] This particular complex is shown in figure 79 and explained on page 387.

If the transverse tie-beams spanning the vault should pass through the pillars in the wall-plane and project beyond them, then these projections can be made to act as simple bracket-arms staying the lowest pair of purlins, the eaves-purlins (Ch. *liao yen fang*), and so the eaves. This is the arrangement used in the construction of the Imperial Shōsō-in at the Tōdaiji Temple, Nara, Japan [p. 268], a comparatively small wooden building of log-cabin type dating from the eighth century AD.

A natural advance is to manifold the single horizontal transverse stay as a regular series of bracket-arms rising in successive steps and tiers from a point fairly low down on the pillar, until the topmost bracket-arm catches the eaves-purlin. More than one member of such a complex may be the projecting end of a transverse tie-beam spanning the vault and passing outwards through each facing pair of pillars. For with massive bracketing making each pillar top-heavy on its outer side, tie-beams actually entering into the bracket-complexes on both sides of the building probably help keep the colonnades from collapsing outwards. The corresponding disadvantage is of course that in using up part of the tie-beam as a bracket-arm, we shorten the length available for actual vaulting, so that the system can be applied only to buildings of small or moderate size.

Development of the multiple transverse stay probably went on during the T'ang and Liao dynasties in north China, and continued in provincial southern architecture during the Sung period. Its monumental forms are well suited for translation into stone, as exemplified by a motif of the granite-built West Pagoda at Ch'üan Chou in Fukien (erected 1228–37) – a two-step, two-tier complex in which the upper bracket-arm directly supports the eaves-purlin above. It is the chief feature of the Tenjikuyō, the so-called 'Indian' style[29], said to have reached Japan from south China in time for the rebuilding of the Tōdaiji Temple at Nara, towards the end of the twelfth century. In the Kaisandō of that temple it takes the form of a three-step, three-tier complex, the highest bracket-arm again directly supporting the eaves-purlin. A new element now makes its appearance, namely a longitudinal tie-beam (Ch. *lo han fang*), which is free except where it passes through each complex. Mechanically this serves to bind the complexes together and give sideways rigidity, while as a design-element it accentuates the strong horizontal line of the elevation.

The fullest elaboration, indeed hypertrophy, of this type of stay is reached in the towering bracket-system of the Nandaimon (South Great Gate) at the Tōdaiji Temple, dating from the thirteenth century. Each complex starts low down on its pillar so as to catch the immense eaves overhang. It consists of no less than seven superimposed bracket-arms and incorporates seven steps and eight tiers. Three of the arms – the second, fourth, and seventh – are actually

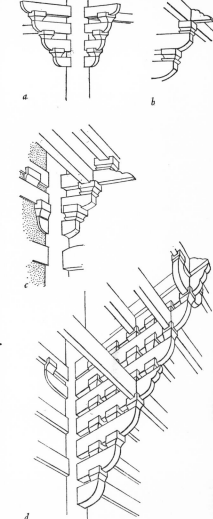

76 The transverse bracket-arm: *a* on the Shui-ching T'ing in the Yung-ch'üan Temple, Fuchow, Fukien; *b* on the West Pagoda, K'ai-yüan Temple, Ch'üan-chou, Fukien; *c* on the Kaisandō of the Tōdaiji Temple, Nara, Japan; *d* on the Nandaimon of the Tōdaiji Temple

fig. 76c

fig. 76d

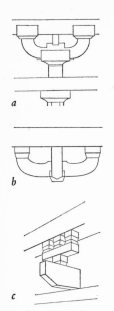

77 Longitudinal and transverse bracketing: *a* bracket-complex from a Han pottery model; *b* upper cross-yoke with bearing blocks and purlin, T'ien-an Mên, Peking; *c* 1-step, 2-tier bracket complex from a Han pottery model

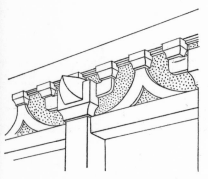

78 Detail of sixth-century AD rock-cut façade, Mai-chi-shan Caves, Kansu

fig. 77b

figs 79–81

the projecting ends of transverse tie-beams spanning the vault, which also continue into the bracket-complex of the opposite side; and there are now three longitudinal tie-beams connecting one complex to the next at the levels of the fourth, sixth, and seventh bracket-arms respectively. Probably China herself had nothing to compare with this titanic system, at least nothing in the official tradition; *Ying tsao fa shih* specifies that 'the maximum number of *t'iao* is limited to five'.[30]

*

It would seem that the Tenjikuyō order, if 'order' it may be called, is in some manner a provincial survivor into Sung and Yüan times of a very much more ancient metropolitan style. In its directness of expression, its masculinity as Soper acutely observes[31], it forcibly conveys the spirit of the early T'ang period, at which time it probably originated. The mechanical arrangement is entirely distinctive, and can be identified by two leading features. First, the bracket-arms pass through, or are mortised into, the body of the pillar, and do not sit on top of it as in later or more advanced systems. Second, the system provides support only at points on the pillar axis.[32] This is an inherent weakness, since the eaves-purlin also needs to be stayed at points *between* the pillars, as does the purlin in the plane of the wall (Ch. *ya ts'ao fang*). In order to provide this sideways support, Chinese bracket-systems incorporated two further complementary principles – cross-bracketing from the pillar complexes themselves, and independent intercolumnar bracketing between.

Cross-bracketing from the pillar-complexes involves use of an architectural member of great antiquity in China, the so-called 'boat-shaped timber' (Ch. *chou mu*, Jap. *funa-hijiki*), its original function being to increase the effective area of stay provided by the pillars in the wall-plane. Typical examples of its form are presented in figure 77. In figure 77a, taken from a pottery model of the Han period, it is placed above the pillar, possibly in the wall-plane, but more probably at or near the end of a projecting transverse beam resting on the architrave, such as is seen in side-view in figure 77c. It consists of a main block below, into which is slotted the curved cross-yoke to which the member owes its name. At each free end the cross-yoke carries a bearing-block of rectangular shape, with grooved upper surface and with sides tapered into a cavetto below. The twin bearing-blocks grip a purlin above (this being either the eaves-purlin or one intermediate between it and the purlin in the plane of the wall), and so support the roof outside the wall-plane. A third block, which stays but does not always grip, sometimes rises from the middle of the bracket, so that the purlin receives three-point support.

If now we isolate the outermost cross-yoke of a typical Ch'ing dynasty bracket-complex on the T'ien-an Mên in Peking, we see that in general form and tectonic purpose this basic element has remained unchanged for the best part of two thousand years. The reader will find it reproduced with minor variations in figures 79 to 81 and will soon be able to recognize it on sight.[33]

The transverse bracket-arm, mounted with a two- or three-point cross-yoke supporting the purlin, represents a one-step, two-tier complex only slightly more advanced than the transverse bracket-arm acting as a direct stay. This seems to have been the ultimate limit of Han bracket development. A second outward step, leading to the two-step, three-tier complex, was never taken in Han times – presumably because the eaves did not project very far and supporting them presented no great problem.

Nor did the four centuries intervening between the Han and T'ang witness any spectacular advance. The carved façades of certain Buddhist caves at T'ien-lung-shan and Mai-

386

chi-shan dating from the sixth century AD, as well as some late fifth- and early sixth-century interiors at Yün-kang [p. 179], show a system still confined essentially to the plane of the wall. But if the Han period marks the beginning of cross-bracketing from the pillar heads, we find on these fifth- and sixth-century façades the first manifest sign of an independent intercolumnar support in the shape of a double-brace strut of unusual aspect[34], alternating with typical three-point cross-yokes mounted above the pillars. This member is a persistent feature of early Chinese architectural orders up to and including the beginning of the T'ang, and its continued reproduction on cave façades and in bas-reliefs strongly suggests that no drastic change in the form of the Chinese roof, such as would have necessitated far-reaching modifications in the method of its support, took place during that time. Indeed everything warrants belief that the problem of supporting deeply projecting roof-eaves did not become critical until the seventh century.

fig. 78

*

At some time near the beginning of the T'ang dynasty (AD 618–906) the forms of metro-politan Chinese architecture were profoundly modified by introduction of curved roofs and deeply overhanging roof-eaves. An incised lintel on the Wild Goose pagoda at Ch'ang-an [p. 395] is believed to date from a rebuilding of that monument which took place between AD 701 and 705. It represents what was presumably a minor palace building of its day. The bracket-complex is still restricted to the pillar; in the transverse plane it extends outwards in two steps and upwards in three tiers, the upper bracket-arm bearing a three-point cross-yoke that grips the eaves-purlin. In the plane of the wall, cross-yokes mounted on wood blocks placed immediately over the tops of the pillars alternate with double-brace struts; both sets of members support a longitudinal bracing-beam by means of grooved bearing-blocks. This beam in turn carries cross-yokes on the pillar axes, the double-brace struts of the lower tier being here replaced by simple vertical posts; both sets of members serve to support a second longitudinal bracing-beam carried up to the same height as the eaves-purlin. With this T'ang arrangement, the architrave beams are for the first time seen to be tenoned into the upper sides of the pillars, not mounted on their tops as in earlier orders.

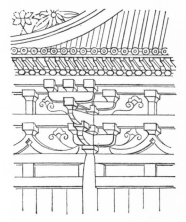

79 Detail of the bracket-system on a Buddhist hall, engraved on a lintel at the Wild Goose Pagoda, Ch'ang-an (c. AD 700)

We have seen that at the Han stage the bracket-complex never projected by more than a single step, nor rose through more than two tiers. At that represented by the Wild Goose pagoda lintel, it has grown into one incorporating two steps and three tiers. Throughout the T'ang dynasty, an ever-deepening eaves-overhang led logically to steady increase in the number of steps and tiers involved.

T'ang architectural traditions evidently persisted in north China long after the end of the dynasty, and the bracket-system of the Liao dynasty Kuan-yin Ko at the Tu-lo Temple in Chi-hsien, Hopei, is probably modelled on late T'ang lines. In its present form the Kuan-yin Ko dates from AD 984, which makes it the second oldest wooden building known to be standing in China. Its lower walls are sheltered by a pent-roof, the eaves of which are stayed by means of complexes comprising four steps and five tiers. The uppermost bracket-arm again bears at its extremity a three-point cross-yoke which, with an interposed spacing-block, carries the eaves-purlin. Between the wall-plane and that of the eaves, each complex helps to support a longitudinal timber corresponding to the free tie-beam of the Tenjikuyō system [p. 385] by means of two superimposed cross-yokes mortised into the third and fourth bracket-arms. Boarding runs downwards from the eaves-purlin to this beam, and from it to a bracing-beam in the plane of the wall, thus forming an 'eaves-ceiling' which serves to hide the rafters above.

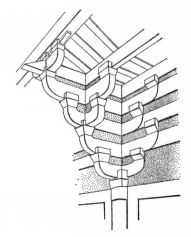

80 Columnar bracket-complex on the lower storey of the Kuan-yin Ko, Chi-hsien, Hopei (AD 984)

In the system represented by the Wild Goose lintel, intercolumnar support is limited to double-brace struts and vertical posts. In that of the Kuan-yin Ko, true intercolumnar bracketing of orthodox type makes its appearance. The elevation is divided into five bays of length by means of six pillars in the wall-plane, and a single intercolumnar complex is inserted on the main architrave beam in each of the middle three bays. Below the lower roof the complexes give support only in the wall-plane; but in the upper storey they extend outwards in a simple two-step, three-tier system to grip, not the eaves-purlin which they cannot reach, but the longitudinal tie-beam. During the Sung period intercolumnar complexes came more and more to resemble those mounted over the pillars and, like them, reached out to stay the eaves-purlin. The number in each bay also increased – at first to two, eventually up to a maximum of six. Placed close together, and rendered on a smaller scale, they now presented the appearance of a continuous cornice whose function was clearly decorative rather than tectonic.

The slanting bracket-arm

Probably well before T'ang times a new member was added to the system supporting the roof-eaves, at all events in buildings of the first class. This was a slanting bracket-arm (Ch. *ang tou*, Jap. *odaruki*), placed directly under the roof and sloping downwards to the eaves at roughly the same angle as the common rafters. The oblique set of this arm made a spirited contrast to the dignified horizontals and verticals of the ordinary complex, while mechanically it brought fresh dynamic interest to the system as a whole. Tethered in the framework above the aisle-pillar within, or made to butt against the underside of a transverse tie-beam, it passed downwards and outwards through the bracket-complex above the wall-pillar serving as a fulcrum, and ended directly beneath the eaves-purlin which it held either by means of a corbel or by a three-point cross-yoke and spacing-block.

The origins of the slanting bracket-arm in China are unknown[35], and for the earliest examples of its actual use we have to turn to Japan. One is in the lower roof of the Kondō of the Hōryūji Temple at Nara, thought to date from the early seventh century AD. The mechanical arrangement is as described above. The massive arm is anchored inside the building above the aisle-pillar. It emerges above the wall-pillar, its fulcrum being a sec-

fig. 81a ond-tier bracing-beam in the plane of the wall. Almost at its extremity, the arm is braced by the projecting end of a transverse beam spanning the nave within and participating also in the complex of the opposite side. Above, the arm carries a cushion member carved in conventional 'cloud pattern' which takes the weight of the eaves-purlin.

Several features about this design suggest a rudimentary stage of development. Soper points out that the sculptural quality lent to it by carved corbels is typical of a pre-T'ang rather than T'ang architectural idiom; in T'ang times such exuberance is usually abandoned in favour of more strictly functional designs. Exposure of raftering and a square-section eaves-purlin are other features seemingly typical of a long-vanished pre-T'ang official style in China.

fig. 81b It is probably rather the lower roof of the Kondō of the Tōshōdaiji Temple at Nara (late eighth century AD) that epitomizes T'ang bracketing science. Designed to stay the enormous T'ang-type eaves, the slanting bracket-arm is here completely integrated both functionally and visually with columnar bracketing of orthodox type. Its balancing functions are much the same as in the Kondō of the Hōryūji. But an ordinary complex comprising two steps and three tiers replaces the transverse stay and carved corbels of the Hōryūji ar-

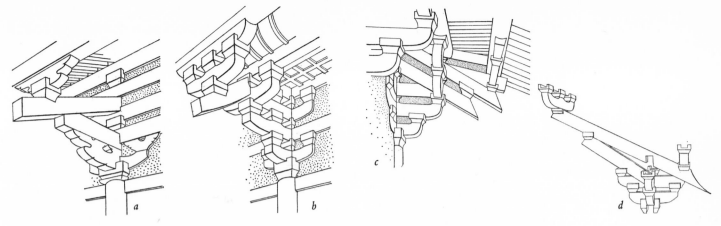

81 The slanting bracket-arm: in Japan: *a* columnar bracket-complex of the Kondō of the Hōryūji, Nara; *b* columnar bracket-complex of the Kondō of the Tōshōdaiji, Nara (adapted from A. C. Soper); in China: *c* columnar bracket-complex of the upper storey of the Kuan-yin Ko, Chi-hsien, Hopei (AD 984); *d* columnar bracket-complex removed from the main hall of the Pao-shêng Ssŭ, Suchow, Chekiang (early eleventh century AD, now demolished)

rangement. The slanting arm now bears the standard three-point cross-yoke with spacing-block above, and the complex also supports a longitudinal tie-beam at its third tier, connected across to eaves- and wall-purlin by means of an 'eaves-ceiling'.

In China the oldest building featuring the slanting bracket-arm, and indeed the oldest wooden building so far discovered, is the main hall of the Fo-kuang Ssŭ on Mount Wu-t'ai in Shansi, which was built in or about the year 857.[36] It is a single-storey building, the eaves of its fully-hipped roof being supported by a bracket-system similar to that of the Tōshōdaiji, and almost identical with that of the upper storey of the Kuan-yin Ko built over a century later. The Chinese arrangement differs from that of the Tōshōdaiji, in that the main slanting arm in each complex is stayed below by a shorter arm which is itself supported by the upper bracket-arm of an ordinary two-step complex. Within, both slanting arms abut against the underside of a transverse tie-beam at a point directly beneath the aisle-purlin. Duplication of lever arms is henceforth a regular feature of Chinese bracket-systems, and so is the convention of terminating the outer ends of the arms with straight slanting arris or curved 'beak'.

pl. 248

fig. 81 c

The Sung period marks a dramatic improvement in the utility and beauty of the slanting bracket-arm. Detached from its moorings above the aisle-pillar, it now functioned as a true lever, while its tectonic qualities were deliberately displayed by omitting the ceiling over the aisle. At its most elemental, in Japanese buildings of the Tenjikuyō, contemporary with late Sung, the arm is employed as an intercolumnar support entirely independent of the columnar complexes. And perhaps that was how it was first conceived of and used.[37]

Figure 81 d shows the elegant and mechanically convincing bracket-complex of the Great Hall at the Pao-shêng Temple, Suchow, probably dating from 1013, when the temple was rebuilt, and now demolished. Here, of course, the arm is intercalated in an ordinary step-and-tier columnar complex. Its fulcrum is provided by the inner end of a short assistant lever which stops against the wall-plane and which is stayed within by two tiers of horizontal arms. At either end the main lever balances aisle- and eaves-purlins by means of three-point cross-yokes. Primitive as the complex is from certain points of view – in later Sung systems and their Japanese derivatives a horizontal member terminates in a beak and so simulates a second slanting arm beneath the true one – it does nevertheless illustrate in a most eloquent and striking manner the basic principle of this type of support.

fig. 81 d

In Ming and Ch'ing times an extra colonnade was placed outside the wall-plane, thus creating an open portico along the front of the building. Standing almost directly beneath the eaves, this colonnade revolutionized the principles of eaves support, for it did away with the need for staying them from points in the wall-plane. The step-and-tier type of complex was now no longer required to perform a mechanical function and gradually fell into obsolescence, and the slanting bracket-arm with its assistant strut beneath was generally abandoned. But it did not disappear without trace. The decorative effect of its diagonal line was no doubt deservedly appreciated. At any rate, the ends of horizontal bracket-arms forming steps in Southern Sung, Ming, and Ch'ing systems are modelled in a conventional form suggesting a bird's beak which, as we have seen, can be traced back to the slanting bracket-arm of T'ang times. They thus perpetuate, in vestigial form, the functional lever of the earlier *pl. 249* systems.

The curved roof

The great roof, elegant not to say rakish in its lines despite its massivity, and lustrous with the enamelled light of its tiles, is the most impressive design-element of the Chinese hall. Its immense overhang, as well as the buoyant upward sweep of its eaves, give to it the appearance of floating free – of hovering over the fabric below. This independence, this magniloquence of the roof, is all the more striking in the case of the hipped roof whose slopes, as they decline smoothly to the eaves on all four sides, mark out a complete and coherent form which gable-ends would only mutilate, by obtruding into the roof, so to speak, the irrelevant qualities of the wall.

Although gable-ends, often enlivened by homely patterns of half-timbering, are typical of much regional domestic architecture in China, the fully-hipped roof has long since been accepted as the *sans pareil* of roofs for buildings of the first class, whether official, religious, or private. It is of extreme antiquity, for we find its form reproduced in full splendour on *pls 74, 115* bronze *fang-i* of the early Chou dynasty as well as on Han bas-reliefs. But while the fully-hipped roof was always given pride of place, a type that may be regarded as structurally intermediate between it and the gabled roof came into fashion during T'ang times if not *pl. 239* before, and has retained a certain popularity ever since. This is the half-hipped roof, wherein end-roofs are pent-roofs hipped to the lower slopes of the main roof below and leaving part of the gable-ends exposed above. Literary allusions make clear that this variety was always regarded as in some way stylistically inferior to the fully-hipped type.

To a European, who may feel as did Christopher Wren that the only roof worthy of being made the dominating feature of a building is the dome, and that others 'had best retire behind a parapet', the Chinese roof is bound to seem something of an oddity. In particular, its exuberant curve is full of fascination for him, arousing greater speculation as to its origin than any other single feature of Chinese architectural design. It is a feature that seems to defy rational explanation, and perhaps that is why scarcely a single writer on Chinese architecture has failed to produce one.

In the earlier edition of this book I reviewed *in extenso* the various theories put forward to account for the concave curve. Many of them can be eliminated by taking into account one indisputable fact, which is that the curve is *not* an indigenous or aboriginal Chinese architectural form. It appears for the first time in Buddhist bas-reliefs of the sixth century, for example one in the Victoria and Albert Museum dated AD 520, and again very prominently *pl. 132* on the limestone slab from Hsiao-t'ang-shan dating from the second half of the century.

390

Association with the foreign religion, complete absence in the repertory of Han and earlier architectural form as preserved in pottery models, bas-reliefs, and other documents, suggests that the curved roof was an importation into north China made during the sixth century AD.

In the light of this evidence we can rule out such ingenious suppositions as that the curved roof perpetuates the memory of an era (hypothetical) when the Chinese lived in tents[38], or that it is an expression of the innate Chinese love for curvilinear form such as is seen in their calligraphy[39], or of their intense feeling for Nature, for living things, and for life itself – an expression so to speak of their national *élan vital*.[40]

Not one of the theories proposed to account for the form of the curved Chinese roof can be regarded as satisfactory. My own view is that the curve is not a result of conscious design composition, but is simply the vestige of a sag caused by the deadweight of roofing materials, unsupported by a developed system of under-roof construction such as we see in figure 75. This would envisage a primitive type of roof in which split bamboo provided the *fig. 75* roofing material, the bamboo lengths being laid side by side from ridge-beam to eaves in the manner of rafters, the hollow inner surfaces uppermost. To seal the joints between them, a second set of bamboo lengths would be laid over them, outer or convex surfaces uppermost, so producing a completely watertight cover with rafters serving as continuous tile-gutters, readily carrying off large quantities of rain-water. Translation of the continuous bamboo tile-gutter into discontinuous short pottery lengths, or tiles, would follow at a later stage.

There is in fact evidence that split bamboo was used as a roofing material in China at least as early as Sung times; and particular reference is made, for instance, by Marco Polo, to use of split bamboo lengths acting as gutters, their inner surfaces uppermost, capped by a second set of bamboo lengths with outer or convex surfaces uppermost.[41] To safeguard such a roof against the effects of a high wind, it would be necessary to secure it in some way, perhaps by weighting it down with baulks of timber or boulders placed upon it, and this would sufficiently account for the sag.

It is a phenomenon observed of all architectural traditions that characteristic features of the primitive domestic dwelling-house, with its wattle-and-daub, its thatched roof, or whatever the material of its construction, become miraculously preserved and given permanence in the structural stone, brick, or, in the case of China, wooden, building construction of the religious or official tradition. Use of pottery tiles of rounded section, laid in doubled rows with inner and outer surfaces uppermost, whether in imitation of split bamboo lengths or no, would produce a deadweight of roofing material sufficient to cause a sag in the absence of a supporting system of under-roof construction, as was first pointed out by Silcock.[42] A conservative tradition would respect such a feature, and the next step would be to preserve and indeed enhance its effect in the forms of the official architecture by providing for it a system of supports within the roof-tree, a system which, as we have seen, was absolutely distinctive of Chinese building construction.

All this is speculation. It leaves open the question as to the form in which the curved roof was received in China, and the direction from which it came. If we are right in regarding it as in some way connected with Buddhist innovation, then the obvious source would be India; but after a five-year stay in that country I can point to nothing in the Indian architectural tradition that could be considered a possible ancestor, whether in the forms of domestic buildings, or in those of the few surviving structural temples of the sixth century AD or earlier, or as depicted in contemporary bas-relief carving or mural art. Possibly it was a form adopted by north from south China, where bamboo is still a roofing material in some parts, and possibly a south Chinese form was itself derived from a contemporary mode of construction in south-east Asia. The nineteenth-century writer Davis observes that 'the mode in which they [the Chinese] tile their roofs is evidently derived from the use of split bamboo for the same purpose as it is practised to this day by the Malays'.[43]

There we must leave a most vexed question. We are agreed, of course, that whatever the origins of the curve, the Chinese made it a form peculiarly their own, and that in developing it to the degree of elaboration found, say, on the great pagodas south of the Yangtze, they were consciously exercising a genius abundantly displayed in every department of Chinese plastic art. What we still cannot tell is how the form arose on Chinese soil in the first place.

Pagodas

pls 250–255 The word 'pagoda' is a corruption of *bhagavati*, 'divine female', the name by which the Mother-Goddess (*alias* Parvati, Devi, etc.) is known on the Malabar coast of south India. It was first applied by the Portuguese early in the sixteenth century to temples dedicated to the worship of Bhagavati, but since the towers of such temples often formed conspicuous landmarks, the word 'pagoda' gradually came to mean any prominent religious monument, not only in India but in any part of the East Indies. The region of the Canton estuary, the point of entry for European shipping to China in the early days, is thick with 'pagodas' which were systematically used by local pilots as seamarks to bring vessels through the maze of creeks and backwaters of the Pearl river up to their anchorages off Canton.

What we call 'pagoda' the Chinese know as *t'a*. The word designates a tall tower, divided into horizontal partitions marked on the outside either by pent-roofs, above which are balconies, or by simple cornices of corbelled masonry. We know that the Chinese pagoda is first and foremost a Buddhist monument; yet its early history hangs on no single thread, but raises many perplexing issues of architectural and religious derivations. These we can do little more than touch on here.[44]

It is nevertheless clear that the Chinese pagoda, in its present diversity of form, has two roots – the native Chinese and the Indian or Western. For discussion of the former we may take as starting-point an early sixth-century AD wood-built pagoda, one of many represented in bas-relief at the Yün-kang and Lung-mên caves [p. 196]. It is a four-sided storeyed tower

fig. 82f which, except for the structure at its crown, is altogether Chinese in mode of construction and architectural form. Such pagodas are, so to speak, built up of several superimposed four-sided open wooden pavilions of traditional type (*t'ing*), each slightly smaller than the one beneath; they have therefore been given the generic name *t'ing*-type. A surviving Japanese example is the five-storeyed wooden pagoda at the Hōryūji Temple, Nara, built at the beginning of the seventh century AD.

pl. 250, fig. 82a Chinese ancestry for the *t'ing*-type pagoda is demonstrated by Han pottery models of watch-towers called *t'ai*. Rectangular in plan, these comprised two or three tall storeys, each slightly smaller than the one below, with floors laid between and connected by an interior stair. Each storey was marked on the outside by a pent-roof and a balcony to which access could be gained from inside through vaulted openings.

Behind the Han watch-tower lies a long tradition of tower-building in China. Pre-Han *t'ai*, according to classical writings, were the pleasure-towers, hunting-towers, observatories, or treasuries of the feudal princes. They were a favourite cause of discontent among the populace whose labour built them, and called forth the strictures of social reformers like Mo Tzŭ for whom they exemplified the extravagance of the age. We today would probably call them 'follies'; they have long since completely disappeared.

82 The architectural origins of the Chinese pagoda: *a* Han dynasty pottery watch-tower; *b* the Great Stūpa at Sāñchī (*c.* 50 BC); *c* stūpa in the form of a reliquary casket, from Gandhāra (*c.* AD 200) in the British Museum; *d* 'Indian' pagoda from a mural at Tun-huang (fifth–sixth centuries AD); *e* pagoda from a mural at Tun-huang (same date as *d*); *f* bas-relief pagoda in Cave 2 at Yün-kang (early sixth century AD)

How did this tradition of secular tower-building in China come into association with Buddhism? For answer we must turn to India, to a Buddhist monument which, like the chapel (*chaitya*-hall) and the hall of residence (*vihāra* or *layana*), was an integral part of the monastic foundation (*mahāvihāra*) – was indeed its most sacred spot. This was the memorial burial mound called *stūpa*, built to stand over the ashes or other relics of a dead personage – in the Buddhist context, of course, over the actual bodily remains (*śarīra dhātu*) of the Buddha himself. When Buddha entered *nirvāṇa* his relics were divided among the chiefs of eight tribes, each of whom built a *stūpa* over them. But authentic relics have a way of multiplying, and no *stūpa* in India need have been without a tiny fragment of bone salvaged from the cremation of Buddha or one of his leading disciples. The *stūpa* thus came to symbolize the Buddha's *nirvāṇa*; and, at a time when images of the Buddha were not allowed to be made, it also supplied a concrete symbol of his actual person.

Had not injunctions in scriptures like Lotus of the True Law [p. 190] called upon devotees to build *stūpas* wherever Buddhism was carried, there would probably have been no Chinese pagoda at all. In the eyes of the Chinese Buddhists, the pagoda *was* a *stūpa*,

393

since it fulfilled precisely the same role as a votive and devotional symbol; nor were they aware of any disparity between Indian and Chinese forms. Moreover, everyone who has written on the subject agrees that the Indian *stūpa* did at some stage of its evolution contribute at least *some* architectural elements to the form of the pagoda. Let us examine the extent of this contribution.

fig. 82b   The Indian prototype, as represented by the Great Stūpa at Sānchī in Madhya Pradesh, comprises a brick dome, *aṇḍa*, surmounted by a square stone coffer, or *harmikā*. Above the *harmikā* rises a mast which originally bore a single royal umbrella or *chhatra* offering protection to the relics in their relic casket, buried at the bottom of a masonry shaft deep within the body of the *stūpa*. At first a single *chhatra* sufficed. In its present form the Great Stūpa has three, strung out as a series of discs along a still puny mast. The tendency was to increase the number of discs and at the same time to enhance the proportions of the mast until it fig. 82c–f   took on the appearance of a regular spire. This spire is the most constant feature of the *stūpa* and its derivatives, although since its elements are not tectonic they are liable to varying degrees of stylization.

During the first few centuries of our era, the practice of building Buddhist *stūpas* spread into north-west India; those built by Kanishka and other Kushān rulers incorporated the same elements as the Sānchī *stūpa*, but in markedly different proportions. The *stūpa* now stood on a high square base or podium serving as a terrace for circumambulation and surrounded by a typical balustrade or *stūpa* railing, while the dome, now comparatively insignificant, was elevated on a cylindrical drum often divided by string-courses into a succession of storeys of gradually diminishing size. The *harmikā* was given several courses of corbelled brickwork above, while the spire became taller and more massive so that it must have looked positively phallic. The umbrellas, increasing in number to as many as thirteen in the case of Kanishka's *stūpa* at Peshawar (according to the sixth-century Chinese pilgrim Sung-yün), were set close together so as not to interrupt the contour of the spire. As its proportions became more imposing, more towerlike, the form of the *stūpa* began to resemble that of the *śikhara* tower built over the sanctum of the Indian Brahmanical temple from the fifth century onwards [p. 396].

fig. 82c   The *stūpas* of north-west India have long since become featureless heaps of rubble; but we can get some idea of what they looked like, partly from small votive bronze models of Indian manufacture, and partly through the publicity they received in the Far East. Chinese Buddhist pilgrims have left reports of them, and they seem also to have been modelled in bronze for export from at least as early as the sixth century AD.[45] An Indian-type *stūpa* is fig. 82d   featured in one of the Tun-huang frescoes; another fresco shows something more recogniz-fig. 82e   ably like the pagoda as we know it, the *stūpa* being raised aloft on a single-storeyed open fig. 82f   pavilion of *t'ing* type. On turning once more to the Yün-kang bas-relief pagoda, we find that this is in all respects similar, except for multiplication of storeys below so that it takes on the appearance of a Han *t'ai*.

Quite why the form of the Indian-type *stūpa* was not regarded as sufficient in itself to provide the model for its Chinese counterpart is hard to say; but the accident of history had made available a native storeyed tower, which Buddhism saw fit to appropriate and convert into the distinctive *t'ing*-type pagoda. Of the original *stūpa* above, only the spire retained its true identity; below, the Chinese tower assumed triumphant proportions, and the main body of the *stūpa* dwindled to a mere vestige at the base of the spire.[46]

But this was not the end of Indian Buddhist influence on Chinese architecture. Other forms were imported, providing models for what has been called the Indian or Western

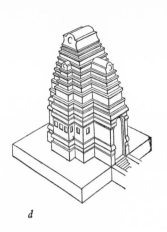

a   b   c   d   e

83 Chinese pagodas and Indian towers; *a* the Wild Goose Pagoda, Ch'ang-an (plate 251) (AD 701–705); *b* tower, probably of the Mahābodhi Temple at Bodh-Gayā, from a terracotta plaque of the second century AD; *c* the Sat Mahal Pāsāda, Polonnaruva, Ceylon (twelfth century AD); *d* restoration, partly conjectural, of the *śikhara* at Bhitagaon near Kanpur; *e* pagoda at Sung-shan, Honan (AD 523)

type of pagoda. Towers were built that were definitely *not* Chinese in inspiration; for the first and almost only time in the history of Chinese architecture, a true eclecticism seems to have been at work.

In AD 652 the project of building a huge pagoda at Ch'ang-an was mooted by no less a person than the famous Chinese pilgrim Hsüan-tsang. The circumstances attending its construction, and details of its specification, are described by his contemporary biographers as follows: 'In the third moon of the third year [AD 652] Dr Hiüan [Hsüan] wished to construct a *Fan-tu* (un Stoupa) [i.e. a *stūpa*] of stone, wherein to deposit the books and statues he had brought back from the Western countries ... This tower was to be 300 feet high, in order that it might be worthy of the Majesty of a great kingdom, and that it might become one of the finest monuments of the Buddhist religion. Before commencing it, he addressed a memorial to the Emperor, who immediately ... gave the necessary orders for carrying out the pious intentions of the Doctor, without causing him any trouble or fatigue. Each face of the tower was 140 feet in size, and *the form adopted in India was faithfully followed in its construction.* ... Its total height was 180 feet. It had five staircases, and was surmounted by a cupola.'[47]

The Wild Goose Pagoda still stands essentially as the biographers describe, despite the   *pl. 251, fig. 83a* extensive restoration of AD 701 to 705, when its original five storeys were increased to seven. Built of yellowish bricks on a mud core, the pagoda is more or less solid, although an interior staircase gives access to vaulted openings at each storey, marked externally by several rows of corbelled bricks forming a simple cornice. It is some 190 feet high.

What *was* the form adopted in India, which Hsüan-tsang so carefully followed in designing the Wild Goose Pagoda? A hint is offered by the appearance of such buildings as the shrines at Bodh-Gayā and Sārnāth, the two holiest places of Buddhism, as reconstructed from contemporary replica models and sealings. Thus a terracotta plaque found at Patna and believed to date from the second century AD shows what is apparently the tower of the Mahā-   *fig. 83b* bodhi Temple at Bodh-Gayā, brick-built and comprising five storeys of diminishing size. Each storey, except the lowest, is marked by a row of five dummy *chaitya*-arches or sun-windows beneath which is a band of *stūpa* railing, a combination which we find carved on the façades of rock-cut *chaityas* in India dating back to the second century BC. The tower is surmounted by a finial in the shape of a balustraded domical *stūpa*, with *harmikā* above, support-

395

ing a mast on which are mounted five disc-shaped honorific umbrellas; the parapet appears to have a miniature *stūpa* at each corner.

The surface treatment of the Wild Goose is a good deal more sober than this. It in fact bears a strong resemblance to the twelfth-century Sat Mahal Pāsāda forming part of the complex of Buddhist buildings at Polonnaruva in Ceylon, with seven original storeys, each stepped inwards and marked by a cornice of corbelled brick. But Hsüan-tsang himself saw the Mahābodhi shrine at Bodh-Gayā; and I think there can be no doubt but that it, or some other much like it, was the actual model he had in mind. Let us enumerate the features the two towers have in common: square on plan; built of brick in the shape of a tall, truncated pyramid; divided, originally, into five horizontal zones by string-courses of corbelled brick; the zones with niches or openings on each face serving as repositories for Buddha images. The present height of the Mahābodhi, we may note, is about 160 feet; that of the original Wild Goose was 175 feet.

It must be admitted that the history of structural architecture in India during the centuries prior to the breakthrough of Buddhism in the Far East is particularly obscure. The suggestion that towers of the Mahābodhi type were inspired by a western Asiatic prototype in the form of the well-known *ziggurat* of Mesopotamia – brick-built with battered walls, square on plan, pyramidal in form, and with seven storeys – has not been favourably received. And indeed the fact that no trace of such a building has yet been found on Indian soil, datable that is within the thousand years before the Gupta period, would seem almost to rule it out. On the other hand a type of tower closely related in architectural form to that of the Mahābodhi, namely the *śikhara* over the shrine of the Brahmanical temple, was developing during the second half of the first millennium AD and was throwing out many variant types. Echoes of some of these can I believe be detected in the forms of many Chinese pagodas of the sixth to eighth centuries. All such, like the Wild Goose, should be sharply differentiated from the native Chinese or *t'ing*-type pagoda; for while even at this early date pagodas with features intermediate between the two were being built, the Indian or Western type is distinguished absolutely from the Chinese in that it is built of brick or stone, not wood, and inasmuch as its divisions are marked by simple string-courses or cornices of brick, as opposed to pent-roofs serving to define actual storeys.

Already by the sixth century AD, Chinese pagodas were being built on a radial plan, and wood gradually gave place to brick or stone. Historically this transfiguration reflects the influence of Indian architectural form of the sort we have just discussed. Thus the celebrated pagoda built in AD 516 for the Yung-ning Temple at Lo-yang, which no longer stands but which was probably between 300 and 400 feet tall, still followed the earlier undiluted Chinese style. Nine-storeyed, it was built on a square plan and of wood, and was perhaps not unlike pagodas represented in contemporary bas-reliefs at the nearby Lung-mên caves, which in turn resemble those at Yün-kang. Very different is the conception embodied in the twelve-sided brick-built Sung-shan Pagoda, dating from only seven years later. Of this building Soper remarks[48] that it 'doubtless ... represented an exceptionally faithful reproduction of some Indian model of the contemporary Gupta style'. Its decorative detailing is clearly fashioned on the Indian mode; use of a motif resembling the *chaitya*-arch to frame a recess containing a niche is especially revealing, and so is the tightly-packed arrangement of fifteen string-courses. In general form this pagoda might be described as a sort of *pastiche* of the curvilinear type of *śikhara*, such as reached maturity at Bhubaneswar in Orissa a few centuries later. If this really is the connexion, then we may say that the Sung-shan Pagoda bears the same sort of stylistic relationship to temples of the Bhitagaon model, or to their descendants at Bhubaneswar, as does the Kew Pagoda in London to the Dragon Blossom Pagoda at Shanghai.

fig. 83d

pls 252, 253

fig. 82f
fig. 83e

fig. 83d

Inevitably, Chinese and Indian architectural forms merged, and by the end of the sixth century had fused into a new and vital synthesis. A most exquisite example, built of white stone and on a radial plan, is the six-sided pagoda on Shê-shan, Kiangsu, said to date from about AD 600.⁴⁹ Indian influence is conspicuous; yet with its five storeys strongly *pl. 254* defined by four pent-roofs and a main roof over, this pagoda speaks eloquently of descent from the native four-sided wooden storeyed tower.

Thus transfigured, the native type of pagoda began to take on an abstract and sculptural quality that asserted, so to speak, its immunity from the practical requirements of a secular architecture, and befitted its higher destiny as a symbol of the life and death of Śākyamuni Buddha. Pent-roofs, balconies, and brackets were customarily retained; but they were now treated simply as design-elements of a monument whose primary purpose was to catch the eye and direct the mind. As pagodas increased in size, the technique was adopted of building them round a solid and more or less independent masonry core that largely filled the interior space. And here again no real contradiction between form and function arose, since the building was never intended for human occupation. An aisle was left at ground level, by means of which devotees could circumambulate round images placed in niches in the core, and where they were closest to the holy relics deposited in its base. And while a staircase might usefully provide access to other ambulatories on the upper storeys, no particular purpose would have been served by making a central floor-space available at each.

We shall say no more about the forms and construction of Chinese pagodas. But a word may be added concerning their siting in larger architectural layouts; and another about the role they increasingly came to play, as the influence of Buddhism in China waned, in the life of the people at large.

The earliest formal layout of Chinese Buddhist temples was axial. The pagoda occupied a dominating position on the axis, forming a central nucleus containing also the great assembly-hall which lay to its north and which it partly hid; north again, and still on axis, was the hall containing the living quarters of the monks. Literary evidence shows that this plan was carried out in building the Ho-tung Temple, Ting-chou, Hopei, the pagoda of which was built in the early fifth century AD, and in the above-mentioned Yung-ning Temple at Lo-yang.⁵⁰

No complete Chinese example of such a layout remains today. In Korea it is represented by temple sites dating from the seventh century AD; and from Korea it passed to Japan where it survives unimpaired in the precinct of the Shitennōji Temple at Nara, belonging to the Asuka period (AD 593–644). The same elements are repeated, and in the same order – pagoda (Jap. *to*) to the south, Buddha hall (Jap. *kondō*) beyond, and living quarters (Jap. *kōdō*) to the north. In China, surviving single pagodas at the Fo-kung Temple, Ying- *pl. 253* hsien, Shansi, and at the P'u-shou Temple in Hopei, both dating from the eleventh century AD, no doubt indicate persistence of this earliest plan under the architecturally conservative Liao [p. 387] long after it had disappeared in more metropolitan areas.

By Sui or early T'ang times the supremacy of the pagoda was being challenged. A first step in its demotion was to remove it from the main axis, thus allowing an unrestricted view of the Buddha hall beyond. Still within the central precinct, it was duplicated to east and west of the main axis, and the twin pagoda plan was born. Later, the twin pagodas were uprooted from the main enclosure and given separate precincts of their own outside. Numbers of twin pagodas still stand in China, particularly in the South where they seem to represent the second great architectural backwater to which we have referred [p. 385]. Those of the Shuang-t'a

(Twin Pagoda) Temple near Suchow, for instance, were first built as late as AD 982. They stand close together, and so were probably originally enclosed in the precinct of the main Buddha hall, remains of which lie some fifty yards behind them on the south–north axis.

A last attempt to integrate the pagoda in the temple plan was to restore it to the main precinct, but relegating it to the rear of the Buddha hall, or to a site well off the main axis. As Soper remarks, in such cases the pagoda seems to have been built long after the first completion of the temple as a whole. In Japan this last move was never made. In China, it is represented by many surviving Liao and Chin dynasty pagodas in the north. Finally, as Buddhism lost its hold on China, the pagoda dissociated itself entirely from the Buddhist temple property, and even from the religion itself. Its meaning was forgotten. China, 'the sea that salts all rivers', appropriated the monument to her own purposes; for several centuries past the pagoda has stood primarily as a tutelary deity and as a venue for local popular festivities – functions equally unconnected with the religion to which it owed its origin.

To a landscape already essentially humanized, pagodas add their own dignity and charm. Freed from the restricting influence of the formal plan, their placing often proved an inspired act of artistic foresight, although in theory determined only by the exigencies of the *fêng shui* system.[51] Much might be written about the local legends that have gathered around them, and especially of the ways in which they were thought to exercise their beneficial influence. Since the shape of the Yangtze port of An-ching resembled a junk, for instance, the fancy arose that the great pagoda there was its mast. To this day two enormous anchors hang on its walls, their original purpose having been to prevent the city from drifting away downstream – in other words to give it magical protection against flood. The inhabitants of the city of Ch'üan-chou had long been the victims of depredation by the people of a nearby town; since Ch'üan-chou was shaped like a carp, and the neighbouring town like a fishing-net, who could have expected things to have been otherwise? Building the twin pagodas saved the situation for Ch'üan-chou, since the hypothetical fishing-net could now no longer be trawled over the heads of its inhabitants.

Something of the latter-day significance of pagodas as tutelary deities in Chinese eyes is, I think, brought out by a proclamation made at Macao in the year 1821. It runs as follows: 'The Chinese and Foreign merchants have hitherto been prosperous, their wealth abounding, and the destinies of the place altogether felicitous. Of late, however, its fortunes have waxed lean, and the influence of the atmosphere has been unlucky, so that the acquisition of riches has become less certain. A proposal is accordingly made to erect a pagoda, in order to renovate and improve the commercial fortunes of the island on which Macao lies. ... He [the architect] declares that a high Pagoda should be built on the eastern arm of "Monkey island", and affirms that prosperity and riches will be the result, and that both Chinese and Foreigners at Macao will share in the felicity.'[52] Impressed by these arguments, the Portuguese Resident Magistrate apparently donated the sum of one hundred dollars towards the project, but the pagoda was never built.

pl. 255

P'ai-lou

pls 256, 257; col. 55

Commemorative in function, these arches were often built to celebrate the virtue of a widow in not remarrying, or to stand at the entrance to a processional way leading to a palace or tomb. By a sort of architectural convergence, the form comes closely to resemble that of the *torana*, or monumental gate-way such as adorned the first- and second-century BC

Buddhist *stūpas* at Sāñchī and Bhārhūt in India, and no historical connexion between the two need be mooted.

P'ai-lou are almost always built of stone, in close imitation of a wooden prototype and with carpentry technique. They have one, three, or five openings. The square-section pillars stand on long transverse stone plinths and are buttressed by means of ornamental brackets on either side, often carved into animal forms or 'cloud pattern'. Where round-section wood pillars are used, these are set in tall stone bases. Stone beams, usually either elaborately carved or bearing inscriptions, are tenoned through the upper sides of the pillars at varying heights, forming a pattern that is symmetrical about the centre line. Sometimes these beams are stayed by means of stone brackets set in the pillars. Carved stone slabs set in the bays between the lintels help to give the structure sideways rigidity. Above the topmost lintel of each bay stand rows of stone brackets, exactly imitating wooden prototypes, and serving to support miniature tiles or stone roofs hipped into exotic shapes. As has been pointed out, the ubiquitous staggering of lintels and roofs at varying levels above each opening gives to the line of the roofs a stepped appearance, and creates a rather restless, Baroque, effect.

Bridges

No news brought by Marco Polo out of Tartary more strained the credulity of his Venetian audience than that of the 12,000 bridges of Hangchow. Exaggerated though it no doubt was, the number may yet have run into thousands; for China – and particularly the great delta plain of the Yangtze on the edge of which Hangchow stands – offers every incentive to the bridge-builder. Throughout eastern China, the countryside is a regular maze of traffic- and irrigation-canals, creeks, and ditches, amounting in parts to twenty-six miles of waterway per square mile of cultivated land. The topography of the south-west, where rivers run in deep and precipitous gorges, presents pressing problems of bridge-building. And while in the north-west waterways are fewer and bridges less in evidence than elsewhere, great rivers such as the Wei and Yellow River have still to be crossed in the course of north-south road and rail communication. A cautious estimate is that there may be some 2,500,000 bridges of every sort and size in China today.[53]

Chinese bridges belong to five constructional types – the pontoon, girder, cantilever, arch, and suspension. The pontoon, whether temporary or for seasonal use only, is probably as ancient as any, since the idea of it would have arisen naturally from that of the ferry. Pontoon bridges were known to Confucius, and a few are still to be found in China today; but they hardly come into the category of architecture, and we need say no more about them here. Of the four others, cantilever and suspension bridges are typical of the west and south-west; the south-east has a unique and splendid tradition of stone beam bridge-building; and in the east and north-east stone arch bridges predominate. There are thus three great regional centres of bridge-building in China. But whereas that of the south-west developed more or less in isolation, the stone arch and beam traditions of eastern China have mingled throughout history, while sharing features derived ultimately from a primitive type of wood beam bridge that has existed from time immemorial in China. Notwithstanding inevitable differences in mechanical construction, therefore, the stone beam and arch bridges of China show similarities of architectural form, made more pronounced by use of distinctive masonry techniques. In their beautiful and noble shapes a lasting unity of engineering design and aesthetic expression has been arrived at. Indeed, they are the finest achievements of monumental stone construction in China.

pls 258–263

399

fig. 84

Where rivers run in deep gorges, or where for any other reason intermediate piers cannot be erected, cantilever and suspension bridges come into their own. In China, cantilever bridges are built with single spans up to 130 feet or so, and suspension bridges with larger spans up to 300 feet. Both are built largely of wood, and both are typical of the well-forested and ravinous hill-country of the south-west. In their more elaborate forms cantilever bridges are given masonry abutments and rest-houses at each bank; a bridge-deck of transverse planks is usually laid on top of the wood girders that form the truss, and a horizontal hand-rail runs along each side, supported at intervals by vertical posts. Posts may also support a continuous tiled roof overhead, or protective bamboo matting hung above the hand-rails.

The Chinese suspension bridge, which is restricted almost entirely to the south-west[54], probably evolved from the single-rope bridge which the traveller crosses in a basket or some similar contraption attached to the rope by a wooden ring. Bamboo cable, the breaking stress of which is something like 26,000 lb. per square inch, is the obvious material for this type of bridge, its only disadvantage being that it rots quickly in the humid air, necessitating frequent replacements. As soon as iron became available, therefore, iron chains began to be used in place of bamboo cables.

pl. 259

Use of iron for bridge-building came to China from India, perhaps during that vital period of cultural acquisition, the seventh century AD, and the idea of spanning deep gorges by means of suspended cables may also have originally reached China from India. But the principles of construction of Chinese and Indian suspension bridges are totally dissimilar. In the Chinese type, between six and twelve main cables span the gorge side by side, being tightened and kept more or less uniformly taut by means of rotary capstans built into bridge-houses at each end. The cables are pegged together sideways, and over them are laid transverse planks forming the bridge-deck; other cables hang above the deck on either side to act as handrails. In this type of bridge, then, the main cables form the foundation of the bridge-deck, and are therefore kept as taut as possible. In the true suspension bridge of the Himalayas, by contrast, the deck hangs suspended from two slack main cables which carry it by means of vertical rope slings or iron chains.[56]

In the vicinity of Ch'ang-an may be seen one or two massive continuous stone beam bridges that probably represent a primitive tradition of bridge-building in the north-west going back to well before Han times.[57] Such bridges are perennial; the elementary post-and-beam principle they incorporate is likely to be applied, under suitable conditions, at any time or place where steel has not made traditional methods of bridge-construction obsolete. Their utility is limited by the fact that intermediate piers have to be built, their number depending on the width to be spanned and the maximum length of the stone beams forming the spans; piers obstruct the waterway, while their construction seldom allows for any considerable free height for passage of boats underneath the bridge.

fig. 84b

In Fukien a number of stone beam bridges were built during the Southern Sung period, of a scale unknown anywhere else in the world. Continuous up to nearly 4,000 feet in one case, and with intermediate boat-shaped piers whose tops are slightly cantilevered out, these bridges have as many as forty-seven spans. But the really impressive thing about them is the colossal size of their granite beams, which are megaliths measuring up to 70 feet in length and weighing as much as 200 tons; each span comprises three such beams laid side by side. It is difficult to imagine how such huge stones were ever got into place, but easy to see that the secret of cutting and laying them died not long after the bridges were first built.

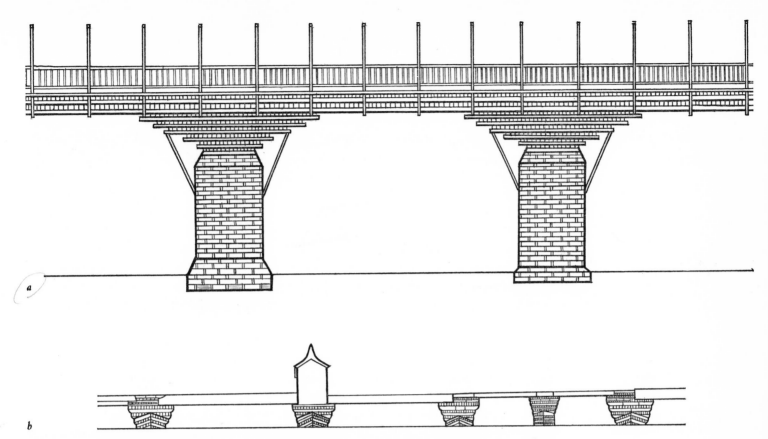

84 *a* part of a continuous cantilever bridge at Li-ling-hsien, Hunan; *b* part of the Poh-lam Bridge, Amoy, Fukien. Distance between the mid-points of piers: *a c.* 70 feet; *b c.* 85 feet

For when the spans failed, as occasionally happened[58], later builders were unable to replace them and were forced to construct secondary intermediate piers spanned by shorter beams.

The ordinary stone beam bridge of eastern China is a much more modest affair, imitating in its design a wood beam bridge of standard form and great antiquity such as appears several times on Han bas-reliefs. A typical modern wood beam bridge is shown in figure 85 a. *fig. 85a* Its flat central section is flanked by ramps leading up over the side spans and continuing down over masonry abutments that fit their backs to the river-bank at each side and are retained there by means of wooden piles. Poles driven into the river bed in pairs act as intermediate piers. Cross-pieces with projecting ends are inserted into their tops, serving as stays for the wooden beams forming the spans, and as bases into which are socketed vertical posts supporting a horizontal hand-rail along each side. Over the beams are laid short transverse staves or planks, and on top of them a clay sheathing makes the actual deck. Needless to say, such constructions are not very lasting. The deck is liable to rot below its clay surface, and so are the supporting poles at points a few feet above low water.

But the model takes permanent shape when reproduced in stone. How literal such translations are, can be seen by comparing the stone beam foot-bridge of figure 85 b with its *fig. 85b* wood prototype. The cross-pieces, by which the vertical slabs forming the piers are assembled, project outwards on both sides exactly as do those of the wood beam bridge. And the stone slabs that form the spans are mortised together by an ordinary carpentry technique; mortar was rarely used and hydraulic mortar never, according to Fugl-Meyer, in traditional Chinese masonry.

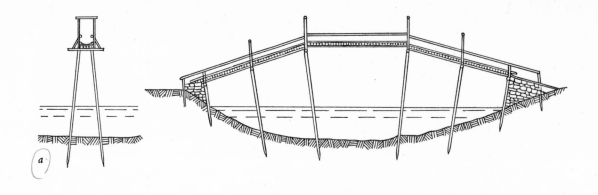

85 *a* wood beam bridge of traditional type; *b* stone beam bridge

This particular design, charming in its simplicity, is executed in single spans up to about twenty feet, and with a free height above the waterway of some six feet. Abutments with masonry retaining-walls are laid back to the banks – as in the wood prototype – and carry ramps which are wider at the land ends and narrower where they enter the bridge, the two sides of which run parallel. The ramps slope with a rise of as much as one in two and a half, and in consequence are usually stepped. Such bridges are, of course, quite useless for wheeled traffic, for which they were never intended; heavy goods were transported by water rather than by road.

ARCH BRIDGES The stone arch bridge represents the culmination of the art of bridge-building in China, but we cannot say exactly when the tradition was inaugurated or whence it came. The typical form, with semicircular arch-opening, is so distinctively Chinese, and incorporates such unusual engineering features, that we may be sure the main development took place in China itself, though the principle of true arch construction may perhaps have found its way in from western Asia. If so, this must have happened not later than the first few centuries AD.

Most Chinese stone arch bridges have single spans of up to some thirty feet, and with about the same free height above the waterway. Usually they are built with semicircular arch-openings, but the two-centred or Gothic arch is occasionally met with; and, rarely, the segmental arch. Other odd-number spans up to nine are quite common, the centre span over the middle of the water being of larger dimensions than those at the sides; sometimes there are many more – the celebrated Pao-tai ('Precious Belt') on Lake T'ai in Kiangsu, for *pl. 262* example, has fifty-three.

fig. 86 Figure 86 shows a typical example of the arch bridge with semicircular opening; it shows, too, the three constructional features that render these bridges unique among the arch bridges

402

of the world. First is the arch-shell itself. In the western provinces of China arch bridges are to be found with radiating voussoirs of conventional type – arch-stones, that is, with their long axis lying radially with respect to the centre of the arch-opening. But the shells of most Chinese arch bridges are built of thin slabs, cut slightly in curves to fit the curvature of the arch, and set with their long axis lying along its perimeter.

The arch is a flexible chain. Arch-stones are cut so as to fit closely together; but in the absence of mortar, they are held in place only by the pressure they exert on one another, although they may also be linked together by means of double dove-tailed iron keys socketed into their ends exactly in the manner of a linked chain. So far from being a disadvantage, this flexibility allows the arch to distort freely under pressure put on various parts of the shell, without actually collapsing. Within limits, the arch will take up any shape required of it. As a rule the arch-shell comprises only a single thickness of these deceptively fragile-looking slabs, but in the case of wide spans two thicknesses may be used. Even so the shell is still surprisingly thin, its depth varying between a thirtieth and a fortieth of the span – proportions which compare favourably, it has been said, with those of modern Western reinforced concrete shells.

The second distinctive feature of the Chinese stone arch bridge lies in the construction of the long abutments on either side of the arch-opening beneath the ramped part of the deck. For economy's sake masonry is used only for retaining walls on the two faces of the bridge, the space between them being filled with rammed clay and stone chips. To give stability to this fill, binder-stones are run deep into it from the side walls. Thus each course of masonry consists of alternate stretchers and binders, the latter lying with their short end-faces in the surface plane of the wall, each being slightly dove-tailed into the stretchers on either side of it.

The third and perhaps most interesting constructional feature is a vertical masonry wall built through the abutments on either side of the arch-opening. The design of this 'shear-wall' closely resembles that of the intermediate piers of traditional stone beam bridges such as that of figure 85b, the vertical slabs comprising them being assembled at the top, and *fig. 85b* sometimes below, by means of transverse beams with projecting ends. Indeed, persistence of this and other tectonic elements in the form of the stone arch bridge allows us to visualize it *pl. 258* simply as a stone beam bridge wherein the span has been replaced by an arch, and emphasizes an underlying unity in the stone bridge-building tradition.

The shear walls serve to isolate the arch mechanically from the ramps on either side of it. Figure 86 shows that the foundations provided for this type of bridge are deeper beneath *fig. 86* the channel arch, where they have to support the vertical downward thrust of the arch and its load, and shallower towards the landward sides of the bridge. It was to counteract the effect upon the arch-shell of more rapid settling on the landward side that the shear wall was designed. Without it the forces of settlement would be transmitted to the arch. Were the latter built rigid it would collapse; being a flexible chain, the effect of such forces would simply be to deform it. The intervention of shear-walls, however, usually prevented the forces of distortion from ever reaching the actual arch.

The whole construction of the arch-bridge is thus a neat illustration of the principle of flexibility, or relative mechanical independence of a building from its foundations, or of one part from another, which we noticed in the case of the hall [see p. 383], and which in a broader sense underlies the whole architectural tradition [p. 362].

Pains were often spent on the decorative detailing of these bridges, and particularly on parapets carved in the traditional patterns of marble balustrades and adorned with sculptured figures of *ch'i-lin* [p. 156] on their portals. An account of such a bridge by Marco Polo

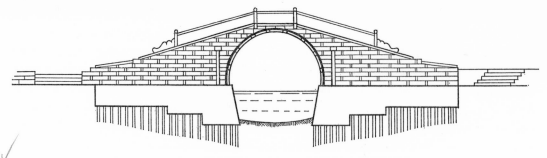

86 Elevation of a single-span stone arch bridge (the foundations shown in sectional view)

pl. 260

probably refers to the original of one still standing over the Hun river some seven miles west of Peking, that known to the Chinese as the Lo-ku Ch'iao, and to Europeans as the Marco Polo Bridge. It is well named; for Marco's description of its general character and decorative detailing is remarkably accurate, despite an error, probably produced by confusing in his mind one bridge with another, as to the number of its arches. 'Over this river [the Hun] there is a very handsome bridge of stone', he writes, 'perhaps unequalled by another in the world. Its length is three hundred paces, and its width eight paces; so that ten men can, without inconvenience, ride abreast. It has twenty-four arches, supported by twenty-five piers erected in the water, all of serpentine stone, and built with great skill. On each side, and from one extremity to the other, there is a handsome parapet, formed of marble slabs and pillars arranged in masterly style. At the commencement of the ascent the bridge is something wider than at the summit, but from the part where the ascent terminates, the sides run in straight lines and parallel to each other ... all the spaces between one pillar and another, throughout the whole length of the bridge, are filled up with slabs of marble, curiously sculptured, and mortised into the next adjoining pillars, which are ... surmounted with lions,

pl. 261

forming altogether a beautiful spectacle. These parapets serve to prevent accidents that might otherwise happen to passengers.'[59]

fig. 87

We can hardly leave the subject of Chinese stone arch bridges without some mention of the venerable Ta-shih Ch'iao, Great Stone Bridge, in Chao-hsien, Hopei. Built during the Sui period (AD 589–618), this bridge stands witness to the engineering genius of its age and of its architect Li Chun. From the point of view of utility there is everything to be said in favour of the single span segmental arch bridge, as against one comprising several spans with round arches and intermediate piers. For one thing, a single span leaves the waterway entirely clear for traffic. For another, intermediate piers are liable to the scouring action of the current; while in time of flood, debris may block the arches and floodwater pile up against the masonry of the bridge, causing it to collapse. Moreover, a flat arch leads more easily to a flat bridge-deck, and involves far less expenditure of building materials.

On the other hand, the constructional difficulties attached to building a single-span seg-mental arch bridge are forbidding. For the flatter the arch, the greater the outward thrust of its haunches. To resist this thrust, and so keep the arch from sliding out, bridge abutments are made solid and unyielding. So long as the arch is in position, the thrust gets transmitted to its weakest point, the crown, which has to withstand an enormous pressure exerted on it from both sides, equivalent to almost the whole system of forces set up by the arch; the danger is that the bridge may crumble or split upwards at this vital point. It is evident that any dead weight placed on a flat arch will increase the pressure at its crown, and corres-pondingly that the pressure will be relieved if such a weight is removed. In constructing such a bridge, therefore, the aim will be to lighten the weight of materials in the spandrels over the haunches to an absolute minimum, while retaining a relatively flat deck.

Successive attempts made by the eighteenth-century engineer Edwards to construct a stone arch bridge over the river at Pontypridd in Wales perfectly illustrate the difficulties we have been discussing. His first, a three-span structure with round arch-openings, collapsed when flood debris choked the arches and floodwater, unable to escape, rose above the level of the parapets. To ensure a free waterway, Edwards now built a single-span flat-arch bridge. This, too, failed; the dead weight of masonry in the spandrels above the haunches exerted too much pressure on the crown, and the arch collapsed upwards. His third, built in 1746, embodied a revolutionary principle. By boring three tunnels through the spandrels on each side, he was able to reduce the dead weight of the bridge by ninety-six tons and still allow for a relatively flat deck. The bridge, lightened but not weakened, is still standing today.

Revolutionary in Europe – but the principle was being applied in China well over 1,000 years earlier. Li Chun's bridge, so reminiscent in form of ferro-concrete bridges built during the present century by the Swiss architect Robert Maillart, has two pairs of subsidiary arch-openings above the main arch, on this same 'open spandrel' principle. The arch is stabilized, and materials saved, while at the same time the smaller arches serve the subsidiary purpose of acting as spillways for floodwater; that this was so in the case of the Great Stone Bridge is proved by the water-marks still to be seen on their walls.

To appreciate to the full the miraculous engineering of the Great Stone Bridge, we must envisage a single channel-arch, a flexible chain thrown like a rainbow across a gap of 123 feet, yet rising no more than twenty-three feet from abutments to crown, while the deck is almost horizontal. The span in itself is impressive enough; but the ratio of rise to span is phenomenally low for a masonry arch, judged even by modern standards.[60] Taken all in all, the Great Stone Bridge, which is now being thoroughly renovated, must be reckoned one of the most impressive in the world.

87 The Great Stone Bridge in Chao-hsien, Hopei province (sixth century AD)

POSTSCRIPT: ARCHITECTURE IN MODERN CHINA

pl. 264   We may suitably end this book on Chinese art with a brief account of architecture in pre-sent-day China; for recent developments in Chinese architecture throw light on what is happening, and what may be expected to happen, to other Chinese art-forms for which counterparts exist in the West. Western cultural influences have of course been invading China for hundreds of years. But not until 1911, the year of the republican revolution, was their existence officially recognized and some attempt started to absorb them into the frame-work of national life. The moment was bound to arrive; for it had been an article of faith among bureaucratic and *bourgeois* reformist elements in Chinese politics, ever since the late nineteenth-century reform movement of K'ang Yu-wei, that Westernization and social reform went hand in hand. Thus the idea of China forever embalmed in her own past, if it were ever true at all, has certainly been invalid for the last fifty years.

The first examples of 'foreign-style' architecture were closely modelled on Western build-ings already standing in China, most of which were of the heterogeneous order politely labelled Eclectic. The extent to which China had lapsed into 'colonial' status *vis-à-vis* the Foreign Powers, psychologically as well as politically, can be measured by the spread of this sort of architecture from modern Western built commercial centres like Shanghai, where it was at least to be expected, to traditional Chinese cities like Nanking and Hangchow. The Lecture Hall of Nanking University is a fair sample. Eulogized in the guide-book as 'a magnificent piece of modern architecture', it incorporates an eighteenth-century façade with attached Classical portico, backed by a squat eight-sided dome, in best Corn Exchange style; the National Government buildings in the same city are no less ludicrous. Fortunately for China, the subservient spirit and intellectual poverty manifested by such buildings is so dead that there seems no possibility of its ever being resurrected.

The wave of nationalist sentiment that followed on the revolutionary struggles of the Kuomintang during the early 'twenties washed up a new national style in architecture com-monly known as Chinese Renaissance. A lead had already been provided by the enter-prise of foreign missionaries, who sinified their Western style mission hospitals and college buildings by decking them with superficial Chinese features and so advertised the fact that Chinese, too, were numbered among Protestantism's far-flung dominion; much as Com-monwealth subjects wear the picturesque headgear of their respective homelands when serving in the British Army or attending a Scout Jamboree. Typical examples of 'Missionary Renaissance' are Ginling College, Nanking; the Peking Union Medical College and Library; and the buildings of Yenching University, Peking.

Realization of a historical style such as Chinese Renaissance should theoretically have depended on careful mating of traditional Chinese architectural form with modern materials and techniques, and have drawn on the combined experience of practical builders and historians of architecture. In practice its sponsors were content with very much less. Chinese design-elements were crudely grafted on to buildings whose construction and form remained inflexibly Western. Neither East nor West could make the least concession to the other; and the result was a half-baked architecture which Liang Ssŭ-ch'êng dismisses as 'nothing but foreign buildings with Chinese roofs put on'.

By 1925 Chinese Renaissance had acquired the status of an official architecture. In that year the conditions of entry for an open competition, held to select a design for the National University Library, Peking, stipulated that the building should be in the so-called 'palace style', the purest manifestation of Chinese Renaissance. The successful design is in fact a moderately satisfactory academic essay, although it gains nothing by intrusion of a conspicuous Western-style doorway into a façade otherwise unexceptionably Chinese. But results generally were bad. For instance, the Municipal Government Building at Shanghai, built in 1930, is designed to feature the three main elements of the traditional Chinese elevation – platform, main storey, and curved roof. But the platform is a sham; for although a stairway gives access to a terrace enclosed by a balustrade of traditional design above, windowing below reveals that it is simply a Western-type ground floor in disguise.

The Sun Yat-sen Memorial on Purple Mountain outside Nanking is another typical *mésalliance*. Superficially this is a Chinese design, following the general layout of the nearby Ming tombs, and incorporating traditional features such as memorial pillars and half-hipped sagged roofs. But massive masonry stairs and foundations artlessly wedged into the hillside, and the formal triumphal avenue of decidedly Western character by which it is approached, contrive to give it an obtrusive monumentality entirely out of keeping with the true spirit of Chinese architecture. The main building, the Hall of the Mausoleum, is altogether uninflected with respect to other parts of the design, while its own oddly distorted proportions make it look like a caricature of a Chinese building – 'as tawdry as a music-hall Mandarin', as Charles Chen remarks of a similar contemporary design in the same style.[61] The shadow of San Francisco, not to say Hollywood, lies heavy on this pretentious, fussy, and fundamentally bogus design.

The ideological outlook which gave birth to Chinese Renaissance was reactionary and unsound. Arguments put forward in favour of adopting it as the style for the Shanghai Civic Centre (1930), at once aggressive and apologetic, are typical of the 'colonial' mentality of the period. It was said that a national style would help to foster a national (i.e. anti-foreign) spirit. At the same time it was suggested that any attempt to build Western-style multi-storey fabrics capable of challenging the Western-built commercial skyscrapers of Shanghai would make its sponsors a laughing-stock, and would in any case be foredoomed to failure because of shortage of funds. The one positive reason for imparting a definitely historical character to official Chinese architecture – that the tradition was a fine one and should by all means be perpetuated so long as it could be adapted to modern materials and techniques – was never stated. The Shanghai ensemble perfectly symbolizes in its incoherent layout the indecisive mentality that lay behind it.

During all these years, and especially after the resumption of Sino-Japanese hostilities in 1937, political and economic chaos in China made planned architectural development impossible. When in 1949 a strong central government at last came into power, the situation changed completely. Municipal planning commissions, set up under the authority of the Ministry of Buildings, quickly got to work in all the major cities. While these boards are inevitably mainly concerned with immediate and large-scale public works such as housing, factories, schools, hospitals, public utilities, and town-planning generally, the question of evolving a new national style in architecture is also being discussed with intense seriousness. Under the tutorship of outstanding scholars like Liang Ssǔ-ch'êng, architectural students are receiving a thorough grounding in the history of Chinese architecture as part of their basic education. If it is decided to reinstate Chinese Renaissance in some form as a style for public buildings, there is good guarantee that the puerilities of its first phase will be avoided.

407

The situation is made more complicated by the presence of two potentially very powerful influences recently arrived from abroad. One is the Soviet-Classic style emanating from Russia; the other is the International style, whose leading exponents are today mostly in America. The former seems at the moment to be represented only by the Soviet Exhibition Centre in the western suburbs outside Peking (1954), although a recent proposal to erect a series of tall towers at various points in the capital was no doubt inspired by the Kremlin-style towers that have so radically altered the townscape of modern Moscow. The International style, on the other hand, is already implanted on Chinese soil in the form of modern Western multi-storey buildings at Shanghai and the Yangtze ports. It may be hoped that this type of building, with its intrinsic freedom from ideological content despite its present political associations, may provide the raw material for a new national architecture that is still recognizably Chinese. The decision to build the eight-storey 'Peace Hotel' (1952) in International style is perhaps an indication that Chinese architects do recognize its essentially international character. The Hotel was not an unqualified success. As R. T. F. Skinner says, it 'has been justly criticized for rearing its imperfectly organized slab forms ... eight storeys high and rudely challenging the palaces and gate-houses'.[62]

Undoubtedly one result of assimilating either foreign style will be to cause Chinese architects to build high, and so make an end to the age-old tradition of low building in urban China. This may not prove to be the case with Peking, where the Planning Board has decreed that no building is to be more than nine storeys high, but in other major industrial centres it is inevitable. In that case the tiled roof, the most conspicuous single design-element hitherto, will probably have to go and a flat roof take its place. One of the most successful examples of Chinese Renaissance to date, the seven-storey Chung Shan Hospital at Shanghai (1937), has its walls battered and terraced inwards, so that the width diminishes at each storey, the topmost being covered by a relatively inconspicuous tiled roof. In a provocative article wherein he speaks of Chinese Renaissance during the 'twenties as 'pigtail' architecture – the tiled roof being the pigtail – Chuin Tung observes that precisely this combination of tiled roof and terraced sides is typical of buildings in the borderlands of China, for example Tibet and Inner Mongolia.[63] Yet such buildings nevertheless retain an unmistakably Chinese character. The tiled roof, in other words, is expendable; if Chinese architecture is to retain a national character, reliance must be placed rather on the fact, noticed above, that the basic principles of Chinese architectural planning and building construction are entirely compatible with use of modern materials and techniques.

The prospect is no less uncertain in the cases of art-forms other than architecture, especially perhaps those of graphic art and sculpture. The immediate future is bound to be determined largely by the course of political events with which the art historian is not directly concerned. The long-term future of Chinese art will in any case be decided by a third factor – the growing confidence that the Chinese repose in their own artistic inheritance, and in their civilization as embodying a distinctive, self-contained, and near-ideal social order. Their task is now to acquire technical and scientific equality with the West without losing hold of this inheritance of beautiful and biologically successful living, accumulated over so many generations. In the past they have never failed to assimilate foreign influences and revitalize their own tradition thereby. What they now have to do may prove to be more painful and protracted than ever before, and if we in the West are to play a full part in the critical history of our times, it is up to us to try to understand the nature of the situation that China is facing in every department of her national life, and to watch and work in expectation of a happy outcome.

227 Town in Shensi showing, from its centre, one-quarter of an axial town plan and the courtyard modular. See page 364.

228 Street in Peking, showing axial residential street, or corridor of houses.

THE TEMPLE OF HEAVEN, PEKING

230 The Temple of Heaven ensemble from the air looking north. See page 375.

231 (right above) The Hall for Prayers for an Abundant Harvest, Ch'i-nien Tien, housing the Altar where Prayer for Grain is Offered, Ch'i-ku T'an, at the end of the Temple of Heaven ensemble; view looking north.

232 (right centre) The Imperial Lofty Throne, Huang-ch'iung Yü. The middle of the Temple of Heaven ensemble; view looking north.

233 (right below) The Altar of Heaven, T'ien T'an, at the south end of the Temple of Heaven ensemble, Peking. The southern entrance; view looking north.

opposite page

229 Peking from the air: view looking south. See pages 374–375.

234 Wu Mên, the southern entrance to the former Forbidden City, Peking; view
looking north. See page 376.

235 The Three Great Halls, San Ta Tien, in the former Forbidden City, Peking; view looking south. See page 377, plates 238–240, and colour plate 58.

opposite page

236 (above) T'ai-ho Mên, interior, showing
columnar bracketing and coffered and painted
ceilings.

237 (below) T'ai-ho Mên, the right end bay
of the south façade showing painted and carved
decorative detailing.

238 Courtyard of T'ai-ho Mên, in the former Forbidden City, Peking, showing the marble conduit through which flows the Chin Shui Ho, River of Golden Water; view looking east.

239 T'ai-ho Mên; view looking north across the Chin Shui Ho. See page 376.

opposite page

240 T'ai-ho Tien (1627), showing marble balustrades leading up to the Dragon Pavement, platform of the Three Great Halls [see also col. 58]; view looking west. See page 377.

THE CHINESE TOWN
GARDEN

241 Rocks in the Shih-tzŭ Lin (Lion Grove), Suchow, Kiangsu. See page 379.

242 (far right) Part of the Shih-tzŭ Lin.

243 Shih-tzŭ Lin, two parts of a landscape scroll in ink on paper by Ni Tsan (1301–1374), painted in 1373. The place was then a sort of Buddhist retreat. Ni Tsan had himself built a garden elsewhere in Suchow. The present whereabouts and dimensions of this painting are unknown.

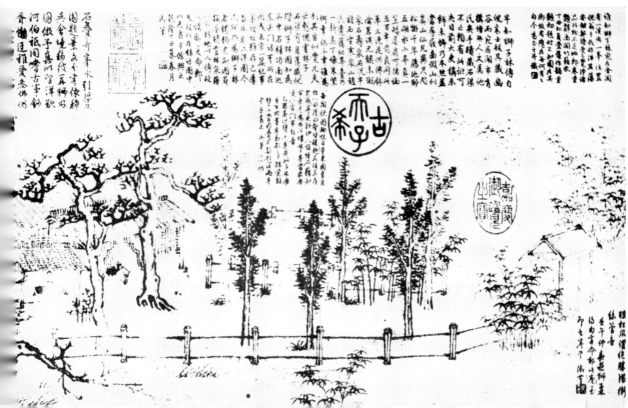

244 Window at Liu Yüan ('Lingering Garden'), Suchow, Kiangsu.

245 The Liu Yüan (sixteenth century). See pages 379–380.

opposite page

246 K'un-ming Lake, with its seventeen-arch bridge (1755) connecting the shore with an island. View looking south [see also col. 55].

247 (below) The covered gallery, *lang*, on the K'un-ming Lake shore (nineteenth century).

THE CURVED ROOF
AND ITS
BRACKETING-
SYSTEM

248 (above) Hall of the Fo-kuang ssŭ, Wu-t'ai-shan, Shansi (AD 857), showing eaves and bracketing-system. This is the oldest known surviving wooden building in China. See page 389.

249 (right) The Drum Tower, Ch'ang-an (= Sian), with the Bell Tower in the background.

Above from left to right

250 Pottery watch-tower, Han dynasty. See page 393. Height: 34 in. British Museum.

251 The Ta-yen T'a, Great Wild Goose Pagoda, at Ch'ang-an (= Sian). Built at the behest of the Chinese pilgrim Hsüan-tsang in AD 652. In its present state it dates from AD 701-705. See pages 395-396.

252 Brick pagoda of the Hsing-chiao Ssŭ near Ch'ang-an (= Sian). Built about AD 669 to receive the remains of the pilgrim Hsüan-tsang. Rebuilt AD 828.

253 Octagonal wooden pagoda of the Fo-kung Ssŭ at Ying-hsien, Shansi. See page 397. Liao dynasty (AD 1058).

254 The Marble Pagoda, with the Jade Pagoda behind it, Western Hills near Peking. It is an eighteenth-century paraphrase of the Shê-shan pagoda built in AD 600 [see p. 397].

5 The Great Pagoda at An-ching, Anhwei. See page 398.

MEMORIAL ARCHES (P'AI-LOU)

256 Memorial Arch, *p'ai-lou,* at the entrance to the tomb of the Ming Emperor Yung-lo (1403–1424), outside Peking. Marble, with blue-glazed tiled roofs. Built 1522–1566 [See also col. 55].

257 (left) Memorial Arch, *p'ai-lou,* at Suchow, Kiangsu.

BRIDGE

opposite p

258 (above) The Yin-shan bridge over the Grand Canal near Sucho Kiangsu. See page 403.

259 (below) Suspension bridge over the Mekong river, Yunnan. S page 400.

260 (above) The Lo-ku Ch'iao or Marco Polo Bridge over the Hun river near Peking. See pages 403–404.

261 (left) Lion on pillar of Lo-ku Ch'iao. See page 403.

opposite page

262 (above) The Pao-t'ai (Precious belt) Bridge across part of Lake T'ai near Suchow, Kiangsu. See page 402. This bridge has fifty-three arches. Note the protecting pagoda built against one of the piers at the far end.

263 (below) The Pao-t'ai (Precious belt) Bridge. Carved flanking lions at the bridgehead.

264 Government Offices, Peking.

The full titles of the works mentioned are given in the relevant chapter section or the general section of the bibliography

INTRODUCTION

1 Bushell, 1904
2 For reasons that will be discussed later [pp. 307–8] these two will be treated as a single art-form.
3 Binyon *et al.*, 1935, p. 1

CHAPTER I

1 Cressey, 1934
2 P'ei Wên-chung, 1957
3 Andersson, 1934
4 Brodrick, 1948, p. 116
5 A recent find of rock paintings in the far South, in Kwangsi province, has yet to be evaluated, but Chinese scholars do not see any connexion between this gallery, attributed to the minority people called Chuang, and the classical culture of north China.
6 Wu, G.D., 1938
7 Hsia Nai, 1956
8 Chêng Tê-k'un, 1959, p. 84
9 Watson, 1961, pp. 46–7
10 Kaplan, 1948–9
11 Sullivan, 1961, pp. 31–2 and 61

CHAPTER II

1 Yüan K'ang (ed.), 1926–36, p. 93 b
2 Andersson, 1943, p. 261
3 Our word 'jade' seems to be derived from the Spanish *piedra de ijada*, 'stone of the loin', so called because the Spaniards came across jade, or rather jadeite, being worn in America in the form of amulets giving protection against kidney diseases. Our word 'nephrite', for true jade, incorporates this belief in jade as a cure for nephritic disorders.
4 Hansford, 1950
5 Translated in Hansford, 1950, p. 31
6 Hansford, 1950, p. 90
7 Haloun, 1937
8 Bergman, 1939, pp. 13–37
9 Ramsden, 1940, p. 21
10 Translated by Biot, 1851
11 Wu Ta-ch'êng, 1889, and Laufer, 1912
12 Childe, 1950, pp. 14–5
13 Laufer, 1912, figures 25–7
14 Laufer, 1912, p. 87 and figure 20
15 Twelve Chou inches were approximately equal to ten English inches. The present specimen is 9½ inches high.

16 Translated by Legge, 1872, as the commentary to *Ch'un Ch'iu*, 'Spring and Autumn Annals'.
17 Henri Michel has recently produced a theory that these jades, like the *hsüan chi* [see p. 57], were astronomical instruments. He would identify them as *t'ou kuei*, which the Chinese Classics say were used to fix the date of the summer solstice by ascertaining the shortest length of shadow cast at midday by a vertical gnomon. See Michel, 1962
18 Karlgren, 1945
19 Andersson, 1943, pp. 252–5, compares incisions on a Neolithic ceremonial stone axe with indentations on a jade axe of the Chou period.
20 Fêng, fasc. 20, p. 17 b
21 Laufer, 1912, p. 21
22 Creel, 1936, pp. 342–3
23 Hentze, 1928–9
24 Michel, 1950
25 Dye, 1930–1

CHAPTER III

1 For an account of circumstances connected with the An-yang finds, and a summary of evidence linking Hsiao-t'un with a late Shang capital, see Yetts, 1942.
2 Sullivan, 1961, p. 36
3 I anticipate here by introducing a style period. Briefly, the First Phase of Chinese bronze art lasts until about 950 BC, the Second Phase from 950 to 600 BC, and the Third Phase from about 600 to 250 BC, as more fully explained on pp. 94–5.
4 Creel, 1936, p. 129
5 Watson, 1961, p. 81
6 Stephen, 1962
7 Li Chi, 1957, pp. 46–8; for more facts and figures on ancient Chinese bronze alloys see Watson, 1962, p. 103; and Garner, Winter 1960.
8 Karlbeck, 1935
9 Watson, 1962, pp. 101–2
10 Hansford, Spring 1958, pp. 3–4; and Hsia Nai, January and December 1957
11 For help received in translating this inscription I am indebted to Mr Wu Shih-ch'ang.
12 Yetts, 1929, p. 44
13 Watson, 1962, p. 108
14 Watson, 1962, p. 20
15 Karlgren's classification introduces the geographical term 'Huai', but it is otherwise roughly the same as Yetts's; viz.: 1. Archaic Period (*ab origine* to 950 BC); 2. Middle Chou (950–650 BC); 3. Huai (650–200 BC).

16 Karlgren, 1936; 1937; 1944; 1946; 1951; 1959; 1961; 1962
17 Watson, 1962, p. 42; for some gallic views of the matter see Brion, 1961, pp. 86–7
18 Waley, 1926, p. 104
19 Karlgren, 1937, p. 19
20 Watson, 1962, p. 169, hints at an inter-state 'trade in finished bronzes'.
21 Karlgren, 1937

CHAPTER IV

1 Translated in part by É. Chavannes, 1895–1905
2 By Pan Ku (died AD 92). The Imperial Annals, with which this work opens have been translated in part by Dubs, 1938–55.
3 By Fan Yeh (AD 420–77). This work is untranslated except for a few isolated chapters. For full bibliographical information on these, as for translations of isolated chapters of *Shih chi* and *Ch'ien Han shu*, see Needham, 1954, pp. 253–62 and 268–98.
4 Hudson, 1931, p. 99
5 Hirth, 1885, p. 42
6 Hirth, 1885, pp. 40–3
7 See Trever, 1932. The best and most accessible short account of the Koslóv finds in English is Yetts's, 1926.
8 Koizumi, 1934, vol. I, p. 4
9 Mänchen-Helfen, 1937
10 White, W.C., 1934, p. 19
11 Chiang Yüen Yi (Yüan-i), 1949, forward (in Chinese) and plates 11 and 12
12 Mänchen-Helfen, 1937
13 Ibid.
14 Bushell, 1904–6, vol. ii, p. 92
15 Sylwan, 1949, p. 1
16 Sylwan, 1949, p. 17
17 Sylwan, 1937
18 Anon., 'A glance at the interior of China, obtained during a journey through the silk and green tea districts', being *The Chinese Miscellany*, no. 1, p. 64
19 Voskresensky and Tikhonov (transl. Tolmachoff), 1936
20 *Lieh tzŭ* is a compilation of literary fragments dating from the fifth to first centuries BC, put together in final form at the end of the fifth century AD. *Huai nan tzŭ*, attributed to the Prince of Huai-nan, Liu An, dates from about 120 BC.
21 Waley, 1939, p. 77
22 Gyllensvärd, 1962
23 Löw-Beer, 1947
24 Karlgren, 1934
25 Löw-Beer, 1937
26 Charleston, 1948
27 Yetts, 1939, p. 134
28 T'ai-i is regarded as the Han equivalent of the Shang dynasty Shang Ti [p. 56].
29 For post-Han portrayals of the Ssŭ Shên, see Cohn, 1940–1.
30 Rudolph and Wen Yu, 1951, plate 73. Two other sides of this coffin are decorated with portrayals of Tiger and Tortoise, and the sculptor undoubtedly had in mind the Ssŭ Shên. But the fourth side, incongruously, has a portrayal of a human figure bearing what may be wings. See also Waley, February 1953, for further comments on this portrayal.
31 The uplifted forepaw is featured, for example, on mirrors of Karlgren's C category, dating from the fourth century BC. It also occurs on the 'bird-dragons' of plate 108.
32 de Saussure, 1909, p. 264
33 Yetts, 1927–8, pp. 35 and 37. A parallel to this division into 'head', 'heart', and 'tail' will be found in the case of the Stellar Mansions in the East Quadrant, corresponding to the head, heart, and tail of the Green Dragon [p. 151].
34 Charleston, 1948
35 Yetts, 1939, p. 142
36 Yetts, 1927–8, p. 32
37 de Groot, 1892–1910, vol. ii, p. 824
38 The similarity is particularly marked in the treatment of the winged arm. Another important document bearing on the Han *t'ao-t'ieh* is the bronze door-handle from the 'Chinese House' discovered recently at Abakan, south-west of Minusinsk, apparently dating from the first century BC. The mask is human, with bull's horns, pointed ears with volutes, upstanding tufts of hair on the forehead, grizzled hair tufts on the cheeks, flowing moustache, flared nostrils, open jaws through which a bronze ring passes, and prominent teeth. See Mongait, 1959, p. 181
39 Gallois, October 1932, p. 648
40 Chavannes, 1913, figure 24
41 Laufer, 1909, plates 48–51 and pp. 213–4
42 Pfister, 1934, p. 53. Yetts, 1926, p. 176, had previously drawn attention to the Iranian influence traceable to this scene.
43 See Sullivan, 1961, plate 45 and pp. 85 and 92–3

CHAPTER V

1 Watson, 1961, pp. 178–80, and Salmony, 1954
2 Chanda, 1936, p. 18
3 Restriction of psychological interest to the mask in Chinese Buddhist sculpture helps to explain why we find so many heads in Western collections and so few complete statues. Dealers' agents, who during the first decades of the century steadily despoiled the great cave-shrines of north China, rarely bothered to take away more than the heads. What they left behind was not only more difficult to remove but also commercially far less valuable.
4 Fry, R., 1920, p. 66
5 Sullivan, 1961, p. 111
6 Sirén, 1938
7 Grousset, 1959, p. 145
8 For example, T'ien-lung-shan, well within range of the capital, in T'ai-yüan-hsien, Shensi; North and South Hsiang-t'ang-shan in Hopei; Shên-t'ung-ssŭ in Shantung; Ting-chou in Hopei; and Lung-mên in Honan.
9 In AD 555 the Northern Ch'i Emperor became officially Buddhist. In AD 573 the Northern Chou Emperor became Confucianist and disbanded Buddhist and Taoist foundations in his territory. This was the so-called 'Second Great Persecution'.
10 For instance, on the eastern of the twin pagodas at Ch'üan-chou (Marco Polo's 'Zayton') in Fukien, dating from the thirteenth century. See Ecke and Demiéville, 1935, plate 49
11 See Sirén, 1925, vol. i, p. lxiii
12 Sirén, 1925, vol. i, p. xcii
13 Waley, 1931, p. xxix, says that in AD 690 she ordered the translation of *Mahāmogha* or 'Great Cloud' sūtra (*Ta yün ch'ing yu ching*) in which passages were inserted to prove that Maitreya would one day descend to earth and rule as a woman.
14 Yetts, 1932, pp. 1–8
15 Soper, Summer 1949, p. 29
16 Passage translated by Soper, Summer 1949, p. 28, from *Kao sêng chüan*, 'Lives of the Famous Priests', written in AD 519 by the monk Hui-chiao. From this source are taken the other details of K'ang Sêng-hui's life recorded above.
17 Henderson and Hurvitz, 1956
18 Chanda, 1936, p. 15
19 Münsterberg, 1956

20 Sir John Marshall, 1960, p. 30

21 See p. 203 for the meaning of Sanskrit terms used to name the positions of the hands (*mudrā*) and of the legs (*āsana*) of Buddhist images.

22 Lohuizen-de Leeuw, 1949, p. 184

23 Ingholt, 1957, pp. 22–3

24 Unfortunately this inscription is probably a modern Japanese fake. Doubts have also been cast on the genuineness of the image itself; I personally do not share them. As regards both style and iconography, the New York Maitreya closely resembles another in a private collection in Tientsin, cast in AD 443, the more polished appearance of the New York piece being no doubt due to the fact that it was intended for a major work. Genuine or no, it undoubtedly reproduces faithfully a type of cult-image popular in the late fifth century, and the date attributed to it is as plausible as any. See Münsterberg, 1946

25 Kern, 1884

26 Wegner, 1929, pp. 156–78, 216–29, 252–70. This is probably the most detailed monograph on the iconography of a Buddhist personage ever to have been made.

27 See Chavannes, 1915. This huge work includes a full translation of all the Lung-mên inscriptions known to Chavannes.

28 Müller, 1894, part 2, pp. 1–85 and 89–107

29 Chavannes, 1915, p. 388

30 Not for the first time, I am using the word 'gods' to name the higher order of beings to whom Mahāyāna Buddhists accorded worship. In Buddhist cosmology gods properly so called (*dēvas*) are of vastly inferior status to Buddhas and their kind. Indeed they are inferior to humans, since they have to be reborn in the human condition before they can hope to attain Buddhahood.

31 Chavannes, 1904, p. 264

32 Waley, 1931, p. xix

33 See Chavannes, 1915, vols ii and iii; Sirén, 1925; Tokiwa and Sekino, 1925–31; Mizuno and Nagahiro, 1941; Mizuno, 1951–4.

34 Of 54 dated sculptures made between AD 390 and 500 listed by Rowland, 1937, pp. 106–7, 25 are of this class and only 15 are made of stone.

35 Sirén, 1925, vol. i, p. lix

36 Rowland, 1937, p. 92

37 It should perhaps be said that production continued at Mathurā through the fourth and fifth centuries; but whereas at Mathurā the cord-mesh formula is adopted for the gown, at Sārnāth this expedient is dropped and the body is rendered virtually as though nude.

38 Ashton and Gray, 1951, p. 136. It is a product of the nearly Ch'ü-yang school. No fewer than a thousand complete sculptures and fragments, of which some two hundred are inscribed, were brought to light as a result of excavations conducted at Ch'ü-yang in 1953. They range in date from AD 520 to 750, and so provide examples from all three of the stylistic phases discussed here.

39 For a discussion of the Lung-mên Amitābha (usually called Vairocana) and its iconographic relations with the group at P'ing-ling-ssŭ, and particularly on the significance of Vaiśravana present in both groups, see Willetts, 1954.

40 They portray the Bodhisattva Kshitigarbha, but he is invariably shown wearing the mantle (*sanghāti*) of a Buddha.

CHAPTER VI

1 Shepherd, 1956

2 I owe this vision of the dragon to Rhodes, 1959, p. 6.

3 Leach, 1940, pp. 188–9. The steep temperature gradient presupposes no stoking through blow-holes at the sides of the kiln. As described by Rhodes, 1959, the Chinese kiln is fired both continuously and serially. When chamber 1 is at peak temperature and has absorbed sufficient heat, firing at the fire-box is halted; side-stoking now raises the temperature in chamber 2 to its peak; then chamber 3 is fired, and so on. In this way all wares throughout the kiln receive the same amount of heat, and attain the same peak temperature. Side-stoking is one way of dealing with temperature variations; another is to vary the refractoriness of pottery bodies to suit a wide range of different temperatures.

4 Assuming Han glazes were based on Near Eastern formulae, they would have contained high percentages of the alkalis soda and lime. The brilliance and relative durability of the T'ang lead-silicate glazes suggests that these alkalis had been largely eliminated from the formula by T'ang times.

5 For a detailed discussion see Hetherington, 1948.

6 The Chün glazes of Sung times, which display an opalescent pale blue or lavender splashed with strawberry, present a major problem in diagnosis. If the blue is an effect of reduced colloidal copper similar to that of the splashes on the T'ang stoneware of colour plate 40, then the strawberry splashes could have been produced by local oxidation at a late stage of cooling. They would thus be *flambé* effects. Some Sung seggars, or protective containers for the bowls in the kilns, have holes in their sides; a fact which might support this interpretation. The holes would admit oxygen to localized areas of the pot's surface, while the rest would remain reduced. It is generally held, however, that the blue of these wares is due to reduced iron, perhaps in the presence of phosphorous, and that the strawberry splashes are due to the merely local application of copper. In any case oxygen must have been let into the kiln during the final stages of cooling, in order to produce the copper red; whereas in the case of the T'ang black and bluish-white glazes, the reducing atmosphere must have been maintained throughout the firing operation.

7 The Turks knew north China by the name of her Ch'i-tan conquerors, in their language 'Khitai'. Hence Marco Polo's name for China, Cathay.

8 'Why T'ang?' is the title of a short paper by the late Sir Herbert Ingram, 1946.

9 For further information on the gradual opening-up of the pre-Ming field see Rackham, 1923–4.

10 See Gray, B., 1953, pp. 11–2

11 'One might almost imagine', says Sir Herbert Ingram, 1946, 'that an edict had gone forth that a complete breakaway from T'ang forms and decoration should be made by Sung potters.'

12 Honey, 1946, p. 20

13 Bachhofer, 1934

14 *T'ao shuo* was translated by Bushell, 1910; *Ching-tê-chên t'ao lu* (usually abbreviated as *T'ao lu*) by Julien, 1856. A recent definitive translation of *T'ao lu* is by Sayer, 1949.

15 Bushell (transl.), 1910, p. 108

16 This is not the Ting-chou where Sung Ting wares were reputedly made, but a place near Ch'ang-an in Shensi.

17 This town is omitted in the *Ch'a ching* notice as quoted in *T'ao shuo*, and consequently does not appear in Bushell's translation. The present translation is made from the extant *Ch'a ching* in the Yüan dynasty compilation *Po ch'uan hsüeh hai*.

18 Bushell (transl.), 1910, pp. 107–8

19 Kahle, 1940–1

20 For the Middle and Near East, see Kahle, 1940–1; Hobson, R. L., 1922–23, 1928–30, and August 1932; Ashton, 1933–4; Sarre, 1925; Plumer, 1937; Willetts, Spring 1960; for Singapore, Sullivan, Winter 1957; for Siam and Malaya, Quaritch-Wales, 1935 and 1940; for Indonesia, Ottema, 1946; de Flines, 1949; for Sarawak, Harrison, T., September 1950, December 1951, Summer 1959, and many other papers in the *Sarawak Museum Journal*; Harrison, B., December 1958; Pope, 1956; for the Philippines, Sullivan, 1956; for Japan, Koyama, 1951

21 Plumer, 1937

22 Gompertz, 1958, p. 14

23 Hsia Nai, October 1959, p. 46

24 Karlbeck, Summer 1949 and 1949–50

25 See a feature, 'Revival of famous Lungchuan porcelain', in *China Pictorial*, Autumn 1962, pp. 24–5.

26 Lindberg, Spring 1950, and see also 1955

27 Sarre, 1925

28 Honey, 1945, p. 78

29 The few facts available about Yo *yao* are set forth in a paper by Roger Bluett entitled 'A note on the wares of Yo Chou', which the author kindly allowed me to see unpublished. Hitchman, Winter 1951, should be read keeping in mind the limited number of pieces then known to its author.

30 While in Ceylon in 1960 the present writer saw at the Colombo Museum a typical Yo *yao* bowl said to have been dug up at the hill-fortress of Sigiriya about 1932. It had the usual dark-grey body and finely-crackled olive-green glaze, and showed conspicuous wreathing marks on the sides of the body. This was a *trouvaille*, since Yo has not hitherto been reported outside China. Strangely enough, the bowl was heavily stained with red earth, exactly as are the Chinese specimens, imparting a curious bluish-red bloom to the olive-green glaze. This might have opened the door to interesting speculations, but in fact the earth in which the bowl had lain at Sigiriya is a liver-red alluvium, and the resemblance is simply due to burial in similar conditions.

31 Bushell (transl.), 1910, pp. 103–4

32 Chêng Tê-k'un, 1957, pp. xvi–xvii and 155–60, and plates 83–91

33 See Thorpe, 1949, p. 29, where he says: 'Students of Chinese pottery will think at once of a lovely T'ang shape which sometimes wears a golden-brown glaze'. The Colchester jar referred to is made of lemon-amber glass.

34 Gallois, 1935–6

35 Smirnov, 1909, plate 41 (No. 75)

36 Smirnov, 1909, nos 75–8. See also Orbeli and Trever, 1935, plate 63

37 Quoted in *T'ao shu*, Bushell (transl.), 1910, p. 115

38 See David, 1931–2, plate vi

39 'The vessel should be made so that the tip always connects with (i.e. is permanently fixed to, or is continuous with) the mouth (of the vessel); the tip is pointed above a flange and should be two fingers (i.e. finger-breadths) high; in it a hole as small as a bronze chopstick is made. Fresh water should be kept in such a vessel. At the side of the vessel is another round opening; it has a pipe (i.e. a funnel) rising two fingers high and is as large as a small "cash". This opening is used for pouring water in; two or three *shêng* (pints) may be put in.' For this translation see Coomaraswamy and Kershaw, 1928–9

40 Sullivan, 1961, pp. 187–8

41 Coomaraswamy and Kershaw, 1928–9

42 Prodan, 1960, p. 24 and colour plate 10

43 For more detailed discussions on the Chinese pilgrim bottle and its Western affiliations see Gray, 1953, pp. 6 and 11; see also Bell, 1914; also Gallois, October 1932, and 1935–6

44 The piece which I would cite in order to demonstrate a Chiu-yen provenance for this ewer is a model of a ram in Yüeh ware in the Barlow collection and illustrated by Gompertz, 1958, plate 7a. One is tempted to say that these two pieces were modelled in the same workshop, so great is the stylistic resemblance between them.

45 Gallois, October 1932, p. 648

46 For example, Prodan, 1960; Gray, 1953; Honey, 1945; see also Oriental Ceramic Society, 1958, and Institute of Ceramics, Tokyo, 1928

47 Smirnov, 1909, plate 62 (No. 100)

48 Smirnov, 1909, plate 78 (No. 137)

49 Lane, 1939, p. 59

50 Compare at this point the gold and silver handled cup from Malaya Perestchepina shown in figure 61c (Orbeli and Trever, 1935, plate 63).

The possibility that this is of actual Chinese manufacture cannot be eliminated.

51 Thorpe, 1949, p. 69

CHAPTER VII

1 Cohn, 1951, pp. 88–9

2 See Sirén, 1956, vol. iii, plate 1; see also Wang Yu-chuan, 1953; Hsia Nai, January–February 1954, figure 5.

3 Mêng may at least have been responsible for introducing the hair writing brush into Ch'in state from the more culturally advanced central states. The *Shuo wên* tells us that the character for 'writing brush' was differently written in different parts of the country. Doubtless, therefore, the form of the writing implement also varied somewhat from state to state, as did the styles of script. In Ch'in a character equated with the modern *pi* [figure 67] was used. Noting the presence of an element signifying 'bamboo' in this character, Erkes, 1941, pp.128–9, suggested that Ch'in state may have been using a wooden stylus long after the hair brush was established elsewhere.

4 Among Sven Hedin's finds in the Lop Nor region was a set of 78 wooden slips of Han date, all nine inches long and half an inch wide, still tied top and bottom in their original order with hemp threads. When opened up, this bundle formed a continuous writing surface four feet long.

5 See Chiang Yuen Yi (Yüan-i), 1950, plate 27

6 Wang Chi-chên, 1930

7 The papers recovered by Sir Aurel Stein at the Tun-huang *limes* in 1911, described as made of pure rag, very white, thin, and transparent, were originally dated to about AD 151 on the evidence of wooden slips. They are letter-papers bearing Sogdian writing, and are now regarded as belonging to the early fourth century AD. For the latest discussion see Carter, revised by Goodrich, 1955.

8 Clapperton, 1934, pp. 23–6. The Tun-huang library was walled up in AD 1035 and not re-opened until 1907.

9 David, 1936

10 See *Ku kung shu hua chi*, 1930 ff., vol. xviii, plate 5

11 See Mayer, 1951, p. 324

12 Petrucci (transl.), 1918

13 Laurie, 1947, p. 62

14 In this connexion Petrucci comments that the Japanese painter Kanaotu is said to have used honey or perhaps propolis as an ingredient in the tempera. Honey mixed with gum in tempering pigments was known to Cennini. See Laurie, 1947, p. 173. Beeswax was a tempera known to Pliny, and to the ninth-century author of the Lucca MS. Actual examples of second- and third-century AD paintings in beeswax tempera have been recovered from Egypt, and it is also known to have been used in making illuminated MSS of the fifteenth century. In China, *Chieh tzŭ yüan* recommends mixing human ear wax with gum in tempering a hard variety of Stone Blue [see p. 302].

15 The two gum-resins were in any case closely alike, being opaque and crumbly in crude form, inodorous but astringent to the taste, insoluble in water but soluble in alcohol and volatile oils. The Chinese believed that *t'êng huang* was the excrement of a serpent. Were they perhaps confusing it with Indian Yellow, a traditional artists' colour that was until comparatively recently produced in India from the urine of cattle?

16 See Gray, 1959, p. 35

17 See Wang Shih-hsiang, 1948–9. Su is actually repeating the dicta of his friend the bamboo-painter Wên T'ung [see pls 197, 198].

18 There is naturally an *a priori* possibility that the eidetic image might be retained by artists, who are entirely concerned with projecting and recording visual images, and Sir Herbert Read suggested in his *Education Through Art*, pp. 44–6, that the visions experienced by the painter Blake, which he conjured up to use as models, were in fact eidetic images.

19 Eidetic children are in fact capable of recording accurately symbols that

can have no possible meaning for them. Thus the German word 'Garten-wirtschaft' appearing in a picture used in an eidetic ability test was spelt out correctly both backwards and forwards by several English children out of a batch taking this test. It would be interesting to see how skilfully non-Chinese eidetic subjects would reproduce the forms of Chinese char-acters similarly used.

20 Waley, January–June 1921, p. 247

21 Contag, 1952

22 Sirén, 1936, p. 188

23 Sirén, 1936, p. 122

24 Sirén, 1936, p. 120

25 There are in fact two entirely different sorts of *p'o mo*, the word *p'o* in each case being written with a different character. The change of meaning to which we refer occurs only in one of these. See Soper (transl.), 1951, p. 122 and footnote 127

26 Cennini's words are: 'Draw ... with willow charcoal, which ... should be bound to a little cane or stick ... Take a vase half full of clear water with a drop of ink, and with a little pointed brush of squirrel strengthen thy drawing everywhere.' See Hiler, 1934, p. 42

27 For example the first character in the sentence written in seven different scripts [figure 69] is a pictogram of a scorpion (*wan*), which is here used to mean *wan*, 'myriad'; the second shows a tree and a field; and so on.

28 The *I wên chih* chapter of 'History of the Former Han Dynasty' says: 'At this time the duties of prison officials became increasingly onerous; a new type of writing was therefore brought into being called *li shu*, originally intended to be used only in the registers of prisoners and exiles.'

29 See Yang Yu-hsün, 1937, plate 2, figure 5. The writing reproduced bears a date corresponding to the year AD 219. For another alleged example of the *k'ai shu* of Chung Yu, see Chiang Yee, 1938, figure 34.

30 Driscoll and Toda, 1935, plate 7. A rubbing from a Sui stone featuring the same *t'ieh* is illustrated by Yang Yu-hsün, 1937, plate 3, figure 6.

31 Chiang Yee, 1938, figure 35

32 For alleged examples of the three Han *ts'ao* styles see Yang Yu-hsün, 1937, plate 3, figure 7; plate 7, figure 18; and plate 7, figure 18 *bis*.

33 Yang Yu-hsün, 1937, plate 8, figure 19

34 Sun Ta-yü (transl.), September 1935

35 Lin Yu-tang, 1935

36 Chiang Yee, 1938

37 Driscoll and Toda, 1935

38 Chiang Yee, 1938, figures 76–82

39 In its present form the body of *Hsüan-ho hua p'u* probably dates from the year 1302. See Ferguson, 1927, p. 19

40 Sakanashi, 1939, pp. 15–6

41 Sirén, 1936

42 Soper (transl.), 1951, p. 21

43 Chang Jên-hsia, 1953

44 Compare Wordsworth's natural philosophy as expressed in *The Excursion* (book ix, 1–5): 'To every Form of being is assigned ... An *active* Prin-ciple; howe'er removed / From sense and observation, it subsists / In all things, in all natures; ...'

45 See Rowland, 1951, p. 7. Chan Wing-tsit, 1940–1, pp. 231–2, helps confirm that this was indeed the Chinese painter's own aim: 'For a painter to express the *ch'i* of a tree, he must express the tree-nature and the rhythmic vital force which gives it spirit and form.'

46 In the first edition of this book I traced the history of the Sung Academy and made an elaborate comparison between its organization and the manner of its functioning and those of the French Académie Royale de Peinture et de Sculpture founded in 1648. The Sung Academy enjoyed a particular esteem under the patronage of Emperor Hui-tsung (reigned 1101–26), who perhaps sought shelter for his own somewhat frail artistic personality behind such big guns as Li T'ang and Ts'ui Po. The Aca-demy was the aversion of the independents, the *wên jên* or 'culture men', who would have nothing to do with professionalism in art.

47 *Assembly of Birds* bears an inscription said to date from the time of Sung Emperor Jên-tsung (1023–63) but there is some question as to whether the painting has not been considerably touched up by some later hand. Judging only from a photographic facsimile my own impression is that the background belongs to the late eleventh century.

48 Had it been the work of a child artist we might be tempted to classify *Assembly of Birds* as an example of 'enumerative' painting. We are prob-ably nearer the truth in seeing it as representing a normal stage in the early development of pictorial composition, for which the European tradition provides parallels; such as the frescoes in the Palace of the Popes at Avignon, and the miniature of rabbits in a wood in the *Livre de Chasse* of Gaston Phébus (*c.* AD 1400), a reproduction of which can be found in Clark, 1949, pl. 6a. In this case the question of a Near Eastern and perhaps ultimately Chinese influence crops up. Speaking of this and similar miniatures from hunting MSS, Clark observes that some were copied from Perso-Arabic originals.

49 Rowland, 1962

50 Soper (transl.), 1951, p. 131, quoting from Shên Kua's *Mêng ch'i pi ts'an*

51 Petrucci (transl.), 1918, pp. 417–8. While the term *hsieh shêng* is here used with reference to painting in the 'boneless' style, Shên Kua in the previous quotation makes it refer to contour painting. For present pur-poses this complete contradiction does not matter. The important thing is that a clear distinction is made between painting with outlines (*kou li*) and painting without (*mei ku*).

52 Soper (transl.), 1951, p. 97

53 Rowland, 1951

54 Yonezawa and Shimada, 1952

55 Yonezawa and Shimada, 1952

56 Price, 1953, p. 286

57 Friedländer, 1941, p. 69

58 Wang Shih-hsiang, 1948–9, pp. 49–58

59 Yonezawa and Shimada, 1952, plate 12

60 *Chu p'u hsiang lu*, written at the end of the thirteenth century, has been translated, with additional information about bamboo-painters down to the end of the Yüan dynasty, by Aschwin Lippe, 1942.

61 Wang Shih-hsiang, 1948–9, p. 52

62 Sirén, 1936, p. 114

63 Wang Shih-hsiang, 1948–9, p. 57

64 He is *supposed* to be shooting at the sun (right) and the moon (left), so illustrating the admonition 'In the universe is nothing that after it has reached exaltation is not brought down ... When the sun has reached its mid-course, it begins to sink, and when the moon is full, it begins to wane. The rise to glory is like a heap of dust, the fall into calamity like the sudden rebound of a spring'. See Sullivan, 1961, p. 102

65 So El Greco said of his picture *Our Lady Presenting the Chasuble to St Ildefonso*: 'I justify enlarging the size of the figures for decorative reasons and on the grounds that they are celestial beings which for us are like lights seen from afar that appear large even though they are actually small.' See Loran, 1946, p. 31

66 Friedländer, 1941, p. 115

67 The function of primitive painting in recording concept-symbols by means of boundary lines could hardly be better brought out than by the definition of *hua*, 'painting', given in *Shuo wên*. After noting that the character for *hua* is composed of those for 'brush' and 'field', it continues: 'Painting is made up of limits; it is like the paths that enclose the fields.' The character for 'field', it should be said, is a pictogram showing four plots of land defined by their boundary paths.

68 Clark, 1949, plate 13 a

69 Clark, 1949, p. 7

70 Sakanashi (transl.), 1935, p. 31

71 Friedländer, 1941, p. 66

72 Short, 1948, p. 361

73 Loran, 1946, p. 33

74 Gowing, 1954, p. 8

75 The following remarks on Cézanne's compositional methods are based on an analysis made by Loran, 1946, who also illustrates the pictures referred to here.

76 *Still Life with Fruit Basket, Mill Near Pont des Trois Sautets*, and *Pigeon House at Montbriand*, in Loran, 1946, plates 14, 25, and 15

77 See for instance Petrucci (transl.), 1918, figures 34–7

CHAPTER VIII

1 Soper, in Sickman and Soper, 1956, p. 215, notes that of late Chou town sites excavated by Japanese archaeologists between 1937 and 1943, only that of the small state of Têng approximates to a regular rectangle, with a more or less centrally situated rectangular palace enclosure on the main south–north axis. *Chou li*'s idealized description of the Chou capital runs in part: 'The architects who laid out a capital made it a square nine *li* on a side, each side having three gateways. Within the capital there were nine lengthwise and nine crosswise avenues, each nine chariot-tracks wide.' As Soper points out, the significance of this schema lies in the fact that it provided a canon for the building of later Imperial capitals; the rectangular plan of the agrarian town, on the other hand, may have been favoured simply because of its essentially practical form.

2 Gutkind, 1946, p. 208. This book gives an excellent account of the origin and development of the Chinese town against the background of Chinese society as a whole.

3 Ch'ang-an's population is in fact rising again. From 550,000 in 1950, it had by 1954 climbed to three-quarters of a million. The town is usually known as Sian (Hsi-an, 'Western Peace') and in consistently calling it Ch'ang-an in the present book, we freely admit to historical prejudice; Ch'ang-an has been its name over most of its history.

4 Gutkind, 1946, p. 313

5 Sirén, 1924, p. 27

6 Gutkind, 1946, p. 21

7 It is interesting to observe as another example of traditionalism in Chinese architecture, that this arrangement of private residence to the north and audience-hall to the south has been repeatedly copied in the plans of later Imperial precincts. Thus the 'Outer Court' of the T'ang dynasty T'ai-chi Kung [p. 366] occupied its southern section, and contained the halls of state. The Imperial residence formed its northern section. Similarly, the northern part of the 'Forbidden City' of Peking contained the residence of the Emperor and of his female relatives, while the southern part was where he appeared in his official capacity as ruler [p. 377].

8 In this respect Gutkind, 1946, p. 217, goes so far as to say: 'People living in the Chinese towns are not citizens, not burghers in the European sense ... the conception of a "community" does not enter the minds of the Chinese.'

9 See Yetts, 1927, p. 123

10 Gutkind, 1946, caption to plate 59

11 Marsden (ed.), 1936, pp. 173–4

12 Cordier, in Yule, 1903, vol. i, p. 378. Notice the apparent displacement of these two towers relative to the centre of the Northern City due to contraction of the northern part of Peking in Ming times. See also the two corresponding towers at Ch'ang-an [plate 249].

13 May I add to this an unpublished description by a Western architect, R. T. F. Skinner, who recently visited the Temple of Heaven site? He speaks first of the causeway, raised to tree-top level, which connects the two main enclosures, and then goes on: 'Standing on the topmost terrace [of the Altar of Heaven] the circular enclosure appears to be just contained by the square enclosure, the sides of the square appearing to be almost tangential to the circle. With the unrestricted sky above, and nothing but a rectangle of trees all around, one's feelings are exactly expressed by the phrase the Chinese use: "The earth is square and the sky is round". On these elevated terraces in their perfect architectural settings one has the sensation of rising above the earth.'

14 Today the former is the Central Park, the latter the Working People's Palace of Culture.

15 Sirén, 1926, vol. i, p. 8. To this account of the 'Forbidden City' I am indebted for much of the information which follows.

16 Sirén, 1926, vol. i, p. 10

17 For an excellent description of the Inner Court see Johnston, 1934, pp. 168–79. For other appreciative writings on Peking see Arlington and Lewisohn, 1935; and Lin Yutang, 1961, with an essay on the art of Peking by Swann.

18 Lin Yutang, 1939, p. 301

19 Sirén, 1950, pp. 35–6

20 Sirén, 1950, p. 5

21 Lin Yutang, 1942, p. 312. The quotation is from Shên Tu's *Fou shêng liu chi*, 'Six Chapters from a Floating Life' (*c.*1750).

22 Sirén, 1949, p. 95. The 'Lingering Garden' is today a Rest Centre. See also Chou Shou-chuan, May 1957, pp. 14–7 (with colour plates).

23 Sirén, 1949, p. 19

24 The whole area from Pei Hai in the Imperial City to the Western Hills is planned as a huge cultural and recreational park. It will be possible to go by boat from the Winter Palace in the heart of Peking direct to the Summer Palace five miles distant by the 'River of Golden Water' [p. 376]. 'Thus', says Liang Ssŭ-ch'êng, March–April 1953, 'all the palaces, temples, and pagodas and gardens in and around present-day Peking will be interlaced with waterways. They will become part of a recreational system in the service of the entire population of the city.'

25 Attiret (translated by Sir Harry Beaumont), 1752, pp. 8–10

26 Liang Ssŭ-ch'êng, November 1952, p. 31

27 The overall size of the Kondō of the Tōdaiji Temple at Nara, Japan (eighth century AD), is 290 by 170 feet: that of an equivalent Chinese palace building, the T'ai-ho Tien [p. 377], is 200 by 100 feet. That of the Han dynasty Wei-yang Kung is said to have been 400 by 110 feet, and this is corroborated by the dimensions of its rammed earth platform, the surviving length of which is some 330 feet. The decrease in scale of more recent buildings, such as T'ai-ho Tien, is probably due to difficulty in obtaining beams of suitable length, consequent on deforestation. See Soper, 1942, pp. 12–3

28 Use of the words 'step' and 'tier' is borrowed from Soper, 1942, which contains the first comprehensive and coherent account of Far Eastern bracket-systems given to the West. In what follows I have made much use of it, and would like to acknowledge here the very great help it has been to me.

29 Ecke, 1935–6, p. 258, suggests that this name may be connected with the Chung T'ien-chu (Jap. Tenjiku) Mountain at Hangchow, a famous centre of Chinese Buddhism at the time.

30 Ecke, 1935–6, p. 272

31 Sickman and Soper, 1956, p. 267

32 It is true that in the Nandaimon system a cross-yoke extends the sideways or longitudinal support given to the eaves-purlin by the outermost bracket-arm [figure 76 d]. Cross-bracketing, nevertheless, is not inherent in the Tenjikuyō system as a whole.

33 In the first edition of this book, pp. 705–6 and figures 98 a and b, I presented evidence that strongly suggests a Persian origin for this member. The evidence is supplied by the grave-pillars of Szechwan dating from later Han times, the architectural form of which surprisingly resembles traditional domestic building construction in Persia in which a bracket

with cross-yoke also appears. The comparison was made by Prip-Møller, 1937, pp. 50–1 and figure 15.

34 There is as yet no clear proof that the double-brace strut was known in Han times, although its presence in the sixth-century AD tomb of the Celestial Kings and Earthly Spirits in Korea may suggest that it was. Modern Chinese architects, unable to find a name for it in classical literature, have christened it *jen tzŭ hsing kung*, 'bracket shaped like the character for "man"', which it certainly does resemble; but Soper, 1942, p. 101, believes that it can be identified with the *chih ch'êng*, 'branch-like prop', spoken of in a *fu* poem dating from the second century AD.

35 A third-century AD *fu* speaks of *ang* 'hopping like birds across an interval'; and Soper, 1956, p. 225, presupposes that the slanting arm must be meant.

36 A full description of this building is provided by Soper, 1942, pp. 243–54.

37 Soper, 1942, has this to say of the system as found in the Tenjikuyō: 'the terse directness of the method, and its utter lack of visual co-ordination with the horizontal bracketing in the column axes, make it seem much older than its first appearance in the late twelfth century in Japan'.

38 See the latest edition of Fletcher, 1954, p. 919.

39 Lin Yutang, 1942, p. 300, says that the curved roof expresses a national aesthetic preference, which, he says, 'is due to our training in calligraphy, in which we are taught that when we have a straight main line ... we must contrast it with curved or soft broken lines around it'. Chiang Yee, 1938, pp. 215–8, is even more positive about the dependence of architectural form on that of calligraphy. 'I can affirm', he writes, 'that there is no type of Chinese building ... whose harmony and form are not derived from calligraphy ... one of the most typical forms in Chinese architecture, the sagging roof, must surely have come from calligraphy.'

40 Thus one Dr Lamprey, quoted by Yetts, 1927, p. 131, finds a connexion between the curved profile of the Chinese roof and 'that graceful curve we notice in the branches of fir-trees, and the little dog-like figures sitting on the upper margin [see plate 249] may be intended for squirrels running or sitting on the branch'. So, too, the German architect Boerschmann is quoted by Yetts: 'The impulse which drove the Chinese to use these curving forms came from their desire to express movement in life.' In this way their buildings began 'to approach as nearly as possible the forms of nature – the varied outlines of rocks, trees, etc.'

41 This evidence is presented in the first edition of this book, 1958, pp. 721 and 722, footnote 3.

42 Silcock, 1935, pp. 127–8, says: 'Earthenware roof-tiles ... have always had in common the one attribute of great weight. On the other hand, the rafters on which they were laid were thin strips of wood that tended to sag under their load ... A slight bending of the rafters was therefore recognized as natural in building small roofs, and in the larger it may well have been purposely exaggerated in order to obtain the pleasing effect of a more definite curve.'

43 Davis, 1836, vol. i, p. 366

44 A fairly complete inventory of Chinese pagodas was made by Boerschmann, 1911–31, vol. iii, but this is neither a systematic analysis of origins nor of methods of construction. The work of Ecke, 1935–6, on the structural principles and antecedents of the great twin pagodas of Ch'üan-chou is a model for future work along these lines.

45 Thus the pilgrim Tao-yao (middle fifth century AD), according to surviving fragments of his diary, recorded the exact dimensions of Kanishka's *stūpa* at Peshawar; and Hui-shêng, a monk who accompanied the expedition sent to India by the Northern Wei Empress Hu in AD 518, is said to have commissioned a native Indian artist to produce bronze models of the Peshawar and four other *stūpas* in north India.

46 That is, of course, only one version of what happened. Another view is that the Kanishka-type *stūpa* was a storeyed tower of wood such as Chinese pilgrims allegedly described, and it was this that provided the model for the *t'ing*-type Chinese pagoda, or at least sanctioned them to adopt

their own *t'ai* for that purpose. We must bear in mind that pilgrims' reports, handed down over centuries, do not always record what was seen, but often what the pilgrim or his biographer thought he should have seen. If at any time the Chinese wooden storeyed tower had been converted by the Chinese to serve as a *stūpa*, its Indian counterpart would thenceforward naturally be envisaged, and probably described, as something similar.

47 In Milne, 1855, p. 59

48 Soper, 1956, p. 230

49 The Marble Pagoda in the Western Hills near Peking, seen in the foreground of plate 254, is an eighteenth-century paraphrase of the Shê-shan pagoda, with two storeys added and with much falsification of decorative detailing, which has been executed in the eighteenth-century style. Nevertheless the Marble Pagoda is close enough to the original to give a fair idea of its basic form.

50 The axial layout may have been copied from India. For example, an account of the Jetavana Monastery at Śrāvastī, made by the Chinese pilgrim Tao-hsüan in AD 667, clearly describes a north–south axial plan. After passing through a number of gateways straddled across the main south–north axis, the pilgrim at last reaches 'a great square pond [tank], filled with lotus blossoms ... Directly north of the pond was the great Buddha pagoda ... next to the north was the great Buddha hall'. Soper, 1942, p. 37, says that the axial layout is Chinese rather than Indian, and that Tao-hsüan is describing retrospectively the Chinese temple plan, which by that time had become obsolete.

51 Broadly speaking, this was a system, in the hands of professional geomancers, by which the mutual influences of the spirits of 'wind and water', *fêng shui*, might be determined for a particular locality. In choosing a site for a building, it was necessary to consult the geomancer in order to ensure that the beneficial influence of these two spirits should not be dissipated, but rather augmented, by the intrusion of a new element in the local air.

52 In Milne, 1855, p. 36

53 See Fugl-Meyer, 1937, p. 33. This fascinating book is about the only work on the subject so far written and I am greatly indebted to it for much that follows. Fugl-Meyer, by the way, is at pains to show that the Hangchow of Marco Polo's day might very well have contained *twelve hundred* bridges, a perfectly reasonable number. But that is not what the *Marco Polo* texts say.

54 A few suspension bridges are found in Formosa, but these seem to have reached the island from Indo-China. The method of their construction reveals a remote Indian ancestry, and they are thus unrelated to the tradition of suspension-bridge building in south-west China [p. 400].

55 The fifth-century AD Chinese pilgrim Fa-hsien speaks of a rope suspension bridge over the Indus, having a span of some eighty paces; he makes no reference to iron for bridge-building. By the seventh century AD, Hsüan-tsang is talking of crossing gorges 'by clinging to iron chains', of 'gangways hanging in mid-air', or 'flying bridges flung across precipices', and at one point of an iron bridge. See Fugl-Meyer, 1937, p. 11. Although no single reference is in itself conclusive, taken together they do seem to add up to a fairly clear picture of a suspension bridge.

56 From an engineering point of view the Himalayan type is in every respect superior. It is more economical in materials, and requires fewer replacements. It involves no tightening devices. The deck does not necessarily have to follow the curve of the main cables, and can be built quite flat. Most important, it is much more stable in high winds than is the Chinese.

57 The actual age of these bridges is uncertain. One of them, the Pa Ch'iao, was rebuilt in 1833.

58 The fact is hardly surprising when we learn from experiments that a granite beam of the same cross-section as those employed in the construction of the Fukien bridges, and only four feet longer than the longest of

them (i.e. seventy-four feet), will break under its own weight, without the addition of any live load. The factor of safety of these trusses, in other words, is practically nil. Fugl-Meyer, 1937, pp. 131-7

59 Marsden (ed.), 1936, pp. 223-34. A bridge over the river at the place where the present bridge stands was begun in 1189 and finished five years later. This was probably the one Marco saw, but the oldest Chinese accounts, and an engraving of it in the Ming geographical work *Chi fu tsung chi*, indicate that it had only thirteen arches. It was repaired under the Chia Ching Emperor in 1522, but was destroyed by flood in 1688. It was then rebuilt, presumably on the original lines but with only eleven arches, and was again repaired in the reign of the Ch'ien Lung Emperor.

In its present form it is three hundred and fifty paces long and eighteen broad, built of green sandstone, and with a hundred and forty portals on each side, each crowned by a large sculptured lion-dog. The bays between are filled with carved stone slabs. As is well known, the Marco Polo bridge was the scene of the alleged incident that led to the resumption of Sino-Japanese hostilities in 1937.

60 The actual ratio is 1 : 5.23. For a circular arch bridge it is of course 1 : 2.

61 In reference to the Nanking Development Plan (Murphy, 1930) which perhaps fortunately never materialized. See Chen, 1947, pp. 27-8

62 Skinner, 1953, pp. 255-8

63 Chuin Tung, 1937

BIBLIOGRAPHY

KEY TO PERIODICAL PUBLICATIONS

A.A. Artibus Asiae, Dresden, then Ascona 1925 et seq.
A.C.A.S.A. Archives of the Chinese Art Society of America, New York 1945 et seq.
A.R. The Asiatic Review, Woking 1913, *The Asiatic Quarterly Review*, London 1914 et seq.
B.M. The Burlington Magazine, London 1903 et seq.
B.M.F.E.A. Bulletin of the Museum of Far Eastern Antiquities, Stockholm 1929 et seq.
B.N.R.I.H.P. Bulletin of the National Research Institute of History and Philology, Peking, then Taiwan, 1928 et seq.
B.S.R.C.A. Bulletin of the Society for Research in Chinese Architecture, Peking 1930–7
C.P. China Pictorial, Peking 1954 et seq.
Ch.R. China Reconstructs, Peking 1952 et seq.
J.A.O.S. Journal of the American Oriental Society, Boston 1849 et seq.
J.W.C.B.R.S. Journal of the West China Border Research Society, Chêng tu 1922–46
M.M.S. Metropolitan Museum Studies, New York 1928–36
M.S. Monumenta Serica, Peking, then Tokyo 1935 et seq.
O.A. Oriental Art, London 1948 et seq.
O.Z. Ostasiatische Zeitschrift, Berlin 1912–37
R.A.A. Revue des Arts Asiatiques, Paris 1924–42
S.B.E. Sacred Books of the East, Oxford and London 1879–1910
T.C.B.R.A.S. Transactions of the China Branch of the Royal Asiatic Society, Hong Kong 1848–55
T.H.M. T'ien Hsia Monthly, Shanghai 1935–41
T.O.C.S. Transactions of the Oriental Ceramic Society, London 1921 et seq.
T.P. T'oung Pao, Leiden 1890 et seq.
W.B.K.K.A. Wiener Beiträge zur Kunst und Kultur Asiens, Vienna 1931 et seq.

GENERAL

ASHTON, L., and Gray, B., *Chinese Art*, London 1951
BACHHOFER, L., *A Short History of Chinese Art*, New York 1946
BINYON, L. (ed.), *Chinese Art*; a collection of essays on various art forms by L. Binyon, L. Ashton, R. L. Hobson, V. Pope Hennessy and A. J. Koop, London 1935
BUSHNELL, S. W., *Chinese Art*, 2 vols, London 1904, 1906
CREEL, H. G., *The Birth of China. A Survey of the Formative Period of Chinese Civilization*, London 1936
EBERHARD, W., *A History of China*, London 1950
GROOT, J. J. M. de, *The Religious System of China, its Ancient Forms, Evolution, History and Present Aspect*, 6 vols, Leiden 1892–1910
GROUSSET, R., *Chinese Art and Culture*, London 1959
HUDSON, G. F., *Europe and China: A Survey of their Relations from the Earliest Times to 1800*, London 1931

NEEDHAM, J., *Science and Civilization in China*, vol. i Introductory Orienta tions, vol. ii History of Scientific Thought, Cambridge 1954 and 1956
SICKMAN, L., and Soper, A. C., *The Art and Architecture of China*, London 1956
SILCOCK, A., *An Introduction to Chinese Art*, Oxford 1935
SIRÉN, O., *A History of Early Chinese Art*, 4 vols, London 1928
STRZYGOWSKI, J., *Asiens bildende Kunst*, Augsburg 1930
SULLIVAN, M., *An Introduction to Chinese Art*, London 1961

CHAPTER I

ANDERSSON, J. G., *Children of the Yellow Earth*, London 1934
ANDERSSON, J. G., 'The site of Chu Chia Chai' in *B.M.F.E.A.*, no. 17, 1945
BRODRICK, A. H., *Early Man. A Survey of Human Origins*, London 1948
CHÊNG Te k'un, *Archaeology in China*, vol. 1 Prehistoric China, Cambridge 1959
CRESSEY, G. B., *China's Geographic Foundations. A Survey of the Land and its People*, New York 1934
HSIA Nai, 'Our neolithic ancestors', in *Ch.R.* vol. 5, no. 5, May 1956
KAPLAN, S., 'Early pottery from the Liang Chu site, Chekiang province' in *A.C.A.S.A.*, vol. iii, 1948–9
LATTIMORE, O., *Inner Asian Frontiers*, New York 1940
LIANG Ssŭ yung, 'Je ho ch'a pu kan miao lin hsi ...' in *T'ien yeh k'ao ku pao kao*, no. 1, Shanghai 1936
P'EI Wên chung, 'New links between ape and man', in *Ch.R.* vol. 6, no. 6, June 1957
WATSON, W., *China before the Han Dynasty*, London 1961
WU, G. D., *Prehistoric Pottery in China*, London 1938

CHAPTER II

ANDERSSON, J. G., 'Researches into the prehistory of the Chinese' being *B.M.F.E.A.* no. 15, Stockholm 1943
BERGMAN, F., 'Archaeological researches in Sinkiang: especially the Lop nor region' being publication vii of the *Reports from the Scientific Expedition to the North Western Provinces of China under the Leadership of Dr Sven Hedin*, Stockholm 1939
CHILDE, V. Gordon, *Magic, Craftsmanship and Science*, Liverpool 1950
Chou Li, The Chou (dynasty) Rituals, attributed to the Duke of Chou. A compendium of ceremonial practices and duties for officials. Translated by E. Biot, *Le Tcheou li, ou Rites des Tcheou*, 2 vols, Paris 1851
DYE, D. S., 'Some ancient circles, squares, angles and curves in earth and stone in Szechwan, China', in *J.W.C.B.R.S.* vol. iv, 1930–1
FÊNG Yün p'êng and Fêng Yün yüan, *Chin Shih So* (Reproductions of Inscriptions on Metal and Stone), 24 fasc., Shanghai 1906
HALOUN, G., 'Zur Üe Tsi Frage', in *Zeitschrift der Deutschen Morgenländi schen Gesellschaft*, vol. xci, Leipzig 1937

HANSFORD, S.H., *Chinese Jade Carving*, London 1950

HENTZE, H., 'Les jades archaïques en Chine', in *A.A.*, 1928–9

KARLGREN, B., 'Some weapons and tools of the Yin dynasty', in *B.M.F.E.A.* no. 17, 1945

Ku yü t'u p'u (An illustrated Study of Ancient Jades), attributed to Lung Ta-yüan, 1712

LAUFER, B., *Jade: a Study in Chinese Archaeology and Religion*, Chicago 1912

Li Chi (Record of Rites), 4th century BC: translated by J. Legge as *S.B.E.* XXVII and XXVIII

MICHEL, H., 'Astronomical Jades', in *O.A.* vol. ii, no. 4, 1950

MICHEL, H., 'Encore un jade astronomique inconnu: le T'ou-kuei', in *Ciel et Terre*, vol. lxxviii, Brussels 1962

PAN KU, *Po hu t'ung tê lun* (Universal Discussions at the White Tiger Lodge), AD 80

RAMSDEN, E.H., *An Introduction to Modern Art*, Oxford 1940

SALMONY, A., *Archaic Chinese Jades from the Edward and Louise B. Sonnen-schein Collection*, Chicago 1952

Shu Ching: a history of China of which the most ancient parts were written in the 10th century BC; translated by B. Karlgren as *The Book of Documents*, Stockholm 1950

SSŬ-MA Ch'ien (*c*.135–85 BC), *Shih Chi*; a history of China up to and including the early years of the Han dynasty; translated in part by B. Watson as *Records of the Grand Historian*, 2 vols, Columbia 1962, and also in part by É. Chavannes as *Mémoires Historiques de Se-ma Ts'ien*, 5 vols, Paris 1895–1905

Tso Chuan: a historical record of the period 1722–250 BC written mainly in the 4th century BC with later additions. Translated by J. Legge in *The Chinese Classics*, vol. 5, parts 1 and 2, as the commentary to the *Ch'un Ch'iu* (Spring and Autumn Annals), London 1872

WU Ta-ch'êng, *Ku yü t'u kao* (An illustrated study of ancient jades), Peking 1889

YÜAN k'ang, *Yüeh chüeh shu* (History of the Secession of Yüeh), in *Ssŭ pu ts'ung k'an*, vol. lxii, Shanghai, 1926–36

CHAPTER III

BRION, M., *The World of Archaeology. India – China – America*, London 1961

Êrh Ya, a glossary written in the 3rd or 2nd century BC

GARNER, Sir Harry, 'The composition of Chinese bronzes', in *O.A.* vol. vi, no. 4, Winter 1960

HANSFORD, S.H., 'Pre-Anyang', in *O.A.* vol. iv, no. 1, 1958

HSIA Nai, 'Workshops of the Dawn of History', in *Ch.R.* vol. 6, no. 1, January 1957

HSIA Nai, 'Workshops of China's oldest civilization', in *Ch.R.* vol. 6, no. 12, December 1957

KARLBECK, O., 'Anyang moulds', in *B.M.F.E.A.* no. 7, 1935

KARLGREN, B., 'Yin and Chou in Chinese bronzes', in *B.M.F.E.A.* no. 8, 1936

KARLGREN, B., 'New studies on Chinese bronzes', *B.M.F.E.A.* no. 9, 1937

KARLGREN, B., 'Some early Chinese bronze masters', in *B.M.F.E.A.* no. 16, 1944

KARLGREN, B., 'Once again the A and B styles in Yin ornamentation', in *B.M.F.E.A.* no. 18, 1946

KARLGREN, B., 'Notes on the grammar of early Chinese bronze décor', in *B.M.F.E.A.* no. 23, 1951

KARLGREN, B., 'Marginalia on some bronze albums', in *B.M.F.E.A.* no. 31, 1959

KARLGREN, B., 'Miscellaneous notes on some bronzes', in *B.M.F.E.A.* no. 33, 1961

KARLGREN, B., 'Some characteristics of the Yin Art', in *B.M.F.E.A.* no. 34, 1962

KOOP, A.J., *Early Chinese Bronzes*, London 1924

LI Chi, *The Beginnings of Chinese Civilization*, Seattle 1957

Lü Shih Ch'un ch'iu (Master Lü's Spring and Autumn Annals) a compendium of natural philosophy attributed to Lü Pu-wei, 3rd century BC. Translated into German by R. Wilhelm as *Frühling und Herbst des Lü Bu-wes*, Jena 1928

Shu Ching: a history of China of which the most ancient parts were written in the 10th century BC; translated by B. Karlgren as *The Book of Documents*, Stockholm 1950

SSŬ-MA Ch'ien (*c*.135–85 BC) *Shih Chi*; a history of China up to and including the early years of the Han dynasty; translated in part by B. Watson as *Records of the Grand Historian*, 2 vols, Columbia 1962, and also in part by É. Chavannes as *Les Mémoires Historiques de Se-ma Ts'ien*, 5 vols, Paris 1895–1905

STEPHEN, B., 'Early Chinese Bronzes in the Royal Ontario Museum', in *O.A.* vol. viii, no. 2, 1962

WALEY, A., 'The T'ao-t'ieh', in *B.M.* vol. xliii, 1926

WATSON, W., *China before the Han Dynasty*, London 1961

WATSON, W., *Ancient Chinese Bronzes*, London 1962

YETTS, W.P., 'A Famous Chinese Bronze', in *B.M.* vol. xliii, 1923

YETTS, W.P., *The George Eumorfopoulos Collection Catalogue of the Chinese and Corean Bronzes, Sculpture, Jades, Jewellery and Miscellaneous Objects. Vol. I, Bronzes: Ritual and Other Vessels, Weapons, etc.*, London 1929

YETTS, W.P., *The Cull Chinese Bronzes*, London 1939

YETTS, W.P., *An-yang, a Retrospect*, London 1942

CHAPTER IV

CHARLESTON, R.J., 'Han damasks', in *O.A.* vol. i, 1948

CHAVANNES, É., *Mission Archéologique dans la Chine Septentrionale*. Text; vol. i, part 1, *La Sculpture à l'Époque des Han*, Paris 1913

CHIANG Yuen-yi (Yüan-i) *Changsha, The Chu Tribe and its Art*, vol. i, Lacquer, Shanghai 1949

Ch'u tz'u (Songs of Ch'u), translated by David Hawkes, Oxford 1959

COHN, W., 'The deities of the Four Cardinal Points', in *T.O.C.S.* vol. xviii, 1940–1

de SAUSSURE, L., 'Les origines de l'astronomie chinoise', in *T.P.* vol. x, 1909

FAN Yeh (AD 420–77), *Hou Han Shu* (History of the Later Han dynasty)

FÊNG Yün-p'êng and Fêng Yün-yüan, *Chin Shih So* (Reproductions of Inscriptions on Metal and Stone), 24 fasc., Shanghai 1906

GALLOIS, H.C., 'Mutual Influences between Chinese and Near Eastern ceramics in the T'ang period and before', in *A.R.* vol. xxviii, no. 96, October 1932

GYLLENSVÄRD, B., 'The First Floral Patterns on Chinese Bronzes' in *B.M.F.E.A.* no. 34, 1962

HIRTH, F., *China and the Roman Orient: researches into their ancient and mediaeval relations as represented in old Chinese records*, Leipzig, Munich, Shanghai, and Hong Kong, 1885

HSIA Nai, 'New finds of ancient silk textiles', in *Ch.R.* vol. xi, no. 1, 1962

Huai-Nan Tzu, attributed to Liu An, Prince of Huai-nan, *c*.120 BC: a classic of Taoist natural philosophy

KARLGREN, B., 'Early Chinese mirror inscriptions', in *B.M.F.E.A.* no. 6, 1934

KARLGREN, B., 'Huai and Han', being *B.M.F.E.A.* no. 13, 1941

KOIZUMI, A., *The Tomb of the Painted Basket of Lo Lang, Detailed Report of Archaeological Researches, Volume 1*, Keijo (Seoul) 1934

LAUFER, B., *Chinese Pottery of the Han Period*, Leiden 1909

Lieh Tzu, a compilation of Taoist fragments dating from 5th–1st centuries BC, put together in its extant form at the end of the 5th century AD. Translated by A.C. Graham, London 1960

LÖW-BEER, F., 'Zum Dekor der Han-Lacke', in *W.B.K.K.A.* vol xi, 1937

LÖW-BEER, F., 'Two lacquered boxes from Ch'angsha', in *A.A.* vol. x, 1947, and vol. xi, 1948

MAILEY, J., and Hathaway, C.S., 'A bonnet and a pair of mitts from Ch'ang-sha', in *Chronicle of the Museum for the Arts of Decoration of the Cooper Union*, vol. ii, no. 10, New York 1958

MÄNCHEN-HELFEN, O., 'Zur Geschichte der Lackkunst in China', in *W.B.K.K.A.* vol. xi, 1937

MONGAIT, A., *Archaeology in the U.S.S.R.*, Moscow 1959

PAN Ku (died AD 92), *Ch'ien Han shu*, partly translated by H.H. Dubs as *The History of the Former Han Dynasty*, London 1938–55

PFISTER, R., *Textiles de Palmyre*, 3 vols, Paris 1934, 1937, 1940

PFISTER, R., 'Les Soiries Han de Palmyre', in *R.A.A.* vol. xiii, fasc. 2, 1941

RUDOLPH, R.C., and Wen Yu, *Han Tomb Art of West China*, Berkeley and Los Angeles 1951

SALMONY, A., *Antler and Tongue. An Essay on Ancient Chinese Symbolism and its Implications*, Ascona 1954

SSŬ-MA Ch'ien (*c.*135–85 BC), *Shih chi*; a history of China up to and including the early years of the Han dynasty; translated in part by B. Watson as *Records of the Grand Historian*, 2 vols, Columbia, 1962, and in part by É. Chavannes as *Les Mémoires Historiques de Se-ma Ts'ien*, 5 vols, Paris 1895–1905

STEIN, Sir Aurel, *Innermost Asia. Detailed Report of Excavations in Central Asia, Kan-su and Eastern Iran*, 4 vols, Oxford 1928

SYLWAN V., 'Silk from the Yin dynasty', in *B.M.F.E.A.* no. 9, 1937

SYLWAN, V., 'Investigation of Silk from Edsen-gol and Lop-nor', being publication xxxii of *Reports from the Scientific Expedition to the North-Western Provinces of China under the Leadership of Dr Sven Hedin*, Stockholm 1949

TREVER, C., *Excavations in Northern Mongolia (1924–5)*, Leningrad 1932

VOSKRESENSKY, A.A., and Tikhonov, N.P. (translated by E.Tolmachoff), 'Technical study of textiles from the burial grounds of Noin-ula', in *Bulletin of the Needle and Bobbin Club*, vol. xx, nos 1 and 2, New York 1936

WALEY, A., *Three Ways of Thought in Ancient China*, London 1939

WALEY, A., 'Life under the Han Dynasty', in *History Today*, vol. iii, no.2, February 1953

WHITE, W.C., *Tombs of Old Lo-yang*, Shanghai 1934

YETTS, W.P., 'Discoveries of the Koslóv Expedition', in *B.M.* vol. xlviii, 1926

YETTS, W.P., 'Notes on Chinese roof-tiles', in *T.O.C.S.* vol. vii, 1927–8

YETTS, W.P., *The Cull Chinese Bronzes*, London 1939

CHAPTER V

BROWN, P., *Indian Architecture (Buddhist and Hindu Periods)*, Bombay 1940

CHANDA, R., *Mediaeval Indian Sculpture in the British Museum*, London 1936

CHAVANNES, É., *Dix Inscriptions Chinoises de l'Asie Centrale, d'après les Estampages de M. Ch.-E.Bonin*, Paris 1904

CHAVANNES, É., *Mission Archéologique dans la Chine Septentrionale*. Text; vol. 1, part 2, *La Sculpture bouddhique*, Paris 1915

ECKE, G., and Demiéville, P., *The Twin Pagodas of Zayton*, Cambridge, Mass., 1935

FRY, R., *Vision and Design*, London 1920

HENDERSON, G., and Hurvitz, L., 'The Buddha of Seiryōji. New finds and theories', in *A.A.* vol. xix, part 1, 1956

INGHOLT, H., *Gandhāran Art in Pakistan*, New York 1957

KERN, H., *The Saddharma-pundarīka or the Lotus of the True Law*, being vol.xxi of *S.B.E.*, Oxford 1884

LOHUIZEN-DE LEEUW, J.E. van, *The 'Scythian' Period*, Leiden 1949

Mai-chi-shan shih-k'u, Peking 1954

MARSHALL, Sir John, *The Buddhist Art of Gandhāra*, Cambridge 1960

MIZUNO, S., and Nagahiro, T., *A Study of the Buddhist Cave-Temples of Lung-mên, Ho-nan*, Tokyo 1941

MIZUNO, S., *Unko Sekkutsi; Yün-kang, The Buddhist Cave-Temples of the Fifth Century AD in North China*, 15 vols, Kyoto 1951-4

MÜLLER, M., 'The Larger Sukhāvati-vyūha and the Smaller Sukhāvati-vyūha', in *Buddhist Mahayana Texts*, part 2, being vol. xlix of *S.B.E.*, London 1894

MÜNSTERBERG, H., 'Buddhist bronzes of the Six Dynasties Period', in *A.A.* vol. ix, 1946

MÜNSTERBERG, H., 'Chinese Buddhist bronzes at the Kamakura Museum', in *A.A.* vol. xix, 1956

ROWLAND, B., 'Notes on the dated statues of the Northern Wei dynasty and the beginnings of Buddhist sculpture in China', in *The Art Bulletin*, vol. xix, Providence 1937

ROWLAND, B., *The Art and Architecture of India*, London 1953

SIRÉN, O., *Chinese Sculpture from the Fifth to the Fourteenth Century*, 1 vol. text, 3 vols plates, London 1925

SIRÉN, O., 'The evolution of Chinese Sculpture', in *B.M.* vol. lxxii, 1938

SOPER, A.C., 'Literary evidence for early Buddhist art in China. 1. Foreign images and artists', in *O.A.* vol. ii, no. 1, Summer 1949

TOKIWA, D., and Sekino, T., *Buddhist Monuments in China*, 5 vols text, 5 portfolios plates, Tokyo 1925–31

WALEY, A., *A Catalogue of Paintings recovered from Tun-huang by Sir Aurel Stein, K.C.I.E.*, London 1931

WEGNER, M., 'Ikonographie des Chinesischen Maitreya', in *O.Z.*, vol.xv, 1929

WILLETTS, W., 'Superb Chinese Buddhist sculptures from newly revealed cave-shrines in north-west China', in *Illustrated London News*, vol. ccxxiv, 1954

YETTS, W.P., *The George Eumorfopoulos Collection Catalogue of the Chinese and Corean Bronzes, Sculptures, Jades, Jewellery and Miscellaneous Objects.* Vol. 3, *Buddhist Sculpture*, London 1932

CHAPTER VI

ASHTON, L., 'China and Egypt', in *T.O.C.S.* vol. xi, 1933–4

BACHHOFER, L., 'Characteristics of T'ang and Sung Pottery', in *B.M.* vol. xv, 1934

BELL, H.H., 'T'ang pottery and its late classical affinities', in *B.M.* vol. vi, 1914

BUSHELL, S.W., 'Description of Chinese pottery and Porcelain', being a translation of the *T'ao Shuo*, 1910

Ch'a ching (Tea Classic), attributed to Lu Yü, 8th century AD, to be found in the Yüan dynasty compilation, *Po Ch'uan hsüeh hai*

CHAIT, R.M., 'Some comments on the dating of early Chinese cloisonné', in *O.A.* vol. iii, no. 2, 1950

CHÊNG Tê-k'un, *Archaeological Studies in Szechwan*, Cambridge 1957

CHU Yen, *T'ao Shuo*, 1774; see S. Bushell, 1910

COOMARASWAMY, A., and Kershaw, F., 'A Chinese Buddhist water-vessel and its Indian prototype', in *A.A.* vol. iii, 1928–9

DAVID, Sir Percival, 'The Shōsō-in pottery', in *T.O.C.S.* vol. x, 1931–2

FLINES, E.W. Van Orsoy de, *Gids de Keramische Verzamling*, Batavia 1949

GALLOIS, H.C., 'Mutual influences between Chinese and Near Eastern ceramics in the T'ang period and before', in *A.R.* vol. xxviii, no. 96, October 1932

GALLOIS, H.C., 'About T'ang and Ta Ts'in', in *T.O.C.S.* vol. xiii, 1935–6

GOMPERTZ, G.St.G.M., *Chinese Celadon Wares*, London 1958

GRAY, Sir Basil, *Early Chinese Pottery and Porcelain*, London 1953

HARADA, J., *The Shōsō-in, an Eighth-Century Repository*, Tokyo 1950

HARRISSON, B., 'Niah's Lobang Tulang (Cave of Bones)', in *Sarawak Museum Journal* vol. viii, December 1958

HARRISSON, T., 'Some Borneo ceramic objects', in *Sarawak Museum Journal* vol. v, September 1950

HARRISSON, T., 'Ceramics penetrating Central Borneo', in *Sarawak Museum Journal* vol. vi, December 1951

HARRISSON, T., 'Export wares found in West Borneo', in *O.A.* vol. v, no. 2, Summer 1959

HETHERINGTON, L., *Chinese Ceramic Glazes*, South Pasadena 1948

HITCHMAN, F., and Swann, Peter C., 'Notes on Chinese Ceramics', in *O.A.* vol. iii, no. 4, Winter 1951

HOBSON, R.L., 'The significance of Samarra', in *T.O.C.S.* vol. ii, 1922–3

HOBSON, R.L., 'Potsherds from Brahminabad', in *T.O.C.S.* vol. viii, 1928–30

HOBSON, R.L., 'Chinese porcelain from Fostat', in *B.M.* vol. lxi, August 1932

HONEY, W.B., *The Ceramic Art of China and Other Countries of the Far East*, London 1945

HONEY, W.B., *The Art of the Potter*, London 1946

HSIA Nai, 'Tracing the thread of the past', in *Ch.R.* vol. 8, no. 10, October 1959

INGRAM, Sir Herbert, 'Why T'ang?', in *Röhsska Könstlodjmuseets Arstryck*, Gothenburg 1946

INGRAM, Sir Herbert, 'Form', in *Ethos*, no. 4, Stockholm 1946

Institute of Ceramics, The, Tokyo, *Catalogue of the T'ang Polychromes*, Tokyo 1928

KAHLE, P., 'Chinese porcelain in the lands of Islam', in *T.O.C.S.* vol. xviii, 1940–1

KARLBECK, O., 'Early Yüeh ware', in *O.A.* o.s. vol. ii, no. 1, Summer 1949

KARLBECK, O., 'Proto-porcelain and Yüeh', in *T.O.C.S.* vol. xxv, 1949–50

KOYAMA, F., 'The Yüeh-chou Yao Celadon excavated in Japan', in *A.A.* vol. xiv, parts 1 and 2, 1951

LAMM, C., *Glass from Iran in the National Museum*, Stockholm 1935

LAN P'u, *Ching-tê-chên T'ao Lu*, 1815; see Sayer, 1949

LANE, A., 'Glazed relief ware of the ninth century AD', in *Ars Islamica*, vol. vi, Ann Arbor 1939

LEACH, B., *A Potter's Book*, London 1940

LINDBERG, G., 'Hsing Yao. Attempt at an interpretation of the T'ang Hsing Chou ware', in *O.A.* o.s. vol. ii, no. 4, Spring 1950

LINDBERG, G., 'Hsing-yao and Ting-yao. An investigation and description of some Chinese T'ang and Sung white wares in the Carl Kempe and Gustav Lindberg collections', in *B.M.F.E.A.* no. 25, 1955

ORBELI, J., and Trever, C., *Orfèvrerie Sasanide, objets en or, argent et bronze*, Moscow/Leningrad, 1935

Oriental Ceramic Society, The, (Catalogue of a) *Loan Exhibition of the Arts of the T'ang Dynasty*, London 1958

OTTEMA, N., *Chineesische Ceramik Handboek*, Amsterdam 1946

PICTON, H., *Early German Art and its Origins from the Beginnings to about 1050*, London 1939

PLUMER, J.M., 'Certain celadon potsherds from Samarra traced to their source', in *Ars Islamica*, vol. iv, Ann Arbor 1937

POPE, J.F., 'Chinese ceramics and Tom Harrisson', in *A.A* vol. vi, 1956

PRODAN, M., *The Art of the T'ang Potter*, London 1960

QUARITCH-WALES, H.G., 'A newly-explored route of ancient Indian cultural expansion', in *Indian Art and Letters*, vol. ix, no. 1, London 1935

QUARITCH-WALES, H.G., 'Archaeological researches on ancient Indian colonization in Malaya', in *Journal of the Malayan Branch of the Royal Asiatic Society*, vol. xviii, part 1, Singapore 1940

RACKHAM, B. 'The earliest arrivals of pre-Ming wares in the West', in *T.O.C.S.* vol. iii, 1923–4

RHODES, D., *Stoneware and Porcelain: the Art of High-fired Pottery*, Philadelphia 1959

SARRE, F., *Die Keramik von Samarra*, being vol. 2 of *Die Ausgrabungen von Samarra*, Berlin 1925

SAYER, G., a translation of *Ching-tê-chên T'ao Lu* or *The Potteries of China*, London 1949

SHEPARD, Anna O., *Ceramics for the Archaeologist*, Washington 1956

SMIRNOV, J., *Argenterie orientale, recueil d'anciennes vaisselles orientales en argent et en or trouvées principalement en Russie*, St Petersburg 1909

SUDBURY, E.R., *Annual Report on the Archaeological Survey of Ceylon for 1924–5*, Colombo 1926

SULLIVAN, M., 'Archaeology in the Philippines', in *Antiquity,* vol. xxx, no. 118, London 1956

SULLIVAN, M., 'Chinese export porcelain in Singapore -I', in *O.A.* vol. iii, no. 4, Winter 1957

THORPE, G., *English Glass*, London 1949

WILLETTS, W., 'Excavations at Bhambore. Possible site of the medieval seaport of Debal in Sind', in *O.A.* vol. vi, no. 1, Spring 1960

CHAPTER VII

CARTER, T.F., *The Invention of Printing and its Spread Westwards*, second edition, revised by L. Carrington Goodrich, New York 1955

CHAN Wing-tsit, 'The quintessence of Chinese Art', in *T.H.M.* vol. xi, no. 3, December–January 1940–1

CHANG Jên-hsia, 'Flower-and-bird painting', in *Ch.R.* vol. ii, no. 3, 1953

CHIANG Yee, *Chinese Calligraphy: an Introduction to its Aesthetic and Technique*, London 1938

CHIANG Yuen Yi (Yüan-i) *Changsha; The Chu Tribe and its Art*, vol. ii, Shanghai 1950

Chieh tzu yüan hua chüan (Mustard Seed Garden Painting Manual), 17th century, see R. Petrucci

CLAPPERTON, R.H., *Paper. An Historical Account of its Making by Hand from the Earliest Times down to the Present Day*, Oxford 1934

CLARK, Sir Kenneth, *Landscape into Art*, London 1949

COHN, W., *Chinese Painting*, London 1951

CONTAG, V., 'The unique characteristics of Chinese landscape painting', in *A.C.A.S.A.* vol. iv, 1952

DAVID, Sir Percival, 'The International Exhibition of Chinese art; some reflections', a lecture delivered before the Royal Society 13 January 1936; in *A.R.* vol. xxxii, no. 110, April 1936

DRISCOLL, L., and Toda, K., *Chinese Calligraphy*, Chicago 1935

ERKES, E., 'The use of writing in ancient China', in *J.A.O.S.* vol. lxi, 1941

FERGUSON, J.C., *Chinese Painting*, Chicago 1927

FRIEDLÄNDER, M.J., *On Art and Connoisseurship*, London 1941

GOWING, L., *The Great Transformation* (introduction to a catalogue of an exhibition of paintings by Cézanne), London, 28 September to 27 October 1954

GRAY, Sir Basil, *Buddhist Cave Paintings at Tun-huang*, London 1959

HILER, H., *Notes on the Technique of Painting*, London 1934

HSIA Nai, 'Arts and crafts of 2300 years ago' in *Ch.R.* vol. iii, no. 1, January–February 1954

HSIA Wên-yen, *T'u-hui Pao-chien* (Notes on Painting and Painters), 1365

Ku kung shu hua chi, Reproductions of painting and calligraphy in the Peking Palace Museum Collections, 14 vols, Peking 1930–6

KUO Hsi (c.1020–90), *Lin Ch'üan Kao Chih* (The Great Message of Forests and Streams); see Sakanashi, 1935

KUO Jo-hsü, *T'u-hua chien-wên chih*, 11th century; see A. Soper, 1951

LAURIE, A.P., *The Painter's Methods and Materials*, London 1947

LI K'an, *Chu p'u hsiang lu* (Comprehensive Record of Bamboo), end of 13th century; see Aschwin Lippe

LIN Yutang, 'The aesthetics of Chinese calligraphy' in *T.H.M.* vol. i, 1935

LIPPE, Aschwin (Ernst Aschwin Prince Lippe-Biesterfeld), *Li K'an und seine ausführliche Beschreibung des Bambusses, Beiträge zur Bambusmalerei der Yüan-Zeit*, Berlin 1942

LORAN, A., *Cézanne's Composition. Analysis of his Form with Diagrams and Photographs of his Motifs*, Berkeley and Los Angeles 1946

MAYER, B., *The Artist's Handbook of Materials and Techniques*, London 1951

MI Fei (1051–1107), *Hua Shih* (A Historical Study of Painting), reprint Shanghai 1935–7

PETRUCCI, R., (transl.) *Kiai-tseu-yuan houa tchouan (Chieh tzŭ yüan hua chüan) les Enseignements de la Peinture du Jardin grand comme un Grain de Moutarde. Encyclopédie de la Peinture Chinoise,* Paris 1918

PRICE, H.H., *Thinking and Experience*, London 1953

READ, Sir Herbert, *Education through Art*, London 1943

ROWLAND, B., 'The problem of Hui Tsung', in *A.C.A.S.A.* vol. v, 1951

ROWLAND, B., 'Early Chinese painting in Japan: the problem of Hsü Hsi', in *A.A.* vol. xv, no. 3, 1952

SAKANASHI, S., (transl.). *An Essay on Landscape Painting (Lin Ch'üan Kao Chih* by Kuo Hsi), London 1935

SAKANASHI, S., *The Spirit of the Brush*, London 1939

Shina Meigwa Lokan (The Pageant of Chinese Painting), Tokyo 1936

SHORT, E.H., *The Painter in History*, London 1948

SIRÉN, O., *The Chinese on the Art of Painting*, Peking 1936

SIRÉN, O., *Chinese Painting. Leading Masters and Principles of Style*, Part I: *From the Han to the End of the Sung Dynasty*, London 1956

SOPER, A.C. (transl.), *Kuo Jo-hsü's Experiences in Painting. An eleventh-century history of Chinese painting together with the Chinese text in facsimile,* Washington 1951

SUN Ta-yü (transl.), 'On the fine art of Chinese calligraphy by Sun Kuo-t'ing of the T'ang dynasty', in *T.H.M.* vol. 1, no. 2, September 1935

WALEY, A., 'Chinese philosophy of art – iv', in *B.M.* vol. xxxviii, January–June 1921

WANG Chi-chên, 'Notes on Chinese ink', in *M.M.S.* vol. iii, part 1, December 1930

WANG Shih-hsiang, 'Chinese ink bamboo paintings', in *A.C.A.S.A.* vol. iii, 1948–9

WANG Yu-chuan, 'Relics of the State of Chu', in *C.P.* vol. ii, no. 8, August 1953

YANG Yu-hsün, *La Calligraphie chinoise depuis les Han*, Paris 1937

YONEZAWA, Y., and Shimada, S., *Painting of the Sung and Yüan Dynasties*, Tokyo 1952

CHAPTER VIII AND POSTSCRIPT

ARLINGTON, L.C., and Lewisohn, W., *In Search of Old Peking*, Peking 1935

ATTIRET, F. (translated by Sir Harry Beaumont), *A Particular Account of the Emperor of China's Gardens near Pekin*, London 1752

BOERSCHMANN, E., *Die Baukunst und religiöse Kultur der Chinesen*, 3 vols, Berlin 1911–3

BOYD, A., *Chinese Architecture*, London 1962

CHEN, C., 'Modern Chinese Architecture', in *Architectural Review*, China Number, July 1947

CHOU Shou-chuan, 'The Gardens of Soochow', in *Ch.R.* vol. vi, no. 5, May 1957

CHUIN Tung, 'Architectural Chronicle', in *T.H.M.* vol. v, no. 3, October 1937

CHUIN Tung, 'Foreign influences in Chinese architecture', in *T.H.M.* vol. vi, no. 5, May 1938

DAVIS, J.F., *The Chinese*, 2 vols, London 1836

ECKE, G., and Demiéville, P., *The Twin Pagodas of Zayton*, Cambridge, Mass., 1935

ECKE, G., 'Structural features of the stone-built T'ing-pagoda,' in *M.S.* vol. i, 1935–6

ECKE, G., 'Ergänzungen und Erläuterungen zu Professor Boerschmanns Kritik von "The Twin Pagodas of Zayton"', in *M.S.* vol. ii, 1936–7

FLETCHER, R. Banister, *A History of Architecture*, London 1954

FUGL-MEYER, H., *Chinese Bridges*, Shanghai 1937

GUTKIND, E.A., *Revolution of Environment*, London 1946

JOHNSTON, R.F., *Twilight in the Forbidden City*, London 1934

LI Chieh, *Ying tsao fa shih* (Methods of Building and Construction), first printed 1103; 1925 edition based on this and another of 1145

LIANG Ssŭ-ch'êng, 'China's architectural heritage and the tasks of today', in *People's China*, vol. 1, no. 21, November 1952

LIANG Ssŭ-ch'êng, 'Peking looks ahead', in *Ch.R.* vol. ii, no. 2, March–April 1953

LIN Yutang, *The Importance of Living*, London 1939

LIN Yutang, *My Country and My People*, London 1942

LIN Yutang, *Imperial Peking. Seven Centuries of China*, with an essay on the art of Peking by P.C. Swann, London 1961

MARSDEN, W. (edit.), *The Travels of Marco Polo*, London 1936

MILNE, W.C., 'Pagodas in China', in *T.C.B.R.A.S.*, part. v, 1855

MIRAMS, D.G., *A Brief History of Chinese Architecture*, Shanghai 1940

PRIP-MØLLER, 'Kinas bygningskunst', in *Arkitekten*, vol. xxiv, nos 3–4, Copenhagen 1937

SIRÉN, O., *The Imperial Palaces of Peking*, 3 vols, Paris and Brussels 1926

SIRÉN, O., *Gardens of China*, New York 1949

SIRÉN, O., *China and the Gardens of Europe of the Eighteenth century*, New York 1950

SKINNER, R.T.F., 'Peking 1953', in *Architectural Review*, October 1953

SOPER, A.C., *The Evolution of Buddhist Architecture in Japan*, Princeton 1942

YETTS, W.P., 'Writings on Chinese Architecture', in *B.M.* vol. 1, 1927

YULE, Sir H., *The Book of Ser Merco Polo the Venetian concerning the Kingdoms and Marvels of the East*, third edition revised in the light of recent discoveries by H. Cordier, 2 vols, London 1903

CHRONOLOGICAL TABLE

YEAR	PERIOD	STYLES, SITES AND ARTISTS		POTTERY	
c.500 000	LOWER PALEOLITHIC	Chou-k'ou-tien Loc. 1	Peking Man		
c.400 000		Chou-k'ou-tien Loc. 15	Ting-ts'un Man		
c. 50 000	UPPER PALEOLITHIC	Shui-tung-k'ou and Sjarra-osso-gol	Ordos Man		
c. 25 000		Chou-k'ou-tien Upper Cave	Homo Sapiens		
c. 6 000	PERI-GOBI MESOLITHIC AND NEOLITHIC	Djalai-nor			
c. 5 000		Ang-ang-hsi			
c. 4 000		Lin-hsi Hung-shan-hou			
2 500	CHINESE NEOLITHIC			*Early Yang-shao*	*Lung-shan*
				Hou-kang I	
2 400				Pan-p'o	
2 300				*Middle Yang-shao*	
2 200				Yang-shao-ts'un	Liang-chêng-chên
2 100				Pan-shan	
2 000					Chêng-tzu-yai
1 900					
1 800					
1 700				Ma-ch'ang	
1 600		BRONZE			Hou-kang II
1 500	SHANG DYNASTY	*First Phase*		Ch'i-chia-p'ing	Liang-chu
1 450	capital at Chêng-chou				
1 400	– high-fired and glazed				
1 350	stoneware			*Late Yang-shao*	
1 300				Hsin-tien	
1 250	capital at An-yang				
1 200	– silk textiles	Hsiao-t'un			
1 150					
1 100				Ssŭ-wa	
1 050	CHOU DYNASTY				
1 000	Western Chou (1027–772)	*Second Phase*			
950	capital at Ch'ang-an				
900					
850					
800	Eastern Chou (772–221)				
750	capital at Lo-yang				
700		Hsin-chêng		Sha-ching	
650					
600		Li-yü			
550		*Third Phase*			
500	Warring States				
450					
400					
350					
300		Chin-ts'un (also lacquer painting)			
250	CH'IN DYNASTY (220–207)	Shou-hsien			

SILK AND LACQUER   PAINTING

200   HAN DYNASTY   Ch'ang⁄sha – lacquer   first⁄found painting on silk

150   Former Han (206 BC – AD 9)   first⁄found writing brush   POTTERY

100   capital at Ch'ang⁄an   Pottery of Yüeh⁄type in

BC   – paper   Lacquer and silk at Lo⁄lang, Korea   production at Tê⁄ching

0   Wang Mang Interregnum   Lacquer and silk at Noin⁄ula, Mongolia   and Chiu⁄yen

AD   Later Han (AD 23–220)

100   capital at Lo⁄yang   Silk at Palmyra, Syria

150   Silk at Lou⁄lan, Chinese Turkestan

200   THREE KINGDOMS

250   Wei (230–65) Shu (221–63)

    Wu (222–50)

300   WESTERN CHIN (265–317)   ARCHITECTURE   SCULPTURE

350   EASTERN CHIN (317–420)

400   WEI, NORTHERN (385–535)   *First Phase*

450   EASTERN (535–50) WESTERN (535–57)   First⁄found Chinese Buddha image

500   NORTHERN CH'I (550–77)   The Great Stone Bridge   Work begun at Tun⁄huang

550   NORTHERN CHOU (557–80)   at Chao⁄hsien   Yün⁄kang

    AND FOUR SOUTHERN DYNASTIES   Lung⁄mên

    SUI DYNASTY (589–618)   *Second Phase*

600   capital at Ch'ang⁄an, then Lo⁄yang   Hsiang⁄t'ang⁄shan

650   T'ANG DYNASTY (618–906)   *Third Phase*

700   capital at Ch'ang⁄an   – the Wild Goose Pagoda   T'ien⁄lung⁄shan

750   P'ing⁄ling⁄ssŭ   Yüeh ware in production

800   Ch'ü⁄yang   at Yü⁄wang⁄miao and

850   Shang⁄lin⁄hu

900   FIVE DYNASTIES   Hsing porcelain at

950   SUNG DYNASTY   Hsü Hsi and Huang Ch'üan   Samarra on the Tigris

000   Northern Sung (960–1126)   Ting porcelain and

050   capital at K'ai⁄feng   Lung⁄ch'üan celadon

100   Southern Sung (1126–1277)   Wên T'ung, Kuo Hsi, Mi Fei, Su Shih

150   capital at Hangchow   Emperor Hui⁄tsung's Academy of Painting

200   Emperor Kao⁄tsung's Academy

250   YÜAN (MONGOL) DYNASTY   Hsia Kuei and Ma Yüan

300   (1280–1368) capital at   Ch'ien Hsüan

350   T'ai⁄tu (Peking)   *Wên⁄jên* revival

400   MING DYNASTY (1368–1644)

450   capital at Nanking to 1420

500   at Peking from 1420

550   Forbidden City built

600   CH'ING (MANCHU) DYNASTY

650   (1644–1912)

700   capital at Peking

750

800

850

900   THE REPUBLIC (1912–....)

950

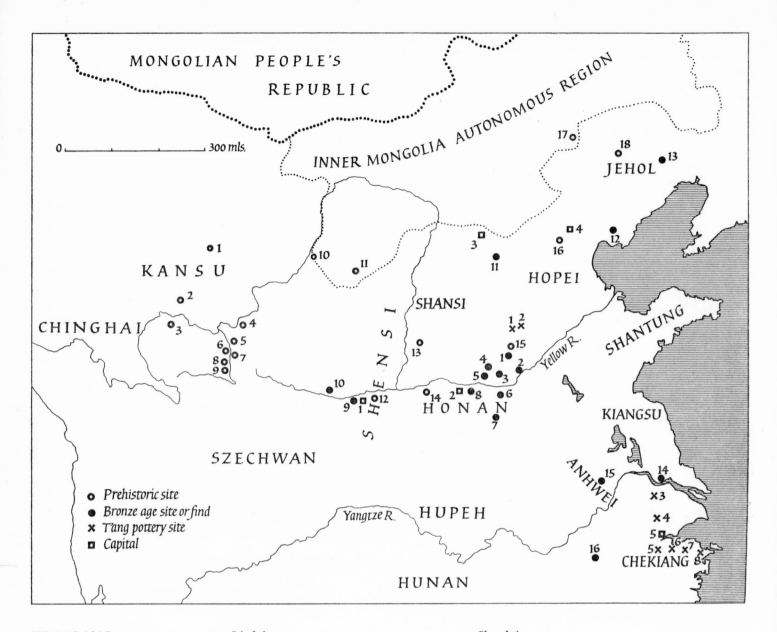

KEY TO MAP

17. Lin-hsi
18. Hung-shan-hou

PREHISTORIC SITES

1. Sha-ching
2. Ma-ch'ang
3. Lo-han-t'ang
4. Pai-tao-kou-p'ing
5. Hsin-tien
6. Pan-shan
7. Ssŭ-wa
8. Ch'i-chia-p'ing
9. Ma-chia-yao
10. Shui-tung-k'ou
11. Sjarra-osso-gol
12. Pan-p'o
13. Ting-ts'un
14. Yang-shao
15. Hou-kang
16. Chou-k'ou-tien

BRONZE AGE SITES

1. An-yang (Ta-ssŭ-k'ung-ts'un,
   Hsiao-t'un, Wu-kuan-ts'un, etc.)
2. Hsün-hsien
3. Hsing-ts'un
4. Hui-hsien (Liu-li-ko, Ku-wei-ts'un)
5. Chao-ku-ts'un
6. Chêng-chou
7. Hsin-chêng
8. Chin-ts'un
9. P'u-tu-ts'un
10. Pao-chi
11. Li-yü
12. T'ang-shan
13. Hsing-lung-hsien
14. Yen-tun-shan

15. Shou-hsien
16. T'un-chi

T'ANG POTTERY SITES

1. Hsing-tai
2. Chü-lu
3. I-hsing
4. Tê-ch'ing
5. Shang-tung
6. Chiu-yen
7. Yü-wang-miao
8. Shang-lin-hu

CAPITALS

1. Ch'ang-an (Sian)
2. Lo-yang
3. Ta-t'ung
4. Peking
5. Hangchow

LIST OF TABLES, MAPS AND FIGURES

For permission to reproduce photographs in this book, the author and publishers are grateful to the following

The Academy of Arts, Honolulu, 89, 194; Art Gallery and Museum, Glasgow, 173; The Art Institute of Chicago (Sonnenschein Collection), *8*, *11*, *26*, *43–5*, (Lucy Maud Buckingham Collection) 68; Art Museum, University of Singapore, *12–4*, *27*, *31*, *34*, *42*; The Trustees of the British Museum, London, *30*, *38*, *44*, *45*, *47*, *5*, 21, 40, 56, 57, 76, 80, 93, 96, 98, 120, 135, 171, 202, 250, (Eumorfopoulos Collection) *9*, *10*, *19*, 27, 28, 36, 38, 92, (Raphael Bequest) 10, *39*; Chinese People's Association for Cultural Relations with Foreign Countries, 191, 229, 249; Chung-kuo chien-chu, 248; City Art Gallery, Bristol (F.P.M. Schiller Bequest), 164; The City Art Museum, St Louis, 82; Mrs A. Clark, Fulmer, England, *36*, *40*, 160, 167, 174, 180; A.C. Cooper Ltd., London, 10, 54, 65, 66, 69, 97, 100, 116, 117, 139, 174, 186, 203, 209, 213; the late Lord Cunliffe, Princes Risborough, England, *28*, *35*, 155, 158; Daitokuji, Kyoto, *52*, 196; The Damascus Museum, 94, 95; The Detroit Institute of Arts, *50*; W.H. Eagle, photographer (British Museum), 245, 254, 256–8, 262, 263; O. Ekberg, photographer, Stockholm, *1–6*; E.N.A., London, 255; T. Fall, photographer, London, 142, 160, 167, 180; Fogg Art Museum, Harvard University (Grenville L. Winthrop Bequest), *18*, 31, 74, 84, 118; J.R. Freeman, photographer, London, *9*, *10*, *19*, *30*, *38*, *44*, 28, 76, 80, 93, 96, 98; Dr F. Funke, photographer, Cologne, *53–8*, 146, 149, 150, 227, 251; E. Hahn, photographer, Zurich, 122, 126; Hakuzuru Art Museum, Kobe, 77; Wallace Heaton Ltd., London, 79; Heibonsha Ltd., Tokyo, 201; The Francis Hopp Museum of Eastern Asiatic Arts, Budapest, 37; Horyuji, Nara, *48*; Hosekawa Collection, Tokyo, *37*; Dr M. Hürlimann, as photographer, Zurich, 228, 231, 264; Institute of Archaeology of the Academy of Sciences, Peking, 1, 8, 11, 19, 20, 62, 72, 81; Dr C. Kempe, Ekolsund, Sweden, 162, 163, 176, 178, 181; Koto-in, Kyoto, 212; Kyoto University, 99; Dr H. Lindberg, Stockholm, 157, 159, 184; Mr and Mrs F. Brodie Lodge, Flore, England, *50*; the late Dato Loke Wan Tho, Singapore, 156, 172; C.T. Loo, Frank Caro Successor, New York, 33, 46; Mr F. Löw-Beer, New York, 105, 112; Mr F.G. Macalpine, Clitheroe, England, 79; Captain D. Malcolm, London, *17*; Professor Mei Chien-yang, Central Academy of Industrial and Handicraft Arts, Peking, 17; The Metropolitan Museum of Art, New York (Rogers Fund), 115, 124, 127, 140, (Kennedy Fund) 121; B. Moosbrugger, photographer, Zurich, 129, 151; The Municipal Museum, Osaka, 209; Musée des Antiquités Nationales, Paris, 22; Musée Guimet, Paris, 170; The Museum of Fine Arts, Boston, *46*, *49*, 67, 103, 133, 136, 187, 205; The Museum of Science, Buffalo, 14, 29, 161, 169; National Museum, New Delhi (The Sir Aurel Stein Collection), 21–5; National Museum, Tokyo, 189; National Palace Museum, Taichung, Taiwan, 190, 192, 193, 195, 197–9, 203, 206–8, 210, 211, 217–21, 223, 225, 226; William Rockhill Nelson Gallery of Art, Kansas City, *39*, 24, 32, 41, 59, 61, 73, 106–8, 200, 214–6; Ostasiatiska Museet, Stockholm, *1–6*, *2–4*, *6*, *7*, *9*, *13*, *15*, *16*, *18*, *23*, *25*, *34*, *51*, *53*; Colin Penn, as photographer, London, 232–4, 236–40, 242, 244, 246, 247, 252, 260, 261; Royal Ontario Museum, University of Toronto, 48, 58, 75, 78, 141, 183; Paul Popper Ltd., London, 259; Rietberg-Museum, Zurich (Von der Heydt Collection), 122, 126, 129, 151; M. Sakamoto, photographer, Tokyo, *15*, *27*, *48*, *51*, 104, 196; T. Schwartz, photographer, London, 179, 182; Seattle Art Museum (Eugene Fuller Memorial Collection), *32*, *35*; Mrs Walter Sedgwick, London, *16*, *42*; the late Mrs B.Z. Seligman, London, 111, 179; C.E. Simmons, photographer, Buffalo, 29, 161, 169; Dr P. Singer, Summit, New Jersey, 109; Dr O. Sirén, as photographer, Stockholm, 131, 241, 253; J. Skeel, photographer, London, 40; Smithsonian Institution, Freer Gallery of Art, Washington DC, 7, 12, 30, 47, 60, 63, 87, 88, 91, 101, 113, 132, 138, 224; Staatliches Museum für Völkerkunde, Munich, 166; A. Stoclet Collection, Brussels, 102; Tenri Museum, Nara, *43*; E. Tweedy, photographer, London, *16*, *17*, *28*, *33*, *35*, *36*, *40*, *41*, *5*, 111, 155; University of Pennsylvania Museum, Philadelphia, 125; S. Vargassov, photographer, 230, 235; Victoria and Albert Museum, London, Crown Copyright, *33*, *41*, 123, 134, 142–4, 165, 168, 177, (Eumorfopoulos Collection) *20*; Victoria Gallery of Art, Melbourne, 130; J. Webb, photographer, London, *20*, 111; Mr C.S. Wilkinson, London, 175; The M.H. de Young Museum, San Francisco (Brundage Collection), 55, 70, 86, 119.

Numbers in italic refer to colour subjects

INDEX

450